get with the programming

Through the power of practice and immediate personalized

feedback, MyProgrammingLab improves your performance.

International Edition contributions by
Anisha Sharma

MyProgrammingLab™

Learn more at www.myprogramminglab.com

INTRODUCTION TO
PROGRAMMING
WITH

Third Edition

International Edition contributions by

Mohit P. Tahiliani
NITK Surathkal

Y. Daniel Liang

Armstrong Atlantic State University

PEARSON

Upper Saddle River   Boston   Columbus   San Francisco   New York
Indianapolis   London   Toronto   Sydney   Singapore   Tokyo   Montreal
Dubai   Madrid   Hong Kong   Mexico City   Munich   Paris   Amsterdam   Cape Town

Editorial Director: Marcia Horton
Executive Editor: Tracy Johnson
Associate Editor: Carole Snyder
Editorial Assistant: Jenah Blitz-Stoehr
Director of Marketing: Christy Lesko
Marketing Manager: Yez Alayan
Marketing Coordinator: Kathryn Ferranti
Director of Production: Erin Gregg
Managing Editor: Scott Disanno
Production Project Manager: Kayla Smith-Tarbox
Publisher, International Edition: Angshuman Chakraborty
Publishing Administrator and Business Analyst,
    International Edition: Shokhi Shah Khandelwal
Associate Print and Media Editor, International Edition:
    Anuprova Dey Chowdhuri

Acquisitions Editor, International Edition: Sandhya Ghoshal
Publishing Administrator, International Edition: Hema Mehta
Project Editor, International Edition: Karthik Subramanian
Operations Supervisor: Nick Sklitsis
Manufacturing Buyer: Lisa McDowell
Art Director: Anthony Gemmellaro
Text and Cover Designer: Anthony Gemmellaro
Manager, Visual Research: Karen Sanatar
Manager, Rights and Permissions: Michael Joyce
Text Permission Coordinator: Brian Wysock
Cover Art: Tetra Images/Glow Images
Lead Media Project Manager: Renata Buetera
Full-Service Project Management: Laserwords
Cover Printer: Lehigh-Phoenix Color/Hagerstown

Pearson Education Limited
Edinburgh Gate
Harlow
Essex CM20 2JE
England

and Associated Companies throughout the world

Visit us on the World Wide Web at:
www.pearsoninternationaleditions.com

© Pearson Education Limited 2014

ISBN 10: 0-273-79324-1
ISBN 13: 978-0-273-79324-3

British Library Cataloguing-in-Publication Data
A catalogue record for this book is available from the British Library

10 9 8 7 6 5 4 3 2 1
14 13

Typeset in Times by Laserwords

Printed and bound by Courier Kendallville in The United States of America
The publisher's policy is to use paper manufactured from sustainable forests.

This book is dedicated to my current and former C++ students. You have inspired and helped me to continue to improve this book.

To Samantha, Michael, and Michelle

DEAR READER,

Many of you have provided feedback on previous editions of *Introduction to Programming with C++*, and your comments and suggestions have greatly improved the book. This edition has been substantially enhanced in presentation, organization, examples, exercises, and supplements—including the following:

■ Reorganized sections and chapters present subjects in a logical order

■ Many new interesting examples and exercises stimulate interest

■ Introduction of the `string` type in Chapter 4 enables students to write programs using strings early

■ Key Points at the beginning of each section highlight important concepts and materials

■ Check Points at the end of each section verify the student's understanding of the material covered

what's new?

Please visit www.cs.armstrong.edu/liang/cpp3e/correlation.html for a complete list of new features as well as correlations to the previous edition.

This book teaches programming using a problem-driven method that focuses on problem solving rather than syntax. We make introductory programming interesting by using thought provoking problems in a broad context. The central thread of early chapters is on problem solving. Appropriate syntax and libraries are introduced to enable readers to write programs to solve problems. To support the teaching of programming in a problem-driven way, the book provides a wide variety of problems at various levels of difficulty to motivate students. To appeal to students in all majors, the problems cover many application areas, including math, science, business, finance, gaming, and animation.

problem driven

The book focuses on fundamentals first by introducing basic programming concepts and techniques before designing custom classes. The fundamental concepts and techniques of loops, functions, and arrays are the basis for programming. Building this strong foundation prepares students to learn object-oriented programming and advanced C++ programming.

fundamentals first

This book teaches C++. The fundamentals of problem solving and programming are the same regardless of which programming language you use. You can learn programming using any high-level programming language such as Python, Java, C++, or C#. Once you know how to program in one language, it is easy to pick up other languages, because the basic techniques for writing programs are the same.

examples and exercises

The best way to teach programming is *by example*, and the only way to learn programming is *by doing*. Basic concepts are explained by example and many exercises with various levels of difficulty are provided for students to practice. In our programming courses, we assign programming exercises after each lecture.

Our goal is to produce a text that teaches problem solving and programming in a broad context using a wide variety of interesting examples. If you have any comments or suggestions for improving this book, please email me.

Sincerely,

Y. Daniel Liang
y.daniel.liang@gmail.com
www.cs.armstrong.edu/liang
www.pearsoninternationaleditions.com/liang

PREFACE

What's New in This Edition?

This third edition substantially improves *Introduction to Programming with C++, Second Edition*. The major improvements are as follows:

complete revision
- A complete revision to enhance clarity, presentation, content, examples, and exercises

new examples and exercises
- New examples and exercises to motivate and stimulate student interest in programming

Key Points
- Key Points that highlight the important concepts covered in each section

Check Points
- Check Points that provide review questions to help students track their learning progress and evaluate their knowledge about a major concept or example

VideoNotes
- New VideoNotes that provide short video tutorials designed to reinforce the key concepts

string objects early
- Introduction of `string` objects in Chapter 4 to enable strings to be used in the early part of the book

simple IO early
- Introduction of simple input and output in Chapter 4 to enable students to write programs using files early

functions in one chapter
- Inclusion of functions in Chapter 6, which now covers all issues related to functions

common error sections
- Chapter sections on common errors and pitfalls to steer students away from common programming errors

simplified examples
- Replacement of complex examples with simpler ones (e.g., Solving the Sudoku problem in Chapter 8 is replaced by a problem of checking whether a solution is correct. The complete solution to the Sudoku problem is moved to the Companion Website.)

algorithm efficiency and techniques
- Expanded bonus Chapter 18 introduces algorithmic techniques: dynamic programming, divide-and-conquer, backtracking, and greedy algorithm with new examples to design efficient algorithms

C++11
- Introduction of new C++11 features of foreach loops and auto type inference in the bonus chapters and of lambda functions in the supplements on the Companion Website

Pedagogical Features

The book uses the following elements to help students gain the most from the material:

- The chapter **Objectives** list what students should learn so that they can determine whether they have met these objectives after completing the chapter.

- The chapter **Introduction** opens the discussion with representative problems to give the reader an overview of what to expect.

- **Key Points** highlight the important concepts covered in each section.

- **Check Points** provide review questions to help students track their progress as they read the chapter and evaluate their learning.

- **Problems and Case Studies**, carefully chosen and presented in an easy-to-follow style, teach problem solving and programming concepts. The book uses many small, simple, and stimulating examples to present important ideas.

- The **Chapter Summary** reviews the important subjects that students should understand and remember. It helps them reinforce the key concepts of the chapter.

■ Self-test quizzes are available online through MyProgrammingLab (www.myprogramminglab .com) for students to self-test on programming concepts and techniques.

■ **Programming Exercises**, grouped by sections, provide students with opportunities to apply their newly acquired skills. The level of difficulty is rated as easy (no asterisk), moderate (*), hard (**), or challenging (***). The trick of learning programming is practice, practice, and practice. To that end, the book provides numerous exercises.

■ **Notes**, **Tips**, **Cautions**, and **Pedagogical Notes** are inserted throughout the text to offer valuable advice and insight on important aspects of program development.

Note
Provides additional information on the subject and reinforces important concepts.

Tip
Teaches good programming style and practice.

Caution
Helps students avoid the pitfalls of programming errors.

Pedagogical Note
Gives advice on how to use the materials in the book effectively.

Flexible Chapter Orderings

The book provides flexible chapter orderings, as shown in the following diagram:

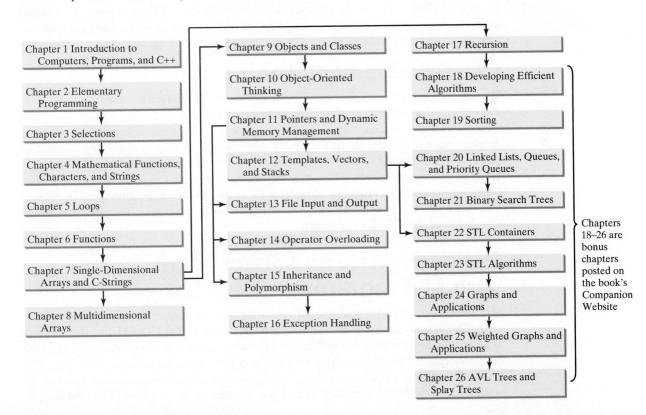

Organization of the Book

The chapters can be grouped into three parts, which together form a solid introduction to problem solving and programming using C++.

Part I: Fundamentals of Programming (Chapters 1–8)

This part is a stepping-stone, which prepares you to embark on the journey of learning programming with C++. You will begin to know C++ (Chapter 1) and will learn elementary programming techniques with primitive data types, expressions, and operators (Chapter 2), selection statements (Chapter 3), mathematical functions, characters, and strings (Chapter 4), loops (Chapter 5), functions (Chapter 6), and arrays (Chapters 7–8).

Part II: Object-Oriented Programming (Chapters 9–16)

This part introduces object-oriented programming. C++ is an object-oriented programming language that uses abstraction, encapsulation, inheritance, and polymorphism to provide great flexibility, modularity, and reusability in developing software. You will learn programming with objects and classes (Chapter 9); design classes (Chapter 10); explore pointers and dynamic memory management (Chapter 11); develop generic classes using templates (Chapter 12); use IO classes for file input and output (Chapter 13); use operators to simplify functions (Chapter 14); define classes from base classes (Chapter 15); and create robust programs using exception handling (Chapter 16).

Part III: Algorithms and Data Structures (Chapter 17 and Bonus Chapters 18–26)

This part introduces the main subjects in a typical data structures course. Chapter 17 introduces recursion to write functions for solving inherently recursive problems. Chapter 18 introduces how to measure algorithm efficiency in order to choose an appropriate algorithm for applications. Chapter 19 presents various sorting algorithms and analyzes their complexities. You will learn how to design and implement linked lists, queues, and priority queues in Chapter 20. Chapter 21 introduces binary search trees. Chapters 22 and 23 cover the standard template library in C++. Chapters 24 and 25 introduce graph algorithms and applications. Chapter 26 introduces balanced binary search trees.

C++ Development Tools

You can use a text editor, such as the Windows Notepad or WordPad, to create C++ programs, and you can compile and run the programs from the command window. You can also use a C++ development tool, such as Visual C++ or Dev-C++. These tools support an integrated development environment (IDE) for rapidly developing C++ programs. Editing, compiling, building, executing, and debugging programs are integrated in one graphical user interface. Using these tools effectively will greatly increase your programming productivity. Creating, compiling, and running programs using Visual C++ and Dev-C++ are introduced in the supplements on the Companion Website. The programs in this book have been tested on Visual C++ 2012 and the GNU C++ compiler.

Online Practice and Assessment with MyProgrammingLab™

MyProgrammingLab helps students fully grasp the logic, semantics, and syntax of programming. Through practice exercises and immediate, personalized feedback, MyProgrammingLab improves the programming competence of beginning students who often struggle with the basic concepts and paradigms of popular high-level programming languages.

A self-study and homework tool, a MyProgrammingLab course consists of hundreds of small practice problems organized around the structure of this textbook. For students, the system automatically detects errors in the logic and syntax of their code submissions and offers targeted hints that enable students to figure out what went wrong—and why. For instructors, a comprehensive gradebook tracks correct and incorrect answers and stores the code inputted by students for review.

MyProgrammingLab is offered to users of this book. For a full demonstration, to see feedback from instructors and students, or to get started using MyProgrammingLab in your course, visit www.myprogramminglab.com.

Student Resource Website

The Student Resource Website, accessible from www.pearsoninternationaleditions.com/liang, contains the following:

- Answers to Check Points

- Solutions to even-numbered Programming Exercises

- Source code for the examples

- Algorithm animations

- Errata

Supplements

The text covers the essential subjects. The supplements extend the text to introduce additional topics that might be of interest to readers. The supplements are available on the Companion Website (www.pearsoninternationaleditions.com/liang).

Instructor Resource Website

The Instructor Resource Website, accessible from www.pearsoninternationaleditions.com/liang, contains the following:

- Microsoft PowerPoint slides with interactive buttons to view full-color, syntax-highlighted source code and to run programs without leaving the slides.

- Solutions to all Programming Exercises. Students have access to the solutions of even-numbered Programming Exercises.

- Sample exams. Most exams have four parts:

  - Multiple-Choice or Short-Answer questions

  - Correct programming errors

  - Trace programs

  - Write programs

- Projects. In general, each project gives a description and asks students to analyze, design, and implement the project.

Some students have requested the materials from the Instructor Resource Website. Please understand that these are for instructors only and such requests will not be honored.

VideoNotes

VideoNote

Twenty percent of the VideoNotes in this edition are brand new! VideoNotes were introduced in the previous edition to provide additional help by presenting examples of key topics and to show how to solve problems completely, from design through coding. VideoNotes can be accessed on the book's Companion Website using the student access code printed on the inside front cover of this book. If you have a used book, you can purchase access to the VideoNotes and other premium content through the Purchase link on the Companion Website (www.pearsoninternationaleditions.com/liang).

Acknowledgments

I would like to thank Armstrong Atlantic State University for enabling me to teach what I write and for supporting me to write what I teach. Teaching is the source of inspiration for continuing to improve the book. I am grateful to the instructors and students who have offered comments, suggestions, bug reports, and praise.

This book was greatly enhanced thanks to outstanding reviews for this and previous editions. The following reviewers contributed: Anthony James Allevato (Virginia Tech); Alton B. Coalter (University of Tennessee, Martin); Linda Cohen (Forsyth Tech); Frank David Ducrest (University of Louisiana, Lafayette); Waleed Farag (Indiana University of Pennsylvania); Max I. Fomitchev (Penn State University); Jon Hanrath (Illinois Institute of Technology); Michael Hennessy (University of Oregon); Debbie Kaneko (Old Dominion University); Henry Ledgard (University of Toledo); Brian Linard (University of California, Riverside); Dan Lipsa (Armstrong Atlantic State University); Jayantha Herath (St. Cloud State University); Daqing Hou (Clarkson University); Hui Liu (Missouri State University); Ronald Marsh (University of North Dakota); Peter Maurer (Baylor University); Jay McCarthy (Brigham Young University); Jay D. Morris (Old Dominion University); Charles Nelson (Rock Valley College); Ronald Del Porto (Pennsylvania State University); Mitch Pryor (University of Texas); Martha Sanchez (University of Texas at Dallas); William B. Seales (University of Kentucky); Kate Stewart (Tallahassee Community College); Ronald Taylor (Wright State University); Matthew Tennyson (Bradley University); David Topham (Ohlone College); Margaret Tseng (Montgomery College); and Barbara Tulley (Elizabethtown College).

It is a great pleasure, honor, and privilege to work with Pearson. I would like to thank Tracy Johnson and her colleagues Marcia Horton, Carole Snyder, Yez Alayan, Scott Disanno, Kayla Smith-Tarbox, Gillian Hall, and their colleagues for organizing, producing, and promoting this project.

As always, I am indebted to my wife, Samantha, for her love, support, and encouragement.

The publishers wish to thank Moumita Mitra (Manna), of Bangabasi College, Kolkata for reviewing the content of the International Edition.

BRIEF CONTENTS

The following bonus chapters are at www
.pearsoninternationaleditions.com/liang.
Access to this premium content requires a
valid student access code. Instructions on how
to obtain an access code are provided on the
Companion Website.

APPENDIXES

CONTENTS

The following bonus chapters are on the book's Companion Website at www.pearsoninternationaleditions.com/liang.

APPENDIXES

VideoNotes

VideoNotes are available at www.pearsoninternationaleditions.com/liang, using the student access code printed on the inside front cover of this book.

VideoNote

Introduction to Computers, Programs, and C++

Objectives

- To understand computer basics, programs, and operating systems (§§1.2–1.4).

- To describe the history of C++ (§1.5).

- To write a simple C++ program for console output (§1.6).

- To understand the C++ program-development cycle (§1.7).

- To know programming style and documentation (§1.8).

- To explain the differences between syntax errors, runtime errors, and logic errors (§1.9).

1.1 Introduction

The central theme of this book is to learn how to solve problems by writing a program.

what is programming?
programming
program

This book is about programming. So, what is programming? The term *programming* means to create (or develop) software, which is also called a *program*. In basic terms, software contains the instructions that tell a computer—or a computerized device—what to do.

Software is all around you, even in devices that you might not think would need it. Of course, you expect to find and use software on a personal computer, but software also plays a role in running airplanes, cars, cell phones, and toasters. On a personal computer, you use word processors to write documents, Web browsers to explore the Internet, and e-mail programs to send messages. These programs are examples of software. Software developers create software with the help of powerful tools called *programming languages*.

This book teaches you how to create programs by using the C++ programming language. There are many programming languages, some of which are decades old. Each language was invented for a specific purpose—to build on the strengths of a previous language, for example, or to give the programmer a new and unique set of tools. Knowing that there are many programming languages available, it would be natural for you to wonder which one is best. But, in truth, there is no "best" language. Each has its strengths and weaknesses. Experienced programmers know that one language might work well in some situations, and another language may be more appropriate in others. Therefore, seasoned programmers try to master many different programming languages, giving them access to a vast arsenal of software development tools.

If you learn to program using one language, it will be easy to pick up other languages. The key is to learn how to solve problems using a programming approach. That is the main theme of this book.

You are about to begin an exciting journey: learning how to program. At the outset, it is helpful to review computer basics, programs, and operating systems. If you are familiar with such terms as CPU, memory, disks, operating systems, and programming languages, you may skip the review in Sections 1.2–1.4.

1.2 What Is a Computer?

A computer is an electronic device that stores and processes data.

hardware
software

A computer includes *hardware* and *software*. In general, hardware comprises the visible, physical elements of a computer, and software provides the invisible instructions that control the hardware and make it perform specific tasks. Knowing computer hardware isn't essential to learning a programming language, but it can help you understand the effects that a program's instructions have on a computer and its components. This section introduces computer hardware components and their functions.

A computer consists of the following major hardware components (see Figure 1.1):

- Central processing unit (CPU)

- Memory (main memory)

- Storage devices (such as disks and CDs)

- Input devices (such as the mouse and keyboard)

- Output devices (such as monitors and printers)

- Communication devices (such as modems and network interface cards)

bus

A computer's components are interconnected by a subsystem called a *bus*. Think of a bus as a system of roads running among the computer's components; data and power travel along the bus from one part of the computer to another. In personal computers, the bus is built into

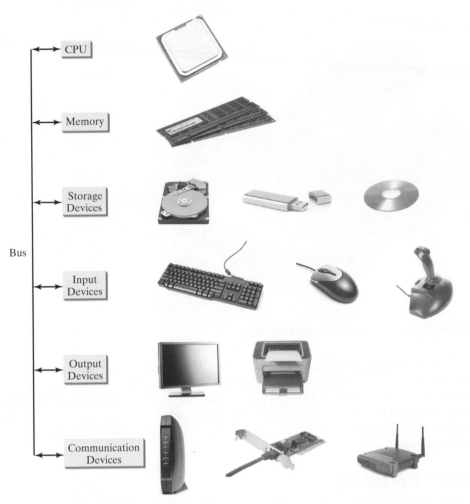

FIGURE 1.1 A computer consists of a CPU, memory, storage devices, input devices, output devices, and communication devices.

the computer's *motherboard*, which is a circuit case that connects the parts of a computer together, as shown in Figure 1.2.

motherboard

1.2.1 Central Processing Unit

The *central processing unit (CPU)* is the computer's brain. It retrieves instructions from memory and executes them. The CPU usually has two components: a *control unit* and an *arithmetic/logic unit*. The control unit controls and coordinates the actions of the other components. The arithmetic/logic unit performs numeric operations (addition, subtraction, multiplication, and division) and logical operations (comparisons).

central processing unit (CPU)

Today's CPUs are built on small silicon semiconductor chips that contain millions of tiny electric switches, called *transistors*, for processing information.

Every computer has an internal clock, which emits electronic pulses at a constant rate. These pulses are used to control and synchronize the pace of operations. A higher clock *speed* enables more instructions to be executed in a given period. The unit of measurement of clock speed is the *hertz (Hz)*, with 1 hertz equaling 1 pulse per second. In the 1990s, computers measured clocked speed in *megahertz (MHz)*, but CPU speed has been continuously improving, and the clock speed of a computer is now usually stated in *gigahertz (GHz)*. Intel's newest processors run at about 3 GHz.

speed

hertz (Hz)
megahertz (MHz)
gigahertz (GHz)

CPU is placed
under the fan

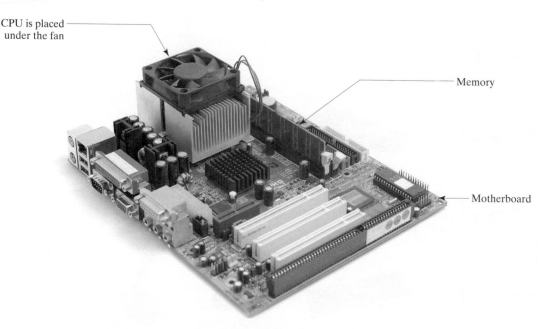

Memory

Motherboard

FIGURE 1.2 The motherboard connects the parts of a computer together.

core

CPUs were originally developed with one core. The *core* is the part of the processor that performs the reading and executing of instructions. To increase CPU processing power, chip manufacturers now produce CPUs that contain multiple cores. A multicore CPU is a single component with two or more independent cores. Today's consumer computers typically have two, three, or even four separate cores. Soon, CPUs with dozens or even hundreds of cores will be affordable.

1.2.2 Bits and Bytes

Before we discuss memory, let's look at how information (data and programs) are stored in a computer.

A computer is really nothing more than a series of switches. Each switch exists in two states: on or off. Storing information in a computer is simply a matter of setting a sequence of switches on or off. If the switch is on, its value is 1. If the switch is off, its value is 0. These 0s and 1s are interpreted as digits in the binary number system and are called *bits* (binary digits).

bit
byte

The minimum storage unit in a computer is a *byte*. A byte is composed of eight bits. A small number such as 3 can be stored as a single byte. To store a number that cannot fit into a single byte, the computer uses several bytes.

Data of various kinds, such as numbers and characters, are encoded as a series of bytes. As a programmer, you don't need to worry about the encoding and decoding of data, which the computer system performs automatically, based on the encoding scheme. An *encoding scheme* is a set of rules that governs how a computer translates characters, numbers, and symbols into data the computer can actually work with. Most schemes translate each character into a predetermined string of bits. In the popular ASCII encoding scheme, for example, the character C is represented as **01000011** in one byte.

encoding scheme

A computer's storage capacity is measured in bytes and multiples of bytes, as follows:

kilobyte (KB)

■ A *kilobyte (KB)* is about 1,000 bytes.

megabyte (MB)

■ A *megabyte (MB)* is about 1 million bytes.

gigabyte (GB)

■ A *gigabyte (GB)* is about 1 billion bytes.

terabyte (TB)

■ A *terabyte (TB)* is about 1 trillion bytes.

A typical one-page Word document might take 20 KB. Therefore, 1 MB can store 50 pages of documents and 1 GB can store 50,000 pages of documents. A typical two-hour high-resolution movie might take 8 GB, so it would require 160 GB to store 20 movies.

1.2.3 Memory

A computer's *memory* consists of an ordered sequence of bytes for storing programs as well as data that the program is working with. You can think of memory as the computer's work area for executing a program. A program and its data must be moved into the computer's memory before they can be executed by the CPU.

memory

Every byte in the memory has a *unique address*, as shown in Figure 1.3. The address is used to locate the byte for storing and retrieving the data. Since the bytes in the memory can be accessed in any order, the memory is also referred to as *random-access memory (RAM)*.

unique address

RAM

Memory address	Memory content	
.	.	
.	.	
.	.	
2000	01000011	Encoding for character 'C'
2001	01110010	Encoding for character 'r'
2002	01100101	Encoding for character 'e'
2003	01110111	Encoding for character 'w'
2004	00000011	Encoding for number 3
.	.	

FIGURE 1.3 Memory stores data and program instructions in uniquely addressed memory locations.

Today's personal computers usually have at least 1 GB of RAM, but more commonly they have 2 to 4 GB installed. Generally speaking, the more RAM a computer has, the faster it can operate, but there are limits to this simple rule of thumb.

A memory byte is never empty, but its initial content may be meaningless to your program. The current content of a memory byte is lost whenever new information is placed in it.

Like the CPU, memory is built on silicon semiconductor chips that have millions of transistors embedded on their surface. Compared to CPU chips, memory chips are less complicated, slower, and less expensive.

1.2.4 Storage Devices

A computer's memory (RAM) is a volatile form of data storage: Information that has been stored in memory (that is, saved) is lost when the system's power is turned off. Programs and data are permanently stored on *storage devices* and are moved, when the computer actually uses them, to memory, which operates at much faster speeds than permanent storage devices can.

storage device

There are three main types of storage devices:

- Magnetic disk drives

- Optical disc drives (CD and DVD)

- USB flash drives

drive

Drives are devices used to operate a storage medium, such as a disk or CD. A storage medium physically stores data and program instructions. The drive reads data from the medium and writes data onto the medium.

Disks

hard disk

A computer usually has at least one hard disk drive (see Figure 1.4). *Hard disks* are used to store data and programs permanently. Newer computers have hard disk drives that can store from 200 to 800 GB of data. Hard disk drives are usually encased inside the computer, but removable hard disks are also available.

FIGURE 1.4   A hard disk drive stores programs and data permanently.

CDs and DVDs

CD-R

CD stands for compact disc. There are two types of CD drives: CD-R and CD-RW. A *CD-R* is for read-only permanent storage; the user cannot modify its contents once they are recorded.

CD-RW

A *CD-RW* can be used like a hard disk; that is, you can write data onto the disc, and then overwrite that data with new data. A single CD can hold up to 700 MB. Most new PCs are equipped with a CD-RW drive that can work with both CD-R and CD-RW discs.

DVD

DVD stands for digital versatile disc or digital video disc. DVDs and CDs look alike, and you can use either to store data. A DVD can hold more information than a CD; a standard DVD's storage capacity is 4.7 GB. Like CDs, there are two types of DVDs: DVD-R (read-only) and DVD-RW (rewritable).

USB Flash Drives

Universal serial bus (USB) connectors allow the user to attach various peripheral devices to the computer. You can use a USB to connect a printer, digital camera, mouse, external hard disk drive, and other devices to the computer.

A USB *flash drive* is a device for storing and transporting data. It's a portable hard drive that can be plugged into your computer's USB port. A flash drive is small—about the size of a pack of gum, as shown in Figure 1.5. USB flash drives are currently available with up to 256 GB storage capacity.

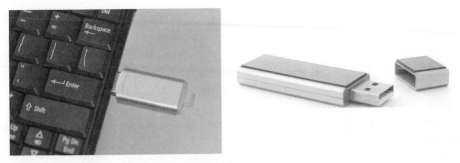

FIGURE 1.5 USB flash drives are portable and can store much data.

1.2.5 Input and Output Devices

Input and output devices let the user communicate with the computer. The most common input devices are *keyboards* and *mice*. The most common output devices are *monitors* and *printers*.

Keyboard

A keyboard is a device for entering input. Figure 1.6 shows a typical keyboard. Compact keyboards are available without a numeric keypad.

FIGURE 1.6 A computer keyboard has keys used to send input to a computer.

Function keys are located across the top of the keyboard and are prefaced with the letter *F*. Their functions depend on the software being used.

A *modifier key* is a special key (such as the *Shift*, *Alt*, or *Ctrl* key) that modifies the normal action of another key when the two are pressed simultaneously.

The *numeric keypad*, located on the right side of most keyboards, is a separate set of keys styled like a calculator and used to enter numbers quickly.

Arrow keys, located between the main keypad and the numeric keypad, are used to move the mouse pointer up, down, left, and right on the screen in many programs.

The *Insert, Delete, Page Up*, and *Page Down keys* are used in word processing and other programs for inserting text and objects, deleting text and objects, and moving up or down through a document one screen at a time.

function key

modifier key

numeric keypad

arrow key
Insert key
Delete key
Page Up key
Page Down key

Mouse

A *mouse* is a pointing device. It is used to move a graphical pointer (usually in the shape of an arrow) called a *cursor* around the screen or to click on-screen objects (such as a button) to trigger them to perform an action.

Monitor

The *monitor* displays information (text and graphics). The screen resolution and dot pitch determine the quality of the display.

screen resolution
pixel

The *screen resolution* specifies the number of pixels in horizontal and vertical dimensions of the display device. *Pixels* (short for "picture elements") are tiny dots that form an image on the screen. A common resolution for a 17-inch screen, for example, is 1,024 pixels wide and 768 pixels high. The resolution can be set manually. The higher the resolution, the sharper and clearer the image.

dot pitch

The *dot pitch* is the amount of space between pixels, measured in millimeters. The smaller the dot pitch, the sharper the display.

1.2.6 Communication Devices

Computers can be networked through communication devices, such as a dial-up modem (*modulator/dem*odulator), a DSL or cable modem, a wired network interface card, or a wireless adapter.

dial-up modem

- A *dial-up modem* uses a phone line and can transfer data at speeds up to 56,000 bps (bits per second).

digital subscriber line (DSL)

- A *digital subscriber line (DSL)* connection also uses a standard phone line, but it can transfer data 20 times faster than a standard dial-up modem.

cable modem

- A *cable modem* uses the cable TV line maintained by the cable company and is generally faster than DSL.

network interface card (NIC)
local area network (LAN)

million bits per second
  (mbps)

- A *network interface card (NIC)* is a device that connects a computer to a *local area network (LAN)*, as shown in Figure 1.7. LANs are commonly used in universities, businesses, and government agencies. A high-speed NIC called *1000BaseT* can transfer data at 1,000 *million bits per second (mbps)*.

- Wireless networking is now extremely popular in homes, businesses, and schools. Every laptop computer sold today is equipped with a wireless adapter that enables the computer to connect to a local area network and the Internet.

Note
Answers to Check Points are on the Companion Website.

Check Point

1.1 Define the terms hardware and software.

1.2 List five major hardware components of a computer.

1.3 What does the acronym "CPU" stand for?

1.4 What unit is used to measure CPU speed?

1.5 What is a bit? What is a byte?

1.6 What is memory used for? What does RAM stand for? Why is memory called RAM?

1.7 What unit is used to measure memory size?

1.8 What unit is used to measure disk size?

1.9 What is the primary difference between memory and a storage device?

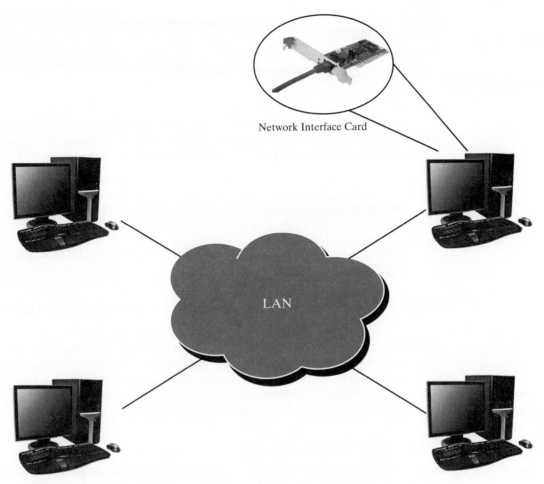

Network Interface Card

FIGURE 1.7 A local area network connects computers in proximity to each other.

1.3 Programming Languages

Computer programs, *known as* software, *are instructions that tell a computer what to do.*

 Key Point

Computers do not understand human languages; so programs must be written in languages computers can understand. There are hundreds of programming languages, developed to make the programming process easier for people. However, all programs must be converted into the instructions the computer can execute.

1.3.1 Machine Language

A computer's native language, which differs among different types of computers, is its *machine language*—a set of built-in primitive instructions. These instructions are in the form of binary code, so if you want to give a computer an instruction in its native language, you have to enter the instruction as binary code. For example, to add two numbers, you might have to write an instruction in binary code, as follows:

machine language

    1101101010011010

1.3.2 Assembly Language

Programming in machine language is a tedious process. Moreover, programs written in machine language are very difficult to read and modify. For this reason, *assembly language* was created in the early days of computing as an alternative to machine languages. Assembly

assembly language

language uses a short descriptive word, known as a *mnemonic*, to represent each of the machine-language instructions. For example, the mnemonic **add** typically means to add numbers and **sub** means to subtract numbers. To add the numbers 2 and 3 and get the result, you might write an instruction in assembly code like this:

```
add 2, 3, result
```

assembler

Assembly languages were developed to make programming easier. However, because the computer cannot execute assembly language, another program—called an *assembler*—is used to translate assembly-language programs into machine code, as shown in Figure 1.8.

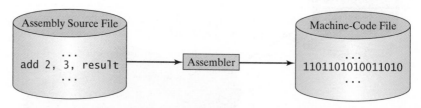

FIGURE 1.8 An assembler translates assembly-language instructions into machine code.

low-level language

Writing code in assembly language is easier than in machine language. However, it is still tedious to write code in assembly language. An instruction in assembly language essentially corresponds to an instruction in machine code. Writing in assembly requires that you know how the CPU works. Assembly language is referred to as a *low-level language*, because assembly language is close in nature to machine language and is machine dependent.

1.3.3 High-Level Language

high-level language

In the 1950s, a new generation of programming languages known as *high-level languages* emerged. They are platform-independent, which means that you can write a program in a high-level language and run it in different types of machines. High-level languages are English-like and easy to learn and use. The instructions in a high-level programming language are called

statement

statements. Here, for example, is a high-level language statement that computes the area of a circle with a radius of 5:

```
area = 5 * 5 * 3.1415
```

There are many high-level programming languages, and each was designed for a specific purpose. Table 1.1 lists some popular ones.

source program
source code
interpreter
compiler

A program written in a high-level language is called a *source program* or *source code*. Because a computer cannot execute a source program, a source program must be translated into machine code for execution. The translation can be done using another programming tool called an *interpreter* or *compiler*.

An interpreter reads one statement from the source code, translates it to the machine code or virtual machine code, and then executes it immediately, as shown in Figure 1.9a. Note that a statement from the source code may be translated into several machine instructions.

A compiler translates the entire source code into a machine-code file, and the machine-code file is then executed, as shown in Figure 1.9b.

Check Point

1.10 What language does the CPU understand?

1.11 What is an assembly language?

1.12 What is an assembler?

1.13 What is a high-level programming language?

1.14 What is a source program?

1.15 What is an interpreter?

1.16 What is a compiler?

1.17 What is the difference between an interpreted language and a compiled language?

TABLE 1.1 Popular High-Level Programming Languages

Language	Description
Ada	Named for Ada Lovelace, who worked on mechanical general-purpose computers. The Ada language was developed for the Department of Defense and is used mainly in defense projects.
BASIC	Beginner's All-purpose Symbolic Instruction Code. It was designed to be learned and used easily by beginners.
C	Developed at Bell Laboratories. C combines the power of an assembly language with the ease of use and portability of a high-level language.
C++	C++ is an object-oriented language, based on C.
C#	Pronounced "C Sharp." It is a hybrid of Java and C++ and was developed by Microsoft.
COBOL	COmmon Business Oriented Language. It is used for business applications.
FORTRAN	FORmula TRANslation. It is popular for scientific and mathematical applications.
Java	Developed by Sun Microsystems, now part of Oracle. It is widely used for developing platform-independent Internet applications.
Pascal	Named for Blaise Pascal, who pioneered calculating machines in the seventeenth century. It is a simple, structured, general-purpose language primarily used for teaching programming.
Python	A simple general-purpose scripting language good for writing short programs.
Visual Basic	Visual Basic was developed by Microsoft and it enables the programmers to rapidly develop graphical user interfaces.

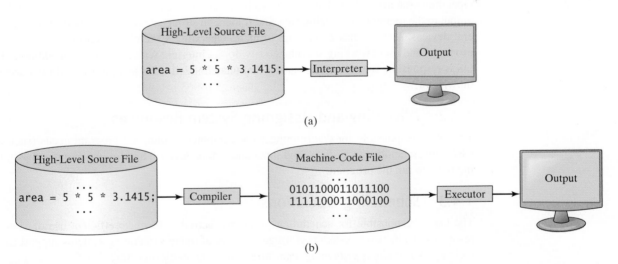

FIGURE 1.9 (a) An interpreter translates and executes a program one statement at a time. (b) A compiler translates the entire source program into a machine-language file for execution.

1.4 Operating Systems

operating
system (OS)

**Key
Point**

The operating system (OS) *is the most important program that runs on a computer.
The OS manages and controls a computer's activities.*

Popular operating systems for general-purpose computers are Microsoft Windows, Mac OS,
and Linux. Application programs, such as a Web browser or a word processor, cannot run
unless an operating system is installed and running on the computer. Figure 1.10 shows the
interrelationship of user, application programs, operating system, and hardware.

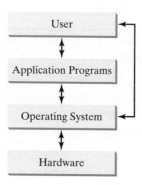

FIGURE 1.10 Users and applications access the computer's hardware via the operating
system.

The following are major tasks of an operating system:

- Controlling and monitoring system activities

- Allocating and assigning system resources

- Scheduling operations

1.4.1 Controlling and Monitoring System Activities

Operating systems perform basic tasks, such as recognizing input from the keyboard, sending
output to the monitor, organizing files and folders on storage devices, and controlling peripheral devices, such as disk drives and printers. Operating systems also ensure that different
programs and users working simultaneously do not interfere with each other. In addition, the
OS is responsible for security, ensuring that unauthorized users and programs do not access
the system.

1.4.2 Allocating and Assigning System Resources

The OS is responsible for determining what computer resources a program needs (such as
CPU time, memory space, disks, and input and output devices) and for allocating and assigning them to run the program.

1.4.3 Scheduling Operations

The OS is responsible for scheduling programs' activities to make efficient use of system
resources. To increase system performance, many of today's operating systems support such
techniques as *multiprogramming*, *multithreading*, and *multiprocessing*.

multiprogramming

Multiprogramming allows multiple programs to run simultaneously by sharing the CPU.
The CPU is much faster than the computer's other components. As a result, it is idle most of

the time—for example, while waiting for data to be transferred from a disk or waiting for other system resources to respond. A multiprogramming OS takes advantage of this situation by allowing multiple programs to use the CPU when it would otherwise be idle. For example, multiprogramming enables you to use a word processor to edit a file at the same time as your Web browser is downloading a file.

Multithreading allows a single program to execute multiple tasks at the same time. For instance, a word-processing program allows users to simultaneously edit text and save it to a disk. In this example, editing and saving are two tasks within the same application. These two tasks may run concurrently.

multithreading

Multiprocessing, or *parallel processing*, uses two or more processors together to perform subtasks concurrently and then combine solutions of the subtasks to obtain a solution for the entire task. It is like a surgical operation where several doctors work together on one patient.

multiprocessing

1.18 What is an operating system? List some popular operating systems.

1.19 What are the major responsibilities of an operating system?

1.20 What are multiprogramming, multithreading, and multiprocessing?

✓ **Check Point**

1.5 History of C++

C++ is a general-purpose, object-oriented programming language.

🔑 **Key Point**

C, C++, Java, and C# are related. C++ evolved from C. Java was modeled after C++. C# is a subset of C++, with some features similar to Java. If you know one of these languages, it is easy to learn the others.

C evolved from the B language, which evolved from the BCPL (Basic Combined Programming Language). Martin Richards developed BCPL in the mid-1960s for writing operating systems and compilers. Ken Thompson incorporated many features from BCPL in his B language and used it to create early versions of the UNIX operating system at Bell Laboratories in 1970 on a DEC PDP-7 computer. Both BCPL and B are typeless—that is, every data item occupies a fixed-length "word" or "cell" in memory. How a data item is treated—for example, as a number or as a string—is the responsibility of the programmer. Dennis Ritchie extended the B language by adding types and other features in 1971 to develop the UNIX operating system on a DEC PDP-11 computer. Today, C is portable and hardware independent. It is widely used for developing operating systems.

BCPL

B

C

C++ is an extension of C, developed by Bjarne Stroustrup at Bell Laboratories during 1983–1985. C++ added a number of features that improved the C language. Most important, it added the support of using classes for object-oriented programming. Object-oriented programming can make programs easy to reuse and easy to maintain. C++ could be considered a superset of C. The features of C are supported by C++. C programs can be compiled using C++ compilers. After learning C++, you will be able to read and understand C programs as well.

C++

An international standard for C++, known as C++98, was created by the International Standard Organization (ISO) in 1998. The ISO standard is an attempt to ensure that C++ is portable—that is, your programs compiled using one vendor's compiler can be compiled without errors from any other vendor's compiler on any platform. Since the standard has been around for a while, all the major vendors now support the ISO standard. Nevertheless, the C++ compiler vendors may add proprietary features into the compiler. So, it is possible that your program may compile fine by one compiler but may need to be modified in order to be compiled by a different compiler.

C++98
ISO standard

A new standard, known as C++11, was approved by ISO in 2011. C++11 added new features into the core language and standard library. These new features are very useful for

C++11

general-purpose
  programming language

object-oriented programming
  (OOP) language

advanced C++ programming. We will introduce some of the new features in the bonus chapters and in the supplements on the Companion Website.

C++ is a general-purpose programming language, which means you can use C++ to write code for any programming task. C++ is an object-oriented programming (OOP) language. Object-oriented programming is a powerful tool for developing reusable software. Object-oriented programming in C++ will be covered in detail starting in Chapter 9.

I.21 What is the relationship between C, C++, Java, and C#?

I.22 Who initially developed C++?

1.6 A Simple C++ Program

A C++ program is executed from the main *function.*

console

console input

console output

Let us begin with a simple C++ program that displays the message Welcome to C++! on the console. (The word console is an old computer term. It refers to a computer's text entry and display device. Console input means to receive input from the keyboard and console output means to display output to the monitor.) The program is shown in Listing 1.1.

LISTING I.I Welcome.cpp

include library

using namespace

main function

comment

output

successful return

```
1  #include <iostream>
2  using namespace std;
3
4  int main()
5  {
6    // Display Welcome to C++ to the console
7    cout << "Welcome to C++!" << endl;
8
9    return 0;
10 }
```

```
Welcome to C++!
```

line numbers

VideoNote

Your first C++ program

The line numbers are not part of the program, but are displayed for reference purposes. So, don't type line numbers in your program.

The first line in the program

```
#include <iostream>
```

preprocessor directive

library

header file

is a compiler *preprocessor directive* that tells the compiler to include the iostream library in this program, which is needed to support console input and output. C++ *library* contains predefined code for developing C++ programs. The library like iostream is called a *header file* in C++, because it is usually included at the head of a program.

The statement in line 2

```
using namespace std;
```

namespace

tells the compiler to use the standard namespace. std is an abbreviation of *standard*. Namespace is a mechanism to avoid naming conflicts in a large program. The names cout and endl in line 7 are defined in the iostream library in the standard namespace. For the compiler to find these names, the statement in line 2 must be used. Namespace is an advanced subject covered in Supplement IV.B. For now, all you need to do is to write line 2 in your program for performing any input and output operations.

Every C++ program is executed from a main function. A function is a construct that contains statements. The main function defined in lines 4–10 contains two statements. They are enclosed in a *block* that starts with a left brace, {, (line 5) and ends with a right brace, } (line 10). Every statement in C++ must end with a semicolon (;), known as the *statement terminator*.

main function

block

statement terminator

The statement in line 7 displays a message to the console. **cout** (pronounced see-out) stands for *console output*. The << operator, referred to as the *stream insertion operator*, sends a string to the console. A string must be enclosed in quotation marks. The statement in line 7 first outputs the string **"Welcome to C++!"** to the console, then outputs **endl**. Note that **endl** stands for *end line*. Sending **endl** to the console ends a line and flushes the output buffer to ensure that the output is displayed immediately.

console output

stream insertion operator

end line

The statement (line 9)

```
return 0;
```

is placed at the end of every main function to exit the program. The value **0** indicates that the program has terminated with a *successful exit*. Some compilers will work fine if this statement is omitted; however, other compilers will not. It is a good practice always to include this statement for your program to work with all C++ compilers.

successful exit

Line 6 is a *comment* that documents what the program is and how it is constructed. Comments help programmers to communicate and understand the program. They are not programming statements and thus are ignored by the compiler. In C++, a comment is preceded by two slashes (//) on a line, called a *line comment*, or enclosed between /* and */ on one or several lines, called a *block comment* or *paragraph comment*. When the compiler sees //, it ignores all text after // on the same line. When it sees /*, it scans for the next */ and ignores any text between /* and */.

comment

line comment

block comment

paragraph comment

Here are examples of the two types of comments:

```
// This application program prints Welcome to C++!
/* This application program prints Welcome to C++! */
/* This application program
   prints Welcome to C++! */
```

Keywords, or *reserved words*, have a specific meaning to the compiler and cannot be used in the program for other purposes. There are four keywords in this program: **using**, **namespace**, **int**, and **return**.

keyword (or reserved word)

Caution

Preprocessor directives are not C++ statements. Therefore, don't put semicolons at the end of preprocessor directives. Doing so may cause subtle errors.

directives are not statements

Caution

Some compilers will not compile if you put extra spaces between < and **iostream** or between **iostream** and >. The extra space will become part of the header file name. To ensure your program will work with all compilers, don't put extra spaces in these cases.

no extra space

Caution

C++ source programs are case sensitive. It would be wrong, for example, to replace **main** in the program with **Main**.

case sensitive

Note

You are probably wondering about such points as why the main function is declared this way and why `cout << "Welcome to C++!" << endl` is used to display a message to the console. Your questions cannot be fully answered yet. For now, you will have to accept that this is how things are done. You will find the answers in subsequent chapters.

special characters

You have seen several special characters (e.g., #, //, <<) in the program. They are used almost in every program. Table 1.2 summarizes their uses.

TABLE 1.2   Special Characters

Character	Name	Description
#	Pound sign	Used in `#include` to denote a preprocessor directive.
<>	Opening and closing angle brackets	Encloses a library name when used with `#include`.
()	Opening and closing parentheses	Used with functions such as `main()`.
{}	Opening and closing braces	Denotes a block to enclose statements.
//	Double slashes	Precedes a comment line.
<<	Stream insertion operator	Outputs to the console.
" "	Opening and closing quotation marks	Wraps a string (i.e., sequence of characters).
;	Semicolon	Marks the end of a statement.

common errors

syntax rules

Most common errors students will encounter in this chapter are syntax errors. Like any other programming language, C++ has its own rules of grammar, called *syntax*, and you need to write code that obeys the syntax rules. If your program violates these rules, the C++ compiler will report syntax errors. Pay close attention to the punctuation. The redirection symbol << is two consecutive <'s. Every statement in the function ends with a semicolon (;).

The program in Listing 1.1 displays one message. Once you understand the program, it is easy to extend it to display more messages. For example, you can rewrite the program to display three messages, as shown in Listing 1.2.

LISTING 1.2   WelcomeWithThreeMessages.cpp

include library

main function

output

successful return

```
 1  #include <iostream>
 2  using namespace std;
 3
 4  int main()
 5  {
 6    cout << "Programming is fun!" << endl;
 7    cout << "Fundamentals First" << endl;
 8    cout << "Problem Driven" << endl;
 9
10    return 0;
11  }
```

```
Programming is fun!
Fundamentals First
Problem Driven
```

Further, you can perform mathematical computations and display the result to the console. Listing 1.3 gives such an example.

LISTING 1.3 ComputeExpression.cpp

```
 1  #include <iostream>                                        include library
 2  using namespace std;
 3
 4  int main()                                                 main function
 5  {
 6    cout << "(10.5 + 2 * 3) / (45 - 3.5) = ";                output
 7    cout << (10.5 + 2 * 3) / (45 - 3.5) << endl;
 8
 9    return 0;                                                successful return
10  }
```

```
(10.5 + 2 * 3) / (45 - 3.5) = 0.39759036144578314
```

The multiplication operator in C++ is *. As you see, it is a straightforward process to translate an arithmetic expression to a C++ expression. We will discuss C++ expressions further in Chapter 2.

You can combine multiple outputs in a single statement. For example, the following statement performs the same function as lines 6–7.

```
cout << "(10.5 + 2 * 3) / (45 - 3.5) = "
  << (10.5 + 2 * 3) / (45 - 3.5) << endl;
```

1.23 Explain the C++ keywords. List some C++ keywords you learned in this chapter.

1.24 Is C++ case sensitive? What is the case for C++ keywords?

1.25 What is the C++ source file name extension, and what is the C++ executable file name extension on Windows?

1.26 What is a comment? What is the syntax for a comment in C++? Is the comment ignored by the compiler?

1.27 What is the statement to display a string on the console?

1.28 What does the namespace `std` stand for?

1.29 Which of the following preprocessor directive is correct?

a. **import** iostream

b. **#include** <iostream>

c. **include** <iostream>

d. **#include** iostream

1.30 Which of the following preprocessor directive will work with all C++ compilers?

a. **#include** < iostream>

b. **#include** <iostream >

c. **include** <iostream>

d. **#include** <iostream>

Check Point

1.31 Show the output of the following code:

```cpp
#include <iostream>
using namespace std;

int main()
{
  cout << "3.5 * 4 / 2 - 2.5 = " << (3.5 * 4 / 2 - 2.5) << endl;

  return 0;
}
```

1.32 Show the output of the following code:

```cpp
#include <iostream>
using namespace std;

int main()
{
  cout << "C++" << "Java"  << endl;
  cout << "C++" << endl << "Java"  << endl;
  cout << "C++, " << "Java, "  << "and C#"  << endl;

  return 0;
}
```

1.7 C++ Program-Development Cycle

Key Point

The C++ program-development process consists of creating/modifying source code, compiling, linking and executing programs.

VideoNote

Compile and run C++

You have to create your program and compile it before it can be executed. This process is repetitive, as shown in Figure 1.11. If your program has compile errors, you have to modify it to fix them and then recompile it. If your program has runtime errors or does not produce the correct result, you have to modify it, recompile it, and execute it again.

The C++ compiler command performs three tasks in sequence: *preprocessing*, *compiling*, and *linking*. Precisely, a C++ compiler contains three separate programs: *preprocessor*, *compiler*, and *linker*. For simplicity, we refer to all three programs together as a C++ compiler.

preprocessor

- A *preprocessor* is a program that processes a source file before it is passed down to the compiler. The preprocessor processes the directives. The directives start with the # sign. For example, #include in line 1 of Listing 1.1 is a directive to tell the compiler to include a library. The preprocessor produces an intermediate file.

object file

- The *compiler* then translates the intermediate file into a machine-code file. The machine-code file is also known as an *object file*. To avoid confusion with C++ objects, we will not use this terminology in the text.

linker

- The *linker* links the machine-code file with supporting library files to form an executable file. On Windows, the machine-code file is stored on disk with an .obj extension, and the executable files are stored with an .exe extension. On UNIX, the machine-code file has an .o extension and the executable files do not have file extensions.

.cpp source file

Note

A C++ source file typically ends with the extension .cpp. Some compilers may accept other file name extensions (e.g., .c, .cp, or .c), but you should stick with the .cpp extension to be compliant with all C++ compilers.

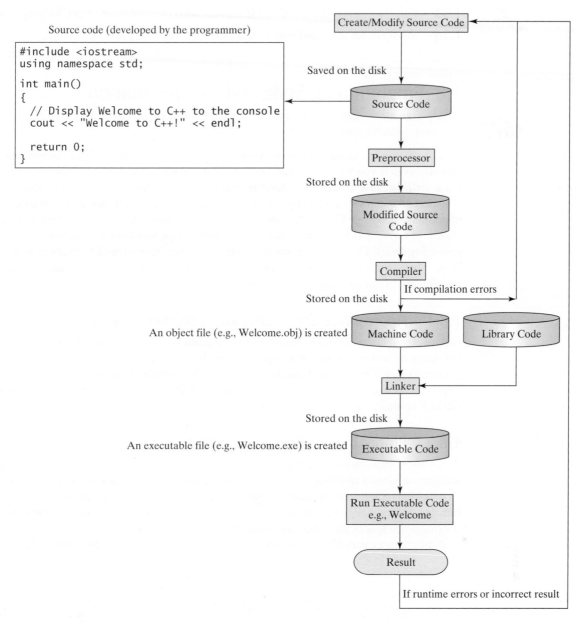

Source code (developed by the programmer)

```cpp
#include <iostream>
using namespace std;

int main()
{
  // Display Welcome to C++ to the console
  cout << "Welcome to C++!" << endl;

  return 0;
}
```

FIGURE 1.11 The C++ program-development process consists of creating/modifying source code, compiling, linking and executing programs.

You can develop a C++ program from a command window or from an IDE. An IDE is software that provides an *integrated development environment* (*IDE*) for rapidly developing C++ programs. Editing, compiling, building, debugging, and online help are integrated in one graphical user interface. Just enter source code or open an existing file in a window, then click a button, menu item, or function key to compile and run the program. Examples of popular IDEs are Microsoft Visual C++, Dev-C++, Eclipse, and NetBeans. All these IDEs can be downloaded free.

integrated development environment (IDE)

Supplement II.B introduces how to develop C++ programs using Visual C++. Supplement II.D introduces how to develop C++ programs using Dev-C++. Supplement II.E introduces how to develop C++ programs from NetBeans IDE. Supplement I.F introduces how to develop C++ programs from a Windows command window. Supplement I.G introduces how to develop C++ on UNIX.

VideoNote
Visual C++ tutorial

1.33 Can C++ run on any machine? What is needed to compile and run C++ programs?

1.34 What are the input and output of a C++ compiler?

1.8 Programming Style and Documentation

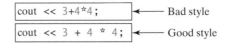

Good programming style and proper documentation make a program easy to read and help programmers prevent errors.

programming style

documentation

Programming style deals with what programs look like. A program could compile and run properly even if you wrote it on one line only, but writing it that way would be bad programming style because it would be hard to read. *Documentation* is the body of explanatory remarks and comments pertaining to a program. Programming style and documentation are as important as coding. Good programming style and appropriate documentation reduce the chance of errors and make programs easy to read. So far you have learned some good programming styles. This section summarizes them and gives several guidelines about how to use them. More detailed guidelines on programming style and documentation can be found in Supplement I.E on the Companion Website.

1.8.1 Appropriate Comments and Comment Styles

Include a summary at the beginning of the program to explain what the program does, its key features, and any unique techniques it uses. In a long program, you should also include comments that introduce each major step and explain anything that is difficult to read. It is important to make comments concise so that they do not crowd the program or make it difficult to read.

1.8.2 Proper Indentation and Spacing

indentation

A consistent indentation style makes programs clear and easy to read, debug, and maintain. *Indentation* is used to illustrate the structural relationships between a program's components or statements. C++ compiler can read the program even if all the statements are in a straight line, but properly aligned code is easier to read and maintain. Indent each subcomponent or statement *two* spaces more than the construct within which it is nested.

A single space should be added on both sides of a binary operator, as shown here:

`cout << 3+4*4;`	◀——— Bad style
`cout << 3 + 4 * 4;`	◀——— Good style

A single line space should be used to separate segments of the code to make the program easier to read.

1.35 Identify and fix the errors in the following code:

```
1   include <iostream>;
2   using namespace std;
3
4   int main
5   {
6     // Display Welcome to C++ to the console
7     cout << Welcome to C++! << endl;
8
9     return 0;
10  }
```

1.36   How do you denote a comment line and a comment paragraph?

1.37   Reformat the following program according to the programming style and documentation guidelines.

```
#include <iostream>
using namespace std;

int main()
{
cout << "2 + 3 = "<<2+3;
  return 0;
}
```

1.9 Programming Errors

Programming errors can be categorized into three types: syntax errors, runtime errors, and logic errors.

Key Point

Programming errors are unavoidable, even for experienced programmers. Errors can be categorized into three types: syntax errors, runtime errors, and logic errors.

1.9.1   Syntax Errors

Errors that are detected by the compiler are called *syntax errors* or *compile errors*. Syntax errors result from errors in code construction, such as mistyping a keyword, omitting necessary punctuation, or using an opening brace without a corresponding closing brace. These errors are usually easy to detect, because the compiler tells you where they are and what caused them. For example, the following program in Listing 1.4 has a syntax error.

syntax error
compile error

LISTING 1.4   ShowSyntaxErrors.cpp

```
1   #include <iostream>
2   using namespace std
3
4   int main()
5   {
6     cout << "Programming is fun << endl;
7
8     return 0;
9   }
```

When you compile this program using Visual C++, it displays the following errors:

compile

```
1>Test.cpp(4): error C2144: syntax error : 'int' should be preceded by ';'
1>Test.cpp(6): error C2001: newline in constant
1>Test.cpp(8): error C2143: syntax error : missing ';' before 'return'
```

Three errors are reported, but the program actually has two errors. First, the semicolon (;) is missing at the end of line 2. Second, the string `Programming is fun` should be closed with a closing quotation mark in line 6.

Since a single error will often display many lines of compile errors, it is a good practice to fix errors from the top line and work downward. Fixing errors that occur earlier in the program may also fix additional errors that occur later.

Tip

fix syntax error

If you don't know how to correct it, compare your program closely, character by character, with similar examples in the text. In the first few weeks of this course, you will probably spend a lot of time fixing syntax errors. Soon you will be familiar with the syntax and can quickly fix syntax errors.

1.9.2 Runtime Errors

runtime error

Runtime errors cause a program to terminate abnormally. They occur while an application is running if the environment detects an operation that is impossible to carry out. Input mistakes typically cause runtime errors. An *input error* occurs when the program is waiting for the user to enter a value, but the user enters a value that the program cannot handle. For instance, if the program expects to read in a number, but instead the user enters a string, this causes data-type errors to occur.

Another common source of runtime errors is division by zero. This happens when the divisor is zero for integer divisions. For instance, the following program in Listing 1.5 would cause a runtime error.

LISTING 1.5 ShowRuntimeErrors.cpp

```
1  #include <iostream>
2  using namespace std;
3
4  int main()
5  {
6      int i = 4;
7      int j = 0;
8      cout << i / j << endl;
9
10     return 0;
11 }
```

runtime error

Here, i and j are called variables. We will introduce variables in Chapter 2. i has a value of 4 and j has a value of 0. i / j in line 8 causes a runtime error of division by zero.

1.9.3 Logic Errors

logic error

Logic errors occur when a program does not perform the way it was intended. Errors of this kind occur for many different reasons. For example, suppose you wrote the following program in Listing 1.6 to convert a Celsius **35** degree to a Fahrenheit degree:

LISTING 1.6 ShowLogicErrors.cpp

```
1  #include <iostream>
2  using namespace std;
3
4  int main()
5  {
6    cout << "Celsius 35 is Fahrenheit degree " << endl;
7    cout << (9 / 5) * 35 + 32 << endl;
8
9    return 0;
10 }
```

```
Celsius 35 is Fahrenheit degree
67
```

You will get Fahrenheit 67 degree, which is wrong. It should be 95. In C++, the division for integers is the quotient. The fractional part is truncated. So 9 / 5 is 1. To get the correct result, you need to use 9.0 / 5, which results in 1.8.

In general, syntax errors are easy to find and easy to correct, because the compiler indicates where the errors were introduced and why they are wrong. Runtime errors are not difficult to find, either, because the reasons and locations for the errors are displayed on the console when the program aborts. Finding logic errors, on the other hand, can be very challenging. In the upcoming chapters, you will learn the techniques of tracing programs and finding logic errors.

1.9.4 Common Errors

Missing a closing brace, missing a semicolon, missing quotation marks for strings, and misspelling names are common errors made by new programmers.

Common Error 1: Missing Braces

Braces are used to denote a block in the program. Each opening brace must be matched by a closing brace. A common error is missing the closing brace. To avoid this error, type a closing brace whenever an opening brace is typed, as shown in the following example.

```
int main()
{

} ◄────── Type this closing brace right away to match the opening brace
```

Common Error 2: Missing Semicolons

Each statement ends with a statement terminator (;). Often, a new programmer forgets to place a statement terminator for the last statement in a block, as shown in the following example:

```
int main()
{
    cout << "Programming is fun!" << endl;
    cout << "Fundamentals First" << endl;
    cout << "Problem Driven" << endl
}                            ↑
                    Missing a semicolon
```

Common Error 3: Missing Quotation Marks

A string must be placed inside the quotation marks. Often, a new programmer forgets to place a quotation mark at the end of a string, as shown in the following example:

```
    cout << "Problem Driven;
                    ↑
        Missing a quotation mark
```

Common Error 4: Misspelling Names

C++ is case-sensitive. Misspelling names is a common error made by new programmers. For example, the word main is misspelled as Main in the following code:

```
1  int Main()
2  {
3      cout << (10.5 + 2 * 3) / (45 – 3.5) << endl;
4      return 0;
5  }
```

1.38 What are syntax errors (compile errors), runtime errors, and logic errors?

1.39 If you forget to put a closing quotation mark on a string, what kind of error will occur?

Check
Point

1.40 If your program needs to read data from a file, but the file does not exist, an error would occur when running this program. What kind of error is this?

1.41 Suppose you write a program for computing the perimeter of a rectangle and you mistakenly write your program so that it computes the area of a rectangle. What kind of error is this?

1.42 Identify and fix the errors in the following code:

```
1  int Main()
2  {
3    cout << 'Welcome to C++!;
4    return 0;
5  )
```

KEY TERMS

assembler 30	linker 38
assembly language 29	logic error 42
bit 24	low-level language 30
block 35	machine language 29
block comment 35	main function 35
bus 22	memory 25
byte 24	modem 28
cable modem 28	motherboard 23
central processing unit (CPU) 23	namespace 34
comment 35	network interface card (NIC) 28
compile error 41	object file 38
compiler 30	operating system (OS) 32
console 34	paragraph comment 35
console input 34	pixel 28
console output 35	preprocessor 38
dot pitch 28	program 22
digital subscriber line (DSL) 28	programming 22
encoding scheme 24	runtime error 42
hardware 22	screen resolution 28
header file 34	software 22
high-level language 30	source code 30
integrated development environment (IDE) 39	source program 30
	statement 30
interpreter 30	statement terminator 35
keyword (or reserved word) 35	storage device 25
library 34	stream insertion operator 35
line comment 35	syntax error 41

 Note
The key terms above are defined in this chapter. Supplement I.A, Glossary, lists all the key terms and descriptions used in the book, organized by chapters.

CHAPTER SUMMARY

1. A computer is an electronic device that stores and processes data.

2. A computer includes both *hardware* and *software*.

3. Hardware is the physical aspect of the computer that can be touched.

4. Computer *programs*, known as *software*, are the invisible instructions that control the hardware and make it perform tasks.

5. Computer *programming* is the writing of instructions (i.e., code) for computers to perform.

6. The *central processing unit* (*CPU*) is a computer's brain. It retrieves instructions from *memory* and executes them.

7. Computers use zeros and ones because digital devices have two stable states, referred to by convention as zero and one.

8. A *bit* is a binary digit 0 or 1.

9. A *byte* is a sequence of 8 bits.

10. A kilobyte is about 1,000 bytes, a megabyte about 1 million bytes, a gigabyte about 1 billion bytes, and a terabyte about 1,000 gigabytes.

11. Memory stores data and program instructions for the CPU to execute.

12. A memory unit is an ordered sequence of bytes.

13. Memory is volatile, because information is lost when the power is turned off.

14. Programs and data are permanently stored on *storage devices* and are moved to memory when the computer actually uses them.

15. *Machine language* is a set of primitive instructions built into every computer.

16. *Assembly language* is a *low-level programming language* in which a mnemonic is used to represent each machine-language instruction.

17. *High-level languages* are English-like and easy to learn and program.

18. A program written in a high-level language is called a *source program*.

19. A *compiler* is a software program that translates the source program into a *machine-language program*.

20. The *operating system* (*OS*) is a program that manages and controls a computer's activities.

21. C++ is an extension of C. C++ added a number of features that improved the C language. Most important, it added the support of using classes for object-oriented programming.

22. C++ source files end with the .cpp extension.

23. `#include` is a preprocessor directive. All preprocessor directives begin with the symbol #.

24. The `cout` object along with the stream insertion operator (`<<`) can be used to display a string on the console.

25. Every C++ program is executed from a main function. A function is a construct that contains statements.

26. Every statement in C++ must end with a semicolon (`;`), known as the *statement terminator*.

27. In C++, a comment is preceded by two slashes (`//`) on a line, called a *line comment*, or enclosed between `/*` and `*/` on one or several lines, called a *block comment* or paragraph comment.

28. Keywords, or reserved words, have a specific meaning to the compiler and cannot be used in the program for other purposes. Examples of keywords are `using`, `namespace`, `int`, and `return`.

29. C++ source programs are case sensitive.

30. You can develop C++ applications from the command window or by using an IDE such as Visual C++ or Dev-C++.

31. Programming errors can be categorized into three types: syntax errors, runtime errors, and logic errors. Errors reported by a compiler are called syntax errors or compile errors. Runtime errors are errors that cause a program to terminate abnormally. Logic errors occur when a program does not perform the way it was intended.

QUIZ

Answer the quiz for this chapter online at www.cs.armstrong.edu/liang/cpp3e/quiz.html.

MyProgrammingLab™

PROGRAMMING EXERCISES

Note
Solutions to even-numbered exercises are provided on the Companion Website. Solutions to all exercises are provided on the Instructor Resource Website. The level of difficulty is rated easy (no star), moderate (*), hard (**), or challenging (***).

level of difficulty

Sections 1.6–1.9

1.1 (*Display two messages*) Write a program that displays `Introduction to Computers` and `Welcome to Object-Oriented Programming`.

VideoNote
Display five messages

1.2 (*Display five messages*) Write a program that displays `Welcome to C++` five times.

*1.3 (*Display a pattern*) Write a program that displays the following pattern:

```
    *                *********
   ***                *******
  *****                *****
 *******                ***
*********                *
```

1.4 (*Print a table*) Write a program that displays the following table:

p	p*5	p*10
5	25	50
10	50	100
25	125	250
50	250	500

1.5 (*Compute Expressions*) Write a program that displays the result of $\dfrac{1.2 \times 0.1 + 3.3 \times 0.3}{0.09 + 0.001}$.

1.6 (*Summation of odd numbers*) Write a program that displays the sum of the first ten odd numbers

1.7 (*Approximate π*) π can be computed using the following formula:

$$\pi = \sqrt{6 \times \left(1 + \frac{1}{4} + \frac{1}{9} + \frac{1}{16} + \frac{1}{25} + \dots \right)}$$

Write a program that displays the result of $\sqrt{6 \times \left(1 + \frac{1}{4} + \frac{1}{9} + \frac{1}{16} + \frac{1}{25}\right)}$ and

$\sqrt{6 \times \left(1 + \frac{1}{4} + \frac{1}{9} + \frac{1}{16} + \frac{1}{25} + \frac{1}{36}\right)}$. Use **1.0** instead of **1** in your program.

1.8 (*Area and perimeter of an equilateral triangle*) Write a program that displays the area and perimeter of an equilateral triangle that has its three sides as **9.2**, using the following formula:

$$area = 1.732 \times (side1)^2 / 4$$

$$perimeter = 3 \times side1$$

1.9 (*Area and perimeter of a square*) Write a program that displays the area and perimeter of a square that has a side of **5.2** using the following formula:

$$area = (side)^2 \text{ and } perimeter = 4 \times side$$

1.10 (*Average sales in grams*) Assume a vendor sells **6** kilograms of grocery in **15** minutes and **30** minutes and 30 seconds. Write a program that displays the average sale in grams per hour (Note that **1** kilogram is **1000** grams).

*1.11 (*Population projection*) The U.S. Census Bureau projects population based on the following assumptions:

- One birth every 7 seconds
- One death every 13 seconds
- One new immigrant every 45 seconds

Write a program that displays the population for each of the next five years. Assume the current population is 312,032,486 and one year has 365 days. *Hint*: In C++, if two integers perform division, the result is the quotient. The fractional part is truncated.

For example, 5 / 4 is 1 (not 1.25) and 10 / 4 is 2 (not 2.5). To get an accurate result with the fractional part, one of the values involved in the division must be a number with a decimal point. For example, 5.0 / 4 is 1.25 and 10 / 4.0 is 2.5.

1.12 (*Average sales in kilograms*) Assume a vendor sells 5553 grams of grocery in 2 hours, 9 minutes and 30 seconds. Write a program that displays the average sale in kilograms per hour (Note that 1 kilogram is 1000 grams).

ELEMENTARY PROGRAMMING

Objectives

- To write C++ programs that perform simple computations (§2.2).
- To read input from the keyboard (§2.3).
- To use identifiers to name elements such as variables and functions (§2.4).
- To use variables to store data (§2.5).
- To program using assignment statements and assignment expressions (§2.6).
- To name constants using the `const` keyword (§2.7).
- To declare variables using numeric data types (§2.8.1).
- To write integer literals, floating-point literals, and literals in scientific notation (§2.8.2).
- To perform operations using operators +, -, *, /, and % (§2.8.3).
- To perform exponent operations using the `pow(a, b)` function (§2.8.4).
- To write and evaluate expressions (§2.9).
- To obtain the current system time using `time(0)` (§2.10).
- To use augmented assignment operators (+=, -=, *=, /=, %=) (§2.11).
- To distinguish between postincrement and preincrement and between postdecrement and predecrement (§2.12).
- To convert numbers to a different type using casting (§2.13).
- To describe the software development process and apply it to develop the loan payment program (§2.14).
- To write a program that converts a large amount of money into smaller units (§2.15).
- To avoid common errors in elementary programming (§2.16).

2.1 Introduction

Key Point

This chapter focuses on learning elementary programming techniques to solve problems.

In Chapter 1, you learned how to create, compile, and run basic programs. Now you will learn how to solve problems by writing programs. Through these problems, you will learn elementary programming using primitive data types, variables, constants, operators, expressions, and input and output.

Suppose, for example, that you want to apply for a student loan. Given the loan amount, loan term, and annual interest rate, how do you write a program to compute your monthly payment and total payment? This chapter shows you how to write such programs. Along the way, you will learn the basic steps involved when analyzing a problem, designing a solution, and implementing the solution by creating a program.

2.2 Writing a Simple Program

Key Point

Writing a program involves designing a strategy for solving a problem and then using a programming language to implement that strategy.

problem

First, let's consider the simple problem of computing the area of a circle. How do we write a program for solving this?

algorithm

Writing a program involves designing algorithms and translating them into programming instructions, or code. An *algorithm* describes how a problem is solved by listing the actions that must be taken and the order of their execution. Algorithms can help the programmer plan a program before writing it in a programming language. Algorithms can

pseudocode

be described in natural languages or in *pseudocode* (natural language mixed with some programming code). The algorithm for calculating the area of a circle can be described as follows:

1. Read in the circle's radius.

2. Compute the area using the following formula:

$$area = radius \times radius \times \pi$$

3. Display the result.

Tip
It's good practice to outline your program (or its underlying problem) in the form of an algorithm before you begin coding.

When you code—that is, when you write a program—you translate an algorithm into a program. You already know that every C++ program begins its execution from the main function. Here, the outline of the main function would look like this:

```
int main()
{
  // Step 1: Read in radius

  // Step 2: Compute area

  // Step 3: Display the area
}
```

The program needs to read the radius entered by the user from the keyboard. This raises two important issues:

- Reading the radius

- Storing the radius in the program

Let's address the second issue first. In order to store the radius, the program needs to declare a symbol called a *variable*. A variable represents a value stored in the computer's memory.

Rather than using x and y as variable names, choose descriptive names: in this case, `radius` for radius, and `area` for area. To let the compiler know what `radius` and `area` are, specify their *data types*. That is the kind of the data stored in a variable, whether integer, *floating-point number,* or something else. This is known as *declaring variables.* C++ provides simple data types for representing integers, floating-point numbers (i.e., numbers with a decimal point), characters, and Boolean types. These types are known as *primitive data types* or *fundamental types.*

Declare `radius` and `area` as double-precision floating-point numbers. The program can be expanded as follows:

```cpp
int main()
{
  double radius;
  double area;

  // Step 1: Read in radius

  // Step 2: Compute area

  // Step 3: Display the area
}
```

The program declares `radius` and `area` as variables. The reserved word `double` indicates that `radius` and `area` are double-precision floating-point values stored in the computer.

The first step is to prompt the user to designate the circle's `radius`. You will learn how to prompt the user for information shortly. For now, to learn how variables work, you can assign a fixed value to `radius` in the program as you write the code; later, you will modify the program to prompt the user for this value.

The second step is to compute `area` by assigning the result of the expression `radius * radius * 3.14159` to `area`.

In the final step, the program will display the value of `area` on the console by using `cout << area`.

The complete program is shown in Listing 2.1.

LISTING 2.1 ComputeArea.cpp

```cpp
1  #include <iostream>
2  using namespace std;
3
4  int main()
5  {
6    double radius;
7    double area;
8
9    // Step 1: Read in radius
10   radius = 20;
11
12   // Step 2: Compute area
13   area = radius * radius * 3.14159;
14
15   // Step 3: Display the area
16   cout << "The area is " << area << endl;
17
18   return 0;
19 }
```

Margin notes: variable; descriptive names; data type; floating-point number; declare variables; primitive data type; include library; declare variable; assign value

```
The area is 1256.64
```

declare a variable
assign a value

Variables such as `radius` and `area` correspond to memory locations. Every variable has a name, type, size, and value. Line 6 declares that `radius` can store a `double` value. The value is not defined until you assign a value. Line 10 assigns `20` into `radius`. Similarly, line 7 declares variable `area` and line 13 assigns a value into `area`. If you comment out line 10, the program will compile and run, but the result is unpredictable, because `radius` is not assigned a proper value. In Visual C++, referencing an uninitialized variable will cause a runtime error. The table below shows the value in the memory for `area` and `radius` when the program is executed. Each row in the table shows the new values of variables after the statement in the corresponding line in the program is executed. This method of reviewing how a program works is called *tracing a program*. Tracing programs can help you understand how programs work and find program errors.

trace a program

Line#	radius	area
6	undefined value	
7		undefined value
10	20	
13		1256.64

Line 16 sends a string `"The area is "` to the console. It also sends the value in variable `area` to the console. Note that quotation marks are not placed around `area`. If they were, the string `"area"` would be sent to the console.

Check Point

2.1 Show the output of the following code:

```
double area = 5.2;
cout << "area";
cout << area;
```

2.3 Reading Input from the Keyboard

Key Point

Reading input from the keyboard enables the program to accept input from the user.

In Listing 2.1, the radius is fixed in the source code. To use a different radius, you have to modify the source code and recompile it. Obviously, this is not convenient. You can use the `cin` object to read input from the keyboard, as shown in Listing 2.2.

VideoNote
Obtain input

LISTING **2.2** ComputeAreaWithConsoleInput.cpp

```
1  #include <iostream>
2  using namespace std;
3
4  int main()
5  {
6    // Step 1: Read in radius
7    double radius;
8    cout << "Enter a radius: ";
```

```
9    cin >> radius;                                              input
10
11   // Step 2: Compute area
12   double area = radius * radius * 3.14159;
13
14   // Step 3: Display the area
15   cout << "The area is " << area << endl;
16
17   return 0;
18 }
```

```
Enter a radius: 2.5 ↵Enter
The area is 19.6349
```

```
Enter a radius: 23 ↵Enter
The area is 1661.9
```

Line 8 displays a string `"Enter a radius: "` to the console. This is known as a *prompt*   prompt
because it directs the user to input something. Your program should always tell the user what
to enter when expecting input from the keyboard.

Line 9 uses the `cin` object to read a value from the keyboard.

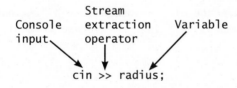

Note that `cin` (pronounced see-in) stands for *console input*. The `>>` symbol, referred to as   console input
the *stream extraction operator,* assigns an input to a variable. As shown in the sample run,   stream extraction operator
the program displays the prompting message `"Enter a radius: "`; the user then enters
number `2`, which is assigned to variable `radius`. The `cin` object causes a program to wait
until data is entered at the keyboard and the *Enter* key is pressed. C++ automatically converts
the data read from the keyboard to the data type of the variable.

 Note

The `>>` operator is the opposite of the `<<` operator. The `>>` indicates that the data flows
from `cin` to a variable. The `<<` shows that the data flows from a variable or a string to
`cout`. You can think of the stream extraction operator `>>` as an arrow that points to
the variable and the stream insertion operator `<<` as an arrow that points to the `cout`,
as shown here:

```
cin >> variable; // cin → variable;
cout << "Welcome "; // cout ← "Welcome";
```

multiple input

You can use a single statement to read multiple input. For example, the following statement reads three values into variable x1, x2, and x3:

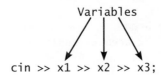

Listing 2.3 gives an example of reading multiple input from the keyboard. The example reads three numbers and displays their average.

LISTING 2.3 ComputeAverage.cpp

```cpp
 1  #include <iostream>
 2  using namespace std;
 3
 4  int main()
 5  {
 6    // Prompt the user to enter three numbers
 7    double number1, number2, number3;
 8    cout << "Enter three numbers: ";
 9    cin >> number1 >> number2 >> number3;
10
11    // Compute average
12    double average = (number1 + number2 + number3) / 3;
13
14    // Display result
15    cout << "The average of " << number1 << " " << number2
16      << " " << number3 << " is " << average << endl;
17
18    return 0;
19  }
```

reading three numbers

enter input in one line

```
Enter three numbers: 1 2 3 ⏎Enter
The average of 1 2 3 is 2
```

enter input in multiple lines

```
Enter three numbers: 10.5 ⏎Enter
11 ⏎Enter
11.5 ⏎Enter
The average of 10.5 11 11.5 is 11
```

Line 8 prompts the user to enter three numbers. The numbers are read in line 9. You may enter three numbers separated by spaces, then press the *Enter* key, or enter each number followed by the *Enter* key, as shown in the sample run of this program.

> **Note**
> Most of the programs in the early chapters of this book perform three steps: input, process, and output, called *IPO*. Input is receiving input from the user; process is producing results using the input; and output is displaying the results.

IPO

2.2 How do you write the statements to let the user enter an integer and a double value from the keyboard?

2.3 What is the printout if you entered **2 2.5** when executing the following code?

```
double width;
double height;
cin >> width >> height;
cout << width * height;
```

2.4 Identifiers

Identifiers are the names that identify elements such as variables and functions in a program.

As you see in Listing 2.3, **main**, **number1**, **number2**, **number3**, and so on are the names of things that appear in the program. In programming terminology, such names are called *identifiers*. All identifiers must obey the following rules:

identifier

identifier naming rules

- An identifier is a sequence of characters comprising letters, digits, and underscores (_).

- An identifier must start with a letter or an underscore; it cannot start with a digit.

- An identifier cannot be a reserved word. (See Appendix A, "C++ Keywords," for a list of reserved words.)

- An identifier can be of any length, but your C++ compiler may impose restriction. Use identifiers of 31 characters or fewer to ensure portability.

For example, **area** and **radius** are legal identifiers, whereas **2A** and **d+4** are illegal identifiers because they do not follow the rules. The compiler detects illegal identifiers and reports syntax errors.

> **Note**
> Since C++ is case-sensitive, **area**, **Area**, and **AREA** are all different identifiers.

case-sensitive

> **Tip**
> Identifiers are used to name variables, functions, and other things in a program. Descriptive identifiers make programs easy to read. Avoid using abbreviations for identifiers—using complete words is more descriptive. For example, **numberOfStudents** is better than **numStuds**, **numOfStuds**, or **numOfStudents**. We use descriptive names for complete programs in the text. However, for brevity occasionally we use variables names such as **i**, **j**, **k**, **x**, and **y** in the code snippets. These names also provide a generic tone to the code snippets.

descriptive names

2.4 Which of the following identifiers are valid? Which are C++ keywords?

```
miles, Test, a++, --a, 4#R, $4, #44, apps
main, double, int, x, y, radius
```

2.5 Variables

Variables are used to represent values that may be changed in the program.

As you see from the programs in the preceding sections, variables are used to store values to be used later in a program. They are called variables because their values can be changed.

why called variables?

In the program in Listing 2.2, `radius` and `area` are variables of the double-precision, floating-point type. You can assign any numerical value to `radius` and `area`, and the values of `radius` and `area` can be reassigned. For example, in the following code, `radius` is initially `1.0` (line 2) and then changed to `2.0` (line 7), and area is set to `3.14159` (line 3) and then reset to `12.56636` (line 8).

```
1  // Compute the first area
2  radius = 1.0;                                    radius:  1.0
3  area = radius * radius * 3.14159;                  area:  3.14159
4  cout << "The area is " << area << " for radius " << radius;
5
6  // Compute the second area
7  radius = 2.0;                                    radius:  2.0
8  area = radius * radius * 3.14159;                  area:  12.56636
9  cout << "The area is " << area << " for radius " << radius;
```

Variables are used to represent data of a certain type. To use a variable, you declare it by telling the compiler its name as well as the type of data it can store. The *variable declaration* tells the compiler to allocate appropriate memory space for the variable based on its data type. The syntax for declaring a variable is

```
datatype variableName;
```

declare variable

Here are some examples of variable declarations:

```
int count;        // Declare count to be an integer variable
double radius;     // Declare radius to be a double variable
double interestRate; // Declare interestRate to be a double variable
```

int type
long type

These examples use the data types `int` and `double`. Later you will be introduced to additional data types, such as `short`, `long`, `float`, `char`, and `bool`.

If variables are of the same type, they can be declared together, as follows:

```
datatype variable1, variable2,..., variablen;
```

The variables are separated by commas. For example,

```
int i, j, k; // Declare i, j, and k as int variables
```

 Note

declare vs. define

We say "*declare* a variable," but not "*define* a variable." We are making a subtle distinction here. A definition defines what the defined item is, but a declaration usually involves allocating memory to store data for the declared item.

 Note

variable naming convention

By convention, variable names are in lowercase. If a name consists of several words, concatenate all of them and capitalize the first letter of each word except the first. Examples of variables are `radius` and `interestRate`.

initialize variables

Variables often have initial values. You can declare a variable and initialize it in one step. Consider, for instance, the following code:

```
int count = 1;
```

This is equivalent to the next two statements:

```
int count;
count = 1;
```

You can also use shorthand to declare and initialize variables of the same type together. For example,

```
int i = 1, j = 2;
```

Note

C++ allows an alternative syntax for declaring and initializing variables, as shown in the following example:

```
int i(1), j(2);
```

which is equivalent to

```
int i = 1, j = 2;
```

Tip

A variable must be declared before it can be assigned a value. A variable declared in a function must be assigned a value. Otherwise, the variable is called *uninitialized* and its value is unpredictable. Whenever possible, declare a variable and assign its initial value in one step. This will make the program easy to read and will avoid programming errors.

uninitialized variable

Every variable has a scope. The *scope of a variable* is the part of the program where the variable can be referenced. The rules that define the scope of a variable will be introduced gradually later in the book. For now, it's sufficient to know that a variable must be declared and initialized before it can be used.

scope of a variable

2.5   Identify and fix the errors in the following code:

Check
Point

```
1   #include<iostream>
2   using namespace std;
3
4   int Main()
5   {
6     int i = k + 1;
7     cout << I << endl;
8
9     int i = 1;
10    cout << i << endl;
11
12    return 0;
13  }
```

2.6 Assignment Statements and Assignment Expressions

An assignment statement designates a value for a variable. An assignment statement can be used as an expression in C++.

Key
Point

assignment statement
assignment operator

After a variable is declared, you can assign a value to it by using an *assignment statement*. In C++, the equal sign (=) is used as the *assignment operator*. The syntax for assignment statements is as follows:

```
variable = expression;
```

expression

An *expression* represents a computation involving values, variables, and operators that, taking them together, evaluates to a value. For example, consider the following code:

```
int y = 1;                    // Assign 1 to variable y
double radius = 1.0;          // Assign 1.0 to variable radius
int x = 5 * (3 / 2);          // Assign the value of the expression to x
x = y + 1;                    // Assign the addition of y and 1 to x
area = radius * radius * 3.14159; // Compute area
```

You can use a variable in an expression. A variable can also be used in both sides of the = operator. For example,

```
x = x + 1;
```

In this assignment statement, the result of x + 1 is assigned to x. If x is 1 before the statement is executed, then it becomes 2 after the statement is executed.

To assign a value to a variable, you must place the variable name to the left of the assignment operator. Thus, the following statement is wrong:

```
1 = x; // Wrong
```

Note

In mathematics, x = 2 * x + 1 denotes an equation. However, in C++, x = 2 * x + 1 is an assignment statement that evaluates the expression 2 * x + 1 and assigns the result to x.

assignment expression

In C++, an assignment statement is essentially an expression that evaluates to the value to be assigned to the variable on the left side of the assignment operator. For this reason, an assignment statement is also known as an *assignment expression*. For example, the following statement is correct:

```
cout << x = 1;
```

which is equivalent to

```
x = 1;
cout << x;
```

If a value is assigned to multiple variables, you can use this syntax:

```
i = j = k = 1;
```

which is equivalent to

```
k = 1;
j = k;
i = j;
```

2.6 Identify and fix the errors in the following code:

```
1  #include <iostream>
2  using namespace std;
```

```
3
4  int main()
5  {
6    int i = j = k = 1;
7
8    return 0;
9  }
```

2.7 Named Constants

A named constant is an identifier that represents a permanent value.

Key Point

The value of a variable may change during the execution of a program, but a *named constant,* or simply *constant,* represents permanent data that never changes. In our ComputeArea program, π is a constant. If you use it frequently, you don't want to keep typing 3.14159; instead, you can declare a constant for π. Here is the syntax for declaring a constant:

constant

```
const datatype CONSTANTNAME = value;
```

A constant must be declared and initialized in the same statement. The word const is a C++ keyword for declaring a constant. For example, you may declare π as a constant and rewrite Listing 2.2 as shown in Listing 2.4.

const keyword

LISTING 2.4 ComputeAreaWithConstant.cpp

```
1  #include <iostream>
2  using namespace std;
3
4  int main()
5  {
6    const double PI = 3.14159;
7
8    // Step 1: Read in radius
9    double radius;
10   cout << "Enter a radius: ";
11   cin >> radius;
12
13   // Step 2: Compute area
14   double area = radius * radius * PI;
15
16   // Step 3: Display the area
17   cout << "The area is ";
18   cout << area << endl;
19
20   return 0;
21 }
```

constant PI

Caution
By convention, constants are named in uppercase: PI, not pi or Pi.

constant naming convention

Note
There are three benefits of using constants: (1) you don't have to repeatedly type the same value; (2) if you have to change the constant value (e.g., from 3.14 to 3.14159 for PI), you need change it only in a single location in the source code; (3) descriptive constant names make the program easy to read.

benefits of constants

2.7 What are the benefits of using named constants? Declare an `int` constant `SIZE` with value `20`.

2.8 Translate the following algorithm into C++ code:

Step 1: Declare a `double` variable named `miles` with initial value `100`.

Step 2: Declare a `double` constant named `KILOMETERS_PER_MILE` with value `1.609`.

Step 3: Declare a `double` variable named `kilometers`, multiply `miles` and `KILOMETERS_PER_MILE`, and assign the result to `kilometers`.

Step 4: Display `kilometers` to the console.

What is `kilometers` after Step 4?

2.8 Numeric Data Types and Operations

C++ has nine numeric types for integers and floating-point numbers with operators $+$, $-$, $*$, $/$, and $\%$.

2.8.1 Numeric Types

Every data type has a range of values. The compiler allocates memory space for each variable or constant according to its data type. C++ provides primitive data types for numeric values, characters, and Boolean values. This section introduces numeric data types and operations.

Table 2.1 lists the numeric data types with their typical ranges and storage sizes.

TABLE 2.1 Numeric Data Types

Name	Synonymy	Range	Storage Size
short	short int	-2^{15} to $2^{15}-1$ ($-32,768$ to $32,767$)	16-bit signed
unsigned short	unsigned short int	0 to $2^{16}-1$ (65535)	16-bit unsigned
int signed		-2^{31} to $2^{31}-1$ (-2147483648 to 2147483647)	32-bit
unsigned	unsigned int	0 to $2^{32}-1$ (4294967295)	32-bit unsigned
long	long int	-2^{31} (-2147483648) to $2^{31}-1$ (2147483647)	32-bit signed
unsigned long	unsigned long int	0 to $2^{32}-1$ (4294967295)	32-bit unsigned
float		Negative range: $-3.4028235E+38$ to $-1.4E-45$ Positive range: $1.4E-45$ to $3.4028235E+38$	32-bit IEEE 754
double		Negative range: $-1.7976931348623157E+308$ to $-4.9E-324$ Positive range: $4.9E-324$ to $1.7976931348623157E+308$	64-bit IEEE 754
long double		Negative range: $-1.18E+4932$ to $-3.37E-4932$ Positive range: $3.37E-4932$ to $1.18E+4932$ Significant decimal digits: 19	80-bit

C++ uses three types for integers: `short`, `int`, and `long`. Each integer type comes in two flavors: *signed* and *unsigned.* Half of the numbers represented by a signed `int` are negative and the other half are non-negative. All the numbers represented by an unsigned `int` are non-negative. Because you have the same storage size for both, the largest number you can store in an unsigned `int` is twice as big as the largest positive number you can store in a signed `int`. If you know the value stored in a variable is always nonnegative, declare it as `unsigned`.

signed versus unsigned

Note

`short int` is synonymous with `short`. `unsigned short int` is synonymous with `unsigned short`. `unsigned` is synonymous with `unsigned int`. `long int` is synonymous with `long`. `unsigned long int` is synonymous with `unsigned long`. For example,

synonymous types

```
short int i = 2;
```

is the same as

```
short i = 2;
```

C++ uses three types for floating-point numbers: `float`, `double`, and `long double`. The `double` type is usually twice as big as `float`. So, the `double` is known as double precision, while `float` is single precision. The `long double` is even bigger than `double`. For most applications, using the `double` type is desirable.

floating-point types

For convenience, C++ defines constants `INT_MIN`, `INT_MAX`, `LONG_MIN`, `LONG_MAX`, `FLT_MIN`, `FLT_MAX`, `DBL_MIN`, and `DBL_MAX` in the `<limits>` header file. These constants are useful in programming. Run the following code in Listing 2.5 and see what constant values are defined by your compiler:

LISTING 2.5 `LimitsDemo.cpp`

```
1   #include <iostream>
2   #include <limits>
3   using namespace std;
4
5   int main()
6   {
7     cout << "INT_MIN is " << INT_MIN << endl;
8     cout << "INT_MAX is " << INT_MAX << endl;
9     cout << "LONG_MIN is " << LONG_MIN << endl;
10    cout << "LONG_MAX is " << LONG_MAX << endl;
11    cout << "FLT_MIN is " << FLT_MIN << endl;
12    cout << "FLT_MIN is " << FLT_MAX << endl;
13    cout << "DBL_MIN is " << DBL_MIN << endl;
14    cout << "DBL_MIN is " << DBL_MAX << endl;
15
16    return 0;
17  }
```

`limits` header

```
INT_MIN is -2147483648
INT_MAX is 2147483647
LONG_MIN is -2147483648
LONG_MAX is 2147483647
FLT_MIN is 1.17549e-038
FLT_MAX is 3.40282e+038
DBL_MIN is 2.22507e-308
DBL_MAX is 1.79769e+308
```

Note these constants may not be defined in some old compilers.

The size of the data types may vary depending on the compiler and computer you are using. Typically, **int** and **long** have the same size. On some systems, **long** requires 8 bytes.

You can use the **sizeof** function to find the size of a type or a variable on your machine. Listing 2.6 gives an example that displays the size of **int**, **long**, and **double**, and variables **age** and **area** on your machine.

LISTING 2.6 SizeDemo.cpp

```cpp
 1  #include <iostream>
 2  using namespace std;
 3
 4  int main()
 5  {
 6    cout << "The size of int: " << sizeof(int) << " bytes" << endl;
 7    cout << "The size of long: " << sizeof(long) << " bytes" << endl;
 8    cout << "The size of double: " << sizeof(double)
 9      << " bytes" << endl;
10
11    double area = 5.4;
12    cout << "The size of variable area: " << sizeof(area)
13      << " bytes" << endl;
14
15    int age = 31;
16    cout << "The size of variable age: " << sizeof(age)
17      << " bytes" << endl;
18
19    return 0;
20  }
```

```
The size of int: 4 bytes
The size of long: 4 bytes
The size of double: 8 bytes
The size of variable area: 8 bytes
The size of variable age: 4 bytes
```

Invoking **sizeof(int)**, **sizeof(long)**, and **sizeof(double)** (lines 6–8) return the number of bytes allocated for the **int**, **long**, and **double** types, respectively. Invoking **sizeof(area)** and **sizeof(age)** return the number of bytes allocated for the variables **area** and **age**, respectively.

2.8.2 Numeric Literals

A *literal* is a constant value that appears directly in a program. In the following statements, for example, **34** and **0.305** are literals:

```cpp
int i = 34;
double footToMeters = 0.305;
```

By default, an integer literal is a decimal integer number. To denote an octal integer literal, use a leading *0* (zero), and to denote a hexadecimal integer literal, use a leading *0x* or *0X* (zero x). For example, the following code displays the decimal value **65535** for hexadecimal number FFFF and decimal value 8 for octal number 10.

```
cout << 0xFFFF << " " << 010;
```

Hexadecimal numbers, binary numbers, and octal numbers are introduced in Appendix D, "Number Systems."

Floating-point literals can be written in scientific notation in the form of a $\times 10^b$. For example, the scientific notation for 123.456 is 1.23456×10^2 and for 0.0123456 it's 1.23456×10^{-2}. A special syntax is used to write scientific notation numbers. For example, 1.23456×10^2 is written as `1.23456E2` or `1.23456E+2` and 1.23456×10^{-2} as `1.23456E-2`. `E` (or `e`) represents an exponent and can be in either lowercase or uppercase.

floating-point literals
scientific notation

Note

The `float` and `double` types are used to represent numbers with a decimal point. Why are they called *floating-point numbers?* These numbers are stored in scientific notation internally. When a number such as `50.534` is converted into scientific notation, such as `5.0534E+1`, its decimal point is moved (i.e., floated) to a new position.

`float` type
`double` type
why called floating-point?

2.8.3 Numeric Operators

The *operators* for numeric data types include the standard arithmetic operators: addition (+), subtraction (−), multiplication (*), division (/), and remainder (%), as shown in Table 2.2. The *operands* are the values operated by an operator.

operator

operands

TABLE 2.2 Numeric Operators

Operator	Name	Example	Result
+	Addition	34 + 1	35
−	Subtraction	34.0 − 0.1	33.9
*	Multiplication	300 * 30	9000
/	Division	1.0 / 2.0	0.5
%	Modulus	20 % 3	2

When both operands of a division are integers, the result of the division is the quotient and the fractional part is truncated. For example, `5 / 2` yields `2`, not `2.5`, and `-5 / 2` yields `-2`, not `-2.5`. To perform regular mathematical division, one of the operands must be a floating-point number. For example, `5.0 / 2` yields `2.5`.

integer division

The `%` operator, known as *modulo* or *remainder* operator, works only with integer operands and yields the remainder after division. The left-hand operand is the dividend and the right-hand operand the divisor. Therefore, `7 % 3` yields `1`, `3 % 7` yields `3`, `12 % 4` yields `0`, `26 % 8` yields `2`, and `20 % 13` yields `7`.

modulo
remainder

The `%` operator is often used with positive integers but also can be used with negative integers. The behavior of the `%` operator involving negative integers is compiler-dependent. In C++, the `%` operator is for integers only.

Modulus is very useful in programming. For example, an even number `% 2` is always `0` and an odd number `% 2` is always `1`. So you can use this property to determine whether a number is even or odd. If today is Saturday, it will be Saturday again in 7 days. Suppose you and your

modulus

friends are going to meet in 10 days. What day is in 10 days? You can find that day is Tuesday using the following expression:

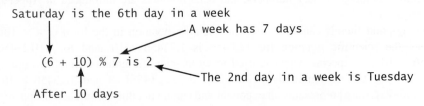

Saturday is the 6th day in a week

A week has 7 days

(6 + 10) % 7 is 2

After 10 days

The 2nd day in a week is Tuesday

The program in Listing 2.7 obtains minutes and remaining seconds from an amount of time in seconds. For example, **500** seconds contains **8** minutes and **20** seconds.

LISTING **2.7** DisplayTime.cpp

```cpp
1  #include <iostream>
2  using namespace std;
3
4  int main()
5  {
6    // Prompt the user for input
7    int seconds;
8    cout << "Enter an integer for seconds: ";
9    cin >> seconds;
10   int minutes = seconds / 60;
11   int remainingSeconds = seconds % 60;
12   cout << seconds << " seconds is " << minutes <<
13     " minutes and " << remainingSeconds << " seconds " << endl;
14
15   return 0;
16 }
```

```
Enter an integer for seconds: 500 ↵Enter
500 seconds is 8 minutes and 20 seconds
```

Line#	seconds	minutes	remainingSeconds
9	500		
10		8	
11			20

Line 9 reads an integer for seconds. Line 10 obtains the minutes using **seconds / 60**. Line 11 (**seconds % 60**) obtains the remaining seconds after taking away minutes.

unary operator
binary operator

The + and − operators can be both unary and binary. A *unary operator* has only one operand; a *binary operator* has two. For example, the − operator in −**5** is a unary operator to negate number **5**, whereas the − operator in **4** − **5** is a binary operator for subtracting **5** from **4**.

2.8.4 Exponent Operations

pow(a, b) function

The **pow(a, b)** function can be used to compute a^b. **pow** is a function defined in the **cmath** library. The function is invoked using the syntax **pow(a, b)** (i.e., **pow(2.0, 3)**) that returns the result of a^b (2^3). Here, **a** and **b** are parameters for the **pow** function and numbers **2.0** and **3** are actual values used to invoke the function. For example,

```cpp
cout << pow(2.0, 3) << endl; // Display 8.0
cout << pow(4.0, 0.5) << endl; // Display 2.0
```

```
cout << pow(2.5, 2) << endl; // Display 6.25
cout << pow(2.5, -2) << endl; // Display 0.16
```

Note that some C++ compilers require that either **a** or **b** in **pow(a, b)** be a decimal value. Here we use **2.0** rather than **2**.

More details on functions will be introduced in Chapter 6. For now, it's sufficient to know how to invoke the **pow** function to perform the exponent operation.

2.9 Find the largest and smallest **short**, **int**, **long**, **float**, and **double** on your machine. Which of these data types requires the least amount of memory?

2.10 Which of the following are correct literals for floating-point numbers?

12.3, 12.3e+2, 23.4e-2, -334.4, 20.5, 39, 40

2.11 Which of the following are the same as 52.534?

5.2534e+1, 0.52534e+2, 525.34e-1, 5.2534e+0

2.12 Show the result of the following remainders:

```
56 % 6
78 % 4
34 % 5
34 % 15
5 % 1
1 % 5
```

2.13 If today is Tuesday, what day will it be in 100 days?

2.14 What is the result of 25 / 4? How would you rewrite the expression if you wished the result to be a floating-point number?

2.15 Show the result of the following code:

```
cout << 2 * (5 / 2 + 5 / 2) << endl;
cout << 2 * 5 / 2 + 2 * 5 / 2 << endl;
cout << 2 * (5 / 2) << endl;
cout << 2 * 5 / 2 << endl;
```

2.16 Are the following statements correct? If so, show the output.

```
cout << "25 / 4 is " << 25 / 4 << endl;
cout << "25 / 4.0 is " << 25 / 4.0 << endl;
cout << "3 * 2 / 4 is " << 3 * 2 / 4 << endl;
cout << "3.0 * 2 / 4 is " << 3.0 * 2 / 4 << endl;
```

2.17 Write a statement to display the result of $2^{3.5}$.

2.18 Suppose **m** and **r** are integers. Write a C++ expression for mr^2 to obtain a floating-point result.

2.9 Evaluating Expressions and Operator Precedence

C++ expressions are evaluated in the same way as arithmetic expressions.

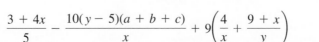

Writing numeric expressions in C++ involves a straightforward translation of an arithmetic expression using C++ operators. For example, the arithmetic expression

$$\frac{3 + 4x}{5} - \frac{10(y - 5)(a + b + c)}{x} + 9\left(\frac{4}{x} + \frac{9 + x}{y}\right)$$

can be translated into a C++ expression as

```
(3 + 4 * x) / 5 - 10 * (y - 5) * (a + b + c) / x +
9 * (4 / x + (9 + x) / y)
```

evaluate an expression

Though C++ has its own way to evaluate an expression behind the scene, the result of a C++ expression and its corresponding arithmetic expression are the same. Therefore, you can safely apply the arithmetic rule for evaluating a C++ expression. Operators contained within pairs of parentheses are evaluated first. Parentheses can be nested, in which case the expression in the inner parentheses is evaluated first. When more than one operator is used

operator precedence rule

in an expression, the following operator precedence rule is used to determine the order of evaluation.

■ Multiplication, division, and remainder operators are applied next. If an expression contains several multiplication, division, and remainder operators, they are applied from left to right.

■ Addition and subtraction operators are applied last. If an expression contains several addition and subtraction operators, they are applied from left to right.

Here is an example of how an expression is evaluated:

```
3 + 4 * 4 + 5 * (4 + 3) - 1
                                        (1) inside parentheses first
3 + 4 * 4 + 5 * 7 - 1
                                        (2) multiplication
3 + 16 + 5 * 7 - 1
                                        (3) multiplication
3 + 16 + 35 - 1
                                        (4) addition
19 + 35 - 1
                                        (5) addition
54 - 1
                                        (6) subtraction
53
```

Listing 2.8 gives a program that converts a Fahrenheit degree to Celsius using the formula $celsius = (\frac{5}{9})(fahrenheit - 32)$.

LISTING 2.8   FahrenheitToCelsius.cpp

```cpp
1  #include <iostream>
2  using namespace std;
3
4  int main()
5  {
6    // Enter a degree in Fahrenheit
7    double fahrenheit;
8    cout << "Enter a degree in Fahrenheit: ";
9    cin >> fahrenheit;
10
11   // Obtain a celsius degree
12   double celsius = (5.0 / 9) * (fahrenheit - 32);
13
```

input fahrenheit

compute celsius

```
14     // Display result
15     cout << "Fahrenheit " << fahrenheit << " is " <<
16         celsius << " in Celsius" << endl;
17
18     return 0;
19 }
```

display output

```
Enter a degree in Fahrenheit: 100  ⏎Enter
Fahrenheit 100 is 37.7778 in Celsius
```

Line#	fahrenheit	celsius
7	undefined	
9	100	
12		37.7778

Be careful when applying division. Division of two integers yields an integer in C++. $\frac{5}{9}$ is translated to `5.0 / 9` instead of `5 / 9` in line 12, because `5 / 9` yields `0` in C++.

integer versus decimal division

2.19 How would you write the following arithmetic expression in C++?

Check Point

a. $\dfrac{4}{3(r + 34)} - 9(a + bc) + \dfrac{3 + d(2 + a)}{a + bd}$

b. $5.5 \times (r + 2.5)^{2.5+t}$

2.10 Case Study: Displaying the Current Time

You can invoke the `time(0)` *function to return the current time.*

Key Point

The problem is to develop a program that displays the current time in GMT (Greenwich Mean Time) in the format hour:minute:second, such as 13:19:8.

The `time(0)` function, in the `ctime` header file, returns the current time in seconds elapsed since the time 00:00:00 on January 1, 1970 GMT, as shown in Figure 2.1. This time is known as the *UNIX epoch*. The epoch is the point when time starts. 1970 was the year when the UNIX operating system was formally introduced.

time(0) function

UNIX epoch

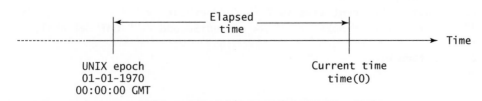

FIGURE 2.1 Invoking `time(0)` returns the number of seconds since the Unix epoch.

You can use this function to obtain the current time, and then compute the current second, minute, and hour as follows:

1. Obtain the total seconds since midnight, January 1, 1970, in **totalSeconds** by invoking **time(0)** (e.g., **1203183086** seconds).

2. Compute the current second from **totalSeconds % 60** (e.g., 1203183086 seconds % 60 = 26, which is the current second).

3. Obtain the total minutes **totalMinutes** by dividing **totalSeconds** by 60 (e.g., **1203183086** seconds / 60 = 20053051 minutes).

4. Compute the current minute from **totalMinutes % 60** (e.g., 20053051 minutes % 60 = 31, which is the current minute).

5. Obtain the total hours **totalHours** by dividing **totalMinutes** by 60 (e.g., 20053051 minutes / 60 = 334217 hours).

6. Compute the current hour from **totalHours % 24** (e.g., 334217 hours % 24 = 17, which is the current hour).

Listing 2.9 shows the complete program followed by a sample run.

VideoNote
Display current time

include ctime

LISTING 2.9 ShowCurrentTime.cpp

```
1   #include <iostream>
2   #include <ctime>
3   using namespace std;
4
5   int main()
6   {
7     // Obtain the total seconds since the midnight, Jan 1, 1970
8     int totalSeconds = time(0);
9
10    // Compute the current second in the minute in the hour
11    int currentSecond = totalSeconds % 60;
12
13    // Obtain the total minutes
14    int totalMinutes = totalSeconds / 60;
15
16    // Compute the current minute in the hour
17    int currentMinute = totalMinutes % 60;
18
19    // Obtain the total hours
20    int totalHours = totalMinutes / 60;
21
22    // Compute the current hour
23    int currentHour = totalHours % 24;
24
25    // Display results
26    cout << "Current time is " << currentHour << ":"
27      << currentMinute << ":" << currentSecond << " GMT" << endl;
28
29    return 0;
30  }
```

totalSeconds

currentSeconds

currentMinutes

currentMinute

totalHours

currentHour

display output

```
Current time is 17:31:26 GMT
```

Line# Variables	8	11	14	17	20	23
totalSeconds	1203183086					
currentSecond		26				
totalMinutes			20053051			
currentMinute				31		
totalHours					334217	
currentHour						17

When `time(0)` (line 8) is invoked, it returns the difference, measured in seconds, between the current GMT and midnight, January 1, 1970 GMT.

2.20 How do you obtain the current second, minute, and hour?

2.11 Augmented Assignment Operators

The operators +, -, *, /, and % can be combined with the assignment operator to form augmented operators.

Often, the current value of a variable is used, modified, and then reassigned back to the same variable. For example, the following statement increases the variable `count` by 1:

```
count = count + 1;
```

C++ allows you to combine assignment and addition operators using an augmented assignment operator. For example, the preceding statement can be written as follows:

```
count += 8;
```

The += is called the *addition assignment operator*. Other augmented operators are shown in Table 2.3.

addition assignment operator

TABLE 2.3 Augmented Assignment Operators

Operator	Name	Example	Equivalent
+=	Addition assignment	i += 8	i = i + 8
-=	Subtraction assignment	i -= 8	i = i - 8
*=	Multiplication assignment	i *= 8	i = i * 8
/=	Division assignment	i /= 8	i = i / 8
%=	Modulus assignment	i %= 8	i = i % 8

The augmented assignment operator is performed last after the other operators in the expression are evaluated. For example,

```
x /= 4 + 5.5 * 1.5;
```

is same as

```
x = x / (4 + 5.5 * 1.5);
```

Caution

There are no spaces in the augmented assignment operators. For example, + = should be +=.

Note

Like the assignment operator (=), the operators (+=, -=, *=, /=, %=) can be used to form an assignment statement as well as an expression. For example, in the following code, x += 2 is a statement in the first line and an expression in the second line.

```
x += 2; // Statement
cout << (x += 2); // Expression
```

Check Point

2.21 Show the printout of the following code:

```
int a = 6;
a -= a + 1;
cout << a << endl;
a *= 6;
cout << a << endl;
a /= 2;
cout << a << endl;
```

2.12 Increment and Decrement Operators

Key Point

The increment (++) and decrement (--) operators are for incrementing and decrementing a variable by 1.

increment operator (++)
decrement operator (--)

The ++ and -- are two shorthand operators for incrementing and decrementing a variable by 1. These are handy, because that's often how much the value needs to be changed in many programming tasks. For example, the following code increments i by 1 and decrements j by 1.

```
int i = 3, j = 3;
i++; // i becomes 4
j--; // j becomes 2
```

postincrement
postdecrement

i++ is pronounced as i plus plus and i-- as i minus minus. These operators are known as *postfix increment (postincrement)* and *postfix decrement (postdecrement)*, because the operators ++ and -- are placed after the variable. These operators can also be placed before the variable. For example,

```
int i = 3, j = 3;
++i; // i becomes 4
--j; // j becomes 2
```

preincrement
predecrement

++i increments i by 1 and --j decrements j by 1. These operators are known as *prefix increment (preincrement)* and *prefix decrement (predecrement)*.

As you see, the effect of i++ and ++i or i-- and --i are the same in the preceding examples. However, their effects are different when they are used in expressions. Table 2.4 describes their differences and gives examples.

TABLE 2.4 Increment and Decrement Operators

Operator	Name	Description	Example (assume i = 1)
++var	preincrement	Increment var by 1 and use the new var value in the statement	`int j = ++i;` `// j is 2, i is 2`
var++	postincrement	Increment var by 1, but use the original var value in the statement	`int j = i++;` `// j is 1, i is 2`
--var	predecrement	Decrement var by 1 and use the new var value in the statement	`int j = --i;` `// j is 0, i is 0`
var--	postdecrement	Decrement var by 1 and use the original var value in the statement	`int j = i--;` `// j is 1, i is 0`

Here are additional examples to illustrate the differences between the prefix form of ++ (or --) and the postfix form of ++ (or --). Consider the following code:

```
int i = 10;
int newNum = 10 * i++;          Same effect as        int newNum = 10 * i;
cout << "i is " << i                                  i = i + 1;
  << ", newNum is " << newNum;
```

```
i is 11, newNum is 100
```

In this case, i is incremented by 1, then the *old* value of i is used in the multiplication. So newNum becomes 100. If i++ is replaced by ++i as follows,

```
int i = 10;
int newNum = 10 * (++i);        Same effect as        i = i + 1;
cout << "i is " << i                                  int newNum = 10 * i;
  << ", newNum is " << newNum;
```

```
i is 11, newNum is 110
```

i is incremented by 1, and the new value of i is used in the multiplication. Thus newNum becomes 110.

Here is another example:

```
double x = 1.1;
double y = 5.4;
double z = x-- + (++y);
```

After all three lines are executed, x becomes 0.1, y becomes 6.4, and z becomes 7.5.

Caution

For most binary operators, C++ does not specify the operand evaluation order. Normally, you assume that the left operand is evaluated before the right operand. This is not guaranteed in C++. For example, suppose i is 1; then the expression

```
++i + i
```

evaluates to 4 (2 + 2) if the left operand (++i) is evaluated first and evaluates to 3 (2 + 1) if the right operand (i) is evaluated first.

operand evaluation order

Since C++ cannot guarantee the operand evaluation order, you should not write code that depends on the operand evaluation order.

2.22 Which of the following statements are true?

a. Any expression can be used as a statement in C++.

b. The expression x++ can be used as a statement.

c. The statement x = x + 5 is also an expression.

d. The statement x = y = x = 0 is illegal.

2.23 Show the printout of the following code:

```
int a = 6;
int b = a++;
cout << a << endl;
cout << b << endl;
a = 6;
b = ++a;
cout << a << endl;
cout << b << endl;
```

2.24 Show the printout of the following code:

```
int a = 6;
int b = a--;
cout << a << endl;
cout << b << endl;
a = 6;
b = --a;
cout << a << endl;
cout << b << endl;
```

2.13 Numeric Type Conversions

Floating-point numbers can be converted into integers using explicit casting.

Can you assign an integer value to a floating-point variable? Yes. Can you assign a floating-point value to an integer variable? Yes. When assigning a floating-point value to an integer variable, the fractional part of the floating-point value is truncated (not rounded). For example:

```
int i = 34.7;      // i becomes 34
double f = i;      // f is now 34
double g = 34.3;   // g becomes 34.3
int j = g;         // j is now 34
```

Can you perform binary operations with two operands of different types? Yes. If an integer and a floating-point number are involved in a binary operation, C++ automatically converts the integer to a floating-point value. So, 3 * 4.5 is the same as 3.0 * 4.5.

C++ also allows you to convert a value from one type to another explicitly by using a *casting operator*. The syntax is

casting operator

```
static_cast<type>(value)
```

where `value` is a variable, a literal, or an expression and `type` is the type you wish to convert the `value` to.

For example, the following statement

```
cout << static_cast<int>(1.7);
```

displays 1. When a `double` value is cast into an `int` value, the fractional part is truncated.

The following statement

```
cout << static_cast<double>(1) / 2;
```

displays 0.5, because 1 is cast to 1.0 first, then 1.0 is divided by 2. However, the statement

```
cout << 1 / 2;
```

displays 0, because 1 and 2 are both integers and the resulting value should also be an integer.

Note

Static casting can also be done using the `(type)` syntax—that is, giving the target type in parentheses, followed by a variable, a literal, or an expression. This is called the *C-style cast*. For example,

C-style cast

```
int i = (int)5.4;
```

This is the same as

```
int i = static_cast<int>(5.4);
```

The C++ `static_cast` operator is recommended by the ISO standard. It is preferable to the C-style cast.

Casting a variable of a type with a small range to a variable of a type with a larger range is known as *widening a type*. Casting a variable of a type with a large range to a variable of a type with a smaller range is known as *narrowing a type*. Narrowing a type, such as assigning a `double` value to an `int` variable, may cause loss of precision. Lost information might lead to inaccurate results. The compiler gives a warning when you narrow a type, unless you use `static_cast` to make the conversion explicit.

widening a type
narrowing a type
loss of precision

Note

Casting does not change the variable being cast. For example, **d** is not changed after casting in the following code:

```
double d = 4.5;
int i = static_cast<int>(d); // i becomes 4, but d is unchanged
```

Listing 2.10 gives a program that displays the sales tax with two digits after the decimal point.

LISTING 2.10   SalesTax.cpp

```
1  #include <iostream>
2  using namespace std;
3
4  int main()
5  {
6    // Enter purchase amount
```

```
 7    double purchaseAmount;
 8    cout << "Enter purchase amount: ";
 9    cin >> purchaseAmount;
10
11    double tax = purchaseAmount * 0.06;
12    cout << "Sales tax is " << static_cast<int>(tax * 100) / 100.0;
13
14    return 0;
15 }
```

casting

```
Enter purchase amount: 197.55  ↵Enter
Sales tax is 11.85
```

Line#	purchaseAmount	tax	Output
7	Undefined		
9	197.55		
11		11.853	
12			Sales tax is 11.85

formatting numbers

Variable purchaseAmount stores the purchase amount entered by the user (lines 7–9). Suppose the user entered 197.55. The sales tax is 6% of the purchase, so the tax is evaluated as 11.853 (line 11). The statement in line 12 displays the tax 11.85 with two digits after the decimal point. Note that

```
tax * 100 is 1185.3
static_cast<int>(tax * 100) is 1185
static_cast<int> (tax * 100) / 100.0 is 11.85
```

So, the statement in line 12 displays the tax 11.85 with two digits after the decimal point.

Check Point

2.25 Can different types of numeric values be used together in a computation?

2.26 What does an explicit casting from a double to an int do with the fractional part of the double value? Does casting change the variable being cast?

2.27 Show the following output:

```
double f = 12.5;
int i = f;
cout << "f is " << f << endl;
cout << "i is " << i << endl;
```

2.28 If you change static_cast<int>(tax * 100) / 100.0 to static_cast<int>(tax * 100) / 100 in line 12 in Listing 2.10, what will be the output for the input purchase amount of 197.556?

2.29 Show the printout of the following code:

```
double amount = 5;
cout << amount / 2 << endl;
cout << 5 / 2 << endl;
```

2.14 Software Development Process

The software development life cycle is a multi-stage process that includes require-ments specification, analysis, design, implementation, testing, deployment, and maintenance.

Key Point

Developing a software product is an engineering process. Software products, no matter how large or how small, have the same life cycle: requirements specification, analysis, design, implementation, testing, deployment, and maintenance, as shown in Figure 2.2.

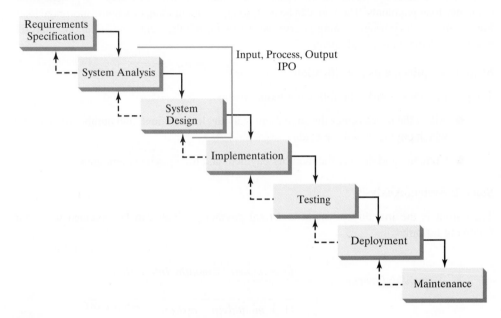

FIGURE 2.2 At any stage of the software development life cycle, it may be necessary to go back to a previous stage to correct errors or deal with other issues that might prevent the software from functioning as expected.

Requirements specification is a formal process that seeks to understand the problem that the software will address and to document in detail what the software system must do. This phase involves close interaction between users and developers. Most of the examples in this book are simple, and their requirements are clearly stated. In the real world, however, prob-lems are not always well defined. Developers need to work closely with their customers (indi-viduals or organizations that will use the software) and study the problem carefully to identify what the software must do.

System analysis seeks to analyze the data flow and to identify the system's input and out-put. Analysis helps to identify what the output is first, and then figure out what input data you need in order to produce the output.

System design is the process for obtaining the output from the input. This phase involves the use of many levels of abstraction to break down the problem into manageable components and design strategies for implementing each component. You can view each component as a subsystem that performs a specific function of the system. The essence of system analysis and design is input, process, and output (IPO).

Implementation involves translating the system design into programs. Separate programs are written for each component and then integrated to work together. This phase requires the use of a programming language such as C++. The implementation involves coding, self-testing, and debugging (that is, finding errors, called *bugs,* in the code).

requirements specification

system analysis

system design

IPO
implementation

testing

deployment

maintenance

VideoNote

Compute loan payments

Testing ensures that the code meets the requirements specification and weeds out bugs. An independent team of software engineers not involved in the design and implementation of the product usually conducts such testing.

Deployment makes the software available for use. Depending on the type of the software, it may be installed on each user's machine or installed on a server accessible on the Internet.

Maintenance is concerned with updating and improving the product. A software product must continue to perform and improve in an ever-evolving environment. This requires periodic upgrades of the product to fix newly discovered bugs and incorporate changes.

To see the software development process in action, we will now create a program that computes loan payments. The loan can be a car loan, a student loan, or a home mortgage loan. For an introductory programming course, we focus on requirements specification, analysis, design, implementation, and testing.

Stage 1: Requirements Specification

The program must satisfy the following requirements:

- Allow the user to enter the annual interest rate, loan amount, and number of years for which payments will be made

- Compute and display the monthly payment and total payment amounts

Stage 2: System Analysis

The output is the monthly payment and total payment, which can be obtained using the following formulas:

$$monthlyPayment = \frac{loanAmount \times monthlyInterestRate}{1 - \dfrac{1}{(1 + monthlyInterestRate)^{numberOfYears \times 12}}}$$

$$totalPayment = monthlyPayment \times numberOfYears \times 12$$

Therefore, the input needed for the program is the monthly interest rate, the length of the loan in years, and the loan amount.

 Note

The requirements specification says that the user must enter the annual interest rate, loan amount, and number of years for which payments will be made. During analysis, however, it's possible that you may discover that input is insufficient or that some values are unnecessary for the output. If this happens, you can modify the requirements specification.

 Note

In the real world, you will work with customers from all occupations. You may develop software for chemists, physicists, engineers, economists, and psychologists. Of course, you will not have (or need) complete knowledge of all these fields. Therefore, you don't have to know how formulas are derived, but given the annual interest rate, the loan amount, and the number of years for which payments will be made, you can compute the monthly payment in this program. You will, however, need to communicate with customers and understand how a mathematical model works for the system.

Stage 3: System Design

During system design, you identify the steps in the program.

Step 1. Prompt the user to enter the annual interest rate, the loan amount, and the number of years. (The interest rate is commonly expressed as a percentage of the principal for a period of one year. This is known as the annual interest rate.)

Step 2. The input for the annual interest rate is a number in percent format, such as 4.5%. The program needs to convert it into a decimal by dividing it by **100**. To obtain the monthly interest rate from the annual interest rate, divide it by **12**, since a year has 12 months. To obtain the monthly interest rate in decimal format, you must divide the annual interest rate in percentage by **1200**. For example, if the annual interest rate is 4.5%, then the monthly interest rate is 4.5/1200 = 0.00375.

Step 3. Compute the monthly payment using the preceding formula.

Step 4. Compute the total payment, which is the monthly payment multiplied by **12** and multiplied by the number of years.

Step 5. Display the monthly payment and total payment.

Stage 4: Implementation

Implementation is also known as *coding* (writing the code). In the formula, you have to compute $(1 + monthlyInterestRate)^{numberOfYears \times 12}$, which can be obtained using **pow(1 + monthlyInterestRate, numberOfYears * 12)**.

Listing 2.11 gives the complete program.

LISTING 2.11 ComputeLoan.cpp

```cpp
1   #include <iostream>
2   #include <cmath>                                          include cmath library
3   using namespace std;
4
5   int main()
6   {
7     // Enter yearly interest rate
8     cout << "Enter yearly interest rate, for example 8.25: ";
9     double annualInterestRate;
10    cin >> annualInterestRate;                              enter interest rate
11
12    // Obtain monthly interest rate
13    double monthlyInterestRate = annualInterestRate / 1200;
14
15    // Enter number of years
16    cout << "Enter number of years as an integer, for example 5: ";
17    int numberOfYears;
18    cin >> numberOfYears;
19
20    // Enter loan amount
21    cout << "Enter loan amount, for example 120000.95: ";
22    double loanAmount;
23    cin >> loanAmount;
24
25    // Calculate payment
26    double monthlyPayment = loanAmount * monthlyInterestRate /     monthlyPayment
27      (1 - 1 / pow(1 + monthlyInterestRate, numberOfYears * 12));
28    double totalPayment = monthlyPayment * numberOfYears * 12;      totalPayment
29
```

```
30      monthlyPayment = static_cast<int>(monthlyPayment * 100) / 100.0;
31      totalPayment = static_cast<int>(totalPayment * 100) / 100.0;
32
33      // Display results
34      cout << "The monthly payment is " << monthlyPayment << endl <<
35        "The total payment is " << totalPayment << endl;
36
37      return 0;
38  }
```

display result

```
Enter annual interest rate, for example 7.25: 3 ↵Enter
Enter number of years as an integer, for example 5: 5 ↵Enter
Enter loan amount, for example 120000.95: 1000 ↵Enter
The monthly payment is 17.96
The total payment is 1078.12
```

Line# Variables	10	13	18	23	26	28	30	31
annualInterestRate	3							
monthlyInterestRate		0.0025						
numberOfYears			5					
loanAmount				1000				
monthlyPayment					17.9687			
totalPayment						1078.12		
monthlyPayment							17.96	
totalPayment								1078.12

pow(a, b) function

To use the pow(a, b) function, you have to include the cmath library in the program (line 2) in the same way you include the iostream library (line 1).

The program prompts the user to enter annualInterestRate, numberOfYears, and loanAmount in lines 7–23. If you entered an input other than a numeric value, a runtime error would occur.

Choose the most appropriate data type for the variable. For example, numberOfYears is better declared as int (line 17), although it could be declared as long, float, or double. Note that unsigned short might be the most appropriate for numberOfYears. For simplicity, however, the examples in this book will use int for integer and double for floating-point values.

The formula for computing the monthly payment is translated into C++ code in lines 26–27. Line 28 obtains the total payment.

Casting is used in lines 30–31 to obtain a new monthlyPayment and totalPayment with two digits after the decimal points.

Stage 5: Testing

After the program is implemented, test it with some sample input data and verify whether the output is correct. Some of the problems may involve many cases, as you will see in later chapters. For these types of problems, you need to design test data that cover all cases.

Tip
The system design phase in this example identified several steps. It is a good approach to *code and test these steps incrementally* by adding them one at a time. This approach makes it much easier to pinpoint problems and debug the program.

incremental code and test

2.30 How would you write the following arithmetic expression?

 Check Point

$$\frac{-b + \sqrt{b^2 - 4ac}}{2a}$$

2.15 Case Study: Counting Monetary Units

This section presents a program that breaks a large amount of money into smaller units.

 Key Point

Suppose you want to develop a program that changes a given amount of money into smaller monetary units. The program lets the user enter an amount as a `double` value representing a total in dollars and cents, and outputs a report listing the monetary equivalent in the maximum number of dollars, quarters, dimes, nickels, and pennies, in this order, to result in the *minimum number of coins,* as shown in the sample run.

minimum number of coins

Here are the steps in developing the program:

1. Prompt the user to enter the amount as a decimal number, such as `11.56`.

2. Convert the amount (e.g., `11.56`) into cents (`1156`).

3. Divide the cents by `100` to find the number of dollars. Obtain the remaining cents using the cents remainder `100`.

4. Divide the remaining cents by `25` to find the number of quarters. Obtain the remaining cents using the remaining cents remainder `25`.

5. Divide the remaining cents by `10` to find the number of dimes. Obtain the remaining cents using the remaining cents remainder `10`.

6. Divide the remaining cents by `5` to find the number of nickels. Obtain the remaining cents using the remaining cents remainder `5`.

7. The remaining cents are the pennies.

8. Display the result.

The complete program is given in Listing 2.12.

LISTING 2.12 ComputeChange.cpp

```cpp
 1  #include <iostream>
 2  using namespace std;
 3
 4  int main()
 5  {
 6    // Receive the amount
 7    cout << "Enter an amount in double, for example 11.56: ";
 8    double amount;
 9    cin >> amount;
10
11    int remainingAmount = static_cast<int>(amount * 100);
```

```
12
dollars          13    // Find the number of one dollars
                 14    int numberOfOneDollars = remainingAmount / 100;
                 15    remainingAmount = remainingAmount % 100;
                 16
                 17    // Find the number of quarters in the remaining amount
quarters         18    int numberOfQuarters = remainingAmount / 25;
                 19    remainingAmount = remainingAmount % 25;
                 20
                 21    // Find the number of dimes in the remaining amount
dimes            22    int numberOfDimes = remainingAmount / 10;
                 23    remainingAmount = remainingAmount % 10;
                 24
                 25    // Find the number of nickels in the remaining amount
nickels          26    int numberOfNickels = remainingAmount / 5;
                 27    remainingAmount = remainingAmount % 5;
                 28
                 29    // Find the number of pennies in the remaining amount
pennies          30    int numberOfPennies = remainingAmount;
                 31
                 32    // Display results
output           33    cout << "Your amount " << amount << " consists of " << endl <<
                 34       "   " << numberOfOneDollars << " dollars" << endl <<
                 35       "   " << numberOfQuarters << " quarters" << endl <<
                 36       "   " << numberOfDimes << " dimes" << endl <<
                 37       "   " << numberOfNickels << " nickels" << endl <<
                 38       "   " << numberOfPennies << " pennies" << endl;
                 39
                 40    return 0;
                 41  }
```

```
Enter an amount in double, for example 11.56: 11.56 ↵Enter
Your amount 11.56 consists of
11 dollars
2 quarters
0 dimes
1 nickels
1 pennies
```

Variables / Line#	9	11	14	15	18	19	22	23	26	27	30
amount	11.56										
remainingAmount		1156		56		6		6		1	
numberOfOneDollars			11								
numberOfQuarters					2						
numberOfDimes							0				
numberOfNickels									1		
numberOfPennies											1

The variable amount stores the amount entered from the keyboard (lines 7–9). This variable should not be changed, because the amount has to be used at the end of the program to display the results. The program introduces the variable remainingAmount (line 11) to store the changing remainingAmount.

The variable `amount` is a `double` decimal representing dollars and cents. It is converted to an `int` variable `remainingAmount`, which represents all the cents. For instance, if `amount` is `11.56`, then the initial `remainingAmount` is `1156`. The division operator yields the integer part of the division. So `1156 / 100` is `11`. The remainder operator obtains the remainder of the division. Therefore, `1156 % 100` is `56`.

The program extracts the maximum number of dollars from the total amount and obtains the remaining amount in the variable `remainingAmount` (lines 14–15). It then extracts the maximum number of quarters from `remainingAmount` and obtains a new `remainingAmount` (lines 18–19). Continuing the same process, the program finds the maximum number of dimes, nickels, and pennies in the remaining amount.

One serious problem with this example is the possible loss of precision when casting a `double` amount to an `int remainingAmount`. This could lead to an inaccurate result. If you try to enter the amount `10.03`, then `10.03 * 100` becomes `1002.9999999999999`. You will find that the program displays `10` dollars and `2` pennies. To fix the problem, enter the amount as an integer value representing cents (see Programming Exercise 2.24).

loss of precision

2.16 Common Errors

Common elementary programming errors often involve undeclared variables, uninitialized variables, integer overflow, unintended integer division, and round-off errors.

 Key Point

Common Error 1: Undeclared/Uninitialized Variables and Unused Variables
A variable must be declared with a type and assigned a value before using it. A common error is not declaring a variable or initializing a variable. Consider the following code:

```
double interestRate = 0.05;
double interest = interestrate * 45;
```

This code is wrong, because `interestRate` is assigned a value `0.05`, but `interestrate` has not been declared and initialized. C++ is case-sensitive, so it considers `interestRate` and `interestrate` to be two different variables.

If a variable is declared, but not used in the program, it might be a potential programming error. So, you should remove the unused variable from your program. For example, in the following code, `taxRate` is never used. Therefore, it should be removed from the code.

```
double interestRate = 0.05;
double taxRate = 0.05;
double interest = interestRate * 45;
cout << "Interest is " << interest << endl;
```

Common Error 2: Integer Overflow
Numbers are stored with a limited number of digits. When a variable is assigned a value that is too large (*in size*) to be stored, it causes *overflow*. For example, executing the following statement causes overflow, because the largest value that can be stored in a variable of the `short` type is `32767`. `32768` is too large.

overflow

```
short value = 32767 + 1; // value will actually become -32768
```

Likewise, executing the following statement causes overflow because the smallest value that can be stored in a variable of the `short` type is –32768. The value –32769 is too large to be stored in a `short` variable.

```
short value = -32768 - 1; // value will actually become 32767
```

C++ does not report errors on overflow. Be careful when working with numbers close to the maximum or minimum range of a given type.

underflow

When a floating-point number is too small (i.e., too close to zero) to be stored, it causes *underflow*. C++ approximates it to zero. So, normally you need not be concerned with underflow.

Common Error 3: Round-off Errors

A *round-off error*, also called a *rounding error*, is the difference between the calculated approximation of a number and its exact mathematical value. For example, 1/3 is approximately 0.333 if you keep three decimal places, and is 0.3333333 if you keep seven decimal places. Since the number of digits that can be stored in a variable is limited, round-off errors are inevitable. Calculations involving floating-point numbers are approximated because these numbers are not stored with complete accuracy. For example,

floating-point approximation

```
float a = 1000.43;
float b = 1000.0;
cout << a - b << endl;
```

displays **0.429993**, not **0.43**. Integers are stored precisely. Therefore, calculations with integers yield a precise integer result.

Common Error 4: Unintended Integer Division

C++ uses the same divide operator, namely /, to perform both integer and floating-point division. When two operands are integers, the / operator performs an integer division. The result of the operation is the quotient. The fractional part is truncated. To force two integers to perform a floating-point division, make one of the integers into a floating-point number. For example, the code in (a) displays that average is **1** and the code in (b) displays that average is **1.5**.

```
int number1 = 1;
int number2 = 2;
double average = (number1 + number2) / 2;
cout << average << endl;
```

(a)

```
int number1 = 1;
int number2 = 2;
double average = (number1 + number2) / 2.0;
cout << average << endl;
```

(b)

Common Error 5: Forgetting Header Files

Forgetting to include appropriate header files is a common compile error. The **pow** function is defined in the **cmath** header file and the **time** function is defined in the **ctime** header file. To use the **pow** function in your program, your program needs to include the **cmath** header. To use the **time** function in your program, your program needs to include the **ctime** header. For every program that uses the console input and output, you need to include the **iostream** header.

KEY TERMS

algorithm 50	constant 59
assignment operator (=) 58	data type 51
assignment statement 58	declare variables 51
C-style cast 73	decrement operator (--) 70
casting operator 72	double type 63
const keyword 59	expression 58

CHAPTER SUMMARY

1. The `cin` object along with the stream extraction operator (>>) can be used to read an input from the console.

2. Identifiers are names for naming elements in a program. An identifier is a sequence of characters that consists of letters, digits, and underscores (_). An identifier must start with a letter or an underscore. It cannot start with a digit. An identifier cannot be a reserved word.

3. Choosing descriptive identifiers can make programs easy to read.

4. Declaring a variable tells the compiler what type of data a variable can hold.

5. In C++, the equal sign (=) is used as the *assignment operator*.

6. A variable declared in a function must be assigned a value. Otherwise, the variable is called *uninitialized* and its value is unpredictable.

7. A *named constant* or simply *constant* represents permanent data that never changes.

8. A named constant is declared by using the keyword `const`.

9. By convention, constants are named in uppercase.

10. C++ provides integer types (`short`, `int`, `long`, `unsigned short`, `unsigned int`, and `unsigned long`) that represent signed and unsigned integers of various sizes.

11. Unsigned integers are nonnegative integers.

12. C++ provides floating-point types (`float`, `double`, and `long double`) that represent floating-point numbers of various precisions.

13. C++ provides operators that perform numeric operations: + (addition), − (subtraction), * (multiplication), / (division), and % (modulus).

14. Integer arithmetic (/) yields an integer result.

15. In C++, the % operator is for integers only.

16. The numeric operators in a C++ expression are applied the same way as in an arithmetic expression.

17. The increment operator (++) and the decrement operator (−−) increment or decrement a variable by 1.

18. C++ provides augmented operators += (addition assignment), −= (subtraction assignment), *= (multiplication assignment), /= (division assignment), and %= (modulus assignment).

19. When evaluating an expression with values of mixed types, C++ automatically casts the operands to appropriate types.

20. You can explicitly cast a value from one type to the other using the `<static_cast>(type)` notation or the legacy c-style `(type)` notation.

21. In computer science, midnight of January 1, 1970 is known as the *UNIX epoch*.

Quiz

Answer the quiz for this chapter online at www.cs.armstrong.edu/liang/cpp3e/quiz.html.

MyProgrammingLab™

Programming Exercises

Note
The compiler usually gives a reason for a syntax error. If you don't know how to correct it, compare your program closely, character by character, with similar examples in the text.

learn from examples

Note
Instructors may ask you to document your analysis and design for selected exercises. Use your own words to analyze the problem, including the input, output, and what needs to be computed, and describe how to solve the problem in pseudocode.

document analysis and design

Sections 2.2–2.12

2.1 (*Convert Celsius to Fahrenheit*) Write a program that reads a Celsius degree in a `double` value from the console, then converts it to Fahrenheit and displays the result. The formula for the conversion is as follows:

```
fahrenheit = (9 / 5) * celsius + 32
```

Hint: In C++, 9 / 5 is 1, but 9.0 / 5 is 1.8.

Here is a sample run:

```
Enter a degree in Celsius: 43 ⏎Enter
43 Celsius is 109.4 Fahrenheit
```

2.2 (*Compute the volume of a cylinder*) Write a program that reads in the radius and length of a cylinder and computes the area and volume using the following formulas:

```
area = radius * radius * π
volume = area * length
```

Here is a sample run:

```
Enter the radius and length of a cylinder: 5.5 12 ⏎Enter
The area is 95.0331
The volume is 1140.4
```

2.3 (*Convert feet into meters*) Write a program that reads a number in feet, converts it to meters, and displays the result. One foot is `0.305` meter. Here is a sample run:

```
Enter a value for feet: 16.5 ⏎Enter
16.5 feet is 5.0325 meters
```

2.4 (*Convert pounds into kilograms*) Write a program that converts pounds into kilograms. The program prompts the user to enter a number in pounds, converts it to kilograms, and displays the result. One pound is `0.454` kilograms. Here is a sample run:

```
Enter a number in pounds: 55.5 ⏎Enter
55.5 pounds is 25.197 kilograms
```

* **2.5** (*Financial application: calculate tips*) Write a program that reads the subtotal and the gratuity rate, then computes the gratuity and total. For example, if the user enters 10 for subtotal and 15% for gratuity rate, the program displays $1.5 as gratuity and $11.5 as total. Here is a sample run:

```
Enter the subtotal and a gratuity rate: 10 15 ⏎Enter
The gratuity is $1.5 and total is $11.5
```

** **2.6** (*Sum the digits in an integer*) Write a program that reads an integer between 0 and 1000 and adds all the digits in the integer. For example, if an integer is 932, the sum of all its digits is 14.

Hint: Use the % operator to extract digits, and use the / operator to remove the extracted digit. For instance, 932 % 10 = 2 and 932 / 10 = 93.

Here is a sample run:

```
Enter a number between 0 and 1000: 999 ⏎Enter
The sum of the digits is 27
```

* **2.7**   (*Find the number of years*) Write a program that prompts the user to enter the minutes (e.g., 1 billion), and displays the number of years and days for the minutes. For simplicity, assume a year has 365 days. Here is a sample run:

```
Enter the number of minutes: 1000000000 ↵Enter
1000000000 minutes is approximately 1902 years and 214 days
```

* **2.8**   (*Current time*) Listing 2.9, ShowCurrentTime.cpp, gives a program that displays the current time in GMT. Revise the program so that it prompts the user to enter the time zone offset to GMT and displays the time in the specified time zone. Here is a sample run:

```
Enter the time zone offset to GMT: -5 ↵Enter
The current time is 4:50:34
```

2.9   (*Physics: acceleration*) Average acceleration is defined as the change of velocity divided by the time taken to make the change, as shown in the following formula:

$$a = \frac{v_1 - v_0}{t}$$

Write a program that prompts the user to enter the starting velocity v_0 in meters/second, the ending velocity v_1 in meters/second, and the time span t in seconds, and displays the average acceleration. Here is a sample run:

```
Enter v0, v1, and t: 5.5 50.9 4.5 ↵Enter
The average acceleration is 10.0889
```

2.10   (*Science: calculating energy*) Write a program that calculates the energy needed to heat water from an initial temperature to a final temperature. Your program should prompt the user to enter the amount of water in kilograms and the initial and final temperatures of the water. The formula to compute the energy is

```
Q = M * (finalTemperature - initialTemperature) * 4184
```

where M is the weight of water in kilograms, temperatures are in degrees Celsius, and energy Q is measured in joules. Here is a sample run:

```
Enter the amount of water in kilograms: 55.5 ↵Enter
Enter the initial temperature: 3.5 ↵Enter
Enter the final temperature: 10.5 ↵Enter
The energy needed is 1625484.0
```

2.11   (*Population projection*) Rewrite Programming Exercise 1.11 to prompt the user to enter the number of years and displays the population after the number of years. Use the hint in Programming Exercise 1.11 for this program. Here is a sample run of the program:

```
Enter the number of years: 5 ↵Enter
The population in 5 years is 325932970
```

2.12 (*Physics: finding runway length*) Given an airplane's acceleration a and take-off speed v, you can compute the minimum runway length needed for an airplane to take off using the following formula:

$$length = \frac{v^2}{2a}$$

Write a program that prompts the user to enter v in meters/second (m/s) and the acceleration a in meters/second squared (m/s^2), and displays the minimum runway length. Here is a sample run:

```
Enter speed and acceleration: 60 3.5  ↵Enter
The minimum runway length for this airplane is 514.286
```

** 2.13 (*Financial application: compound value*) Suppose you save $100 *each* month into a savings account with the annual interest rate 5%. Thus, the monthly interest rate is $0.05/12 = 0.00417$. After the first month, the value in the account becomes

```
100 * (1 + 0.00417) = 100.417
```

After the second month, the value in the account becomes

```
(100 + 100.417) * (1 + 0.00417) = 201.252
```

After the third month, the value in the account becomes

```
(100 + 201.252) * (1 + 0.00417) = 302.507
```

and so on.

Write a program that prompts the user to enter a monthly saving amount and displays the account value after the sixth month. (In Programming Exercise 5.32, you will use a loop to simplify the code and display the account value for any month.)

```
Enter the monthly saving amount: 100  ↵Enter
After the sixth month, the account value is $608.81
```

* 2.14 (*Health application: BMI*) Body Mass Index (BMI) is a measure of health on weight. It can be calculated by taking your weight in kilograms and dividing by the square of your height in meters. Write a program that prompts the user to enter a weight in pounds and height in inches and displays the BMI. Note that one pound is 0.45359237 kilograms and one inch is 0.0254 meters. Here is a sample run:

VideoNote
Compute BMI

```
Enter weight in pounds: 95.5  ↵Enter
Enter height in inches: 50  ↵Enter
BMI is 26.8573
```

2.15 (*Geometry: distance of two points*) Write a program that prompts the user to enter two points (x1, y1) and (x2, y2) and displays their distance between them.

The formula for computing the distance is $\sqrt{(x_2 - x_1)^2 + (y_2 - y_1)^2}$. Note that you can use **pow(a, 0.5)** to compute $\sqrt{a}$. Here is a sample run:

```
Enter x1 and y1: 1.5 -3.4  ↵Enter
Enter x2 and y2: 4 5  ↵Enter
The distance between the two points is 8.764131445842194
```

2.16 (*Geometry: area of a hexagon*) Write a program that prompts the user to enter the side of a hexagon and displays its area. The formula for computing the area of a hexagon is

$$Area = \frac{3\sqrt{3}}{2}s^2,$$

where s is the length of a side. Here is a sample run:

```
Enter the side: 5.5  ↵Enter
The area of the hexagon is 78.5895
```

*2.17 (*Science: wind-chill temperature*) How cold is it outside? The temperature alone is not enough to provide the answer. Other factors including wind speed, relative humidity, and sunshine play important roles in determining coldness outside. In 2001, the National Weather Service (NWS) implemented the new wind-chill temperature to measure the coldness using temperature and wind speed. The formula is:

$$t_{wc} = 35.74 + 0.6215t_a - 35.75v^{0.16} + 0.4275t_av^{0.16}$$

where t_a is the outside temperature measured in degrees Fahrenheit and v is the speed measured in miles per hour. t_{wc} is the wind-chill temperature. The formula cannot be used for wind speeds below 2 mph or temperatures below $-58°F$ or above $41°F$.

Write a program that prompts the user to enter a temperature between $-58°F$ and $41°F$ and a wind speed greater than or equal to **2** and displays the wind-chill temperature. Use **pow(a, b)** to compute $v^{0.16}$. Here is a sample run:

```
Enter the temperature in Fahrenheit: 5.3  ↵Enter
Enter the wind speed in miles per hour: 6  ↵Enter
The wind chill index is -5.56707
```

2.18 (*Print a table*) Write a program that displays the following table:

x	y	pow(x, y)
2.5	1.2	3.00281
5.0	2.4	47.5913
1.2	3.6	1.92776
2.4	5.0	79.6262
3.6	2.5	24.5899

*2.19 (*Geometry: area of a triangle*) Write a program that prompts the user to enter three points (**x1, y1**), (**x2, y2**), (**x3, y3**) of a triangle and displays its area. The formula for computing the area of a triangle is

$$s = (side1 + side2 + side3)/2;$$

$$area = \sqrt{s(s - side1)(s - side2)(s - side3)}$$

Here is a sample run:

```
Enter three points for a triangle: 1.5 -3.4 4.6 5 9.5 -3.4  ↵Enter
The area of the triangle is 33.6
```

*2.20   (*Slope of a line*) Write a program that prompts the user to enter the coordinates of two points (x1, y1) and (x2, y2), and displays the slope of the line that connects the two points. The formula of the slope is $(y_2 - y_1)/(x_2 - x_1)$. Here is a sample run:

```
Enter the coordinates for two points: 4.5 -5.5 6.6 -6.5  ↵Enter
The slope for the line that connects two points (4.5, -5.5) and (6.6,
-6.5) is -0.47619
```

*2.21   (*Cost of driving*) Write a program that prompts the user to enter the distance to drive, the fuel efficiency of the car in miles per gallon, and the price per gallon, and displays the cost of the trip. Here is a sample run:

```
Enter the driving distance: 900.5  ↵Enter
Enter miles per gallon: 25.5  ↵Enter
Enter price per gallon: 3.55  ↵Enter
The cost of driving is $125.36
```

Sections 2.13–2.16

*2.22   (*Financial application: calculate interest*) If you know the balance and the annual percentage interest rate, you can compute the interest on the next monthly payment using the following formula:

```
interest = balance x (annualInterestRate/1200)
```

Write a program that reads the balance and the annual percentage interest rate and displays the interest for the next month. Here is a sample run:

```
Enter balance and interest rate (e.g., 3 for 3%): 1000 3.5  ↵Enter
The interest is 2.91667
```

*2.23   (*Financial application: future investment value*) Write a program that reads in investment amount, annual interest rate, and number of years, and displays the future investment value using the following formula:

```
futureInvestmentValue =
    investmentAmount x (1 + monthlyInterestRate)^{numberOfYears*12}
```

For example, if you enter amount **1000**, annual interest rate **3.25%**, and number of years **1**, the future investment value is **1032.98**. Here is a sample run:

```
Enter investment amount: 1000  ↵Enter
Enter annual interest rate in percentage: 4.25  ↵Enter
Enter number of years: 1  ↵Enter
Accumulated value is $1043.34
```

*2.24   (*Financial application: monetary units*) Rewrite Listing 2.12, ComputeChange.cpp, to fix the possible loss of accuracy when converting a float value to an `int` value. Enter the input as an integer whose last two digits represent the cents. For example, the input **1156** represents **11** dollars and **56** cents.

SELECTIONS

Objectives

- To declare `bool` variables and write Boolean expressions using relational operators (§3.2).

- To implement selection control using one-way `if` statements (§3.3).

- To implement selection control using two-way `if` statements (§3.4).

- To implement selection control using nested `if` and multi-way `if-else` statements (§3.5).

- To avoid common errors and pitfalls in `if` statements (§3.6).

- To program using selection statements for a variety of examples (`BMI`, `ComputeTax`, `SubtractionQuiz`) (§§3.7–3.9).

- To generate random numbers using the `rand` function and set a seed using the `srand` function (§3.9).

- To combine conditions using logical operators (`&&`, `||`, and `!`) (§3.10).

- To program using selection statements with combined conditions (`LeapYear`, `Lottery`) (§§3.11–3.12).

- To implement selection control using `switch` statements (§3.13).

- To write expressions using the conditional expressions (§3.14).

- To examine the rules governing operator precedence and operator associativity (§3.15).

- To debug errors (§3.16).

3.1 Introduction

The program can decide which statements to execute based on a condition.

If you enter a negative value for `radius` in Listing 2.2, ComputeAreaWithConsoleInput.cpp, the program displays an invalid result. If the radius is negative, you don't want the program to compute the area. How can you deal with this situation?

problem

selection statements

Like all high-level programming languages, C++ provides *selection statements*: statements that let you choose actions with alternative courses. You can use the following selection statement to replace lines 12–15 in Listing 2.2:

```cpp
if (radius < 0)
{
  cout << "Incorrect input" << endl;
}
else
{
  area = radius * radius * PI;
  cout << "The area for the circle of radius " << radius
    << " is " << area << endl;
}
```

Boolean expression

Boolean value

Selection statements use conditions that are Boolean expressions. A *Boolean expression* is an expression that evaluates to a *Boolean value*: `true` or `false`. We now introduce Boolean types and relational operators.

3.2 The **bool** Data Type

The **bool** *data type declares a variable with the value either* **true** *or* **false**.

bool data type

relational operator

How do you compare two values, such as whether a radius is greater than 0, equal to 0, or less than 0? C++ provides six *relational operators*, shown in Table 3.1, which can be used to compare two values (assume radius is 5 in the table).

TABLE 3.1 Relational Operators

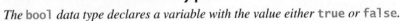

Operator	Mathematics Symbol	Name	Example (radius is 5)	Result
<	<	less than	`radius < 0`	false
<=	≤	less than or equal to	`radius <= 0`	false
>	>	greater than	`radius > 0`	true
>=	≥	greater than or equal to	`radius >= 0`	true
==	=	equal to	`radius == 0`	false
!=	≠	not equal to	`radius != 0`	true

Caution

== vs. =

The equality testing operator is two equal signs (==), not a single equal sign (=). The latter symbol is used for assignment.

Boolean variable

The result of the comparison is a Boolean value: `true` or `false`. A variable that holds a Boolean value is known as a *Boolean variable*. The `bool` data type is used to declare Boolean variables. For example, the following statement assigns `true` to the variable `lightsOn`:

```cpp
bool lightsOn = true;
```

true and **false** are Boolean literals, just like a number such as **10**. They are keywords and cannot be used as identifiers in your program.

Boolean literals

Internally, C++ uses **1** to represent **true** and **0** for **false**. If you display a **bool** value to the console, **1** is displayed if the value is **true** and **0** if it is **false**.

For example,

```
cout << (4 < 5);
```

displays **1**, because **4** < **5** is **true**.

```
cout << (4 > 5);
```

displays **0**, because **4** > **5** is **false**.

> **Note**
>
> In C++, you can assign a numeric value to a **bool** variable. Any nonzero value evaluates to **true** and zero value evaluates to **false**. For example, after the following assignment statements, **b1** and **b3** become **true**, and **b2** becomes **false**.
>
> ```
> bool b1 = -1.5; // Same as bool b1 = true
> bool b2 = 0; // Same as bool b2 = false
> bool b3 = 1.5; // Same as bool b3 = true
> ```

convert numbers to a **bool** value

3.1 List six relational operators.

3.2 Assuming that x is **1**, show the result of the following Boolean expressions:

```
(x > 0)
(x < 0)
(x != 0)
(x >= 0)
(x != 1)
```

3.3 Show the printout of the following code:

```
bool b = true;
int i = b;
cout << b << endl;
cout << i << endl;
```

3.3 **if** Statements

An if statement is a construct that enables a program to specify alternative path of execution.

The programs that you have written so far execute in sequence. However, often there are situations in which you must provide alternative paths. C++ provides several types of selection statements: one-way **if** statements, two-way **if-else** statements, nested **if** statements, **switch** statements, and conditional expressions.

A one-way **if** statement executes an action if and only if the condition is **true**. The syntax for a one-way **if** statement is shown here:

if statement

```
if (boolean-expression)
{
  statement(s);
}
```

flowchart

The flowchart in Figure 3.1a illustrates how C++ executes the syntax of an `if` statement. A *flowchart* is a diagram that describes an algorithm or process, showing the steps as boxes of various kinds, and their order by connecting these with arrows. Process operations are represented in these boxes, and arrows connecting them represent flow of control. A diamond box is used to denote a Boolean condition and a rectangle box is used to represent statements.

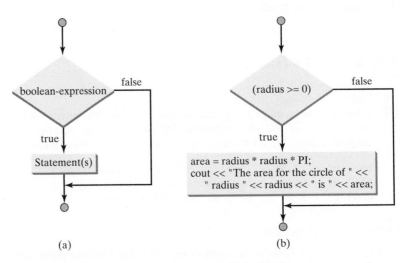

(a)   (b)

FIGURE 3.1   An `if` statement executes statements if the **boolean-expression** evaluates to **true**.

If the **boolean-expression** evaluates to **true**, the statements in the block are executed. As an example, see the following code:

```
if (radius >= 0)
{
  area = radius * radius * PI;
  cout << "The area for the circle of " <<
    " radius " << radius << " is " << area;
}
```

The flowchart of the preceding statement is shown in Figure 3.1b. If the value of **radius** is greater than or equal to **0**, then the **area** is computed and the result is displayed; otherwise, the two statements in the block will not be executed.

The **boolean-expression** is enclosed in parentheses. For example, the code in (a) below is wrong. The corrected version is shown in (b).

```
if i > 0
{
  cout << "i is positive" << endl;
}
```

```
if (i > 0)
{
  cout << "i is positive" << endl;
}
```

(a) Wrong   (b) Correct

The braces can be omitted if they enclose a single statement. For example, the following statements are equivalent.

```
if (i > 0)
{
  cout << "i is positive" << endl;
}
```

(a)

Equivalent

```
if (i > 0)
    cout << "i is positive" << endl;
```

(b)

Listing 3.1 gives a program that prompts the user to enter an integer. If the number is a multiple of **5**, display **HiFive**. If the number is even, display **HiEven**.

LISTING 3.1   SimpleIfDemo.cpp

```
1  #include <iostream>
2  using namespace std;
3
4  int main()
5  {
6    // Prompt the user to enter an integer
7    int number;
8    cout << "Enter an integer: ";
9    cin >> number;                              enter input
10
11   if (number % 5 == 0)                        check 5
12     cout << "HiFive" << endl;
13
14   if (number % 2 == 0)                        check even
15     cout << "HiEven" << endl;
16
17   return 0;
18 }
```

```
Enter an integer: 4 ↵Enter
HiEven
```

```
Enter an integer: 30 ↵Enter
HiFive
HiEven
```

The program prompts the user to enter an integer (line 9) and displays **HiFive** if it is multiple by **5** (lines 11–12) and **HiEven** if it is even (lines 14–15).

3.4   Write an **if** statement that assigns **1** to x if y is greater than **0**.

3.5   Write an **if** statement that increases pay by 3% if **score** is greater than **90**.

✓Check
Point

3.6 What is wrong in the following code?

```
if radius >= 0
{
  area = radius * radius * PI;
  cout << "The area for the circle of " <<
    " radius " << radius << " is " << area;
}
```

3.4 Two-Way **if-else** Statements

Key Point

An if-else statement decides which statements to execute based on whether the condition is true or false.

A one-way if statement performs an action if the specified condition is **true**. If the condition is **false**, nothing is done. But what if you want to perform an alternative action when the condition is **false**? You can use a two-way if statement. A two-way **if-else** statement specifies different actions, depending on whether the condition is **true** or **false**.

Here is the syntax for a two-way **if-else** statement:

```
if (boolean-expression)
{
  statement(s)-for-the-true-case;
}
else
{
  statement(s)-for-the-false-case;
}
```

The flowchart of the statement is shown in Figure 3.2.

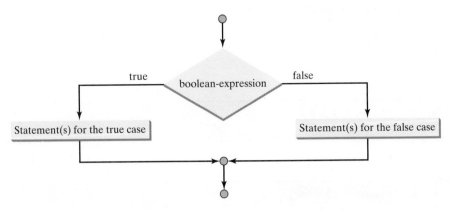

FIGURE 3.2 An if-else statement executes statements for the true case if the Boolean-expression evaluates to true; otherwise, statements for the false case are executed.

If the boolean-expression evaluates to true, the statement(s) for the true case is executed; otherwise, the statement(s) for the false case is executed. For example, consider the following code:

two-way if-else statement

```
if (radius >= 0)
{
  area = radius * radius * PI;
```

```
  cout << "The area for the circle of radius " <<
    radius << " is " << area;
}
else
{
  cout << "Negative radius";
}
```

If `radius >= 0` is `true`, `area` is computed and displayed; if it is `false`, the message `"Negative radius"` is displayed.

As usual, the braces can be omitted if they enclose only one statement. Therefore, in the preceding example, the braces enclosing the `cout << "Negative radius"` statement can be omitted.

Here is another example of the `if-else` statement. The example checks whether a number is even or odd, as follows:

```
if (number % 2 == 0)
  cout << number << " is even.";
else
  cout << number << " is odd.";
```

3.7   Write an `if` statement that increases **pay** by 3% if **score** is greater than **90**, otherwise increases **pay** by 1%.

3.8   What is the printout of the code in (a) and (b) if **number** is 30? What if **number** is 35?

Check Point

```
if (number % 2 == 0)
  cout << number << " is even." << endl;

cout << number << " is odd." << endl;
```
(a)

```
if (number % 2 == 0)
  cout << number << " is even." << endl;
else
  cout << number << " is odd." << endl;
```
(b)

3.5 Nested **if** and Multi-Way **if-else** Statements

An if statement can be inside another if statement to form a nested if statement.

Key Point

The statement in an `if` or `if-else` statement can be any legal C++ statement, including another `if` or `if-else` statement. The inner `if` statement is said to be *nested* inside the outer `if` statement. The inner `if` statement can contain another `if` statement; in fact, there is no limit to the depth of the nesting. For example, the following is a nested `if` statement:

```
if (i > k)
{
  if (j > k)
    cout << "i and j are greater than k" << endl;
}
else
  cout << "i is less than or equal to k" << endl;
```

nested if statement

The `if (j > k)` statement is nested inside the `if (i > k)` statement.

The nested `if` statement can be used to implement multiple alternatives. For example, the statement given in Figure 3.3a assigns a letter grade to the variable **grade** according to the score, with multiple alternatives.

```
if (score >= 90.0)
  cout << "Grade is A";
else
  if (score >= 80.0)
    cout << "Grade is B";
  else
    if (score >= 70.0)
      cout << "Grade is C";
    else
      if (score >= 60.0)
        cout << "Grade is D";
    else
      cout << "Grade is F";
```

(a)

Equivalent

This is better

```
if (score >= 90.0)
  cout << "Grade is A";
else if (score >= 80.0)
  cout << "Grade is B";
else if (score >= 70.0)
  cout << "Grade is C";
else if (score >= 60.0)
  cout << "Grade is D";
else
  cout << "Grade is F";
```

(b)

FIGURE 3.3 A preferred format for multiple alternatives is shown in (b) using a multi-way if-else statement.

The execution of this if statement proceeds as shown in Figure 3.4. The first condition (score >= 90.0) is tested. If it is true, the grade is A. If it is false, the second condition (score >= 80.0) is tested. If the second condition is true, the grade is B. If that condition is false, the third condition and the rest of the conditions (if necessary) are tested until a condition is met or all the conditions are false. In the latter case, the grade is F. Note that a condition is tested only when all the conditions that come before it are false.

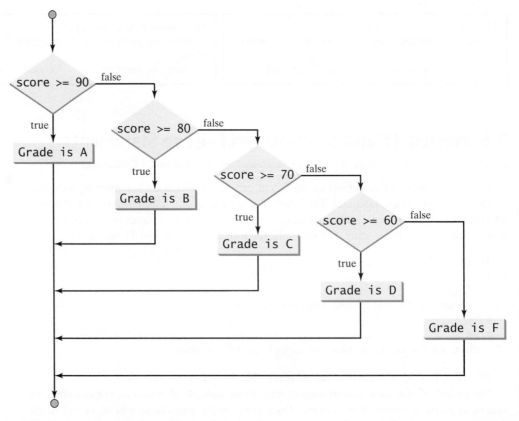

FIGURE 3.4 You can use a multi-way if-else statement to assign a grade.

The `if` statement in Figure 3.3a is equivalent to the `if` statement in Figure 3.3b. In fact, Figure 3.3b is the preferred coding style for multiple alternative `if` statements. This style, called *multi-way* `if-else` *statements*, avoids deep indentation and makes the program easy to read.

multi-way `if` statement

3.9 Suppose x = 3 and y = 2; show the output, if any, of the following code. What is the output if x = 3 and y = 4? What is the output if x = 2 and y = 2? Draw a flowchart of the code.

Check Point

```
if (x > 2)
{
  if (y > 2)
  {
    int z = x + y;
    cout << "z is " << z << endl;
  }
}
else
  cout << "x is " << x << endl;
```

3.10 Suppose x = 2 and y = 3. Show the output, if any, of the following code. What is the output if x = 3 and y = 2? What is the output if x = 3 and y = 3?

```
if (x > 2)
  if (y > 2)
  {
    int z = x + y;
    cout << "z is " << z << endl;
  }
  else
    cout << "x is " << x << endl;
```

3.11 What is wrong in the following code?

```
if (score >= 60.0)
  cout << "Grade is D";
else if (score >= 70.0)
  cout << Grade is C";
else if (score >= 80.0)
  cout << Grade is B";
else if (score >= 90.0)
  cout << "Grade is A";
else
  cout << "Grade is F";
```

3.6 Common Errors and Pitfalls

Forgetting necessary braces, misplacing semicolons in an `if` statement, mistaking `==` for `=`, and dangling `else` clauses are common errors in selection statements. Duplicated statements in `if-else` statements and testing equality of double values are common pitfalls.

 Key Point

Common Error 1: Forgetting Necessary Braces
The braces can be omitted if the block contains a single statement. However, forgetting the braces when they are needed for grouping multiple statements is a common programming

error. If you modify the code by adding new statements in an `if` statement without braces, you will have to insert the braces. For example, the following code in (a) is wrong. It should be written with braces to group multiple statements, as shown in (b).

```
if (radius >= 0)
  area = radius * radius * PI;
  cout << "The area "
    << " is " << area;
```
(a) Wrong

```
if (radius >= 0)
{
  area = radius * radius * PI;
  cout << "The area "
    << " is " << area;
}
```
(b) Correct

In (a), the console output statement is not part of the `if` statement. It is the same as the following code:

```
if (radius >= 0)
  area = radius * radius * PI;

cout << "The area "
  << " is " << area;
```

Regardless of the condition in the `if` statement, the console output statement is always executed.

Common Error 2: Wrong Semicolon at the `if` Line

Adding a semicolon at the end of an `if` line, as shown in (a) below, is a common mistake.

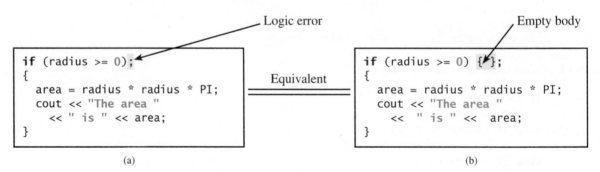

This mistake is hard to find, because it is neither a compile error nor a runtime error; it is a logic error. The code in (a) is equivalent to that in (b) with an empty body.

Common Error 3: Mistakenly Using = for ==

The equality testing operator is two equal signs (==). In C++, if you mistakenly use = for ==, it will lead to a logic error. Consider the following code:

```
if (count = 3)
  cout << "count is zero" << endl;
else
  cout << "count is not zero" << endl;
```

It always displays `"count is zero"`, because `count = 3` assigns 3 to `count` and the assignment expression is evaluated to 3. Since 3 is a nonzero value, it is interpreted as a true condition by the `if` statement. Recall that any nonzero value evaluates to `true` and zero value evaluates to `false`.

Common Error 4: Redundant Testing of Boolean Values
To test whether a `bool` variable is `true` or `false` in a test condition, it is redundant to use the equality testing operator like the code in (a):

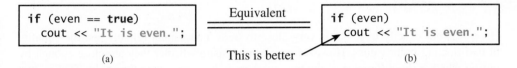

```
if (even == true)
   cout << "It is even.";
```
(a)

Equivalent
―――――――――
This is better

```
if (even)
   cout << "It is even.";
```
(b)

Instead, it is better to test the `bool` variable directly, as in (b). Another good reason for doing this is to avoid errors that are difficult to detect. Using the = operator instead of the == operator to compare equality of two items in a test condition is a common error. It could lead to the following erroneous statement:

```
if (even = true)
   cout << "It is even.";
```

This statement assigns `true` to `even` so that `even` is always `true`. So, the condition for the `if` statement is always `true`.

Common Error 5: Dangling `else` Ambiguity
The code in (a) below has two `if` clauses and one `else` clause. Which `if` clause is matched by the `else` clause? The indentation indicates that the `else` clause matches the first `if` clause. However, the `else` clause actually matches the second `if` clause. This situation is known as the *dangling `else` ambiguity*. The `else` clause always matches the most recent unmatched `if` clause in the same block. So, the statement in (a) is equivalent to the code in (b).

dangling `else` ambiguity

```
int i = 1, j = 2, k = 3;

if (i > j)
  if (i > k)
    cout << "A";
else
    cout << "B";
```
(a)

Equivalent
―――――――――
This is better with correct indentation

```
int i = 1, j = 2, k = 3;

if (i > j)
  if (i > k)
    cout << "A";
  else
    cout << "B";
```
(b)

Since `(i > j)` is false, nothing is displayed from the statements in (a) and (b). To force the `else` clause to match the first `if` clause, you must add a pair of braces:

```
int i = 1, j = 2, k = 3;

if (i > j)
{
  if (i > k)
    cout << "A";
}
else
  cout << "B";
```

This statement displays `B`.

Common Error 6: Equality Test of Two Floating-Point Values
As discussed in Common Error 3 in Section 2.16, floating-point numbers have limited precision and calculations involving floating-point numbers can introduce round-off errors. Therefore, an equality test of two floating-point values is not reliable. For example, you expect the following code to display `x is 0.5`, but surprisingly it displays `x is not 0.5`.

```
double x = 1.0 - 0.1 - 0.1 - 0.1 - 0.1 - 0.1;
if (x == 0.5)
  cout << "x is 0.5" << endl;
else
  cout << "x is not 0.5" << endl;
```

Here, x is not exactly 0.5, but is very close to 0.5. You cannot reliably test the equality of two floating-point values. However, you can compare whether they are close enough by testing whether the difference of the two numbers is less than some threshold. That is, two numbers x and y are very close if $|x - y| < \varepsilon$, for a very small value, ε. ε, a Greek letter pronounced epsilon, is commonly used to denote a very small value. Normally, you set ε to 10^{-14} for comparing two values of the double type and to 10^{-7} for comparing two values of the float type. For example, the following code

```
const double EPSILON = 1E-14;
double x = 1.0 - 0.1 - 0.1 - 0.1 - 0.1 - 0.1;
if (abs(x - 0.5) < EPSILON)
  cout << "x is approximately 0.5" << endl;
```

will display that
    x is approximately 0.5
    The abs(a) function in the cmath library file can be used to return the absolute value of a.

Common Pitfall 1: Simplifying Boolean Variable Assignment

Often, new programmers write the code that assigns a test condition to a bool variable like the code in (a):

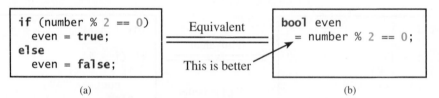

```
if (number % 2 == 0)
  even = true;
else
  even = false;
```
(a)

Equivalent

This is better

```
bool even
  = number % 2 == 0;
```
(b)

This is not an error, but it should be better written as shown in (b).

Common Pitfall 2: Avoiding Duplicate Code in Different Cases

Often, new programmers write the duplicate code in different cases that should be combined in one place. For example, the highlighted code in the following statement is duplicated:

```
if (inState)
{
  tuition = 5000;
  cout << "The tuition is " << tuition << endl;
}
else
{
  tuition = 15000;
  cout << "The tuition is " << tuition << endl;
}
```

This is not an error, but it is better to write it as follows:

```
if (inState)
{
  tuition = 5000;
}
else
```

```
{
  tuition = 15000;
}
cout << "The tuition is " << tuition << endl;
```

The new code removes the duplication and makes the code easy to maintain, because if the print statement is modified you only need to change in one place.

Common Pitfall 3: Integer Values Can Be Used as Boolean Values

In C++, a Boolean `true` is treated as `1` and `false` as `0`. A numeric value can be used as a Boolean value. In particular, C++ converts a nonzero value to `true` and `0` to `false`. A Boolean value can be used as an integer. This may lead to potential logic errors. For example, the following code in (a) has a logic error. Assume `amount` is `40`, the code will display `Amount is more than 50`, because `!amount` evaluates to `0` and `0 <= 50` is `true`. The correct code should be as shown in (b).

```
if (!amount <= 50)
  cout << "Amount is more than 50";
```

(a)

```
if (!(amount <= 50))
  cout << "Amount is more than 50";
```

(b)

3.12 Show the output of the following code:

```
int amount = 5;

if (amount >= 100)
{
  cout << "Amount is " << amount << " ";
  cout << "Tax is " << amount * 0.03;
}
```

(a)

```
int amount = 5;

if (amount >= 100)
  cout << "Amount is " << amount << " ";
  cout << "Tax is " << amount * 0.03;
```

(b)

```
int amount = 5;

if (amount >= 100);
  cout << "Amount is " << amount << " ";
  cout << "Tax is " << amount * 0.03;
```

(c)

```
int amount = 0;

if (amount = 0)
  cout << "Amount is zero";
else
  cout << "Amount is not zero";
```

(d)

3.13 Which of the following statements are equivalent? Which ones are correctly indented?

```
if (i > 0) if
(j > 0)
x = 0; else
if (k > 0) y = 0;
else z = 0;
```

(a)

```
if (i > 0) {
  if (j > 0)
    x = 0;
  else if (k > 0)
    y = 0;
}
else
  z = 0;
```

(b)

```
if (i > 0)
  if (j > 0)
    x = 0;
  else if (k > 0)
    y = 0;
  else
    z = 0;
```

(c)

```
if (i > 0)
  if (j > 0)
    x = 0;
  else if (k > 0)
    y = 0;
else
  z = 0;
```

(d)

3.14 Rewrite the following statement using a Boolean expression:

```
if (count % 10 == 0)
  newLine = true;
else
  newLine = false;
```

3.15 Are the following statements correct? Which one is better?

```
if (age < 16)
  cout <<
    "Cannot get a driver's license";
if (age >= 16)
  cout <<
    "Can get a driver's license";
```

(a)

```
if (age < 16)
  cout <<
    "Cannot get a driver's license";
else
  cout <<
    "Can get a driver's license";
```

(b)

3.16 What is the output of the following code if **number** is 14, 15, and 30?

```
if (number % 2 == 0)
  cout << number << " is even";
if (number % 5 == 0)
  cout << number << " is multiple of 5";
```

(a)

```
if (number % 2 == 0)
  cout << number << " is even";
else if (number % 5 == 0)
  cout << number << " is multiple of 5";
```

(b)

3.7 Case Study: Computing Body Mass Index

Key Point

You can use nested if statements to write a program that interprets Body Mass Index.

Body Mass Index (BMI) is a measure of health based on height and weight. You can calculate your BMI by taking your weight in kilograms and dividing it by the square of your height in meters. The interpretation of BMI for people 20 years or older is as follows:

BMI	Interpretation
BMI $<$ 18.5	Underweight
18.5 $\leq$ BMI $<$ 25.0	Normal
25.0 $\leq$ BMI $<$ 30.0	Overweight
30.0 $\leq$ BMI	Obese

Write a program that prompts the user to enter a weight in pounds and height in inches and displays the BMI. Note that one pound is 0.45359237 kilograms and one inch is 0.0254 meters. Listing 3.2 gives the program.

VideoNote
Compute BMI

LISTING 3.2 ComputeAndInterpreteBMI.cpp

```
1  #include <iostream>
2  using namespace std;
3
4  int main()
5  {
6    // Prompt the user to enter weight in pounds
```

```
 7    cout << "Enter weight in pounds: ";
 8    double weight;
 9    cin >> weight;                                                    input weight
10
11    // Prompt the user to enter height in inches
12    cout << "Enter height in inches: ";
13    double height;
14    cin >> height;                                                    input height
15
16    const double KILOGRAMS_PER_POUND = 0.45359237; // Constant
17    const double METERS_PER_INCH = 0.0254; // Constant
18
19    // Compute BMI
20    double weightInKilograms = weight * KILOGRAMS_PER_POUND;
21    double heightInMeters = height * METERS_PER_INCH;
22    double bmi = weightInKilograms /                                  compute bmi
23      (heightInMeters * heightInMeters);
24
25    // Display result
26    cout << "BMI is " << bmi << endl;                                 display output
27    if (bmi < 18.5)
28      cout << "Underweight" << endl;
29    else if (bmi < 25)
30      cout << "Normal" << endl;
31    else if (bmi < 30)
32      cout << "Overweight" << endl;
33    else
34      cout << "Obese" << endl;
35
36    return 0;
37  }
```

```
Enter weight in pounds: 146 ↵Enter
Enter height in inches: 70 ↵Enter
BMI is 20.9486
Normal
```

Line#	weight	height	weightInKilograms	heightInMeters	bmi	Output
9	146					
14		70				
20			66.22448602			
21				1.778		
22					20.9486	
26						BMI is 20.9486
32						Normal

Two constants KILOGRAMS_PER_POUND and METERS_PER_INCH are defined in lines 16–17. Using constants here makes the program easy to read.

You should test the program by entering the input that covers all possible cases for BMI to ensure that the program works for all cases.   test all cases

3.8 Case Study: Computing Taxes

Key Point

You can use nested if *statements to write a program for computing taxes.*

The United States federal personal income tax is calculated based on filing status and taxable income. There are four filing statuses: single filers, married filing jointly or qualified widow(er), married filing separately, and head of household. The tax rates vary every year. Table 3.2 shows the rates for 2009. If you are, say, single with a taxable income of $10,000, the first $8,350 is taxed at 10% and the other $1,650 is taxed at 15%, so, your total tax is $1,082.50.

TABLE 3.2 2009 U.S. Federal Personal Tax Rates

Marginal Tax Rate	Single	Married Filing Jointly or Qualifying Widow(er)	Married Filing Separately	Head of Household
10%	$0 – $8,350	$0 – $16,700	$0 – $8,350	$0 – $11,950
15%	$8,351 – $33,950	$16,701 – $67,900	$8,351 – $33,950	$11,951 – $45,500
25%	$33,951 – $82,250	$67,901 – $137,050	$33,951 – $68,525	$45,501 – $117,450
28%	$82,251 – $171,550	$137,051 – $208,850	$68,526 – $104,425	$117,451 – $190,200
33%	$171,551 – $372,950	$208,851 – $372,950	$104,426 – $186,475	$190,201 – $372,950
35%	$372,951+	$372,951+	$186,476+	$372,951+

You are to write a program to compute personal income tax. Your program should prompt the user to enter the filing status and taxable income and compute the tax. Enter 0 for single filers, 1 for married filing jointly or qualified widow(er), 2 for married filing separately, and 3 for head of household.

Your program computes the tax for the taxable income based on the filing status. The filing status can be determined using if statements outlined as follows:

```
if (status == 0)
{
  // Compute tax for single filers
}
else if (status == 1)
{
  // Compute tax for married filing jointly or qualifying widow(er)
}
else if (status == 2)
{
  // Compute tax for married filing separately
}
else if (status == 3)
{
  // Compute tax for head of household
}
else {
  // Display wrong status
}
```

For each filing status there are six tax rates. Each rate is applied to a certain amount of taxable income. For example, of a taxable income of $400,000 for single filers, $8,350 is taxed at 10%, (33,950 – 8,350) at 15%, (82,250 – 33,950) at 25%, (171,550 – 82,250) at 28%, (372,950 – 171,550) at 33%, and (400,000 – 372,950) at 35%.

Listing 3.3 gives the solution to compute taxes for single filers. The complete solution is left as an exercise.

LISTING 3.3 ComputeTax.cpp

```cpp
 1  #include <iostream>
 2  using namespace std;
 3
 4  int main()
 5  {
 6    // Prompt the user to enter filing status
 7    cout << "(0-single filer, 1-married jointly, "
 8         << "or qualifying widow(er), " << endl
 9         << "2-married separately, 3-head of household)" << endl
10         << "Enter the filing status: ";
11
12    int status;
13    cin >> status;                                              input status
14
15    // Prompt the user to enter taxable income
16    cout << "Enter the taxable income: ";
17    double income;
18    cin >> income;                                              input income
19
20    // Compute tax
21    double tax = 0;                                             compute tax
22
23    if (status == 0) // Compute tax for single filers
24    {
25      if (income <= 8350)
26        tax = income * 0.10;
27      else if (income <= 33950)
28        tax = 8350 * 0.10 + (income - 8350) * 0.15;
29      else if (income <= 82250)
30        tax = 8350 * 0.10 + (33950 - 8350) * 0.15 +
31          (income - 33950) * 0.25;
32      else if (income <= 171550)
33        tax = 8350 * 0.10 + (33950 - 8350) * 0.15 +
34          (82250 - 33950) * 0.25 + (income - 82250) * 0.28;
35      else if (income <= 372950)
36        tax = 8350 * 0.10 + (33950 - 8350) * 0.15 +
37          (82250 - 33950) * 0.25 + (171550 - 82250) * 0.28 +
38          (income - 171550) * 0.33;
39      else
40        tax = 8350 * 0.10 + (33950 - 8350) * 0.15 +
41          (82250 - 33950) * 0.25 + (171550 - 82250) * 0.28 +
42          (372950 - 171550) * 0.33 + (income - 372950) * 0.35;
43    }
44    else if (status == 1) // Compute tax for married file jointly
45    {
46      // Left as an exercise
47    }
48    else if (status == 2) // Compute tax for married separately
49    {
50      // Left as an exercise
51    }
```

```
52    else if (status == 3) // Compute tax for head of household
53    {
54      // Left as an exercise
55    }
56    else
57    {
```

exit program
```
58      cout << "Error: invalid status";
59      return 0;
60    }
61
62    // Display the result
```

display output
```
63    cout << "Tax is " << static_cast<int>(tax * 100) / 100.0 << endl;
64
65    return 0;
66  }
```

```
(0-single filer, 1-married jointly or qualifying widow(er),
2-married separately, 3-head of household)
Enter the filing status: 0  ↵Enter
Enter the taxable income: 400000  ↵Enter
Tax is 117684
```

Line#	status	income	tax	Output
13	0			
18		400000		
21			0	
40			130599	
63				Tax is 130599

The program receives the filing status and taxable income. The multi-way `if-else` statements (lines 23, 44, 48, 52, 56) check the filing status and compute the tax on which it is based.

test all cases

To test a program, you should provide the input that covers all cases. For this program, your input should cover all statuses (0, 1, 2, 3). For each status, test the tax for each of the six brackets. So, there are a total of 24 cases.

Tip
For all programs, you should write a small amount of code and test it before adding more code. This is called *incremental development and testing*. This approach makes identifying errors easier, because the errors are likely in the new code you just added.

incremental development
and testing

Check Point

3.17 Are the following statements equivalent?

```
if (income <= 10000)
  tax = income * 0.1;
else if (income <= 20000)
  tax = 1000 +
    (income - 10000) * 0.15;
```

```
if (income <= 10000)
  tax = income * 0.1;
else if (income > 10000 &&
        income <= 20000)
  tax = 1000 +
    (income - 10000) * 0.15;
```

3.9 Generating Random Numbers

You can use the `rand()` *function to obtain a random integer.*

Suppose you want to develop a program for a first-grader to practice subtraction. The program randomly generates two single-digit integers, `number1` and `number2`, with `number1` `>=` `number2`, and it displays to the student a question such as `"What is 9 - 2?"` After the student enters the answer, the program displays a message indicating whether it is correct.

To generate a random number, use the `rand()` function in the `cstdlib` header file. This function returns a random integer between `0` and `RAND_MAX`. `RAND_MAX` is platform-dependent constant. In Visual C++, `RAND_MAX` is `32767`.

The numbers `rand()` produces are pseudorandom. That is, every time it is executed on the same system, `rand()` produces the same sequence of numbers. On the author's machine, for example, executing these three statements will always produce the numbers `130`, `10982`, and `1090`.

```
cout << rand() << endl << rand() << endl << rand() << endl;
```

Why? The `rand()` function's algorithm uses a value called the *seed* to control how to generate the numbers. By default, the seed value is `1`. If you change the seed to a different value, the sequence of random numbers will be different. To change the seed, use the `srand(seed)` function in the `cstdlib` header file. To ensure that the seed value is different each time you run the program, use `time(0)`. As discussed in Section 2.10, "Case Study: Displaying the Current Time," invoking `time(0)` returns the current time in seconds elapsed since the time 00:00:00 on January 1, 1970 GMT. So, the following code will display a random integer with a random seed.

```
srand(time(0));
cout << rand() << endl;
```

To obtain a random integer between `0` and `9`, use

```
rand() % 10
```

The program may be set up to work as follows:

Step 1: Generate two single-digit integers into `number1` and `number2`.
Step 2: If `number1` < `number2`, swap `number1` with `number2`.
Step 3: Prompt the student to answer "What is number1 – number2?"
Step 4: Check the student's answer and display whether it is correct.

The complete program is shown in Listing 3.4.

LISTING 3.4 SubtractionQuiz.cpp

```
 1  #include <iostream>
 2  #include <ctime> // for time function
 3  #include <cstdlib> // for rand and srand functions
 4  using namespace std;
 5
 6  int main()
 7  {
 8    // 1. Generate two random single-digit integers
 9    srand(time(0));
10    int number1 = rand() % 10;
11    int number2 = rand() % 10;
12
13    // 2. If number1 < number2, swap number1 with number2
14    if (number1 < number2)
```

Key Point

VideoNote
Subtraction quiz

rand() function

pseudorandom

rsand(seed) function

include `ctime`
include `cstdlib`

set a seed
random `number1`
random `number2`

swap numbers

```
15   {
16     int temp = number1;
17     number1 = number2;
18     number2 = temp;
19   }
20
21   // 3. Prompt the student to answer "what is number1 - number2?"
22   cout << "What is " << number1 << " - " << number2 << "? ";
23   int answer;
```

enter answer
```
24   cin >> answer;
25
```

display result
```
26   // 4. Grade the answer and display the result
27   if (number1 - number2 == answer)
28     cout << "You are correct!";
29   else
30     cout << "Your answer is wrong. " << number1 << " - " << number2
31         << " should be " << (number1 - number2) << endl;
32
33   return 0;
34 }
```

```
What is 5 - 2? 3
You are correct!
```

```
What is 4 - 2? 1
Your answer is wrong.
4 - 2 should be 2
```

Line#	number1	number2	temp	answer	Output
10	2				
11		4			
16			2		
17	4				
18		2			
24				1	
30					Your answer is wrong 4 - 2 should be 2

To swap two variables `number1` and `number2`, a temporary variable `temp` (line 16) is first used to hold the value in `number1`. The value in `number2` is assigned to `number1` (line 17) and the value in `temp` is assigned to `number2` (line 18).

3.18 Which of the following is a possible output from invoking `rand()`?

323.4, 5, 34, 1, 0.5, 0.234

3.19 a. How do you generate a random integer i such that $0 \le i < 20$?

b. How do you generate a random integer i such that $10 \le i < 20$?

c. How do you generate a random integer i such that $10 \le i \le 50$?

    d. Write an expression that returns −1 or 1 randomly.

    e. Find out what RAND_MAX is on your machine.

3.20 Write an expression that obtains a random integer between 34 and 55. Write an expression that obtains a random integer between 0 and 999.

3.10 Logical Operators

The logical operators !, &&, and || can be used to create a compound Boolean expression.

Key Point

Sometimes, a combination of several conditions determines whether a statement is executed. You can use logical operators to combine these conditions. *Logical operators*, also known as *Boolean operators*, operate on Boolean values to create a new Boolean value. Table 3.3 gives a list of Boolean operators. Table 3.4 defines the not (!) operator. The not (!) operator negates true to false and false to true. Table 3.5 defines the and (&&) operator. The and (&&) of two Boolean operands is true if and only if both operands are true. Table 3.6 defines the or (||) operator. The or (||) of two Boolean operands is true if at least one of the operands is true.

TABLE 3.3 Boolean Operators

Operator	Name	Description
!	not	logical negation
&&	and	logical conjunction
||	or	logical disjunction

TABLE 3.4 Truth Table for Operator !

p	!p	Example (assume age = 24, weight = 140)
true	false	!(age > 18) is false, because (age > 18) is true.
false	true	!(weight == 150) is true, because (weight == 150) is false.

TABLE 3.5 Truth Table for Operator &&

p1	p2	p1 && p2	Example (assume age = 24, weight = 140)
false	false	false	(age > 18) && (weight <= 140) is true, because
false	true	false	(age > 18) and (weight <= 140) are both true.
true	false	false	(age > 18) && (weight > 140) is false, because
true	true	true	(weight > 140) is false.

TABLE 3.6 Truth Table for Operator ||

p1	p2	p1 || p2	Example (assume age = 24, weight = 140)
false	false	false	(age > 34) || (weight <= 140) is true, because
false	true	true	(weight <= 140) is true.
true	false	true	(age > 34) || (weight >= 150) is false, because
true	true	true	(age > 34) and (weight >= 150) are both false.

Listing 3.5 gives a program that checks whether a number is divisible by 2 and 3, by 2 or 3, and by 2 or 3 but not both:

LISTING **3.5** TestBooleanOperators.cpp

```
1  #include <iostream>
2  using namespace std;
3
4  int main()
5  {
6    int number;
7    cout << "Enter an integer: ";
8    cin >> number;
9
10   if (number % 2 == 0 && number % 3 == 0)
11     cout << number << " is divisible by 2 and 3." << endl;
12
13   if (number % 2 == 0 || number % 3 == 0)
14     cout << number << " is divisible by 2 or 3." << endl;
15
16   if ((number % 2 == 0 || number % 3 == 0) &&
17       !(number % 2 == 0 && number % 3 == 0))
18     cout << number << " divisible by 2 or 3, but not both." << endl;
19
20   return 0;
21 }
```

input

and

or

```
Enter an integer: 4
4 is divisible by 2 or 3.
4 is divisible by 2 or 3, but not both.
```

```
Enter an integer: 18
18 is divisible by 2 and 3
18 is divisible by 2 or 3.
```

(number % 2 == 0 && number % 3 == 0) (line 10) checks whether the number is divisible by 2 and 3. (number % 2 == 0 || number % 3 == 0) (line 13) checks whether the number is divisible by 2 or 3. So, the Boolean expression in lines 16–17

```
((number % 2 == 0 || number % 3 == 0) &&
  !(number % 2 == 0 && number % 3 == 0))
```

checks whether the number is divisible by 2 or 3 but not both.

 Caution

In mathematics, the expression

```
1 <= numberOfDaysInAMonth <= 31
```

is correct. However, it is incorrect in C++, because 1 <= **numberOfDaysInAMonth** is evaluated to a **bool** value, and then a **bool** value (1 for **true** and 0 for false) is compared with 31, which would lead to a logic error. The correct expression is

    incompatible operands

```
(1 <= numberOfDaysInAMonth) && (numberOfDaysInAMonth <= 31)
```

Note

De Morgan's law, named after Indian-born British mathematician and logician Augustus De Morgan (1806–1871), can be used to simplify Boolean expressions. The law states:

    De Morgan's law

```
!(condition1 && condition2)  is the same as
   !condition1 || !condition2
!(condition1 || condition2)  is the same as
   !condition1 && !condition2
```

For example,

```
!(number % 2 == 0 && number % 3 == 0)
```

can be simplified using an equivalent expression:

```
(number % 2 != 0 || number % 3 != 0)
```

As another example,

```
!(number == 2 || number == 3)
```

is better written as

```
number != 2 && number != 3
```

If one of the operands of an && operator is false, the expression is false; if one of the operands of an || operator is true, the expression is true. C++ uses these properties to improve the performance of these operators. When evaluating p1 && p2, C++ evaluates p1 and, if it is true, evaluates p2; otherwise it does not evaluate p2. When evaluating p1 || p2, C++ evaluates p1 and, if it is false, evaluates p2; otherwise it does not evaluate p2. Therefore, we refer to && as the *conditional* or *short-circuit AND* operator and to || as the *conditional* or *short-circuit OR* operator. C++ also provides the bitwise AND (&) and OR (|) operators, which are covered in Supplement IV.J and IV.K for advanced readers.

    conditional operator
    short-circuit operator

3.21 Assuming that x is 1, show the result of the following Boolean expressions:

```
(true) && (3 > 4)
!(x > 0) && (x > 0)
(x > 0) || (x < 0)
(x != 0) || (x == 0)
(x >= 0) || (x < 0)
(x != 1) == !(x == 1)
```

3.22 (a) Write a Boolean expression that evaluates to true if a number stored in variable num is between 1 and 100. (b) Write a Boolean expression that evaluates to true if a number stored in variable num is between 1 and 100 or the number is negative.

3.23 (a) Write a Boolean expression for $|x - 5| < 4.5$. (b) Write a Boolean expression for $|x - 5| > 4.5$.

3.24 To test whether x is between 10 and 100, which of the following expressions are correct?

a. `100 > x > 10`

b. `(100 > x) && (x > 10)`

c. `(100 > x) || (x > 10)`

d. `(100 > x) and (x > 10)`

e. `(100 > x) or (x > 10)`

3.25 Are the following two expressions the same?

a. `x % 2 == 0 && x % 3 == 0`

b. `x % 6 == 0`

3.26 What is the value of the expression `x >= 50 && x <= 100` if x is `45`, `67`, or `101`?

3.27 Suppose, when you run the program, you enter the input `2 3 6` from the console. What is the output?

```
#include <iostream>
using namespace std;

int main()
{
  double x, y, z;
  cin >> x >> y >> z;

  cout << "(x < y && y < z) is " << (x < y && y < z) << endl;
  cout << "(x < y || y < z) is " << (x < y || y < z) << endl;
  cout << "!(x < y) is " << !(x < y) << endl;
  cout << "(x + y < z) is " << (x + y < z) << endl;
  cout << "(x + y > z) is " << (x + y > z) << endl;

  return 0;
}
```

3.28 Write a Boolean expression that evaluates to `true` if age is greater than 13 and less than 18.

3.29 Write a Boolean expression that evaluates to `true` if weight is greater than 50 pounds or height is greater than 60 inches.

3.30 Write a Boolean expression that evaluates to `true` if weight is greater than 50 pounds and height is greater than 60 inches

3.31 Write a Boolean expression that evaluates to `true` if either weight is greater than 50 pounds or height is greater than 60 inches, but not both.

3.11 Case Study: Determining Leap Year

Key Point

A year is a leap year *if it is divisible by 4 but not by 100, or if it is divisible by 400.*

You can use the following Boolean expressions to check whether a year is a leap year:

```
// A leap year is divisible by 4
bool isLeapYear = (year % 4 == 0);
```

```
// A leap year is divisible by 4 but not by 100
isLeapYear = isLeapYear && (year % 100 != 0);

// A leap year is divisible by 4 but not by 100 or divisible by 400
isLeapYear = isLeapYear || (year % 400 == 0);
```

or you can combine all these expressions into one:

```
isLeapYear = (year % 4 == 0 && year % 100 != 0) || (year % 400 == 0);
```

Listing 3.6 gives a program that lets the user enter a year and checks whether it is a leap year.

LISTING 3.6 LeapYear.cpp

```
1   #include <iostream>
2   using namespace std;
3
4   int main()
5   {
6     cout << "Enter a year: ";
7     int year;
8     cin >> year;                                              input
9
10    // Check if the year is a leap year
11    bool isLeapYear =                                         leap year?
12      (year % 4 == 0 && year % 100 != 0) || (year % 400 == 0);
13
14    // Display the result
15    if (isLeapYear)                                           if statement
16      cout << year << " is a leap year" << endl;
17    else
18      cout << year << " is a not leap year" << endl;
19
20    return 0;
21  }
```

```
Enter a year: 2008 ↵Enter
2008 is a leap year
```

```
Enter a year: 1900 ↵Enter
1900 is not a leap year
```

```
Enter a year: 2002 ↵Enter
2002 is not a leap year
```

3.12 Case Study: Lottery

The lottery program involves generating random numbers, comparing digits, and using Boolean operators.

Key Point

Suppose you are to develop a program to play the lottery. The program randomly generates a lottery of a two-digit number, prompts the user to enter a two-digit number, and determines whether the user wins according to the following rule:

1. If the user input matches the lottery number in the exact order, the award is $10,000.

2. If all the digits in the user input match all the digits in the lottery number, the award is $3,000.

3. If one digit in the user input matches a digit in the lottery number, the award is $1,000.

Note that the digits of a two-digit number may be 0. If a number is less than 10, we assume the number is preceded by a 0 to form a two-digit number. For example, number 8 is treated as 08 and number 0 is treated as 00 in the program. Listing 3.7 gives the complete program.

LISTING 3.7 Lottery.cpp

```
 1  #include <iostream>
 2  #include <ctime> // for time function
 3  #include <cstdlib> // for rand and srand functions
 4  using namespace std;
 5
 6  int main()
 7  {
 8    // Generate a lottery
 9    srand(time(0));
10    int lottery = rand() % 100;
11
12    // Prompt the user to enter a guess
13    cout << "Enter your lottery pick (two digits): ";
14    int guess;
15    cin >> guess;
16
17    // Get digits from lottery
18    int lotteryDigit1 = lottery / 10;
19    int lotteryDigit2 = lottery % 10;
20
21    // Get digits from guess
22    int guessDigit1 = guess / 10;
23    int guessDigit2 = guess % 10;
24
25    cout << "The lottery number is " << lottery << endl;
26
27    // Check the guess
28    if (guess == lottery)
29      cout << "Exact match: you win $10,000" << endl;
30    else if (guessDigit2 == lotteryDigit1
31        && guessDigit1 == lotteryDigit2)
32      cout << "Match all digits: you win $3,000" << endl;
33    else if (guessDigit1 == lotteryDigit1
34          || guessDigit1 == lotteryDigit2
35          || guessDigit2 == lotteryDigit1
36          || guessDigit2 == lotteryDigit2)
37      cout << "Match one digit: you win $1,000" << endl;
38    else
39      cout << "Sorry, no match" << endl;
40
41    return 0;
42  }
```

generate a lottery number (line 10)

enter a guess (line 15)

exact match? (line 28)

match all digits? (line 30)

match one digit? (line 33)

no match (line 38)

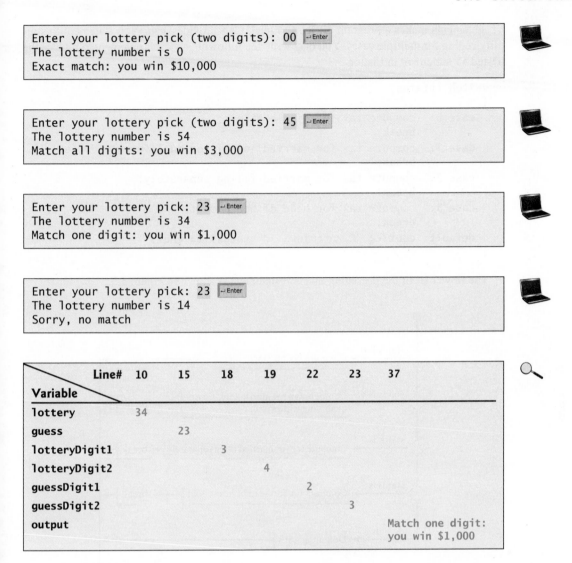

```
Enter your lottery pick (two digits): 00 ↵Enter
The lottery number is 0
Exact match: you win $10,000
```

```
Enter your lottery pick (two digits): 45 ↵Enter
The lottery number is 54
Match all digits: you win $3,000
```

```
Enter your lottery pick: 23 ↵Enter
The lottery number is 34
Match one digit: you win $1,000
```

```
Enter your lottery pick: 23 ↵Enter
The lottery number is 14
Sorry, no match
```

Variable \ Line#	10	15	18	19	22	23	37
lottery	34						
guess		23					
lotteryDigit1			3				
lotteryDigit2				4			
guessDigit1					2		
guessDigit2						3	
output							Match one digit: you win $1,000

The program generates a lottery using the **rand()** function (line 10) and prompts the user to enter a guess (line 15). Note that **guess % 10** obtains the last digit from **guess**, and **guess / 10** obtains the first digit from **guess**, since **guess** is a two-digit number (lines 22–23).

The program checks the guess against the lottery number in this order:

1. First, check whether the guess matches the lottery exactly (line 28).

2. If not, check whether the reversal of the guess matches the lottery (lines 30–31).

3. If not, check whether one digit is in the lottery (lines 33–36).

4. If not, nothing matches and display **"Sorry, no match"** (lines 38–39).

3.13 **switch** Statements

A **switch** *statement executes statements based on the value of a variable or an expression.*

Key Point

The **if** statement in Listing 3.3, ComputeTax.cpp, makes selections based on a single **true** or **false** condition. There are four cases for computing taxes, which depend on the value of **status**. To account fully for all the cases, nested **if** statements were used. Overusing nested `if` statements makes a program difficult to read. C++ provides a `switch` statement to simplify coding for multiple cases. You may write the following `switch` statement to replace the nested `if` statement in Listing 3.3:

```
switch (status)
{
  case 0:  compute tax for single filers;
           break;
  case 1:  compute tax for married jointly or qualifying widow(er);
           break;
  case 2:  compute tax for married filing separately;
           break;
  case 3:  compute tax for head of household;
           break;
  default: cout << "Error: invalid status" << endl;
}
```

The flowchart of the preceding `switch` statement is shown in Figure 3.5.

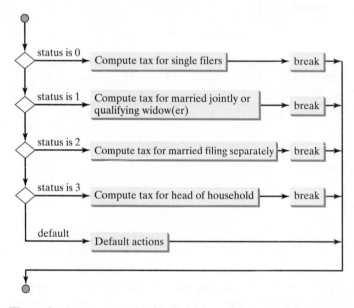

FIGURE 3.5 The `switch` statement checks all cases and executes the statements in the matched case.

This statement checks to see whether the status matches the value 0, 1, 2, or 3, in that order. If there is a match, the corresponding tax is computed; if not, a message is displayed. Here is the full syntax for the `switch` statement:

switch statement

```
switch (switch-expression)
{
  case value1: statement(s)1;
               break;
  case value2: statement(s)2;
               break;
  ...
  case valueN: statement(s)N;
               break;
  default:     statement(s)-for-default;
}
```

The **switch** statement observes the following rules:

- The **switch-expression** must yield an integral value and always be enclosed in parentheses.

- The **value1**, ... , and **valueN** are integral constant expressions, meaning that they cannot contain variables, such as **1 + x**. These values are integers and cannot be floating-point values.

- When the value in a **case** statement matches the value of the **switch-expression**, the statements *starting from this case* are executed until either a **break** statement or the end of the **switch** statement is reached.

- The **default** case, which is optional, can be used to perform actions when none of the specified cases matches the **switch-expression**.

- The keyword **break** is optional. The **break** statement immediately ends the **switch** statement.

Caution

Do not forget to use a **break** statement when necessary. Once a case is matched, the statements starting from the matched case are executed until a **break** statement or the end of the **switch** statement is reached. This is called *fall-through behavior*. For example, the following code displays **Weekdays** for days **1** to **5** and **Weekends** for day **0** and **6**.

```
switch (day)
{
  case 1: // Fall to through to the next case
  case 2: // Fall to through to the next case
  case 3: // Fall to through to the next case
  case 4: // Fall to through to the next case
  case 5: cout << "Weekday"; break;
  case 0: // Fall to through to the next case
  case 6: cout << "Weekend";
}
```

Tip

To avoid programming errors and improve code maintainability, it is a good idea to put a comment in a case clause if **break** is purposely omitted.

Now let us write a program to determine the Chinese Zodiac sign for a given year. The Chinese Zodiac is based on a twelve-year cycle, each year being represented by an animal: rat, ox, tiger, rabbit, dragon, snake, horse, sheep, monkey, rooster, dog, and pig, in this cycle, as shown in Figure 3.6 (next page).

Note that **year % 12** determines the Zodiac sign. 1900 is the year of the rat since **1900 % 12** is **4**. Listing 3.8 gives a program that prompts the user to enter a year and displays the animal for the year.

LISTING 3.8 ChineseZodiac.cpp

```
1  #include <iostream>
2  using namespace std;
3
4  int main()
5  {
6    cout << "Enter a year: ";
```

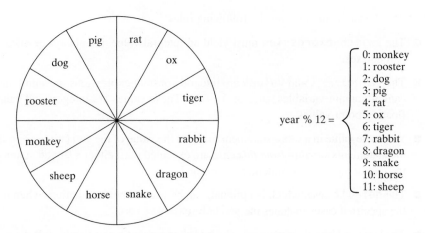

year % 12 =
$\begin{cases} \text{0: monkey} \\ \text{1: rooster} \\ \text{2: dog} \\ \text{3: pig} \\ \text{4: rat} \\ \text{5: ox} \\ \text{6: tiger} \\ \text{7: rabbit} \\ \text{8: dragon} \\ \text{9: snake} \\ \text{10: horse} \\ \text{11: sheep} \end{cases}$

FIGURE 3.6 The Chinese Zodiac is based on a twelve-year cycle.

enter year

determine Zodiac sign

```cpp
7    int year;
8    cin >> year;
9
10   switch (year % 12)
11   {
12     case 0: cout << "monkey" << endl; break;
13     case 1: cout << "rooster" << endl; break;
14     case 2: cout << "dog" << endl; break;
15     case 3: cout << "pig" << endl; break;
16     case 4: cout << "rat" << endl; break;
17     case 5: cout << "ox" << endl; break;
18     case 6: cout << "tiger" << endl; break;
19     case 7: cout << "rabbit" << endl; break;
20     case 8: cout << "dragon" << endl; break;
21     case 9: cout << "snake" << endl; break;
22     case 10: cout << "horse" << endl; break;
23     case 11: cout << "sheep" << endl; break;
24   }
25
26   return 0;
27 }
```

```
Enter a year: 1963 ⏎Enter
rabbit
```

```
Enter a year: 1877 ⏎Enter
ox
```

3.32 What data types are required for a `switch` variable? If the keyword `break` is not used after a case is processed, what is the next statement to be executed? Can you convert a `switch` statement to an equivalent `if` statement, or vice versa? What are the advantages of using a `switch` statement?

3.33 What is y after the following `switch` statement is executed? Rewrite the code using an `if` statement.

```
x = 3; y = 3;
switch (x + 3)
{
  case 6:  y = 1;
  default: y += 1;
}
```

3.34 What is x after the following `if-else` statement is executed? Use a `switch` statement to rewrite it and draw the flowchart for the new `switch` statement.

```
int x = 1, a = 3;
if (a == 1)
  x += 5;
else if (a == 2)
  x += 10;
else if (a == 3)
  x += 16;
else if (a == 4)
  x += 34;
```

3.14 Conditional Expressions

A conditional expression evaluates an expression based on a condition.

Key Point

You might want to assign a variable a value that is restricted by certain conditions. For example, the following statement assigns 1 to y if x is greater than 0, and -1 to y if x is less than or equal to 0.

conditional expression

```
if (x > 0)
  y = 1;
else
  y = -1;
```

Alternatively, as in the next example, you can use a conditional expression to achieve the same result:

```
y = x > 0 ? 1 : -1;
```

Conditional expressions have a completely different structure and do not include an explicit `if`. The syntax is shown here:

```
boolean-expression ? expression1 : expression2;
```

The result of this conditional expression is `expression1` if `boolean-expression` is `true`; otherwise, the result is `expression2`.

Suppose you want to assign the larger number between variable `num1` and `num2` to `max`. You can simply write a statement using the conditional expression:

```
max = num1 > num2 ? num1 : num2;
```

As another example, the following statement displays the message `"num is even"` if `num` is even, and otherwise displays `"num is odd."`

```
cout << (num % 2 == 0 ? "num is even" : "num is odd") << endl;
```

ternary operator

Note
The symbols **?** and **:** appear together in a conditional expression. They form a conditional operator called a *ternary operator* because it uses three operands. It is the only ternary operator in C++.

Check Point

3.35 Suppose that, when you run the following program, you enter the input `2  3  6` from the console. What is the output?

```cpp
#include <iostream>
using namespace std;

int main()
{
  double x, y, z;
  cin >> x >> y >> z;

  cout << (x < y && y < z ? "sorted" : "not sorted") << endl;

  return 0;
}
```

3.36 Rewrite the following `if` statements using the conditional operator:

```cpp
if (ages >= 16)
  ticketPrice = 20;
else
  ticketPrice = 10;
```

```cpp
if (count % 10 == 0)
  cout << count << endl;
else
  cout << count << " ";
```

3.37 Rewrite the following conditional expressions using `if-else` statements:
a. `score = x > 10 ? 3 * scale : 4 * scale;`
b. `tax = income > 10000 ? income * 0.2 : income * 0.17 + 1000;`
c. `cout << (number % 3 == 0 ? i : j) << endl;`

3.15 Operator Precedence and Associativity

Key Point

Operator precedence and associativity determine the order in which operators are evaluated.

operator precedence

Section 2.9, "Evaluating Expressions and Operator Precedence," introduced *operator precedence* involving arithmetic operators. This section discusses operator precedence in more details. Suppose that you have the following expression:

```
3 + 4 * 4 > 5 * (4 + 3) - 1 && (4 - 3 > 5)
```

What is its value? What is the execution order of the operators?

The expression in the parentheses is evaluated first. (Parentheses can be nested, in which case the expression in the inner parentheses is executed first.) When evaluating an expression without parentheses, the operators are applied according to the precedence rule and the associativity rule.

The precedence rule defines precedence for operators, as shown in Table 3.7, which contains the operators you have learned so far. Operators are listed in decreasing order of precedence from top to bottom. The logical operators have lower precedence than the relational operators and the relational operators have lower precedence than the arithmetic operators. Operators with the same precedence appear in the same group. (See Appendix C, Operator Precedence Chart, for a complete list of C++ operators and their precedence.)

TABLE 3.7   Operator Precedence Chart

Precedence	Operator
	`var++` and `var--` (Postfix)
	`+`, `-` (Unary plus and minus), `++var` and `--var` (Prefix)
	`static_cast<type>(v)`, (type) (Casting)
	`!` (Not)
	`*`, `/`, `%` (Multiplication, division, and remainder)
	`+`, `-` (Binary addition and subtraction)
	`<`, `<=`, `>`, `>=` (Relational)
	`==`, `!=` (Equality)
	`&&` (AND)
	`||` (OR)
	`=`, `+=`, `-=`, `*=`, `/=`, `%=` (Assignment operator)

If operators with the same precedence are next to each other, their *associativity* determines the order of evaluation. All binary operators except assignment operators are *left associative*. For example, since + and – are of the same precedence and are left associative, the expression

operator associativity

$$a - b + c - d \quad \overset{\text{is equivalent to}}{=\!=\!=\!=\!=\!=} \quad ((a - b) + c) - d$$

Assignment operators are *right associative*. Therefore, the expression

$$a = b\ +\!=\ c = 5 \quad \overset{\text{is equivalent to}}{=\!=\!=\!=\!=\!=} \quad a = (b\ +\!=\ (c = 5))$$

Suppose a, b, and c are 1 before the assignment; after the whole expression is evaluated, a becomes 6, b becomes 6, and c becomes 5. Note that left associativity for the assignment operator would not make sense.

> **Tip**
> You can use parentheses to force an evaluation order as well as to make a program easy to read. Use of redundant parentheses does not slow down the execution of the expression.

3.38   List the precedence order of the Boolean operators. Evaluate the following expressions:

```
true || true && false

true && true || false
```

3.39   True or false? All the binary operators except = are left associative.

3.40   Evaluate the following expressions:

```
2 * 2 - 3 > 2 && 4 - 2 > 5

2 * 2 - 3 > 2 || 4 - 2 > 5
```

3.41 Is (x > 0 && x < 10) the same as ((x > 0) && (x < 10))? Is (x > 0 ||
x < 10) the same as ((x > 0) || (x < 10))? Is (x > 0 || x < 10 &&
y < 0) the same as (x > 0 || (x < 10 && y < 0))?

3.16 Debugging

Key
Point

Debugging is the process of finding and fixing errors in a program.

As discussed in Section 1.9.1, syntax errors are easy to find and easy to correct because the compiler indicates where the errors came from and why they are wrong. Runtime errors are not difficult to find either, since the operating system displays them on the console when the program aborts. Finding logic errors, on the other hand, can be very challenging.

bugs
debugging
hand-traces

Logic errors are called *bugs*. The process of finding and correcting errors is called *debugging*. A common approach to debugging is to use a combination of methods to narrow down to the part of the program where the bug is located. You can *hand-trace* the program (i.e., catch errors by reading the program), or you can insert print statements in order to show the values of the variables or the execution flow of the program. This approach might work for a short, simple program. However, for a large, complex program, the most effective approach for debugging is to use a debugger utility.

debugging in IDE

The C++ IDE tools, such as Visual C++, include integrated debuggers. The debugger utilities let you follow the execution of a program. They vary from one system to another, but they all support most of the following helpful features:

- **Executing a single statement at a time:** The debugger allows you to execute one statement at a time so that you can see the effect of each statement.

- **Tracing into or stepping over a function:** If a function is being executed, you can ask the debugger to enter the function and execute one statement at a time in the function, or you can ask it to step over the entire function. You should step over the entire function if you know that the function works. For example, always step over system-supplied functions, such as pow(a, b).

- **Setting breakpoints:** You can also set a breakpoint at a specific statement. Your program pauses when it reaches a breakpoint and displays the line with the breakpoint. You can set as many breakpoints as you want. Breakpoints are particularly useful when you know where your programming error starts. You can set a breakpoint at that line and have the program execute until it reaches the breakpoint.

- **Displaying variables:** The debugger lets you select several variables and display their values. As you trace through a program, the content of a variable is continuously updated.

- **Displaying call stacks:** The debugger lets you trace all of the function calls and lists all pending functions. This feature is helpful when you need to see a large picture of the program-execution flow.

- **Modifying variables:** Some debuggers enable you to modify the value of a variable when debugging. This is convenient when you want to test a program with different samples but do not want to leave the debugger.

Tip
If you use Microsoft Visual C++, please refer to *Learning C++ Effectively with Microsoft Visual C++* in Supplement II.C. The supplement shows you how to use a debugger to trace programs and how debugging can help you learn C++ effectively.

KEY TERMS

CHAPTER SUMMARY

1. A `bool` type variable can store a `true` or `false` value.

2. Internally, C++ uses `1` to represent `true` and `0` for `false`.

3. If you display a `bool` value to the console, `1` is displayed if the value is `true` and `0` if the value is `false`.

4. In C++, you can assign a numeric value to a `bool` variable. Any nonzero value evaluates to `true` and zero value evaluates to `false`.

5. The relational operators (<, <=, ==, !=, >, >=) yield a Boolean value.

6. The equality testing operator is two equal signs (==), not a single equal sign (=). The latter symbol is for assignment.

7. *Selection statements* are used for programming with alternative courses of actions. There are several types of selection statements: `if` statements, two-way `if-else` statements, nested `if` statements, multi-way `if-else` statements, `switch` statements, and conditional expressions.

8. The various `if` statements all make control decisions based on a *Boolean expression*. Based on the `true` or `false` evaluation of the expression, these statements take one of two possible courses.

9. The Boolean operators `&&`, `||`, and `!` operate with Boolean values and variables.

10. When evaluating `p1 && p2`, C++ first evaluates `p1` and then evaluates `p2` if `p1` is `true`; if `p1` is `false`, it does not evaluate `p2`. When evaluating `p1 || p2`, C++ first evaluates `p1` and then evaluates `p2` if `p1` is `false`; if `p1` is `true`, it does not evaluate `p2`. Therefore, `&&` is referred to as the *conditional* or *short-circuit AND operator*, and `||` is referred to as the *conditional* or *short-circuit OR operator*.

11. The `switch` statement makes control decisions based on a switch expression.

12. The keyword `break` is optional in a `switch` statement, but it is normally used at the end of each case in order to skip the remainder of the `switch` statement. If the `break` statement is not present, the next `case` statement will be executed.

13. The operators in expressions are evaluated in the order determined by the rules of parentheses, *operator precedence*, and *operator associativity*.

14. Parentheses can be used to force the order of evaluation to occur in any sequence.

15. Operators with higher precedence are evaluated earlier. For operators of the same precedence, their associativity determines the order of evaluation

16. All binary operators except assignment operators are left-associative; assignment operators are right-associative.

QUIZ

Answer the quiz for this chapter online at www.cs.armstrong.edu/liang/cpp3e/quiz.html.

MyProgrammingLab™ ## PROGRAMMING EXERCISES

Note
For each exercise, carefully analyze the problem requirements and design strategies for solving the problem before coding.

think before coding

Note
Before you ask for help, read and understand the program, and trace it using several representative inputs by hand or by using an IDE debugger. You learn how to program by debugging your mistakes.

learn from mistakes

Sections 3.3–3.8

*3.1 (*Algebra: solve quadratic equations*) The two roots of a quadratic equation $ax^2 + bx + c = 0$ can be obtained using the following formula:

$$r_1 = \frac{-b + \sqrt{b^2 - 4ac}}{2a} \quad \text{and} \quad r_2 = \frac{-b - \sqrt{b^2 - 4ac}}{2a}$$

$b^2 - 4ac$ is called the discriminant of the quadratic equation. If it is positive, the equation has two real roots. If it is zero, the equation has one root. If it is negative, the equation has no real roots.

Write a program that prompts the user to enter values for a, b, and c and displays the result based on the discriminant. If the discriminant is positive, display two roots. If the discriminant is 0, display one root. Otherwise, display "The equation has no real roots."

Note that you can use `pow(x, 0.5)` to compute $\sqrt{x}$. Here are some sample runs.

```
Enter a, b, c: 1.0 3 1   ↵Enter
The roots are -0.381966 and -2.61803
```

```
Enter a, b, c: 1 2.0 1   ↵Enter
The root is -1
```

```
Enter a, b, c: 1 2 3   ↵Enter
The equation has no real roots
```

3.2 (*Check numbers*) Write a program that prompts the user to enter two integers and checks whether the first number is divisible by the second. Here is a sample run:

```
Enter two integers: 2 3  ↵Enter
2 is not divisible by 3
```

```
Enter two integers: 22 2  ↵Enter
22 is divisible by 2
```

*3.3 (*Algebra: solve 2 × 2 linear equations*) You can use Cramer's rule to solve the following 2 × 2 system of linear equation:

$$ax + by = e \qquad x = \frac{ed - bf}{ad - bc} \qquad y = \frac{af - ec}{ad - bc}$$
$$cx + dy = f$$

Write a program that prompts the user to enter *a, b, c, d, e,* and *f,* and displays the result. If *ad − bc* is **0**, report that "The equation has no solution."

```
Enter a, b, c, d, e, f: 9.0 4.0 3.0 -5.0 -6.0 -21.0  ↵Enter
x is -2.0 and y is 3.0
```

```
Enter a, b, c, d, e, f: 1.0 2.0 2.0 4.0 4.0 5.0  ↵Enter
The equation has no solution
```

**3.4 (*Check the speed*) Write a program that prompts the user to enter the speed of a vehicle. If speed is less than 20, display `too slow`; if speed is greater than 80, display `too fast`; otherwise, display `just right`.

*3.5 (*Find future dates*) Write a program that prompts the user to enter an integer for today's day of the week (Sunday is 0, Monday is 1, . . . , and Saturday is 6). Also, prompt the user to enter the number of days after today for a future day and display the future day of the week. Here is a sample run:

```
Enter today's day: 1  ↵Enter
Enter the number of days elapsed since today: 3  ↵Enter
Today is Monday and the future day is Thursday
```

```
Enter today's day: 0  ↵Enter
Enter the number of days elapsed since today: 31  ↵Enter
Today is Sunday and the future day is Wednesday
```

*3.6 (*Health application: BMI*) Revise Listing 3.2, ComputeAndInterpretBMI.cpp, to let the user enter weight, feet, and inches. For example, if a person is 5 feet, 10 inches, you will enter **5** for feet and **10** for inches. Here is a sample run:

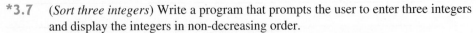

```
Enter weight in pounds: 140   ↵Enter
Enter feet: 5   ↵Enter
Enter inches: 10   ↵Enter
BMI is 20.087702275404553
Normal
```

VideoNote

Sort three integers

*3.7 (*Sort three integers*) Write a program that prompts the user to enter three integers and display the integers in non-decreasing order.

*3.8 (*Comparing Integers*) Write a program that prompts the user to enter the edges of a triangle and compares them. If all edges are equal, display `Equilateral Triangle`; if only two edges are equal, display `Isosceles Triangle` and if none of the edges are equal, display `Scalene Triangle`.

Sections 3.9–3.16

*3.9 (*Display the day and remaining hours*) Write a program that prompts the user to enter the day number of a week and hours passed, and displays the day and remaining hours. For example, if the user entered day number 1 and hours passed 20, the program should display `Today is Sunday` and `Remaining Hours: 4`. If the user entered day number 7 and hours passed 2, the program should display `Today is Saturday` and `Remaining Hours 22`.

3.10 (*Game: Multiplication quiz*) Listing 3.4, `SubtractionQuiz.cpp`, randomly generates a subtraction question. Revise the program to randomly generate a multiplication question with two integers less than 50.

*3.11 (*Loan Interest Rates*) A bank uses the following function to calculate the rate of interest (in percentage) for a particular loan amount (in lakhs of dollars).

$$r(a) = \begin{cases} 15, & if\ 0.1 < a \le 1 \\ 13.5, & if\ 1 < a \le 5 \\ 12.5, & if\ 5 < a \le 10 \\ 11.0, & if\ 10 < a \le 50 \end{cases}$$

Write a program that prompts the user to enter the amount of the loan and displays the rate of interest. If the amount is less than $10,000 or more than $50,00,000, display a message "Loan cannot be provided."

3.12 (*Game: Even or Odd*) Write a program that lets the user guess whether a randomly generated integer would be even or odd. The program randomly generates an integer and divides it by 2. The integer is even if the remainder is 0, otherwise odd. The program prompts the user to enter a guess and reports whether the guess is correct or incorrect.

*3.13 (*Financial application: compute taxes*) Listing 3.3, ComputeTax.cpp, gives the source code to compute taxes for single filers. Complete Listing 3.3 to give the complete source code.

**3.14 (*Game: Prediction*) Write a program that generates a random two-digit integer. The program prompts the user to predict the generated number by entering a two-digit integer, and then determines the accuracy of the user's prediction according to the following rules:

If the user's prediction matches the generated number exactly, the accuracy is 100%. If one digit in the user's predicted number matches a digit in the generated number, the accuracy is 50%. If none of the digits in user's predicted number matches with the generated number, the accuracy is 0%.

*3.15 (*Game: scissor, rock, paper*) Write a program that plays the popular scissor, rock, paper game. (A scissor can cut a paper, a rock can knock a scissor, and a paper can wrap a rock.) The program randomly generates a number **0**, **1**, or **2** representing scissor, rock, or paper. The program prompts the user to enter a number **0**, **1**, or **2** and displays a message indicating whether the user or the computer wins, loses, or draws. Here are sample runs:

```
scissor (0), rock (1), paper (2): 1  ↵Enter
The computer is scissor. You are rock. You won
```

```
scissor (0), rock (1), paper (2): 2  ↵Enter
The computer is paper. You are paper too. It is a draw
```

**3.16 (*Compute the area of an equilateral triangle*) Write a program that reads three edges of a triangle and computes the area if the input is valid. Otherwise, it displays that the input is invalid. The input is valid if all the edges of the triangle are equal.

*3.17 (*Sum the digits in an integer*) Programming Exercise 2.6 prompts the user to enter an integer between **0** and **1000**, and displays the sum of all digits in the integer. Write a program that prompts the user to enter a three-digit integer. The program displays the sum of all digits in the integer if the input is valid; otherwise, it displays a message indicating that the integer is not a three-digit number and hence, is invalid.

3.18 (*Game: Multiplication for four numbers*) Listing 3.4, `SubtractionQuiz.cpp`, randomly generates a subtraction question. Revise the program to randomly generate a multiplication question with four integers less than **5**.

Comprehensive

3.19 (*Geometry: point in a circle?*) Write a program that prompts the user to enter a point (x**, **y**) and checks whether the point is within the circle centered at (**0**, **0**) with radius **10**. For example, (**4**, **5**) is inside the circle and (**9**, **9**) is outside the circle, as shown in Figure 3.7a.

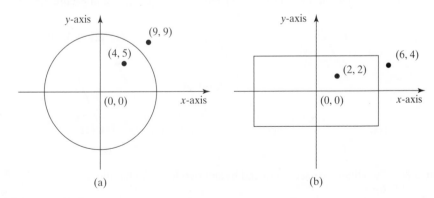

FIGURE 3.7 (a) Points inside and outside of the circle. (b) Points inside and outside of the rectangle.

(*Hint*: A point is in the circle if its distance to (**0**, **0**) is less than or equal to **10**. The formula for computing the distance is $\sqrt{(x_2 - x_1)^2 + (y_2 - y_1)^2}$. Test your program to cover all cases.) Two sample runs are shown here:

```
Enter a point with two coordinates: 4 5  ↵Enter
Point (4, 5) is in the circle
```

```
Enter a point with two coordinates: 9 9  ↵Enter
Point (9, 9) is not in the circle
```

**3.20 (*Geometry: point in a rectangle?*) Write a program that prompts the user to enter a point (x, y) and checks whether the point is within the rectangle centered at (0, 0) with width 10 and height 5. For example, (2, 2) is inside the rectangle and (6, 4) is outside the rectangle, as shown in Figure 3.7b. (*Hint*: A point is in the rectangle if its horizontal distance to (0, 0) is less than or equal to 10 / 2 and its vertical distance to (0, 0) is less than or equal to 5 / 2. Test your program to cover all cases.) Here are two sample runs.

```
Enter a point with two coordinates: 2 2  ↵Enter
Point (2, 2) is in the rectangle
```

```
Enter a point with two coordinates: 6 4  ↵Enter
Point (6, 4) is not in the rectangle
```

**3.21 (*Game: pick a card*) Write a program that simulates picking a card from a deck of 52 cards. Your program should display the rank (Ace, 2, 3, 4, 5, 6, 7, 8, 9, 10, Jack, Queen, King) and suit (Clubs, Diamonds, Hearts, Spades) of the card. Here is a sample run of the program:

```
The card you picked is Jack of Hearts
```

*3.22 (*Geometry: intersecting point*) Two points on line 1 are given as (x1, y1) and (x2, y2) and on line 2 as (x3, y3) and (x4, y4), as shown in Figure 3.8a–b.

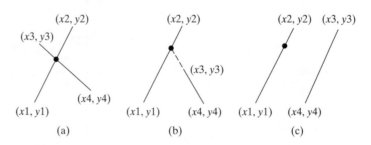

FIGURE 3.8 Two lines intersect in (a and b) and two lines are parallel in (c).

The intersecting point of the two lines can be found by solving the following linear equation:

$$(y_1 - y_2)x - (x_1 - x_2)y = (y_1 - y_2)x_1 - (x_1 - x_2)y_1$$

$$(y_3 - y_4)x - (x_3 - x_4)y = (y_3 - y_4)x_3 - (x_3 - x_4)y_3$$

This linear equation can be solved using Cramer's rule (see Programming Exercise 3.3). If the equation has no solutions, the two lines are parallel (Figure 3.8c). Write a program that prompts the user to enter four points and displays the intersecting point. Here are some sample runs:

```
Enter x1, y1, x2, y2, x3, y3, x4, y4: 2 2 5 -1.0 4.0 2.0 -1.0 -2.0 ↵Enter
The intersecting point is at (2.88889, 1.1111)
```

```
Enter x1, y1, x2, y2, x3, y3, x4, y4: 2 2 7 6.0 4.0 2.0 -1.0 -2.0 ↵Enter
The two lines are parallel
```

**3.23 (*Geometry: points in triangle?*) Suppose a right triangle is placed in a plane as shown below. The right-angle point is placed at (0, 0), and the other two points are placed at (200, 0), and (0, 100). Write a program that prompts the user to enter a point with x- and y-coordinates and determines whether the point is inside the triangle.

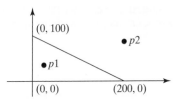

Here are the sample runs:

```
Enter a point's x- and y-coordinates: 100.5 25.5 ↵Enter
The point is in the triangle
```

```
Enter a point's x- and y-coordinates: 100.5 50.5 ↵Enter
The point is not in the triangle
```

3.24 (*Use the && and || operators*) Write a program that prompts the user to enter an integer and determines whether it is divisible by 5 and 6, whether it is divisible by 5 or 6, and whether it is divisible by 5 or 6, but not both. Here is a sample run of this program:

```
Enter an integer: 10 ↵Enter
Is 10 divisible by 5 and 6? false
Is 10 divisible by 5 or 6? true
Is 10 divisible by 5 or 6, but not both? true
```

**3.25 (*Geometry: two rectangles*) Write a program that prompts the user to enter the center x-, y-coordinates, width, and height of two rectangles and determines whether the second rectangle is inside the first or overlaps with the first, as shown in Figure 3.9. Test your program to cover all cases.

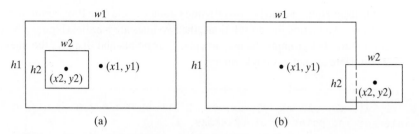

FIGURE 3.9 (a) A rectangle is inside another one. (b) A rectangle overlaps another one.

Here are the sample runs:

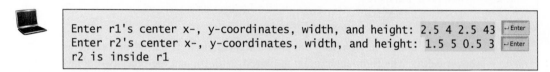

```
Enter r1's center x-, y-coordinates, width, and height: 2.5 4 2.5 43  ↵Enter
Enter r2's center x-, y-coordinates, width, and height: 1.5 5 0.5 3  ↵Enter
r2 is inside r1
```

```
Enter r1's center x-, y-coordinates, width, and height: 1 2 3 5.5  ↵Enter
Enter r2's center x-, y-coordinates, width, and height: 3 4 4.5 5  ↵Enter
r2 overlaps r1
```

```
Enter r1's center x-, y-coordinates, width, and height: 1 2 3 3  ↵Enter
Enter r2's center x-, y-coordinates, width, and height: 40 45 3 2  ↵Enter
r2 does not overlap r1
```

**3.26 (*Geometry: two circles*) Write a program that prompts the user to enter the center coordinates and radii of two circles and determines whether the second circle is inside the first or overlaps with the first, as shown in Figure 3.10. (*Hint*: circle2 is inside circle1 if the distance between the two centers <= |r1 - r2| and circle2 overlaps circle1 if the distance between the two centers <= r1 + r2. Test your program to cover all cases.)

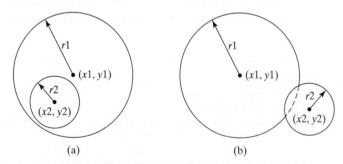

FIGURE 3.10 (a) A circle is inside another circle. (b) A circle overlaps another circle.

Here are the sample runs:

```
Enter circle1's center x-, y-coordinates, and radius: 0.5 5.1 13 ⏎Enter
Enter circle2's center x-, y-coordinates, and radius: 1 1.7 4.5 ⏎Enter
circle2 is inside circle1
```

```
Enter circle1's center x-, y-coordinates, and radius: 3.4 5.7 5.5 ⏎Enter
Enter circle2's center x-, y-coordinates, and radius: 6.7 3.5 3 ⏎Enter
circle2 overlaps circle1
```

```
Enter circle1's center x-, y-coordinates, and radius: 3.4 5.5 1 ⏎Enter
Enter circle2's center x-, y-coordinates, and radius: 5.5 7.2 1 ⏎Enter
circle2 does not overlap circle1
```

*3.27 (*Current time*) Revise Programming Exercise 2.8 to display the hour using a 12-hour clock. Here is a sample run:

```
Enter the time zone offset to GMT: -5 ⏎Enter
The current time is 4:50:34 AM
```

*3.28 (*Financials: currency exchange*) Write a program that prompts the user to enter the exchange rate from currency in U.S. dollars to Chinese RMB. Prompt the user to enter 0 to convert from U.S. dollars to Chinese RMB and 1 to convert from Chinese RMB and U.S. dollars. Prompt the user to enter the amount in U.S. dollars or Chinese RMB to convert it to Chinese RMB or U.S. dollars, respectively. Here are the sample runs:

```
Enter the exchange rate from dollars to RMB: 6.81 ⏎Enter
Enter 0 to convert dollars to RMB and 1 vice versa: 0 ⏎Enter
Enter the dollar amount: 100 ⏎Enter
$100 is 681 yuan
```

```
Enter the exchange rate from dollars to RMB: 6.81 ⏎Enter
Enter 0 to convert dollars to RMB and 1 vice versa: 1 ⏎Enter
Enter the RMB amount: 10000 ⏎Enter
10000.0 yuan is $1468.43
```

```
Enter the exchange rate from dollars to RMB: 6.81 ⏎Enter
Enter 0 to convert dollars to RMB and 1 vice versa: 5 ⏎Enter
Incorrect input
```

*3.29 (*Geometry: point position*) Given a directed line from point $p0(x0, y0)$ to $p1(x1, y1)$, you can use the following condition to decide whether a point $p2(x2, y2)$ is on the left of the line, on the right, or on the same line (see Figure 3.11):

$$(x1 - x0) * (y2 - y0) - (x2 - x0) * (y1 - y0) \begin{cases} > 0 \ p2 \text{ is on the left side of the line} \\ = 0 \ p2 \text{ is on the same line} \\ < 0 \ p2 \text{ is on the right side of the line} \end{cases}$$

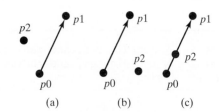

FIGURE 3.11 (a) $p2$ is on the left of the line. (b) $p2$ is on the right of the line. (c) p2 is on the same line.

Write a program that prompts the user to enter the three points for $p0$, $p1$, and $p2$ and displays whether $p2$ is on the left of the line from $p0$ to $p1$, to the right, or on the same line. Here are some sample runs:

```
Enter three points for p0, p1, and p2: 4.4 2 6.5 9.5 -5 4  ↵Enter
p2 is on the left side of the line
```

```
Enter three points for p0, p1, and p2: 1 1 5 5 2 2  ↵Enter
p2 is on the same line
```

```
Enter three points for p0, p1, and p2: 3.4 2 6.5 9.5 5 2.5  ↵Enter
p2 is on the right side of the line
```

*3.30 (*Financial: compare costs*) Suppose you shop for two different packages of rice. You would like to write a program to compare the cost. The program prompts the user to enter the weight and price of each package and displays the one with the better price. Here is a sample run:

```
Enter weight and price for package 1: 50 24.59  ↵Enter
Enter weight and price for package 2: 25 11.99  ↵Enter
Package 2 has a better price.
```

```
Enter weight and price for package 1: 50 25  ↵Enter
Enter weight and price for package 2: 25 12.5  ↵Enter
Two packages have the same price.
```

*3.31 (*Geometry: point on line segment*) Programming Exercise 3.29 shows how to test whether a point is on an unbounded line. Revise Programming Exercise 3.29 to test whether a point is on a line segment. Write a program that prompts the user to enter the three points for *p*0, *p*1, and *p*2 and displays whether *p*2 is on the line segment from *p*0 to *p*1. Here are some sample runs:

```
Enter three points for p0, p1, and p2: 1 1 2.5 2.5 1.5 1.5 ↵Enter
(1.5, 1.5) is on the line segment from (1, 1) to (2.5, 2.5)
```

```
Enter three points for p0, p1, and p2: 1 1 2 2 3.5 3.5 ↵Enter
(3.5, 3.5) is not on the line segment from (1, 1) to (2, 2)
```

*3.32 (*Algebra: slope-intercept form*) Write a program that prompts the user to enter the coordinates of two points ($x1$, $y1$) and ($x2$, $y2$), and displays the line equation in the slope-intercept form, i.e., $y = mx + b$. For a review of line equations, see www.purplemath.com/modules/strtlneq.htm. *m* and *b* can be computed using the following formula:

$$m = (y_2 - y_1)/(x_2 - x_1) \quad b = y_1 - mx_1$$

Don't display *m* if it is 1 and don't display *b* if it is 0. Here is a sample run:

```
Enter the coordinates for two points: 1 1 0 0 ↵Enter
The line equation for two points (1, 1) and (0, 0) is y = x
```

```
Enter the coordinates for two points: 4.5 –5.5 6.6 –6.5 ↵Enter
The line equation for two points (4.5, –5.5) and (6.6, –6.5) is
    y = –0.47619 x –3.35714
```

**3.33 (*Science: day of the week*) Zeller's congruence is an algorithm developed by Christian Zeller to calculate the day of the week. The formula is

$$h = \left(q + \frac{26(m + 1)}{10} + k + \frac{k}{4} + \frac{j}{4} + 5j \right) \% 7$$

where

- h is the day of the week (0: Saturday, 1: Sunday, 2: Monday, 3: Tuesday, 4: Wednesday, 5: Thursday, 6: Friday).
- q is the day of the month.
- m is the month (3: March, 4: April, . . . , 12: December). January and February are counted as months 13 and 14 of the previous year.
- j is the century (i.e., $\frac{year}{100}$).
- k is the year of the century (i.e., *year* % 100).

Note that the division in the formula performs an integer division. Write a program that prompts the user to enter a year, month, and day of the month, and displays the name of the day of the week. Here are some sample runs:

```
Enter year: (e.g., 2012): 2015 ↵Enter
Enter month: 1-12: 1 ↵Enter
Enter the day of the month: 1-31: 25 ↵Enter
Day of the week is Sunday
```

```
Enter year: (e.g., 2012): 2012 ↵Enter
Enter month: 1-12: 5 ↵Enter
Enter the day of the month: 1-31: 12 ↵Enter
Day of the week is Saturday
```

(*Hint*: January and February are counted as 13 and 14 in the formula, so you need to convert the user input 1 to 13 and 2 to 14 for the month and change the year to the previous year.)

3.34 (*Random point*) Write a program that displays two random coordinates in a square. The square is centered at (0, 0) with a side of 300.

**3.35 (*Business: check ISBN-10*) An ISBN-10 (International Standard Book Number) consists of 10 digits: $d_1d_2d_3d_4d_5d_6d_7d_8d_9d_{10}$. The last digit, d_{10}, is a checksum, which is calculated from the other nine digits using the following formula:

$$(d_1 \times 1 + d_2 \times 2 + d_3 \times 3 + d_4 \times 4 + d_5 \times 5 + d_6 \times 6 + d_7 \times 7$$

$$+ d_8 \times 8 + d_9 \times 9) \% 11$$

If the checksum is **10**, the last digit is denoted as X according to the ISBN-10 convention. Write a program that prompts the user to enter the first 9 digits and displays the 10-digit ISBN (including leading zeros). Your program should read the input as an integer. Here are sample runs:

```
Enter the first 9 digits of an ISBN as integer: 013601267 ↵Enter
The ISBN-10 number is 0136012671
```

```
Enter the first 9 digits of an ISBN as integer: 013031997 ↵Enter
The ISBN-10 number is 013031997X
```

3.36 (*Palindrome number*) Write a program that prompts the user to enter a three-digit integer and determines whether it is a palindrome number. A number is palindrome if it reads the same from right to left and from left to right. Here is a sample run of this program:

```
Enter a three-digit integer: 121 ↵Enter
121 is a palindrome
```

```
Enter a three-digit integer: 123 ↵Enter
123 is not a palindrome
```

CHAPTER

4

MATHEMATICAL FUNCTIONS, CHARACTERS, AND STRINGS

Objectives

- To solve mathematics problems by using the C++ mathematical functions (§4.2).
- To represent characters using the `char` type (§4.3).
- To encode characters using ASCII code (§4.3.1).
- To read a character from the keyboard (§4.3.2).
- To represent special characters using the escape sequences (§4.3.3).
- To cast a numeric value to a character and cast a character to an integer (§4.3.4).
- To compare and test characters (§4.3.5).
- To program using characters (`DisplayRandomCharacter`, `GuessBirthday`) (§§4.4–4.5).
- To test and convert characters using the C++ character functions (§4.6).
- To convert a hexadecimal character to a decimal value (`HexDigit2Dec`) (§4.7).
- To represent strings using the `string` type and introduce objects and instance functions (§4.8).
- To use the subscript operator for accessing and modifying characters in a string (§4.8.1).
- To use the + operator to concatenate strings (§4.8.2).
- To compare strings using the relational operators (§4.8.3).
- To read strings from the keyboard (§4.8.4).
- To revise the lottery program using strings (`LotteryUsingStrings`) (§4.9).
- To format output using stream manipulators (§4.10).
- To read/write data from/to a file (§4.11).

4.1 Introduction

The focus of this chapter is to introduce mathematical functions, characters, and string objects, and use them to develop programs.

The preceding chapters introduced fundamental programming techniques; you learned how to write simple programs to solve basic problems. This chapter introduces functions for performing common mathematical operations. You will learn how to create custom functions in Chapter 6.

problem

Suppose you need to estimate the area enclosed by four cities, given the GPS locations (latitude and longitude) of these cities, as shown in the following diagram. How would you write a program to solve this problem? You will be able to write such a program after completing this chapter.

Charlotte (35.2270869, −80.8431267)

Atlanta
(33.7489954, −84.3879824)

Savannah (32.0835407, −81.0998342)

Orlando (28.5383355, −81.3792365)

Because strings are frequently used in programming, it is beneficial to introduce them early so that you can begin to use them to develop useful programs. This chapter gives a brief introduction to string objects; you will learn more about objects and strings in Chapter 10.

4.2 Mathematical Functions

C++ provides many useful functions in the cmath header for performing common mathematical functions.

A function is a group of statements that performs a specific task. You have already used the `pow(a, b)` function to compute a^b in Section 2.8.4, "Exponent Operations," and the `rand()` function to generate a random number in Section 3.9, "Generating Random Numbers." This section introduces other useful functions. They can be categorized as *trigonometric functions*, *exponent functions*, and *service functions*. Service functions include the rounding, min, max, and absolute functions.

4.2.1 Trigonometric Functions

C++ provides the following functions as shown in Table 4.1 for performing trigonometric functions in the cmath header:

TABLE 4.1 Trigonometric Functions in the cmath Header

Function	Description
sin(radians)	Returns the trigonometric sine of an angle in radians.
cos(radians)	Returns the trigonometric cosine of an angle in radians
tan(radians)	Returns the trigonometric tangent of an angle in radians.
asin(a)	Returns the angle in radians for the inverse of sine.
acos(a)	Returns the angle in radians for the inverse of cosine.
atan(a)	Returns the angle in radians for the inverse of tangent.

The parameter for `sin`, `cos`, and `tan` is an angle in radians. The return value for `asin`, `acos`, and `atan` is an angle in radians in the range between $-\pi/2$ and $\pi/2$. One degree is equal to $\pi/180$ in radians, 90 degrees is equal to $\pi/2$ in radians, and 30 degrees is equal to $\pi/6$ in radians.

Assume `PI` is a constant with value `3.14159`. Here are some examples of using these functions:

```
sin(0) returns 0.0
sin(270 * PI / 180) returns -1.0
sin(PI / 6) returns 0.5
sin(PI / 2) returns 1.0
cos(0) returns 1.0
cos(PI / 6) returns 0.866
cos(PI / 2) returns 0
asin(0.5) returns 0.523599  (same as π/6)
acos(0.5) returns 1.0472  (same as π/3)
atan(1.0) returns 0.785398  (same as π/4)
```

4.2.2 Exponent Functions

There are five functions related to exponents in the `cmath` header as shown in Table 4.2.

TABLE 4.2 Exponent Functions in the `cmath` Header

Function	Description
`exp(x)`	Returns e raised to power of x (e^x).
`log(x)`	Returns the natural logarithm of x ($\ln(x) = \log_e(x)$).
`log10(x)`	Returns the base 10 logarithm of x ($\log_{10}(x)$).
`pow(a, b)`	Returns a raised to the power of b (a^b).
`sqrt(x)`	Returns the square root of x ($\sqrt{x}$) for x $>= 0$.

Assume `E` is a constant with value `2.71828`. Here are some examples of using these functions:

```
exp(1.0) returns 2.71828
log(E) returns 1.0
log10(10.0) returns 1.0
pow(2.0, 3) returns 8.0
sqrt(4.0) returns 2.0
sqrt(10.5) returns 3.24
```

4.2.3 Rounding Functions

The `cmath` header contains the functions for obtaining rounding as shown in Table 4.3.

TABLE 4.3 Rounding Functions in the `cmath` Header

Function	Description
`ceil(x)`	x is rounded up to its nearest integer. This integer is returned as a double value.
`floor(x)`	x is rounded down to its nearest integer. This integer is returned as a double value.

For example,

```
ceil(2.1) returns 3.0
ceil(2.0) returns 2.0
ceil(-2.0) returns -2.0
ceil(-2.1) returns -2.0
floor(2.1) returns 2.0
floor(2.0) returns 2.0
floor(-2.0) returns -2.0
floor(-2.1) returns -3.0
```

4.2.4   The **min**, **max**, and **abs** Functions

The min and max functions return the minimum and maximum numbers of two numbers (int, long, float, or double). For example, max(4.4, 5.0) returns 5.0, and min(3, 2) returns 2.

The abs function returns the absolute value of the number (int, long, float, or double). For example,

```
max(2,  3) returns 3
max(2.5,  3.0) returns 3.0
min(2.5,  4.6) returns 2.5
abs(-2) returns 2
abs(-2.1) returns 2.1
```

Note

The functions min, max, and abs are defined in the cstdlib header.

4.2.5   Case Study: Computing Angles of a Triangle

You can use the math functions to solve many computational problems. Given the three sides of a triangle, for example, you can compute the angles by using the following formula:

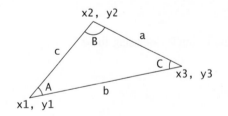

```
A = acos((a * a - b * b - c * c) / (-2 * b * c))
B = acos((b * b - a * a - c * c) / (-2 * a * c))
C = acos((c * c - b * b - a * a) / (-2 * a * b))
```

Don't be intimidated by the mathematic formula. As we discussed in Listing 2.11, ComputeLoan.cpp, you don't have to know how the mathematical formula is derived in order to write a program for computing the loan payments. In this example, given the length of three sides, you can use this formula to write a program to compute the angles without knowing how the formula is derived. In order to compute the lengths of the sides, we need to know the coordinates of three corner points and compute the distances between the points.

Listing 4.1 is an example of a program that prompts the user to enter the x- and y-coordinates of the three corner points in a triangle and then displays the triangle's angles.

LISTING 4.1   ComputeAngles.cpp

include cmath header

```
1  #include <iostream>
2  #include <cmath>
3  using namespace std;
4
```

```
5   int main()
6   {
7       // Prompt the user to enter three points
8       cout << "Enter three points: ";
9       double x1, y1, x2, y2, x3, y3;
10      cin >> x1 >> y1 >> x2 >> y2 >> x3 >> y3;                    enter three points
11
12      // Compute three sides
13      double a = sqrt((x2 - x3) * (x2 - x3) + (y2 - y3) * (y2 - y3));   compute sides
14      double b = sqrt((x1 - x3) * (x1 - x3) + (y1 - y3) * (y1 - y3));
15      double c = sqrt((x1 - x2) * (x1 - x2) + (y1 - y2) * (y1 - y2));
16
17      // Obtain three angles in radians
18      double A = acos((a * a - b * b - c * c) / (-2 * b * c));          compute angles
19      double B = acos((b * b - a * a - c * c) / (-2 * a * c));
20      double C = acos((c * c - b * b - a * a) / (-2 * a * b));
21
22      // Display the angles in degress
23      const double PI = 3.14159;                                        display result
24      cout << "The three angles are " << A * 180 / PI << " "
25           << B * 180 / PI << " " << C * 180 / PI << endl;
26
27      return 0;
28  }
```

```
Enter three points: 1 1 6.5 1 6.5 2.5  ⏎Enter
The three angles are 15.2551 90.0001 74.7449
```

The program prompts the user to enter three points (line 10). This prompting message is not clear. You should give the user explicit instructions on how to enter these points as follows:

```
cout << "Enter the coordinates of three points separated "
     << "by spaces like x1 y1 x2 y2 x3 y3: ";
```

Note that the distance between two points (x1, y1) and (x2, y2) can be computed using the formula $\sqrt{(x_2 - x_1)^2 + (y_2 - y_1)^2}$. The program applies this formula to compute the three sides (lines 13–15), and then applies the formula to compute the angles in radians (lines 18–20). The angles are displayed in degrees (lines 24–25). Note that 1 radian is $180/\pi$ degrees.

4.1   Assume PI is 3.14159 and E is 2.71828, evaluate the following function calls:

    (a) sqrt(4.0)   (j) floor(-2.5)

    (b) sin(2 * PI)   (k) asin(0.5)

    (c) cos(2 * PI)   (l) acos(0.5)

    (d) pow(2.0, 2)   (m) atan(1.0)

    (e) log(E)   (n) ceil(2.5)

    (f) exp(1.0)   (o) floor(2.5)

    (g) max(2, min(3, 4))   (p) log10(10.0)

    (h) sqrt(125.0)   (q) pow(2.0, 3)

    (i) ceil(-2.5)

4.2   True or false? The argument for trigonometric functions is an angle in radians.

4.3 Write a statement that converts 47 degrees to radians and assigns the result to a variable.

4.4 Write a statement that converts π / 7 to an angle in degrees and assigns the result to a variable.

4.3 Character Data Type and Operations

A character data type represents a single character.

char type

In addition to processing numeric values, you can process characters in C++. The character data type, **char**, is used to represent a single character. A character literal is enclosed in single quotation marks. Consider the following code:

```
char letter = 'A';
char numChar = '4';
```

The first statement assigns character **A** to the **char** variable **letter**. The second statement assigns digit character **4** to the **char** variable **numChar**.

char literal

> **Caution**
> A string literal must be enclosed in quotation marks (" "). A character literal is a single character enclosed in single quotation marks (' '). Therefore, **"A"** is a string and **'A'** is a character.

4.3.1 ASCII Code

Computers use binary numbers internally. A character is stored in a computer as a sequence of 0s and 1s. Mapping a character to its binary representation is called *encoding*. There are different ways to encode a character. How characters are encoded is defined by an *encoding scheme*.

encoding

ASCII

Most computers use *ASCII (American Standard Code for Information Interchange)*, an 8-bit encoding scheme for representing all uppercase and lowercase letters, digits, punctuation marks, and control characters. Table 4.4 shows the ASCII code for some commonly used characters. Appendix B, "The ASCII Character Set," gives a complete list of ASCII characters and their decimal and hexadecimal codes. On most systems, the size of the **char** type is 1 byte.

TABLE 4.4 ASCII Code for Commonly Used Characters

Characters	ASCII Code
'0' to '9'	48 to 57
'A' to 'Z'	65 to 90
'a' to 'z'	97 to 122

char increment and decrement

> **Note**
> The increment and decrement operators can also be used on **char** variables to get the next or preceding ASCII code character. For example, the following statements display character **b**.
>
> ```
> char ch = 'a';
> cout << ++ch;
> ```

4.3.2 Reading a Character from the Keyboard

To read a character from the keyboard, use

read character

```
cout << "Enter a character: ";
char ch;
cin >> ch; // Read a character
cout << "The character read is " << ch << endl;
```

4.3.3 Escape Sequences for Special Characters

Suppose you want to print a message with quotation marks in the output. Can you write a statement like this?

```
cout << "He said "Programming is fun"" << endl;
```

No, this statement has a compile error. The compiler thinks the second quotation character is the end of the string and does not know what to do with the rest of the characters.

To overcome this problem, C++ uses a special notation to represent special characters, as shown in Table 4.5. This special notation, called an *escape sequence*, consists of a backslash (\) followed by a character or a combination of digits. For example, \t is an escape sequence for the Tab character. The symbols in an escape sequence are interpreted as a whole rather than individually. An escape sequence is considered as a single character.

escape sequence

TABLE 4.5 Escape Sequences

Escape Sequence	Name	ASCII Code	Escape Sequence	Name	ASCII Code
\b	Backspace	8	\r	Carriage Return	13
\t	Tab	9	\\	Backslash	92
\n	Linefeed	10	\"	Double Quote	34
\f	Formfeed	12			

So, now you can print the quoted message using the following statement:

```
cout << "He said \"Programming is fun\"" << endl;
```

The output is

```
He said "Programming is fun"
```

Note that the symbols \ and " together represent one character.

The backslash \ is called an *escape character*. It is a special character. To display this character, you have to use an escape sequence \\. For example, the following code

escape character

```
cout << "\\t is a tab character" << endl;
```

displays

```
\t is a tab character
```

Note

The characters ' ', '\t', '\f', '\r', and '\n' are known as the *whitespace characters*.

whitespace character

Note

Both of the following statements display a string and move the cursor to the next line:

```
cout << "Welcome to C++\n";
cout << "Welcome to C++" << endl;
```

However, using **endl** ensures that the output is displayed immediately on all platforms.

\n vs. endl

4.3.4   Casting between **char** and Numeric Types

A **char** can be cast into any numeric type, and vice versa. When an integer is cast into a **char**, only its lower 8 bits of data are used; the other part is ignored. For example,

```
char c = 0XFF41; // The lower 8 bits hex code 41 is assigned to c
cout << c;       // variable c is character A
```

When a floating-point value is cast into a **char**, the floating-point value is first cast into an **int**, which is then cast into a **char**.

```
char c = 65.25;  // 65 is assigned to variable c
cout << c;       // variable c is character A
```

When a **char** is cast into a numeric type, the character's ASCII is cast into the specified numeric type. For example:

```
int i = 'A';     // The ASCII code of character A is assigned to i
cout << i;       // variable i is 65
```

numeric operators on characters

The **char** type is treated as if it were an integer of the byte size. All numeric operators can be applied to **char** operands. A **char** operand is automatically cast into a number if the other operand is a number or a character. For example, the following statements

```
// The ASCII code for '2' is 50 and for '3' is 51
int i = '2' + '3';
cout << "i is " << i << endl; // i is now 101

int j = 2 + 'a'; // The ASCII code for 'a' is 97
cout << "j is " << j << endl;
cout << j << " is the ASCII code for character " <<
  static_cast<char>(j) << endl;
```

display

```
i is 101
j is 99
99 is the ASCII code for character c
```

Note that the **static_cast<char>(value)** operator explicitly casts a numeric value into a character.

As shown in Table 4.4, ASCII codes for lowercase letters are consecutive integers starting from the ASCII code for **'a'**, then for **'b'**, **'c'**, ..., and **'z'**. The same is true for the uppercase letters and numeric characters. Furthermore, the ASCII code for **'a'** is greater than the code for **'A'**. You can use these properties to convert an uppercase letter to lowercase or vice versa. Listing 4.2 gives a program that prompts the user to enter a lowercase letter and finds its corresponding uppercase letter.

LISTING 4.2   ToUppercase.cpp

```
1  #include <iostream>
2  using namespace std;
3
4  int main()
5  {
6    cout << "Enter a lowercase letter: ";
7    char lowercaseLetter;
8    cin >> lowercaseLetter;
```

enter a character

```
9
10    char uppercaseLetter =
11      static_cast<char>('A' + (lowercaseLetter - 'a'));
12
13    cout << "The corresponding uppercase letter is "
14      << uppercaseLetter << endl;
15
16    return 0;
17  }
```

convert to uppercase

```
Enter a lowercase letter: b  ↵Enter
The corresponding uppercase letter is B
```

Note that for a lowercase letter **ch1** and its corresponding uppercase letter **ch2**, **ch1** - **'a'** is the same as **ch2** - **'A'**. Hence, **ch2** = **'A'** + **ch1** - **'a'**. Therefore, the corresponding uppercase letter for **lowercaseLetter** is **static_cast<char>('A' + (lowercaseLetter - 'a'))** (line 11). Note that lines 10–11 can be replaced by

```
char uppercaseLetter = 'A' + (lowercaseLetter - 'a');
```

Since **uppercaseLetter** is declared as a char type value, C++ automatically converts the **int** value **'A'** + **(lowercaseLetter - 'a')** to a **char** value.

4.3.5 Comparing and Testing Characters

Two characters can be compared using the relational operators just like comparing two numbers. This is done by comparing the ASCII codes of the two characters. For example,

'a' < **'b'** is true because the ASCII code for **'a'** (**97**) is less than the ASCII code for **'b'** (**98**).

'a' < **'A'** is false because the ASCII code for **'a'** (**97**) is greater than the ASCII code for **'A'** (**65**).

'1' < **'8'** is true because the ASCII code for **'1'** (**49**) is less than the ASCII code for **'8'** (**56**).

Often in the program, you need to test whether a character is a number, a letter, an uppercase letter, or a lowercase letter. For example, the following code tests whether a character **ch** is an uppercase letter.

```
if (ch >= 'A' && ch <= 'Z')
  cout << ch << " is an uppercase letter" << endl;
else if (ch >= 'a' && ch <= 'z')
  cout << ch << " is a lowercase letter" << endl;
else if (ch >= '0' && ch <= '9')
  cout << ch << " is a numeric character" << endl;
```

4.5 Use console print statements to determine the ASCII code for **'1'**, **'A'**, **'B'**, **'a'**, and **'b'**. Use print statements to determine the character for the decimal codes 40, 59, 79, 85, and 90. Use print statements to determine the character for the hexadecimal code 40, 5A, 71, 72, and 7A.

Check Point

4.6 Are the following correct literals for characters?

'1', **'\t'**, **'&'**, **'\b'**, **'\n'**

4.7 How do you display the characters \ and "?

4.8 Show the printout of the following code:

```
int i = '1';
int j = '1' + '2';
int k = 'a';
char c = 90;
cout << i << " " << j << " " << k << " " << c << endl;
```

4.9 Show the printout of the following code:

```
char c = 'A';
int i = c;

float f = 1000.34f;
int j = f;

double d = 1000.34;
int k = d;

int l = 97;
char ch = l;

cout << c << endl;
cout << i << endl;
cout << f << endl;
cout << j << endl;
cout << d << endl;
cout << k << endl;
cout << l << endl;
cout << ch << endl;
```

4.10 Show the output of the following program:

```
#include <iostream>
using namespace std;

int main()
{
  char x = 'a';
  char y = 'c';

  cout << ++x << endl;
  cout << y++ << endl;
  cout << (x - y) << endl;

  return 0;
}
```

4.4 Case Study: Generating Random Characters

**Key
Point**

*A character is coded using an integer. Generating a random character is to generate
an integer.*

Computer programs process numeric data and characters. You have seen many examples
involving numeric data. It is also important to understand characters and how to process them.
This section gives an example of generating random characters.

Every character has a unique ASCII code between 0 and 127. To generate a random character is to generate a random integer between 0 and 127. In Section 3.9, you learned how to
generate a random number. Recall that you can use the srand(seed) function to set a seed

and use **rand()** to return a random integer. You can use it to write a simple expression to generate random numbers in any range. For example,

rand() % 10 ⟶ Returns a random integer between 0 and 9.

50 + rand() % 50 ⟶ Returns a random integer between 50 and 99.

In general,

a + rand() % b ⟶ Returns a random number between a and a + b, excluding a + b.

So, you can use the following expression to generate a random integer between 0 and 127:

rand() % 128

Now let us consider how to generate a random lowercase letter. The ASCII codes for lowercase letters are consecutive integers starting with the code for **'a'**, then that for **'b'**, **'c'**, ..., and **'z'**. The code for **'z'** is

static_cast<int>('a')

So a random integer between **static_cast<int>('a')** and **static_cast<int>('z')** is

static_cast<int>('a') +
    rand() % (static_cast<int>('z') - static_cast<int>('a') + 1)

Recall that all numeric operators can be applied to the **char** operands. The **char** operand is cast into a number if the other operand is a number or a character. Thus, the preceding expression can be simplified as follows:

('a' + rand) % ('z' - 'a' + 1)

and a random lowercase letter is

static_cast<char>('a' + rand() % ('z' - 'a' + 1))

To generalize the foregoing discussion, a random character between any two characters **ch1** and **ch2** with **ch1 < ch2** can be generated as follows:

static_cast<char>(ch1 + rand() % (ch2 - ch1 + 1))

This is a simple but useful discovery. Listing 4.3 gives a program that prompts the user to enter two characters x and y with x <= y and displays a random character between x and y.

LISTING 4.3 DisplayRandomCharacter.cpp

```
 1  #include <iostream>
 2  #include <cstdlib>
 3  using namespace std;
 4
 5  int main()
 6  {
 7    cout << "Enter a starting character: ";
 8    char startChar;
 9    cin >> startChar;
10
11    cout << "Enter an ending character: ";
```

```
12    char endChar;
13    cin >> endChar;
14
15    // Get a random character
16    char randomChar = static_cast<char>(startChar + rand() %
17            (endChar - startChar + 1));
18
19    cout << "The random character between " << startChar << " and "
20            << endChar << " is " << randomChar << endl;
21
22    return 0;
23 }
```

```
Enter a starting character: a  ↵Enter
Enter an ending character: z  ↵Enter
The random character between a and z is p
```

The program prompts the user to enter a starting character (line 9) and an ending character (line 13). It obtains a random character between these two characters (may include these two characters) in lines 16–17.

4.11 If the input for a starting character and an ending character are the same, what a random character will the program display?

4.5 Case Study: Guessing Birthdays

Guessing birthdays is an interesting problem with a simple programming solution.

You can determine the day of the month when your friend was born by asking five questions. Each question asks whether the day is in one of the following five sets of numbers.

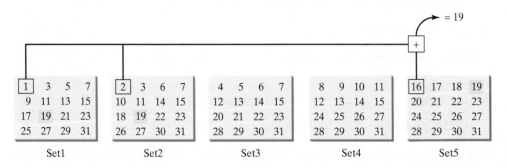

The birthday is the sum of the first numbers in the sets where the day appears. For example, if the birthday is 19, it appears in Set1, Set2, and Set5. The first numbers in these three sets are 1, 2, and 16. Their sum is 19.

Listing 4.4 gives a program that prompts the user to answer whether the day is in Set1 (lines 10–16), in Set2 (lines 22–28), in Set3 (lines 34–40), in Set4 (lines 46–52), and in Set5 (lines 58–64). If the number is in the set, the program adds the first number in the set to day (lines 19, 31, 43, 55, 67).

VideoNote
Guess birthday

LISTING 4.4 GuessBirthday.cpp

```
1  #include <iostream>
2  using namespace std;
3
4  int main()
```

```
 5  {
 6      int day = 0; // Day to be determined
 7      char answer;
 8
 9      // Prompt the user for Set1
10      cout << "Is your birthday in Set1?" << endl;
11      cout << " 1  3  5  7\n" <<
12              " 9 11 13 15\n" <<
13              "17 19 21 23\n" <<
14              "25 27 29 31" << endl;
15      cout << "Enter N/n for No and Y/y for Yes: ";
16      cin >> answer;
17
18      if (answer == 'Y' || answer == 'y')
19        day += 1;
20
21      // Prompt the user for Set2
22      cout << "\nIs your birthday in Set2?" << endl;
23      cout << " 2  3  6  7\n" <<
24              "10 11 14 15\n" <<
25              "18 19 22 23\n" <<
26              "26 27 30 31" << endl;
27      cout << "Enter N/n for No and Y/y for Yes: ";
28      cin >> answer;
29
30      if (answer == 'Y' || answer == 'y')
31        day += 2;
32
33      // Prompt the user for Set3
34      cout << "\nIs your birthday in Set3?" << endl;
35      cout << " 4  5  6  7\n" <<
36              "12 13 14 15\n" <<
37              "20 21 22 23\n" <<
38              "28 29 30 31" << endl;
39      cout << "Enter N/n for No and Y/y for Yes: ";
40      cin >> answer;
41
42      if (answer == 'Y' || answer == 'y')
43        day += 4;
44
45      // Prompt the user for Set4
46      cout << "\nIs your birthday in Set4?" << endl;
47      cout << " 8  9 10 11\n" <<
48              "12 13 14 15\n" <<
49              "24 25 26 27\n" <<
50              "28 29 30 31" << endl;
51      cout << "Enter N/n for No and Y/y for Yes: ";
52      cin >> answer;
53
54      if (answer == 'Y' || answer == 'y')
55        day += 8;
56
57      // Prompt the user for Set5
58      cout << "\nIs your birthday in Set5?" << endl;
59      cout << "16 17 18 19\n" <<
60              "20 21 22 23\n" <<
61              "24 25 26 27\n" <<
62              "28 29 30 31" << endl;
63      cout << "Enter N/n for No and Y/y for Yes: ";
64      cin >> answer;
65
```

day to be determined

in Set1?

in Set2?

in Set3?

in Set4?

in Set5?

```
66    if (answer == 'Y' || answer == 'y')
67        day += 16;
68
69    cout << "Your birthday is " << day << endl;
70
71    return 0;
72  }
```

```
Is your birthday in Set1?
 1  3  5  7
 9 11 13 15
17 19 21 23
25 27 29 31
Enter N/n for No and Y/y for Yes: Y ↵Enter

Is your birthday in Set2?
 2  3  6  7
10 11 14 15
18 19 22 23
26 27 30 31
Enter N/n for No and Y/y for Yes: Y ↵Enter

Is your birthday in Set3?
 4  5  6  7
12 13 14 15
20 21 22 23
28 29 30 31
Enter N/n for No and Y/y for Yes: N ↵Enter

Is your birthday in Set4?
 8  9 10 11
12 13 14 15
24 25 26 27
28 29 30 31
Enter N/n for No and Y/y for Yes: N ↵Enter

Is your birthday in Set5?
16 17 18 19
20 21 22 23
24 25 26 27
28 29 30 31
Enter N/n for No and Y/y for Yes: Y ↵Enter
Your birthday is 19
```

Line#	day	answer	Output
6	0		
7		undefined value	
16		Y	
19	1		
28		Y	
31	3		
40		N	
52		N	

Line#	day	answer	Output
64		Y	
67	19		
69			Your birthday is 19

This game is easy to program. You may wonder how the game was created. The mathematics behind the game is actually quite simple. The numbers are not grouped together by accident— the way they are placed in the five sets is deliberate. The starting numbers in the five sets are 1, 2, 4, 8, and 16, which correspond to 1, 10, 100, 1000, and 10000 in binary (binary numbers are introduced in Appendix D, Number Systems). A binary number for decimal integers between 1 and 31 has at most five digits, as shown in Figure 4.1a. Let it be $b_5b_4b_3b_2b_1$. Thus, $b_5b_4b_3b_2b_1 = b_50000 + b_4000 + b_300 + b_20 + b_1$, as shown in Figure 4.1b. If a day's binary number has a digit 1 in b_k, the number should appear in Set$k$. For example, number 19 is binary 10011, so it appears in Set1, Set2, and Set5. It is binary 1 + 10 + 10000 = 10011 or decimal 1 + 2 + 16 = 19. Number 31 is binary 11111, so it appears in Set1, Set2, Set3, Set4, and Set5. It is binary 1 + 10 + 100 + 1000 + 10000 = 11111 or decimal 1 + 2 + 4 + 8 + 16 = 31.

mathematics behind the game

Decimal	Binary
1	00001
2	00010
3	00011
...	
19	10011
...	
31	11111

$$b_5\ 0\ 0\ 0$$
$$b_4\ 0\ 0\ 0$$
$$b_3\ 0\ 0$$
$$b_2\ 0$$
$$+\underline{\qquad b_1}$$
$$b_5\ b_4\ b_3\ b_2\ b_1$$

$$\begin{array}{r}10000\\10\\1\\+\underline{\quad}\\10011\\19\end{array}$$

$$\begin{array}{r}10000\\1000\\100\\10\\1\\+\underline{\quad}\\11111\\31\end{array}$$

(a)   (b)

FIGURE 4.1 (a) A number between 1 and 31 can be represented using a 5-digit binary number. (b) A 5-digit binary number can be obtained by adding binary numbers 1, 10, 100, 1000, or 10000.

4.12 If you run Listing 4.4 GuessBirthday.cpp with input Y for Set1, Set3, and Set4 and N for Set2 and Set5, what will be the birthday?

Check Point

4.6 Character Functions

C++ contains the functions for working with characters.

Key Point

C++ provides several functions for testing a character and for converting a character in the <cctype> header file, as shown in Table 4.6. The testing functions test a single character and return true or false. Note that they actually return an int value. A nonzero integer corresponds to true and zero to false. C++ also provides two functions for converting cases.

TABLE 4.6 Character Functions

Function	Description
isdigit(ch)	Returns true if the specified character is a digit.
isalpha(ch)	Returns true if the specified character is a letter.
isalnum(ch)	Returns true if the specified character is a letter or digit.

(continued)

TABLE 4.6 (*continued*)

Function	Description
islower(ch)	Returns true if the specified character is a lowercase letter.
isupper(ch)	Returns true if the specified character is an uppercase letter.
isspace(ch)	Returns true if the specified character is a whitespace character.
tolower(ch)	Returns the lowercase of the specified character.
toupper(ch)	Returns the uppercase of the specified character.

Listing 4.5 is a program to use character functions.

LISTING 4.5 CharacterFunctions.cpp

include cctype

input character

is lowercase?

convert to uppercase

is uppercase?

convert to lowercase

is digit?

```cpp
 1  #include <iostream>
 2  #include <cctype>
 3  using namespace std;
 4
 5  int main()
 6  {
 7    cout << "Enter a character: ";
 8    char ch;
 9    cin >> ch;
10
11    cout << "You entered " << ch << endl;
12
13    if (islower(ch))
14    {
15      cout << "It is a lowercase letter " << endl;
16      cout << "Its equivalent uppercase letter is " <<
17        static_cast<char>(toupper(ch)) << endl;
18    }
19    else if (isupper(ch))
20    {
21      cout << "It is an uppercase letter " << endl;
22      cout << "Its equivalent lowercase letter is " <<
23        static_cast<char>(tolower(ch)) << endl;
24    }
25    else if (isdigit(ch))
26    {
27      cout << "It is a digit character " << endl;
28    }
29
30    return 0;
31  }
```

```
Enter a character: a  ↵Enter
You entered a
It is a lowercase letter
Its equivalent uppercase letter is A
```

```
Enter a character: T  ↵Enter
You entered T
It is an uppercase letter
Its equivalent lowercase letter is t
```

```
Enter a character: 8 ↵Enter
You entered 8
It is a digit character
```

4.13 Which function do you use to test whether a character is a digit? a letter? a lower-case letter? an uppercase letter? a digit or a letter?

4.14 Which function do you use to convert a letter to lowercase or to uppercase?

Check
Point

4.7 Case Study: Converting a Hexadecimal Digit to a Decimal Value

This section presents a program that converts a hexadecimal digit into a decimal value.

Key
Point

The hexadecimal number system has 16 digits: 0–9, A–F. The letters A, B, C, D, E, and F correspond to the decimal numbers 10, 11, 12, 13, 14, and 15. We now write a program that prompts the user to enter a hex digit and display its corresponding decimal value, as shown in Listing 4.6.

LISTING 4.6 HexDigit2Dec.cpp

```
1   #include <iostream>
2   #include <cctype>
3   using namespace std;
4
5   int main()
6   {
7     cout << "Enter a hex digit: ";
8     char hexDigit;
9     cin >> hexDigit;                                          input a character
10
11    hexDigit = toupper(hexDigit);                            to uppercase
12    if (hexDigit <= 'F' && hexDigit >= 'A')                  is A-F?
13    {
14      int value = 10 + hexDigit - 'A';
15      cout << "The decimal value for hex digit "
16        << hexDigit << " is " << value << endl;
17    }
18    else if (isdigit(hexDigit))                              is 0-9?
19    {
20      cout << "The decimal value for hex digit "
21        << hexDigit << " is " << hexDigit << endl;
22    }
23    else                                                     not a valid hex digit
24    {
25      cout << hexDigit << " is an invalid input" << endl;
26    }
27
28    return 0;
29  }
```

```
Enter a hex digit: b ↵Enter
The decimal value for hex digit B is 11
```

```
Enter a hex digit: B  ↵Enter
The decimal value for hex digit B is 11
```

```
Enter a hex digit: 8  ↵Enter
The decimal value for hex digit 8 is 8
```

```
Enter a hex digit: T  ↵Enter
T is an invalid input
```

The program reads a hex digit as a character from the console (line 9) and obtains the upper-case letter for the character (line 11). If the character is between `'A'` and `'F'` (line 12), the corresponding decimal value is `hexDigit - 'A' + 10` (line 14). Note that `hexDigit - 'A'` is 0 if `hexDigit` is `'A'`, `hexDigit - 'A'` is 1 if `hexDigit` is `'B'`, and so on. When two characters perform a numerical operation, the characters' ASCII codes are used in the computation.

The program invokes the `isdigit(hexDigit)` function to check if `hexDigit` is between `'0'` and `'9'` (line 18). If so, the corresponding decimal digit is the same as `hexDigit` (lines 20–21).

If `hexDigit` is not between `'A'` and `'F'` nor a digit character, the program displays an error message (line 25).

4.15 Which line in the code tests if the character is between `'0'` and `'9'`?

4.16 If the input is f, what is the value displayed?

4.8 The **string** Type

A string is a sequence of characters.

The `char` type represents only one character. To represent a string of characters, use the data type called `string`. For example, the following code declares that `message` to be a string with the value `Programming is fun`.

```
string message = "Programming is fun";
```

The `string` type is not a primitive type. It is known as an *object type*. Here `message` represents a `string` object with contents `Programming is fun`.

Objects are defined using classes. `string` is a predefined class in the `<string>` header file. An object is also known as an instance of a class. Objects and classes will be thoroughly discussed in Chapter 9. For now, you need to know only how to create a `string` object, and how to use the simple functions in the `string` class, as shown in Table 4.7.

TABLE 4.7 Simple Functions for **string** Objects

Function	Description
length()	Returns the number of characters in this string.
size()	Same as length().
at(index)	Returns the character at the specified index from this string.

The functions in the `string` class can only be invoked from a specific `string` instance. For this reason, these functions are called *instance functions*. For example, you can use the `size()` function in the `string` class to return the size of a string object and use the `at(index)` function to return the character at the specified index, as shown in the following code:

instance function

```cpp
string message = "ABCD";
cout << message.length() << endl;
cout << message.at(0) << endl;
string s = "Bottom";
cout << s.length() << endl;
cout << s.at(1) << endl;
```

Invoking `message.length()` returns 4 and invoking `message.at(0)` returns character A. Invoking `s.length()` returns 6 and invoking `s.at(1)` returns character o.

The syntax to invoke an instance function is `objectName.functionName(arguments)`. A function may have many arguments or no arguments. For example, the `at(index)` function has one argument, but the `length()` function has no arguments.

Note

By default, a string is initialized to an *empty string*, i.e., a string containing no characters. An empty string literal can be written as "". Therefore, the following two statements have the same effect:

empty string

```cpp
string s;
string s = "";
```

Note

To use the string type, you need to include the `<string>` header file in your program.

4.8.1 String Index and Subscript Operator

The `s.at(index)` function can be used to retrieve a specific character in a string `s`, where the index is between 0 and `s.length()-1`. For example, `message.at(0)` returns the character W, as shown in Figure 4.2. Note that the index for the first character in the string is 0.

at(index)

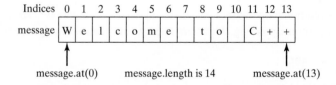

FIGURE 4.2 The characters in a `string` object can be accessed using its index.

For convenience, C++ provides the subscript operator for accessing the character at a specified index in a string using the syntax `stringName[index]`. You can use this syntax to retrieve and modify the character in a string. For example, the following code sets a new character P at index 0 using `s[0] = 'P'` and displays it.

subscript operator

```cpp
string s = "ABCD";
s[0] = 'P';
cout << s[0] << endl;
```

string index range

Caution

Attempting to access characters in a string s out of bounds is a common programming error. To avoid it, make sure that you do not use an index beyond `s.length() - 1`. For example, `s.at(s.length())` or `s[s.length()]` would cause an error.

4.8.2 Concatenating Strings

string concatenation

C++ provides the + operator for concatenating two strings. The statement shown below, for example, concatenates strings s1 and s2 into s3:

```
string s3 = s1 + s2;
```

The augmented += operator can also be used for string concatenation. For example, the following code appends the string `"and programming is fun"` with the string `"Welcome to C++"` in message.

```
message += " and programming is fun";
```

Therefore, the new message is `"Welcome to C++ and programming is fun"`. You can also concatenate a character with a string. For example,

```
string s = "ABC";
s += 'D';
```

Therefore, the new s is `"ABCD"`.

Caution

It is illegal to concatenate two string literals. For example, the following code is incorrect:

```
string cites = "London" + "Paris";
```

However, the following code is correct, because it first concatenates string s with `"London"` and then the new string is concatenated with `"Paris"`.

```
string s = "New York";
string cites = s + "London" + "Paris";
```

4.8.3 Comparing Strings

You can use the relational operators ==, !=, <, <=, >, >= to compare two strings. This is done by comparing their corresponding characters one by one from left to right. For example,

```
string s1 = "ABC";
string s2 = "ABE";
cout << (s1 == s2) << endl; // Displays 0 (means false)
cout << (s1 != s2) << endl; // Displays 1 (means true)
cout << (s1 > s2) << endl; // Displays 0 (means false)
cout << (s1 >= s2) << endl; // Displays 0 (means false)
cout << (s1 < s2) << endl; // Displays 1 (means true)
cout << (s1 <= s2) << endl; // Displays 1 (means true)
```

Consider evaluating s1 > s2. The first two characters (A versus A) from s1 and s2 are compared. Because they are equal, the second two characters (B versus B) are compared. Because they are also equal, the third two characters (C versus E) are compared. Since the character C is less than E, the comparison returns 0.

4.8.4   Reading Strings

A string can be read from the keyboard using the `cin` object. For example, see the following code:

```
1  string city;
2  cout << "Enter a city: ";
3  cin >> city; // Read to string city
4  cout << "You entered " << city << endl;
```

Line 3 reads a string to `city`. This approach to reading a string is simple, but there is a problem. The input ends with a whitespace character. If you want to enter New York, you have to use an alternative approach. C++ provides the `getline` function in the `string` header file, which reads a string from the keyboard using the following syntax:

```
getline(cin, s, delimitCharacter)
```

The function stops reading characters when the delimiter character is encountered. The delimiter is read but not stored into the string. The third argument `delimitCharacter` has a default value (`'\n'`).

The following code uses the `getline` function to read a string.

```
1  string city;                                    declare a string
2  cout << "Enter a city: ";
3  getline(cin, city, '\n'); // Same as getline(cin, city)    read a string
4  cout << "You entered " << city << endl;
```

Since the default value for the third argument in the `getline` function is `'\n'`, line 3 can be replaced by

```
getline(cin, city); // Read a string
```

Listing 4.7 gives a program that prompts the user to enter two cities and displays them alphabetically.

LISTING 4.7   OrderTwoCities.cpp

```
1  #include <iostream>
2  #include <string>                               include string
3  using namespace std;
4
5  int main()
6  {
7    string city1, city2;
8    cout << "Enter the first city: ";
9    getline(cin, city1);                          input city1
10   cout << "Enter the second city: ";
11   getline(cin, city2);                          input city2
12
13   cout << "The cities in alphabetical order are ";
14   if (city1 < city2)                            compare two cities
15     cout << city1 << " " << city2 << endl;
16   else
17     cout << city2 << " " << city1 << endl;
18
19   return 0;
20 }
```

```
Enter the first city: New York ↵Enter
Enter the second city: Boston ↵Enter
The cities in alphabetical order are Boston New York
```

When using strings in the program, you should always include the **string** header file (line 2). If line 9 is replaced by **cin >> city1**, you cannot enter a string with spaces for **city1**. Since a city name may contain multiple words separated by spaces, the program uses the **getline** function to read a string (lines 9, 11).

**Check
Point**

4.17 Write a statement that declares a string named **city** with value **Chicago**.

4.18 Write a statement that displays the number of characters in string **s**.

4.19 Write a statement that changes the first character in string **s** to **'P'**.

4.20 Show the output of the following code:

```
string s1 = "Good morning";
string s2 = "Good afternoon";
cout << s1[0] << endl;
cout << (s1 == s2 ? "true": "false") << endl;
cout << (s1 != s2 ? "true": "false") << endl;
cout << (s1 > s2 ? "true": "false") << endl;
cout << (s1 >= s2 ? "true": "false") << endl;
cout << (s1 < s2 ? "true": "false") << endl;
cout << (s1 <= s2 ? "true": "false") << endl;
```

4.21 How do you read a string that contains spaces?

4.9 Case Study: Revising the Lottery Program Using Strings

**Key
Point**

A problem can be solved using many different approaches. This section rewrites the lottery program in Listing 3.7, Lottery.cpp, using strings. Using strings simplifies this program.

The lottery program in Listing 3.7 generates a random two-digit number, prompts the user to enter a two-digit number, and determines whether the user wins according to the following rules:

1. If the user input matches the lottery number in the exact order, the award is $10,000.

2. If all the digits in the user input match all the digits in the lottery number, the award is $3,000.

3. If one digit in the user input matches a digit in the lottery number, the award is $1,000.

The program in Listing 3.7 uses an integer to store the number. Listing 4.8 gives a new program that generates a random two-digit string instead of a number and receives the user input as a string instead of a number.

LISTING 4.8 LotteryUsingStrings.cpp

```
1  #include <iostream>
2  #include <string> // for using strings
```

```
3   #include <ctime> // for time function
4   #include <cstdlib> // for rand and srand functions
5   using namespace std;
6
7   int main()
8   {
9     string lottery;
10    srand(time(0));
11    int digit = rand() % 10; // Generate first digit          generate first digit
12    lottery += static_cast<char>(digit + '0');               concatenate to a string
13    digit = rand() % 10; // Generate second digit            generate second digit
14    lottery += static_cast<char>(digit + '0');               concatenate to a string
15
16    // Prompt the user to enter a guess
17    cout << "Enter your lottery pick (two digits): ";
18    string guess;                                             enter a guess
19    cin >> guess;
20
21    cout << "The lottery number is " << lottery << endl;
22
23    // Check the guess
24    if (guess == lottery)                                     exact match?
25      cout << "Exact match: you win $10,000" << endl;
26    else if (guess[1] == lottery[0] && guess[0] == lottery[1])  match all digits?
27      cout << "Match all digits: you win $3,000" << endl;
28    else if (guess[0] == lottery[0] || guess[0] == lottery[1]    match one digit?
29            || guess[1] == lottery[0] || guess[1] == lottery[1])
30      cout << "Match one digit: you win $1,000" << endl;
31    else                                                      no match
32      cout << "Sorry, no match" << endl;
33
34    return 0;
35  }
```

```
Enter your lottery pick (two digits): 00  [↵ Enter]
The lottery number is 00
Exact match: you win $10,000
```

```
Enter your lottery pick (two digits): 45  [↵ Enter]
The lottery number is 54
Match all digits: you win $3,000
```

```
Enter your lottery pick: 23  [↵ Enter]
The lottery number is 34
Match one digit: you win $1,000
```

```
Enter your lottery pick: 23  [↵ Enter]
The lottery number is 14
Sorry, no match
```

The program generates the first random digit (line 11), casts it to a character, and concatenates the character to the string **lottery** (line 12). The program then generates the second random digit (line 13), casts it to a character, and concatenates the character to the string **lottery** (line 14). After this, **lottery** contains two random digits.

The program prompts the user to enter a guess as a two-digit string (line 19) and checks the guess against the lottery number in this order:

1. First, check whether the guess matches the lottery exactly (line 24).

2. If not, check whether the reversal of the guess matches the lottery (line 26).

3. If not, check whether one digit is in the lottery (lines 28–29).

4. If not, nothing matches and display "Sorry, no match" (lines 31–32).

4.10 Formatting Console Output

Key Point

You can use the stream manipulators to display formatted output on the console.

Often it is desirable to display numbers in a certain format. For example, the following code computes interest, given the amount and the annual interest rate.

```
double amount = 12618.98;
double interestRate = 0.0013;
double interest = amount * interestRate;
cout << "Interest is " << interest << endl;
```

```
Interest is 16.4047
```

Because the interest amount is currency, it is desirable to display only two digits after the decimal point. To do this, you may write the code as follows:

```
double amount = 12618.98;
double interestRate = 0.0013;
double interest = amount * interestRate;
cout << "Interest is "
  << static_cast<char>(interest * 100) / 100.0 << endl;
```

```
Interest is 16.4
```

However, the format is still not correct. There should be two digits after the decimal point (i.e., **16.40** rather than **16.4**). You can fix it by using formatting functions, like this:

```
double amount = 12618.98;
double interestRate = 0.0013;
double interest = amount * interestRate;
cout << "Interest is " << fixed << setprecision(2)
  << interest << endl;
```

```
Interest is 16.40
```

You already know how to display console output using the **cout** object. C++ provides additional functions for formatting how a value is displayed. These functions are called stream manipulators and are included in the `iomanip` header file. Table 4.8 summarizes several useful stream manipulators.

stream manipulator

TABLE 4.8 Frequently Used Stream Manipulators

Operator	Description
`setprecision(n)`	sets the precision of a floating-point number
`fixed`	displays floating-point numbers in fixed-point notation
`showpoint`	causes a floating-point number to be displayed with a decimal point with trailing zeros even if it has no fractional part
`setw(width)`	specifies the width of a print field
`left`	justifies the output to the left
`right`	justifies the output to the right

4.10.1 `setprecision(n)` Manipulator

You can specify the total number of digits displayed for a floating-point number using the `setprecision(n)` manipulator, where n is the number of significant digits (i.e., the total number of digits that appear before and after the decimal point). If a number to be displayed has more digits than the specified precision, it will be rounded. For example, the code

```
double number = 12.34567;
cout << setprecision(3) << number << " "
     << setprecision(4) << number << " "
     << setprecision(5) << number << " "
     << setprecision(6) << number << endl;
```

displays

```
12.3□12.35□12.346□12.3457
```

where the square box (□) denotes a blank space.

The value of **number** is displayed using precision **3**, **4**, **5**, and **6**, respectively. Using precision **3**, `12.34567` is rounded to `12.3`. Using precision **4**, `12.34567` is rounded to `12.35`. Using precision **5**, `12.34567` is rounded to `12.346`. Using precision **6**, `12.34567` is rounded to `12.3457`.

The `setprecision` manipulator remains in effect until the precision is changed. So,

```
double number = 12.34567;
cout << setprecision(3) << number << " ";
cout << 9.34567 << " " << 121.3457 << " " << 0.2367 << endl;
```

displays

```
12.3□9.35□121□ 0.237
```

The precision is set to **3** for the first value, and it remains effective for the next two values, because it has not been changed.

If the width is not sufficient for an integer, the **setprecision** manipulator is ignored. For example,

```
cout << setprecision(3) << 23456 << endl;
```

displays

```
23456
```

4.10.2 **fixed** Manipulator

Sometimes, the computer automatically displays a large floating-point number in scientific notation. On the Windows machine, for example, the statement

```
cout << 232123434.357;
```

displays

```
2.32123e+08
```

You can use the `fixed` manipulator to force the number to be displayed in nonscientific notation with a fixed number of digits after the decimal point. For example,

```
cout << fixed << 232123434.357;
```

displays

```
232123434.357000
```

By default, the fixed number of digits after the decimal point is 6. You can change it using the `fixed` manipulator along with the `setprecision` manipulator. When it is used after the `fixed` manipulator, the `setprecision` manipulator specifies the number of digits after the decimal point. For example,

```
double monthlyPayment = 345.4567;
double totalPayment = 78676.887234;
cout << fixed << setprecision(2)
     << monthlyPayment << endl
     << totalPayment << endl;
```

displays

```
345.46
78676.89
```

4.10.3 **showpoint** Manipulator

By default, floating-point numbers that do not have a fractional part are not displayed with a decimal point. You can use the `fixed` manipulator to force the floating-point numbers to be displayed with a decimal point and a fixed number of digits after the decimal point. Alternatively, you can use the `showpoint` manipulator together with the `setprecision` manipulator.

For example,

```
cout << setprecision(6);
cout << 1.23 << endl;
cout << showpoint << 1.23 << endl;
cout << showpoint << 123.0 << endl;
```

displays

```
1.23
1.23000
123.000
```

The `setprecision(6)` function sets the precision to 6. So, the first number 1.23 is displayed as 1.23. Because the `showpoint` manipulator forces the floating-point number to be displayed with a decimal point and trailing zeros if necessary to fill in the positions, the second number 1.23 is displayed as 1.23000 with trailing zeros, and the third number 123.0 is displayed as 123.000 with a decimal point and trailing zeros.

4.10.4 setw(width) Manipulator

By default, cout uses just the number of the positions needed for an output. You can use setw(width) to specify the minimum number of columns for an output. For example,

```
cout << setw(8) << "C++" << setw(6) << 101 << endl;
cout << setw(8) << "Java" << setw(6) << 101 << endl;
cout << setw(8) << "HTML" << setw(6) << 101 << endl;
```

displays

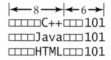

The output is right-justified within the specified columns. In line 1, setw(8) specifies that "C++" is displayed in eight columns. So, there are five spaces before C++. setw(6) specifies that 101 is displayed in six columns. So, there are three spaces before 101.

Notice that the setw manipulator affects only the next output. For example,

```
cout << setw(8) << "C++" << 101 << endl;
```

displays

```
     C++101
```

The setw(8) manipulator affects only the next output "C++", not 101.

Note that the argument n for setw(n) and setprecision(n) can be an integer variable, expression, or constant.

If an item requires more spaces than the specified width, the width is automatically increased. For example, the following code

```
cout << setw(8) << "Programming" << "#" << setw(2) << 101;
```

displays

```
Programming#101
```

The specified width for Programming is 8, which is smaller than its actual size 11. The width is automatically increased to 11. The specified width for 101 is 2, which is smaller than its actual size 3. The width is automatically increased to 3.

4.10.5 left and right Manipulators

Note that the setw manipulator uses right justification by the default. You can use the left manipulator to left-justify the output and use the right manipulator to right-justify the output. For example,

```
cout << right;
cout << setw(8) << 1.23 << endl;
cout << setw(8) << 351.34 << endl;
```

displays

```
␣␣␣␣1.23
␣␣351.34
```

```cpp
cout << left;
cout << setw(8) << 1.23;
cout << setw(8) << 351.34 << endl;
```

displays

```
1.23␣␣␣351.34␣␣
```

4.22 To use stream manipulators, which header file must you include?

4.23 Show the output of the following statements.

```cpp
cout << setw(10) << "C++" << setw(6) << 101 << endl;
cout << setw(8) << "Java" << setw(5) << 101 << endl;
cout << setw(6) << "HTML" << setw(4) << 101 << endl;
```

4.24 Show the output of the following statements:

```cpp
double number = 93123.1234567;
cout << setw(10) << setprecision(5) << number;
cout << setw(10) << setprecision(4) << number;
cout << setw(10) << setprecision(3) << number;
cout << setw(10) << setprecision(8) << number;
```

4.25 Show the output of the following statements:

```cpp
double monthlyPayment = 1345.4567;
double totalPayment = 866.887234;

cout << setprecision(7);
cout << monthlyPayment << endl;
cout << totalPayment << endl;

cout << fixed << setprecision(2);
cout << setw(8) << monthlyPayment << endl;
cout << setw(8) << totalPayment << endl;
```

4.26 Show the output of the following statements:

```cpp
cout << right;
cout << setw(6) << 21.23 << endl;
cout << setw(6) << 51.34 << endl;
```

4.27 Show the output of the following statements.

```cpp
cout << left;
cout << setw(6) << 21.23 << endl;
cout << setw(6) << 51.34 << endl;
```

4.11 Simple File Input and Output

You can save data to a file and read data from the file later.

You used the `cin` to read input from the keyboard and the `cout` to write output to the console. You can also read/write data from/to a file. This section introduces simple file input and output. Detailed coverage of file input and output will be presented in Chapter 13.

stream manipulator

4.11.1 Writing to a File

To write data to a file, first declare a variable of the **ofstream** type:

```
ofstream output;
```

To specify a file, invoke the **open** function from **output** object as follows:

```
output.open("numbers.txt");
```

This statement creates a file named **numbers.txt**. If this file already exists, the contents are destroyed and a new file is created. Invoking the **open** function is to associate a file with the stream. In Chapter 13, you will learn how to check whether a file exists before creating the file.

Optionally, you can create a file output object and open the file in one statement like this:

```
ofstream output("numbers.txt");
```

To write data, use the stream insertion operator (<<) in the same way that you send data to the **cout** object. For example,

```
output << 95 << " " << 56 << " " << 34 << endl;
```

This statement writes numbers **95**, **56**, and **34** to the file. Numbers are separated spaces, as shown in Figure 4.3.

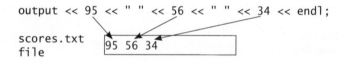

FIGURE 4.3 The output stream sends data to the file.

After you are done with the file, invoke the **close** function from **output** as follows:

```
output.close();
```

Invoking the **close** function is necessary to ensure the data is written to the file before the program exits.

Listing 4.9 gives the complete program for writing data to a file.

LISTING 4.9 SimpleFileOutput.cpp

```
1  #include <iostream>
2  #include <fstream>              include fstream header
3  using namespace std;
4
5  int main()
6  {
7    ofstream output;              declare output
8
9    // Create a file
10   output.open("numbers.txt");   open file
11
12   // Write numbers
13   output << 95 << " " << 56 << " " << 34;   output to file
14
15   // close file
16   output.close();              close file
```

```
17
18    cout << "Done" << endl;
19
20    return 0;
21 }
```

including <fstream> header

Since `ofstream` is defined in the `fstream` header file, line 2 includes this header file.

4.11.2 Reading from a File

To read data from a file, first declare a variable of the `ifstream` type:

```
ifstream input;
```

To specify a file, invoke the **open** function from **input** as follows:

```
input.open("numbers.txt");
```

This statement opens a file named `numbers.txt` for input. If a file you attempt to open does not exist, unexpected error may arise. In Chapter 13, you will learn how to check whether a file exists when opening a file for input.

Optionally, you can create a file input object and open the file in one statement like this:

```
ifstream input("numbers.txt");
```

To read data, use the stream extraction operator (>>) in the same way that you read data from the `cin` object. For example,

```
input << score1;
input << score2;
input << score3;
```

or

```
input << score1 << score2 << score3;
```

These statements read three numbers from the file into variables `score1`, `score2`, and `score3`, as shown in Figure 4.4.

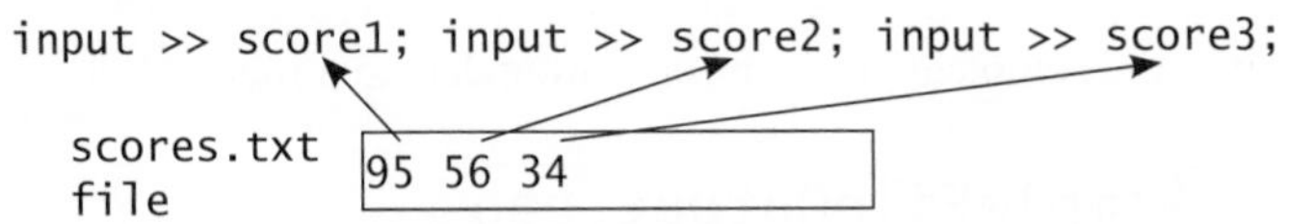

```
input >> score1; input >> score2; input >> score3;

scores.txt    95 56 34
file
```

FIGURE 4.4   The input stream reads data from the file.

After you have done with the file, invoke the **close** function from **input** as follows:

```
input.close();
```

Listing 4.10 gives the complete program for writing data to a file:

LISTING 4.10   SimpleFileInput.cpp

include fstream header

```
1  #include <iostream>
2  #include <fstream>
3  using namespace std;
4
5  int main()
```

```
 6  {
 7    ifstream input;                                           declare output
 8
 9    // Open a file
10    input.open("numbers.txt");                                open file
11
12    int score1, score2, score3;
13
14    // Read data
15    input >> score1;                                          input from file
16    input >> score2;
17    input >> score3;
18
19    cout << "Total score is " << score1 + score2 + score3 << endl;
20
21    // Close file
22    input.close();                                            close file
23
24    cout << "Done" << endl;
25
26    return 0;
27  }
```

```
Total score is 185
Done
```

Since `ifstream` is defined in the `fstream` header file, line 2 includes this header file. You can simplify the statements in lines 15–17 using the following one statement: including <fstream> header

```
input >> score1 >> score2 >> score3;
```

4.28 How do you create an object for reading data from file **test.txt**? How do you create an object for writing data to file **test.txt**?

Check Point

4.29 Can you replace the statements in lines 7–10 in Listing 4.10 using one statement?

4.30 What happens if the file already exists when you open a file for output?

KEY TERMS

ASCII code   142
char type   142
empty string   155
encoding   142
escape character   143

escape sequence   145
instance function   155
subscript operator   155
whitespace character   143

CHAPTER SUMMARY

1. C++ provides the mathematical functions `sin`, `cos`, `tan`, `asin`, `acos`, `atan`, `exp`, `log`, `log10`, `pow`, `sqrt`, `cell`, `floor`, `min`, `max`, and `abs` for performing mathematical functions.

2. Character type (`char`) represents a single character.

3. The character \ is an escape character and an escape sequence starts with the escape character followed by another character or a combination of digits.

4. C++ allows you to use escape sequences to represent special characters such as '\t' and '\n'.

5. The characters ' ', '\t', '\f', '\r', and '\n' are known as the whitespace characters.

6. C++ provides the functions isdigit, isalpha, isalnum, islower, isupper, isspace for testing whether a character is a digit, letter, digit or letter, lowercase, uppercase, and whitespace. It also contains the tolower and toupper functions for returning a lowercase or uppercase letter.

7. A *string* is a sequence of characters. A string value is enclosed in matching double quotes ("). A character value is enclosed in matching single quotes (').

8. You can declare a string object using the string type. A function that is invoked from a specific object is called an *instance function*.

9. You can get the length of a string by invoking its length() function, and retrieve a character at the specified index in the string using the at(index).

10. You can use the subscript operator to retrieve or modify the character in a string and can use the + operator to concatenate two strings.

11. You can use the relational operators to compare two strings.

12. You can format output using stream manipulators defined in the iomanip header.

13. You can create an ifstream object for reading data from a file and an ofstream object for writing data to a file.

QUIZ

Answer the quiz for this chapter online at www.cs.armstrong.edu/liang/cpp3e/quiz.html.

MyProgrammingLab™ **PROGRAMMING EXERCISES**

Section 4.2

4.1 (*Geometry: area of a pentagon*) Write a program that prompts the user to enter the length from the center of a pentagon to a vertex and computes the area of the pentagon, as shown in the following figure.

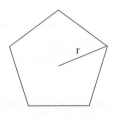

The formula for computing the area of a pentagon is $Area = \dfrac{5 \times s^2}{4 \times \tan\left(\dfrac{\pi}{5}\right)}$, where

s is the length of a side. The side can be computed using the formula $s = 2r \sin\dfrac{\pi}{5}$, where r is the length from the center of a pentagon to a vertex. Round up two digits after the decimal point. Here is a sample run:

```
Enter the length from the center to a vertex: 5.5  ↵Enter
The area of the pentagon is 71.92
```

*4.2 (*Geometry: great circle distance*) The great circle distance is the distance between two points on the surface of a sphere. Let $(x1, y1)$ and $(x2, y2)$ be the geographical latitude and longitude of two points. The great circle distance between the two points can be computed using the following formula:

VideoNote
Great circle distance

$$d = radius \times \arccos(\sin(x_1) \times \sin(x_2) + \cos(x_1) \times \cos(x_2) \times \cos(y_1 - y_2))$$

Write a program that prompts the user to enter the latitude and longitude of two points on the earth in degrees and displays its great circle distance. The average earth radius is 6,378.1 km. The latitude and longitude degrees in the formula are for north and west. Use negative to indicate south and east degrees. Here is a sample run:

```
Enter point 1 (latitude and longitude) in degrees:
39.55, -116.25  ↵Enter
Enter point 2 (latitude and longitude) in degrees:
41.5, 87.37  ↵Enter
The distance between the two points is 10691.79183231593 km
```

*4.3 (*Computing angles of triangles*) Listing 4.1, **ComputeAngles.cpp**, prompts the user to enter the x- and y- coordinates of the three corner points in a triangle and then displays the triangle's angles. Write a program that prompts the user to enter the x- and y- coordinates of three corner points of two triangles, displays the triangle's angles, and then compares whether the angles of both the triangles are equal.

4.4 (*Geometry: area of a hexagon*) The area of a *hexagon* can be computed using the following formula (**s** is the length of a side):

$$Area = \dfrac{6 \times s^2}{4 \times \tan\left(\dfrac{\pi}{6}\right)}$$

Write a program that prompts the user to enter the side of a *hexagon* and displays its area. Here is a sample run:

```
Enter the side: 5.5  ↵Enter
The area of the hexagon is 78.59
```

*4.5 (*Geometry: area of a regular polygon*) A regular polygon is an *n*-sided polygon in which all sides are of the same length and all angles have the same degree (i.e., the polygon is both equilateral and equiangular). The formula for computing the area of a regular polygon is

$$Area = \frac{n \times s^2}{4 \times \tan\left(\dfrac{\pi}{n}\right)}$$

Here, s is the length of a side. Write a program that prompts the user to enter the number of sides and their length of a regular polygon and displays its area. Here is a sample run:

```
Enter the number of sides: 5 ↵Enter
Enter the side: 6.5 ↵Enter
The area of the polygon is 72.69
```

*4.6 (*Random point on a circle*) Write a program that generates three random points on a circle centered at (0, 0) with radius 40 and display three angles in a triangle formed by these three points, as shown in Figure 4.5a. (*Hint*: Generate a random angle α in radians between 0 and 2π, as shown in Figure 4.5b and the point determined by this angle is (r*cos(α), r*sin(α)).)

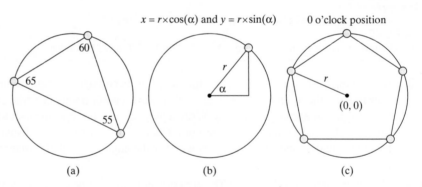

FIGURE 4.5 (a) A triangle is formed from three random points on the circle. (b) A random point on the circle can be generated using a random angle α. (c) A pentagon is centered at (0, 0) with one point at the 0 o'clock position.

*4.7 (*Corner point coordinates*) Suppose a pentagon is centered at (0, 0) with one point at the 0 o'clock position, as shown in Figure 4.5c. Write a program that prompts the user to enter the radius of the bounding circle of a pentagon and displays the coordinates of the five corner points on the pentagon. Here is a sample run:

```
Enter the radius of the bounding circle: 100 ↵Enter
The coordinates of five points on the pentagon are
(95.1057, 30.9017)
(0.000132679, 100)
(-95.1056, 30.9019)
(-58.7788, -80.9015)
(58.7782, -80.902)
```

Sections 4.3–4.7

*4.8 (*Find the character of an ASCII code*) Write a program that receives an ASCII code (an integer between 0 and 127) and displays its character. Here is a sample run:

```
Enter an ASCII code: 69 ↵Enter
The character is E
```

*4.9 (*Find the ASCII code of a character*) Write a program that receives a character and displays its ASCII code. Here is a sample run:

```
Enter a character: E ↵Enter
The ASCII code for the character is 69
```

*4.10 (*Vowel or consonant?*) Assume letters A/a, E/e, I/i, O/o, and U/u as the vowels. Write a program that prompts the user to enter a letter and check whether the letter is a vowel or consonant. Here is a sample run:

```
Enter a letter: B ↵Enter
B is a consonant
```

```
Enter a letter grade: a ↵Enter
a is a vowel
```

```
Enter a letter grade: # ↵Enter
# is an invalid input
```

*4.11 (*Convert an uppercase letter to lowercase*) Write a program that prompts the user to enter an uppercase letter and converts it to a lowercase letter. Here is a sample run:

```
Enter an uppercase letter: T ↵Enter
The lowercase letter is t
```

*4.12 (*Convert letter grade to number*) Write a program that prompts the user to enter a letter grade A/a, B/b, C/c, D/d, or F/f and displays its corresponding numeric value 4, 3, 2, 1, or 0. Here is a sample run:

```
Enter a letter grade: B ↵Enter
The numeric value for grade B is 3
```

```
Enter a letter grade: b ↵Enter
The numeric value for grade b is 3
```

```
Enter a letter grade: T ↵Enter
T is an invalid grade
```

4.13 (*Hex to binary*) Write a program that prompts the user to enter a hex digit and displays its corresponding binary number. Here is a sample run:

```
Enter a hex digit: B  ↵Enter
The binary value is 1011
```

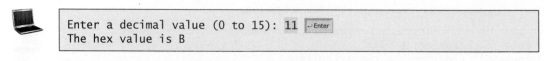

```
Enter a hex digit: G  ↵Enter
G is an invalid input
```

*4.14 (*Decimal to hex*) Write a program that prompts the user to enter an integer between 0 and 15 and displays its corresponding hex number. Here are some sample runs:

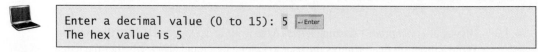

```
Enter a decimal value (0 to 15): 11  ↵Enter
The hex value is B
```

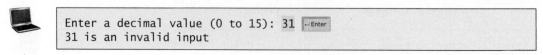

```
Enter a decimal value (0 to 15): 5  ↵Enter
The hex value is 5
```

```
Enter a decimal value (0 to 15): 31  ↵Enter
31 is an invalid input
```

*4.15 (*Phone key pads*) The international standard letter/number mapping found on the telephone is shown below:

Write a program that prompts the user to enter a letter and displays its corresponding number.

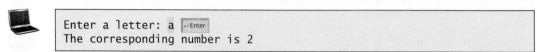

```
Enter a letter: A  ↵Enter
The corresponding number is 2
```

```
Enter a letter: a  ↵Enter
The corresponding number is 2
```

```
Enter a letter: +  ↵Enter
+ is an invalid input
```

Sections 4.8–4.11

4.16 (*Process two string*) Write a program that prompts the user to enter two strings and displays the length and the last character of each.

4.17 (*Palindrome string*) Write a program that prompts the user to enter a string with five lowercase letters and determines whether it is a palindrome.

*4.18 (*Random strings*) Write a program that generates a random string with six lowercase letters.

*4.19 (*Order three cities*) Write a program that prompts the user to enter three cities and displays them in ascending order. Here is a sample run:

```
Enter the first city: Chicago  ↵Enter
Enter the second city: Los Angeles  ↵Enter
Enter the third city: Atlanta  ↵Enter
The three cities in alphabetical order are Atlanta Chicago Los Angeles
```

*4.20 (*Days of a month*) Write a program that prompts the user to enter the year and the first three letters of a month name (with the first letter in uppercase) and displays the number of days in the month. Here is a sample run:

```
Enter a year: 2001  ↵Enter
Enter a month: Jan  ↵Enter
Jan 2001 has 31 days
```

```
Enter a year: 2001  ↵Enter
Enter a month: jan  ↵Enter
jan is not a correct month name
```

*4.21 (*Student major and status*) Write a program that prompts the user to enter two characters and displays the major and status represented in the characters. The first character indicates the major and the second is number character 1, 2, 3, 4, which indicates whether a student is a freshman, sophomore, junior, or senior. Suppose the following characters are used to denote the majors:

M: Mathematics
C: Computer Science
I: Information Technology

Here is a sample run:

```
Enter two characters: M1  ↵Enter
Mathematics Freshman
```

```
Enter two characters: C3  ↵Enter
Computer Science Junior
```

```
Enter two characters: T3  ↵Enter
Invalid major code
```

```
Enter two characters: M7  ↵Enter
Invalid status code
```

*4.22 (*Financial application: payroll*) Write a program that reads the following informa-tion and prints a payroll statement:

> Employee's name (e.g., Smith)
>
> Number of hours worked in a week (e.g., 10)
>
> Hourly pay rate (e.g., 9.75)
>
> Federal tax withholding rate (e.g., 20%)
>
> State tax withholding rate (e.g., 9%)

A sample run is shown below:

```
Enter employee's name: Smith  ↵Enter
Enter number of hours worked in a week: 10  ↵Enter
Enter hourly pay rate: 9.75  ↵Enter
Enter federal tax withholding rate: 0.20  ↵Enter
Enter state tax withholding rate: 0.09  ↵Enter

Employee Name: Smith
Hours Worked: 10.0
Pay Rate: $9.75
Gross Pay: $97.50
Deductions:
  Federal Withholding (20.0%): $19.5
  State Withholding (9.0%): $8.77
  Total Deduction: $28.27
Net Pay: $69.22
```

*4.23 (*Check SSN*) Write a program that prompts the user to enter a Social Security number in the format ddd-dd-dddd, where d is a digit. Here are sample runs:

```
Enter a SSN: 232-23-5435  ↵Enter
232-23-5435 is a valid social security number
```

```
Enter a SSN: 23-23-5435  ↵Enter
23-23-5435 is an invalid social security number
```

CHAPTER

5

LOOPS

Objectives

■ To write programs that execute statements repeatedly using a `while` loop (§5.2).

■ To follow the loop design strategy to develop loops (§§5.2.1–5.2.3).

■ To control a loop with the user confirmation (§5.2.4).

■ To control a loop with a sentinel value (§5.2.5).

■ To obtain input from a file using input redirection rather than typing from the keyboard (§5.2.6).

■ To read all data from a file (§5.2.7).

■ To write loops using `do-while` statements (§5.3).

■ To write loops using `for` statements (§5.4).

■ To discover the similarities and differences of three types of loop statements (§5.5).

■ To write nested loops (§5.6).

■ To learn the techniques for minimizing numerical errors (§5.7).

■ To learn loops from a variety of examples (`GCD`, `FutureTuition`, `MonteCarloSimulation`, `Dec2Hex`) (§5.8).

■ To implement program control with `break` and `continue` (§5.9).

■ To write a program that tests palindromes (§5.10).

■ To write a program that displays prime numbers (§5.11).

5.1 Introduction

A loop can be used to tell a program to execute statements repeatedly.

problem

Suppose that you need to display a string (e.g., `"Welcome to C++!"`) 100 times. It would be tedious to write the following statements 100 times:

$$100 \text{ times} \begin{cases} \texttt{cout << "Welcome to C++!\textbackslash n";} \\ \texttt{cout << "Welcome to C++!\textbackslash n";} \\ \texttt{...} \\ \texttt{cout << "Welcome to C++!\textbackslash n";} \end{cases}$$

why loop?

So, how do you solve this problem?

C++ provides a powerful construct called a *loop* that controls how many times an operation or a sequence of operations is performed in succession. Using a loop statement, you simply tell the computer to display a string 100 times without having to code the print statement 100 times, as follows:

```
int count = 0;
while (count < 100)
{
  cout << "Welcome to C++!\n";
  count++;
}
```

The variable `count` is initially 0. The loop checks whether `(count < 100)` is `true`. If so, it executes the loop body to display the message `Welcome to C++!` and increments `count` by 1. It repeatedly executes the loop body until `(count < 100)` becomes `false` (i.e., when `count` reaches 100). At this point, the loop terminates and the next statement after the loop statement is executed.

Loops are constructs that control repeated executions of a block of statements. The concept of looping is fundamental to programming. C++ provides three types of loop statements: `while` loops, `do-while` loops, and `for` loops.

5.2 The `while` Loop

A `while` loop executes statements repeatedly while the condition is true.

The syntax for the `while` loop is

while loop

```
while (loop-continuation-condition)
{
  // Loop body
  Statement(s);
}
```

loop body
iteration
loop-continuation-condition

Figure 5.1a shows the `while`-loop flowchart. The part of the loop that contains the statements to be repeated is called the *loop body*. A one-time execution of a loop body is referred to as an *iteration (or repetition) of the loop*. Each loop contains a *loop-continuation-condition*, a Boolean expression that controls the execution of the body. It is evaluated each time to determine if the loop body is executed. If its evaluation is `true`, the loop body is executed; if its evaluation is `false`, the entire loop terminates and the program control turns to the statement that follows the `while` loop.

The loop for displaying `Welcome to C++!` 100 times introduced in the preceding section is an example of a `while` loop. Its flowchart is shown in Figure 5.1b. The `loop-continuation-condition` is `count < 100` and the loop body contains the following two statements:

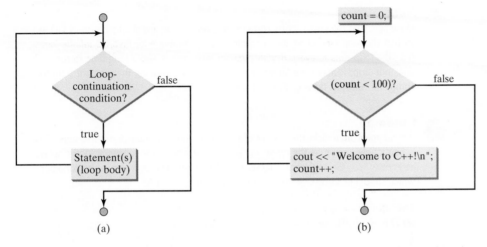

FIGURE 5.1 The while loop repeatedly executes the statements in the loop body when the loop-continuation-condition evaluates to true.

```
int count = 0;          ←———————— loop-continuation-condition
while (count < 100)
{
  cout << "Welcome to C++!\n";  } loop body
  count++;
}
```

In this example, you know exactly how many times the loop body needs to be executed because the control variable **count** is used to count the number of executions. This type of loop is known as a *counter-controlled loop*.

counter-controlled loop

Note
The **loop-continuation-condition** must always appear inside the parentheses. The braces enclosing the loop body can be omitted only if the loop body contains one statement or none.

Here is another example to help understand how a loop works:

```
int sum = 0, i = 1;
while (i < 10)
{
  sum = sum + i;
  i++;
}

cout << "sum is " << sum; // sum is 45
```

If **i < 10** is **true**, the program adds **i** to **sum**. Variable **i** is initially set to **1**, then is incremented to **2**, **3**, and up to **10**. When **i** is **10**, **i < 10** is **false**, so the loop exits. Therefore, the sum is **1 + 2 + 3 + ... + 9 = 45**.

What happens if the loop is incorrectly written as follows?

```
int sum = 0, i = 1;
while (i < 10)
{
  sum = sum + i;
}
```

This loop is infinite, because **i** is always **1** and **i < 10** will always be **true**.

infinite loop

Note
Make sure that the `loop-continuation-condition` eventually becomes `false` so that the loop will terminate. A common programming error involves *infinite loops* (i.e., the loop runs forever). If your program takes an unusually long time to run and does not stop, it may have an infinite loop. If you are running the program from the command window, press *CTRL+C* to stop it.

Caution
Programmers often make the mistake of executing a loop one more or one less time. This is commonly known as the *off-by-one error*. For example, the following loop displays `Welcome to C++` 101 times rather than 100 times. The error lies in the condition, which should be `count < 100` rather than `count <= 100`.

off-by-one error

```
int count = 0;
while (count <= 100)
{
  cout << "Welcome to C++!\n";
  count++;
}
```

VideoNote
Repeat subtraction quiz

Recall that Listing 3.4 SubtractionQuiz.cpp gives a program that prompts the user to enter an answer for a question on subtraction. Using a loop, you can rewrite the program to let the user enter a new answer until it is correct, as shown in Listing 5.1.

LISTING 5.1 RepeatSubtractionQuiz.cpp

include ctime
include cstdlib

set a seed
generate number1
generate number2

swap numbers

enter answer

check answer

enter answer

```
 1  #include <iostream>
 2  #include <ctime> // for time function
 3  #include <cstdlib> // for rand and srand functions
 4  using namespace std;
 5
 6  int main()
 7  {
 8    // 1. Generate two random single-digit integers
 9    srand(time(0));
10    int number1 = rand() % 10;
11    int number2 = rand() % 10;
12
13    // 2. If number1 < number2, swap number1 with number2
14    if (number1 < number2)
15    {
16      int temp = number1;
17      number1 = number2;
18      number2 = temp;
19    }
20
21    // 3. Prompt the student to answer "What is number1 - number2"
22    cout << "What is " << number1 << " - " << number2 << "? ";
23    int answer;
24    cin >> answer;
25
26    // 4. Repeatedly ask the user the question until it is correct
27    while (number1 - number2 != answer)
28    {
29      cout << "Wrong answer. Try again. What is "
30        << number1 << " - " << number2 << "? ";
31      cin >> answer;
32    }
33
```

```
34    cout << "You got it!" << endl;
35
36    return 0;
37 }
```

```
What is 4 - 3? 4 ↵Enter
Wrong answer. Try again. What is 4 - 3? 5 ↵Enter
Wrong answer. Try again. What is 4 - 3? 1 ↵Enter
You got it!
```

The loop in lines 27–32 repeatedly prompts the user to enter an answer when **number1 - number2 != answer** is true. Once **number1 - number2 != answer** is false, the loop exits.

5.2.1 Case Study: Guessing Numbers

The problem is to guess what number a computer has in mind. You will write a program that randomly generates an integer between **0** and **100**, inclusive. The program prompts the user to enter a number continuously until the number matches the randomly generated number. For each user input, the program tells the user whether the input is too low or too high, so the user can make the next guess intelligently. Here is a sample run:

VideoNote
Guess a number

```
Guess a magic number between 0 and 100

Enter your guess: 50 ↵Enter
Your guess is too high

Enter your guess: 25 ↵Enter
Your guess is too low

Enter your guess: 42 ↵Enter
Your guess is too high

Enter your guess: 39 ↵Enter
Yes, the number is 39
```

The magic number is between **0** and **100**. To minimize the number of guesses, first enter **50**. If your guess is too high, the magic number is between **0** and **49**. If your guess is too low, the magic number is between **51** and **100**. So, you can eliminate half of the numbers from consideration after one guess.

intelligent guess

How do you write this program? Do you immediately begin coding? No. It is important to *think before coding*. Think how you would solve the problem without writing a program. First you need to generate a random number between **0** and **100**, inclusive, then prompt the user to enter a guess, and then compare the guess with the random number.

think before coding

It is a good practice to *code incrementally* one step at a time. For programs involving loops, if you don't know how to write a loop, you may first write the code for executing the loop one time, and then figure out how to execute the code repeatedly in a loop. For this program, you may create an initial draft, as shown in Listing 5.2.

code incrementally

LISTING 5.2 GuessNumberOneTime.cpp

```
1  #include <iostream>
2  #include <cstdlib>
```

```
3  #include <ctime> // Needed for the time function
4  using namespace std;
5
6  int main()
7  {
8    // Generate a random number to be guessed
9    srand(time(0));
10   int number = rand() % 101;
11
12   cout << "Guess a magic number between 0 and 100";
13
14   // Prompt the user to guess the number
15   cout << "\nEnter your guess: ";
16   int guess;
17   cin >> guess;
18
19   if (guess == number)
20     cout << "Yes, the number is " << number << endl;
21   else if (guess > number)
22     cout << "Your guess is too high" << endl;
23   else
24     cout << "Your guess is too low" << endl;
25
26   return 0;
27 }
```

generate a number (line 10)

enter a guess (line 17)

correct guess? (line 19)

too high? (line 21)

too low? (line 23)

When you run this program, it prompts the user to enter one guess. To let the user enter a guess repeatedly, you may put the code in lines 15–24 in a loop as follows:

```
while (true)
{
  // Prompt the user to guess the number
  cout << "\nEnter your guess: ";
  cin >> guess;

  if (guess == number)
    cout << "Yes, the number is " << number << endl;
  else if (guess > number)
    cout << "Your guess is too high" << endl;
  else
    cout << "Your guess is too low" << endl;
} // End of loop
```

This loop repeatedly prompts the user to enter a guess. However, this loop is incorrect, because it never terminates. When **guess** matches **number**, the loop should end. So, the loop can be revised as follows:

```
while (guess != number)
{
  // Prompt the user to guess the number
  cout << "\nEnter your guess: ";
  cin >> guess;

  if (guess == number)
    cout << "Yes, the number is " << number << endl;
  else if (guess > number)
    cout << "Your guess is too high" << endl;
  else
    cout << "Your guess is too low" << endl;
} // End of loop
```

The complete code is given in Listing 5.3.

LISTING 5.3 GuessNumber.cpp

```cpp
1   #include <iostream>
2   #include <cstdlib>
3   #include <ctime> // Needed for the time function
4   using namespace std;
5
6   int main()
7   {
8     // Generate a random number to be guessed
9     srand(time(0));
10    int number = rand() % 101;                              generate a number
11
12    cout << "Guess a magic number between 0 and 100";
13
14    int guess = -1;
15    while (guess != number)
16    {
17      // Prompt the user to guess the number
18      cout << "\nEnter your guess: ";
19      cin >> guess;                                         enter a guess
20
21      if (guess == number)                                  correct guess?
22        cout << "Yes, the number is " << number << endl;
23      else if (guess > number)                              too high?
24        cout << "Your guess is too high" << endl;
25      else                                                  too low?
26        cout << "Your guess is too low" << endl;
27    } // End of loop
28
29    return 0;
30  }
```

	Line#	number	guess	Output
	10	39		
	14		-1	
iteration 1	19		50	
	24			Your guess is too high
iteration 2	19		25	
	26			Your guess is too low
iteration 3	19		12	
	24			Your guess is too high
iteration 4	19		39	
	22			Yes, the number is 39

The program generates the magic number in line 10 and prompts the user to enter a guess repeatedly in a loop (lines 15–27). For each guess, the program checks if it is correct, too high, or too low (lines 21–26). When the guess is correct, the program exits the loop (line 15). Note that **guess** is initialized to -1. Initializing it to a value between 0 and 100 would be wrong, because that could be the number guessed.

5.2.2 Loop Design Strategies

Writing a correct loop is not an easy task for novice programmers. Consider three steps when writing a loop.

Step 1: Identify the statements that need to be repeated.

Step 2: Wrap these statements in a loop as follows:

```
while (true)
{
  Statements;
}
```

Step 3: Code the loop-continuation-condition and add appropriate statements for controlling the loop.

```
while (loop-continuation-condition)
{
  Statements;
  Additional statements for controlling the loop;
}
```

5.2.3 Case Study: Multiple Subtraction Quiz

The subtraction quiz program in Listing 3.4, SubtractionQuiz.cpp, generates just one question for each run. You can use a loop to generate questions repeatedly. How do you write the code to generate five questions? Follow the loop design strategy. First, identify the statements that need to be repeated. They are the statements for obtaining two random numbers, prompting the user with a subtraction question, and grading the question. Second, wrap the statements in a loop. Third, add a loop control variable and the loop-continuation-condition to execute the loop five times.

Listing 5.4 gives a program that generates five questions and, after a student answers them, reports the number of correct answers. The program also displays the time spent taking the test, as shown in the sample run.

LISTING 5.4 SubtractionQuizLoop.cpp

```
1  #include <iostream>
2  #include <ctime> // Needed for time function
3  #include <cstdlib> // Needed for the srand and rand functions
4  using namespace std;
5
6  int main()
7  {
8    int correctCount = 0; // Count the number of correct answers
9    int count = 0; // Count the number of questions
10   long startTime = time(0);
11   const int NUMBER_OF_QUESTIONS = 5;
12
13   srand(time(0)); // Set a random seed
14
15   while (count < NUMBER_OF_QUESTIONS)
16   {
17     // 1. Generate two random single-digit integers
18     int number1 = rand() % 10;
19     int number2 = rand() % 10;
20
21     // 2. If number1 < number2, swap number1 with number2
```

correct count
total count
get start time

loop

```
22        if (number1 < number2)
23        {
24          int temp = number1;
25          number1 = number2;
26          number2 = temp;
27        }
28
29        // 3. Prompt the student to answer "what is number1 - number2?"
30        cout << "What is " << number1 << " - " << number2 << "? ";      display a question
31        int answer;
32        cin >> answer;
33
34        // 4. Grade the answer and display the result
35        if (number1 - number2 == answer)                                 grade an answer
36        {
37          cout << "You are correct!\n";
38          correctCount++;                                                increase correct count
39        }
40        else
41          cout << "Your answer is wrong.\n" << number1 << " - " <<
42            number2 << " should be " << (number1 - number2) << endl;
43
44        // Increase the count
45        count++;                                                         increase control variable
46      }
47
48      long endTime = time(0);                                            get end time
49      long testTime = endTime - startTime;                               test time
50
51      cout << "Correct count is " << correctCount << "\nTest time is "   display result
52          << testTime << " seconds\n";
53
54      return 0;
55  }
```

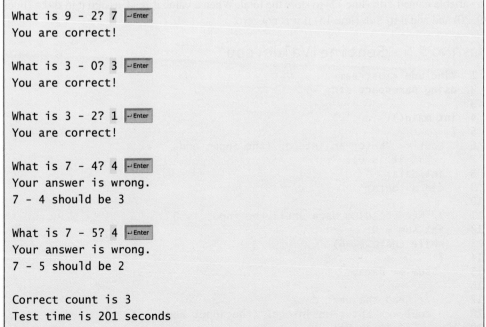

```
What is 9 - 2? 7 ↵Enter
You are correct!

What is 3 - 0? 3 ↵Enter
You are correct!

What is 3 - 2? 1 ↵Enter
You are correct!

What is 7 - 4? 4 ↵Enter
Your answer is wrong.
7 - 4 should be 3

What is 7 - 5? 4 ↵Enter
Your answer is wrong.
7 - 5 should be 2


Correct count is 3
Test time is 201 seconds
```

The program uses the control variable **count** to control the execution of the loop. **count** is initially **0** (line 9) and is increased by **1** in each iteration (line 45). A subtraction question is displayed and processed in each iteration. The program obtains the time before the test starts in line 10, the time after the test ends in line 48, and computes the test time in line 49.

5.2.4 Controlling a Loop with User Confirmation

confirmation

The preceding example executes the loop five times. If you want the user to decide whether to continue, you can offer a user *confirmation*. The template of the program can be coded as follows:

```
char continueLoop = 'Y';
while (continueLoop == 'Y')
{
  // Execute the loop body once
  ...

  // Prompt the user for confirmation
  cout << "Enter Y to continue and N to quit: ";
  cin >> continueLoop;
}
```

You can rewrite Listing 5.4 with user confirmation to let the user decide whether to advance to the next question.

5.2.5 Controlling a Loop with a Sentinel Value

sentinel value

sentinel-controlled loop

Another common technique for controlling a loop is to designate a special value when reading and processing a set of values. This special input value, known as a *sentinel value*, signifies the end of the input. A loop that uses a sentinel value to control its execution is called a *sentinel-controlled loop*.

Listing 5.5 gives a program that reads and calculates the sum of an unspecified number of integers. The input **0** signifies the end of the input. Do you need to declare a new variable for each input value? No. Just use a variable named **data** (line 8) to store the input value and use a variable named **sum** (line 12) to store the total. When a value is read, assign it to **data** (lines 9, 20) and add it to **sum** (line 15) if it is not zero.

LISTING 5.5 SentinelValue.cpp

input

loop

```
1  #include <iostream>
2  using namespace std;
3
4  int main()
5  {
6    cout << "Enter an integer (the input ends " <<
7      "if it is 0): ";
8    int data;
9    cin >> data;
10
11   // Keep reading data until the input is 0
12   int sum = 0;
13   while (data != 0)
14   {
15     sum += data;
16
17     // Read the next data
18     cout << "Enter an integer (the input ends " <<
19       "if it is 0): ";
20     cin >> data;
```

```
21   }
22
23   cout << "The sum is " << sum << endl;                              display result
24
25   return 0;
26 }
```

```
Enter an integer (the input ends if it is 0): 2  ↵Enter
Enter an integer (the input ends if it is 0): 3  ↵Enter
Enter an integer (the input ends if it is 0): 4  ↵Enter
Enter an integer (the input ends if it is 0): 0  ↵Enter
The sum is 9
```

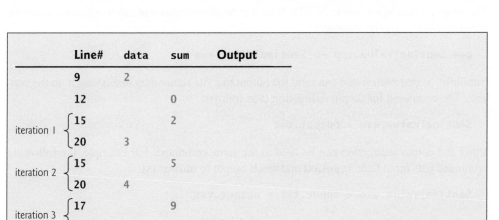

	Line#	data	sum	Output
	9	2		
	12		0	
iteration 1 {	15		2	
	20	3		
iteration 2 {	15		5	
	20	4		
iteration 3 {	17		9	
	20	0		
	23			The sum is 9

If **data** is not **0**, it is added to the **sum** (line 15) and the next items of input data are read (lines 18–20). If **data** is **0**, the loop terminates. The input value **0** is the sentinel value for this loop. Note that if the first input read is **0**, the loop body never executes, and the resulting sum is **0**.

Caution

Don't use floating-point values for equality checking in a loop control expression. Because floating-point values are approximations for some values, using them can result in imprecise counter values and inaccurate results.   numeric error

Consider the following code for computing $1 + 0.9 + 0.8 + \ldots + 0.1$:

```
double item = 1; double sum = 0;
while (item != 0) // No guarantee item will be 0
{
  sum += item;
  item -= 0.1;
}
cout << sum << endl;
```

Variable **item** starts with **1** and is reduced by **0.1** each time the loop body is executed. The loop should terminate when **item** becomes **0**. However, there is no guarantee that item will be exactly **0**, because the floating-point arithmetic is approximated. This loop seems fine, but actually, it is an infinite loop.

VideoNote
Redirect input and output

5.2.6 Input and Output Redirections

In the preceding example, if you have a lot of data to enter, it would be cumbersome to type from the keyboard. You may store the data separated by whitespaces in a text file, say **input.txt**, and run the program using the following command:

```
SentinelValue.exe < input.txt
```

input redirection

This command is called *input redirection*. The program takes the input from the file **input.txt** rather than having the user type the data from the keyboard at runtime. Suppose the contents of the file are

```
2 3 4 5 6 7 8 9 12 23 32
23 45 67 89 92 12 34 35 3 1 2 4 0
```

The program should set `sum` to be `518`. Note that **SentinelValue.exe** can be obtained using the command-line compiler command:

```
g++ SentinelValue.cpp -o SentinelValue.exe
```

output redirection

Similarly, *output redirection* can send the output to a file rather than displaying it on the console. The command for output redirection is as follows:

```
SentinelValue.exe > output.txt
```

Input and output redirection can be used in the same command. For example, the following command gets input from **input.txt** and sends output to **output.txt**:

```
SentinelValue.exe < input.txt > output.txt
```

Run the program to see what contents are in **output.txt**.

5.2.7 Reading All Data from a File

VideoNote
Read file
eof function

Listing 4.11 reads three numbers from the data file. If you have many numbers to read, you will have to write a loop to read all of them. If you don't know how many numbers are in the file and want to read them all, how do you know the end of file? You can invoke the `eof()` function on the input object to detect it. Listing 5.6 revises Listing 4.10 SimpleFileInput.cpp to read all numbers from the file **numbers.txt**.

LISTING 5.6 ReadAllData.cpp

include `fstream` header

open file

end of file?

```
 1  #include <iostream>
 2  #include <fstream>
 3  using namespace std;
 4
 5  int main()
 6  {
 7    // Open a file
 8    ifstream input("score.txt");
 9
10    double sum = 0;
11    double number;
12    while (!input.eof()) // Continue if not end of file
```

```
13   {
14     input >> number;  // Read data                              input from file
15     cout << number << " ";  // Display data
16     sum += number;
17   }
18
19   input.close();                                                close file
20
21   cout << "\nSum is " << sum << endl;
22
23   return 0;
24 }
```

```
95 56 34
Total score is 185
Done
```

The program reads data in a loop (lines 12–17). Each iteration of the loop reads one number.
The loop terminates when the input reaches the end of file.   end of file?

When there is nothing more to read, **eof()** returns **true**. For this program to work correctly, there shouldn't be any blank characters after the last number in the file. In Chapter 13,
we will discuss how to improve the program for handling the unusual cases with blank characters after the last number in the file.

5.1 Analyze the following code. Is **count** < 100 always **true**, always **false**, or
sometimes **true** or sometimes **false** at Point A, Point B, and Point C?   ✓**Check Point**

```
int count = 0;
while (count < 100)
{
  // Point A
  cout << "Welcome to C++!\n";
  count++;
  // Point B
}
// Point C
```

5.2 What is wrong if **guess** is initialized to **0** in line 14 in Listing 5.3?

5.3 How many times are the following loop bodies repeated? What is the printout of
each loop?

```
int i = 1;
while (i < 10)
  if (i % 2 == 0)
    cout << i << endl;
```
(a)

```
int i = 1;
while (i < 10)
  if (i % 2 == 0)
    cout << i++ << endl;
```
(b)

```
int i = 1;
while (i < 10)
  if (i++ % 2 == 0)
    cout << i << endl;
```
(c)

5.4 Suppose the input is 2 3 4 5 0. What is the output of the following code?

```cpp
#include <iostream>
using namespace std;

int main()
{
  int number, max;
  cin >> number;
  max = number;

  while (number != 0)
  {
    cin >> number;
    if (number > max)
      max = number;
  }

  cout << "max is " << max << endl;
  cout << "number " << number << endl;

  return 0;
}
```

5.5 What is the output of the following code? Explain.

```cpp
int x = 80000000;

while (x > 0)
  x++;

cout << "x is " << x << endl;
```

5.6 How do you test end of the file when reading data from a file?

5.3 The do-while Loop

 Key Point

A do-while *loop is the same as a* while *loop except that it executes the loop body first and then checks the loop continuation condition.*

The do-while loop is a variation of the while loop. Its syntax is as follows:

do-while loop

```cpp
do
{
  // Loop body;
  Statement(s);
} while (loop-continuation-condition);
```

Its execution flowchart is shown in Figure 5.2.

The loop body is executed first. Then the loop-continuation-condition is evaluated. If the evaluation is true, the loop body is executed again; otherwise the do-while loop terminates. The major difference between a while and a do-while loop is the order in which the loop-continuation-condition is evaluated and the loop body executed. The while and do-while loops have equal expressive power. Sometimes one is more convenient than the other. For example, you can rewrite the while loop in Listing 5.5 using a do-while loop, as shown in Listing 5.7.

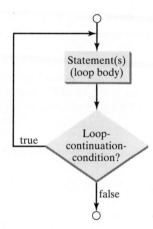

FIGURE 5.2 The do-while loop executes the loop body first, then checks the loop-continuation-condition to determine whether to continue or terminate the loop.

LISTING 5.7 TestDoWhile.cpp

```
1   #include <iostream>
2   using namespace std;
3
4   int main()
5   {
6     // Keep reading data until the input is 0
7     int sum = 0;
8     int data = 0;
9
10    do                                                              loop
11    {
12      sum += data;
13
14      // Read the next data
15      cout << "Enter an integer (the input ends " <<
16        "if it is 0): ";
17      cin >> data;                                                  input
18    }
19    while (data != 0);
20
21    cout << "The sum is " << sum << endl;
22
23    return 0;
24  }
```

```
Enter an integer (the input ends if it is 0): 3 ↵Enter
Enter an integer (the input ends if it is 0): 5 ↵Enter
Enter an integer (the input ends if it is 0): 6 ↵Enter
Enter an integer (the input ends if it is 0): 0 ↵Enter
The sum is 14
```

What would happen if **sum** and **data** were not initialized to 0? Would it cause a syntax error? No. It would cause a logic error, because **sum** and **data** could be initialized to any value.

Tip

Use the **do-while** loop if you have statements inside the loop that must be executed *at least once*, as in the case of the **do-while** loop in the preceding TestDoWhile program. These statements must appear before the loop as well as inside it if you use a **while** loop.

5.7 Suppose the input is 2 3 4 5 0. What is the output of the following code?

```cpp
#include <iostream>
using namespace std;

int main()
{
  int number, max;
  cin >> number;
  max = number;

  do
  {
    cin >> number;
    if (number > max)
      max = number;
  } while (number != 0);

  cout << "max is " << max << endl;
  cout << "number " << number << endl;

  return 0;
}
```

5.8 What are the differences between a **while** loop and a **do-while** loop? Convert the following **while** loop into a **do-while** loop.

```cpp
int sum = 0;
int number;
cin >> number;
while (number != 0)
{
  sum += number;
  cin >> number;
}
```

5.9 What is wrong in the following code?

```cpp
int total = 0, num = 0;

do
{
  // Read the next data
  cout << "Enter an int value, " <<
    "\nexit if the input is 0: ";
  int num;
  cin >> num;

  total += num;
} while (num != 0);

cout << "Total is " << total << endl;
```

5.4 The **for** Loop

A for *loop has a concise syntax for writing loops.*

Often you write a loop in the following common form:

```
i = initialValue;  // Initialize loop-control variable
while (i < endValue)
{
  // Loop body
  ...
  i++; // Adjust loop-control variable
}
```

A for loop can be used to simplify the above loop:

```
for (i = initialValue; i < endValue; i++)
{
  // Loop body
  ...
}
```

In general, the syntax of a for loop is as shown below:

```
for (initial-action; loop-continuation-condition;
     action-after-each-iteration)
{
  // Loop body;
  Statement(s);
}
```

for loop

The flowchart of the for loop is shown in Figure 5.3a.

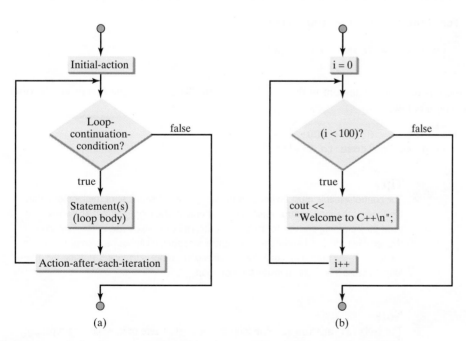

(a)   (b)

FIGURE 5.3   A for loop performs an initial action once, then repeatedly executes the statements in the loop body, and performs an action after an iteration when the loop-continuation-condition evaluates to true.

The for-loop statement starts with the keyword **for**, followed by a pair of parentheses enclosing initial-action, loop-continuation-condition, and action-after-each-iteration, followed by the loop body enclosed inside braces. initial-action, loop-continuation-condition, and action-after-each-iteration are separated by semicolons.

control variable

A **for** loop generally uses a variable to control how many times the loop body is executed and when the loop terminates. This is called a *control variable*. The initial-action often initializes a control variable, the action-after-each-iteration usually increments or decrements the control variable, and the loop-continuation-condition tests whether the control variable has reached a termination value. For example, the following **for** loop displays Welcome to C++! 100 times:

```cpp
int i;
for (i = 0; i < 100; i++)
{
  cout << "Welcome to C++!\n";
}
```

The flowchart of the statement is shown in Figure 5.3b. The **for** loop initializes i to 0, then repeatedly executes the output statement and evaluates i++ while i is less than 100.

initial-action

The initial-action, i = 0, initializes the control variable, i. The loop-continuation-condition, i < 100, is a Boolean expression. The expression is evaluated right after the initialization and at the beginning of each iteration. If this condition is **true**, the loop body is executed. If it is **false**, the loop terminates and the program control turns to the line following the loop.

action-after-each-iteration

The action-after-each-iteration, i++, is a statement that adjusts the control variable. This statement is executed after each iteration. It increments the control variable. Eventually, the value of the control variable should force the loop-continuation-condition to become **false**. Otherwise, the loop is infinite.

The loop control variable can be declared and initialized in the **for** loop. Here is an example:

```cpp
for (int i = 0; i < 100; i++)
{
  cout << "Welcome to C++!\n";
}
```

omitting braces

If there is only one statement in the loop body, as in this example, the braces can be omitted as shown below:

```cpp
for (int i = 0; i < 100; i++)
  cout << "Welcome to C++!\n";
```

declare control variable

Tip

The control variable must be declared inside the control structure of the loop or before the loop. If the loop control variable is used only in the loop, and not elsewhere, it is good programming practice to declare it in the initial-action of the **for** loop. If the variable is declared inside the loop control structure, it cannot be referenced outside the loop. In the preceding code, for example, you cannot reference i outside the **for** loop, because it is declared inside the **for** loop.

for loop variations

Note

The initial-action in a **for** loop can be a list of zero or more comma-separated variable declaration statements or assignment expressions. For example:

```
for (int i = 0, j = 0; i + j < 10; i++, j++)
{
   // Do something
}
```

The **action-after-each-iteration** in a **for** loop can be a list of zero or more comma-separated statements. For example:

```
for (int i = 1; i < 100; cout << i << endl, i++);
```

This example is correct, but it is a bad example, because it makes the code difficult to read. Normally, you declare and initialize a control variable as an initial action and increment or decrement the control variable as an action after each iteration.

 Note

If the **loop-continuation-condition** in a **for** loop is omitted, it is implicitly **true**. Thus, the statement given below in (a), which is an infinite loop, is the same as in (b). To avoid confusion, though, it is better to use the equivalent loop in (c).

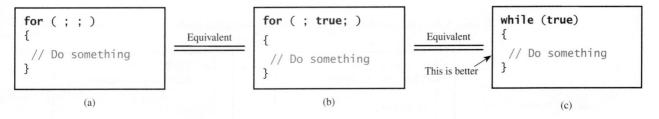

```
for ( ; ; )
{
   // Do something
}
```
(a)

Equivalent

```
for ( ; true; )
{
   // Do something
}
```
(b)

Equivalent

This is better

```
while (true)
{
   // Do something
}
```
(c)

5.10 Do the following two loops result in the same value in **sum**?

```
for (int i = 0; i < 10; ++i)
{
   sum += i;
}
```
(a)

```
for (int i = 0; i < 10; i++)
{
   sum += i;
}
```
(b)

✓ Check Point

5.11 What are the three parts of a **for** loop control? Write a **for** loop that prints the numbers from **1** to **100**.

5.12 Suppose the input is **2 3 4 5 0**. What is the output of the following code?

```
#include <iostream>
using namespace std;

int main()
{
   int number, sum = 0, count;

   for (count = 0; count < 5; count++)
   {
      cin >> number;
      sum += number;
   }
```

```
cout << "sum is " << sum << endl;
cout << "count is " << count << endl;

return 0;
}
```

5.13   What does the following statement do?

```
for ( ; ; )
{
   // Do something
}
```

5.14   If a variable is declared in the **for** loop control, can it be used after the loop exits?

5.15   Convert the following **for** loop statement to a **while** loop and to a **do-while** loop:

```
long sum = 0;
for (int i = 0; i <= 1000; i++)
   sum = sum + i;
```

5.16   Count the number of iterations in the following loops:

```
int count = 0;
while (count < n)
{
   count++;
}
```
(a)

```
for (int count = 0;
     count <= n; count++)
{
}
```
(b)

```
int count = 5;
while (count < n)
{
   count++;
}
```
(c)

```
int count = 5;
while (count < n)
{
   count = count + 3;
}
```
(d)

5.5 Which Loop to Use?

Key Point

pretest loop
posttest loop

You can use a **for** *loop, a* **while** *loop, or a* **do-while** *loop, whichever is convenient.*

The **while** loop and **for** loop are called *pretest loops* because the continuation condition is checked before the loop body is executed. The **do-while** loop is called a *posttest loop* because the condition is checked after the loop body is executed. The three forms of loop statements—**while**, **do-while**, and **for**—are expressively equivalent; that is, you can write a loop in any of these three forms. For example, a **while** loop in (a) in the following figure can always be converted into the **for** loop in (b).

```
while (loop-continuation-condition)
{
   // Loop body
}
```
(a)

Equivalent

```
for ( ; loop-continuation-condition; )
{
   // Loop body
}
```
(b)

A **for** loop in (a) in the next figure can generally be converted into the **while** loop in (b) except in certain special cases (see Check Point 5.24 for such a case).

```
for (initial-action;
     loop-continuation-condition;
     action-after-each-iteration)
{
    // Loop body;
}
```
(a)

Equivalent
———————————

```
initial-action;
while (loop-continuation-condition)
{
    // Loop body;
    action-after-each-iteration;
}
```
(b)

Use the loop statement that is most intuitive and comfortable for you. In general, a **for** loop may be used if the number of repetitions is known in advance, as, for example, when you need to display a message 100 times. A **while** loop may be used if the number of repetitions is not fixed, as in the case of reading the numbers until the input is 0. A **do-while** loop can be used to replace a **while** loop if the loop body has to be executed before the continuation condition is tested.

Caution
Adding a semicolon at the end of the **for** clause before the loop body is a common error, as shown below. In (a), the semicolon signifies the end of the loop prematurely. The loop body is actually empty, as shown in (b). (a) and (b) are equivalent.

Error

```
for (int i = 0; i < 10; i++);
{
    cout << "i is " << i << endl;
}
```
(a)

Empty Body

```
for (int i = 0; i < 10; i++) { };
{
    cout << "i is " << i << endl;
}
```
(b)

Similarly, the loop in (c) is also wrong. (c) is equivalent to (d).

Error

```
int i = 0;
while (i < 10);
{
    cout << "i is " << i << endl;
    i++;
}
```
(c)

Empty Body

```
int i = 0;
while (i < 10) { };
{
    cout << "i is " << i << endl;
    i++;
}
```
(d)

In the case of the **do-while** loop, the semicolon is needed to end the loop.

```
int i = 0;
do
{
    cout << "i is " << i << endl;
    i++;
} while (i < 10);  ←——— Correct
```

5.17 Can you convert a `for` loop to a `while` loop? List the advantages of using `for` loops.

5.18 Can you always convert a `while` loop into a `for` loop? Convert the following `while` loop into a `for` loop.

```
int i = 1;
int sum = 0;
while (sum < 10000)
{
   sum = sum + i;
   i++;
}
```

5.19 Identify and fix the errors in the following code:

```
1   int main()
2   {
3      for (int i = 0; i < 10; i++);
4         sum += i;
5
6      if (i < j);
7         cout << i << endl;
8      else
9         cout << j << endl;
10
11     while (j < 10);
12     {
13        j++;
14     }
15
16     do {
17        j++;
18     }
19     while (j < 10)
20  }
```

5.20 What is wrong with the following programs?

```
1   int main()
2   {
3      for (int i = 0; i < 10; i++);
4         cout << i + 4 << endl;
5   }
```

5.6 Nested Loops

A loop can be nested inside another loop.

nested loop

Nested loops consist of an outer loop and one or more inner loops. Each time the outer loop is repeated, the inner loops are reentered, and started anew.

Listing 5.8 presents a program that uses nested `for` loops to display a multiplication table.

LISTING 5.8 MultiplicationTable.cpp

```
1   #include <iostream>
2   #include <iomanip>
3   using namespace std;
4
```

```
 5  int main()
 6  {
 7    cout << "        Multiplication Table\n";          table title
 8    cout << "-------------------------------\n";
 9
10    // Display the number title
11    cout << "  | ";
12    for (int j = 1; j <= 9; j++)
13      cout << setw(3) << j;
14
15    cout << "\n";
16
17    // Display table body
18    for (int i = 1; i <= 9; i++)                        outer loop
19    {
20      cout << i << " | ";
21      for (int j = 1; j <= 9; j++)                      inner loop
22      {
23        // Display the product and align properly
24        cout << setw(3) << i * j;
25      }
26      cout << "\n";
27    }
28
29    return 0;
30  }
```

```
        Multiplication Table
        1   2   3   4   5   6   7   8   9
-------------------------------------------
1 |     1   2   3   4   5   6   7   8   9
2 |     2   4   6   8  10  12  14  16  18
3 |     3   6   9  12  15  18  21  24  27
4 |     4   8  12  16  20  24  28  32  36
5 |     5  10  15  20  25  30  35  40  45
6 |     6  12  18  24  30  36  42  48  54
7 |     7  14  21  28  35  42  49  56  63
8 |     8  16  24  32  40  48  56  64  72
9 |     9  18  27  36  45  54  63  72  81
```

The program displays a title (line 7) on the first line and dashes (-) (line 8) on the second line. The first **for** loop (lines 12–13) displays the numbers 1 through 9 on the third line.

The next loop (lines 18–27) is a nested **for** loop with the control variable i in the outer loop and j in the inner loop. For each i, the product i * j is displayed on a line in the inner loop, with j being 1, 2, 3, ... , 9. The **setw(3)** manipulator (line 24) specifies the width for each number to be displayed.

 Note

Be aware that a nested loop may take a long time to run. Consider the following loop nested in three levels:

```
for (int i = 0; i < 10000; i++)
  for (int j = 0; j < 10000; j++)
    for (int k = 0; k < 10000; k++)
        Perform an action
```

The action is performed 1 trillion times. If it takes 1 microsecond to perform the action, the total time to run the loop would be more than 277 hours. Note that 1 microsecond is one millionth (10^{-6}) of a second.

5.21 How many times is the print statement executed?

```
for (int i = 0; i < 10; i++)
  for (int j = 0; j < i; j++)
    cout << i * j << endl;
```

5.22 Show the output of the following programs. (*Tip*: Draw a table and list the variables in the columns to trace these programs.)

```
for (int i = 1; i < 5; i++)
{
  int j = 0;
  while (j < i)
  {
    cout << j << " ";
    j++;
  }
}
```
(a)

```
int i = 0;
while (i < 5)
{
  for (int j = i; j > 1; j--)
    cout << j << " ";
  cout << "****" << endl;
  i++;
}
```
(b)

```
int i = 5;
while (i >= 1)
{
  int num = 1;
  for (int j = 1; j <= i; j++)
  {
    cout << num << "xxx";
    num *= 2;
  }

  cout << endl:
  i--;
}
```
(c)

```
int i = 1;
do
{
  int num = 1
  for (int j = 1; j <= i; j++)
  {
    cout << num << "G";
    num += 2;
  }

  cout << endl;
  i++;
} while (i <= 5);
```
(d)

5.7 Minimizing Numeric Errors

Using floating-point numbers in the loop continuation condition may cause numeric errors.

numeric error

Numeric errors involving floating-point numbers are inevitable. This section discusses how to minimize such errors.

Listing 5.9 presents an example summing a series that starts with **0.01** and ends with **1.0**. The numbers in the series will increment by **0.01**, as follows: **0.01 + 0.02 + 0.03** and so on.

LISTING 5.9   TestSum.cpp

```
1  #include <iostream>
2  using namespace std;
```

```
3
4    int main()
5    {
6      // Initialize sum
7      double sum = 0;
8
9      // Add 0.01, 0.02, ... , 0.99, 1 to sum
10     for (double i = 0.01; i <= 1.0; i = i + 0.01)          loop
11       sum += i;
12
13     // Display result
14     cout << "The sum is " << sum << endl;
15
16     return 0;
17   }
```

```
The sum is 49.5
```

The result is **49.5**, but the correct result should be **50.5**. What happened? For each iteration in the loop, i is incremented by **0.01**. When the loop ends, the i value is slightly larger than **1** (not exactly **1**). This causes the last i value not to be added into **sum**. The fundamental problem is that the floating-point numbers are represented by approximation.

To fix the problem, use an integer count to ensure that all the numbers are added to **sum**. Here is the new loop:

```
double currentValue = 0.01;

for (int count = 0; count < 100; count++)
{
  sum += currentValue;
  currentValue += 0.01;
}
```

After this loop, **sum** is **50.5**.

5.8 Case Studies

Loops are fundamental in programming. The ability to write loops is essential in learning programming.

Key Point

If you can write programs using loops, you know how to program! For this reason, this section presents four additional examples of solving problems using loops.

5.8.1   Case Study: Finding the Greatest Common Divisor

The greatest common divisor (GCD) of the two integers **4** and **2** is **2**. The GCD of the two integers **16** and **24** is **8**. How do you determine the GCD? Let the two input integers be **n1** and **n2**. You know that number **1** is a common divisor, but it may not be the greatest one. So, you can check whether **k** (for **k = 2, 3, 4,** and so on) is a common divisor for **n1** and **n2**, until **k** is greater than **n1** or **n2**. Store the common divisor in a variable named **gcd**. Initially, **gcd** is **1**. Whenever a new common divisor is found, it becomes the new GCD. When you have checked all the possible common divisors from **2** up to **n1** or **n2**, the value in variable **gcd** is the GCD. The idea can be translated into the following loop:

GCD

```
int gcd = 1; // Initial gcd is 1
int k = 2; // Possible gcd
```

```
while (k <= n1 && k <= n2)
{
  if (n1 % k == 0 && n2 % k == 0)
    gcd = k; // Update gcd
  k++; // Next possible gcd
}

// After the loop, gcd is the greatest common divisor for n1 and n2
```

Listing 5.10 presents the program that prompts the user to enter two positive integers and finds their GCD.

LISTING 5.10 GreatestCommonDivisor.cpp

```
1  #include <iostream>
2  using namespace std;
3
4  int main()
5  {
6    // Prompt the user to enter two integers
7    cout << "Enter first integer: ";
8    int n1;
9    cin >> n1;
10
11   cout << "Enter second integer: ";
12   int n2;
13   cin >> n2;
14
15   int gcd = 1;
16   int k = 2;
17   while (k <= n1 && k <= n2)
18   {
19     if (n1 % k == 0 && n2 % k == 0)
20       gcd = k;
21     k++;
22   }
23
24   cout << "The greatest common divisor for " << n1 << " and "
25        << n2 << " is " << gcd << endl;
26
27   return 0;
28 }
```

input (line 9)

input (line 13)

gcd (line 15)

check divisor (line 19)

output (line 24)

```
Enter first integer: 125 ⏎Enter
Enter second integer: 2525 ⏎Enter
The greatest common divisor for 125 and 2525 is 25
```

think before you type

How would you write this program? Would you immediately begin to write the code? No. It is important to *think before you type*. Thinking enables you to generate a logical solution for the problem before writing the code. Once you have a logical solution, type the code to translate the solution into a program. The translation is not unique. For example, you could use a **for** loop to rewrite the code as follows:

```
for (int k = 2; k <= n1 && k <= n2; k++)
{
  if (n1 % k == 0 && n2 % k == 0)
    gcd = k;
}
```

A problem often has multiple solutions, and the gcd problem can be solved in many ways. Programming Exercise 5.16 suggests another solution. A more efficient solution is to use the classic Euclidean algorithm (see www.cut-the-knot.org/blue/Euclid.shtml for more information).

multiple solutions

You might think that a divisor for a number **n1** cannot be greater than **n1 / 2**, prompting you to try to improve the program using the following loop:

erroneous solutions

```
for (int k = 2; k <= n1 / 2 && k <= n2 / 2; k++)
{
  if (n1 % k == 0 && n2 % k == 0)
    gcd = k;
}
```

This revision is wrong. Can you find the reason? See Check Point 5.23 for the answer.

5.8.2 Case Study: Predicting the Future Tuition

Suppose that the tuition for a university is $10,000 this year and tuition increases 7% every year. In how many years will the tuition be doubled?

Before you can write a program to solve this problem, first consider how to solve it by hand. The tuition for the second year is the tuition for the first year * 1.07. The tuition for a future year is the tuition of its preceding year * 1.07. Thus, the tuition for each year can be computed as follows:

```
double tuition = 10000;   int year = 0; // Year 0
tuition = tuition * 1.07; year++;       // Year 1
tuition = tuition * 1.07; year++;       // Year 2
tuition = tuition * 1.07; year++;       // Year 3
...
```

Keep computing the tuition for a new year until it is at least **20000**. By then you will know how many years it will take for the tuition to be doubled. You can now translate the logic into the following loop:

```
double tuition = 10000;   // Year 0
int year = 0;
while (tuition < 20000)
{
  tuition = tuition * 1.07;
  year++;
}
```

The complete program is shown in Listing 5.11.

LISTING 5.11 FutureTuition.cpp

```
1  #include <iostream>
2  #include <iomanip>
3  using namespace std;
4
5  int main()
6  {
7    double tuition = 10000;   // Year 1
8    int year = 1;
9    while (tuition < 20000)
10   {
11     tuition = tuition * 1.07;
12     year++;
13   }
```

loop

next year's tuition

```
14
15    cout << "Tuition will be doubled in " << year << " years" << endl;
16    cout << setprecision(2) << fixed << showpoint <<
17          "Tuition will be $" << tuition << " in "
18          << year << " years" << endl;
19
20    return 0;
21  }
```

```
Tuition will be doubled in 11 years
Tuition will be $21048.52 in 11 years
```

The `while` loop (lines 9–13) is used to repeatedly compute the tuition for a new year. The loop terminates when tuition is greater than or equal to `20000`.

5.8.3 Case Study: Monte Carlo Simulation

Monte Carlo simulation uses random numbers and probability to solve problems. This method has a wide range of applications in computational mathematics, physics, chemistry, and finance. This section gives an example of using Monte Carlo simulation for estimating π.

To estimate π using the Monte Carlo method, draw a circle with its bounding square as shown below:

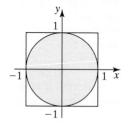

Assume the radius of the circle is 1. Therefore, the circle area is π and the square area is 4. Randomly generate a point in the square. The probability for the point to fall in the circle is `circleArea / squareArea = ` π ` / 4`.

Write a program that randomly generates $1,000,000$ points in the square and let `numberOfHits` denote the number of points that fall in the circle. Thus, `numberOfHits` is approximately `1000000` $*$ `(`π` / 4)`. π can be approximated as `4 * numberOfHits / 1000000`. The complete program is shown in Listing 5.12.

LISTING 5.12 MonteCarloSimulation.cpp

```
1   #include <iostream>
2   #include <cstdlib>
3   #include <ctime>
4   using namespace std;
5
6   int main()
7   {
8     const int NUMBER_OF_TRIALS = 1000000;
9     int numberOfHits = 0;
10    srand(time(0));
11
12    for (int i = 0; i < NUMBER_OF_TRIALS; i++)
13    {
```

generate random points
```
14      double x = rand() * 2.0 / RAND_MAX - 1;
```

```
15       double y = rand() * 2.0 / RAND_MAX - 1;
16       if (x * x + y * y <= 1)                              check inside circle
17          numberOfHits++;
18     }
19
20     double pi = 4.0 * numberOfHits / NUMBER_OF_TRIALS;     estimate pi
21     cout << "PI is " << pi << endl;
22
23     return 0;
24  }
```

```
PI is 3.14124
```

The program repeatedly generates a random point (x, y) in the square in lines 14–15. Note that RAND_MAX is the maximum number that may be returned from invoking the `rand()` function. So, `rand() * 1.0 / RAND_MAX` is a random number between 0.0 and 1.0, and `2.0 * rand() / RAND_MAX` is a random number between 0.0 and 2.0. Therefore, `2.0 * rand() / RAND_MAX - 1` is a random number between -1.0 and 1.0.

If $x^2 + y^2 \le 1$, the point is inside the circle and `numberOfHits` is incremented by 1. π is approximately `4 * numberOfHits / NUMBER_OF_TRIALS` (line 20).

5.8.4 Case Study: Converting Decimals to Hexadecimals

Hexadecimals are often used in computer systems programming (see Appendix D for an introduction to number systems). How do you convert a decimal number to a hexadecimal number? To convert a decimal number d to a hexadecimal number is to find the hexadecimal digits $h_n, h_{n-1}, h_{n-2}, \ldots, h_2, h_1,$ and h_0 such that

$$d = h_n \times 16^n + h_{n-1} \times 16^{n-1} + h_{n-2} \times 16^{n-2} + \ldots$$
$$+ h_2 \times 16^2 + h_1 \times 16^1 + h_0 \times 16^0$$

These hexadecimal digits can be found by successively dividing d by 16 until the quotient is 0. The remainders are $h_0, h_1, h_2, \ldots, h_{n-2}, h_{n-1},$ and h_n. The hexadecimal digits include the decimal digits 0, 1, 2, 3, 4, 5, 6, 7, 8, and 9, plus A, which is the decimal value 10; B, which is the decimal value 11; C, which is 12; D, which is 13; E, which is 14; and F, which is 15.

For example, the decimal number 123 is 7B in hexadecimal. The conversion is done as follows. Divide 123 by 16. The remainder is 11 (B in hexadecimal) and the quotient is 7. Continue divide 7 by 16. The remainder is 7 and the quotient is 0. Therefore, 7B is the hexadecimal number for 123.

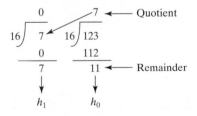

Listing 5.13 gives a program that prompts the user to enter a decimal number and converts it into a hex number as a string.

LISTING 5.13 Dec2Hex.cpp

```
1  #include <iostream>
2  #include <string>
```

```
3   using namespace std;
4
5   int main()
6   {
7     // Prompt the user to enter a decimal integer
8     cout << "Enter a decimal number: ";
9     int decimal;
10    cin >> decimal;
11
12    // Convert decimal to hex
13    string hex = "";
14
15    while (decimal != 0)
16    {
17      int hexValue = decimal % 16;
18
19      // Convert a decimal value to a hex digit
20      char hexChar = (hexValue <= 9 && hexValue >= 0) ?
21        static_cast<char>(hexValue + '0') :
22        static_cast<char>(hexValue - 10 + 'A');
23
24      hex = hexChar + hex;
25      decimal = decimal / 16;
26    }
27
28    cout << "The hex number is " << hex << endl;
29
30    return 0;
31  }
```

input decimal

decimal to hex

get a hex char

add to hex string

```
Enter a decimal number: 1234 [↵ Enter]
The hex number is 4D2
```

	Line#	decimal	hex	hexValue	hexChar
	13	1234	""		
iteration 1	17			2	
	24		"2"		2
	25	77			
iteration 2	17			13	
	24		"D2"		D
	25	4			
iteration 3	17			4	
	24		"4D2"		4
	25	0			

The program prompts the user to enter a decimal integer (line 10), converts it to a hex number as a string (lines 13–26), and displays the result (line 28). To convert a decimal to a hex number, the program uses a loop to successively divide the decimal number by **16** and obtain its remainder (line 17). The remainder is converted into a hex character (lines 20–22). The character is then appended to the hex string (line 24). The hex string is initially empty (line 13). Divide the decimal number by 16 to remove a hex digit from the number (line 25). The loop ends when the remaining decimal number becomes 0.

The program converts a hexValue between 0 and 15 into a hex character. If hexValue is between 0 and 9, it is converted to static_cast<char>(hexValue + '0') (line 21). Recall that when adding a character with an integer, the character's ASCII code is used in the evaluation. For example, if hexValue is 5, static_cast<char>(hexValue + '0') returns character 5 (line 21). Similarly, if hexValue is between 10 and 15, it is converted to static_cast<char>(hexValue - 10 + 'A') (line 22). For instance, if hexValue is 11, static_cast<char>(hexValue - 10 + 'A') returns character B.

5.23 Will the program work if n1 and n2 are replaced by n1 / 2 and n2 / 2 in line 17 in Listing 5.10?

5.24 In Listing 5.13, is it correct if you change the code static_cast <char>(hexValue + '0') to hexValue + '0' in line 21?

5.25 In Listing 5.13, how many times the loop body is executed for a decimal number 245 and how many times the loop body is executed for a decimal number 3245?

5.9 Keywords **break** and **continue**

The break *and* continue *keywords provide additional controls in a loop.*

> **Pedagogical Note**
> Two keywords, break and continue, can be used in loop statements to provide additional controls. Using break and continue can simplify programming in some cases. Overusing or improperly using them, however, can make programs difficult to read and debug. (*Note to instructors*: You may skip this section without affecting students' understanding of the rest of the book.)

You have used the keyword break in a switch statement. You can also use break in a loop to immediately terminate the loop. Listing 5.14 presents a program to demonstrate the effect of using break in a loop.

break statement

LISTING 5.14 TestBreak.cpp

```cpp
1  #include <iostream>
2  using namespace std;
3
4  int main()
5  {
6    int sum = 0;
7    int number = 0;
8
9    while (number < 20)
10   {
11     number++;
12     sum += number;
13     if (sum >= 100)
14       break;
15   }
16
17   cout << "The number is " << number << endl;
18   cout << "The sum is " << sum << endl;
19
20   return 0;
21 }
```

break

```
The number is 14
The sum is 105
```

The program adds integers from 1 to 20 in this order to **sum** until **sum** is greater than or equal to 100. Without lines 13–14, this program would calculate the sum of the numbers from 1 to 20. But with lines 13–14, the loop terminates when **sum** becomes greater than or equal to 100. Without lines 13–14, the output would be

```
The number is 20
The sum is 210
```

continue

You can also use the **continue** keyword in a loop. When encountered, it ends the current iteration. Program control goes to the end of the loop body. In other words, **continue** breaks out of an iteration, while the **break** keyword breaks out of a loop. The program in Listing 5.15 shows the effect of using **continue** in a loop.

LISTING 5.15 TestContinue.cpp

continue

```
1   #include <iostream>
2   using namespace std;
3
4   int main()
5   {
6     int sum = 0;
7     int number = 0;
8
9     while (number < 20)
10    {
11      number++;
12      if (number == 10 || number == 11)
13        continue;
14      sum += number;
15    }
16
17    cout << "The sum is " << sum << endl;
18
19    return 0;
20  }
```

```
The sum is 189
```

continue statement

The program adds the integers from 1 to 20 except 10 and 11 to **sum**. The **continue** statement is executed when **number** becomes 10 or 11. The **continue** statement ends the current iteration so that the rest of the statement in the loop body is not executed; therefore, **number** is not added to **sum** when it is 10 or 11.

Without lines 12–13, the output would be as follows:

```
The sum is 210
```

In this case, all the numbers are added to **sum**, even when **number** is 10 or 11. Therefore, the result is 210.

Note

The `continue` statement is always inside a loop. In the **while** and **do-while** loops, the `loop-continuation-condition` is evaluated immediately after the `continue` statement. In the **for** loop, the `action-after-each-iteration` is performed, then the `loop-continuation-condition` is evaluated, immediately after the `continue` statement.

You can always write a program without using **break** or `continue` in a loop. See Check Point 5.28. In general, it is appropriate to use **break** and `continue` if their use simplifies coding and makes programs easy to read.

Suppose you need to write a program to find the smallest factor other than 1 for an integer n (assume n >= 2). You can write a simple and intuitive code using the **break** statement as follows:

```
int factor = 2;
while (factor <= n)
{
  if (n % factor == 0)
    break;
  factor++;
}
cout << "The smallest factor other than 1 for "
  << n << " is " << factor << endl;
```

You may rewrite the code without using **break** as follows:

```
bool found = false;
int factor = 2;
while (factor <= n && !found)
{
  if (n % factor == 0)
    found = true;
  else
    factor++;
}
cout << "The smallest factor other than 1 for "
  << n << " is " << factor << endl;
```

Obviously, the **break** statement makes this program simpler and easier to read. However, you should use **break** and `continue` with caution. Too many **break** and `continue` statements will produce a loop with many exit points and make the program difficult to read.

Note

Some programming languages including C++ have a **goto** statement. The **goto** statement indiscriminately transfers control to any statement in the program and executes it. This makes your program vulnerable to errors. The **break** and `continue` statements in C++ are different from **goto** statements. They operate only in a loop or a **switch** statement. The **break** statement breaks out of the loop, and the `continue` statement breaks out of the current iteration in the loop.

goto

5.26 What is the keyword **break** for? What is the keyword `continue` for? Will the following programs terminate? If so, give the output.

Check Point

```
int balance = 1000;
while (true)
{
  if (balance < 9)
    break;
  balance = balance - 9;
}

cout << "Balance is " <<
  balance << endl;
```

(a)

```
int balance = 1000;
while (true)
{
  if (balance < 9)
    continue;
  balance = balance - 9;
}

cout << "Balance is "
  << balance << endl;
```

(b)

5.27   The `for` loop on the left is converted into the `while` loop on the right. What is wrong? Correct it.

```
for (int i = 0; i < 4; i++)
{
  if (i % 3 == 0) continue;
  sum += i;
}
```

Converted →

Wrong conversion

```
int i = 0;
while (i < 4)
{
  if (i % 3 == 0) continue;
  sum += i;
  i++;
}
```

5.28   Rewrite the programs `TestBreak` and `TestContinue` in Listings 5.14 and 5.15 without using `break` and `continue`.

5.29   After the `break` statement in (a) is executed in the following loop, which statement is executed? Show the output. After the `continue` statement in (b) is executed in the following loop, which statement is executed? Show the output.

```
for (int i = 1; i < 4; i++)
{
  for (int j = 1; j < 4; j++)
  {
    if (i * j > 2)
      break;

    cout << i * j << endl;
  }

  cout << i << endl;
}
```

(a)

```
for (int i = 1; i < 4; i++)
{
  for (int j = 1; j < 4; j++)
  {
    if (i * j > 2)
      continue;

    cout << i * j << endl;
  }

  cout << i << endl;
}
```

(b)

5.10 Case Study: Checking Palindromes

Key Point

This section presents a program that tests whether a string is a palindrome.

A string is a palindrome if it reads the same forward and backward. The words "mom," "dad," and "noon," for example, are palindromes.

How do you write a program to check whether a string is a palindrome? One solution is to check whether the first character in the string is the same as the last character. If so, check whether the second character is the same as the second-last character. This process continues until a mismatch is found or all the characters in the string are checked, except for the middle character if the string has an odd number of characters.

To implement this idea, use two variables, say `low` and `high`, to denote the position of two characters at the beginning and the end in a string `s`, as shown in Listing 5.16 (lines 13, 16). Initially, `low` is 0 and `high` is `s.length()` − 1. If the two characters at these positions match, increment `low` by 1 and decrement `high` by 1 (lines 27–28). This process continues until (`low >= high`) or a mismatch is found.

LISTING 5.16 TestPalindrome.cpp

```
1   #include <iostream>
2   #include <string>
3   using namespace std;
4
5   int main()
6   {
7     // Prompt the user to enter a string
8     cout << "Enter a string: ";
9     string s;
10    getline(cin, s);                                    input string
11
12    // The index of the first character in the string
13    int low = 0;
14
15    // The index of the last character in the string
16    int high = s.length() - 1;
17
18    bool isPalindrome = true;
19    while (low < high)
20    {
21      if (s[low] != s[high])                            compare two characters
22      {
23        isPalindrome = false; // Not a palindrome       not palindrome
24        break;                                          exit loop
25      }
26
27      low++;
28      high--;
29    }
30
31    if (isPalindrome)
32      cout << s << " is a palindrome" << endl;
33    else
34      cout << s << " is not a palindrome" << endl;
35
36    return 0;
37  }
```

```
Enter a string: abccba [↵Enter]
abccba is a palindrome
```

```
Enter a string: abca [↵Enter]
abca is not a palindrome
```

The program declares a string (line 9), reads a string from the console (line 10), and checks whether the string is a palindrome (lines 13–29).

The `bool` variable `isPalindrome` is initially set to `true` (line 18). When comparing two corresponding characters from both ends of the string, `isPalindrome` is set to `false` if the two characters differ (line 23). In this case, the `break` statement is used to exit the `while` loop (line 24).

If the loop terminates when `low >= high`, `isPalindrome` is true, which indicates that the string is a palindrome.

5.11 Case Study: Displaying Prime Numbers

 Key Point

This section presents a program that displays the first 50 prime numbers in 5 lines, each containing 10 numbers.

An integer greater than 1 is *prime* if its only positive divisor is 1 or itself. For example, 2, 3, 5, and 7 are prime numbers, but 4, 6, 8, and 9 are not.

The program can be broken into the following tasks:

- Determine whether a given number is prime.

- For number = 2, 3, 4, 5, 6, . . . , test whether it is prime.

- Count the prime numbers.

- Display each prime number, and display ten numbers per line.

Obviously, you need to write a loop and repeatedly test whether a new **number** is prime. If the **number** is prime, increase the count by 1. The **count** is 0 initially. When it reaches 50, the loop terminates.

Here is the algorithm:

```
Set the number of prime numbers to be printed as
  a constant NUMBER_OF_PRIMES;
Use count to track the number of prime numbers and
  set an initial count to 0;
Set an initial number to 2;

while (count < NUMBER_OF_PRIMES)
{
  Test whether number is prime;

  if number is prime
  {
    Display the prime number and increase the count;
  }

  Increment number by 1;
}
```

To test whether a number is prime, check whether it is divisible by 2, 3, 4, up to **number/2**. If a divisor is found, the number is not a prime. The algorithm can be described as follows:

```
Use a bool variable isPrime to denote whether
  the number is prime; Set isPrime to true initially;

for (int divisor = 2; divisor <= number / 2; divisor++)
{
  if (number % divisor == 0)
  {
    Set isPrime to false
    Exit the loop;
  }
}
```

The complete program is given in Listing 5.17.

LISTING 5.17 PrimeNumber.cpp

```cpp
1   #include <iostream>
2   #include <iomanip>
3   using namespace std;
4
5   int main()
6   {
7     const int NUMBER_OF_PRIMES = 50; // Number of primes to display
8     const int NUMBER_OF_PRIMES_PER_LINE = 10; // Display 10 per line
9     int count = 0; // Count the number of prime numbers
10    int number = 2; // A number to be tested for primeness
11
12    cout << "The first 50 prime numbers are \n";
13
14    // Repeatedly find prime numbers
15    while (count < NUMBER_OF_PRIMES)
16    {
17      // Assume the number is prime
18      bool isPrime = true; // Is the current number prime?
19
20      // Test if number is prime
21      for (int divisor = 2; divisor <= number / 2; divisor++)
22      {
23        if (number % divisor == 0)
24        {
25          // If true, the number is not prime
26          isPrime = false; // Set isPrime to false
27          break; // Exit the for loop
28        }
29      }
30
31      // Display the prime number and increase the count
32      if (isPrime)
33      {
34        count++; // Increase the count
35
36        if (count % NUMBER_OF_PRIMES_PER_LINE == 0)
37          // Display the number and advance to the new line
38          cout << setw(4) << number << endl;
39        else
40          cout << setw(4) << number;
41      }
42
43      // Check if the next number is prime
44      number++;
45    }
46
47    return 0;
48  }
```

count prime numbers

check primeness

exit loop

display if prime

```
The first 50 prime numbers are
   2    3    5    7   11   13   17   19   23   29
  31   37   41   43   47   53   59   61   67   71
  73   79   83   89   97  101  103  107  109  113
 127  131  137  139  149  151  157  163  167  173
 179  181  191  193  197  199  211  223  227  229
```

subproblem

This is a complex program for novice programmers. The key to developing a program-matic solution for this problem, and for many other problems, is to break it into subproblems and develop solutions for each of them in turn. Do not attempt to develop a complete solution in the first trial. Instead, begin by writing the code to determine whether a given number is prime, then expand the program to test whether other numbers are prime in a loop.

To determine whether a number is prime, check whether it is divisible by a number between 2 and number/2 inclusive. If so, it is not a prime number; otherwise, it is a prime number. For a prime number, display it. If the count is divisible by 10, advance to a new line. The program ends when the count reaches 50.

The program uses the break statement in line 27 to exit the for loop as soon as the number is found to be a nonprime. You can rewrite the loop (lines 21–29) without using the break statement, as follows:

```
for (int divisor = 2; divisor <= number / 2 && isPrime;
    divisor++)
{
  // If true, the number is not prime
  if (number % divisor == 0)
  {
    // Set isPrime to false, if the number is not prime
    isPrime = false;
  }
}
```

However, using the break statement makes the program simpler and easier to read in this case.

KEY TERMS

break statement   205
continue statement   206
do-while loop   188
for loop   191
infinite loop   178
input redirection   186
iteration   176
loop   176
loop body   176

loop-continuation-condition   176
nested loop   196
off-by-one error   178
output redirection   186
posttest loop   194
pretest loop   194
sentinel value   184
while loop   176

CHAPTER SUMMARY

1. There are three types of repetition statements: the while loop, the do-while loop, and the for loop.

2. The part of the loop that contains the statements to be repeated is called the *loop body*.

3. A one-time execution of a loop body is referred to as an *iteration of the loop*.

4. An *infinite loop* is a loop statement that executes infinitely.

5. In designing loops, you need to consider both the *loop control structure* and the loop body.

6. The `while` loop checks the `loop-continuation-condition` first. If the condition is `true`, the loop body is executed; if it is `false`, the loop terminates.

7. The `do-while` loop is similar to the `while` loop, except that the `do-while` loop executes the loop body first and then checks the `loop-continuation-condition` to decide whether to continue or to terminate.

8. The `while` loop and the `do-while` loop often are used when the number of repetitions is not predetermined.

9. A *sentinel value* is a special value that signifies the end of the loop.

10. The `for` loop generally is used to execute a loop body a fixed number of times.

11. The `for` loop control has three parts. The first part is an initial action that often initializes a control variable. The second part, the loop-continuation-condition, determines whether the loop body is to be executed. The third part is executed after each iteration and is often used to adjust the control variable. Usually, the loop control variables are initialized and changed in the control structure.

12. The `while` loop and `for` loop are called *pretest loops* because the continuation condition is checked before the loop body is executed.

13. The `do-while` loop is called a *posttest loop* because the condition is checked after the loop body is executed.

14. Two keywords, `break` and `continue`, can be used in a loop.

15. The `break` keyword immediately ends the innermost loop, which contains the break.

16. The `continue` keyword only ends the current iteration.

Quiz

Answer the quiz for this chapter online at www.cs.armstrong.edu/liang/cpp3e/quiz.html.

Programming Exercises

Pedagogical Note
Read each problem several times until you understand it. Think how to solve the problem before starting to write code. Translate your logic into a program. A problem often can be solved in many different ways. Students are encouraged to explore various solutions.

read and think before coding

explore solutions

Sections 5.2–5.7

*5.1 (*Count positive and negative numbers and compute the average of numbers*) Write a program that reads an unspecified number of integers, determines how many positive and negative values have been read, and computes the total and average of the input values (not counting zeros). Your program ends with the input 0. Display the average as a floating-point number. Here is a sample run:

```
Enter an integer, the input ends if it is 0: 1 2 -1 3 0  ↵Enter
The number of positives is 3
The number of negatives is 1
The total is 5
The average is 1.25
```

```
Enter an integer, the input ends if it is 0: 0  ↵Enter

No numbers are entered except 0
```

5.2 (*Repeat multiplications*) Listing 5.4, `SubtractionQuizLoop.cpp`, generates five random subtraction questions. Revise the program to generate nine random multiplication questions for three integers between 1 and 5. Display the correct count and test time.

5.3 (*Conversion from millimeters to inches*) Write a program that displays the following table (note that 1 millimeter is 0.039 inches):

Millimeters	Inches
2	0.078
4	0.156
...	
96	3.744
98	3.822

5.4 (*Conversion from meters to feet*) Write a program that displays the following table (note that 1 meter is 3.280 feet):

Meters	Feet
1	3.280
2	6.560
...	
14	45.920
15	49.200

5.5 (*Conversion from millimeters to inches and inches to millimeters*) Write a program that displays the following tables side by side (note that 1 millimeter is 0.039 inches):

Millimeters	Inches		Inches	Millimeters
2	0.078	|	1	25.641
4	0.156	|	2	51.282
...				
98	3.822	|	49	1256.410
100	3.900	|	50	1282.051

5.6 (*Conversion from meters to feet*) Write a program that displays the following tables side by side (note that 1 meter is 3.280 feet):

Meters	Feet		Feet	Meters
1	3.280	|	3	0.915
2	6.560	|	6	1.829
...				
14	45.920	|	42	12.805
15	49.200	|	45	13.720

5.7 (*Use trigonometric functions*) Print the following table to display the **tan** and **cot** values of degrees from 0 to 60 with increments of 10 degrees. Round the value to keep four digits after the decimal point.

Degree	Sin/Cos	Cos/Sin
10	0.0000	inf
20	0.1736	5.6713
...		
50	1.1918	0.8391
60	1.7320	0.5774

5.8 (*Use the* exp *function*) Write a program that prints the following table using the exp function:

Number	Exponent
0	1
1	2.71828
...	
9	8103.08
10	22026.5

**5.9 (*Financial application: compute future apartment rent*) Suppose that the rent for an apartment is $1000 this year and increases 3% every year. Write a program that computes the rent in five years and the total rent for one year starting five years from now.

5.10 (*Find the lowest price*) Write a program that prompts the user to enter the number of items and each item's name and price, and finally displays the name and price of the item with the lowest price.

*5.11 (*Find the two lowest prices*) Write a program that prompts the user to enter the number of items and each item's name and price, and finally displays the name and price of the item with the lowest score and the item with the second-lowest price.

5.12 (*Find numbers divisible by 3 and 4*) Write a program that displays all the numbers from 1 to 500, 5 per line, that are divisible by 3 and 4. Numbers are separated by exactly one space.

5.13 (*Find numbers divisible by 3 or 6, but not both*) Write a program that displays all the numbers from 300 to 400, 5 per line, that are divisible by 3 or 6, but not both. Numbers are separated by exactly one space.

5.14 (*Find the largest* n *such that* $2^n < 30,000$) Use a while loop to find the largest integer n such that 2^n is less than 30,000.

5.15 (*Find the smallest* n *such that* $3^n > 30,000$) Use a while loop to find the smallest integer n such that 3^n is greater than 30,000.

Sections 5.8–5.11

*5.16 (*Compute the greatest common divisor*) Another solution for Listing 5.10 to find the greatest common divisor (GCD) of two integers n1 and n2 is as follows: First find d to be the minimum of n1 and n2, then check whether d, d-1, d-2, ..., 2, or 1 is a divisor for both n1 and n2 in this order. The first such common divisor is the greatest common divisor for n1 and n2. Write a program that prompts the user to enter two positive integers and displays the GCD.

*5.17 (*Display the ASCII character table*) Write a program that prints all the uppercase characters of the ASCII character table. Display 5 characters per line. The ASCII table is shown in Appendix B. Characters are separated by exactly one space.

*5.18 (*First five multiples of an integer*) Write a program that reads an integer and displays its first five multiples. For example, if the input integer is 10, the output should be as follows: 10, 20, 30, 40, 50.

5.19 (*Display pyramid*) Write a program that prompts the user to enter an integer from 1 to 15 and displays a pyramid, as shown in the following sample run:

```
Enter the number of lines: 7 ↵Enter
                  1
                2 1 2
              3 2 1 2 3
            4 3 2 1 2 3 4
          5 4 3 2 1 2 3 4 5
        6 5 4 3 2 1 2 3 4 5 6
      7 6 5 4 3 2 1 2 3 4 5 6 7
```

*5.20 (*Display four patterns using loops*) Use nested loops that display the following patterns in four separate programs:

```
Pattern A      Pattern B              Pattern C          Pattern D
123456             1                     3                        1
1    6           1 2 3                  3 3                      1 2
1    6         1 2 3 4 5              3 3 3                    1 2 3
1    6       1 2 3 4 5 6 7            3 3                    1 2 3 4
1    6       1 2 3 4 5 6 8 9           3                   1 2 3 4 5
123456                                                   1 2 3 4 5 6
```

5.21 (*Display numbers in a pyramid pattern*) Write a nested **for loop that prints the following output:

```
a  b  c  d  e  f  g  h  h  g  f  e  d  c  b  a
   a  b  c  d  e  f  g  g  f  e  d  c  b  a
      a  b  c  d  e  f  f  e  d  c  b  a
         a  b  c  d  e  e  d  c  b  a
            a  b  c  d  d  c  b  a
               a  b  c  c  b  a
                  a  b  b  a
                     a  a
```

*5.22 (*Display non-prime numbers between 1 and 100*) Modify Listing 5.17 to display all the non-prime numbers between 1 and 100. Display five non-prime numbers per line. Numbers are separated by exactly one space.

Comprehensive

**5.23 (*Financial application: compare loans with various interest rates*) Write a program that lets the user enter the loan amount and loan period in number of years and displays the monthly and total payments for each interest rate starting from 5% to 8%, with an increment of 1/8. Here is a sample run:

```
Loan Amount: 10000 ↵Enter
Number of Years: 5 ↵Enter
Interest Rate    Monthly Payment    Total Payment
5.000%              188.71             11322.74
5.125%              189.28             11357.13
5.250%              189.85             11391.59
...
7.875%              202.17             12129.97
8.000%              202.76             12165.83
```

For the formula to compute monthly payment, see Listing 2.11, ComputeLoan.cpp.

**5.24 (*Financial application: loan amortization schedule*) The monthly payment for a given loan pays the principal and the interest. The monthly interest is computed by multiplying the monthly interest rate and the balance (the remaining principal). The principal paid for the month is therefore the monthly payment minus the monthly interest. Write a program that lets the user enter the loan amount, number of years, and interest rate and displays the amortization schedule for the loan. Here is a sample run:

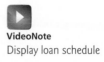

VideoNote
Display loan schedule

```
Loan Amount: 10000 ↵Enter
Number of Years: 1 ↵Enter
Annual Interest Rate: 7 ↵Enter

Monthly Payment: 865.26
Total Payment: 10383.21

Payment#   Interest   Principal   Balance
1          58.33      806.93      9193.07
2          53.62      811.64      8381.43
...
11         10.00      855.26      860.27
12          5.01      860.25        0.01
```

> **Note**
> The balance after the last payment may not be zero. If so, the last payment should be the normal monthly payment plus the final balance.

Hint: Write a loop to display the table. Since the monthly payment is the same for each month, it should be computed before the loop. The balance is initially the loan amount. For each iteration in the loop, compute the interest and principal, and update the balance. The loop may look like this:

```
for (i = 1; i <= numberOfYears * 12; i++)
{
  interest = monthlyInterestRate * balance;
  principal = monthlyPayment - interest;
  balance = balance - principal;
  cout << i << "\t\t" << interest
    << "\t\t" << principal << "\t\t" << balance << endl;
}
```

*5.25 (*Demonstrate cancellation errors*) A cancellation error occurs when you are manipulating a very large number with a very small number. The large number may cancel out the smaller number. For example, the result of `100000000.0 + 0.000000001` is equal to `100000000.0`. To avoid cancellation errors and obtain more accurate results, carefully select the order of computation. For example, in computing the following series, you will obtain more accurate results by computing from right to left rather than from left to right:

$$1 + \frac{1}{2} + \frac{1}{3} + \ldots + \frac{1}{n}$$

Write a program that compares the results of the summation of the preceding series, computing from left to right and from right to left with `n = 50000`.

*5.26 (*Product of a series*) Write a program to calculate the product of the following series:

$$\frac{1}{5} \times \frac{1}{9} \times \frac{1}{13} \times \frac{1}{17} \times \frac{1}{21} \times \frac{1}{25} \times \cdots \times \frac{1}{93} \times \frac{1}{97}$$

**5.27 (*Compute π*) You can approximate π by using the following series:

$$\pi = \sqrt{6 \times \left(1 + \frac{1}{4} + \frac{1}{9} + \frac{1}{16} + \frac{1}{25} + \cdots + \frac{1}{n^2}\right)}$$

Write a program that displays the π value for $n = 100, 200, \ldots$, and 600.

**5.28 (*Compute e^x*) You can approximate e^x using the following series:

$$e^x = 1 + \frac{x}{1!} + \frac{x^2}{2!} + \frac{x^3}{3!} + \frac{x^4}{4!} + \cdots + \frac{x^n}{n!}$$

Write a program that prompts the user to enter x and displays the e^x value for n = 15. (*Hint*: Because $n! = n \times (n - 1) \times \cdots \times 2 \times 1$, then

$$\frac{1}{n!} \text{ is } \frac{1}{n(n-1)!}$$

Initialize e^x and item to be 1 and keep adding a new item to e^x. The new item is the previous item multiplied by x and divided by n for n = 2, 3, 4, ..., 15).

**5.29 (*Display multiples of 10*) Write a program that displays all the multiples of 10, 15 per line, from 4000 to 4500, separated by exactly one space.

**5.30 (*Display the Sundays in a month*) Write a program that prompts the user to enter the month and first day of the month, and displays all the Sundays in that month. For example, if the user entered the month 7 for July, and the first day 4 for Wednesday, your program should display the following output:

```
The first day of this month is Wednesday!
...
Next Sunday of this month is on 26.
```

**5.31 (*Display calendars*) Write a program that prompts the user to enter the year and first day of the year and displays the calendar table for the year on the console. For example, if the user entered the year 2013 and 2 for Tuesday, January 1, 2013, your program should display the calendar for each month in the year, as follows:

```
                        January 2013
      -----------------------------------------------
       Sun    Mon    Tue    Wed    Thu    Fri    Sat
                       1      2      3      4      5
        6      7      8      9     10     11     12
       13     14     15     16     17     18     19
       20     21     22     23     24     25     26
       27     28     29     30     31

                           ...
```

December 2013

Sun	Mon	Tue	Wed	Thu	Fri	Sat
1	2	3	4	5	6	7
8	9	10	11	12	13	14
15	16	17	18	19	20	21
22	23	24	25	26	27	28
29	30	31				

*5.32 (*Financial application: compound value*) Suppose you save $100 *each* month into a savings account with the annual interest rate 5%. So, the monthly interest rate is `0.05 / 12 = 0.00417`. After the first month, the value in the account becomes

$$100 * (1 + 0.00417) = 100.417$$

After the second month, the value in the account becomes

$$(100 + 100.417) * (1 + 0.00417) = 201.252$$

After the third month, the value in the account becomes

$$(100 + 201.252) * (1 + 0.00417) = 302.507$$

and so on.

Write a program that prompts the user to enter an amount (e.g., 100), the annual interest rate (e.g., 5), and the number of months (e.g., 6) and displays the amount in the savings account after the given month.

*5.33 (*Financial application: compute CD value*) Suppose you put $10,000 into a CD with an annual percentage yield of 5.75%. After one month, the CD is worth

$$10000 + 10000 * 5.75 / 1200 = 10047.91$$

After two months, the CD is worth

$$10047.91 + 10047.91 * 5.75 / 1200 = 10096.06$$

After three months, the CD is worth

$$10096.06 + 10096.06 * 5.75 / 1200 = 10144.43$$

and so on.

Write a program that prompts the user to enter an amount (e.g., 10000), the annual percentage yield (e.g., 5.75), and the number of months (e.g., 18) and displays a table as shown in the sample run.

```
Enter the initial deposit amount: 10000 ↵Enter
Enter annual percentage yield: 5.75 ↵Enter
Enter maturity period (number of months): 18 ↵Enter

Month CD Value
1      10047.91
2      10096.06
...
17     10846.56
18     10898.54
```

*5.34 (*Game: Prediction*) Revise Exercise 3.14 to generate a random three-digit number. The three digits in the number must be distinct. (*Hint*: Generate the first digit. Use a loop to repeatedly generate the second and third digits until they are different from other digits.)

**5.35 (*Fibonacci Series*) The Fibonacci series is a series that begins with 0 and 1 and has the property that each succeeding term is the sum of the two preceding terms. For example, the third Fibonacci number is 1 which is sum of 0 and 1. The next is 2, which is a sum of 1 + 1. Write a program that displays the first ten numbers in a Fibonacci series.

***5.36 (*Game: scissor, rock, paper*) Revise Programming Exercise 3.15 to let the user continuously play ten games. The program must display the number of times a user wins, the computer wins and the number of draws.

*5.37 (*Summation*) Write a program to compute the following summation:

$$\frac{1}{\sqrt[3]{99} - \sqrt[3]{93}} + \frac{1}{\sqrt[3]{93} - \sqrt[3]{87}} + \frac{1}{\sqrt[3]{87} - \sqrt[3]{81}} + \dots + \frac{1}{\sqrt[3]{9} - \sqrt[3]{3}}$$

**5.38 (*Palindrome number*) Write a program that prompts the user to enter an integer and uses loops to simplify Programming Exercise 3.36.

*5.39 (*Financial application: find the profit-per-item*) You have just started a new stationary shop. Your profit-per-item depends on the total quantity of item sold. The scheme shown below is used to determine the total profit:

Quantity	Profit-per-item
0–1000	$1
1001–5000	$2
5001 and above	$5

Note that this is a graduated profit. The profit for selling up to 1000 items is $1, for next 4000 items is $2 and beyond that is $5. If the total quantity of item sold is 10000, the profit is 1000 * $1 + 4000 * $2 + 5000 * $5 = $34000.

Your goal is to make $50,000 a year. Write a program that uses a `do-while` loop to find out the minimum quantity of item you have to sell in order to make $50,000.

5.40 (*Simulation: Even or Odd*) Write a program that generates a random integer 1 hundred thousand times and displays the number of even and odd integers.

**5.41 (*Occurrence of max numbers*) Write a program that reads integers, finds the largest of them, and counts its occurrences. Assume that the input ends with number 0. Suppose that you entered 3 5 2 5 5 5 0; the program finds that the largest is 5 and the occurrence count for 5 is 4.

(*Hint*: Maintain two variables, `max` and `count`. `max` stores the current max number, and `count` stores its occurrences. Initially, assign the first number to `max` and 1 to `count`. Compare each subsequent number with `max`. If the number is greater than `max`, assign it to `max` and reset `count` to 1. If the number is equal to `max`, increment `count` by 1.)

```
Enter numbers: 3 5 2 5 5 5 0 ↵Enter
The largest number is 5
The occurrence count of the largest number is 4
```

*5.42 (*Financial application: find the profit-per-item*) Rewrite Programming Exercise 5.39 as follows:

- Use a `while` loop instead of a `do-while` loop.
- Let the shop owner enter `PROFIT_DESIRED` instead of fixing it as a constant.

*5.43 (*Simulation: clock countdown*) Write a program that prompts the user to enter the number of seconds, displays a message at every second, and terminates when the time expires. Here is a sample run:

```
Enter the number of seconds: 3 ↵Enter
2 seconds remaining
1 second remaining
Stopped
```

**5.44 (*Monte Carlo simulation*) A square is divided into four smaller regions as shown below in (a). If you throw a dart into the square 1,000,000 times, what is the probability for a dart to fall into an odd-numbered region? Write a program to simulate the process and display the result.

(*Hint*: Place the center of the square in the center of a coordinate system, as shown in (b). Randomly generate a point in the square and count the number of times for a point to fall into an odd-numbered region.)

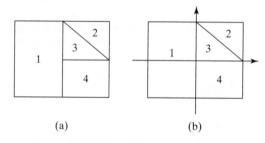

(a)　　　　　(b)

*5.45 (*Math: combinations*) Write a program that displays all possible combinations for picking two numbers from integers 1 to 7. Also, display the total number of all combinations.

```
1 2
1 3
...
...

The total number of all combinations is 21
```

*5.46 (*Computer architecture: bit-level operations*) A `short` value is stored in 16 bits. Write a program that prompts the user to enter a short integer and displays the 16 bits for the integer. Here are sample runs:

```
Enter an integer: 5 ↵Enter
The bits are 0000000000000101
```

```
Enter an integer: -5 ↵Enter
The bits are 1111111111111011
```

(*Hint*: You need to use the bitwise right shift operator (`>>`) and the bitwise AND operator (`&`), which are covered in Appendix E.)

5.47 (*Statistics: compute mean and standard deviation*) In business applications, you are often asked to compute the mean and standard deviation of data. The mean is simply the average of the numbers. The standard deviation is a statistic that tells you how tightly all the various data are clustered around the mean in a set of data. For example, what is the average age of the students in a class? How close are the ages? If all the students are the same age, the deviation is **0.

Write a program that prompts the user to enter 10 numbers, and displays the mean and standard deviations of these numbers using the following formula:

$$mean = \frac{\sum_{i=1}^{n} x_i}{n} = \frac{x_1 + x_2 + \ldots + x_n}{n} \qquad deviation = \sqrt{\frac{\sum_{i=1}^{n} x_i^2 - \frac{\left(\sum_{i=1}^{n} x_i\right)^2}{n}}{n - 1}}$$

Here is a sample run:

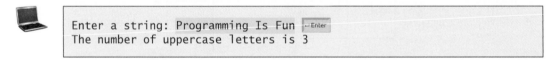

```
Enter ten numbers: 1 2 3 4.5 5.6 6 7 8 9 10  ↵Enter
The mean is 5.61
The standard deviation is 2.99794
```

*5.48 (*Count uppercase letters*) Write a program that prompts the user to enter a string and displays the number of the uppercase letters in the string. Here is a sample run:

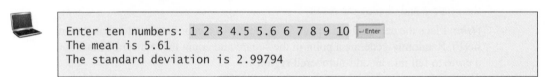

```
Enter a string: Programming Is Fun  ↵Enter
The number of uppercase letters is 3
```

*5.49 (*Longest common prefix*) Write a program that prompts the user to enter two strings and displays the largest common prefix of the two strings. Here are sample runs:

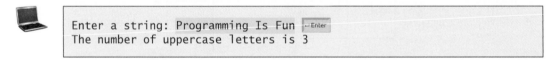

```
Enter s1: Programming is fun  ↵Enter
Enter s2: Program using a language  ↵Enter
The common prefix is Program
```

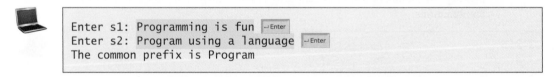

```
Enter s1: ABC  ↵Enter
Enter s2: CBA  ↵Enter
ABC and CBA have no common prefix
```

*5.50 (*Reverse a string*) Write a program that prompts the user to enter a string and displays the string in reverse order.

```
Enter a string: ABCD  ↵Enter
The reversed string is DCBA
```

*5.51 (*Business: check ISBN-13*) ISBN-13 is a new standard for identifying books. It uses 13 digits $d_1d_2d_3d_4d_5d_6d_7d_8d_9d_{10}d_{11}d_{12}d_{13}$. The last digit d_{13} is a checksum, which is calculated from the other digits using the following formula:

$$10 - (d_1 + 3d_2 + d_3 + 3d_4 + d_5 + 3d_6 + d_7 + 3d_8 + d_9 + 3d_{10} + d_{11} + 3d_{12})\%10$$

If the checksum is **10**, replace it with **0**. Your program should read the input as a string. Here are sample runs:

```
Enter the first 12 digits of an ISBN-13 as a string: 978013213080  ↵Enter
The ISBN-13 number is 9780132130806
```

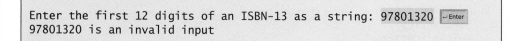
```
Enter the first 12 digits of an ISBN-13 as a string: 978013213079  ↵Enter
The ISBN-13 number is 9780132130790
```

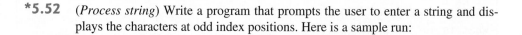
```
Enter the first 12 digits of an ISBN-13 as a string: 97801320  ↵Enter
97801320 is an invalid input
```

*5.52 (*Process string*) Write a program that prompts the user to enter a string and displays the characters at odd index positions. Here is a sample run:

```
Enter a string: ABeijing Chicago  ↵Enter
BiigCiao
```

*5.53 (*Count vowels and consonants*) Assume letters A, E, I, O, and U as the vowels. Write a program that prompts the user to enter a string and displays the number of vowels and consonants in the string.

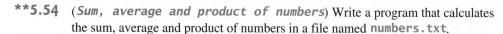
```
Enter a string: Programming is fun  ↵Enter
The number of vowels is 5
The number of consonants is 11
```

**5.54 (*Sum, average and product of numbers*) Write a program that calculates the sum, average and product of numbers in a file named `numbers.txt`.

**5.55 (*Math tutor*) Write a program that displays a menu as shown in the sample run. You can enter 1, 2, 3, or 4 for choosing an addition, subtraction, multiplication, or division test. After a test is finished, the menu is redisplayed. You may choose another test or enter 5 to exit the system. Each test generates two random single-digit numbers to form a question for addition, subtraction, multiplication, or division. For a subtraction such as `number1 - number2`, `number1` is greater than or equal to `number2`. For a division question such as `number1 / number2`, `number2` is not zero.

```
Main menu
1: Addition
2: Subtraction
3: Multiplication
4: Division
5: Exit
Enter a choice: 1 ↵Enter
What is 1 + 7? 8 ↵Enter
Correct

Main menu
1: Addition
2: Subtraction
3: Multiplication
4: Division
5: Exit
Enter a choice: 1 ↵Enter
What is 4 + 0? 5 ↵Enter
Your answer is wrong. The correct answer is 4

Main menu
1: Addition
2: Subtraction
3: Multiplication
4: Division
5: Exit
Enter a choice: 4 ↵Enter
What is 4 / 5? 1 ↵Enter
Your answer is wrong. The correct answer is 0

Main menu
1: Addition
2: Subtraction
3: Multiplication
4: Division
5: Exit
Enter a choice:
```

*5.56 (*Corner point coordinates*) Suppose an n-sided regular polygon is centered at (0, 0) with one point at the 3 o'clock position, as shown in Figure 5.4. Write a program that prompts the user to enter the number of the sides, the radius of the bounding circle of a polygon, and displays the coordinates of the corner points on the polygon.

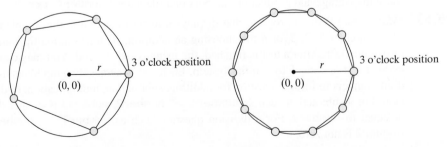

FIGURE 5.4 An n-sided polygon is centered at (0, 0) with one point at the 3 o'clock position.

Here is a sample run:

```
Enter the number of the sides: 6  ↵Enter
Enter the radius of the bounding circle: 100  ↵Enter
The coordinates of the points on the polygon are
(100, 0)
(50.0001, 86.6025)
(-49.9998, 86.6026)
(-100, 0.000265359)
(-50.0003, -86.6024)
(49.9996, -86.6028)
```

**5.57 (*Check Student ID*) Some colleges impose certain rules for Student ID. Suppose the Student ID rules are as follows:

- A Student ID must have exactly ten characters.
- A Student ID must consist of only digits and letters.
- A Student ID must always start with a digit.

Write a program that prompts the student to enter a Student ID and displays `valid Student ID` if the rules are followed or `invalid Student ID` otherwise.

FUNCTIONS

Objectives

- To define functions with formal parameters (§6.2).
- To define/invoke value-returning functions (§6.3).
- To define/invoke void functions (§6.4).
- To pass arguments by value (§6.5).
- To develop reusable code that is modular, easy to read, easy to debug, and easy to maintain (§6.6).
- To use function overloading and understand ambiguous overloading (§6.7).
- To use function prototypes to declare function headers (§6.8).
- To define functions with default arguments (§6.9).
- To improve runtime efficiency for short functions using inline functions (§6.10).
- To determine the scope of local and global variables (§6.11).
- To pass arguments by reference and understand the differences between pass-by-value and pass-by-reference (§6.12).
- To declare `const` parameters to prevent them from being modified accidentally (§6.13).
- To write a function that converts a hexadecimal number to a decimal number (§6.14).
- To design and implement functions using stepwise refinement (§6.15).

6.1 Introduction

Key
Point

Functions can be used to define reusable code and organize and simplify code.

problem

Suppose that you need to find the sum of integers from 1 to 10, from 20 to 37, and from 35 to 49, respectively. You may write the code as follows:

```cpp
int sum = 0;
for (int i = 1; i <= 10; i++)
  sum += i;
cout << "Sum from 1 to 10 is " << sum << endl;

sum = 0;
for (int i = 20; i <= 37; i++)
  sum += i;
cout << "Sum from 20 to 37 is " << sum << endl;

sum = 0;
for (int i = 35; i <= 49; i++)
  sum += i;
cout << "Sum from 35 to 49 is " << sum << endl;
```

You may have observed that computing these sums from 1 to 10, from 20 to 37, and from 35 to 49 are very similar except that the starting and ending integers are different. Wouldn't it be nice if we could write the common code once and reuse it? We can do so by defining a function and invoking it.

why use functions?

The preceding code can be simplified as follows:

define sum function

```cpp
1  int sum(int i1, int i2)
2  {
3    int sum = 0;
4    for (int i = i1; i <= i2; i++)
5      sum += i;
6
7    return sum;
8  }
9
```

main function

```cpp
10  int main()
11  {
```

invoke sum function

```cpp
12    cout << "Sum from 1 to 10 is " << sum(1, 10) << endl;
13    cout << "Sum from 20 to 37 is " << sum(20, 37) << endl;
14    cout << "Sum from 35 to 49 is " << sum(35, 49) << endl;
15
16    return 0;
17  }
```

Lines 1–8 defines the function named sum with two parameters i1 and i2. The statements in the main function invokes sum(1, 10) to compute sum from 1 to 10, and sum(20, 37) to compute sum from 20 to 37, and sum(35, 49) to compute sum from 35 to 49.

function

A *function* is a collection of statements grouped together to perform an operation. In earlier chapters, you learned about such functions as pow(a, b), rand(), srand(seed), time(0), and main(). When you call the pow(a, b) function, for example, the system actually executes the statements in the function and returns the result. In this chapter, you will learn how to define and use functions and apply function abstraction to solve complex problems.

6.2 Defining a Function

A function definition consists of its function name, parameters, return value type, and body.

Key Point

The syntax for defining a function is as follows:

```
returnValueType functionName(list of parameters)
{
  // Function body;
}
```

Let's look at a function created to find which of two integers is bigger. This function, named max, has two **int** parameters, **num1** and **num2**, the larger of which is returned by the function. Figure 6.1 illustrates the components of this function.

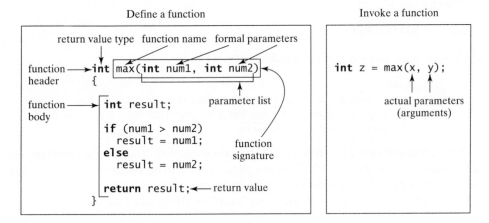

FIGURE 6.1 You can define a function and invoke it with arguments.

The *function header* specifies the function's *return value type*, *function name*, and *parameters*.

A function may return a value. The **returnValueType** is the data type of that value. Some functions perform desired operations without returning a value. In this case, the **returnValueType** is the keyword **void**. For example, the **returnValueType** in the **srand** function is **void**. The function that returns a value is called a *value-returning function* and the function that does not return a value is called a *void function*.

The variables declared in the function header are known as *formal parameters* or simply *parameters*. A parameter is like a placeholder. When a function is invoked, you pass a value to the parameter. This value is referred to as an *actual parameter* or *argument*. The *parameter list* refers to the type, order, and number of the parameters of a function. The function name and the parameter list together constitute the *function signature*. Parameters are optional; that is, a function may contain no parameters. For example, the **rand()** function has no parameters.

The function body contains a collection of statements that define what the function does. The function body of the max function uses an **if** statement to determine which number is larger and returns the value of that number. A return statement using the keyword **return** is required for a value-returning function to return a result. The function exits when a return statement is executed.

(margin terms: function header; value-returning function; void function; formal parameter; parameter; actual parameter; argument; parameter list; function signature)

Caution

In the function header, you need to declare each parameter separately. For instance, `max(int num1, int num2)` is correct, but `max(int num1, num2)` is wrong.

6.3 Calling a Function

Key Point

Calling a function executes the code in the function.

In creating a function, you define what it should do. To use a function, you have to *call* or *invoke* it. There are two ways to call a function, depending on whether or not it returns a value.

If the function returns a value, a call to that function is usually treated as a value. For example,

```
int larger = max(3, 4);
```

calls `max(3, 4)` and assigns the result of the function to the variable `larger`. Another example of such a call is

```
cout << max(3, 4);
```

which prints the return value of the function call `max(3, 4)`.

Note

A value-returning function can also be invoked as a statement in C++. In this case, the caller simply ignores the return value. This is not often done, but it is permitted if the caller is not interested in the return value.

When a program calls a function, program control is transferred to the called function. The called function is executed. A called function returns control to the caller when its return statement is executed or when its function-ending closing brace is reached.

Listing 6.1 shows a complete program that is used to test the `max` function.

VideoNote

The **max** function

LISTING 6.1 TestMax.cpp

```
1  #include <iostream>
2  using namespace std;
3
4  // Return the max between two numbers
5  int max(int num1, int num2)
6  {
7    int result;
8
9    if (num1 > num2)
10     result = num1;
11   else
12     result = num2;
13
14   return result;
15 }
16
17 int main()
18 {
19   int i = 5;
20   int j = 2;
21   int k = max(i, j);
22   cout << "The maximum between " << i <<
23     " and " << j << " is " << k << endl;
24
25   return 0;
26 }
```

define max function

main function

invoke max

```
The maximum between 5 and 2 is 5
```

Line#	i	j	k	num1	num2	result
19	5					
20		2				
5				5	2	
7						undefined
10						5
21			5			

Invoking max ← (braces grouping lines 5, 7, 10)

This program contains the `max` function and the `main` function. The `main` function is just — main function
like any other function except that it is invoked by the operating system to execute the program. All other functions must be executed by function call statements.

A function must be defined before it is invoked. Since the `max` function is invoked by the — order of function
`main` function, it must be defined before the `main` function.

When the `max` function is invoked (line 21), variable `i`'s value 5 is passed to `num1`, and — max function
variable `j`'s value 2 is passed to `num2` in the `max` function. The flow of control transfers to the
`max` function. The `max` function is executed. When the `return` statement in the `max` function
is executed, the `max` function returns the control to its caller (in this case the caller is the `main`
function). This process is illustrated in Figure 6.2.

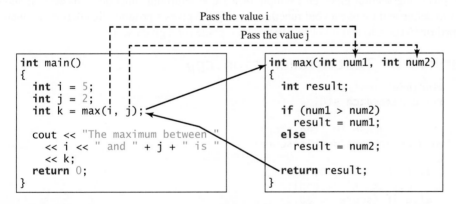

Pass the value i
Pass the value j

```
int main()                        int max(int num1, int num2)
{                                 {
   int i = 5;                        int result;
   int j = 2;
   int k = max(i, j);                if (num1 > num2)
                                       result = num1;
   cout << "The maximum between "  else
      << i << " and " + j + " is "       result = num2;
      << k;
   return 0;                         return result;
}                                 }
```

FIGURE 6.2 When the `max` function is invoked, the flow of control transfers to it. Once the
`max` function is finished, it returns control to the caller.

Each time a function is invoked, the system creates an *activation record* (also called an — activation record
activation frame) that stores its arguments and variables for the function and places the activation record in an area of memory known as a *call stack*. A call stack is also known as an — stack
execution stack, runtime stack, or machine stack, and is often shortened to just "the stack."
When a function calls another function, the caller's activation record is kept intact and a new
activation record is created for the new function call. When a function finishes its work and
returns control to its caller, its activation record is removed from the call stack.

A call stack stores the activation records in a last-in, first-out fashion. The activation record
for the function that is invoked last is removed first from the stack. Suppose function `m1` calls
function `m2`, and then `m2` calls `m3`. The runtime system pushes `m1`'s activation record into the

stack, then m2's, and then m3's. After m3 is finished, its activation record is removed from the stack. After m2 is finished, its activation record is removed from the stack. After m1 is finished, its activation record is removed from the stack.

Understanding call stacks helps us comprehend how functions are invoked. The variables defined in the main function are i, j, and k. The variables defined in the max function are num1, num2, and result. The variables num1 and num2 are defined in the function signature and are parameters of the function. Their values are passed through function invocation. Figure 6.3 illustrates the activation records in the stack.

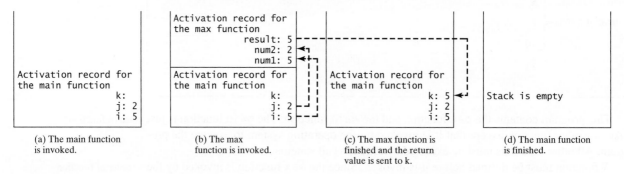

(a) The main function is invoked.

(b) The max function is invoked.

(c) The max function is finished and the return value is sent to k.

(d) The main function is finished.

FIGURE 6.3 When the max function is invoked, the flow of control transfers to the max function. Once the max function is finished, it returns control to the caller.

6.4 void Functions

A void function does not return a value.

Key Point

The preceding section gives an example of a value-returning function. This section shows how to define and invoke a void function. Listing 6.2 gives a program that defines a function named printGrade and invokes it to print the grade for a given score.

VideoNote
void vs. value-return function

printGrade function

main function

LISTING 6.2 TestVoidFunction.cpp

```cpp
1  #include <iostream>
2  using namespace std;
3
4  // Print grade for the score
5  void printGrade(double score)
6  {
7    if (score >= 90.0)
8      cout << 'A' << endl;
9    else if (score >= 80.0)
10     cout << 'B' << endl;
11   else if (score >= 70.0)
12     cout << 'C' << endl;
13   else if (score >= 60.0)
14     cout << 'D' << endl;
15   else
16     cout << 'F' << endl;
17 }
18
19 int main()
20 {
21   cout << "Enter a score: ";
22   double score;
23   cin >> score;
24
```

```
25     cout << "The grade is ";
26     printGrade(score);                                    invoke printGrade
27
28     return 0;
29  }
```

```
Enter a score: 78.5  ⏎Enter
The grade is C
```

The **printGrade** function is a void function. It does not return any value. A call to a void   invoke void function
function must be a statement. So, it is invoked as a statement in line 26 in the main function.
Like any C++ statement, it is terminated with a semicolon.

To see the differences between a void and a value-returning function, let us redesign the   void vs. value-returned
printGrade function to return a value. We call the new function that returns the grade, as
shown in Listing 6.3, **getGrade**.

LISTING 6.3 TestReturnGradeFunction.cpp

```
1   #include <iostream>
2   using namespace std;
3
4   // Return the grade for the score
5   char getGrade(double score)                              getGrade function
6   {
7     if (score >= 90.0)
8       return 'A';
9     else if (score >= 80.0)
10      return 'B';
11    else if (score >= 70.0)
12      return 'C';
13    else if (score >= 60.0)
14      return 'D';
15    else
16      return 'F';
17  }
18
19  int main()                                               main function
20  {
21    cout << "Enter a score: ";
22    double score;
23    cin >> score;
24
25    cout << "The grade is ";
26    cout << getGrade(score) << endl;                       invoke getGrade
27
28    return 0;
29  }
```

```
Enter a score: 78.5  ⏎Enter
The grade is C
```

The **getGrade** function defined in lines 5–17 returns a character grade based on the
numeric score value. The caller invokes this function in line 26.

The **getGrade** function can be invoked by a caller wherever a character may appear. The
printGrade function does not return any value. It must be invoked as a statement.

return in void function

Note

A return statement is not needed for a void function, but it can be used for terminating the function and returning control to the function's caller. The syntax is simply

```
return;
```

This is rare but sometimes is useful for circumventing the normal flow of control in a void function. For example, the following code has a return statement to terminate the function when the score is invalid.

```cpp
// Print grade for the score
void printGrade(double score)
{
  if (score < 0 || score > 100)
  {
    cout << "Invalid score";
    return;
  }

  if (score >= 90.0)
    cout << 'A';
  else if (score >= 80.0)
    cout << 'B';
  else if (score >= 70.0)
    cout << 'C';
  else if (score >= 60.0)
    cout << 'D';
  else
    cout << 'F';
}
```

Note

Occasionally you may need to terminate the program from the function immediately if an abnormal condition occurs. This can be done by invoking the `exit(int)` function defined in the `cstdlib` header. You can pass any integer to invoke this function to indicate an error in the program. For example, the following function terminates the program if an invalid score is passed to the function.

```cpp
// Print grade for the score
void printGrade(double score)
{
  if (score < 0 || score > 100)
  {
    cout << "Invalid score" << endl;
    exit(1);
  }

  if (score >= 90.0)
    cout << 'A';
  else if (score >= 80.0)
    cout << 'B';
  else if (score >= 70.0)
    cout << 'C';
  else if (score >= 60.0)
    cout << 'D';
  else
    cout << 'F';
}
```

6.1 What are the benefits of using a function?

6.2 How do you define a function? How do you invoke a function?

6.3 How do you simplify the `max` function in Listing 6.1 using a conditional expression?

6.4 True or false? A call to a function with a `void` return type is always a statement itself, but a call to a value-returning function cannot be a statement by itself.

6.5 What is the `return` type of a `main` function?

6.6 What would be wrong with not writing a `return` statement in a value-returning function? Can you have a `return` statement in a `void` function? Does the `return` statement in the following function cause syntax errors?

```
void p(double x, double y)
{
  cout << x << " " << y << endl;
  return x + y;
}
```

6.7 Define the terms parameter, argument, and function signature.

6.8 Write function headers (not the bodies) for the following functions:

  a. Return a sales commission, given the sales amount and the commission rate.

  b. Display the calendar for a month, given the month and year.

  c. Return a square root of a number.

  d. Test whether a number is even, and return `true` if it is.

  e. Display a message a specified number of times.

  f. Return the monthly payment, given the loan amount, number of years, and annual interest rate.

  g. Return the corresponding uppercase letter, given a lowercase letter.

6.9 Identify and correct the errors in the following program:

```
int function1(int n)
{
  cout << n;
}

function2(int n, m)
{
  n += m;
  function1(3.4);
}
```

6.5 Passing Arguments by Value

By default, the arguments are passed by value to parameters when invoking a function.

The power of a function is its ability to work with parameters. You can use `max` to find the maximum between any two `int` values. When calling a function, you need to provide arguments, which must be given in the same order as their respective parameters in the function signature. This is known as *parameter order association*. For example, the following function prints a character `n` times:

parameter order association

```
void nPrint(char ch, int n)
{
  for (int i = 0; i < n; i++)
    cout << ch;
}
```

You can use **nPrint('a', 3)** to print **'a'** three times. The **nPrint('a', 3)** statement passes the actual **char** parameter, **'a'**, to the parameter, **ch**; passes 3 to **n**; and prints **'a'** three times. However, the statement **nPrint(3, 'a')** has a different meaning. It passes 3 to **ch** and **'a'** to **n**.

Check Point

6.10 Can the argument have the same name as its parameter?

6.11 Identify and correct the errors in the following program:

```
1   void nPrintln(string message, int n)
2   {
3     int n = 1;
4     for (int i = 0; i < n; i++)
5       cout << message << endl;
6   }
7
8   int main()
9   {
10    nPrintln(5, "Welcome to C++!");
11  }
```

6.6 Modularizing Code

Key Point

Modularizing makes the code easy to maintain and debug and enables the code to be reused.

Functions can be used to reduce redundant code and enable code reuse. Functions can also be used to modularize code and improve the program's quality.

Listing 5.10, GreatestCommonDivisor.cpp, gives a program that prompts the user to enter two integers and displays their greatest common divisor. You can rewrite the program using a function, as shown in Listing 6.4.

VideoNote
Modularize code

LISTING 6.4 GreatestCommonDivisorFunction.cpp

```
1   #include <iostream>
2   using namespace std;
3
4   // Return the gcd of two integers
5   int gcd(int n1, int n2)
6   {
7     int gcd = 1; // Initial gcd is 1
8     int k = 2;   // Possible gcd
9
10    while (k <= n1 && k <= n2)
11    {
12      if (n1 % k == 0 && n2 % k == 0)
13        gcd = k; // Update gcd
14      k++;
15    }
16
17    return gcd; // Return gcd
18  }
```

compute gcd

return gcd

```
19
20   int main()
21   {
22     // Prompt the user to enter two integers
23     cout << "Enter first integer: ";
24     int n1;
25     cin >> n1;
26
27     cout << "Enter second integer: ";
28     int n2;
29     cin >> n2;
30
31     cout << "The greatest common divisor for " << n1 <<
32       " and " << n2 << " is " << gcd(n1, n2) << endl;        invoke gcd
33
34     return 0;
35   }
```

```
Enter first integer: 45  ↵Enter
Enter second integer: 75  ↵Enter
The greatest common divisor for 45 and 75 is 15
```

By encapsulating the code for obtaining the GCD in a function, this program has several advantages:

1. It isolates the problem for computing the GCD from the rest of the code in the main function. Thus, the logic becomes clear and the program is easier to read.

2. If there are errors on computing GCD, they will be confined in the gcd function, which narrows the scope of debugging.

3. The gcd function now can be reused by other programs.

Listing 6.5 applies the concept of code modularization to improve Listing 5.17, PrimeNumber.cpp. The program defines two new functions isPrime and printPrimeNumbers. The isPrime function checks whether a number is prime and the printPrimeNumbers function prints prime numbers.

LISTING 6.5 PrimeNumberFunction.cpp

```
1   #include <iostream>
2   #include <iomanip>
3   using namespace std;
4
5   // Check whether number is prime
6   bool isPrime(int number)                                   isPrime function
7   {
8     for (int divisor = 2; divisor <= number / 2; divisor++)
9     {
10      if (number % divisor == 0)
11      {
12        // If true, number is not prime
13        return false; // number is not a prime
14      }
15    }
16
17    return true; // number is prime
18  }
```

```
                              19
printPrimeNumbers            20    void printPrimeNumbers(int numberOfPrimes)
   function                  21    {
                             22      const int NUMBER_OF_PRIMES = 50; // Number of primes to display
                             23      const int NUMBER_OF_PRIMES_PER_LINE = 10; // Display 10 per line
                             24      int count = 0; // Count the number of prime numbers
                             25      int number = 2; // A number to be tested for primeness
                             26
                             27      // Repeatedly find prime numbers
                             28      while (count < numberOfPrimes)
                             29      {
                             30        // Print the prime number and increase the count
invoke isPrime               31        if (isPrime(number))
                             32        {
                             33          count++; // Increase the count
                             34
                             35          if (count % NUMBER_OF_PRIMES_PER_LINE == 0)
                             36          {
                             37            // Print the number and advance to the new line
                             38            cout << setw(4) << number << endl;
                             39          }
                             40          else
                             41            cout << setw(4) << number;
                             42        }
                             43
                             44        // Check if the next number is prime
                             45        number++;
                             46      }
                             47    }
                             48
                             49    int main()
                             50    {
                             51      cout << "The first 50 prime numbers are \n";
invoke printPrimeNumbers     52      printPrimeNumbers(50);
                             53
                             54      return 0;
                             55    }
```

```
The first 50 prime numbers are
   2   3   5   7  11  13  17  19  23  29
  31  37  41  43  47  53  59  61  67  71
  73  79  83  89  97 101 103 107 109 113
 127 131 137 139 149 151 157 163 167 173
 179 181 191 193 197 199 211 223 227 229
```

We divided a large problem into two subproblems. As a result, the new program is easier to read and easier to debug. Moreover, the functions `printPrimeNumbers` and `isPrime` can be reused by other programs.

6.7 Overloading Functions

Key Point

Overloading functions enables you to define the functions with the same name as long as their signatures are different.

The `max` function that was used earlier works only with the `int` data type. But what if you need to determine which of two floating-point numbers has the larger value? The solution is to create another function with the same name but different parameters, as shown in the following code:

```
double max(double num1, double num2)
{
  if (num1 > num2)
    return num1;
  else
    return num2;
}
```

If you call `max` with `int` parameters, the `max` function that expects `int` parameters will be invoked; if you call `max` with `double` parameters, the `max` function that expects `double` parameters will be invoked. This is referred to as *function overloading*; that is, two functions have the same name but different parameter lists within one file. The C++ compiler determines which function is used based on the function signature.

function overloading

The program in Listing 6.6 creates three functions. The first finds the maximum integer, the second finds the maximum double, and the third finds the maximum among three double values. All three functions are named `max`.

LISTING 6.6 TestFunctionOverloading.cpp

```
 1  #include <iostream>
 2  using namespace std;
 3
 4  // Return the max between two int values
 5  int max(int num1, int num2)                              max function
 6  {
 7    if (num1 > num2)
 8      return num1;
 9    else
10      return num2;
11  }
12
13  // Find the max between two double values
14  double max(double num1, double num2)                     max function
15  {
16    if (num1 > num2)
17      return num1;
18    else
19      return num2;
20  }
21
22  // Return the max among three double values
23  double max(double num1, double num2, double num3)        max function
24  {
25    return max(max(num1, num2), num3);
26  }
27
28  int main()                                               main function
29  {
30    // Invoke the max function with int parameters
31    cout << "The maximum between 3 and 4 is " << max(3, 4) << endl;   invoke max
32
33    // Invoke the max function with the double parameters
34    cout << "The maximum between 3.0 and 5.4 is "
35      << max(3.0, 5.4) << endl;                            invoke max
36
37    // Invoke the max function with three double parameters
```

invoke max

```
38      cout << "The maximum between 3.0, 5.4, and 10.14 is "
39        << max(3.0, 5.4, 10.14) << endl;
40
41      return 0;
42  }
```

When calling max(3, 4) (line 31), the max function for finding the maximum of two integers is invoked. When calling max(3.0, 5.4) (line 35), the max function for finding the maximum of two doubles is invoked. When calling max(3.0, 5.4, 10.14) (line 39), the max function for finding the maximum of three double values is invoked.

Can you invoke the max function with an int value and a double value, such as max(2, 2.5)? If you can, which of the max functions is invoked? The answer to the first question is yes. The answer to the second is that the max function for finding the maximum of two double values is invoked. The argument value 2 is automatically converted into a double value and passed to this function.

You may be wondering why the function max(double, double) is not invoked for the call max(3, 4). Both max(double, double) and max(int, int) are possible matches for max(3, 4). The C++ compiler finds the most specific function for a function invocation. Since the function max(int, int) is more specific than max(double, double), max(int, int) is used to invoke max(3, 4).

Tip
Overloading functions can make programs clearer and more readable. Functions that perform the same task with different types of parameters should be given the same name.

Note
Overloaded functions must have different parameter lists. You cannot overload functions based on different return types.

ambiguous invocation

Sometimes there are two or more possible matches for an invocation of a function, and the compiler cannot determine the most specific match. This is referred to as *ambiguous invocation*. Ambiguous invocation causes a compile error. Consider the following code:

```
#include <iostream>
using namespace std;

int maxNumber(int num1, double num2)
{
  if (num1 > num2)
    return num1;
  else
    return num2;
}

double maxNumber(double num1, int num2)
{
  if (num1 > num2)
    return num1;
  else
    return num2;
}

int main()
{
  cout << maxNumber(1, 2) << endl;

  return 0;
}
```

Both maxNumber(int, double) and maxNumber(double, int) are possible candidates to match maxNumber(1, 2). Since neither is more specific, the invocation is ambiguous, resulting in a compile error.

If you change maxNumber(1, 2) to maxNumber(1, 2.0), it will match the first maxNumber function. So, there will be no compile error.

Caution

Math functions are overloaded in the <cmath> header file. For example, there are three overloaded functions for sin:

```
float sin(float)
double sin(double)
long double sin(long double)
```

6.12 What is function overloading? Can we define two functions that have the same name but different parameter types? Can we define two functions in one program that have identical function names and parameter lists but different return value types?

Check Point

6.13 What is wrong in the following program?

```
void p(int i)
{
  cout << i << endl;
}

int p(int j)
{
  cout << j << endl;
}
```

6.14 Given two function definitions,

```
double m(double x, double y)
double m(int x, double y)
```

answer the following questions:

a. Which of the two functions is invoked for
   ```
   double z = m(4, 5);
   ```
b. Which of the two functions is invoked for
   ```
   double z = m(4, 5.4);
   ```
c. Which of the two functions is invoked for
   ```
   double z = m(4.5, 5.4);
   ```

6.8 Function Prototypes

A function prototype declares a function without having to implement it.

Before a function is called, its header must be declared. One way to ensure this is to place the definition before all function calls. Another approach is to define a function prototype before the function is called. A function prototype, also known as *function declaration*, is a function header without implementation. The implementation is given later in the program.

Key Point

function prototype

function declaration

Listing 6.7 rewrites Listing 6.6, TestFunctionOverloading.cpp, using function prototypes. Three `max` function prototypes are defined in lines 5–7. These functions are called later in the `main` function. The functions are implemented in lines 27, 36, and 45.

LISTING 6.7 TestFunctionPrototype.cpp

```
1  #include <iostream>
2  using namespace std;
3
4  // Function prototype
5  int max(int num1, int num2);
6  double max(double num1, double num2);
7  double max(double num1, double num2, double num3);
8
9  int main()
10 {
11   // Invoke the max function with int parameters
12   cout << "The maximum between 3 and 4 is " <<
13     max(3, 4) << endl;
14
15   // Invoke the max function with the double parameters
16   cout << "The maximum between 3.0 and 5.4 is "
17     << max(3.0, 5.4) << endl;
18
19   // Invoke the max function with three double parameters
20   cout << "The maximum between 3.0, 5.4, and 10.14 is "
21     << max(3.0, 5.4, 10.14) << endl;
22
23   return 0;
24 }
25
26 // Return the max between two int values
27 int max(int num1, int num2)
28 {
29   if (num1 > num2)
30     return num1;
31   else
32     return num2;
33 }
34
35 // Find the max between two double values
36 double max(double num1, double num2)
37 {
38   if (num1 > num2)
39     return num1;
40   else
41     return num2;
42 }
43
44 // Return the max among three double values
45 double max(double num1, double num2, double num3)
46 {
47   return max(max(num1, num2), num3);
48 }
```

Margin notes:
- function prototype (line 5)
- function prototype (line 6)
- function prototype (line 7)
- main function (line 9)
- invoke max (line 13)
- invoke max (line 17)
- invoke max (line 21)
- function implementation (line 27)
- function implementation (line 36)
- function implementation (line 45)

Tip

omitting parameter names

In the prototype, you need not list the parameter names, only the parameter types. C++ compiler ignores the parameter names. The prototype tells the compiler the name of the function, its return type, the number of parameters, and each parameter's type. So lines 5–7 can be replaced by

```
int max(int, int);
double max(double, double);
double max(double, double, double);
```

Note

We say "*define* a function" and "*declare* a function." Declaring a function specifies   define vs. declare functions
what a function is without implementing it. Defining a function gives a function body
that implements the function.

6.9 Default Arguments

You can define default values for parameters in a function.

**Key
Point**

C++ allows you to declare functions with default argument values. The default values are
passed to the parameters when a function is invoked without the arguments.

Listing 6.8 demonstrates how to declare functions with default argument values and how
to invoke such functions.

LISTING 6.8   DefaultArgumentDemo.cpp

```
1   #include <iostream>
2   using namespace std;
3
4   // Display area of a circle
5   void printArea(double radius = 1)
6   {
7     double area = radius * radius * 3.14159;
8     cout << "area is " << area << endl;
9   }
10
11  int main()
12  {
13    printArea();
14    printArea(4);
15
16    return 0;
17  }
```

default argument

invoke with default
invoke with argument

```
area is 3.14159
area is 50.2654
```

Line 5 declares the `printArea` function with the parameter `radius`. `radius` has a default
value `1`. Line 13 invokes the function without passing an argument. In this case, the default
value `1` is assigned to `radius`.

When a function contains a mixture of parameters with and without default values, those
with default values must be declared last. For example, the following declarations are illegal: default arguments last

```
void t1(int x, int y = 0, int z); // Illegal
void t2(int x = 0, int y = 0, int z); // Illegal
```

However, the following declarations are fine:

```
void t3(int x, int y = 0, int z = 0); // Legal
void t4(int x = 0, int y = 0, int z = 0); // Legal
```

When an argument is left out of a function, all arguments that come after it must be left out as well. For example, the following calls are illegal:

```
t3(1,  , 20);
t4(,  , 20);
```

but the following calls are fine:

```
t3(1); // Parameters y and z are assigned a default value
t4(1, 2); // Parameter z is assigned a default value
```

6.15 Which of the following function declarations are illegal?

```
void t1(int x, int y = 0, int z);
void t2(int x = 0, int y = 0, int z);
void t3(int x, int y = 0, int z = 0);
void t4(int x = 0, int y = 0, int z = 0);
```

6.10 Inline Functions

C++ provides inline functions for improving performance for short functions.

efficiency

inline function

Implementing a program using functions makes the program easy to read and easy to maintain, but function calls involve runtime overhead (i.e., pushing arguments and CPU registers into the stack and transferring control to and from a function). C++ provides *inline functions* to avoid function calls. Inline functions are not called; rather, the compiler copies the function code *in line* at the point of each invocation. To specify an inline function, precede the function declaration with the `inline` keyword, as shown in Listing 6.9.

LISTING 6.9 InlineDemo.cpp

inline function

```
 1  #include <iostream>
 2  using namespace std;
 3
 4  inline void f(int month, int year)
 5  {
 6    cout << "month is " << month << endl;
 7    cout << "year is " << year << endl;
 8  }
 9
10  int main()
11  {
12    int month = 10, year = 2008;
13    f(month, year);  // Invoke inline function
14    f(9, 2010); // Invoke inline function
15
16    return 0;
17  }
```

invoke inline function
invoke inline function

```
month is 10
year is 2008
month is 9
year is 2010
```

As far as programming is concerned, inline functions are the same as regular functions, except they are preceded with the `inline` keyword. However, behind the scenes, the C++ compiler expands the inline function call by copying the inline function code. So, Listing 6.9 is essentially equivalent to Listing 6.10.

LISTING 6.10 `InlineExpandedDemo.cpp`

```
1   #include <iostream>
2   using namespace std;
3
4   int main()
5   {
6     int month = 10, year = 2008;
7     cout << "month is " << month << endl;
8     cout << "year is " << year << endl;
9     cout << "month is " << 9 << endl;
10    cout << "year is " << 2010 << endl;
11
12    return 0;
13  }
```

Inline function expanded

```
month is 10
year is 2008
month is 9
year is 2010
```

 Note

Inline functions are desirable for short functions but not for long ones that are called in multiple places in a program, because making multiple copies will dramatically increase the executable code size. For this reason, C++ allows the compilers to ignore the `inline` keyword if the function is too long. So, the `inline` keyword is merely a request; it is up to the compiler to decide whether to honor or ignore it.

for short functions
not for long functions

compiler decision

6.16 What is an inline function? How do you define an inline function?

6.17 When should you use an inline function?

 Check Point

6.11 Local, Global, and Static Local Variables

A variable can be declared as a local, a global, or a static local in C++.

Key Point

As mentioned in Section 2.5, "Variables," the *scope of a variable* is the part of the program where the variable can be referenced. A variable defined inside a function is referred to as a *local variable*. C++ also allows you to use *global variables*. They are declared outside all functions and are accessible to all functions in their scope. Local variables do not have default values, but global variables are defaulted to zero.

scope of variable
local variable
global variable

A variable must be declared before it can be used. The scope of a local variable starts from its declaration and continues to the end of the block that contains the variable. The scope of a global variable starts from its declaration and continues to the end of the program.

A parameter is actually a local variable. The scope of a function parameter covers the entire function.

Listing 6.11 demonstrates the scope of local and global variables.

LISTING 6.11 VariableScopeDemo.cpp

```
1   #include <iostream>
2   using namespace std;
3
4   void t1(); // Function prototype
5   void t2(); // Function prototype
6
7   int main()
8   {
9     t1();
10    t2();
11
12    return 0;
13  }
14
15  int y; // Global variable, default to 0
16
17  void t1()
18  {
19    int x = 1;
20    cout << "x is " << x << endl;
21    cout << "y is " << y << endl;
22    x++;
23    y++;
24  }
25
26  void t2()
27  {
28    int x = 1;
29    cout << "x is " << x << endl;
30    cout << "y is " << y << endl;
31  }
```

function prototype — lines 4, 5
global variable — line 15
local variable — line 19
increment x — line 22
increment y — line 23
local variable — line 28

```
x is 1
y is 0
x is 1
y is 1
```

A global variable y is declared in line 15 with default value 0. This variable is accessible in functions t1 and t2, but not in the main function, because the main function is declared before y is declared.

When the main function invokes t1() in line 9, the global variable y is incremented (line 23) and becomes 1 in t1. When the main function invokes t2() in line 10, the global variable y is now 1.

A local variable x is declared in t1 in line 19 and another is declared in t2 in line 28. Although they are named the same, these two variables are independent. So, incrementing x in t1 does not affect the variable x defined in t2.

If a function has a local variable with the same name as a global variable, only the local variable can be seen from the function.

Caution

It is tempting to declare a variable globally once and then use it in all functions. However, this is a bad practice, because modifying the global variables could lead to errors that are hard to debug. Avoid using global variables. Using global constants is permitted, since constants are never changed.

avoid global variables
use global constants

6.11.1 The Scope of Variables in a **for** Loop

A variable declared in the initial-action part of a **for**-loop header has its scope in the entire loop. However, a variable declared inside a **for**-loop body has its scope limited in the loop body from its declaration to the end of the block that contains the variable, as shown in Figure 6.4.

for loop control variable

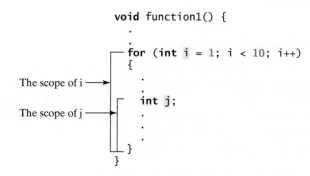

FIGURE 6.4 A variable declared in the initial action part of a **for**-loop header has its scope in the entire loop.

It is commonly acceptable to declare a local variable with the same name in different nonnesting blocks in a function, as shown in Figure 6.5a, but it is not a good practice to declare a local variable twice in nested blocks, even though it is allowed in C++, as shown in Figure 6.5b. In this case, **i** is declared in the function block and also in the **for** loop. The program can compile and run, but it is easy to make mistakes. Therefore, you should avoid declaring the same variable in nested blocks.

multiple declarations

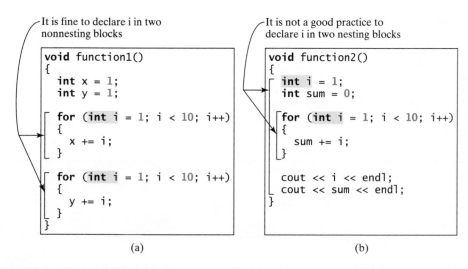

FIGURE 6.5 A variable can be declared multiple times in nonnesting blocks, but you should avoid declaring them in nesting blocks.

Caution

Do not declare a variable inside a block and then attempt to use it outside the block. Here is an example of a common mistake:

```
for (int i = 0; i < 10; i++)
{
}

cout << i << endl;
```

The last statement would cause a syntax error, because variable i is not defined outside the for loop.

6.11.2 Static Local Variables

automatic variable

static local variable

After a function completes its execution, all its local variables are destroyed. These variables are also known as *automatic variables*. Sometimes it is desirable to retain the values stored in local variables so that they can be used in the next call. C++ allows you to declare static local variables. *Static local variables* are permanently allocated in the memory for the lifetime of the program. To declare a static variable, use the keyword **static**.

Listing 6.12 demonstrates using static local variables.

LISTING 6.12 StaticVariableDemo.cpp

```
 1  #include <iostream>
 2  using namespace std;
 3
 4  void t1(); // Function prototype
 5
 6  int main()
 7  {
 8    t1();
 9    t1();
10
11    return 0;
12  }
13
14  void t1()
15  {
16    static int x = 1;
17    int y = 1;
18    x++;
19    y++;
20    cout << "x is " << x << endl;
21    cout << "y is " << y << endl;
22  }
```

function prototype

invoke t1

static local variable
local variable
increment x
increment y

```
x is 2
y is 2
x is 3
y is 2
```

A static local variable x is declared in line 16 with initial value 1. The initialization of static variables happens only once in the first call. When t1() is invoked for the first time in line 8, static variable x is initialized to 1 (line 16). x is incremented to 2 (line 18). Since x is a static local variable, x is retained in memory after this call. When t1() is invoked again in line 9, x is 2 and is incremented to 3 (line 18).

A local variable y is declared in line 17 with initial value 1. When t1() is invoked for the first time in line 8, y is incremented to 2 (line 19). Since y is a local variable, it is destroyed after this call. When t1() is invoked again in line 9, y is initialized to 1 and is incremented to 2 (line 19).

6.18 Show the output of the following code:

```cpp
#include <iostream>
using namespace std;

const double PI = 3.14159;

double getArea(double radius)
{
  return radius * radius * PI;
}

void displayArea(double radius)
{
  cout << getArea(radius) << endl;
}

int main()
{
  double r1 = 1;
  double r2 = 10;
  cout << getArea(r1) << endl;
  displayArea(r2);
}
```

6.19 Identify global and local variables in the following program. Does a global variable have a default value? Does a local variable have a default value? What will be the output of the code?

```cpp
#include <iostream>
using namespace std;

int j;

int main()
{
  int i;
  cout << "i is " << i << endl;
  cout << "j is " << j << endl;
}
```

6.20 Identify global variables, local variables, and static local variables in the following program. What will be the output of the code?

```cpp
#include <iostream>
using namespace std;

int j = 40;

void p()
```

```
    {
      int i = 5;
      static int j = 5;
      i++;
      j++;

      cout << "i is " << i << endl;
      cout << "j is " << j << endl;
    }

    int main()
    {
      p();
      p();
    }
```

6.21   Identify and correct the errors in the following program:

```
    void p(int i)
    {
      int i = 5;

      cout << "i is " << i << endl;
    }
```

6.12 Passing Arguments by Reference

Key Point

Parameters can be passed by reference, which makes the formal parameter an alias of the actual argument. Thus, changes made to the parameters inside the function also made to the arguments.

pass-by-value

When you invoke a function with a parameter, as described in the preceding sections, the value of the argument is passed to the parameter. This is referred to as *pass-by-value*. If the argument is a variable rather than a literal value, the value of the variable is passed to the parameter. The variable is not affected, regardless of the changes made to the parameter inside the function. As shown in Listing 6.13, the value of x (1) is passed to the parameter n when invoking the **increment** function (line 14). n is incremented by 1 in the function (line 6), but x is not changed no matter what the function does.

LISTING 6.13   Increment.cpp

```
1   #include <iostream>
2   using namespace std;
3
4   void increment(int n)
5   {
6     n++;
7     cout << "\tn inside the function is " << n << endl;
8   }
9
10  int main()
11  {
12    int x = 1;
13    cout << "Before the call, x is " << x << endl;
14    increment(x);
15    cout << "after the call, x is " << x << endl;
16
17    return 0;
18  }
```

increment n

invoke increment

```
Before the call, x is 1
  n inside the function is 2
after the call, x is 1
```

Pass-by-value has serious limitations. Listing 6.14 illustrates these. The program creates a function for swapping two variables. The **swap** function is invoked by passing two arguments. However, the values of the arguments are not changed after the function is invoked.

limitations of pass-by-value

LISTING 6.14   SwapByValue.cpp

```cpp
1   #include <iostream>
2   using namespace std;
3
4   // Attempt to swap two variables does not work!
5   void swap(int n1, int n2)                              swap function
6   {
7     cout << "\tInside the swap function" << endl;
8     cout << "\tBefore swapping n1 is " << n1 <<
9       " n2 is " << n2 << endl;
10
11    // Swap n1 with n2
12    int temp = n1;
13    n1 = n2;
14    n2 = temp;
15
16    cout << "\tAfter swapping n1 is " << n1 <<
17      " n2 is " << n2 << endl;
18  }
19
20  int main()                                             main function
21  {
22    // Declare and initialize variables
23    int num1 = 1;
24    int num2 = 2;
25
26    cout << "Before invoking the swap function, num1 is "
27      << num1 << " and num2 is " << num2 << endl;
28
29    // Invoke the swap function to attempt to swap two variables
30    swap(num1, num2);                                    false swap
31
32    cout << "After invoking the swap function, num1 is " << num1 <<
33      " and num2 is " << num2 << endl;
34
35    return 0;
36  }
```

```
Before invoking the swap function, num1 is 1 and num2 is 2
    Inside the swap function
    Before swapping n1 is 1 n2 is 2
    After swapping n1 is 2 n2 is 1
After invoking the swap function, num1 is 1 and num2 is 2
```

Before the **swap** function is invoked (line 30), **num1** is 1 and **num2** is 2. After the **swap** function is invoked, **num1** is still 1 and **num2** is still 2. Their values have not been swapped.

As shown in Figure 6.6, the values of the arguments **num1** and **num2** are passed to **n1** and **n2**, but **n1** and **n2** have their own memory locations independent of **num1** and **num2**. Therefore, changes in **n1** and **n2** do not affect the contents of **num1** and **num2**.

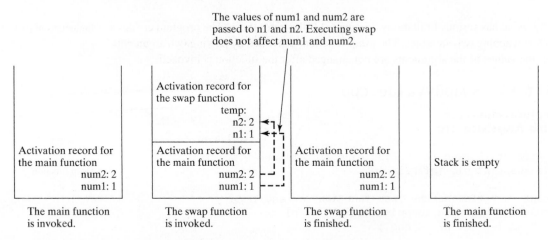

FIGURE 6.6 The values of the variables are passed to the parameters of the function.

Another twist is to change the parameter name **n1** in **swap** to **num1**. What effect does this have? No change occurs, because it makes no difference whether the parameter and the argument have the same name. The parameter is a variable in the function with its own memory space. The variable is allocated when the function is invoked, and it disappears when the function is returned to its caller.

The **swap** function attempts to swap two variables. After the function is invoked, though, the values of the variables are not swapped, because the values of variables are passed to the parameters. The original variables and parameters are independent. Even though the values in the called function are changed, the values in the original variables are not.

reference variable

So, can we write a function to swap two variables? Yes. The function can accomplish this by passing a reference to the variables. C++ provides a special type of variable—a *reference variable*—which can be used as a function parameter to reference the original variable. You can access and modify the original data stored in that variable through its reference variable. A reference variable is an alias for another variable. To declare a reference variable, place the ampersand (&) in front of the variable or after the data type for the variable. For example, the following code declares a reference variable **r** that refers to variable **count**.

```
int &r = count;
```

or equivalently,

```
int& r = count;
```

 Note

equivalent notation

The following notations for declaring reference variables are equivalent:

```
dataType &refVar;
dataType & refVar;
dataType& refVar;
```

The last notation is more intuitive and it clearly states that the variable **refVar** is of the type **dataType&**. For this reason, the last notation will be used in this book.

Listing 6.15 gives an example of using reference variables.

LISTING 6.15 TestReferenceVariable.cpp

```
1   #include <iostream>
2   using namespace std;
3
4   int main()
5   {
6     int count = 1;
7     int& r = count;                              declare reference variable
8     cout << "count is " << count << endl;
9     cout << "r is " << r << endl;
10
11    r++;                                         use reference variable
12    cout << "count is " << count << endl;
13    cout << "r is " << r << endl;
14
15    count = 10;                                  change count
16    cout << "count is " << count << endl;
17    cout << "r is " << r << endl;
18
19    return 0;
20  }
```

```
count is 1
r is 1
count is 2
r is 2
count is 10
r is 10
```

Line 7 declares a reference variable named r that is merely an alias for count. As shown in Figure 6.7a, r and count reference the same value. Line 11 increments r, which in effect increments count, since they share the same value, as shown in Figure 6.7b.

(a)   (b)

FIGURE 6.7   r and count share the same value.

Line 15 assigns 10 to count. Since count and r refer to the same value. Both count and r are now 10.

You can use a reference variable as a parameter in a function and pass a regular variable to invoke the function. The parameter becomes an alias for the original variable. This is known as *pass-by-reference*. You can access and modify the value stored in the original variable   pass-by-reference
through the reference variable. To demonstrate the effect of pass-by-reference, let us rewrite the increment function in Listing 6.13 as shown in Listing 6.16.

LISTING **6.16** IncrementWithPassByReference.cpp

```
1  #include <iostream>
2  using namespace std;
3
4  void increment(int& n)
5  {
6    n++;
7    cout << "n inside the function is " << n << endl;
8  }
9
10 int main()
11 {
12   int x = 1;
13   cout << "Before the call, x is " << x << endl;
14   increment(x);
15   cout << "After the call, x is " << x << endl;
16
17   return 0;
18 }
```

increment n

invoke increment

```
Before the call, x is 1
  n inside the function is 2
After the call, x is 2
```

Invoking increment(x) in line 14 passes the reference of variable x to the reference variable n in the increment function. Now n and x are the same, as shown in the output. Incrementing n in the function (line 6) is the same as incrementing x. So, before the function is invoked, x is 1, and afterward, x becomes 2.

Pass-by-value and pass-by-reference are two ways of passing arguments to the parameters of a function. Pass-by-value passes the value to an independent variable and pass-by-reference shares the same variable. Semantically pass-by-reference can be described as *pass-by-sharing*.

Now you can use reference parameters to implement a correct swap function, as shown in Listing 6.17.

pass-by-sharing

VideoNote

Pass-by-reference

LISTING **6.17** SwapByReference.cpp

reference variables

```
1  #include <iostream>
2  using namespace std;
3
4  // Swap two variables
5  void swap(int& n1, int& n2)
6  {
7    cout << "\tInside the swap function" << endl;
8    cout << "\tBefore swapping n1 is " << n1 <<
9      " n2 is " << n2 << endl;
10
11   // Swap n1 with n2
12   int temp = n1;
13   n1 = n2;
14   n2 = temp;
15
16   cout << "\tAfter swapping n1 is " << n1 <<
17     " n2 is " << n2 << endl;
18 }
```

swap

```
19
20  int main()
21  {
22    // Declare and initialize variables
23    int num1 = 1;
24    int num2 = 2;
25
26    cout << "Before invoking the swap function, num1 is "
27      << num1 << " and num2 is " << num2 << endl;
28
29    // Invoke the swap function to attempt to swap two variables
30    swap(num1, num2);
31
32    cout << "After invoking the swap function, num1 is " << num1 <<
33      " and num2 is " << num2 << endl;
34
35    return 0;
36  }
```

invoke swap function

```
Before invoking the swap function, num1 is 1 and num2 is 2
  Inside the swap function
  Before swapping n1 is 1 n2 is 2
  After swapping n1 is 2 n2 is 1
After invoking the swap function, num1 is 2 and num2 is 1
```

Before the swap function is invoked (line 30), num1 is 1 and num2 is 2. After the swap function is invoked, num1 becomes 2 and num2 becomes 1. Their values have been swapped. As shown in Figure 6.8, the references of num1 and num2 are passed to n1 and n2, so n1 and num1 are alias and n2 and num2 are alias. Swapping values between n1 and n2 is the same as swapping values between num1 and num2.

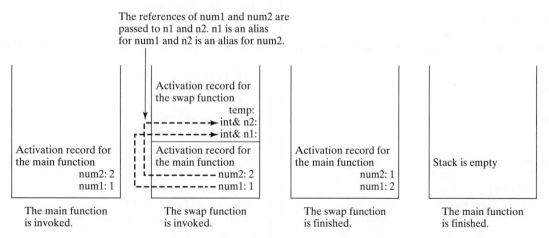

FIGURE 6.8 The references of the variables are passed to the parameters of the function.

When you pass an argument by reference, the formal parameter and the argument must have the same type. For example, in the following code, the reference of variable x is passed

require same type

to the function, which is fine. However, the reference of variable **y** is passed to the function, which is wrong, since **y** and **n** are of different types.

```cpp
#include <iostream>
using namespace std;

void increment(double& n)
{
  n++;
}

int main()
{
  double x = 1;
  int y = 1;

  increment(x);
  increment(y); // Cannot invoke increment(y) with an int argument

  cout << "x is " << x << endl;
  cout << "y is " << y << endl;

  return 0;
}
```

require variable   When you pass an argument by reference, the argument must be a variable. When you pass an argument by value, the argument can be a literal, a variable, an expression, or even the return value of another function.

Check Point

6.22 What is pass-by-value? What is pass-by-reference? Show the result of the following programs:

```cpp
#include <iostream>
using namespace std;

void maxValue(int value1, int value2, int max)
{
  if (value1 > value2)
    max = value1;
  else
    max = value2;
}

int main()
{
  int max = 0;
  maxValue(1, 2, max);
  cout << "max is " << max << endl;

  return 0;
}
```

(a)

```cpp
#include <iostream>
using namespace std;

void maxValue(int value1, int value2, int& max)
{
  if (value1 > value2)
    max = value1;
  else
    max = value2;
}

int main()
{
  int max = 0;
  maxValue(1, 2, max);
  cout << "max is " << max << endl;

  return 0;
}
```

(b)

```cpp
#include <iostream>
using namespace std;

void f(int i, int num)
{
  for (int j = 1; j <= i; j++)
  {
    cout << num << " ";
    num *= 2;
  }

  cout << endl;
}

int main()
{
  int i = 1;
  while (i <= 6)
  {
    f(i, 2);
    i++;
  }

  return 0;
}
```

(c)

```cpp
#include <iostream>
using namespace std;

void f(int& i, int num)
{
  for (int j = 1; j <= i; j++)
  {
    cout << num << " ";
    num *= 2;
  }

  cout << endl;
}

int main()
{
  int i = 1;
  while (i <= 6)
  {
    f(i, 2);
    i++;
  }

  return 0;
}
```

(d)

6.23 A student wrote the following function to find the minimum and maximum number between two values **a** and **b**. What is wrong in the program?

```cpp
#include <iostream>
using namespace std;

void minMax(double a, double b, double min, double max)
{
  if (a < b)
  {
    min = a;
    max = b;
  }
  else
  {
    min = b;
    max = a;
  }
}

int main()
{
  double a = 5, b = 6, min, max;
  minMax(a, b, min, max);

  cout << "min is " << min << " and max is " << max << endl;

  return 0;
}
```

6.24   A student wrote the following function to find the minimum and maximum number between two values **a** and **b**. What is wrong in the program?

```cpp
#include <iostream>
using namespace std;

void minMax(double a, double b, double& min, double& max)
{
  if (a < b)
  {
    double min = a;
    double max = b;
  }
  else
  {
    double min = b;
    double max = a;
  }
}

int main()
{
  double a = 5, b = 6, min, max;
  minMax(a, b, min, max);

  cout << "min is " << min << " and max is " << max << endl;

  return 0;
}
```

6.25   For Check Point 6.24, show the contents of the stack just before the function minMax is invoked, just after entering minMax, just before minMax returns, and right after minMax returns.

6.26   Show the output of the following code:

```cpp
#include <iostream>
using namespace std;

void f(double& p)
{
  p += 2;
}

int main()
{
  double x = 10;
  int y = 10;

  f(x);
  f(y);

  cout << "x is " << x << endl;
  cout << "y is " << y << endl;

  return 0;
}
```

6.27 What is wrong in the following program?

```cpp
#include <iostream>
using namespace std;

void p(int& i)
{
  cout << i << endl;
}

int p(int j)
{
  cout << j << endl;
}

int main()
{
  int k = 5;
  p(k);

  return 0;
}
```

6.13 Constant Reference Parameters

You can specify a constant reference parameter to prevent its value from being changed by accident.

Key Point

If your program uses a pass-by-reference parameter and the parameter is not changed in the function, you should mark it constant to tell the compiler that the parameter should not be changed. To do so, place the **const** keyword before the parameter in the function declaration. Such a parameter is known as *constant reference parameter*. For example, **num1** and **num2** are declared as constant reference parameters in the following function.

const

constant reference parameter

```cpp
// Return the max between two numbers
int max(const int& num1, const int& num2)
{
  int result;

  if (num1 > num2)
    result = num1;
  else
    result = num2;

  return result;
}
```

In pass-by-value, the actual parameter and its formal parameter are independent variables. In pass-by-reference, the actual parameter and its formal parameter refer to the same variable. Pass-by-reference is more efficient than pass-by-value for object types such as strings, because objects can take a lot of memory. However, the difference is negligible for parameters of primitive types such as **int** and **double**. So, *if a primitive data type parameter is not changed in the function, you should simply declare it as pass-by-value parameter.*

use pass-by-value or pass-by-reference?

6.14 Case Study: Converting Hexadecimals to Decimals

This section presents a program that converts a hexadecimal number into a decimal number.

Key Point

Section 5.8.4, "Case Study: Converting Decimals to Hexadecimals," gives a program that converts a decimal to a hexadecimal. How do you convert a hex number into a decimal?

Given a hexadecimal number $h_n h_{n-1} h_{n-2} \ldots h_2 h_1 h_0$, the equivalent decimal value is

$$h_n \times 16^n + h_{n-1} \times 16^{n-1} + h_{n-2} \times 16^{n-2} + \ldots + h_2 \times 16^2 + h_1 \times 16^1 + h_0 \times 16^0$$

For example, the hex number AB8C is

$$10 \times 16^3 + 11 \times 16^2 + 8 \times 16^1 + 12 \times 16^0 = 43916$$

Our program will prompt the user to enter a hex number as a string and convert it into a decimal using the following function:

```
int hex2Dec(const string& hex)
```

A brute-force approach is to convert each hex character into a decimal number, multiply it by 16^i for a hex digit at the i's position, and then add all the items together to obtain the equivalent decimal value for the hex number.

Note that

$$h_n \times 16^n + h_{n-1} \times 16^{n-1} + h_{n-2} \times 16^{n-2} + \ldots + h_1 \times 16^1 + h_0 \times 16^0$$

$$= (\ldots((h_n \times 16 + h_{n-1}) \times 16 + h_{n-2}) \times 16 + \ldots + h_1) \times 16 + h_0$$

Horner's algorithm

This observation, known as the Horner's algorithm, leads to the following efficient code for converting a hex string to a decimal number:

```
int decimalValue = 0;
for (int i = 0; i < hex.size(); i++)
{
  char hexChar = hex[i];
  decimalValue = decimalValue * 16 + hexCharToDecimal(hexChar);
}
```

Here is a trace of the algorithm for hex number AB8C:

	i	hexChar	hexCharToDecimal (hexChar)	decimalValue
before the loop				0
after the 1st iteration	0	A	10	10
after the 2nd iteration	1	B	11	10 * 16 + 11
after the 3rd iteration	2	8	8	(10 * 16 + 11) * 16 + 8
after the 4th iteration	3	C	12	((10 * 16 + 11) * 16 + 8) * 16 + 12

Listing 6.18 gives the complete program.

LISTING 6.18 Hex2Dec.cpp

```
1  #include <iostream>
2  #include <string>
3  #include <cctype>
4  using namespace std;
5
6  // Converts a hex number as a string to decimal
7  int hex2Dec(const string& hex);
```

```
 8
 9    // Converts a hex character to a decimal value
10    int hexCharToDecimal(char ch);
11
12    int main()
13    {
14      // Prompt the user to enter a hex number as a string
15      cout << "Enter a hex number: ";
16      string hex;
17      cin >> hex;                                                   input string
18
19      cout << "The decimal value for hex number " << hex
20        << " is " << hex2Dec(hex) << endl;                          hex to decimal
21
22      return 0;
23    }
24
25    int hex2Dec(const string& hex)
26    {
27      int decimalValue = 0;
28      for (unsigned i = 0; i < hex.size(); i++)
29        decimalValue = decimalValue * 16 + hexCharToDecimal(hex[i]);
30
31      return decimalValue;
32    }
33
34    int hexCharToDecimal(char ch)                                   hex char to decimal
35    {
36      ch = toupper(ch); // Change it to uppercase                   to uppercase
37      if (ch >= 'A' && ch <= 'F')
38        return 10 + ch - 'A';
39      else // ch is '0', '1', ..., or '9'
40        return ch - '0';
41    }
```

```
Enter a hex number: AB8C  ↵Enter
The decimal value for hex number AB8C is 43916
```

```
Enter a hex number: af71  ↵Enter
The decimal value for hex number af71 is 44913
```

The program reads a string from the console (line 17), and invokes the **hex2Dec** function to convert a hex string to decimal number (line 20).

The **hex2Dec** function is defined in lines 25–32 to return an integer. The string parameter is declared as a **const** and passed by reference, because the string is not changed in the function and it saves memory by passing it as reference. The length of the string is determined by invoking **hex.size()** in line 28.

The **hexCharToDecimal** function is defined in lines 34–41 to return a decimal value for a hex character. The character can be in either lowercase or uppercase. It is converted to uppercase in line 36. Recall that to subtract two characters is to subtract their ASCII codes. For example, `'5' - '0'` is 5.

6.15 Function Abstraction and Stepwise Refinement

The key to developing software is to apply the concept of abstraction.

VideoNote
Stepwise refinement

function abstraction
information hiding

You will learn many levels of abstraction from this book. *Function abstraction* is achieved by separating the use of a function from its implementation. The client can use a function without knowing how it is implemented. The details of the implementation are encapsulated in the function and hidden from the client who invokes the function. This is known as *information hiding* or *encapsulation*. If you decide to change the implementation, the client program will not be affected, provided that you do not change the function signature. The implementation of the function is hidden from the client in a "black box," as shown in Figure 6.9.

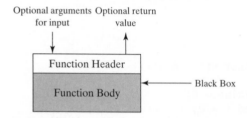

FIGURE 6.9 The function body can be thought of as a black box that contains the detailed implementation for the function.

You have already used the **rand()** function to return a random number, the **time(0)** function to obtain the current time, and the **max** function to find the maximum number. You know how to write the code to invoke these functions in your program, but as a user of these functions, you are not required to know how they are implemented.

divide and conquer
stepwise refinement

The concept of function abstraction can be applied to the process of developing programs. When writing a large program, you can use the "*divide-and-conquer*" strategy, also known as *stepwise refinement*, to decompose it into subproblems. The subproblems can be further decomposed into smaller, more manageable ones.

Suppose you write a program that displays the calendar for a given month of the year. The program prompts the user to enter the year and the month, and then displays the entire calendar for the month, as shown in Figure 6.10.

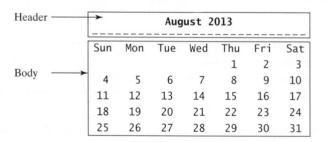

FIGURE 6.10 After prompting the user to enter the year and the month, the program displays the calendar for that month.

Let us use this example to demonstrate the divide-and-conquer approach.

6.15.1 Top-Down Design

How would you start such a program? Would you immediately start coding? Beginning programmers often start by trying to work out the solution to every detail. Although details are important in the final program, concern for detail in the early stages may block the problem-solving process. To make problem-solving flow smoothly, this example begins by using function abstraction to isolate details from design; only later does it implement the details.

For this example, the problem is first broken into two subproblems: get input from the user, and print the calendar for the month. At this stage, you should be concerned with what the subproblems will achieve, not with how to get input and print the calendar for the month. You can draw a structure chart to help visualize the decomposition of the problem (see Figure 6.11a).

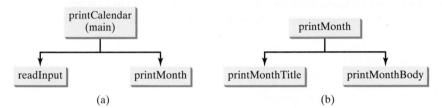

(a)   (b)

FIGURE 6.11   (a) The structure chart shows that the `printCalendar` problem is divided into two subproblems, `readInput` and `printMonth`. (b) `printMonth` is divided into two smaller subproblems, `printMonthTitle` and `printMonthBody`.

You can use the `cin` object to read input for the year and the month. The problem of printing the calendar for a given month can be broken into two subproblems: print the month title, and print the month body, as shown in Figure 6.11b. The month title consists of three lines: month and year, a dashed line, and the names of the seven days of the week. You need to get the month name (e.g., January) from the numeric month (e.g., 1). This is accomplished in `printMonthName` (see Figure 6.12a).

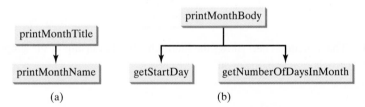

(a)   (b)

FIGURE 6.12   (a) To accomplish `printMonthTitle`, you need `printMonthName`. (b) The `printMonthBody` problem is refined into several smaller problems.

To print the month body, you need to know which day of the week is the first day of the month (`getStartDay`) and how many days the month has (`getNumberOfDaysInMonth`), as shown in Figure 6.12b. For example, August 2013 has thirty-one days, and the first day of the month is Thursday, as shown in Figure 6.10.

How would you get the start day for a month? There are several ways to find it. Assume that you know that the start day (`startDay1800 = 3`) for January 1, 1800, was Wednesday. You could compute the total number of days (`totalNumberOfDays`) between January 1, 1800, and the start day of the calendar month. The computation is (`totalNumberOfDays + startDay1800`) `% 7`, because every week has seven days. So the `getStartDay` problem can be further refined as `getTotalNumberOfDays`, as shown in Figure 6.13a.

To get the total number of days, you need to know whether a year is a leap year and how many days are in each month. So `getTotalNumberOfDays` is further refined into two subproblems: `isLeapYear` and `getNumberOfDaysInMonth`, as shown in Figure 6.13b. The complete structure chart is shown in Figure 6.14.

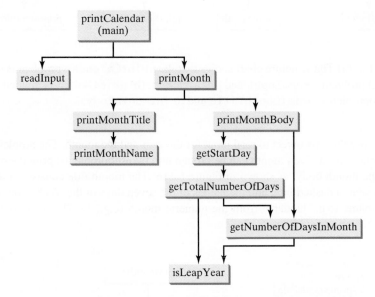

FIGURE 6.13 (a) To accomplish `getStartDay`, you need `getTotalNumberOfDays`. (b) The `getTotalNumberOfDays` problem is refined into two smaller problems.

FIGURE 6.14 The structure chart shows the hierarchical relationship of the subproblems in the program.

6.15.2 Top-Down or Bottom-Up Implementation

Now we turn our attention to implementation. In general, a subproblem corresponds to a function in the implementation, although some subproblems are so simple that this is unnecessary. You must decide which modules to implement as functions and which to combine in other functions. Such decisions should be based on whether the overall program will be easier to read because of your choice. In this example, the subproblem `readInput` can be simply implemented in the `main` function.

top-down implementation
bottom-up implementation
stub

You can use either a "*top-down*" or a "*bottom-up*" implementation. The top-down approach implements one function at a time in the structure chart from top to bottom. Stubs can be used for the functions waiting to be implemented. A *stub* is a simple, but incomplete, version of a function. Usually a stub displays a test message indicating that it was called, and nothing more. The use of stubs enables you to test invoking the function from a caller. Implement the `main` function first, then use a stub for the `printMonth` function. For example, let `printMonth` display the year and the month in the stub. Thus, your program may begin like this:

```
#include <iostream>
#include <iomanip>
using namespace std;
```

```
void printMonth(int year, int month);
void printMonthTitle(int year, int month);
void printMonthName(int month);
void printMonthBody(int year, int month);
int getStartDay(int year, int month);
int getTotalNumberOfDays(int year, int month);
int getNumberOfDaysInMonth(int year, int month);
bool isLeapYear(int year);

int main()
{
  // Prompt the user to enter year
  cout << "Enter full year (e.g., 2001): ";
  int year;
  cin >> year;

  // Prompt the user to enter month
  cout << "Enter month in number between 1 and 12: ";
  int month;
  cin >> month;

  // Print calendar for the month of the year
  printMonth(year, month);

  return 0;
}

void printMonth(int year, int month)
{
  cout << month << "   " << year << endl;
}
```

Compile and test the program and fix any errors. You can now implement the `printMonth` function. For functions invoked from the `printMonth` function, you can use stubs.

The bottom-up approach implements one function at a time in the structure chart from bottom to top. For each function implemented, write a test program, known as the *driver*, to test it. The top-down and bottom-up approaches are both fine. Both implement functions incrementally, help to isolate programming errors, and facilitate debugging. Sometimes they can be used together.

bottom-up approach
driver

6.15.3 Implementation Details

The `isLeapYear(int year)` function can be implemented using the following code:

```
return (year % 400 == 0 || (year % 4 == 0 && year % 100 != 0));
```

Use the following information to implement `getTotalNumberOfDaysInMonth(int year, int month)`:

- January, March, May, July, August, October, and December have 31 days.
- April, June, September, and November have 30 days.
- February has 28 days in a regular year and 29 days in a leap year. A regular year, therefore, has 365 days, and a leap year has 366.

To implement `getTotalNumberOfDays(int year, int month)`, you need to compute the total number of days (`totalNumberOfDays`) between January 1, 1800, and the first day of the calendar month. You could find the total number of days between the year 1800 and the calendar year and then figure out the total number of days prior to the calendar month in the calendar year. The sum of these two totals is `totalNumberOfDays`.

To print a body, first add some space before the start day and then print the lines for every week, as shown for August 2013 (see Figure 6.10).

The complete program is given in Listing 6.19.

LISTING 6.19   PrintCalendar.cpp

```cpp
1   #include <iostream>
2   #include <iomanip>
3   using namespace std;
4
5   // Function prototypes
6   void printMonth(int year, int month);
7   void printMonthTitle(int year, int month);
8   void printMonthName(int month);
9   void printMonthBody(int year, int month);
10  int getStartDay(int year, int month);
11  int getTotalNumberOfDays(int year, int month);
12  int getNumberOfDaysInMonth(int year, int month);
13  bool isLeapYear(int year);
14
15  int main()
16  {
17    // Prompt the user to enter year
18    cout << "Enter full year (e.g., 2001): ";
19    int year;
20    cin >> year;
21
22    // Prompt the user to enter month
23    cout << "Enter month in number between 1 and 12: ";
24    int month;
25    cin >> month;
26
27    // Print calendar for the month of the year
28    printMonth(year, month);
29
30    return 0;
31  }
32
33  // Print the calendar for a month in a year
34  void printMonth(int year, int month)
35  {
36    // Print the headings of the calendar
37    printMonthTitle(year, month);
38
39    // Print the body of the calendar
40    printMonthBody(year, month);
41  }
42
43  // Print the month title, e.g., May, 1999
44  void printMonthTitle(int year, int month)
45  {
46    printMonthName(month);
47    cout << " " << year << endl;
48    cout << "-----------------------------" << endl;
49    cout << " Sun Mon Tue Wed Thu Fri Sat" << endl;
```

function prototype

main function

input year

input month

print calendar

print month

print month title

```
50  }
51
52  // Get the English name for the month
53  void printMonthName(int month)
54  {
55    switch (month)
56    {
57      case 1:
58        cout << "January";
59        break;
60      case 2:
61        cout << "February";
62        break;
63      case 3:
64        cout << "March";
65        break;
66      case 4:
67        cout << "April";
68        break;
69      case 5:
70        cout << "May";
71        break;
72      case 6:
73        cout << "June";
74        break;
75      case 7:
76        cout << "July";
77        break;
78      case 8:
79        cout << "August";
80        break;
81      case 9:
82        cout << "September";
83        break;
84      case 10:
85        cout << "October";
86        break;
87      case 11:
88        cout << "November";
89        break;
90      case 12:
91        cout << "December";
92    }
93  }
94
95  // Print month body
96  void printMonthBody(int year, int month)
97  {
98    // Get start day of the week for the first date in the month
99    int startDay = getStartDay(year, month);
100
101   // Get number of days in the month
102   int numberOfDaysInMonth = getNumberOfDaysInMonth(year, month);
103
104   // Pad space before the first day of the month
105   int i = 0;
106   for (i = 0; i < startDay; i++)
107     cout << "    ";
```

print month body

```
108
109     for (i = 1; i <= numberOfDaysInMonth; i++)
110     {
111       cout << setw(4) << i;
112
113       if ((i + startDay) % 7 == 0)
114         cout << endl;
115     }
116   }
117
118   // Get the start day of the first day in a month
119   int getStartDay(int year, int month)
120   {
121     // Get total number of days since 1/1/1800
122     int startDay1800 = 3;
123     int totalNumberOfDays = getTotalNumberOfDays(year, month);
124
125     // Return the start day
126     return (totalNumberOfDays + startDay1800) % 7;
127   }
128
129   // Get the total number of days since January 1, 1800
130   int getTotalNumberOfDays(int year, int month)
131   {
132     int total = 0;
133
134     // Get the total days from 1800 to year - 1
135     for (int i = 1800; i < year; i++)
136       if (isLeapYear(i))
137         total = total + 366;
138       else
139         total = total + 365;
140
141     // Add days from Jan to the month prior to the calendar month
142     for (int i = 1; i < month; i++)
143       total = total + getNumberOfDaysInMonth(year, i);
144
145     return total;
146   }
147
148   // Get the number of days in a month
149   int getNumberOfDaysInMonth(int year, int month)
150   {
151     if (month == 1 || month == 3 || month == 5 || month == 7 ||
152         month == 8 || month == 10 || month == 12)
153       return 31;
154
155     if (month == 4 || month == 6 || month == 9 || month == 11)
156       return 30;
157
158     if (month == 2) return isLeapYear(year) ? 29 : 28;
159
160     return 0; // If month is incorrect
161   }
162
163   // Determine if it is a leap year
164   bool isLeapYear(int year)
```

get start day

getTotalNumberOfDays

getNumberOfDaysInMonth

isLeapYear

```
165  {
166    return year % 400 == 0 || (year % 4 == 0 && year % 100 != 0);
167  }
```

```
Enter full year (e.g., 2012): 2012 ⏎Enter
Enter month as a number between 1 and 12: 3 ⏎Enter
          March 2012
-------------------------------
 Sun Mon Tue Wed Thu Fri Sat
                   1   2   3
   4   5   6   7   8   9  10
  11  12  13  14  15  16  17
  18  19  20  21  22  23  24
  25  26  27  28  29  30  31
```

The program does not validate user input. For instance, if the user entered a month not in the range between 1 and 12, or a year before 1800, the program would display an erroneous calendar. To avoid this error, add an `if` statement to check the input before printing the calendar.

This program prints calendars for a month but could easily be modified to print calendars for a year. Although it can only print months after January 1800, it could be modified to trace the day of a month before 1800.

6.15.4 Benefits of Stepwise Refinement

Stepwise refinement breaks a large problem into smaller manageable subproblems. Each subproblem can be implemented using a function. This approach makes the program easier to write, reuse, debug, test, modify, and maintain.

Simpler Program

The print calendar program is long. Rather than writing a long sequence of statements in one function, stepwise refinement breaks it into smaller functions. This simplifies the program and makes the whole program easier to read and understand.

Reusing Functions

Stepwise refinement promotes code reuse within a program. The `isLeapYear` function is defined once and invoked from the `getTotalNumberOfDays` and `getNumberOfDaysInMonth` functions. This reduces redundant code.

Easier Developing, Debugging, and Testing

Since each subproblem is solved in a function, a function can be developed, debugged, and tested individually. This isolates the errors and makes developing, debugging, and testing easier.

incremental development and testing

When implementing a large program, use the top-down or bottom-up approach. Do not write the entire program at once. Using these approaches seems to take more development time (because you repeatedly compile and run the program), but actually it saves time and facilitates debugging.

Better Facilitating Teamwork

Since a large problem is divided into subprograms, the subproblems can be assigned to other programmers. This makes it easier for programmers to work in teams.

KEY TERMS

actual parameter 229
ambiguous invocation 240
argument 229
automatic variable 248
bottom-up implementation 264
divide and conquer 262
formal parameter (i.e., parameter) 229
function abstraction 262
function declaration 241
function header 229
function overloading 239
function prototype 241
function signature 229

global variable 245
information hiding 262
inline function 244
local variable 245
parameter list 229
pass-by-reference 253
pass-by-value 250
reference variable 252
scope of variable 245
static local variable 248
stepwise refinement 262
stub 264
top-down implementation 264

CHAPTER SUMMARY

1. Making programs modular and reusable is a goal of software engineering. Functions can be used to develop modular and reusable code.

2. The function header specifies the *return value type*, *function name*, and *parameters* of the function.

3. A function may return a value. The `returnValueType` is the data type of the value that the function returns.

4. If the function does not return a value, the `returnValueType` is the keyword `void`.

5. The *parameter list* refers to the type, order, and number of the parameters of a function.

6. The arguments that are passed to a function should have the same number, type, and order as the parameters in the function signature.

7. The function name and the parameter list together constitute the *function signature*.

8. Parameters are optional; that is, a function may contain no parameters.

9. A value-returning function must return a value when the function is finished.

10. A return statement can be used in a void function for terminating the function and returning control to the function's caller.

11. When a program calls a function, program control is transferred to the called function.

12. A called function returns control to the caller when its return statement is executed or its function-ending closing brace is reached.

13. A value-returning function also can be invoked as a statement in C++. In this case, the caller simply ignores the return value.

14. A function can be overloaded. This means that two functions can have the same name as long as their function parameter lists differ.

15. Pass-by-value passes the value of the argument to the parameter.

16. Pass-by-reference passes the reference of the argument.

17. If you change the value of a pass-by-value argument in a function, the value is not changed in the argument after the function finishes.

18. If you change the value of a pass-by-reference argument in a function, the value is changed in the argument after the function finishes.

19. A *constant reference parameter* is specified using the `const` keyword to tell the compiler that its value cannot be changed in the function.

20. The *scope of a variable* is the part of the program where the variable can be used.

21. Global variables are declared outside functions and are accessible to all functions in their scope.

22. Local variables are defined inside a function. After a function completes its execution, all of its local variables are destroyed.

23. Local variables are also called automatic variables.

24. Static local variables can be defined to retain the local variables for use by the next function call.

25. C++ provides *inline functions* to avoid function calls for fast execution.

26. Inline functions are not called; rather, the compiler copies the function code *in line* at the point of each invocation.

27. To specify an inline function, precede the function declaration with the `inline` keyword.

28. C++ allows you to declare functions with default argument values for pass-by-value parameters.

29. The default values are passed to the parameters when a function is invoked without the arguments.

30. *Function abstraction* is achieved by separating the use of a function from its implementation.

31. Programs written as collections of concise functions are easier to write, debug, maintain, and modify than would otherwise be the case.

32. When implementing a large program, use the top-down or bottom-up coding approach.

33. Do not write the entire program at once. This approach seems to take more time for coding (because you are repeatedly compiling and running the program), but it actually saves time and facilitates debugging.

QUIZ

Answer the quiz for this chapter online at www.cs.armstrong.edu/liang/cpp3e/quiz.html.

PROGRAMMING EXERCISES

Sections 6.2–6.11

6.1 (*Math: Triangular numbers*) A triangular number is defined as $m(m + 1)/2$ for $m = 1, 2, \ldots$, and so on. Therefore, the first few numbers are 1, 5, 12, 22, ... Write a function with the following header that returns a triangular number:

```
int getTriangularNumber(int n)
```

Write a test program that uses this function to display the first 75 triangular numbers with 5 numbers on each line.

*6.2 (*Average of digits in an integer*) Write a function that computes the average of the digits in an integer. Use the following function header:

```
double averageDigits(long n)
```

For example, `averageDigits(936)` returns `6.0` ((9 + 3 + 6)/3). (*Hint*: Use the `%` operator to extract digits, and the `/` operator to remove the extracted digit. For instance, to extract 6 from 936, use `936 % 10` (= 6). To remove 6 from 936, use `936 / 10` (= 93). Use a loop to repeatedly extract and remove the digit until all the digits are extracted. Write a test program that prompts the user to enter an integer and displays the sum of all its digits.

**6.3 (*Armstrong integer*) Write the functions with the following headers:

```
// Return the sum of the cubes of the digits in an integer,
// i.e., cubeOfDigits(131) returns 1³ + 3³ + 1³ = 29
int cubeOfDigits(int number)
```

```
// Displays if integer is an Armstrong integer
void isArmstrong(int sum, int number)
```

Use `cubeOfDigits` to implement `isArmstrong`. An integer is an Armstrong integer if the sum of the cubes of its digits is equal to the number itself. Write a test program that prompts the user to enter an integer and reports whether it is an Armstrong integer.

*6.4 (*Display even digits in an integer*) Write a function with the following header to display the even digits in an integer:

```
void displayEven(int number)
```

For example, `displayEven(345)` displays 4. Write a test program that prompts the user to enter an integer and displays the even digits in it.

*6.5 (*Largest of three numbers*) Write a function with the following header to display the largest of three numbers:

```
void displayLargest(
  double num1, double num2, double num3)
```

Write a test program that prompts the user to enter three numbers and invokes the function to display the largest of them.

*6.6 (*Display patterns*) Write a function to display a pattern as follows:

```
****************
**************
************
...
*
```

The function header is

void displayPattern(**int** n)

*6.7 (*Financial application: compute the future investment value*) Write a function that computes future investment value at a given interest rate for a specified number of years. The future investment is determined using the formula in Programming Exercise 2.23.

Use the following function header:

double futureInvestmentValue(
    double investmentAmount, **double** monthlyInterestRate, **int** years)

For example, futureInvestmentValue(10000, 0.05/12, 5) returns 12833.59.

Write a test program that prompts the user to enter the investment amount (e.g., 1000) and the interest rate (e.g., 9%) and prints a table that displays future value for the years from 1 to 30, as shown below:

```
The amount invested: 1000 ↵Enter
Annual interest rate: 9 ↵Enter

Years    Future Value
1        1093.80
2        1196.41
...
29       13467.25
30       14730.57
```

6.8 (*Conversions between Millimeters and Inches*) Write the following two functions:

```
// Convert from millimeters to inches
double millimetersToInches(double millimeters)

// Convert from inches to millimeters
double inchesToMillimeters(double inches)
```

The formula for the conversion is

```
millimeter = 0.39 * inches
```

Write a test program that invokes these functions to display the following tables:

Millimeters	Inches		Inches	Millimeters
2	0.078		1	65.574
4	0.156		2	81.967
...				
98	3.822		49	1256.41
100	3.900		50	1282.05

6.9 (*Conversions between Pounds and Ounces*) Write the following two functions:

```
// Convert from pounds to ounces
double poundsToOunces(double pounds)

// Convert from ounces to pounds
double ouncesToPounds(double inches)
```

The formula for the conversion is

```
pound = 16 * ounces
celsius = 0.0625 * pound
```

Write a test program that invokes these functions to display the following tables:

Pounds	Ounces		Ounces	Pounds
11	176	|	1	0.0625
12	192	|	2	0.125
...				
19	304	|	9	0.5625
20	320	|	10	0.625

6.10 (*Financial application: find the profit-per-item*) Use the scheme in programming Exercise 5.39 to write a function that computes the profit-per-item. The header of the function is:

double computeProfitPerItem(**double** quantity)

Write a test program that displays the following table:

Quantity	Profit-per-item (in $)
1000	1000
2000	3000
...	
9000	29000
10000	34000

6.11 (*Display ASCII values*) Write a function that prints the ASCII values of the characters using the following header:

void printASCII(**char** ch1, **char** ch2, **int** numberPerLine)

This function prints the ASCII values of characters between **ch1** and **ch2** with the specified number of characters per line. Write a test program that prints 6 ASCII values per line of characters from 'a' to 'm'.

*6.12 (*Sum series*) Write a function to compute the following series:

$$f(n) = \frac{1}{3} + \frac{1}{8} + \frac{1}{15} \cdots + \frac{1}{n(n + 2)}$$

Write a test program that displays the following table:

n	f(n)
2	0.458333
4	0.566667
...	
12	0.675824
14	0.685417

*6.13   (*Estimate π*) π can be computed using the following series:

$$f(n) = \sqrt{6 * \left(1 + \frac{1}{4} + \frac{1}{9} + \frac{1}{16} + \frac{1}{25} + \ldots + \frac{1}{n^2} \right)}$$

Write a function that returns **f(n)** for a given **n** and write a test program that displays the following table:

n	f(n)
2	2.73861
4	2.92261
6	2.99138
8	3.0273
10	3.04936
12	3.06429
14	3.07506
16	3.08319
18	3.08956
20	3.09467

*6.14   (*Financial application: print a tax table*) Listing 3.3, ComputeTax.cpp, is a program to compute tax. Write a function for computing tax using the following header:

double computeTax(**int** status, **double** taxableIncome)

Use this function to write a program that prints a tax table for taxable income from $50,000 to $60,000 with intervals of $50 for all four statuses, as follows:

Taxable Income	Single	Married Joint or Qualifying Widow(er)	Married Separate	Head of a House
50000	8688	6665	8688	7352
50050	8700	6673	8700	7365
...				
59950	11175	8158	11175	9840
60000	11188	8165	11188	9852

*6.15   (*Number of days in February*) Write a function that returns the number of days in February using the following header:

int numberOfDaysInFebruary(**int** year)

Write a test program that displays the number of days in February from year **1985**, . . . , upto **1983**.

*6.16   (*Display matrix of 0s and 1s*) Write a function that displays an *n*-by-*n* matrix using the following header:

void printMatrix(**int** n)

Each element is 0 or 1, which is generated randomly. Write a test program that prompts the user to enter **n** and displays an *n*-by-*n* matrix. Here is a sample run:

```
Enter n: 3  ↵Enter
0 1 0
0 0 0
1 1 1
```

6.17 (*Equilateral Triangle validation and perimeter*) Implement the following two functions:

```
// Returns true if all the sides of the triangle
// are same.
bool isValid(double side1, double side2, double side3)

// Returns the perimeter of an equilateral triangle.
double perimeter(double side1)
```

The formula for computing the perimeter is `perimeter = 3 * side`. Write a test program that reads three sides for a triangle and computes the perimeter if the input is valid. Otherwise, display that the input is invalid.

6.18 (*Modify the gcd function*) Listing 6.4, `GreatestCommonDivisorFunction.cpp`, provides the `gcd(int n1, int n2)` function for calculating the GCD of two numbers. Modify this function to calculate the Least Common Multiple (LCM) of two numbers.

**6.19 (*Reverse Armstrong number*) Write a test program that prompts the user to enter an integer and checks whether it is an Armstrong integer. If it is an Armstrong number, the program reverses the digits of the integer and checks whether the reversed integer is also an Armstrong number. Otherwise, display that the integer entered by the user is not an Armstrong number.

*6.20 (*Geometry: point position*) Programming Exercise 3.29 shows how to test whether a point is on the left side of a directed line, right, or on the same line. Write the following functions:

```
/** Return true if point (x2, y2) is on the left side of the
 *  directed line from (x0, y0) to (x1, y1) */
bool leftOfTheLine(double x0, double y0,
  double x1, double y1, double x2, double y2)

/** Return true if point (x2, y2) is on the same
 *  line from (x0, y0) to (x1, y1) */
bool onTheSameLine(double x0, double y0,
  double x1, double y1, double x2, double y2)

/** Return true if point (x2, y2) is on the
 *  line segment from (x0, y0) to (x1, y1) */
bool onTheLineSegment(double x0, double y0,
  double x1, double y1, double x2, double y2)
```

Write a program that prompts the user to enter the three points for p0, p1, and p2 and displays whether p2 is on the left of the line from p0 to p1, right, the same line, or on the line segment. Here are some sample runs:

```
Enter three points for p0, p1, and p2: 1 1 2 2 1.5 1.5 ↵Enter
(1.5, 1.5) is on the line segment from (1.0, 1.0) to (2.0, 2.0)
```

```
Enter three points for p0, p1, and p2: 1 1 2 2 3 3 ↵Enter
(3.0, 3.0) is on the same line from (1.0, 1.0) to (2.0, 2.0)
```

```
Enter three points for p0, p1, and p2: 1 1 2 2 1 1.5 ↵Enter
(1.0, 1.5) is on the left side of the line
  from (1.0, 1.0) to (2.0, 2.0)
```

```
Enter three points for p0, p1, and p2: 1 1 2 2 1 -1 ↵Enter
(1.0, -1.0) is on the right side of the line
  from (1.0, 1.0) to (2.0, 2.0)
```

**6.21 (*Even Palindrome number*) A number is a palindrome if its reversal is the same as itself. An even palindrome number is a number which is even and also a palindrome. Write a program that displays the first 50 even palindrome numbers. Display 5 numbers per line and align the numbers properly, as follows:

```
 2    4    6    8   22
44   66   88  202  212
...
```

**6.22 (*Game: craps*) Craps is a popular dice game played in casinos. Write a program to play a variation of the game, as follows:

Roll two dice. Each die has six faces representing values 1, 2, ... , and 6, respectively. Check the sum of the two dice. If the sum is 2, 3, or 12 (called *craps*), you lose; if the sum is 7 or 11 (called *natural*), you win; if the sum is another value (i.e., 4, 5, 6, 8, 9, or 10), a *point* is established. Continue until you roll either a 7 (you lose) or the same point value (you win).

Your program acts as a single player. Here are some sample runs:

```
You rolled 5 + 6 = 11
You win
```

```
You rolled 1 + 2 = 3
You lose
```

```
You rolled 4 + 4 = 8
point is 8
You rolled 6 + 2 = 8
You win
```

```
You rolled 3 + 2 = 5
point is 5
You rolled 2 + 5 = 7
You lose
```

**6.23 (*Emirp*) An *emirp* (prime spelled backward) is a nonpalindromic prime number whose reversal is also a prime. For example, 17 is a prime and 71 is a prime. So 17 and 71 are emirps. Write a program that displays the first 100 emirps. Display 10 numbers per line and align the numbers properly, as follows:

VideoNote
Find emirp prime

```
 13   17   31   37   71   73   79   97  107  113
149  157  167  179  199  311  337  347  359  389
...
```

**6.24 (*Game: Win to lose ratio at craps*) Revise Programming Exercise 6.22 to run it 5000 times and display the win to lose ratio.

**6.25 (*Additive prime*) A prime number is called an Additive prime if the sum of its digits is also a prime number. Write a program that finds the first 25 additive prime numbers and displays the output in the following format:

Prime number	Sum of its digits
2	2
3	3
...	
11	2
...	

**6.26 (*Day and remaining hours*) Programming Exercise 3.9 displays the current day and remaining hours. Simplify Programming Exercise 3.9 by using a function to get the day number of a week and hours passed.

**6.27 (*Math: approximate the square root*) How is the `sqrt` function in the `cmath` library implemented? There are several techniques for implementing it. One such technique is known as the *Babylonian method*. It approximates the square root of a number, `n`, by repeatedly performing a calculation using the following formula:

```
nextGuess = (lastGuess + (n / lastGuess)) / 2
```

When `nextGuess` and `lastGuess` are almost identical, `nextGuess` is the approximated square root. The initial guess can be any positive value (e.g., `1`). This value will be the starting value for `lastGuess`. If the difference between `nextGuess` and `lastGuess` is less than a very small number, such as `0.0001`, you can claim that `nextGuess` is the approximated square root of n. If not, `nextGuess` becomes `lastGuess` and the approximation process continues. Implement the following function that returns the square root of `n`:

double sqrt(**int** n)

*6.28 (*Even or Odd digit integer*) Write a function that checks whether an integer is an even digit or an odd digit integer using the following header:

int getType(**int** n)

For example, `getType(39)` is an even digit integer and `getType(5)` is an odd digit integer. Write a test program that prompts the user to enter an integer and displays its type.

*6.29 (*Average of even places*) Write a function that returns the average of the digits in the even places in an integer using the following header:

double avgOfEvenPlaces(**int** n)

For example, `avgOfEvenPlaces(5856)` returns `7.0` and `avgOfEvenPlaces(131)` returns `3.0`. Write a test program that prompts the user to enter an integer and displays the average of the digits in the even places of this integer.

Sections 6.12–6.15

*6.30 (*Search a character*) Write a function that searches for a particular character in a string using the following header:

void search(string& s, char& key)

Write a test program that prompts the user to enter the string and a character and displays if the character is found.

*6.31 (*Multiply by a constant value*) Write a function with the following header to multiply the three numbers with a constant value:

void multiply(**double**& num1, **double**& num2, **double**& num3 int constant)

Write a test program that prompts the user to enter three numbers and a constant to multiply them with, and displays the result.

*6.32 (*Algebra: solve quadratic equations*) The two roots of a quadratic equation $ax^2 + bx + x = 0$ can be obtained using the following formula:

$$r_1 = \frac{-b + \sqrt{b^2 - 4ac}}{2a} \quad \text{and} \quad r_2 = \frac{-b - \sqrt{b^2 - 4ac}}{2a}$$

Write a function with the following header

```
void solveQuadraticEquation(double a, double b, double c,
    double& discriminant, double& r1, double& r2)
```

$b^2 - 4ac$ is called the discriminant of the quadratic equation. If the discriminant is less than 0, the equation has no roots. In this case, ignore the value in r1 and r2.

Write a test program that prompts the user to enter values for *a*, *b*, and *c* and displays the result based on the discriminant. If the discriminant is greater than or equal to 0, display the two roots. If the discriminant is equal to 0, display the one root. Otherwise, display "the equation has no roots". See Programming Exercise 3.1 for sample runs.

*6.33 (*Algebra: solve 2 × 2 linear equations*) You can use Cramer's rule to solve the following 2 × 2 system of linear equations:

$$\begin{array}{ll} ax + by = e \\ cx + dy = f \end{array} \quad x = \frac{ed - bf}{ad - bc} \quad y = \frac{af - ec}{ad - bc}$$

Write a function with the following header:

```
void solveEquation(double a, double b, double c, double d,
    double e, double f, double& x, double& y, bool& isSolvable)
```

If $ad - bc$ is 0, the equation has no solution and isSolvable should be false. Write a program that prompts the user to enter a, b, c, d, e, and f and displays the result. If $ad - bc$ is 0, report that "The equation has no solution." See Programming Exercise 3.3 for sample runs.

***6.34 (*Current date and time*) Invoking time(0) returns the elapse time in milliseconds since midnight January 1, 1970. Write a program that displays the date and time. Here is a sample run:

```
Current date and time is May 16, 2009 10:34:23
```

**6.35 (*Geometry: intersection*) Suppose two line segments intersect. The two endpoints for the first line segment are (x1, y1) and (x2, y2) and for the second line segment are (x3, y3) and (x4, y4). Write the following function that returns the intersecting point if the two lines intersect:

VideoNote
Find intersecting point

```
void intersectPoint(double x1, double y1, double x2, double y2,
    double x3, double y3, double x4, double y4,
    double& x, double& y, bool& isIntersecting)
```

Write a program that prompts the user to enter these four endpoints and displays the intersecting point. (*Hint*: Use the function for solving 2 × 2 linear equations in Programming Exercise 6.33.)

```
Enter the endpoints of the first line segment: 2.0 2.0 0 0 ↵Enter
Enter the endpoints of the second line segment: 0 2.0 2.0 0 ↵Enter
The intersecting point is: (1, 1)
```

```
Enter the endpoints of the first line segment: 2.0 2.0 0 0 ↵Enter
Enter the endpoints of the second line segment: 3 3 1 1 ↵Enter
The two lines do not cross
```

6.36 (*Format an integer*) Write a function with the following header to format a positive integer with the specified width:

```
string format(int number, int width)
```

The function returns a string for the number with one or more prefix 0s. The size of the string is the width. For example, format(34, 4) returns 0034 and format(34, 5) returns 00034. If the number is longer than the width, the function returns the string representation for the number. For example, format(34, 1) returns 34.

Write a test program that prompts the user to enter a number and its width and displays a string returned by invoking format(number, width).

**6.37 (*Financial: credit card number validation*) Credit card numbers follow certain patterns. A credit card number must have between 13 and 16 digits. The number must start with the following:

- 4 for Visa cards
- 5 for MasterCard cards
- 37 for American Express cards
- 6 for Discover cards

In 1954, Hans Luhn of IBM proposed an algorithm for validating credit card numbers. The algorithm is useful to determine whether a card number is entered correctly or is scanned correctly by a scanner. Almost all credit card numbers are generated following this validity check, commonly known as the *Luhn check* or the *Mod 10 check*. It can be described as follows. (For illustration, consider the card number 4388576018402626.)

1. Double every second digit from right to left. If doubling of a digit results in a two-digit number, add the two digits to get a single digit number.

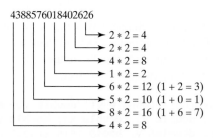

2. Now add all single-digit numbers from Step 1.
   $4 + 4 + 8 + 2 + 3 + 1 + 7 + 8 = 37$

3. Add all digits in the odd places from right to left in the card number.
   $6 + 6 + 0 + 8 + 0 + 7 + 8 + 3 = 38$

4. Sum the results from Step 2 and Step 3.

$$37 + 38 = 75$$

5. If the result from Step 4 is divisible by 10, the card number is valid; otherwise, it is invalid. For example, the number 4388576018402626 is invalid, but the number 4388576018410707 is valid.

Write a program that prompts the user to enter a credit card number as a string. Display whether the number is valid. Design your program to use the following functions:

```
// Return true if the card number is valid
bool isValid(const string& cardNumber)

// Get the result from Step 2
int sumOfDoubleEvenPlace(const string& cardNumber)

// Return this number if it is a single digit, otherwise,
// return the sum of the two digits
int getDigit(int number)

// Return sum of odd-place digits in the card number
int sumOfOddPlace(const string& cardNumber)

// Return true if substr is the prefix for cardNumber
bool startsWith(const string& cardNumber, const string& substr)
```

*6.38 (*Decimal to octal*) Write a function that parses a decimal number into an octal number. The function header is as follows:

```
int dec2Octal(const int& decimal)
```

Write a test program that prompts the user to enter a decimal number, uses the dec2Octal function to parse it into an equivalent octal number and displays the octal number.

*6.39 (*Octal to decimal*) Write a function that returns a decimal number from an octal number. The function header is as follows:

```
int octal2Dec(const int& octalNumber)
```

For example, octalNumber 345 is 229 ($3 \times 8^2 + 4 \times 8^1 + 5 \times 8^0 = 229$). So, octal2Dec("345") returns 229. Write a test program that prompts the user to enter an octal number and displays its decimal equivalent value.

**6.40 (*Binary to Octal*) Write a function that returns an octal number from a binary number. The function header is as follows:

```
int bin2Octal(const string& binaryString)
```

Write a test program that prompts the user to enter a binary number as a string and displays the corresponding octal value as a string.

**6.41 (*Octal to binary*) Write a function that returns a binary string from an octal number. The function header is as follows:

```
string octal2Binary(const int& octalNumber)
```

Write a test program that prompts the user to enter an octal number, uses octal-2Binary function to parse it into an equivalent binary string and displays the binary string.

*6.42 (*Display longest string*) Write the longest function using the following function header to return the longest string among two strings:

```
string longest(const string& s1, const string& s2)
```

Write a test program that prompts the user to enter two strings and displays the longest string if the input is valid. For example, if two strings are Welcome and Programming, output is Programming.

**6.43 (*Check substrings*) Write the following function to check whether string s1 is a substring of string s2. The function returns the first index in s2 if there is a match. Otherwise, return -1.

```
int indexOf(const string& s1, const string& s2)
```

Write a test program that reads two strings and checks whether the first string is a substring of the second string. Here is a sample run of the program:

```
Enter the first string: welcome ↵Enter
Enter the second string: We welcome you! ↵Enter
indexOf("welcome", "We welcome you!") is 3
```

```
Enter the first string: welcome ↵Enter
Enter the second string: We invite you! ↵Enter
indexOf("welcome", "We invite you!") is -1
```

*6.44 (*Occurrences of a specified character*) Write a function that finds the number of occurrences of a specified character in the string using the following header:

```
int count(const string& s, char a)
```

For example, count("Welcome", 'e') returns 2. Write a test program that reads a string and a character and displays the number of occurrences of the character in the string. Here is a sample run of the program:

```
Enter a string: Welcome to C++ ↵Enter
Enter a character: o ↵Enter
o appears in Welcome to C++ 2 times
```

***6.45 (*Current year, month, and day*) Write a program that displays the current year, month, and day using the time(0) function. Here is a sample run of the program:

```
The current date is May 17, 2012
```

**6.46 (*Swap case*) Write the following function that returns a new string in which the uppercase letters are changed to lowercase and lowercase to uppercase.

```
string swapCase(const string& s)
```

Write a test program that prompts the user to enter a string and invokes this function, and displays the return value from this function. Here is a sample run:

```
Enter a string: I'm here
The new string is: i'M HERE
```

**6.47 (*Phone keypads*) The international standard letter/number mapping for telephones is shown in Programming Exercise 4.15. Write a function that returns a number, given an uppercase letter, as follows:

```
int getNumber(char uppercaseLetter)
```

Write a test program that prompts the user to enter a phone number as a string. The input number may contain letters. The program translates a letter (uppercase or lowercase) to a digit and leaves all other characters intact. Here is a sample run of the program:

```
Enter a string: 1-800-Flowers ↵Enter
1-800-3569377
```

```
Enter a string: 1800flowers ↵Enter
18003569377
```

CHAPTER

7

SINGLE-DIMENSIONAL ARRAYS AND C-STRINGS

Objectives

- To describe why an array is necessary in programming (§7.1).

- To declare arrays (§7.2.1).

- To access array elements using indexes (§7.2.2).

- To initialize the values in an array (§7.2.3).

- To program common array operations (displaying arrays, summing all elements, finding min and max elements, random shuffling, shifting elements) (§7.2.4).

- To apply arrays in application development (LottoNumbers, DeckOfCards) (§§7.3–7.4).

- To define and invoke functions with array arguments (§7.5).

- To define a const array parameter to prevent it from being changed (§7.6).

- To return an array by passing it as an argument (§7.7).

- To count occurrences of each letter in an array of characters (CountLettersInArray) (§7.8).

- To search elements using the linear (§7.9.1) or binary search algorithm (§7.9.2).

- To sort an array using the selection sort (§7.10).

- To represent strings using C-strings and use C-string functions (§7.11).

7.1 Introduction

**Key
Point**

A single array can store a large collection of data.

problem

Often, you will have to store a large number of values during the execution of a program. Suppose, for instance, that you need to read 100 numbers, compute their average, and determine how many numbers are above the average. First, your program reads the numbers and computes their average, and then compares each number with the average to determine whether it is above the average. To accomplish this, the numbers must all be stored in variables. You have to declare 100 variables and repeatedly write almost identical code 100 times. Writing a program this way would be impractical. So, how do you solve this problem?

array?

An efficient, organized approach is needed. C++ and most other high-level languages provide a data structure, the *array*, which stores a fixed-size sequential collection of elements of the same type. In the present case, you can store all 100 numbers into an array and access them through a single array variable. The solution is given in Listing 7.1.

LISTING 7.1 AnalyzeNumbers.cpp

```
 1  #include <iostream>
 2  using namespace std;
 3
 4  int main()
 5  {
 6    const int NUMBER_OF_ELEMENTS = 100;
 7    double numbers[NUMBER_OF_ELEMENTS];
 8    double sum = 0;
 9
10    for (int i = 0; i < NUMBER_OF_ELEMENTS; i++)
11    {
12      cout << "Enter a new number: ";
13      cin >> numbers[i];
14      sum += numbers[i];
15    }
16
17    double average = sum / NUMBER_OF_ELEMENTS;
18
19    int count = 0; // The number of elements above average
20    for (int i = 0; i < NUMBER_OF_ELEMENTS; i++)
21      if (numbers[i] > average)
22        count++;
23
24    cout << "Average is " << average << endl;
25    cout << "Number of elements above the average " << count << endl;
26
27    return 0;
28  }
```

declare array

store number in array

get average

above average?

numbers   array

numbers[0]:
numbers[1]:
numbers[2]:

numbers[i]:

numbers[97]:
numbers[98]:
numbers[99]:

The program declares an array of **100** elements in line 7, stores numbers into the array in line 13, adds each number to **sum** in line 11, and obtains the average in line 17. Then it compares each number in the array with the average to count the number of values above the average (lines 19–22).

You will be able to write this program after completing this chapter. This chapter introduces single-dimensional arrays. Chapter 8 will introduce two-dimensional and multidimensional arrays.

7.2 Array Basics

An array is used to store multiple values of the same type. An element in an array can be accessed using an index.

Key Point

An array is used to store a collection of data, but often it is more useful to think of an array as a collection of variables of the same type. Instead of declaring individual variables, such as `number0`, `number1`, . . . , and `number99`, you declare one array with a name such as numbers and use `numbers[0]`, `numbers[1]`, . . . , and `numbers[99]` to represent individual variables. This section introduces how to declare arrays and access array elements using indexes.

index

7.2.1 Declaring Arrays

To declare an array, you need to specify its *element type* and size using the following syntax:

```
elementType arrayName[SIZE];
```

The `elementType` can be any data type, and all elements in the array will have the same data type. The `SIZE`, known as *array size declarator*, must be an expression that evaluates to a constant integer greater than zero. For example, the following statement declares an array of 10 `double` elements:

array size declarator

```
double myList[10];
```

The compiler allocates the space for 10 `double` elements for array `myList`. When an array is declared, its elements are assigned arbitrary values. To assign values we use the following syntax:

arbitrary initial values

```
arrayName[index] = value;
```

For example, the following code initializes the array:

```
myList[0] = 5.6;
myList[1] = 4.5;
myList[2] = 3.3;
myList[3] = 13.2;
myList[4] = 4.0;
myList[5] = 34.33;
myList[6] = 34.0;
myList[7] = 45.45;
myList[8] = 99.993;
myList[9] = 111.23;
```

The array is pictured in Figure 7.1.

Note

The array size used to declare an array must be a constant expression in standard C++. For example, the following code is illegal:

constant size

```
int size = 4;
double myList[size]; // Wrong
```

But it is all right if `SIZE` is a constant as follows:

```
const int SIZE = 4;
double myList[SIZE]; // Correct
```

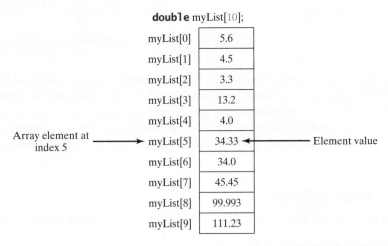

FIGURE 7.1 The array `myList` has 10 elements of `double` type and `int` indices from 0 to 9.

declaring together

Tip

If arrays have the same element type, they can be declared together, as follows:

```
elementType arrayName1[size1], arrayName2[size2], ...,
    arrayNamen[sizeN];
```

The arrays are separated by commas. For example,

```
double list1[10], list2[25];
```

7.2.2 Accessing Array Elements

array index
0-based

The array elements are accessed through the integer index. Array indices are *0-based*; that is, they run from 0 to `arraySize-1`. The first element is assigned the index 0, the second element is assigned 1, and so on. In the example in Figure 7.1, `myList` holds 10 `double` values, and the indices are from 0 to 9.

Each element in the array is represented using the following syntax:

```
arrayName[index];
```

For example, `myList[9]` represents the last element in the array `myList`. Note that the *size declarator* is used to indicate the number of elements when declaring the *array*. An array index is used to access a specific element in an array.

Each element in the array, when accessed by its index, can be used in the same way as a regular variable. For example, the following code adds the values in `myList[0]` and `myList[1]` to `myList[2]`.

```
myList[2] = myList[0] + myList[1];
```

The following code increments `myList[0]` by 1:

```
myList[0]++;
```

The following code invokes the `max` function to return the larger number between `myList[1]` and `myList[2]`:

```
cout << max(myList[1], myList[1]) << endl;
```

The following loop assigns 0 to myList[0], 1 to myList[1], ..., and 9 to myList[9]:

```
for (int i = 0; i < 10; i++)
{
  myList[i] = i;
}
```

Caution

Accessing array elements using indexes beyond the boundaries (e.g., myList[-1] and myList[10]) causes an out-of-bounds error. Out of bounds is a serious error. Unfortunately, the C++ compiler does not report it. Be careful to ensure that array indexes are within bounds.

out-of-bounds error

7.2.3 Array Initializers

C++ has a shorthand notation, known as the *array initializer*, which declares and initializes an array in a single statement, using the following syntax:

array initializer

```
elementType arrayName[arraySize] = {value0, value1, ..., valuek};
```

For example,

```
double myList[4] = {1.9, 2.9, 3.4, 3.5};
```

This statement declares and initializes the array **myList** with four elements, making it equivalent to the statements shown below:

```
double myList[4];
myList[0] = 1.9;
myList[1] = 2.9;
myList[2] = 3.4;
myList[3] = 3.5;
```

Caution

Using an array initializer, you must declare and initialize the array in one statement. Splitting it would cause a syntax error. Thus, the next statement is wrong:

```
double myList[4];
myList = {1.9, 2.9, 3.4, 3.5};
```

Note

C++ allows you to omit the array size when declaring and creating an array using an initializer. For example, the following declaration is fine:

implicit size

```
double myList[] = {1.9, 2.9, 3.4, 3.5};
```

The compiler automatically figures out how many elements are in the array.

Note

C++ allows you to initialize a part of the array. For example, the following statement assigns values 1.9, 2.9 to the first two elements of the array. The other two elements will be set to zero.

partial initialization

```
double myList[4] = {1.9, 2.9};
```

Note that if an array is declared, but not initialized, all its elements will contain "garbage," like all other local variables.

7.2.4 Processing Arrays

When processing array elements, you will often use a **for** loop—for the following reasons:

- All of the elements in an array are of the same type. They are evenly processed in the same way using a loop.

- Since the size of the array is known, it is natural to use a **for** loop.

Assume the array is declared as follows:

```
const int ARRAY_SIZE = 10;
double myList[ARRAY_SIZE];
```

Here are 10 examples of processing arrays:

1. *Initialing arrays with input values*: The following loop initializes the array **myList** with user input values:

```
cout << "Enter " << ARRAY_SIZE << " values: ";
for (int i = 0; i < ARRAY_SIZE; i++)
  cin >> myList[i];
```

2. *Initializing arrays with random values*: The following loop initializes the array **myList** with random values between **0** and **99**:

```
for (int i = 0; i < ARRAY_SIZE; i++)
{
  myList[i] = rand() % 100;
}
```

3. *Printing arrays*: To print an array, you must print each element in it, using a loop like the following:

```
for (int i = 0; i < ARRAY_SIZE; i++)
{
  cout << myList[i] << " ";
}
```

4. *Copying arrays*: Suppose you have two arrays, **list** and **myList**. Can you copy **myList** to **list** using a syntax like the following?

```
list = myList;
```

This is not allowed in C++. You must copy individual elements from one array to the other as follows:

```
for (int i = 0; i < ARRAY_SIZE; i++)
{
  list[i] = myList[i];
}
```

5. *Summing all elements*: Use a variable named **total** to store the sum. Initially, **total** is **0**. Add each element in the array to **total** using a loop like this:

```
double total = 0;
for (int i = 0; i < ARRAY_SIZE; i++)
{
  total += myList[i];
}
```

6. *Finding the largest element*: Use a variable named **max** to store the largest element. Initially, **max** is **myList[0]**. To find the largest element in the array **myList**, compare each element in it with **max**, and then update **max** if the element is greater than **max**.

```
double max = myList[0];
for (int i = 1; i < ARRAY_SIZE; i++)
{
  if (myList[i] > max) max = myList[i];
}
```

7. *Finding the smallest index of the largest element*: Often you need to locate the largest element in an array. If an array has multiple elements with the same largest value, find the smallest index of such an element. Suppose the array `myList` is {1, 5, 3, 4, 5, 5}. So, the largest element is 5 and the smallest index for 5 is 1. Use a variable named `max` to store the largest element and a variable named `indexOfMax` to denote the index of the largest element. Initially `max` is `myList[0]` and `indexOfMax` is 0. Compare each element in `myList` with `max`. If the element is greater than `max`, update `max` and `indexOfMax`.

```
double max = myList[0];
int indexOfMax = 0;

for (int i = 1; i < ARRAY_SIZE; i++)
{
  if (myList[i] > max)
  {
    max = myList[i];
    indexOfMax = i;
  }
}
```

What is the consequence if `(myList[i] > max)` is replaced by `(myList[i] >= max)`?

8. *Random shuffling*: In many applications, you need to reorder the elements in an array randomly. This is called *shuffling*. To accomplish this, for each element `myList[i]`, randomly generate an index `j` and swap `myList[i]` with `myList[j]`, as follows:

```
srand(time(0));

for (int i = ARRAY_SIZE - 1; i > 0; i--)
{
  // Generate an index j randomly with 0 <= j <=i
  int j = rand() % (i + 1);

  // Swap myList[i] with myList[j]
  double temp = myList[i];
  myList[i] = myList[j]
  myList[j] = temp;
}
```

9. *Shifting elements*: Sometimes you need to shift the elements left or right. For example, you may shift the elements one position to the left and fill the last element with the first element:

```
double temp = myList[0]; // Retain the first element

// Shift elements left
for (int i = 1; i < ARRAY_SIZE; i++)
{
  myList[i - 1] = myList[i];
}

// Move the first element to fill in the last position
myList[ARRAY_SIZE - 1] = temp;
```

10. *Simplifying coding*: Arrays can be used to simplify coding for certain tasks. For example, suppose you want to obtain the English name of a given month by its number. If the month names are stored in an array, the month name for a given month can be accessed simply via the index. The following code prompts the user to enter a month number and displays its month name:

```
string months[] = {"January", "February", ..., "December"};
cout << "Enter a month number (1 to 12): ";
int monthNumber;
cin >> monthNumber;
cout << "The month is " << months[monthNumber - 1] << endl;
```

If you didn't use the `months` array, you would have to determine the month name using a lengthy multiway `if-else` statement as follows:

```
if (monthNumber == 1)
  cout << "The month is January" << endl;
else if (monthNumber == 2)
  cout << "The month is February" << endl;
...
else
  cout << "The month is December" << endl;
```

Caution

off-by-one error

Programmers often mistakenly reference the first element in an array with index 1. This is called the *off-by-one error*. It is a common error in a loop to use <= where < should be used. For example, the following loop is wrong:

```
for (int i = 0; i <= ARRAY_SIZE; i++)
  cout << list[i] << " ";
```

The <= should be replaced by <.

Tip

checking index bounds

Since C++ does not check the array's bound, you should pay special attention to ensure that the indexes are within the range. Check the first and the last iteration in a loop to see whether the indexes are in the permitted range.

Check Point

7.1 How do you declare an array? What is the difference between an array size declarator and an array index?

7.2 How do you access elements of an array? Can you copy an array **a** to **b** using **b** = **a**?

7.3 Is memory allocated when an array is declared? Do the elements in the array have default values? What happens when the following code is executed?

```
int numbers[30];
cout << "numbers[0] is " << numbers[0] << endl;
cout << "numbers[29] is " << numbers[29] << endl;
cout << "numbers[30] is " << numbers[30] << endl;
```

7.4 Indicate true or false for the following statements:
- Every element in an array has the same type.
- The array size is fixed after it is declared.
- The array size declarator must be a constant expression.
- The array elements are initialized when an array is declared.

7.5 Which of the following statements are valid array declarations?

```
double d[30];
char[30] r;
int i[] = (3, 4, 3, 2);
float f[] = {2.3, 4.5, 6.6};
```

7.6 What is the array index type? What is the smallest index? What is the representation of the third element in an array named a?

7.7 Write C++ statements to do the following:

a. Declare an array to hold 10 double values.

b. Assign value 5.5 to the last element in the array.

c. Display the sum of the first two elements.

d. Write a loop that computes the sum of all elements in the array.

e. Write a loop that finds the minimum element in the array.

f. Randomly generate an index and display the element at this index in the array.

g. Use an array initializer to declare another array with initial values 3.5, 5.5, 4.52, and 5.6.

7.8 What happens when your program attempts to access an array element with an invalid index?

7.9 Identify and fix the errors in the following code:

```
1  int main()
2  {
3     double[100] r;
4
5     for (int i = 0; i < 100; i++);
6        r(i) = rand() % 100;
7  }
```

7.10 What is the output of the following code?

```
int list[] = {1, 2, 3, 4, 5, 6};

for (int i = 1; i < 6; i++)
  list[i] = list[i - 1];

for (int i = 0; i < 6; i++)
  cout << list[i] << " ";
```

7.3 Problem: Lotto Numbers

The problem is to write a program that checks if all the input numbers cover 1 to 99.

Key Point

Each Pick-10 lotto ticket has 10 unique numbers ranging from 1 to 99. Suppose you buy a lot of tickets and would like to have them cover all numbers from 1 to 99. Write a program that reads the ticket numbers from a file and checks whether all numbers are covered. Assume the last number in the file is 0. Suppose the file contains the numbers

```
80 3 87 62 30 90 10 21 46 27
12 40 83 9 39 88 95 59 20 37
80 40 87 67 31 90 11 24 56 77
11 48 51 42 8 74 1 41 36 53
```

```
52 82 16 72 19 70 44 56 29 33
54 64 99 14 23 22 94 79 55 2
60 86 34 4 31 63 84 89 7 78
43 93 97 45 25 38 28 26 85 49
47 65 57 67 73 69 32 71 24 66
92 98 96 77 6 75 17 61 58 13
35 81 18 15 5 68 91 50 76
0
```

Your program should display

```
The tickets cover all numbers
```

Suppose the file contains the numbers

```
11 48 51 42 8 74 1 41 36 53
52 82 16 72 19 70 44 56 29 33
0
```

Your program should display

```
The tickets don't cover all numbers
```

How do you mark a number as covered? You can declare an array with **99 bool** elements. Each element in the array can be used to mark whether a number is covered. Let the array be **isCovered**. Initially, each element is **false**, as shown in Figure 7.2a. Whenever a number is read, its corresponding element is set to **true**. Suppose the numbers entered are **1, 2, 3, 99, 0**. When number **1** is read, **isCovered[1 - 1]** is set to **true** (see Figure 7.2b). When number **2** is read, **isCovered[2 - 1]** is set to **true** (see Figure 7.2c). When number **3** is read, **isCovered[3 - 1]** is set to **true** (see Figure 7.2d). When number **99** is read, set **isCovered[99 - 1]** to **true** (see Figure 7.2e).

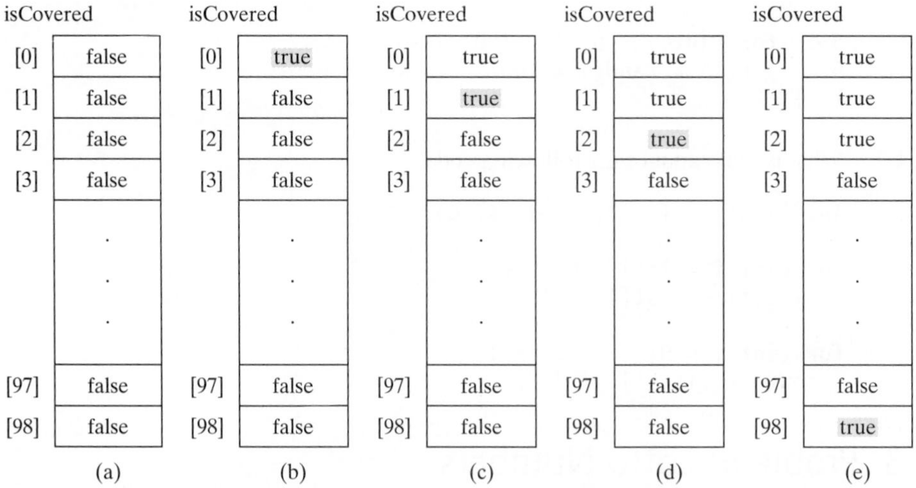

isCovered		isCovered		isCovered		isCovered		isCovered	
[0]	false	[0]	true	[0]	true	[0]	true	[0]	true
[1]	false	[1]	false	[1]	true	[1]	true	[1]	true
[2]	false	[2]	false	[2]	false	[2]	true	[2]	true
[3]	false	[3]	false	[3]	false	[3]	false	[3]	false
	.		.		.		.		.
	.		.		.		.		.
	.		.		.		.		.
[97]	false	[97]	false	[97]	false	[97]	false	[97]	false
[98]	false	[98]	false	[98]	false	[98]	false	[98]	true
(a)		(b)		(c)		(d)		(e)	

FIGURE 7.2 If number i appears in a lotto ticket, isCovered[i-1] is set to true.

The algorithm for the program can be described as follows:

```
for each number k read from the file,
  mark number k as covered by setting isCovered[k - 1] true;

if every isCovered[i] is true
  The tickets cover all numbers
else
  The tickets don't cover all numbers
```

The complete program is given in Listing 7.2.

LISTING 7.2   LottoNumbers.cpp

VideoNote
Lotto numbers

```cpp
 1  #include <iostream>
 2  using namespace std;
 3
 4  int main()
 5  {
 6    bool isCovered[99];                                    declare array
 7    int number; // number read from a file
 8
 9    // Initialize the array
10    for (int i = 0; i < 99; i++)
11      isCovered[i] = false;                               initialize array
12
13    // Read each number and mark its corresponding element covered
14    cin >> number;                                        read number
15    while (number != 0)
16    {
17      isCovered[number - 1] = true;                       mark number covered
18      cin >> number;                                      read number
19    }
20
21    // Check if all covered
22    bool allCovered = true; // Assume all covered initially
23    for (int i = 0; i < 99; i++)
24      if (!isCovered[i])                                  check allCovered?
25      {
26        allCovered = false; // Find one number not covered
27        break;
28      }
29
30    // Display result
31    if (allCovered)
32      cout << "The tickets cover all numbers" << endl;
33    else
34      cout << "The tickets don't cover all numbers" << endl;
35
36    return 0;
37  }
```

Suppose you have created a text file named LottoNumbers.txt that contains the input data 2 5 6 5 4 3 23 43 2 0. You can run the program using the following command:

```
g++ LottoNumbers.cpp -o LottoNumbers.exe
LottoNumbers.exe < LottoNumbers.txt
```

The program can be traced as follows:

Line#	Representative elements in array isCovered							number	allCovered
	[1]	[2]	[3]	[4]	[5]	[22]	[42]		
11	false	false	false	false	false	false	false		
14								2	
17	true								
18								5	
17				true					

(continued)

	Representative elements in array `isCovered`								
Line#	[1]	[2]	[3]	[4]	[5]	[22]	[42]	number	allCovered
18								6	
17					true				
18								5	
17				true					
18								4	
17			true						
18								3	
17		true							
18								23	
17						true			
18								43	
17							true		
18								2	
17	true								
18								0	
22									true
24(i=0)									false

The program declares an array of **99 bool** elements (line 6) and initializes each element to **false** (lines 10–11). It reads the first number from the file (line 14). The program then repeats the following operations in a loop:

- If the number is not zero, set its corresponding value in array `isCovered` to `true` (line 17);

- Read the next number (line 18).

When the input is **0**, the input ends. The program checks whether all numbers are covered in lines 22–28 and displays the result in lines 31–34.

7.4 Problem: Deck of Cards

Key Point

The problem is to create a program that will randomly select four cards from a deck of 52 cards.

All the cards can be represented using an array named **deck**, filled with initial values 0 to 51, as follows:

```
int deck[52];

// Initialize cards
for (int i = 0; i < NUMBER_OF_CARDS; i++)
  deck[i] = i;
```

Card numbers **0** to **12**, **13** to **25**, **26** to **38**, **39** to **51** represent 13 spades, 13 hearts, 13 diamonds, and 13 clubs, respectively, as shown in Figure 7.3. **cardNumber / 13** determines the suit of the card and **cardNumber % 13** determines the rank of the card, as shown in Figure 7.4. After shuffling the array **deck**, pick the first four cards from **deck**.

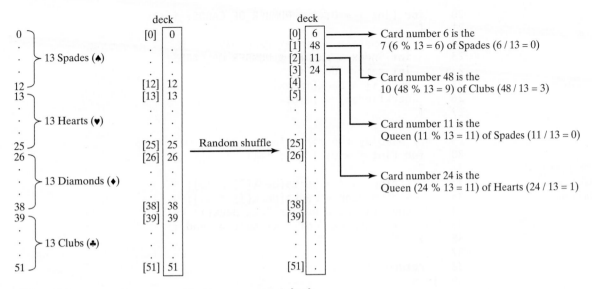

FIGURE 7.3 Fifty-two cards are stored in an array named **deck**.

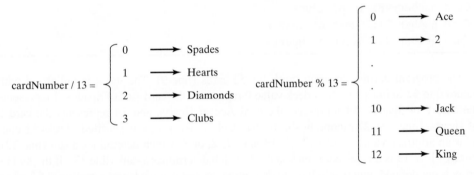

FIGURE 7.4 A card number identifies to a card.

Listing 7.3 gives the solution to the problem.

LISTING 7.3 DeckOfCards.cpp

```cpp
1   #include <iostream>
2   #include <ctime>
3   #include <string>
4   using namespace std;
5
6   int main()
7   {
8     const int NUMBER_OF_CARDS = 52;
9     int deck[NUMBER_OF_CARDS];                                    declare array deck
10    string suits[] = {"Spades", "Hearts", "Diamonds", "Clubs"};   declare array suits
11    string ranks[] = {"Ace", "2", "3", "4", "5", "6", "7", "8", "9",   declare array ranks
12      "10", "Jack", "Queen", "King"};
13
14    // Initialize cards
15    for (int i = 0; i < NUMBER_OF_CARDS; i++)
16      deck[i] = i;                                                initialize deck
17
18    // Shuffle the cards                                          shuffle deck
19    srand(time(0));
```

```
20     for (int i = 0; i < NUMBER_OF_CARDS; i++)
21     {
22       // Generate an index randomly
23       int index = rand() % NUMBER_OF_CARDS;
24       int temp = deck[i];
25       deck[i] = deck[index];
26       deck[index] = temp;
27     }
28
29     // Display the first four cards
30     for (int i = 0; i < 4; i++)
31     {
32       string suit = suits[deck[i] / 13];
33       string rank = ranks[deck[i] % 13];
34       cout << "Card number " << deck[i] << ": "
35         << rank << " of " << suit << endl;
36     }
37
38     return 0;
39   }
```

display suit
display rank

```
Card number 6: 7 of Spades
Card number 48: 10 of Clubs
Card number 11: Queen of Spades
Card number 24: Queen of Hearts
```

The program defines an array deck for 52 cards (line 9). The deck is initialized with values 0 to 51 in lines 15–16. A deck value 0 represents the card Ace of Spades, 1 represents the card 2 of Spades, 13 represents the card Ace of Hearts, and 14 represents the card 2 of Hearts. Lines 20–27 randomly shuffle the deck. After a deck is shuffled, deck[i] contains an arbitrary value. deck[i] / 13 is 0, 1, 2, or 3, which determines a suit (line 32). deck[i] % 13 is a value between 0 and 12, which determines a rank (line 33). If the suits array is not defined, you would have to determine the suit using a lengthy multiway if-else statement as follows:

```
if (deck[i] / 13 == 0)
  cout << "suit is Spades" << endl;
else if (deck[i] / 13 == 1)
  cout << "suit is Heart" << endl;
else if (deck[i] / 13 == 2)
  cout << "suit is Diamonds" << endl;
else
  cout << "suit is Clubs" << endl;
```

With suits = {"Spades", "Hearts", "Diamonds", "Clubs"} declared as an array, suits[deck / 13] gives the suit for the deck. Using arrays greatly simplifies the solution for this program.

7.5 Passing Arrays to Functions

Key Point

When an array argument is passed to a function, its starting address is passed to the array parameter in the function. Both parameter and argument refer to the same array.

Just as you can pass single values to a function, you also can pass an entire array to a function. Listing 7.4 gives an example to demonstrate how to declare and invoke this type of function.

LISTING 7.4   PassArrayDemo.cpp

```cpp
1   #include <iostream>
2   using namespace std;
3
4   void printArray(int list[], int arraySize); // Function prototype
5
6   int main()
7   {
8     int numbers[5] = {1, 4, 3, 6, 8};
9     printArray(numbers, 5); // Invoke the function
10
11    return 0;
12  }
13
14  void printArray(int list[], int arraySize)
15  {
16    for (int i = 0; i < arraySize; i++)
17    {
18      cout << list[i] << " ";
19    }
20  }
```

function prototype

declare array
invoke function

function implementation

```
1 4 3 6 8
```

In the function header (line 14), `int list[]` specifies that the parameter is an integer array of any size. Therefore, you can pass any integer array to invoke this function (line 9). Note that the parameter names in function prototypes can be omitted. So, the function prototype may be declared without the parameter names `list` and `arraySize` as follows:

```cpp
void printArray(int [], int); // Function prototype
```

> **Note**
>
> Normally when you pass an array to a function, you should also pass its size in another argument, so that the function knows how many elements are in the array. Otherwise, you will have to hard code this into the function or declare it in a global variable. Neither is flexible or robust.

passing size along with array

C++ uses *pass-by-value* to pass array arguments to a function. There are important differences between passing the values of variables of primitive data types and passing arrays.

pass-by-value

- For an argument of a primitive type, the argument's value is passed.

- For an argument of an array type, the value of the argument is the starting memory address to an array; this value is passed to the array parameter in the function. Semantically, it can be best described as *pass-by-sharing*, that is, the array in the function is the same as the array being passed. Thus, if you change the array in the function, you will see the change outside the function. Listing 7.5 gives an example that demonstrates this effect.

LISTING 7.5   EffectOfPassArrayDemo.cpp

```cpp
1   #include <iostream>
2   using namespace std;
3
4   void m(int, int []);
5
```

function prototype

```
6  int main()
7  {
8    int x = 1; // x represents an int value
9    int y[10]; // y represents an array of int values
10   y[0] = 1; // Initialize y[0]
11
12   m(x, y); // Invoke m with arguments x and y
13
14   cout << "x is " << x << endl;
15   cout << "y[0] is " << y[0] << endl;
16
17   return 0;
18 }
19
20 void m(int number, int numbers[])
21 {
22   number = 1001; // Assign a new value to number
23   numbers[0] = 5555; // Assign a new value to numbers[0]
24 }
```

pass array y (line 12)

modify array (line 23)

```
x is 1
y[0] is 5555
```

You will see that after function m is invoked, x remains 1, but y[0] is 5555. This is because the value of x is copied to number, and x and number are independent variables, but y and numbers reference to the same array. numbers can be considered as an alias for array y.

7.6 Preventing Changes of Array Arguments in Functions

Key Point

You can define const *array parameter in a function to prevent it from being changed in a function.*

Passing an array merely passes the starting memory address of the array. The array elements are not copied. This makes sense for conserving memory space. However, using array arguments could lead to errors if your function accidentally changed the array. To prevent this, you can put the const keyword before the array parameter to tell the compiler that the array cannot be changed. The compiler will report errors if the code in the function attempts to modify the array.

const array

Listing 7.6 gives an example that declares a const *array* argument list in the function p (line 4). In line 7, the function attempts to modify the first element in the array. This error is detected by the compiler, as shown in the sample output.

LISTING 7.6 ConstArrayDemo.cpp

```
1  #include <iostream>
2  using namespace std;
3
4  void p(const int list[], int arraySize)
5  {
6    // Modify array accidentally
7    list[0] = 100; // Compile error!
8  }
9
```

const array argument (line 4)

attempt to modify (line 7)

```
10  int main()
11  {
12    int numbers[5] = {1, 4, 3, 6, 8};
13    p(numbers, 5);
14
15    return 0;
16  }
```

Compiled using
Visual C++ 2012

```
error C3892: "list": you cannot assign to a variable that is const
```

Compiled using
GNU C++

```
ConstArrayDemo.cpp:7: error: assignment of read-only location
```

 Note

If you define a **const** parameter in a function **f1** and this parameter is passed to
another function **f2**, then the corresponding parameter in function **f2** must be declared
const for consistency. Consider the following code:

cascading **const** parameters

```
void f2(int list[], int size)
{
    // Do something
}

void f1(const int list[], int size)
{
    // Do something
    f2(list, size);
}
```

The compiler reports an error, because **list** is **const** in **f1** and it is passed to **f2**, but
it is not **const** in **f2**. The function declaration for **f2** should be

```
void f2(const int list[], int size)
```

7.7 Returning Arrays from Functions

To return an array from a function, pass it as a parameter in a function.

 Key Point

You can declare a function to return a primitive type value or an object. For example,

```
// Return the sum of the elements in the list
int sum(const int list[], int size)
```

Can you return an array from a function using a similar syntax? For example, you may
attempt to declare a function that returns a new array that is a reversal of an array, as follows:

```
// Return the reversal of list
int[] reverse(const int list[], int size)
```

This is not allowed in C++. However, you can circumvent this restriction by passing two
array arguments in the function:

```
// newList is the reversal of list
void reverse(const int list[], int newList[], int size)
```

The program is given in Listing 7.7.

VideoNote
Reverse array

LISTING 7.7 ReverseArray.cpp

```
 1  #include <iostream>
 2  using namespace std;
 3
 4  // newList is the reversal of list
 5  void reverse(const int list[], int newList[], int size)
 6  {
 7    for (int i = 0, j = size - 1; i < size; i++, j--)
 8    {
 9      newList[j] = list[i];
10    }
11  }
12
13  void printArray(const int list[], int size)
14  {
15    for (int i = 0; i < size; i++)
16      cout << list[i] << " ";
17  }
18
19  int main()
20  {
21    const int SIZE = 6;
22    int list[] = {1, 2, 3, 4, 5, 6};
23    int newList[SIZE];
24
25    reverse(list, newList, SIZE);
26
27    cout << "The original array: ";
28    printArray(list, SIZE);
29    cout << endl;
30
31    cout << "The reversed array: ";
32    printArray(newList, SIZE);
33    cout << endl;
34
35    return 0;
36  }
```

reverse function

reverse to newList

print array

declare original array
declare new array

invoke reverse

print original array

print reversed array

```
The original array: 1 2 3 4 5 6
The reversed array: 6 5 4 3 2 1
```

The **reverse** function (lines 5–11) uses a loop to copy the first element, second, . . . , and so on in the original array to the last element, second last, . . . , in the new array, as shown in the following diagram:

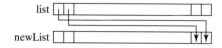

To invoke this function (line 25), you have to pass three arguments. The first argument is the original array, whose contents are not changed in the function. The second argument is the new array, whose contents are changed in the function. The third argument indicates the size of the array.

7.11 When an array is passed to a function, a new array is created and passed to the function. Is this true?

Check
Point

7.12 Show the output of the following two programs:

```cpp
#include <iostream>
using namespace std;

void m(int x, int y[])
{
  x = 3;
  y[0] = 3;
}

int main()
{
  int number = 0;
  int numbers[1];

  m(number, numbers);

  cout << "number is " << number
    << " and numbers[0] is " << numbers[0];

  return 0;
}
```
(a)

```cpp
#include <iostream>
using namespace std;

void reverse(int list[], int size)
{
  for (int i = 0; i < size / 2; i++)
  {
    int temp = list[i];
    list[i] = list[size - 1 - i];
    list[size - 1 - i] = temp;
  }
}

int main()
{
  int list[] = {1, 2, 3, 4, 5};
  int size = 5;
  reverse(list, size);
  for (int i = 0; i < size; i++)
    cout << list[i] << " ";

  return 0;
}
```
(b)

7.13 How do you prevent the array from being modified accidentally in a function?

7.14 Suppose the following code is written to reverse the characters in a string, explain why it is wrong.

```cpp
string s = "ABCD";
for (int i = 0, j = s.size() - 1; i < s.size(); i++, j--)
{
  // Swap s[i] with s[j]
  char temp = s[i];
  s[i] = s[j];
  s[j] = temp;
}

cout << "The reversed string is " << s << endl;
```

7.8 Problem: Counting the Occurrences of Each Letter

This section presents a program to count the occurrences of each letter in an array of characters.

The program does the following:

1. Generate 100 lowercase letters randomly and assign them to an array of characters, as shown in Figure 7.5a. As discussed in Section 4.4, "Case Study: Generating Random Characters," a random lowercase letter can be generated using

   static_cast<char>('a' + rand() % ('z' - 'a' + 1))

2. Count the occurrences of each letter in the array. To do so, declare an array, say **counts** of 26 **int** values, each of which counts the occurrences of a letter, as shown in Figure 7.5b. That is, **counts[0]** counts the number of **a**'s, **counts[1]** counts the number of **b**'s, and so on.

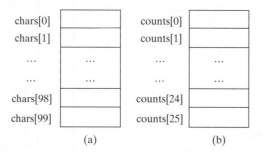

FIGURE 7.5 The **chars** array stores **100** characters and the **counts** array stores **26** counts, each counting the occurrences of a letter.

Listing 7.8 gives the complete program.

LISTING 7.8 CountLettersInArray.cpp

```cpp
1  #include <iostream>
2  #include <ctime>
3  using namespace std;
4
5  const int NUMBER_OF_LETTERS = 26;
6  const int NUMBER_OF_RANDOM_LETTERS = 100;
7  void createArray(char []);
8  void displayArray(const char []);
9  void countLetters(const char [], int []);
10 void displayCounts(const int []);
11
12 int main()
13 {
14   // Declare and create an array
15   char chars[NUMBER_OF_RANDOM_LETTERS];
16
17   // Initialize the array with random lowercase letters
18   createArray(chars);
19
20   // Display the array
21   cout << "The lowercase letters are: " << endl;
22   displayArray(chars);
```

26 letters
hundred letters
function prototypes

chars array

assign random letters

display array

```
23
24     // Count the occurrences of each letter
25     int counts[NUMBER_OF_LETTERS];                                      counts array
26
27     // Count the occurrences of each letter
28     countLetters(chars, counts);                                        count letters
29
30     // Display counts
31     cout << "\nThe occurrences of each letter are: " << endl;
32     displayCounts(counts);                                              display counts
33
34     return 0;
35   }
36
37   // Create an array of characters
38   void createArray(char chars[])
39   {                                                                     initialize array
40     // Create lowercase letters randomly and assign
41     // them to the array
42     srand(time(0));                                                     set a new seed
43     for (int i = 0; i < NUMBER_OF_RANDOM_LETTERS; i++)
44       chars[i] = static_cast<char>('a' + rand() % ('z' - 'a' + 1));     random letter
45   }
46
47   // Display the array of characters
48   void displayArray(const char chars[])
49   {
50     // Display the characters in the array 20 on each line
51     for (int i = 0; i < NUMBER_OF_RANDOM_LETTERS; i++)
52     {
53       if ((i + 1) % 20 == 0)
54         cout << chars[i] << " " << endl;
55       else
56         cout << chars[i] << " ";
57     }
58   }
59
60   // Count the occurrences of each letter
61   void countLetters(const char chars[], int counts[])                   count letter
62   {
63     // Initialize the array
64     for (int i = 0; i < NUMBER_OF_LETTERS; i++)
65       counts[i] = 0;
66
67     // For each lowercase letter in the array, count it
68     for (int i = 0; i < NUMBER_OF_RANDOM_LETTERS; i++)
69       counts[chars[i] - 'a'] ++;
70   }
71
72   // Display counts
73   void displayCounts(const int counts[])
74   {
75     for (int i = 0; i < NUMBER_OF_LETTERS; i++)
76     {
77       if ((i + 1) % 10 == 0)
78         cout << counts[i] << " " << static_cast<char>(i + 'a') << endl;  cast to char
79       else
80         cout << counts[i] << " " << static_cast<char>(i + 'a') << " ";
81     }
82   }
```

```
The lowercase letters are:
p y a o u n s u i b t h y g w q l b y o
x v b r i g h i x w v c g r a s p y i z
n f j v c j c a c v l a j r x r d t w q
m a y e v m k d m e m o j v k m e v t a
r m o u v d h f o o x d g i u w r i q h

The occurrences of each letter are:
6 a 3 b 4 c 4 d 3 e 2 f 4 g 4 h 6 i 4 j
2 k 2 l 6 m 2 n 6 o 2 p 3 q 6 r 2 s 3 t
4 u 8 v 4 w 4 x 5 y 1 z
```

The `createArray` function (lines 38–45) generates an array of 100 random lowercase letters and assigns them in array `chars`. The `countLetters` function (lines 61–70) counts the occurrence of letters in `chars` and stores the counts in the array `counts`. Each element in `counts` stores the number of occurrences of a letter. The function processes each letter in the array and increases its count by one. A brute force approach to count the occurrences of each letter might be as follows:

```
for (int i = 0; i < NUMBER_OF_RANDOM_LETTERS; i++)
  if (chars[i] == 'a')
    counts[0]++;
  else if (chars[i] == 'b')
    counts[1]++;
  ...
```

But a better solution is given in lines 68–69.

```
for (int i = 0; i < NUMBER_OF_RANDOM_LETTERS; i++)
  counts[chars[i] - 'a']++;
```

If the letter (`chars[i]`) is `'a'`, the corresponding count is `counts['a' - 'a']` (i.e., `counts[0]`). If the letter is `'b'`, the corresponding count is `counts['b' - 'a']` (i.e., `counts[1]`) since the ASCII code of `'b'` is one more than that of `'a'`. If the letter is `'z'`, the corresponding count is `counts['z' - 'a']` (i.e., `counts[25]`) since the ASCII code of `'z'` is 25 more than that of `'a'`.

7.9 Searching Arrays

Key Point

If an array is sorted, binary search is more efficient than linear search for finding an element in the array.

Searching is the process of looking for a specific element in an array—for example, discovering whether a certain score is included in a list of scores. Searching is a common task in computer programming. Many algorithms and data structures are devoted to searching. This section discusses two commonly used approaches: *linear search* and *binary search*.

linear search
binary search

7.9.1 The Linear Search Approach

The linear search approach compares the key element `key` sequentially with each element in the array. The function continues to do so until the key matches an element in the array or the array is exhausted. If a match is made, the linear search returns the index of the element in the array that matches the key. Otherwise, the search returns -1. The linearSearch function in Listing 7.9 gives the solution:

Linear search animation on Companion Website

LISTING 7.9   LinearSearch.cpp

```
int linearSearch(const int list[], int key, int arraySize)
{
  for (int i = 0; i < arraySize; i++)
  {
    if (key == list[i])
      return i;
  }
  return -1;
}
```

[0] [1] [2] ...

list

key Compare key with list[i] for i = 0, 1, ...

Please trace the function using the following statements:

```
int list[] = {1, 4, 4, 2, 5, -3, 6, 2};
int i = linearSearch(list, 4, 8);   // Returns 1
int j = linearSearch(list, -4, 8);  // Returns -1
int k = linearSearch(list, -3, 8);  // Returns 5
```

The linear search function compares the key with each element in the array. The elements in the array can be in any order. On average, the algorithm will have to compare half of the elements before finding the key if it exists. Since the execution time of a linear search increases linearly as the number of array elements increases, linear search is inefficient for a large array.

7.9.2   The Binary Search Approach

Binary search is the other common search approach for a list of values. It requires that the elements in the array already be ordered. Assume that the array is in ascending order. The binary search first compares the key with the element in the middle of the array. Consider the following cases:

- If the key is less than the middle element, you only need to continue to search in the first half of the array.

- If the key is equal to the middle element, the search ends with a match.

- If the key is greater than the middle element, you only need to continue to search in the second half of the array.

Clearly, the binary search function eliminates at least half of the array after each comparison. Sometimes you eliminate half of the elements, and sometimes you eliminate half plus one. Suppose that the array has n elements. For convenience, let n be a power of 2. After the first comparison, $n/2$ elements are left for further search; after the second comparison, $(n/2)/2$ elements are left for further search. After the kth comparison, $n/2^k$ elements are left for further search. When $k = \log_2 n$, only one element is left in the array, and you need only one more comparison. In the worst case, therefore, when using the binary search approach, you need $\log_2 n+1$ comparisons to find an element in the sorted array. In the worst case, for a list of 1024 (2^{10}) elements, binary search requires only eleven comparisons whereas a linear search requires 1024. The portion of the array being searched shrinks by half after each comparison. Let low and high denote, respectively, the first index and last index of the subarray. Initially, low is 0 and high is listSize-1. Let mid denote the index of the middle element. So mid is (low + high)/2. Figure 7.6 shows how to find key 11 in the list {2, 4, 7, 10, 11, 45, 50, 59, 60, 66, 69, 70, 79} using binary search.

Binary search animation on the Companion Website

308 Chapter 7   Single-Dimensional Arrays and C-Strings

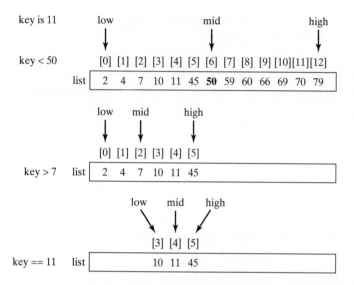

FIGURE 7.6   Binary search eliminates half of the list from further consideration after each comparison.

You now know how the binary search works. The next task is to implement it. Don't rush to give a complete implementation. Implement it incrementally, one step at a time. You may start with the first iteration of the search, as shown in Figure 7.7a. It compares the key with the middle element in the list whose `low` index is `0` and `high` index is `listSize - 1`. If `key < list[mid]`, set the `high` index to `mid - 1`; if `key == list[mid]`, a match is found and return `mid`; if `key > list[mid]`, set the `low` index to `mid + 1`.

```
int binarySearch(const int
    list[], listSize)
{
  int low = 0;
  int high = listSize - 1;


  int mid = (low + high) / 2;
  if (key < list[mid])
    high = mid - 1;
  else if (key == list[mid])
    return mid;
  else
    low = mid + 1;



}
```

(a) Version 1

```
int binarySearch(const int
    list[], listSize)
{
  int low = 0;
  int high = listSize - 1;

  while (low <= high)
  {
    int mid = (low + high) / 2;
    if (key < list[mid])
      high = mid - 1;
    else if (key == list[mid])
      return mid;
    else
      low = mid + 1;
  }

  return -1;
}
```

(b) Version 2

FIGURE 7.7   Binary search is implemented incrementally.

Next, consider how to implement the function to perform the search repeatedly by adding a loop, as shown in Figure 7.7b. The search ends if the key is found or the key is not found. Note that when `low > high`, the key is not in the array.

When the key is not found, `low` is the insertion point where a key would be inserted to maintain the order of the list. It is more useful to return the insertion point than −1. The function must return a negative value to indicate that the key is not in the list. Can it simply return −`low`? No. If key is less than `list[0]`, `low` would be 0. -0 is 0. This would indicate that key matches `list[0]`. A good choice is to let the function return −`low` − 1 if the key is not in the list. Returning −`low` − 1 not only indicates that the key is not in the list, but also where the key would be inserted in the list.

The binary search function is implemented in Listing 7.10.

LISTING 7.10 BinarySearch.cpp

```
1  int binarySearch(const int list[], int key, int listSize)
2  {
3    int low = 0;
4    int high = listSize - 1;
5
6    while (high >= low)
7    {
8      int mid = (low + high) / 2;
9      if (key < list[mid])
10       high = mid - 1;
11     else if (key == list[mid])
12       return mid;                              match found
13     else
14       low = mid + 1;
15   }
16
17   return -low - 1;                             no match
18 }
```

The binary search returns the index of the search key if it is contained in the list (line 12). Otherwise, it returns −`low` − 1 (line 17). What happens if `(high >= low)` in line 6 is replaced by `(high > low)`? The search would miss a possible matching element. Consider a list with just one element. The search would miss the element. Does the function still work if there are duplicate elements in the list? Yes, as long as the elements are sorted in non-decreasing order in the list. The function returns the index of one of the matching elements if the element is in the list.

To understand this function better, trace it with the following statements and identify `low` and `high` when the function returns.

```
int list[] = {2, 4, 7, 10, 11, 45, 50, 59, 60, 66, 69, 70, 79};
int i = binarySearch(list, 2, 13); // Returns 0
int j = binarySearch(list, 11, 13); // Returns 4
int k = binarySearch(list, 12, 13); // Returns −6
int l = binarySearch(list, 1, 13); // Returns −1
int m = binarySearch(list, 3, 13); // Returns −2
```

Here is the table that lists the `low` and `high` values when the function exits and the value returned from invoking the function.

Function	low	high	Value Returned
binarySearch (list, 2, 13)	0	1	0
binarySearch (list, 11, 13)	3	5	4
binarySearch (list, 12, 13)	5	4	−6
binarySearch (list, 1, 13)	0	−1	−1
binarySearch (list, 3, 13)	1	0	−2

binary search benefits

Note
Linear search is useful for finding an element in a small array or an unsorted array, but it is inefficient for large arrays. Binary search is more efficient, but requires that the array be presorted.

7.10 Sorting Arrays

 Key Point

selection sort

Selection sort animation on the Companion Website

Sorting, like searching, is a common task in computer programming. Many different algorithms have been developed for sorting. This section introduces an intuitive sorting algorithm: selection sort.

Suppose that you want to sort a list in ascending order. Selection sort finds the smallest number in the list and swaps it with the first. It then finds the smallest number remaining and swaps it with the next to first, and so on, until only a single number remains. Figure 7.8 shows how to sort the list {2, 9, 5, 4, 8, 1, 6} using selection sort.

VideoNote
Selection sort

		swap						

Select 1 (the smallest) and swap it with 2 (the first) in the list

2 9 5 4 8 1 6

The number 1 is now in the correct position and thus no longer needs to be considered.

1 9 5 4 8 2 6

Select 2 (the smallest) and swap it with 9 (the first) in the remaining list

The number 2 is now in the correct position and thus no longer needs to be considered.

1 2 5 4 8 9 6

Select 4 (the smallest) and swap it with 5 (the first) in the remaining list

The number 4 is now in the correct position and thus no longer needs to be considered.

1 2 4 5 8 9 6

5 is the smallest and in the right position. No swap is necessary

The number 5 is now in the correct position and thus no longer needs to be considered.

1 2 4 5 8 9 6

Select 6 (the smallest) and swap it with 8 (the first) in the remaining list

The number 6 is now in the correct position and thus no longer needs to be considered.

1 2 4 5 6 9 8

Select 8 (the smallest) and swap it with 9 (the first) in the remaining list

The number 8 is now in the correct position and thus no longer needs to be considered.

1 2 4 5 6 8 9

Since there is only one element remaining in the list, sort is completed

FIGURE 7.8 Selection sort repeatedly selects the smallest number and swaps it with the first number in the remaining list.

You know how the selection sort approach works. The task now is to implement it in C++. For beginners, it is difficult to develop a complete solution on the first attempt. You may start to write the code for the first iteration to find the smallest element in the list and swap it with the first element, and then observe what would be different for the second iteration, the third, and so on. The insight this gives will enable you to write a loop that generalizes all the iterations.

The solution can be described as follows:

```
for (int i = 0; i < listSize - 1; i++)
{
  select the smallest element in list[i..listSize-1];
  swap the smallest with list[i], if necessary;
  // list[i] is in its correct position.
  // The next iteration apply on list[i+1..listSize-1]
}
```

Listing 7.11 implements the solution.

LISTING 7.11 SelectionSort.cpp

```
1  void selectionSort(double list[], int listSize)
2  {
3    for (int i = 0; i < listSize - 1; i++)
4    {
5      // Find the minimum in the list[i..listSize-1]
6      double currentMin = list[i];
7      int currentMinIndex = i;
8
9      for (int j = i + 1; j < listSize; j++)
10     {
11       if (currentMin > list[j])
12       {
13         currentMin = list[j];
14         currentMinIndex = j;
15       }
16     }
17
18     // Swap list[i] with list[currentMinIndex] if necessary;
19     if (currentMinIndex != i)
20     {
21       list[currentMinIndex] = list[i];
22       list[i] = currentMin;
23     }
24   }
25 }
```

The `selectionSort(double list[], int listSize)` function sorts any array of `double` elements. The function is implemented with a nested `for` loop. The outer loop (with the loop-control variable `i`) (line 3) is iterated in order to find the smallest element in the list, which ranges from `list[i]` to `list[listSize - 1]`, and exchange it with `list[i]`.The variable `i` is initially `0`. After each iteration of the outer loop, `list[i]` is in the right place. Eventually, all the elements are put in the right place; therefore, the whole list is sorted. To understand this function better, trace it with the following statements:

```
double list[] = {1, 9, 4.5, 6.6, 5.7, -4.5};
selectionSort(list, 6);
```

Check
Point

7.15 Use Figure 7.6 as an example to show how to apply the binary search approach to search for key **10** and key **12** in list {**2**, **4**, **7**, **10**, **11**, **45**, **50**, **59**, **60**, **66**, **69**, **70**, **79**}.

7.16 Use Figure 7.8 as an example to show how to apply the selection-sort approach to sort {**3.4**, **5**, **3**, **3.5**, **2.2**, **1.9**, **2**}.

7.17 How do you modify the `selectionSort` function in Listing 7.11 to sort numbers in decreasing order?

7.11 C-Strings

Key Point

C-string is an array of characters that ends with the null terminator character `'\0'`. You can process C-strings using C-string functions in the C++ library.

C-strings vs. `string` type

Pedagogical Note

C-string is popular in the C language, but it has been replaced by a more robust, convenient, and useful **string** type in C++. For this reason, the **string** type, introduced in Chapter 4 is used to process strings in this book. The purpose of introducing C-strings in this section is to give additional examples and exercises using arrays and to enable you to work with the legacy C programs.

C-string
null terminator

A *C-string* is an array of characters ending with the *null terminator* (`'\0'`), which indicates where a string terminates in memory. Recall that a character that begins with the backslash symbol (\) is an escape sequence in Section 4.3.3, "Escape Sequences for Special Characters." The symbols \ and **0** (zero) together represent one character. This character is the first character in the ASCII table.

Every string literal is a C-string. You can declare an array initialized with a string literal. For example, the following statement creates an array for a C-string that contains characters `'D'`, `'a'`, `'l'`, `'l'`, `'a'`, `'s'`, and `'\0'`, as shown in Figure 7.9.

```
char city[7] = "Dallas";
```

'D'	'a'	'l'	'l'	'a'	's'	'\0'
city[0]	city[1]	city[2]	city[3]	city[4]	city[5]	city[6]

FIGURE 7.9 A character array can be initialized with a C-string.

Note that the size of the array is **7** and the last character in the array is `'\0'`. There is a subtle difference between a C-string and an array of characters. For example, the following two statements are different:

```
char city1[] = "Dallas"; // C-string
char city2[] = {'D', 'a', 'l', 'l', 'a', 's'}; // Not a C-string
```

The first statement is a C-string and the second statement is just an array of characters. The former has **7** characters including the last null terminator and the latter has **6** characters.

7.11.1 Input and Output of C-Strings

To output a C-string is simple. Suppose **s** is an array for a C-string. To display it to the console, simply use

```
cout << s;
```

You can read a C-string from the keyboard just as you do a number. For example, consider the following code:

```
1  char city[7];
2  cout << "Enter a city: ";
3  cin >> city; // Read to array city
4  cout << "You entered " << city << endl;
```

declare an array

read C-string

When you read a string to an array, be sure to leave room for the null terminator character. Since `city` has a size 7, your input should not exceed 6 characters. This approach to reading a string is simple, but there is a problem. The input ends with a whitespace character. You cannot read a string that contains a space. Suppose you want to enter New York; then you have to use an alternative approach. C++ provides the `cin.getline` function in the `iostream` header file, which reads a string into an array. The syntax of the function is as follows:

input size

```
cin.getline(char array[], int size, char delimitChar)
```

The function stops reading characters when the delimiter character is encountered or when the `size - 1` number of characters have been read. The last character in the array is reserved for the null terminator (`'\0'`). If the delimiter is encountered, it is read but is not stored in the array. The third argument `delimitChar` has a default value (`'\n'`). The following code uses the `cin.getline` function to read a string:

```
1  char city[30];
2  cout << "Enter a city: "; // i.e., New York
3  cin.getline(city, 30, '\n'); // Read to array city
4  cout << "You entered " << city << endl;
```

declare array

string to array

Since the default value for the third argument in the `cin.getline` function is `'\n'`, line 3 can be replaced by

```
cin.getline(city, 30); // Read to array city
```

7.11.2 C-String Functions

Given that a C-string ends with a null terminator, C++ can utilize this fact to process C-strings efficiently. When you pass a C-string to a function, you don't have to pass its length, because the length can be obtained by counting all characters from left to right in the array until the null terminator character is reached. Here is the function for obtaining the length of a C-string:

processing C-string

```
unsigned int strlen(char s[])
{
   int i = 0;
   for ( ; s[i] != '\0'; i++);
   return i;
}
```

In fact, `strlen` and several other functions are provided in the C++ library for processing C-strings, as shown in Table 7.1.

Note

`size_t` is a C++ type. For most compilers, it is the same as `unsigned int`.

type `size_t`

All these functions are defined in the `cstring` header file except that conversion functions `atoi`, `atof`, `atol`, and `itoa` are defined in the `cstdlib` function.

TABLE 7.1 String Functions

Function	Description
`size_t strlen(char s[])`	Returns the length of the string, i.e., the number of the characters before the null terminator.
`strcpy(char s1[], const char s2[])`	Copies string s2 to string s1.
`strncpy(char s1[], const char s2[], size_t n)`	Copies the first n characters from string s2 to string s1.
`strcat(char s1[], const char s2[])`	Appends string s2 to s1.
`strncat(char s1[], const char s2[], size_t n)`	Appends the first n characters from string s2 to s1.
`int strcmp(char s1[], const char s2[])`	Returns a value greater than 0, 0, or less than 0 if s1 is greater than, equal to, or less than s2 based on the numeric code of the characters.
`int strncmp(char s1[], const char s2[], size_t n)`	Same as strcmp, but compares up to n number of characters in s1 with those in s2.
`int atoi(char s[])`	Returns an int value for the string.
`double atof(char s[])`	Returns a double value for the string.
`long atol(char s[])`	Returns a long value for the string.
`void itoa(int value, char s[], int radix)`	Obtains an integer value to a string based on specified radix.

7.11.3 Copying Strings Using **strcpy** and **strncpy**

strcpy

Function **strcpy** can be used to copy a source string in the second argument to a target string in the first argument. The target string must have already been allocated sufficient memory for the function to work. A common mistake is to copy a C-string using code like this:

```
char city[30] = "Chicago";
city = "New York"; // Copy New York to city. Wrong!
```

In order to copy "New York" to city, you have to use

```
strcpy(city, "New York");
```

strncpy

The **strncpy** function works like **strcpy**, except that it takes a third argument specifying the number of the characters to be copied. For example, the following code copies the first three characters "New" to city.

```
char city[9];
strncpy(city, "New York", 3);
```

There is a problem with this code. The **strncpy** function does not append a null terminator to the target string if the specified number of characters is less than or equal to the length of the source string. If the specified number of characters is greater than the length of the source string, the source string is copied to the target padded with null terminators all the way up to the end of the target string. Both **strcpy** and **strncpy** can potentially override the bounds of an array. To ensure safe copying, check bounds before using these functions.

7.11.4 Concatenating Strings Using **strcat** and **strncat**

Function `strcat` can be used to append the string in the second argument to the string in the first argument. For the function to work, the first string must have already been allocated sufficient memory. For example, the following code works fine to append `s2` into `s1`.

`strcat`

```
char s1[7] = "abc";
char s2[4] = "def";
strcat(s1, s2);
cout << s1 << endl; // The printout is abcdef
```

However, the following code does not work, because there is no space to add `s2` into `s1`.

```
char s1[4] = "abc";
char s2[4] = "def";
strcat(s1, s2);
```

The `strncat` function works like `strcat`, except that it takes a third argument specifying the number of the characters to be concatenated from the target string with the source string. For example, the following code concatenates the first three characters `"ABC"` to `s`:

`strncat`

```
char s[9] = "abc";
strncat(s, "ABCDEF", 3);
cout << s << endl; // The printout is abcABC
```

Both `strcat` and `strncat` can potentially override the bounds of an array. To ensure safe concatenating, check bounds before using these functions.

7.11.5 Comparing Strings Using **strcmp**

Function `strcmp` can be used to compare two strings. How do you compare two strings? You compare their corresponding characters according to their numeric codes. Most compilers use the ASCII code for characters. The function returns the value 0 if `s1` is equal to `s2`, a value less than 0 if `s1` is less than `s2`, and a value greater than 0 if `s1` is greater than `s2`. For example, suppose `s1` is `"abc"` and `s2` is `"abg"`, and `strcmp(s1, s2)` returns a negative value. The first two characters (a vs. a) from `s1` and `s2` are compared. Because they are equal, the second two characters (b vs. b) are compared. Because they are also equal, the third two characters (c vs. g) are compared. Since the character c is 4 less than g, the comparison returns a negative value. Exactly what value is returned depends on the compiler. Visual C++ and GNU compilers return −1, but Borland C++ compiler returns −4 since the character c is 4 less than g.

`strcmp`

Here is an example of using the `strcmp` function:

```
char s1[] = "Good morning";
char s2[] = "Good afternoon";
if (strcmp(s1, s2) > 0)
  cout << "s1 is greater than s2" << endl;
else if (strcmp(s1, s2) == 0)
  cout << "s1 is equal to s2" << endl;
else
  cout << "s1 is less than s2" << endl;
```

It displays `s1 is greater than s2`.

The `strncmp` function works like `strcmp`, except that it takes a third argument specifying the number of the characters to be compared. For example, the following code compares the first four characters in the two strings.

`strncmp`

```
char s1[] = "Good morning";
char s2[] = "Good afternoon";
cout << strncmp(s1, s2, 4) << endl;
```

It displays 0.

7.11.6 Conversion between Strings and Numbers

atoi
atol

Function `atoi` can be used to convert a C-string into an integer of the `int` type and function `atol` can be used to convert a C-string into an integer of the `long` type. For example, the following code converts numerical strings `s1` and `s2` to integers:

```
char s1[] = "65";
char s2[] = "4";
cout << atoi(s1) + atoi(s2) << endl;
```

It displays 69.

atof

Function `atof` can be used to convert a C-string into a floating-point number. For example, the following code converts numerical strings `s1` and `s2` to floating-point numbers:

```
char s1[] = "65.5";
char s2[] = "4.4";
cout << atof(s1) + atof(s2) << endl;
```

It displays 69.9.

itoa

Function `itoa` can be used to convert an integer into a C-string based on a specified radix. For example, the following code

```
char s1[15];
char s2[15];
char s3[15];
itoa(100, s1, 16);
itoa(100, s2, 2);
itoa(100, s3, 10);
cout << "The hex number for 100 is " << s1 << endl;
cout << "The binary number for 100 is " << s2 << endl;
cout << "s3 is " << s3 << endl;
```

displays

```
The hex number for 100 is 64
The binary number for 100 is 1100100
s3 is 100
```

Note that some C++ compilers may not support the `itoa` function.

Check
Point

7.18 What are the differences between the following arrays?

```
char s1[] = {'a', 'b', 'c'};
char s2[] = "abc";
```

7.19 Suppose `s1` and `s2` are defined as follows:

```
char s1[] = "abc";
char s2[] = "efg";
```

Are the following expressions/statements correct?

a. `s1 = "good"`

b. `s1 < s2`

  c. `s1[0]`

  d. `s1[0] < s2[0]`

  e. `strcpy(s1, s2)`

  f. `strcmp(s1, s2)`

  g. `strlen(s1)`

KEY TERMS

array 286	C-string 312
array size declaratory 287	index 287
array index 288	linear search 306
array initializer 289	null terminator (`'\0'`) 312
binary search 306	selection sort 310
`const` array 300	

CHAPTER SUMMARY

1. An array stores a list of value of the same type.

2. An array is declared using the syntax

   ```
   elementType arrayName[size]
   ```

3. Each element in the array is represented using the syntax `arrayName[index]`.

4. An index must be an integer or an integer expression.

5. Array index is 0-based, meaning that the index for the first element is 0.

6. Programmers often mistakenly reference the first element in an array with index 1 rather than 0. This causes the *index off-by-one error*.

7. Accessing array elements using indexes beyond the boundaries causes out-of-bounds error.

8. Out of bounds is a serious error, but it is not checked automatically by the C++ compiler.

9. C++ has a shorthand notation, known as the *array initializer*, which declares and initializes an array in a single statement using the syntax:

   ```
   elementType arrayName[] = {value0, value1, ..., valuek};
   ```

10. When an array is passed to a function, the starting address of the array is passed to the array parameter in the function.

11. When you pass an array argument to a function, often you also should pass the size in another argument, so the function knows how many elements are in the array.

12. You can specify `const` array parameters to prevent arrays from being accidentally modified.

13. An array of characters that ends with a null terminator is called a C-string.

14. A string literal is a C-string.

15. C++ provides several functions for processing C-strings.

16. You can obtain a C-string length using the **strlen** function.

17. You can copy a C-string to another C-string using the **strcpy** function.

18. You can compare two C-strings using the **strcmp** function.

19. You can use the **itoa** function to convert an integer to a C-string, and use **atoi** to convert a string to an integer.

QUIZ

Answer the quiz for this chapter online at www.cs.armstrong.edu/liang/cpp3e/quiz.html.

PROGRAMMING EXERCISES

Sections 7.2–7.4

*7.1   (*Assign grades*) Write a program that reads student scores, gets the best score, and then assigns grades based on the following scheme:

Grade is A if score is $>=$ best $-$ 10;
Grade is B if score is $>=$ best $-$ 20;
Grade is C if score is $>=$ best $-$ 30;
Grade is D if score is $>=$ best $-$ 40;
Grade is F otherwise.

The program prompts the user to enter the total number of students, then prompts the user to enter all of the scores, and concludes by displaying the grades. Here is a sample run:

```
Enter the number of students: 4 ↵Enter
Enter 4 scores: 40 55 70 58 ↵Enter
Student 0 score is 40 and grade is C
Student 1 score is 55 and grade is B
Student 2 score is 70 and grade is A
Student 3 score is 58 and grade is B
```

7.2   (*Largest and Smallest integers*) Write a program that reads 6 integers and displays the largest and the smallest amongst those integers.

*7.3   (*Count occurrence of numbers*) Write a program that reads at most 100 integers between **1** and **100** and counts the occurrence of each number. Assume the input ends with **0**. Here is a sample run of the program:

```
Enter the integers between 1 and 100: 2 5 6 5 4 3 23 43 2 0 ↵Enter
2 occurs 2 times
3 occurs 1 time
4 occurs 1 time
5 occurs 2 times
6 occurs 1 time
23 occurs 1 time
43 occurs 1 time
```

Note that if a number occurs more than once, the plural word "times" is used in the output.

7.4 (*Count the number of Vowels and Consonants*) Write a program that reads an unspecified number of uppercase or lowercase alphabets, and determines how many of them are vowels and how many are consonants. Enter zero to signify the end of the input.

**7.5 (*Print distinct numbers*) Write a program that reads in 10 numbers and displays distinct numbers (i.e., if a number appears multiple times, it is displayed only once). (*Hint*: Read a number and store it to an array if it is new. If the number is already in the array, discard it. After the input, the array contains the distinct numbers.) Here is a sample run of the program:

```
Enter ten numbers: 1 2 3 2 1 6 3 4 5 2 ↵Enter
The distinct numbers are: 1 2 3 6 4 5
```

*7.6 (*Revise Listing 5.17, PrimeNumber.cpp*) Listing 5.17 determines whether a number n is prime by checking whether 2, 3, 4, 5, 6, . . . , n/2 is a divisor. If a divisor is found, n is not prime. A more efficient approach to determine whether n is prime is to check whether any of the prime numbers less than or equal to $\sqrt{n}$ can divide n evenly. If not, n is prime. Rewrite Listing 5.17 to display the first 50 prime numbers using this approach. You need to use an array to store the prime numbers and later use them to check whether they are possible divisors for n.

*7.7 (*Sum of Even random numbers*) Write a program that generates twenty five random integers between 0 and 25 and displays the sum of even integers. (*Hint*: Use rand() % 25 to generate a random integer between 0 and 25. Use an array of 25 integers, say num, to store the random integers generated between 0 and 25.)

Sections 7.5–7.7

7.8 (*Product of an array*) Write two overloaded functions that return the product of elements in an array with the following headers:

```
int product(const int array[], int size);
double product(const double array[], int size);
```

Write a test program that prompts the user to enter 3 double values, invokes this function, and displays the product of these values.

7.9 (*Find the smallest element*) Write a function that finds the smallest element in an array of double values using the following header:

```
double min(double array[], int size)
```

Write a test program that prompts the user to enter 10 numbers, invokes this function, and displays the minimum value. Here is a sample run of the program:

```
Enter ten numbers: 1.9 2.5 3.7 2 1.5 6 3 4 5 2  ↵Enter
The minimum number is 1.5
```

7.10 (*Find the index of the largest element*) Write a function that returns the index of the largest element in an array of integers. If there are more such elements than one, return the largest index. Use the following header:

```
int indexOfLargestElement(double array[], int size)
```

Write a test program that prompts the user to enter 15 numbers, invokes this function to return the index of the largest element, and displays the index.

VideoNote
Find standard deviation

*7.11 (*Statistics: compute deviation*) Programming Exercise 5.47 computes the standard deviation of numbers. This exercise uses a different but equivalent formula to compute the standard deviation of **n** numbers.

$$mean = \frac{\sum_{i=1}^{n} x_i}{n} = \frac{x_1 + x_2 + \ldots + x_n}{n} \quad deviation = \sqrt{\frac{\sum_{i=1}^{n}(x_i - mean)^2}{n - 1}}$$

To compute deviation with this formula, you have to store the individual numbers using an array, so that they can be used after the mean is obtained.

Your program should contain the following functions:

```
// Compute the mean of an array of double values
double mean(const double x[], int size)
```

```
// Compute the deviation of double values
double deviation(const double x[], int size)
```

Write a test program that prompts the user to enter 10 numbers and displays the mean and deviation, as shown in the following sample run:

```
Enter ten numbers: 1.9 2.5 3.7 2 1 6 3 4 5 2  ↵Enter
The mean is 3.11
The standard deviation is 1.55738
```

Sections 7.8–7.9

7.12 (*Execution time*) Write a program that randomly generates an array of **100000** integers and a key. Estimate the execution time of invoking the **linearSearch** function in Listing 7.9. Sort the array and estimate the execution time of invoking the **binarySearch** function in Listing 7.10. You may use the following code template to obtain the execution time:

```
long startTime = time(0);
perform the task;
long endTime = time(0);
long executionTime = endTime - startTime;
```

7.13 (*Game: Rolling a die*) A die has six faces representing values 1, 2, . . . , 6, respectively. Write a program that rolls a die **10000**, times and displays the number of occurrences of each value.

**7.14 (*Bubble sort*) Write a sort function that uses the bubble-sort algorithm. The algorithm makes several passes through the array. On each pass, successive neighboring pairs are compared. If a pair is in decreasing order, its values are swapped; otherwise, the values remain unchanged. The technique is called a *bubble sort* or *sinking sort* because the smaller values gradually "bubble" their way to the top and the larger values sink to the bottom.

The algorithm can be described as follows:

```
bool changed = true;
do
{
  changed = false;
  for (int j = 0; j < listSize - 1; j++)
    if (list[j] > list[j + 1])
    {
      swap list[j] with list[j + 1];
      changed = true;
    }
} while (changed);
```

Clearly, the list is in increasing order when the loop terminates. It is easy to show that the **do** loop executes at most **listSize - 1** times.

Write a test program that reads in an array of ten double numbers, invokes the function, and displays the sorted numbers.

*7.15 (*Game: locker puzzle*) A school has 100 lockers and 100 students. All lockers are closed on the first day of school. As the students enter, the first student, denoted S1, opens every locker. Then the second student, S2, begins with the second locker, denoted L2, and closes every other locker. Student S3 begins with the third locker and changes every third locker (closes it if it was open, and opens it if it was closed). Student S4 begins with locker L4 and changes every fourth locker. Student S5 starts with L5 and changes every fifth locker, and so on, until student S100 changes L100.

After all the students have passed through the building and changed the lockers, which lockers are open? Write a program to find your answer and display all open locker numbers separated by exactly one space.

(*Hint*: Use an array of **100 bool** elements, each of which indicates whether a locker is open (**true**) or closed (**false**). Initially, all lockers are closed.)

7.16 (*Reverse bubble sort*) In Programming Exercise 7.14, you used bubble sort to sort an array. The bubble sort function repeatedly compares the successive neighboring pairs in the array and swaps them if they are in decreasing order. Modify this program by swapping successive neighboring pairs if they are in increasing order. Write a test program that reads in an array of 15 integers, invokes the function, and displays the numbers sorted in decreasing order.

***7.17 (*Game: bean machine*) The bean machine, also known as a quincunx or the Galton box, is a device for statistic experiments named after English scientist Sir Francis Galton. It consists of an upright board with evenly spaced nails (or pegs) in a triangular form, as shown in Figure 7.10.

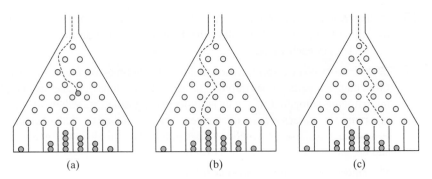

FIGURE 7.10 Each ball takes a random path and falls into a slot.

Balls are dropped from the opening of the board. Every time a ball hits a nail, it has a 50% chance to fall to the left or to the right. The piles of balls are accumulated in the slots at the bottom of the board.

Write a program that simulates the bean machine. Your program should prompt the user to enter the number of the balls and the number of the slots (maximum 50) in the machine. Simulate the falling of each ball by printing its path. For example, the path for the ball in Figure 7.10b is LLRRLLR and the path for the ball in Figure 7.10c is RLRRLRR. Display the final buildup of the balls in the slots in a histogram. Here is a sample run of the program:

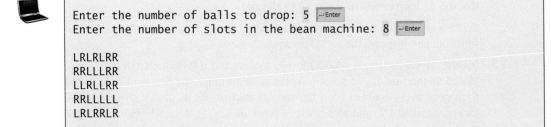

```
Enter the number of balls to drop: 5  ↵Enter
Enter the number of slots in the bean machine: 8  ↵Enter

LRLRLRR
RRLLLRR
LLRLLRR
RRLLLLL
LRLRRLR

     0
     0
   000
```

(*Hint*: Create an array named `slots`. Each element in `slots` stores the number of balls in a slot. Each ball falls into a slot via a path. The number of R's in a path is the position of the slot where the ball falls. For example, for the path LRLRLRR, the ball falls into `slots[4]`, and for the path RRLLLLL, the ball falls into `slots[2]`.)

***7.18 (*Game: Eight Queens*) The classic Eight Queens puzzle is to place eight queens on a chessboard such that no two can attack each other (i.e., no two queens are on the same row, same column, or same diagonal). There are many possible solutions. Write a program that displays one such solution. A sample output is shown below:

***7.19   (*Game: multiple Eight Queens solutions*) Programming Exercise 7.18 finds one solution for the Eight Queens problem. Write a program to count all possible solutions for the Eight Queens problem and displays all solutions.

7.20   (*Strictly identical arrays*) Two arrays `list1` and `list2` are *strictly identical* if they have the same length and `list1[i]` is equal to `list2[i]` for each `i`. Write a function that returns `true` if `list1` and `list2` are strictly identical using the following header:

```
bool strictlyEqual(const int list1[], const int list2[],
  int size)
```

Write a test program that prompts the user to enter two lists of integers and displays whether the two are strictly identical. The sample runs follow. Note that the first number in the input indicates the number of the elements in the list. This number is not part of the list. Assume the list size is maximum `20`.

```
Enter list1: 5 2 5 6 1 6  ↵Enter
Enter list2: 5 2 5 6 1 6  ↵Enter
Two lists are strictly identical
```

```
Enter list1: 5 2 5 6 6 1  ↵Enter
Enter list2: 5 2 5 6 1 6  ↵Enter
Two lists are not strictly identical
```

**7.21   (*Simulation: coupon collector's problem*) Coupon collector is a classic statistic problem with many practical applications. The problem is to pick objects from a set of objects repeatedly and determine how many picks are needed for all the objects to be picked at least once. A variation of the problem is to pick cards from a shuffled deck of `52` cards repeatedly and find out how many picks are needed before you see one of each suit. Assume a picked card is placed back in the deck before picking another. Write a program to simulate the number of picks needed to get four cards from each suit and display the four cards picked (it is possible that a card may be picked twice). Here is a sample run of the program:

```
Queen of Spades
5 of Clubs
Queen of Hearts
4 of Diamonds
Number of picks: 12
```

7.22   (*Math: Combinations*) Write a program that prompts the user to enter an integer and displays all combinations to get that integer as a sum of two dice.

7.23   (*Identical arrays*) Two arrays `list1` and `list2` are *identical* if they have the same contents. Write a function that returns `true` if `list1` and `list2` are identical using the following header:

```
bool isEqual(const int list1[], const int list2[], int size)
```

Write a test program that prompts the user to enter two lists of integers and displays whether the two are identical. Here are the sample runs. Note that the first number in the input indicates the number of the elements in the list. This number is not part of the list. Assume the list size is maximum `20`.

```
Enter list1: 5 2 5 6 6 1 ↵Enter
Enter list2: 5 5 2 6 1 6 ↵Enter
Two lists are identical
```

```
Enter list1: 5 5 5 6 6 1 ↵Enter
Enter list2: 5 2 5 6 1 6 ↵Enter
Two lists are not identical
```

*7.24 (*Pattern recognition: consecutive four equal numbers*) Write the following function that tests whether the array has four consecutive numbers with the same value.

```
bool isConsecutiveFour(const int values[], int size)
```

Write a test program that prompts the user to enter a series of integers and displays if the series contains four consecutive numbers with the same value. Your program should first prompt the user to enter the input size—i.e., the number of values in the series. Assume the maximum number of values is 80. Here are sample runs:

```
Enter the number of values: 8 ↵Enter
Enter the values: 3 4 5 5 5 5 4 5 ↵Enter
The list has consecutive fours
```

```
Enter the number of values: 9 ↵Enter
Enter the values: 3 4 5 5 5 6 5 4 5 ↵Enter
The list has no consecutive fours
```

7.25 (*Game: Sum of even or odd faces*) Write a program that rolls three dice and displays the sum of faces of the three dice if either all the faces have an even number or all the faces have an odd number. Otherwise, the program displays the largest number amongst the faces of the three dice.

**7.26 (*Merge two sorted*) Write the following function that merges two sorted lists into a new sorted list:

```
void merge(const int list1[], int size1, const int list2[],
    int size2, int list3[])
```

Implement the function in a way that takes size1 + size2 comparisons. Write a test program that prompts the user to enter two sorted lists and display the merged list. Here is a sample run. Note that the first number in the input indicates the number of the elements in the list. This number is not part of the list. Assume the maximum list size is 80.

```
Enter list1: 5 1 5 16 61 111 ↵Enter
Enter list2: 4 2 4 5 6 ↵Enter
The merged list is 1 2 4 5 5 6 16 61 111
```

**7.27 (*Sorted?*) Write the following function that returns true if the list is already sorted in increasing order:

```
bool isSorted(const int list[], int size)
```

Write a test program that prompts the user to enter a list and displays whether the list is sorted or not. Here is a sample run. Note that the first number in the input indicates the number of the elements in the list. This number is not part of the list. Assume the maximum list size is 80.

```
Enter list: 8 10 1 5 16 61 9 11 1  ↵Enter
The list is not sorted
```

```
Enter list: 10 1 1 3 4 4 5 7 9 11 21  ↵Enter
The list is already sorted
```

**7.28 (*Partition of a list*) Write the following function that partitions the list using the first element, called a *pivot*:

```
int partition(int list[], int size)
```

After the partition, the elements in the list are rearranged so that all the elements before the pivot are less than or equal to the pivot and the element after the pivot are greater than the pivot. The function also returns the index where the pivot is located in the new list. For example, suppose the list is {5, 2, 9, 3, 6, 8}. After the partition, the list becomes {3, 2, 5, 9, 6, 8}. Implement the function in a way that takes `size` number of comparisons.

Write a test program that prompts the user to enter a list and displays the list after the partition. Here is a sample run. Note that the first number in the input indicates the number of the elements in the list. This number is not part of the list. Assume the maximum list size is 80.

```
Enter list: 8 10 1 5 16 61 9 11 1  ↵Enter
After the partition, the list is 9 1 5 1 10 61 11 16
```

*7.29 (*Area of a polygon*) Write a program that prompts the user to enter the points of a convex polygon and display its area. Assume that the polygon has six end points and the points are entered clockwise. For the definition of a convex polygon, see www.mathopenref.com/polygonconvex.html. *Hint*: The total area of a polygon is the sum of the areas of the small triangles as shown in Figure 7.11.

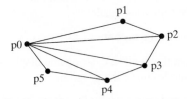

FIGURE 7.11 A convex polygon can be divided into small nonoverlapping triangles.

Here is a sample run of the program:

```
Enter the coordinates of six points:
  -8.5 10 0 11.4 5.5 7.8 6 -5.5 0 -7 -3.5 -3.5  ↵Enter
The total area is 183.95
```

*7.30 (*Replace: space with underscore*) Write a program that prompts the user to enter a string and replaces all spaces in it with underscores.

**7.31 (*Common elements*) Write a program that prompts the user to enter two arrays of 10 integers and displays the common elements that appear in both arrays. Here is a sample run.

```
Enter list1: 8 5 10 1 6 16 61 9 11 2  ↵Enter
Enter list2: 4 2 3 10 3 34 35 67 3 1  ↵Enter
The common elements are 10 1 2
```

Section 7.11

*7.32 (*Display longest string*) Rewrite the longest function in Programming Exercise 6.42 to find the longest amongst the two strings using C-strings with the following header:

```
string longest(const char s1[], const char s2[],
    char longestString[])
```

Write a test program that prompts the user to enter two C-strings and displays the longest one. For example, if two strings are Welcome and Programming, the output is Programming.

*7.33 (*Palindrome string*) Modify Programming Exercise 4.17 by using the following function to find the whether C-string s is a palindrome or not. The function returns the length of the string if it is a palindrome. Otherwise, it returns -1.

```
int isPalindrome(const char s[])
```

Write a test program that reads a C-string, invokes the function and checks whether the string is a palindrome or not. The program returns the length of the string if it is a palindrome.

*7.34 (*Occurrences of a specified character*) Rewrite the count function in Programming Exercise 6.44 to find the number of occurrences of a specified character in a C-string using the following header:

```
int count(const char s[], char a)
```

Write a test program that reads a string and a character and displays the number of occurrences of the character in the string. The sample run is the same as in Programming Exercise 6.44.

*7.35 (*Count the letters in a string*) Write a function that counts the number of letters in a C-string using the following header:

```
int countLetters(const char s[])
```

Write a test program that reads a C-string and displays the number of letters in the string. Here is a sample run of the program:

```
Enter a string: 2010 is coming  ↵Enter
The number of letters in 2010 is coming is 8
```

**7.36 (*Swap case*) Rewrite the swapCase function in Programming Exercise 6.46 to obtain a new string s2 in which the uppercase letters are changed to lowercase and lowercase to uppercase in s1 using the following function header:

```
void swapCase(const char s1[], char s2[])
```

Write a test program that prompts the user to enter a string and invokes this function, and displays the new string. The sample run is the same as in Programming Exercise 6.46.

*7.37 (*Count occurrence of each letter in a string*) Write a function that counts the occurrence of each letter in the string using the following header:

```
void count(const char s[], int counts[])
```

where counts is an array of 26 integers. counts[0], counts[1], . . . , and counts[25] count the occurrence of a, b, . . . , and z, respectively. Letters are not case-sensitive, i.e., letter A and a are counted the same as a.

Write a test program that reads a string, invokes the count function, and displays the non-zero counts. Here is a sample run of the program:

```
Enter a string: Welcome to New York! ↵Enter
c: 1 times
e: 3 times
k: 1 times
l: 1 times
m: 1 times
n: 1 times
o: 3 times
r: 1 times
t: 1 times
w: 2 times
y: 1 times
```

* 7.38 (*Convert float to string*) Write a function that converts a floating-point number to a C-String using the following header:

```
void ftoa(double f, char s[])
```

Write a test program that prompts the user to enter a floating-point number and displays each digit and the decimal point separated by a space. Here is a sample run:

```
Enter a number: 232.45 ↵Enter
The number is 2 3 2 . 4 5
```

*7.39 (*Business: check ISBN-13*) Rewrite Programming Exercise 5.51 using a C-string rather than a string for storing the ISBN numbers. Write the following function that obtains the checksum from the first 12 digits:

```
int getChecksum(const char s[])
```

Your program should read the input as a C-string. The sample runs are the same as in Programming Exercise 5.51.

*7.40   (*Decimal to Binary*) Use the `itoa` function described in Table 7.1 to convert a decimal number to a binary number using C-strings with the following header:

```
void itoaUse(int value, char s[], int radix)
```

Write a test program that prompts the user to enter a decimal number and displays the corresponding binary value as a string.

*7.41   (*Decimal to Octal or Hex*) Use the itoa function described in Table 7.1 to convert a decimal number to an octal number or a hex number using C-strings with the following header:

```
void itoaUse(int value, char s[], int radix)
```

Write a test program that prompts the user to enter a decimal number and radix, and displays the corresponding octal number or hex value.

**7.42   (*Binary to Octal*) Rewrite the `bin2Octal` function in Programming Exercise 6.40 to convert a binary string into an octal number with the following header:

```
void bin2Octal(char binaryString[], int octalNumber)
```

Write a test program that prompts the user to enter a binary string and displays its equivalent octal value.

**7.43   (*Octal to binary*) Rewrite the `octal2Binary` function in Programming Exercise 6.41 to convert an octal number into a binary string with the following header:

```
void octal2Binary(int octalNumber, char binaryString[])
```

Write a test program that prompts the user to enter an octal number and displays its equivalent binary string.

CHAPTER

8

MULTIDIMENSIONAL ARRAYS

Objectives

- To give examples of representing data using two-dimensional arrays (§8.1).

- To declare two-dimensional arrays and access array elements in a two-dimensional array using row and column indexes (§8.2).

- To program common operations for two-dimensional arrays (displaying arrays, summing all elements, finding min and max elements, and random shuffling) (§8.3).

- To pass two-dimensional arrays to functions (§8.4).

- To write a program for grading multiple-choice questions using two-dimensional arrays (§8.5).

- To solve the closest-pair problem using two-dimensional arrays (§8.6).

- To check a Sudoku solution using two-dimensional arrays (§8.7).

- To declare and use multidimensional arrays (§8.8).

8.1 Introduction

Key Point

Data in a table or a matrix can be represented using a two-dimensional array.

Chapter 7 introduced how to use one-dimensional arrays to store linear collections of elements. You can use a two-dimensional array to store a matrix or a table. For example, the following table that describes the distances between the cities can be stored using a two-dimensional array.

Distance Table (in miles)

	Chicago	Boston	New York	Atlanta	Miami	Dallas	Houston
Chicago	0	983	787	714	1375	967	1087
Boston	983	0	214	1102	1763	1723	1842
New York	787	214	0	888	1549	1548	1627
Atlanta	714	1102	888	0	661	781	810
Miami	1375	1763	1549	661	0	1426	1187
Dallas	967	1723	1548	781	1426	0	239
Houston	1087	1842	1627	810	1187	239	0

8.2 Declaring Two-Dimensional Arrays

Key Point

An element in a two-dimensional array is accessed through a row and column index.

The syntax for declaring a two-dimensional array is

```
elementType arrayName[ROW_SIZE][COLUMN_SIZE];
```

As an example, here is how to declare a two-dimensional array `matrix` of `int` values:

```
int matrix[5][5];
```

Two subscripts are used in a two-dimensional array, one for the row and the other for the column. As in a one-dimensional array, the index for each subscript is of the `int` type and starts from `0`, as shown in Figure 8.1a.

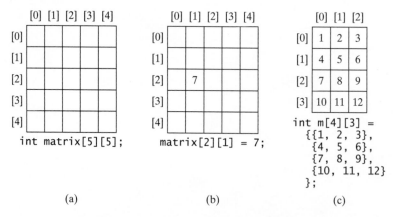

FIGURE 8.1 The index of each subscript of a two-dimensional array is an `int` value starting from `0`.

To assign the value 7 to a specific element at row 2 and column 1, as shown in Figure 8.1b, you can use the following:

```
matrix[2][1] = 7;
```

Caution
It is a common mistake to use `matrix[2, 1]` to access the element at row 2 and column 1. In C++, each subscript must be enclosed in a pair of square brackets.

You also can use an array initializer to declare and initialize a two-dimensional array. For example, the code in (a) below declares an array with the specified initial values, as shown in Figure 8.1c. This is equivalent to the code in (b).

```
int m[4][3] =
{  {1, 2, 3},
   {4, 5, 6},
   {7, 8, 9},
   {10, 11, 12}
};
```

Equivalent

```
int m[4][3];
m[0][0] = 1; m[0][1] = 2; m[0][2] = 3;
m[1][0] = 4; m[1][1] = 5; m[1][2] = 6;
m[2][0] = 7; m[2][1] = 8; m[2][2] = 9;
m[3][0] = 10; m[3][1] = 11; m[3][2] = 12;
```

(a)   (b)

8.1   Declare and create a 4 × 5 `int` matrix.

Check Point

8.2   What is the output of the following code?

```
int m[5][6];
int x[] = {1, 2};
m[0][1] = x[1];
cout << "m[0][1] is " << m[0][1];
```

8.3   Which of the following statements are valid array declarations?

```
int r[2];
int x[];
int y[3][];
```

8.3 Processing Two-Dimensional Arrays

Nested for loops are often used to process a two-dimensional array.

Key Point

Suppose an array `matrix` is declared as follows:

```
const int ROW_SIZE = 10;
const int COLUMN_SIZE = 10;
int matrix[ROW_SIZE][COLUMN_SIZE];
```

Here are some examples of processing two-dimensional arrays:

1. (*Initializing arrays with input values*) The following loop initializes the array with user input values:

VideoNote

Process 2-D arrays

```
   cout << "Enter " << ROW_SIZE << " rows and "
     << COLUMN_SIZE << " columns: " << endl;
   for (int i = 0; i < ROW_SIZE; i++)
     for (int j = 0; j < COLUMN_SIZE; j++)
       cin >> matrix[i][j];
```

2. (*Initializing arrays with random values*) The following loop initializes the array with random values between 0 and 99:

```
for (int row = 0; row < ROW_SIZE; row++)
{
  for (int column = 0; column < COLUMN_SIZE; column++)
  {
    matrix[row][column] = rand() % 100;
  }
}
```

3. (*Displaying arrays*) To display a two-dimensional array, you have to display each element in the array using a loop like the following:

```
for (int row = 0; row < ROW_SIZE; row++)
{
  for (int column = 0; column < COLUMN_SIZE; column++)
  {
    cout << matrix[row][column] << " ";
  }

  cout << endl;
}
```

4. (*Summing all elements*) Use a variable named total to store the sum. Initially total is 0. Add each element in the array to total using a loop like this:

```
int total = 0;
for (int row = 0; row < ROW_SIZE; row++)
{
  for (int column = 0; column < COLUMN_SIZE; column++)
  {
    total += matrix[row][column];
  }
}
```

5. (*Summing elements by column*) For each column, use a variable named total to store its sum. Add each element in the column to total using a loop like this:

```
for (int column = 0; column < COLUMN_SIZE; column++)
{
  int total = 0;
  for (int row = 0; row < ROW_SIZE; row++)
    total += matrix[row][column];
  cout << "Sum for column " << column << " is " << total << endl;
}
```

6. (*Which row has the largest sum?*) Use variables maxRow and indexOfMaxRow to track the largest sum and index of the row. For each row, compute its sum and update maxRow and indexOfMaxRow if the new sum is greater.

```
int maxRow = 0;
int indexOfMaxRow = 0;

// Get sum of the first row in maxRow
for (int column = 0; column < COLUMN_SIZE; column++)
  maxRow += matrix[0][column];

for (int row = 1; row < ROW_SIZE; row++)
```

```
  {
    int totalOfThisRow = 0;
    for (int column = 0; column < COLUMN_SIZE; column++)
      totalOfThisRow += matrix[row][column];

    if (totalOfThisRow > maxRow)
    {
      maxRow = totalOfThisRow;
      indexOfMaxRow = row;
    }
  }

  cout << "Row " << indexOfMaxRow
       << " has the maximum sum of " << maxRow << endl;
```

7. (*Random shuffling*) Shuffling the elements in a one-dimensional array was introduced in Section 7.2.4, "Processing Arrays." How do you shuffle all the elements in a two-dimensional array? To accomplish this, for each element `matrix[i][j]`, randomly generate indices `i1` and `j1` and swap `matrix[i][j]` with `matrix[i1][j1]`, as follows:

```
srand(time(0));

for (int i = 0; i < ROW_SIZE; i++)
{
  for (int j = 0; j < COLUMN_SIZE; j++)
  {
    int i1 = rand() % ROW_SIZE;
    int j1 = rand() % COLUMN_SIZE;

    // Swap matrix[i][j] with matrix[i1][j1]
    double temp = matrix[i][j];
    matrix[i][j] = matrix[i1][j1];
    matrix[i1][j1] = temp;
  }
}
```

8.4   What is the output of the following code?

```
#include <iostream>
using namespace std;

int main()
{
  int matrix[4][4] =
    {{1, 2, 3, 4},
     {4, 5, 6, 7},
     {8, 9, 10, 11},
     {12, 13, 14, 15}};

  int sum = 0;

  for (int i = 0; i < 4; i++)
    sum += matrix[i][i];

  cout << sum << endl;

  return 0;
}
```

8.5 What is the output of the following code?

```cpp
#include <iostream>
using namespace std;

int main()
{
  int matrix[4][4] =
    {{1, 2, 3, 4},
     {4, 5, 6, 7},
     {8, 9, 10, 11},
     {12, 13, 14, 15}};

  int sum = 0;

  for (int i = 0; i < 4; i++)
    cout << matrix[i][1] << " ";

  return 0;
}
```

8.4 Passing Two-Dimensional Arrays to Functions

Key Point

When passing a two-dimensional array to a function, C++ requires that the column size be specified in the function parameter type declaration.

VideoNote

Pass 2D array arguments

Listing 8.1 gives an example with a function that returns the sum of all the elements in a matrix.

LISTING 8.1 PassTwoDimensionalArray.cpp

fixed column size

```cpp
1  #include <iostream>
2  using namespace std;
3
4  const int COLUMN_SIZE = 4;
5
6  int sum(const int a[][COLUMN_SIZE], int rowSize)
7  {
8    int total = 0;
9    for (int row = 0; row < rowSize; row++)
10   {
11     for (int column = 0; column < COLUMN_SIZE; column++)
12     {
13       total += a[row][column];
14     }
15   }
16
17   return total;
18 }
19
20 int main()
21 {
22   const int ROW_SIZE = 3;
23   int m[ROW_SIZE][COLUMN_SIZE];
24   cout << "Enter " << ROW_SIZE << " rows and "
25     << COLUMN_SIZE << " columns: " << endl;
26   for (int i = 0; i < ROW_SIZE; i++)
27     for (int j = 0; j < COLUMN_SIZE; j++)
28       cin >> m[i][j];
```

```
29
30    cout << "\nSum of all elements is " << sum(m, ROW_SIZE) << endl;        pass array
31
32    return 0;
33  }
```

```
Enter 3 rows and 4 columns:
1 2 3 4   ↵Enter
5 6 7 8   ↵Enter
9 10 11 12   ↵Enter
Sum of all elements is 78
```

The function sum (line 6) has two arguments. The first specifies a two-dimensional array with a fixed column size. The second specifies the row size for the two-dimensional array.

8.6   Which of the following function declarations are wrong?

Check
Point

```
int f(int[][] a, int rowSize, int columnSize);
int f(int a[][], int rowSize, int columnSize);
int f(int a[][3], int rowSize);
```

8.5 Problem: Grading a Multiple-Choice Test

The problem is to write a program that will grade multiple-choice tests.

Key
Point

Suppose there are 8 students and 10 questions, and the answers are stored in a two-dimensional array. Each row records a student's answers to the questions. For example, the following array stores the test.

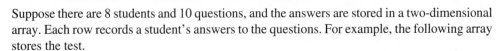

Students' Answers to the Questions:

	0	1	2	3	4	5	6	7	8	9
Student 0	A	B	A	C	C	D	E	E	A	D
Student 1	D	B	A	B	C	A	E	E	A	D
Student 2	E	D	D	A	C	B	E	E	A	D
Student 3	C	B	A	E	D	C	E	E	A	D
Student 4	A	B	D	C	C	D	E	E	A	D
Student 5	B	B	E	C	C	D	E	E	A	D
Student 6	B	B	A	C	C	D	E	E	A	D
Student 7	E	B	E	C	C	D	E	E	A	D

The key is stored in a one-dimensional array, as follows:

Key to the Questions:

	0	1	2	3	4	5	6	7	8	9
key	D	B	D	C	C	D	A	E	A	D

Your program grades the test and displays the result. The program compares each student's answers with the key, counts the number of correct answers, and displays it. Listing 8.2 gives the program.

LISTING 8.2 GradeExam.cpp

two-dimensional array

array

```cpp
 1  #include <iostream>
 2  using namespace std;
 3
 4  int main()
 5  {
 6    const int NUMBER_OF_STUDENTS = 8;
 7    const int NUMBER_OF_QUESTIONS = 10;
 8
 9    // Students' answers to the questions
10    char answers[NUMBER_OF_STUDENTS][NUMBER_OF_QUESTIONS] =
11    {
12      {'A', 'B', 'A', 'C', 'C', 'D', 'E', 'E', 'A', 'D'},
13      {'D', 'B', 'A', 'B', 'C', 'A', 'E', 'E', 'A', 'D'},
14      {'E', 'D', 'D', 'A', 'C', 'B', 'E', 'E', 'A', 'D'},
15      {'C', 'B', 'A', 'E', 'D', 'C', 'E', 'E', 'A', 'D'},
16      {'A', 'B', 'D', 'C', 'C', 'D', 'E', 'E', 'A', 'D'},
17      {'B', 'B', 'E', 'C', 'C', 'D', 'E', 'E', 'A', 'D'},
18      {'B', 'B', 'A', 'C', 'C', 'D', 'E', 'E', 'A', 'D'},
19      {'E', 'B', 'E', 'C', 'C', 'D', 'E', 'E', 'A', 'D'}
20    };
21
22    // Key to the questions
23    char keys[] = {'D', 'B', 'D', 'C', 'C', 'D', 'A', 'E', 'A', 'D'};
24
25    // Grade all answers
26    for (int i = 0; i < NUMBER_OF_STUDENTS; i++)
27    {
28      // Grade one student
29      int correctCount = 0;
30      for (int j = 0; j < NUMBER_OF_QUESTIONS; j++)
31      {
32        if (answers[i][j] == keys[j])
33          correctCount++;
34      }
35
36      cout << "Student " << i << "'s correct count is " <<
37        correctCount << endl;
38    }
39
40    return 0;
41  }
```

```
Student 0's correct count is 7
Student 1's correct count is 6
Student 2's correct count is 5
Student 3's correct count is 4
Student 4's correct count is 8
Student 5's correct count is 7
Student 6's correct count is 7
Student 7's correct count is 7
```

The statement in lines 10–20 declares and initializes a two-dimensional array of characters. The statement in line 23 declares and initializes an array of **char** values.

Each row in the array **answers** stores a student's answer, which is graded by comparing it with the key in the array **keys**. Immediately after a student is graded, the result for the student is displayed.

8.6 Problem: Finding a Closest Pair

This section presents a geometric problem for finding the closest pair of points.

Key Point

Given a set of points, the closest-pair problem is to find the two points that are nearest to each other. In Figure 8.2, for example, points **(1, 1)** and **(2, 0.5)** are closest to each other. There are several ways to solve this problem. An intuitive approach is to compute the distances between all pairs of points and find the pair with the minimum distance, as implemented in Listing 8.3.

Closest-pair animation on the Companion Website

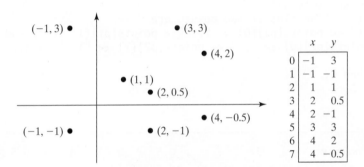

FIGURE 8.2   Points can be represented in a two-dimensional array.

LISTING 8.3   FindNearestPoints.cpp

VideoNote
Nearest points

```cpp
1  #include <iostream>
2  #include <cmath>
3  using namespace std;
4
5  // Compute the distance between two points (x1, y1) and (x2, y2)
6  double getDistance(double x1, double y1, double x2, double y2)
7  {
8    return sqrt((x2 - x1) * (x2 - x1) + (y2 - y1) * (y2 - y1));
9  }
10
11  int main()
12  {
13    const int NUMBER_OF_POINTS = 8;
14
15    // Each row in points represents a point
16    double points[NUMBER_OF_POINTS][2];
17
18    cout << "Enter " << NUMBER_OF_POINTS << " points: ";
19    for (int i = 0; i < NUMBER_OF_POINTS; i++)
20      cin >> points[i][0] >> points[i][1];
21
22    // p1 and p2 are the indices in the points array
23    int p1 = 0, p2 = 1; // Initial two points
24    double shortestDistance = getDistance(points[p1][0], points[p1][1],
25      points[p2][0], points[p2][1]); // Initialize shortestDistance
```

distance between two points

2-D array

read all points

track shortestDistance

```
26
27      // Compute distance for every two points
28      for (int i = 0; i < NUMBER_OF_POINTS; i++)
29      {
30        for (int j = i + 1; j < NUMBER_OF_POINTS; j++)
31        {
32          double distance = getDistance(points[i][0], points[i][1],
33            points[j][0], points[j][1]); // Find distance
34
35          if (shortestDistance > distance)
36          {
37            p1 = i; // Update p1
38            p2 = j; // Update p2
39            shortestDistance = distance; // Update shortestDistance
40          }
41        }
42      }
43
44      // Display result
45      cout << "The closest two points are " <<
46        "(" << points[p1][0] << ", " << points[p1][1] << ") and (" <<
47        points[p2][0] << ", " << points[p2][1] << ")" << endl;
48
49      return 0;
50    }
```

Labels on left margin:
- for each point i (line 28)
- for each point j (line 30)
- distance between i and j (line 32)
- update shortestDistance (line 35)

```
Enter 8 points: -1 3  -1 -1  1 1  2 0.5  2 -1  3 3 4 2 4 -0.5  ↵Enter
The closest two points are (1, 1) and (2, 0.5)
```

The points are read from the console and stored in a two-dimensional array named **points** (lines 19–20). The program uses variable **shortestDistance** (line 24) to store the distance between two nearest points, and the indices of these two points in the **points** array are stored in **p1** and **p2** (line 23).

For each point at index i, the program computes the distance between **points[i]** and **points[j]** for all j > i (lines 28–42). Whenever a shorter distance is found, the variable **shortestDistance**, **p1**, and **p2** are updated (lines 37–39).

The distance between two points **(x1, y1)** and **(x2, y2)** can be computed using the formula $\sqrt{(x_2 - x_1)^2 + (y_2 - y_1)^2}$ in function **getDistance** (lines 6–9).

The program assumes that the plain has at least two points. You can easily modify the program to handle the case if the plain has one point or none.

multiple closest pairs

Note that there might be more than one closest pair of points with the same minimum distance. The program finds one such pair. You may modify the program to find all closest pairs in Programming Exercise 8.10.

Tip

input file

It is cumbersome to enter all points from the keyboard. You may store the input in a file, say FindNearestPoints.txt, and compile and run the program using the following command:

g++ FindNearestPoints.cpp –o FindNearestPoints.exe
FindNearestPoints.exe < FindNearestPoints.txt

8.7 Problem: Sudoku

The problem is to check whether a given Sudoku solution is correct.

Key
Point

This book teaches how to program using a wide variety of problems with various levels of difficulty. We use simple, short, and stimulating examples to introduce programming and problem-solving techniques and use interesting and challenging examples to motivate students. This section presents an interesting problem of a sort that appears in the newspaper every day. It is a number-placement puzzle, commonly known as *Sudoku*. This is a very challenging problem. To make it accessible to novices, this section presents a solution to a simplified version of the Sudoku problem, which is to verify whether a solution is correct. How to find a solution to the Sudoku problem is given in Supplement VI.A.

Sudoku is a 9 × 9 grid divided into smaller 3 × 3 boxes (also called regions or blocks), as shown in Figure 8.3a. Some cells, called *fixed cells*, are populated with numbers from 1 to 9. The objective is to fill the empty cells, also called *free cells*, with numbers 1 to 9 so that every row, every column, and every 3 × 3 box contains the numbers 1 to 9, as shown in Figure 8.3b.

fixed cells
free cells

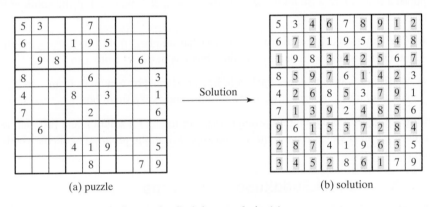

(a) puzzle   Solution →   (b) solution

FIGURE 8.3 (b) is the solution to the Sudoku puzzle in (a).

For convenience, we use value 0 to indicate a free cell, as shown in Figure 8.4a. The grid can be naturally represented using a two-dimensional array, as shown in Figure 8.4b.

representing a grid

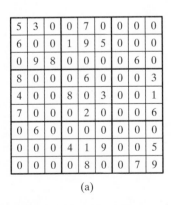

(a)

```
int grid[9][9] =
  {{5, 3, 0, 0, 7, 0, 0, 0, 0},
   {6, 0, 0, 1, 9, 5, 0, 0, 0},
   {0, 9, 8, 0, 0, 0, 0, 6, 0},
   {8, 0, 0, 0, 6, 0, 0, 0, 3},
   {4, 0, 0, 8, 0, 3, 0, 0, 1},
   {7, 0, 0, 0, 2, 0, 0, 0, 6},
   {0, 6, 0, 0, 0, 0, 2, 8, 0},
   {0, 0, 0, 4, 1, 9, 0, 0, 5},
   {0, 0, 0, 0, 8, 0, 0, 7, 9},
  };
```

(b)

FIGURE 8.4 A grid can be represented using a two-dimensional array.

To find a solution for the puzzle is to replace 0 in the grid with appropriate numbers between 1 and 9. For the solution in Figure 8.3b, the `grid` should be as shown in Figure 8.5.

```
A solution grid is
  {{5, 3, 4, 6, 7, 8, 9, 1, 2},
   {6, 7, 2, 1, 9, 5, 3, 4, 8},
   {1, 9, 8, 3, 4, 2, 5, 6, 7},
   {8, 5, 9, 7, 6, 1, 4, 2, 3},
   {4, 2, 6, 8, 5, 3, 7, 9, 1},
   {7, 1, 3, 9, 2, 4, 8, 5, 6},
   {9, 6, 1, 5, 3, 7, 2, 8, 4},
   {2, 8, 7, 4, 1, 9, 6, 3, 5},
   {3, 4, 5, 2, 8, 6, 1, 7, 9}
  };
```

FIGURE 8.5　A solution is stored in `grid`.

Suppose a solution to a Sudoku puzzle is found, how do you check if the solution is correct? Here are two approaches:

- One way to check it is to see if every row has numbers from 1 to 9, every column has numbers from 1 to 9, and every small box has numbers from 1 to 9.

- The other way is to check each cell. Each cell must be a number from 1 to 9 and the cell is unique on every row, every column, and every small box.

Listing 8.4 gives a program that prompts the user to enter a solution and program reports true if the solution is valid. We use the second approach in the program to check whether the solution is correct.

LISTING 8.4　CheckSudokuSolution.cpp

```cpp
 1  #include <iostream>
 2  using namespace std;
 3
 4  void readASolution(int grid[][9]);
 5  bool isValid(const int grid[][9]);
 6  bool isValid(int i, int j, const int grid[][9]);
 7
 8  int main()
 9  {
10    // Read a Sudoku puzzle
11    int grid[9][9];
12    readASolution(grid);
13
14    cout << (isValid(grid) ? "Valid solution" : "Invalid solution");
15
16    return 0;
17  }
18
19  // Read a Sudoku puzzle from the keyboard
20  void readASolution(int grid[][9])
21  {
22    cout << "Enter a Sudoku puzzle:" << endl;
23    for (int i = 0; i < 9; i++)
24      for (int j = 0; j < 9; j++)
25        cin >> grid[i][j];
26  }
```

read input

solution valid?

read solution

```
27
28  // Check whether the fixed cells are valid in the grid
29  bool isValid(const int grid[][9])
30  {
31    for (int i = 0; i < 9; i++)
32      for (int j = 0; j < 9; j++)
33        if (grid[i][j] < 1 || grid[i][j] > 9 ||
34            !isValid(i, j, grid))
35          return false;
36
37    return true; // The fixed cells are valid
38  }
39
40  // Check whether grid[i][j] is valid in the grid
41  bool isValid(int i, int j, const int grid[][9])
42  {
43    // Check whether grid[i][j] is valid at the i's row
44    for (int column = 0; column < 9; column++)
45      if (column != j && grid[i][column] == grid[i][j])
46        return false;
47
48    // Check whether grid[i][j] is valid at the j's column
49    for (int row = 0; row < 9; row++)
50      if (row != i && grid[row][j] == grid[i][j])
51        return false;
52
53    // Check whether grid[i][j] is valid in the 3-by-3 box
54    for (int row = (i / 3) * 3; row < (i / 3) * 3 + 3; row++)
55      for (int col = (j / 3) * 3; col < (j / 3) * 3 + 3; col++)
56        if (row != i && col != j && grid[row][col] == grid[i][j])
57          return false;
58
59    return true; // The current value at grid[i][j] is valid
60  }
```

check solution

check rows

check columns

check small boxes

```
Enter a Sudoku puzzle solution:
9 6 3 1 7 4 2 5 8  ↵Enter
1 7 8 3 2 5 6 4 9  ↵Enter
2 5 4 6 8 9 7 3 1  ↵Enter
8 2 1 4 3 7 5 9 6  ↵Enter
4 9 6 8 5 2 3 1 7  ↵Enter
7 3 5 9 6 1 8 2 4  ↵Enter
5 8 9 7 1 3 4 6 2  ↵Enter
3 1 7 2 4 6 9 8 5  ↵Enter
6 4 2 5 9 8 1 7 3  ↵Enter
Valid solution
```

The program invokes the `readASolution(grid)` function (line 12) to read a Sudoku solution into a two-dimensional array representing a Sudoku grid.

The `isValid(grid)` function checks whether the values in the grid are valid. It checks whether each value is between 1 and 9 and each value is valid in the grid (lines 31–35).

The `isValid(i, j, grid)` function checks whether the value at `grid[i][j]` is valid. It checks whether `grid[i][j]` appears more than once at row i (lines 44–46), at column j (lines 49–51), and in the 3 × 3 box (lines 54–57).

isValid function

overloaded isValid function

How do you locate all the cells in the same box? For any `grid[i][j]`, the starting cell of the 3 × 3 box that contains it is `grid[(i / 3) * 3][(j / 3) * 3]`, as illustrated in Figure 8.6.

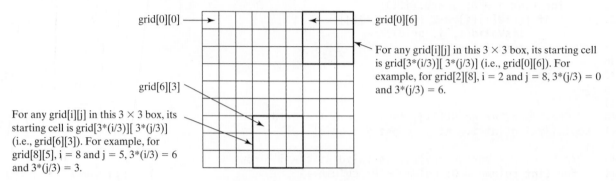

grid[0][0]

grid[0][6]

For any grid[i][j] in this 3 × 3 box, its starting cell is grid[3*(i/3)][3*(j/3)] (i.e., grid[0][6]). For example, for grid[2][8], i = 2 and j = 8, 3*(j/3) = 0 and 3*(j/3) = 6.

grid[6][3]

For any grid[i][j] in this 3 × 3 box, its starting cell is grid[3*(i/3)][3*(j/3)] (i.e., grid[6][3]). For example, for grid[8][5], i = 8 and j = 5, 3*(i/3) = 6 and 3*(j/3) = 3.

FIGURE 8.6 The location of the first cell in a 3 × 3 box determines the locations of other cells in the box.

With this observation, you can easily identify all the cells in the box. Suppose `grid[r][c]` is the starting cell of a 3 × 3 box, the cells in the box can be traversed in a nested loop as follows:

```
// Get all cells in a 3 by 3 box starting at grid[r][c]
for (int row = r; row < r + 3; row++)
  for (int col = c; col < c + 3; col++)
    // grid[row][col] is in the box
```

input file

It is cumbersome to enter 81 numbers from the keyboard. You may store the input in a file, say CheckSudokuSolution.txt (see www.cs.armstrong.edu/liang/data/CheckSudokuSolution.txt), and compile and run the program using the following command:

**g++ CheckSudokuSolution.cpp –o CheckSudokuSolution.exe
CheckSudokuSolution.exe < CheckSudokuSolution.txt**

8.8 Multidimensional Arrays

**Key
Point**

You can create an array of any dimension in C++.

In the preceding section, you used a two-dimensional array to represent a matrix or a table. Occasionally, you will need to represent *n*-dimensional data structures. In C++, you can create *n*-dimensional arrays for any integer *n*.

Declaring a two-dimensional array can be generalized to declaring an *n*-dimensional array for *n* >= 3. For example, you may use a three-dimensional array to store exam scores for a class of six students with five exams and each exam has two parts (multiple-choice and essay). The following syntax declares a three-dimensional array variable `scores`.

```
double scores[6][5][2];
```

You can also use the short-hand notation to create and initialize the array as follows:

```
double scores[6][5][2] = {
  {{7.5, 20.5}, {9.0, 22.5}, {15, 33.5}, {13, 21.5}, {15, 2.5}},
  {{4.5, 21.5}, {9.0, 22.5}, {15, 34.5}, {12, 20.5}, {14, 9.5}},
```

```
     {{6.5, 30.5}, {9.4, 10.5}, {11, 33.5}, {11, 23.5}, {10, 2.5}},
     {{6.5, 23.5}, {9.4, 32.5}, {13, 34.5}, {11, 20.5}, {16, 7.5}},
     {{8.5, 26.5}, {9.4, 52.5}, {13, 36.5}, {13, 24.5}, {16, 2.5}},
     {{9.5, 20.5}, {9.4, 42.5}, {13, 31.5}, {12, 20.5}, {16, 6.5}}};
```

scores[0][1][0] refers to the multiple-choice score for the first student's second exam, which is 9.0. scores[0][1][1] refers to the essay score for the first student's second exam, which is 22.5. This is depicted in the following figure:

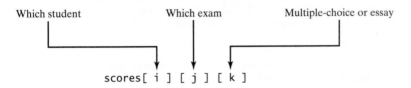

8.8.1 Problem: Daily Temperature and Humidity

Suppose a meteorology station records the temperature and humidity at each hour of every day and stores the data for the past 10 days in a text file named weather.txt (see www.cs.armstrong .edu/liang/data/Weather.txt). Each line of the file consists of four numbers that indicate the day, hour, temperature, and humidity. The contents of the file may appear as in (a):

```
1    1   76.4   0.92          10   24   98.7   0.74
1    2   77.7   0.93          1    2   77.7   0.93
...                           ...
10   23  97.7   0.71          10   23   97.7   0.71
10   24  98.7   0.74          1    1   76.4   0.92
```
              (a)   (b)

Note that the lines in the file are not necessary in order. For example, the file may appear as shown in (b).

Your task is to write a program that calculates the average daily temperature and humidity for the 10 days. You can use the input redirection to read the data from the file and store them in a three-dimensional array, named **data**. The first index of **data** in the range from 0 to 9 represents 10 days, the second index from 0 to 23 represents 24 hours, and the third index from 0 to 1 represents temperature and humidity, respectively. Note that the days are numbered from 1 to 10 and hours are numbered from 1 to 24 in the file. Since the array index starts from 0, data[0][0][0] stores the temperature in day 1 at hour 1 and data[9][23][1] stores the humidity in day 10 at hour 24.

The program is given in Listing 8.5.

Listing 8.5 Weather.cpp

```
1   #include <iostream>
2   using namespace std;
3
4   int main()
5   {
```

```
6     const int NUMBER_OF_DAYS = 10;
7     const int NUMBER_OF_HOURS = 24;
8     double data[NUMBER_OF_DAYS][NUMBER_OF_HOURS][2];
9
10    // Read input using input redirection from a file
11    int day, hour;
12    double temperature, humidity;
13    for (int k = 0; k < NUMBER_OF_DAYS * NUMBER_OF_HOURS; k++)
14    {
15      cin >> day >> hour >> temperature >> humidity;
16      data[day - 1][hour - 1][0] = temperature;
17      data[day - 1][hour - 1][1] = humidity;
18    }
19
20    // Find the average daily temperature and humidity
21    for (int i = 0; i < NUMBER_OF_DAYS; i++)
22    {
23      double dailyTemperatureTotal = 0, dailyHumidityTotal = 0;
24      for (int j = 0; j < NUMBER_OF_HOURS; j++)
25      {
26        dailyTemperatureTotal += data[i][j][0];
27        dailyHumidityTotal += data[i][j][1];
28      }
29
30      // Display result
31      cout << "Day " << i << "'s average temperature is "
32        << dailyTemperatureTotal / NUMBER_OF_HOURS << endl;
33      cout << "Day " << i << "'s average humidity is "
34        << dailyHumidityTotal / NUMBER_OF_HOURS << endl;
35    }
36
37    return 0;
38  }
```

three-dimensional array

```
Day 0's average temperature is 77.7708
Day 0's average humidity is 0.929583
Day 1's average temperature is 77.3125
Day 1's average humidity is 0.929583
...
Day 9's average temperature is 79.3542
Day 9's average humidity is 0.9125
```

You can use the following command to compile the program:

g++ Weather.cpp -o Weather

Use the following command to run the program:

Weather.exe < Weather.txt

A three-dimensional array **data** is declared in line 8. The loop in lines 13–18 reads the input to the array. You could enter the input from the keyboard, but it would be awkward. For convenience, we store the data in a file and use the input redirection to read the data from the file. The loop in lines 24–28 adds all temperatures for each hour in a day to **dailyTemperatureTotal** and all humidity for each hour to **dailyHumidityTotal**. The average daily temperature and humidity are displayed in lines 31–34.

8.8.2 Problem: Guessing Birthdays

Listing 4.4, GuessBirthday.cpp, gives a program that guesses a birthday. The program can be simplified by storing the numbers in five sets in a three-dimensional array and prompting the user for the answers using a loop, as shown in Listing 8.6.

LISTING 8.6 GuessBirthdayUsingArray.cpp

```cpp
 1  #include <iostream>
 2  #include <iomanip>
 3  using namespace std;
 4
 5  int main()
 6  {
 7    int day = 0; // Day to be determined
 8    char answer;
 9
10    int dates[5][4][4] = {                                          three-dimensional array
11      {{ 1,  3,  5,  7},
12       { 9, 11, 13, 15},
13       {17, 19, 21, 23},
14       {25, 27, 29, 31}},
15      {{ 2,  3,  6,  7},
16       {10, 11, 14, 15},
17       {18, 19, 22, 23},
18       {26, 27, 30, 31}},
19      {{ 4,  5,  6,  7},
20       {12, 13, 14, 15},
21       {20, 21, 22, 23},
22       {28, 29, 30, 31}},
23      {{ 8,  9, 10, 11},
24       {12, 13, 14, 15},
25       {24, 25, 26, 27},
26       {28, 29, 30, 31}},
27      {{16, 17, 18, 19},
28       {20, 21, 22, 23},
29       {24, 25, 26, 27},
30       {28, 29, 30, 31}}};
31
32    for (int i = 0; i < 5; i++)
33    {
34      cout << "Is your birthday in Set" << (i + 1) << "?" << endl;    Set 1, 2, 3, 4, 5?
35      for (int j = 0; j < 4; j++)
36      {
37        for (int k = 0; k < 4; k++)
38          cout << setw(3) << dates[i][j][k] << " ";
39        cout << endl;
40      }
41      cout << "\nEnter N/n for No and Y/y for Yes: ";
42      cin >> answer;
43      if (answer == 'Y' || answer == 'y')
44        day += dates[i][0][0];
45    }
46
47    cout << "Your birthday is " << day << endl;
48
49    return 0;
50  }
```

A three-dimensional array `dates` is created in lines 10–30. This array stores five sets of numbers. Each set is a 4-by-4 two-dimensional array.

The loop starting from line 32 displays the numbers in each set and prompts the user to answer whether the day is in the set (lines 37–38). If it is, the first number (dates[i][0][0]) in the set is added to variable day (line 44).

8.7 Declare and create a 4 × 6 × 5 int array.

CHAPTER SUMMARY

1. A two-dimensional array can be used to store a table.

2. A two-dimensional array can be created using the syntax: elementType arrayName [ROW_SIZE][COLUMN_SIZE].

3. Each element in a two-dimensional array is represented using the syntax: arrayName [rowIndex][columnIndex].

4. You can create and initialize a two-dimensional array using an array initializer with the syntax: elementType arrayName[][COLUMN_SIZE] = {{row values}, ..., {row values}}.

5. You can pass a two-dimensional array to a function; however, C++ requires that the column size be specified in the function declaration.

6. You can use arrays of arrays to form multidimensional arrays. For example, a three-dimensional array is declared as an array of arrays using the syntax elementType arrayName[size1][size2][size3].

QUIZ

Answer the quiz for this chapter online at www.cs.armstrong.edu/liang/cpp3e/quiz.html.

PROGRAMMING EXERCISES

Sections 8.2–8.5

*8.1 (*Sum elements column by columns*) Write a function that returns the sum of all the elements in a specified column in a matrix using the following header:

```
const int SIZE = 4;
double sumColumn(const double m[][SIZE], int rowSize,
  int columnIndex);
```

Write a test program that reads a 3-by-4 matrix and displays the sum of each column. Here is a sample run:

```
Enter a 3-by-4 matrix row by row:
1.5 2 3 4 ↵Enter
5.5 6 7 8 ↵Enter
9.5 1 3 1 ↵Enter
Sum of the elements at column 0 is 16.5
Sum of the elements at column 1 is 9
Sum of the elements at column 2 is 13
Sum of the elements at column 3 is 13
```

*8.2 (*Sum the major diagonal in a matrix*) Write a function that sums all the double values in the major diagonal in an $n \times n$ matrix of double values using the following header:

```
const int SIZE = 4;
double sumMajorDiagonal(const double m[][SIZE]);
```

Write a test program that reads a 4-by-4 matrix and displays the sum of all its elements on the major diagonal. Here is a sample run:

```
Enter a 4-by-4 matrix row by row:
1 2 3 4  ↵Enter
5 6 7 8  ↵Enter
9 10 11 12  ↵Enter
13 14 15 16  ↵Enter
Sum of the elements in the major diagonal is 34
```

*8.3 (*Sort and display students*) Rewrite Listing 8.2, GradeExam.cpp, to sort students in reverse order and display only those having more than six correct answers.

*8.4 (*Compute total marks for each student*) Suppose the marks obtained by all students are stored in a two-dimensional array. Each row records a student's marks for five tests. For example, the following array stores the test marks for eight students. Write a program that displays students and the total marks they obtained in five tests, in decreasing order of the total marks.

	T1	T2	T3	T4	T5
Student 0	12	14	13	14	15
Student 1	17	13	14	13	13
Student 2	13	13	14	13	13
Student 3	19	13	14	17	13
Student 4	13	15	14	13	16
Student 5	13	14	14	16	13
Student 6	13	17	14	18	13
Student 7	16	13	15	19	12

8.5 (*Algebra: add two matrices*) Write a function to add two matrices a and b and save the result in c.

$$\begin{pmatrix} a_{11} & a_{12} & a_{13} \\ a_{21} & a_{22} & a_{23} \\ a_{31} & a_{32} & a_{33} \end{pmatrix} + \begin{pmatrix} b_{11} & b_{12} & b_{13} \\ b_{21} & b_{22} & b_{23} \\ b_{31} & b_{32} & b_{33} \end{pmatrix} = \begin{pmatrix} a_{11} + b_{11} & a_{12} + b_{12} & a_{13} + b_{13} \\ a_{21} + b_{21} & a_{22} + b_{22} & a_{23} + b_{23} \\ a_{31} + b_{31} & a_{32} + b_{32} & a_{33} + b_{33} \end{pmatrix}$$

The header of the function is

```
const int N = 3;

void addMatrix(const double a[][N],
  const double b[][N], double c[][N]);
```

Each element c_{ij} is $a_{ij} + b_{ij}$. Write a test program that prompts the user to enter two 3×3 matrices and displays their addition. Here is a sample run:

```
Enter matrix1: 1 2 3 4 5 6 7 8 9  ↵Enter
Enter matrix2: 0 2 4 1 4.5 2.2 1.1 4.3 5.2  ↵Enter
The addition of the matrices is
 1 2 3      0 2 4          1 4 7
 4 5 6  +   1 4.5 2.2  =   5 9.5 8.2
 7 8 9      1.1 4.3 5.2    8.1 12.3 14.2
```

**8.6 (*Financial application: compute tax*) Rewrite Listing 3.3, ComputeTax.cpp, using arrays. For each filing status, there are six tax rates. Each rate is applied to a certain amount of taxable income. For example, from the taxable income of \$400,000 for a single filer, \$8,350 is taxed at 10%, (33,950–8,350) at 15%, (82,250–33,950) at 25%, (171,550–82,550) at 28%, (372,550–82,250) at 33%, and (400,000–372,950) at 36%. The six rates are the same for all filing statuses, which can be represented in the following array:

```
double rates[] = {0.10, 0.15, 0.25, 0.28, 0.33, 0.36};
```

The brackets for each rate for all the filing statuses can be represented in a two-dimensional array as follows:

```
int brackets[4][5] =
{
   {8350, 33950, 82250, 171550, 372950},   // Single filer
   {16700, 67900, 137050, 20885, 372950},  // Married jointly
                                            // or qualifying
                                            // widow(er)
   {8350, 33950, 68525, 104425, 186475},   // Married separately
   {11950, 45500, 117450, 190200, 372950}  // Head of household
};
```

Suppose the taxable income is \$400,000 for single filers. The tax can be computed as follows:

```
tax = brackets[0][0] * rates[0] +
   (brackets[0][1] - brackets[0][0]) * rates[1] +
   (brackets[0][2] - brackets[0][1]) * rates[2] +
   (brackets[0][3] - brackets[0][2]) * rates[3] +
   (brackets[0][4] - brackets[0][3]) * rates[4] +
   (400000 - brackets[0][4]) * rates[5]
```

**8.7 (*Explore matrix*) Write a program that randomly fills in 0s and 1s into a 4-by-4 square matrix, prints the matrix, and finds the rows, columns, and diagonals with all 0s or 1s. Here is a sample run of the program:

```
0111
0000
0100
1111
All 0's on row 1
All 1's on row 3
No same numbers on a column
No same numbers on the major diagonal
No same numbers on the sub-diagonal
```

***8.8   (*Shuffle columns*) Write a function that shuffles the columns in a two-dimensional int array using the following header:

```
void shuffle(int m[3][columnSize]);
```

Write a test program that shuffles the following matrix:

```
int m[3][5] = {{1, 2, 3, 4, 5}, {3, 4, 5, 6, 7}, {5, 6, 7, 8, 9}};
```

**8.9   (*Algebra: multiply two matrices*) Write a function to multiply two matrices a and b and save the result in c.

$$\begin{pmatrix} a_{11} & a_{12} & a_{13} \\ a_{21} & a_{22} & a_{23} \\ a_{31} & a_{32} & a_{33} \end{pmatrix} \times \begin{pmatrix} b_{11} & b_{12} & b_{13} \\ b_{21} & b_{22} & b_{23} \\ b_{31} & b_{32} & b_{33} \end{pmatrix} = \begin{pmatrix} c_{11} & c_{12} & c_{13} \\ c_{21} & c_{22} & c_{23} \\ c_{31} & c_{32} & c_{33} \end{pmatrix}$$

The header of the function is

```
const int N = 3;
void multiplyMatrix(const double a[][N],
  const double b[][N], double c[][N]);
```

Each element c_{ij} is $a_{i1} \times b_{1j} + a_{i2} \times b_{2j} + a_{i3} \times b_{3j}$.

Write a test program that prompts the user to enter two 3×3 matrices and displays their product. Here is a sample run:

```
Enter matrix1: 1 2 3 4 5 6 7 8 9  ↵Enter
Enter matrix2: 0 2 4 1 4.5 2.2 1.1 4.3 5.2  ↵Enter
The multiplication of the matrices is
 1 2 3     0 2.0 4.0        5.3 23.9 24
 4 5 6  *  1 4.5 2.2   =   11.6 56.3 58.2
 7 8 9     1.1 4.3 5.2     17.9 88.7 92.4
```

Section 8.6

**8.10   (*All closest pairs*) Listing 8.3, FindNearestPoints.cpp, finds one closest pair. Revise the program to display all closest pairs with the same minimum distance. Here is a sample run:

```
Enter the number of points: 8  ↵Enter
Enter 8 points: 0 0 1 1 -1 -1  2 2 -2 -2 -3 -3 -4 -4 5 5  ↵Enter
The closest two points are (0.0, 0.0) and (1.0, 1.0)
The closest two points are (0.0, 0.0) and (-1.0, -1.0)
The closest two points are (1.0, 1.0) and (2.0, 2.0)
The closest two points are (-1.0, -1.0) and (-2.0, -2.0)
The closest two points are (-2.0, -2.0) and (-3.0, -3.0)
The closest two points are (-3.0, -3.0) and (-4.0, -4.0)
Their distance is 1.4142135623730951
```

**8.11   (*Game: nine heads and tails*) Nine coins are placed in a 3×3 matrix with some face up and some face down. You can represent the state of the coins using a 3×3 matrix with values 0 (head) and 1 (tail). Here are some examples:

```
0 0 0     1 0 1     1 1 0     1 0 1     1 0 0
0 1 0     0 0 1     1 0 0     1 1 0     1 1 1
0 0 0     1 0 0     0 0 1     1 0 0     1 1 0
```

Each state can also be represented using a binary number. For example, the preceding matrices correspond to the numbers

000010000 101001100 110100001 101110100 100111110

The total number of possibilities is 512. So you can use decimal numbers 0, 1, 2, 3, . . . , and 511 to represent all states of the matrix. Write a program that prompts the user to enter a number between 0 and 511 and displays the corresponding matrix with characters H and T. Here is a sample run:

```
Enter a number between 0 and 511: 7 ↵ Enter
H H H
H H H
T T T
```

The user entered 7, which corresponds to 000000111. Since 0 stands for H and 1 for T, the output is correct.

VideoNote
3-D nearest points

*8.12 (*Points nearest to each other*) Listing 8.3, FindNearestPoints.cpp, is a program that finds two points in a two-dimensional space nearest to other. Revise the program so that it finds two points in a three-dimensional space nearest to other. Use a two-dimensional array to represent the points. Test the program using the following points:

```
double points[][3] = {{-1, 0, 3}, {-1, -1, -1}, {4, 1, 1},
    {2, 0.5, 9}, {3.5, 2, -1}, {3, 1.5, 3}, {-1.5, 4, 2},
    {5.5, 4, -0.5}};
```

The formula for computing the distance between two points (x1, y1, z1) and (x2, y2, z2) is $\sqrt{(x_2 - x_1)^2 + (y_2 - y_1)^2 + (z_2 - z_1)^2}$.

*8.13 (*Sort two-dimensional array in reverse order*) Write a function to sort a two-dimensional array in reverse order using following header:

```
void reverseSort(int m[][2], int numberOfRows)
```

The function performs a sort primarily on the first element in the rows and then secondarily on the second element in the rows if the first elements are equal. For example, the array {{9, 7}, {6, 12}, {9, 10}, {6, 7}, {6, 6}, {9, 6}} will be sorted to {{9, 10}, {9, 7}, {9, 6}, {6, 12}, {6, 7}, {6, 6}}. Write a test program that prompts the user to enter 12 points, invokes this function, and displays the sorted points.

*8.14 (*Smallest row and column*) Write a program that randomly fills in 0s and 1s into a 6 × 6 matrix, prints the matrix, and finds the first row and first column with the least 1s. Here is a sample run of the program:

```
1 1 0 1 0 1
1 1 0 1 1 1
1 0 0 0 1 0
1 1 1 1 1 0
1 1 0 1 0 1
1 0 0 1 0 0
The smallest row's index: 2
The smallest column's index: 2
```

*8.15 (*Algebra: 2 × 2 matrix inverse*) The inverse of a square matrix A is denoted A^{-1}, such that $A \times A^{-1} = I$, where I is the identity matrix with all 1s on the diagonal and 0 on all other cells. For example, the inverse of matrix $\begin{bmatrix} 1 & 2 \\ 3 & 4 \end{bmatrix}$ is, $\begin{bmatrix} -2 & 1 \\ 1.5 & -0.5 \end{bmatrix}$, i.e.,

$$\begin{bmatrix} 1 & 2 \\ 3 & 4 \end{bmatrix} \times \begin{bmatrix} -2 & 1 \\ 1.5 & -0.5 \end{bmatrix} = \begin{bmatrix} 1 & 0 \\ 0 & 1 \end{bmatrix}$$

The inverse of a 2 × 2 matrix A can be obtained using the following formula if `ad - bc != 0`:

$$A = \begin{bmatrix} a & b \\ c & d \end{bmatrix} \qquad A^{-1} = \frac{1}{ad - bc} \begin{bmatrix} d & -b \\ -c & a \end{bmatrix}$$

Implement the following function to obtain an inverse of the matrix:

void inverse(**const double** A[][2], **double** inverseOfA[][2])

Write a test program that prompts the user to enter a, b, c, d for a matrix, and displays its inverse matrix. Here is a sample run:

```
Enter a, b, c, d: 1 2 3 4 ↵Enter
-2.0 1.0
1.5 -0.5
```

```
Enter a, b, c, d: 0.5 2 1.5 4.5 ↵Enter
-6.0 2.6666666666666665
2.0 -0.6666666666666666
```

*8.16 (*Geometry: same line?*) Programming Exercise 6.20 gives a function for testing whether three points are on the same line. Write the following function to test whether all the points in **points** array are on the same line.

```
const int SIZE = 2;
bool sameLine(const double points[][SIZE], int numberOfPoints)
```

Write a program that prompts the user to enter five points and displays whether they are on the same line. Here are sample runs:

```
Enter five points: 3.4 2 6.5 9.5 2.3 2.3 5.5 5 -5 4 ↵Enter
The five points are not on same line
```

```
Enter five points: 1 1 2 2 3 3 4 4 5 5 ↵Enter
The five points are on same line
```

Sections 8.7–8.8

***8.17   (*Locate the largest element*) Write the following function that finds the location of the largest element in a two-dimensional array.

```
void locateLargest(const double a[][4], int location[])
```

The location is stored in a one-dimensional array **location** that contains two elements. These two elements indicate the row and column indices of the largest element in the two-dimensional array. Write a test program that prompts the user to enter a 3 × 4 two-dimensional array and displays the location of the largest element in the array. Here is a sample run:

```
Enter the array:
23.5 35 2 10 ↵Enter
4.5 3 45 3.5 ↵Enter
35 44 5.5 9.6 ↵Enter
The location of the largest element is at (1, 2)
```

*8.18   (*Algebra: 3 × 3 matrix inverse*) The inverse of a square matrix **A** is denoted A^{-1}, such that $A \times A^{-1} = I$, where **I** is the identity matrix with all **1**s on the diagonal and **0** on all other cells. For example, the inverse of matrix $\begin{bmatrix} 1 & 2 & 1 \\ 2 & 3 & 1 \\ 4 & 5 & 3 \end{bmatrix}$ is $\begin{bmatrix} -2 & 0.5 & 0.5 \\ 1 & 0.5 & -0.5 \\ 1 & -1.5 & 0.5 \end{bmatrix}$, i.e.,

$$\begin{bmatrix} 1 & 2 & 1 \\ 2 & 3 & 1 \\ 4 & 5 & 3 \end{bmatrix} \times \begin{bmatrix} -2 & 0.5 & 0.5 \\ 1 & 0.5 & -0.5 \\ 1 & -1.5 & 0.5 \end{bmatrix} = \begin{bmatrix} 1 & 0 & 0 \\ 0 & 1 & 0 \\ 0 & 0 & 1 \end{bmatrix}$$

The inverse of a 3 × 3 matrix $A = \begin{bmatrix} a_{11} & a_{12} & a_{13} \\ a_{21} & a_{22} & a_{23} \\ a_{31} & a_{32} & a_{33} \end{bmatrix}$ can be obtained using the following formula if $|A| \neq 0$:

$$A^{-1} = \frac{1}{|A|} \begin{bmatrix} a_{22}a_{33} - a_{23}a_{32} & a_{13}a_{32} - a_{12}a_{33} & a_{12}a_{23} - a_{13}a_{22} \\ a_{23}a_{31} - a_{21}a_{33} & a_{11}a_{33} - a_{13}a_{31} & a_{13}a_{21} - a_{11}a_{23} \\ a_{21}a_{32} - a_{22}a_{31} & a_{12}a_{31} - a_{11}a_{32} & a_{11}a_{22} - a_{12}a_{21} \end{bmatrix}$$

$$|A| = \begin{vmatrix} a_{11} & a_{12} & a_{13} \\ a_{21} & a_{22} & a_{23} \\ a_{31} & a_{32} & a_{33} \end{vmatrix} = a_{11}a_{22}a_{33} + a_{31}a_{12}a_{23} + a_{13}a_{21}a_{32}$$

$$- a_{13}a_{22}a_{31} - a_{11}a_{23}a_{32} - a_{33}a_{21}a_{12}.$$

Implement the following function to obtain an inverse of the matrix:

```
void inverse(const double A[][3], double inverseOfA[][3])
```

Write a test program that prompts the user to enter $a_{11}, a_{12}, a_{13}, a_{21}, a_{21},$ $a_{23}, a_{31}, a_{32}, a_{33},$ for a matrix, and displays its inverse matrix. Here is a sample run:

```
Enter a11, a12, a13, a21, a22, a23, a31, a32, a33: 1 2 1 2 3 1 4 5 3  ↵Enter
-2 0.5 0.5
1 0.5 -0.5
1 -1.5 0.5
```

```
Enter a11, a12, a13, a21, a22, a23, a31, a32, a33: 1 4 2 2 5 8 2 1 8  ↵Enter
2.0 -1.875 1.375
0.0 0.25 -0.25
-0.5 0.4375 -0.1875
```

***8.19   (*Financial tsunami*) Banks loan money to each other. In tough economic times, if a bank goes bankrupt, it may not be able to pay back the loan. A bank's total asset is its current balance plus its loans to other banks. Figure 8.7 is a diagram that shows five banks. The banks' current balances are **25**, **125**, **175**, **75**, and **181** million dollars, respectively. The directed edge from node 1 to node 2 indicates that bank 1 loans **40** million dollars to bank 2.

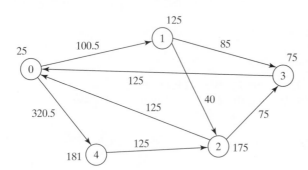

FIGURE 8.7   Banks loan money to each other.

If a bank's total asset is under a certain limit, the bank is unsafe. If a bank is unsafe, the money it borrowed cannot be returned to the lender, and the lender cannot count the loan in its total asset. Consequently, the lender may also be unsafe, if its total asset is under the limit. Write a program to find all unsafe banks. Your program reads the input as follows. It first reads two integers **n** and **limit**, where **n** indicates the number of banks and **limit** is the minimum asset for keeping a bank safe. It then reads **n** lines that describe the information for **n** banks with id from **0** to **n-1**. The first number in the line is the bank's balance, the second number indicates the number of banks that borrowed money from the bank, and the rest are pairs of two numbers. Each pair describes a borrower. The first number in the pair is the borrower's id and the second is the amount borrowed. Assume that the maximum number of the banks is **100**. For example, the input for the five banks in Figure 8.7 is as follows (the limit is **201**):

```
5 201
25 2 1 100.5 4 320.5
125 2 2 40 3 85
175 2 0 125 3 75
75 1 0 125
181 1 2 125
```

The total asset of bank 3 is (**75** + **125**), which is under **201**. So bank 3 is unsafe. After bank 3 becomes unsafe, the total asset of bank 1 becomes **125** + **40**. So bank 1 is also unsafe. The output of the program should be

```
Unsafe banks are 3 1
```

(*Hint*: Use a two-dimensional array **borrowers** to represent loans. **loan[i][j]** indicates the loan that bank **i** loans to bank **j**. Once bank j becomes unsafe, **loan[i][j]** should be set to **0**.)

***8.20 (*TicTacToe game*) In a game of TicTacToe, two players take turns marking an available cell in a 3 × 3 grid with their respective tokens (either X or O). When one player has placed three tokens in a horizontal, vertical, or diagonal row on the grid, the game is over and that player has won. A draw (no winner) occurs when all the cells on the grid have been filled with tokens and neither player has achieved a win. Create a program for playing TicTacToe. The program prompts the first player to enter an X token, and then prompts the second player to enter an O token. Whenever a token is entered, the program redisplays the board on the console and determines the status of the game (win, draw, or unfinished). Here is a sample run:

```
-------------
|   |   |   |
-------------
|   |   |   |
-------------
|   |   |   |
-------------
Enter a row (0, 1, or 2) for player X: 1 ⏎Enter
Enter a column (0, 1, or 2) for player X: 1 ⏎Enter

-------------
|   |   |   |
-------------
|   | X |   |
-------------
|   |   |   |
-------------
Enter a row (0, 1, or 2) for player O: 1 ⏎Enter
Enter a column (0, 1, or 2) for player O: 2 ⏎Enter

-------------
|   |   |   |
-------------
|   | X | O |
-------------
|   |   |   |
-------------
Enter a row (0, 1, or 2) for player X:

...

-------------
| X |   |   |
-------------
| O | X | O |
-------------
|   |   | X |
-------------
X player won
```

**8.21 (*Pattern recognition: consecutive four equal numbers*) Write the following function that tests whether a two-dimensional array has four consecutive numbers of the same value, either horizontally, vertically, or diagonally.

```
bool isConsecutiveFour(int values[][7])
```

Write a test program that prompts the user to enter the number of rows and columns of a two-dimensional array and then the values in the array and displays true if the array contains four consecutive numbers with the same value. Otherwise, display false. Here are some examples of the true cases:

```
0 1 0 3 1 6 1      0 1 0 3 1 6 1      0 1 0 3 1 6 1      0 1 0 3 1 6 1
0 1 6 8 6 0 1      0 1 6 8 6 0 1      0 1 6 8 6 0 1      0 1 6 8 6 0 1
5 6 2 1 8 2 9      5 5 2 1 8 2 9      5 6 2 1 6 2 9      9 6 2 1 8 2 9
6 5 6 1 1 9 1      6 5 6 1 1 9 1      6 5 6 6 1 9 1      6 9 6 1 1 9 1
1 3 6 1 4 0 7      1 5 6 1 4 0 7      1 3 6 1 4 0 7      1 3 9 1 4 0 7
3 3 3 3 4 0 7      3 5 3 3 4 0 7      3 6 3 3 4 0 7      3 3 3 9 4 0 7
```

***8.22 (*Game: connect four*) Connect four is a two-player board game in which the players alternately drop colored disks into a seven-column, six-row vertically-suspended grid, as shown below.

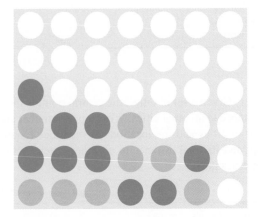

The objective of the game is to connect four same-colored disks in a row, a column, or a diagonal before your opponent can do likewise. The program prompts two players to drop a RED (shown in dark blue) or YELLOW (shown in light blue) disk alternately. Whenever a disk is dropped, the program redisplays the board on the console and determines the status of the game (win, draw, or continue). Here is a sample run:

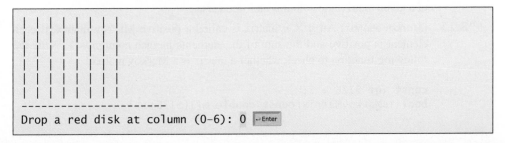

```
| | | | | | | |
| | | | | | | |
| | | | | | | |
| | | | | | | |
| | | | | | | |
| | | | | | | |
---------------------
Drop a red disk at column (0-6): 0 ⏎Enter
```

```
| | | | | | | |
| | | | | | | |
| | | | | | | |
| | | | | | | |
| | | | | | | |
|R| | | | | | |
----------------------
Drop a yellow disk at column (0-6): 3 ⏎Enter

| | | | | | | |
| | | | | | | |
| | | | | | | |
| | | | | | | |
| | | | | | | |
|R| | |Y| | | |

...
...
...

Drop a yellow disk at column (0-6): 6 ⏎Enter
| | | | | | | |
| | | | | | | |
| | | |R| | | |
| | | |Y|R|Y| |
| | | |R|Y|Y|Y|Y|
|R|Y|R|Y|R|R|R|
----------------------
The yellow player won
```

*8.23 (*Central city*) Given a set of cities, the central point is the city that has the shortest total distance to all other cities. Write a program that prompts the user to enter the number of cities and the locations of the cities (coordinates), and finds the central city and its total distance to all other cities. Assume that the maximum number of cities is 20.

```
Enter the number of cities: 5 ⏎Enter
Enter the coordinates of the cities: 2.5 5 5.1 3 1 9 5.4 54 5.5 2.1 ⏎Enter
The central city is at (2.5, 5.0)
The total distance to all other cities is 60.81
```

*8.24 (*Transpose of a matrix*) Write a program that inputs a matrix and displays the transpose of that matrix. A transpose of a matrix is obtained by converting all the rows of a given matrix into columns and vice versa.

*8.25 (*Markov matrix*) An $n \times n$ matrix is called a positive Markov matrix, if each element is positive and the sum of the elements in each column is 1. Write the following function to check whether a matrix is a Markov matrix:

```
const int SIZE = 3;
bool isMarkovMatrix(const double m[][SIZE]);
```

Write a test program that prompts the user to enter a 3 × 3 matrix of double values and tests whether it is a Markov matrix. Here are sample runs:

```
Enter a 3 by 3 matrix row by row:
0.15 0.875 0.375  ↵Enter
0.55 0.005 0.225  ↵Enter
0.30 0.12 0.4  ↵Enter
It is a Markov matrix
```

```
Enter a 3 by 3 matrix row by row:
0.95 -0.875 0.375  ↵Enter
0.65 0.005 0.225  ↵Enter
0.30 0.22 -0.4  ↵Enter
It is not a Markov matrix
```

*8.26 (*Row sorting*) Implement the following function to sort the rows in a two-dimensional array. A new array is returned. The original array is intact.

```
const int SIZE = 3;
void sortRows(const double m[][SIZE], double result[][SIZE]);
```

Write a test program that prompts the user to enter a 3 × 3 matrix of double values and display a new row-sorted matrix. Here is a sample run:

```
Enter a 3 by 3 matrix row by row:
0.15 0.875 0.375  ↵Enter
0.55 0.005 0.225  ↵Enter
0.30 0.12 0.4  ↵Enter
The row-sorted array is
0.15 0.375 0.875
0.005 0.225 0.55
0.12 0.30 0.4
```

*8.27 (*Column sorting*) Implement the following function to sort the columns in a two-dimensional array. A new array is returned. The original array is intact.

```
const int SIZE = 3;
void sortColumns(const double m[][SIZE], double result[][SIZE]);
```

Write a test program that prompts the user to enter a 3 × 3 matrix of double values and display a new column-sorted matrix. Here is a sample run:

```
Enter a 3 by 3 matrix row by row:
0.15 0.875 0.375  ↵Enter
0.55 0.005 0.225  ↵Enter
0.30 0.12 0.4  ↵Enter
The column-sorted array is
0.15 0.0050 0.225
0.3  0.12   0.375
0.55 0.875  0.4
```

8.28   (*Strictly identical arrays*) Two two-dimensional arrays m1 and m2 are *strictly identical* if their corresponding elements are equal. Write a function that returns true if m1 and m2 are strictly identical, using the following header:

```
const int SIZE = 3;
bool equals(const int m1[][SIZE], const int m2[][SIZE]);
```

Write a test program that prompts the user to enter two 3 × 3 arrays of integers and displays whether the two are strictly identical. Here are the sample runs.

```
Enter m1: 51 22 25 6 1 4 24 54 6  ↵Enter
Enter m2: 51 22 25 6 1 4 24 54 6  ↵Enter
Two arrays are strictly identical
```

```
Enter m1: 51 25 22 6 1 4 24 54 6  ↵Enter
Enter m2: 51 22 25 6 1 4 24 54 6  ↵Enter
Two arrays are not strictly identical
```

8.29   (*Identical arrays*) Two two-dimensional arrays m1 and m2 are *identical* if they have the same contents. Write a function that returns true if m1 and m2 are identical, using the following header:

```
const int SIZE = 3;
bool equals(const int m1[][SIZE], const int m2[][SIZE]);
```

Write a test program that prompts the user to enter two 3 × 3 arrays of integers and displays whether the two are identical. Here are the sample runs.

```
Enter m1: 51 25 22 6 1 4 24 54 6  ↵Enter
Enter m2: 51 22 25 6 1 4 24 54 6  ↵Enter
Two arrays are identical
```

```
Enter m1: 51 5 22 6 1 4 24 54 6  ↵Enter
Enter m2: 51 22 25 6 1 4 24 54 6  ↵Enter
Two arrays are not identical
```

*8.30   (*Algebra: solve linear equations*) Write a function that solves the following 2 × 2 system of linear equation:

$$a_{00}x + a_{01}y = b_0 \qquad x = \frac{b_0 a_{11} - b_1 a_{01}}{a_{00}a_{11} - a_{01}a_{10}} \qquad y = \frac{b_1 a_{00} - b_0 a_{10}}{a_{00}a_{11} - a_{01}a_{10}}$$
$$a_{10}x + a_{11}y = b_1$$

The function header is

```
const int SIZE = 2;
bool linearEquation(const double a[][SIZE], const double b[],
    double result[]);
```

The function returns false if $a_{00}a_{11} - a_{01}a_{10}$ is 0; otherwise, returns true. Write a test program that prompts the user to enter a_{00}, a_{01}, a_{10}, a_{11}, b_0, b_1, and display the result. If $a_{00}a_{11} - a_{01}a_{10}$ is 0, report that "The equation has no solution". A sample run is similar to Programming Exercise 3.3.

*8.31 (*Geometry: intersecting point*) Write a function that returns the intersecting point of the two lines. The intersecting point of the two lines can be found by using the formula shown in Programming Exercise 3.22. Assume that (x1, y1) and (x2, y2) are the two points in line 1 and (x3, y3) and (x4, y4) on line 2. If the equation has no solutions, the two lines are parallel. The function header is

```
const int SIZE = 2;
bool getIntersectingPoint(const double points[][SIZE],
  double result[]);
```

The points are stored in a 4 × 2 two-dimensional array `points` with (`points[0][0]`, `points[0][1]`) for (x1, y1). The function returns the intersecting point and true, if the two lines are parallel. Write a program that prompts the user to enter four points and display the intersecting point. See Programming Exercise 3.22 for a sample run.

*8.32 (*Geometry: area of a triangle*) Write a function that returns the area of a triangle using the following header:

```
const int SIZE = 2;
double getTriangleArea(const double points[][SIZE]);
```

The points are stored in a 3 × 2 two-dimensional array `points` with (`points[0][0]`, `points[0][1]`) for (x1, y1). The triangle area can be computed using the formula in Programming Exercise 2.19. The function returns 0, if the three points are on the same line. Write a program that prompts the user to enter two lines and display the intersecting point. Here is a sample run of the program:

```
Enter x1, y1, x2, y2, x3, y3: 2.5 2 5 -1.0 4.0 2.0 ↵Enter
The area of the triangle is 2.25
```

```
Enter x1, y1, x2, y2, x3, y3: 2 2 4.5 4.5 6 6 ↵Enter
The three points are on the same line
```

*8.33 (*Geometry: polygon subareas*) A convex 4-vertex polygon is divided into four triangles, as shown in Figure 8.8.

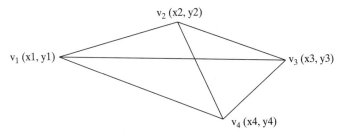

FIGURE 8.8 A 4-vertex polygon is defined by four vertices.

Write a program that prompts the user to enter the coordinates of the four vertices and displays the areas of the four triangles in increasing order. Here is a sample run:

```
Enter x1, y1, x2, y2, x3, y3, x4, y4: -2.5 2 4 4 3 -2 -2 -3.5 ↵Enter
The areas are 1.390 1.517 8.082 8.333
```

*8.34   (*Geometry: rightmost lowest point*) In computational geometry, often you need to find the rightmost lowest point in a set of points. Write the following function that returns the rightmost lowest point in a set of points.

```
const int SIZE = 2;
void getRightmostLowestPoint(const double points[][SIZE],
    int numberOfPoints, double rightMostPoint[]);
```

Write a test program that prompts the user to enter the coordinates of six points and displays the rightmost lowest point. Here is a sample run:

```
Enter 6 points: 1.5 2.5 -3 4.5 5.6 -7 6.5 -7 8 1 10 2.5 ↵Enter
The rightmost lowest point is (6.5, -7.0)
```

*8.35   (*Game: find the flipped cell*) Suppose you are given a 6 × 6 matrix filled with 0 and 1. All rows and all columns have the even number of 1s. Let the user flip one cell (i.e., flip from 1 to 0 or from 0 to 1) and write a program to find which cell was flipped. Your program should prompt the user to enter a 6 × 6 array with 0 and 1 and find the first row r and first column c where the parity is violated (i.e., the number of 1's is not even). The flipped cell is at (r, c). Here is a sample run:

```
Enter a 6-by-6 matrix row by row:
1 1 1 0 1 1 ↵Enter
1 1 1 1 0 0 ↵Enter
0 1 0 1 1 1 ↵Enter
1 1 1 1 1 1 ↵Enter
0 1 1 1 1 0 ↵Enter
1 0 0 0 0 1 ↵Enter
The first row and column where the parity is violated is at (0, 1)
```

*8.36   (*Parity checking*) Write a program that generates a 9 × 9 two-dimensional matrix filled with 0s and 1s, displays the matrix, and checks if every row and every column have the odd number of 1s.

OBJECTS AND CLASSES

Objectives

- To describe objects and classes, and to use classes to model objects (§9.2).

- To use UML graphical notations to describe classes and objects (§9.2).

- To demonstrate defining classes and creating objects (§9.3).

- To create objects using constructors (§9.4).

- To access data fields and invoke functions using the object member access operator (.) (§9.5).

- To separate a class definition from a class implementation (§9.6).

- To prevent multiple inclusions of header files using the `#ifndef` inclusion guard directive (§9.7).

- To know what inline functions in a class are (§9.8).

- To declare private data fields with appropriate `get` and `set` functions for data field encapsulation and make classes easy to maintain (§9.9).

- To understand the scope of data fields (§9.10).

- To apply class abstraction to develop software (§9.11).

9.1 Introduction

Object-oriented programming enables you to develop large-scale software effectively.

why OOP?

Having learned the material in earlier chapters, you are able to solve many programming problems using selections, loops, functions, and arrays. However, these features are not sufficient for developing large-scale software systems. This chapter begins the introduction of object-oriented programming, which will enable you to develop large-scale software systems effectively.

9.2 Defining Classes for Objects

A class defines the properties and behaviors for objects.

object-oriented programming
object

Object-oriented programming (OOP) involves programming using objects. An *object* represents an entity in the real world that can be distinctly identified. For example, a student, a desk, a circle, a button, and even a loan can all be viewed as objects. An object has a unique identity, state, and behavior.

state
property
data field

- The *state* of an object (also known as *properties* or *attributes*) is represented by *data fields* with their current values. A circle object, for example, has a data field, `radius`, which is the property that characterizes a circle. A rectangle object, for example, has data fields, `width` and `height`, which are the properties that characterize a rectangle.

behavior

- The *behavior* of an object (also known as *actions*) is defined by functions. To invoke a function on an object is to ask the object to perform an action. For example, you may define a function named `getArea()` for circle objects. A circle object may invoke `getArea()` to return its area.

class
contract

instantiation
object
instance

Objects of the same type are defined using a common class. A *class* is a template, blueprint, or *contract* that defines what an object's data fields and functions will be. An object is an instance of a class. You can create many instances of a class. Creating an instance is referred to as *instantiation*. The terms *object* and *instance* are often interchangeable. The relationship between classes and objects is analogous to the relationship between apple pie recipes and apple pies. You can make as many apple pies as you want from a single recipe. Figure 9.1 shows a class named `Circle` and its three objects.

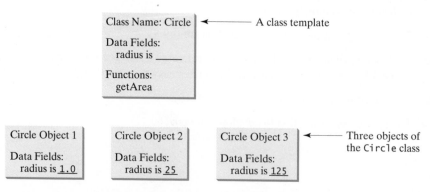

FIGURE 9.1 A class is a blueprint for creating objects.

class
data field
function

A C++ *class* uses variables to define *data fields* and *functions* to define behaviors. Additionally, a class provides functions of a special type, known as *constructors*, which are invoked when a new object is created. A constructor is a special kind of function. Constructors can

perform any action, but they are designed to perform initializing actions, such as initializing   constructor
the data fields of objects. Figure 9.2 shows an example of the class for `Circle` objects.

```
class Circle
{
public:
  // The radius of this circle
  double radius;  ◄──────────── Data field

  // Construct a circle object
  Circle()
  {
    radius = 1;
  }
                                ◄──────────── Constructors
  // Construct a circle object
  Circle(double newRadius)
  {
    radius = newRadius;
  }

  // Return the area of this circle
  double getArea()  ◄──────────── Function
  {
    return radius * radius * 3.14159;
  }
};
```

FIGURE 9.2   A class is a blueprint that defines objects of the same type.

The illustration of class and objects in Figure 9.1 can be standardized using UML (Unified
Modeling Language) notation, as shown in Figure 9.3. This is called a *UML class diagram*, or   UML class diagram
simply *class diagram*. The data field is denoted as

`dataFieldName: dataFieldType`

The constructor is denoted as

`ClassName(parameterName: parameterType)`

The function is denoted as

`functionName(parameterName: parameterType): returnType`

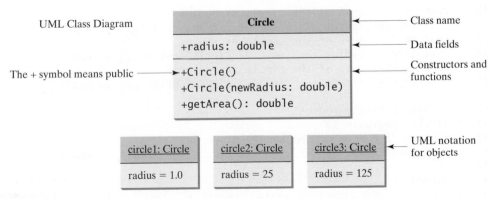

FIGURE 9.3   Classes and objects can be represented using UML notations.

9.3 Example: Defining Classes and Creating Objects

Key
Point

Classes are definitions for objects and objects are created from classes.

Listing 9.1 is a program that demonstrates classes and objects. It constructs three circle objects with radius 1.0, 25, and 125 and displays the radius and area of each. Change the radius of the second object to 100 and display its new radius and area.

VideoNote
Use classes

define class

data field

no-arg constructor

second constructor

function

don't omit

main function

creating object
creating object
creating object

accessing radius
invoking getArea

modify radius

LISTING 9.1   TestCircle.cpp

```cpp
1  #include <iostream>
2  using namespace std;
3
4  class Circle
5  {
6  public:
7     // The radius of this circle
8     double radius;
9
10    // Construct a default circle object
11    Circle()
12    {
13       radius = 1;
14    }
15
16    // Construct a circle object
17    Circle(double newRadius)
18    {
19       radius = newRadius;
20    }
21
22    // Return the area of this circle
23    double getArea()
24    {
25       return radius * radius * 3.14159;
26    }
27 };   // Must place a semicolon here
28
29 int main()
30 {
31    Circle circle1(1.0);
32    Circle circle2(25);
33    Circle circle3(125);
34
35    cout << "The area of the circle of radius "
36       << circle1.radius << " is " << circle1.getArea() << endl;
37    cout << "The area of the circle of radius "
38       << circle2.radius << " is " << circle2.getArea() << endl;
39    cout << "The area of the circle of radius "
40       << circle3.radius << " is " << circle3.getArea() << endl;
41
42    // Modify circle radius
43    circle2.radius = 100;
44    cout << "The area of the circle of radius "
45       << circle2.radius << " is " << circle2.getArea() << endl;
46
47    return 0;
48 }
```

```
The area of the circle of radius 1 is 3.14159
The area of the circle of radius 25 is 1963.49
The area of the circle of radius 125 is 49087.3
The area of the circle of radius 100 is 31415.9
```

The class is defined in lines 4–27. Don't forget that the semicolon (`;`) in line 27 is required.

The `public` keyword in line 6 denotes that all data fields, constructors, and functions can be accessed from the objects of the class. If you don't use the `public` keyword, the visibility is private by default. Private visibility will be introduced in Section 9.8.

The main function creates three objects named `circle1`, `circle2`, and `circle3` with radius `1.0`, `25`, and `125`, respectively (lines 31–33). These objects have different radii but the same functions. Therefore, you can compute their respective areas by using the `getArea()` function. The data fields can be accessed via the object using `circle1.radius`, `circle2.radius`, and `circle3.radius`, respectively. The functions are invoked using `circle1.getArea()`, `circle2.getArea()`, and `circle3.getArea()`, respectively.

These three objects are independent. The radius of `circle2` is changed to `100` in line 43. The object's new radius and area are displayed in lines 44–45.

As another example, consider TV sets. Each TV is an object with state (current channel, current volume level, power on or off) and behaviors (change channels, adjust volume, turn on/off). You can use a class to model TV sets. The UML diagram for the class is shown in Figure 9.4.

margin notes:
ending class definition
public
private by default

TV	
channel: int	The current channel (1 to 120) of this TV.
volumeLevel: int	The current volume level (1 to 7) of this TV.
on: boolean	Indicates whether this TV is on/off.
+TV()	Constructs a default TV object.
+turnOn(): void	Turns on this TV.
+turnOff(): void	Turns off this TV.
+setChannel(newChannel: int): void	Sets a new channel for this TV.
+setVolume(newVolumeLevel: int): void	Sets a new volume level for this TV.
+channelUp(): void	Increases the channel number by 1.
+channelDown(): void	Decreases the channel number by 1.
+volumeUp(): void	Increases the volume level by 1.
+volumeDown(): void	Decreases the volume level by 1.

FIGURE 9.4   The TV class models TV sets.

Listing 9.2 gives a program that defines the TV class and uses the TV class to create two objects.

LISTING 9.2   TV.cpp

```
1   #include <iostream>
2   using namespace std;
3
4   class TV                                          define a class
5   {
6   public:
```

data fields	7	`int channel;`
	8	`int volumeLevel; // Default volume level is 1`
	9	`bool on; // By default TV is off`
	10	
constructor	11	`TV()`
	12	`{`
	13	`  channel = 1; // Default channel is 1`
	14	`  volumeLevel = 1; // Default volume level is 1`
	15	`  on = false; // By default TV is off`
	16	`}`
	17	
turn on TV	18	`void turnOn()`
	19	`{`
	20	`  on = true;`
	21	`}`
	22	
turn off TV	23	`void turnOff()`
	24	`{`
	25	`  on = false;`
	26	`}`
set a new channel	27	
	28	`void setChannel(int newChannel)`
	29	`{`
	30	`  if (on && newChannel >= 1 && newChannel <= 120)`
	31	`    channel = newChannel;`
	32	`}`
	33	
set a new volume	34	`void setVolume(int newVolumeLevel)`
	35	`{`
	36	`  if (on && newVolumeLevel >= 1 && newVolumeLevel <= 7)`
	37	`    volumeLevel = newVolumeLevel;`
	38	`}`
	39	
increase channel	40	`void channelUp()`
	41	`{`
	42	`  if (on && channel < 120)`
	43	`    channel++;`
	44	`}`
	45	
decrease channel	46	`void channelDown()`
	47	`{`
	48	`  if (on && channel > 1)`
	49	`    channel--;`
	50	`}`
	51	
increase volume	52	`void volumeUp()`
	53	`{`
	54	`  if (on && volumeLevel < 7)`
	55	`    volumeLevel++;`
	56	`}`
	57	
decrease volume	58	`void volumeDown()`
	59	`{`
	60	`  if (on && volumeLevel > 1)`
	61	`    volumeLevel--;`
	62	`}`
	63	`};`
	64	
main function	65	`int main()`
	66	`{`

```
67   TV tv1;                                          create a TV
68   tv1.turnOn();                                    turn on
69   tv1.setChannel(30);                              set a new channel
70   tv1.setVolume(3);                                set a new volume
71
72   TV tv2;                                          create a TV
73   tv2.turnOn();                                    turn on
74   tv2.channelUp();                                 increase channel
75   tv2.channelUp();
76   tv2.volumeUp();                                  increase volume
77
78   cout << "tv1's channel is " << tv1.channel       display state
79     << " and volume level is " << tv1.volumeLevel << endl;
80   cout << "tv2's channel is " << tv2.channel
81     << " and volume level is " << tv2.volumeLevel << endl;
82
83   return 0;
84 }
```

```
tv1's channel is 30 and volume level is 3
tv2's channel is 3 and volume level is 2
```

Note that the channel and volume level are not changed if the TV is not on. Before changing a channel or volume level, the current values are checked to ensure that the channel and volume level are within the correct range.

The program creates two objects in lines 67 and 72, and invokes the functions on the objects to perform actions for setting channels and volume levels and for increasing channels and volumes. The program displays the state of the objects in lines 78–81. The functions are invoked using a syntax such as `tv1.turnOn()` (line 68). The data fields are accessed using a syntax such as `tv1.channel` (line 78).

These examples have given you a glimpse of classes and objects. You may have many questions about constructors and objects, accessing data fields and invoking objects' functions. The sections that follow discuss these issues in detail.

9.4 Constructors

A constructor is invoked to create an object.

Key Point

Constructors are a special kind of function, with three peculiarities:

- Constructors must have the same name as the class itself.   constructor's name

- Constructors do not have a return type—not even `void`.   no return type

- Constructors are invoked when an object is created. Constructors play the role of   invoke constructor
  initializing objects.

The constructor has exactly the same name as the defining class. Like regular functions, constructors can be overloaded (i.e., multiple constructors with the same name but different   constructor overloading signatures), making it easy to construct objects with different sets of data values.

It is a common mistake to put the `void` keyword in front of a constructor. For example,   no void

```
void Circle()
{
}
```

Most C++ compilers will report an error, but some will treat this as a regular function, not as a constructor.

Constructors are for initializing data fields. The data field **radius** does not have an initial value, so it must be initialized in the constructor (lines 13 and 19 in Listing 9.1). Note that a variable (local or global) can be declared and initialized in one statement, but as a class member, a data field cannot be initialized when it is declared. For example, it would be wrong to replace line 8 in Listing 9.1 by

```
double radius = 5; // Wrong for data field declaration
```

A class normally provides a constructor without arguments (e.g., **Circle()**). Such constructor is called a *no-arg* or *no-argument constructor*.

A class may be defined without constructors. In this case, a no-arg constructor with an empty body is implicitly defined in the class. Called a *default constructor*, it is provided automatically *only if no constructors are explicitly defined in the class*.

Data fields may be initialized in the constructor using an initializer list in the following syntax:

```
ClassName(parameterList)
  : datafield1(value1), datafield2(value2) // Initializer list
{
  // Additional statements if needed
}
```

The initializer list initializes **datafield1** with **value1** and **datafield2** with **value2**. For example,

```
Circle::Circle()
  : radius(1)
{
}
```
same as
```
Circle::Circle()
{
  radius = 1;
}
```

(a)   (b)

Constructor in (b), which does not use an initializer list, is actually more intuitive than the one in (a). However, using an initializer list is necessary to initialize object data fields that don't have a no-arg constructor. This is an advanced topic covered in Supplement IV.E on the Companion Website.

9.5 Constructing and Using Objects

Key Point

An object's data and functions can be accessed through the dot (.) operator via the object's name.

A constructor is invoked when an object is created. The syntax to create an object using the no-arg constructor is

```
ClassName objectName;
```

For example, the following declaration creates an object named **circle1** by invoking the **Circle** class's no-arg constructor.

```
Circle circle1;
```

The syntax to create an object using a constructor with arguments is

```
ClassName objectName(arguments);
```

For example, the following declaration creates an object named `circle2` by invoking the `Circle` class's constructor with a specified radius `5.5`.

```
Circle circle2(5.5);
```

In OOP term, an object's member refers to its data fields and functions. Newly created objects are allocated in the memory. After an object is created, its data can be accessed and its functions invoked using the *dot operator* (`.`), also known as the *object member access operator*:

dot operator

member access operator

- `objectName.dataField` references a data field in the object.

- `objectName.function(arguments)` invokes a function on the object.

For example, `circle1.radius` references the radius in `circle1`, and `circle1.getArea()` invokes the `getArea` function on `circle1`. Functions are invoked as operations on objects.

The data field `radius` is referred to as an *instance member variable* or simply *instance variable*, because it is dependent on a specific instance. For the same reason, the function `getArea` is referred to as an *instance member function* or *instance function*, because you can invoke it only on a specific instance. The object on which an instance function is invoked is called a *calling object*.

instance variable

member function

instance function

calling object

Note

When you define a custom class, capitalize the first letter of each word in a class name—for example, the class names `Circle`, `Rectangle`, and `Desk`. The class names in the C++ library are named in lowercase. The objects are named like variables.

class naming convention

object naming convention

The following points on classes and objects are worth noting:

- You can use primitive data types to define variables. You can also use class names to declare object names. In this sense, a class is also a data type.

class is a type

- In C++, you can use the assignment operator `=` to copy the contents from one object to the other. By default, each data field of one object is copied to its counterpart in the other object. For example,

memberwise copy

```
circle2 = circle1;
```

copies the `radius` in `circle1` to `circle2`. After the copy, `circle1` and `circle2` are still two different objects but have the same radius.

- Object names are like array names. Once an object name is declared, it represents an object. It cannot be reassigned to represent another object. In this sense, an object name is a constant, though the contents of the object may change. Memberwise copy can change an object's contents but not its name.

constant object name

- An object contains data and may invoke functions. This may lead you to think that an object is quite large. It isn't, though. Data are physically stored in an object, but functions are not. Since functions are shared by all objects of the same class, the compiler creates just one copy for sharing. You can find out the actual size of an object using the `sizeof` function. For example, the following code displays the size of objects `circle1` and `circle2`. Their size is **8**, since the data field radius is **double**, which takes **8** bytes.

object size

```
Circle circle1;
Circle circle2(5.0);

cout << sizeof(circle1) << endl;
cout << sizeof(circle2) << endl;
```

anonymous objects

Usually you create a named object and later access its members through its name. Occasionally you may create an object and use it only once. In this case, you don't have to name it. Such objects are called *anonymous objects*.

The syntax to create an anonymous object using the no-arg constructor is

```
ClassName()
```

The syntax to create an anonymous object using the constructor with arguments is

```
ClassName(arguments)
```

For example,

```
circle1 = Circle();
```

creates a `Circle` object using the no-arg constructor and copies its contents to `circle1`.

```
circle1 = Circle(5);
```

creates a `Circle` object with radius 5 and copies its contents to `circle1`.

For example, the following code creates `Circle` objects and invokes their `getArea()` function.

```
cout << "Area is " << Circle().getArea() << endl;
cout << "Area is " << Circle(5).getArea() << endl;
```

As you see from these examples, you may create an anonymous object if it will not be referenced later.

no-arg constructor

Caution

Please note that in C++, to create an anonymous object using the *no-arg constructor*, you have to add parentheses after the constructor name (e.g., `Circle()`). To create a named object using the no-arg constructor, you cannot use the parentheses after the constructor name (e.g., you use `Circle circle1` rather than `Circle circle1()`). This is the required syntax, which you just have to accept.

9.1 Describe the relationship between an object and its defining class. How do you define a class? How do you declare and create an object?

9.2 What are the differences between constructors and functions?

9.3 How do you create an object using a no-arg constructor? How do you create an object using a constructor with arguments?

9.4 Once an object name is declared, can it be reassigned to reference another object?

9.5 Assuming that the `Circle` class is defined as in Listing 9.1, show the printout of the following code:

```
Circle c1(5);
Circle c2(6);
c1 = c2;
cout << c1.radius << " " << c2.radius << endl;
```

9.6 What is wrong in the following code? (Use the `Circle` class defined in Listing 9.1, TestCircle.cpp.)

```
int main()
{
  Circle c1();
  cout << c1.getRadius() << endl;

  return 0;
}
```
(a)

```
int main()
{
  Circle c1(5);
  Circle c1(6);

  return 0;
}
```
(b)

9.7 What is wrong in the following code?

```
class Circle
{
public:
  Circle()
  {
  }
  double radius = 1;
};
```

9.8 Which of the following statements is correct?

```
Circle c;
```

```
Circle c();
```

9.9 Suppose the following two are independent statements. Are they correct?

```
Circle c;
```

```
Circle c = Circle();
```

VideoNote

Separate class definition

Key Point

9.6 Separating Class Definition from Implementation

Separating class definition from class implementation makes the class easy to maintain.

C++ allows you to separate class definition from implementation. The class definition describes the *contract* of the class and the class implementation carries out the contract. The class definition simply lists all the data fields, constructor prototypes, and function prototypes. The class implementation implements the constructors and functions. The class definition and implementation may be in two separate files. Both files should have the same name but different extension names. The class definition file has an extension name **.h** (h means header) and the class implementation file an extension name **.cpp**.

Listings 9.3 and 9.4 present the **Circle** class definition and implementation.

LISTING 9.3 Circle.h

```
1  class Circle
2  {
3  public:
4    // The radius of this circle
5    double radius;
6
7    // Construct a default circle object
8    Circle();
```

data field

no-arg constructor

```
9
10    // Construct a circle object
11    Circle(double);
12
13    // Return the area of this circle
14    double getArea();
15  };
```

second constructor

function prototype
semicolon required

don't omit semicolon

> **Caution**
> It is a common mistake to omit the semicolon (;) at the end of the class definition.

LISTING 9.4   Circle.cpp

include class definition

implement constructor

implement constructor

implement function

```
1  #include "Circle.h"
2
3  // Construct a default circle object
4  Circle::Circle()
5  {
6    radius = 1;
7  }
8
9  // Construct a circle object
10 Circle::Circle(double newRadius)
11 {
12   radius = newRadius;
13 }
14
15 // Return the area of this circle
16 double Circle::getArea()
17 {
18   return radius * radius * 3.14159;
19 }
```

binary scope resolution operator

The :: symbol, known as the *binary scope resolution operator*, specifies the scope of a class member in a class.

Here, Circle:: preceding each constructor and function in the Circle class tells the compiler that these constructors and functions are defined in the Circle class.

Listing 9.5 is a program that uses the Circle class. Such a program that uses the class is often referred to as a *client* of the class.

client

LISTING 9.5   TestCircleWithHeader.cpp

include class definition

construct circle
construct circle

set a new radius

```
1  #include <iostream>
2  #include "Circle.h"
3  using namespace std;
4
5  int main()
6  {
7    Circle circle1;
8    Circle circle2(5.0);
9
10   cout << "The area of the circle of radius "
11     << circle1.radius << " is " << circle1.getArea() << endl;
12   cout << "The area of the circle of radius "
13     << circle2.radius << " is " << circle2.getArea() << endl;
14
15   // Modify circle radius
16   circle2.radius = 100;
```

```
17    cout << "The area of the circle of radius "
18      << circle2.radius << " is " << circle2.getArea() << endl;
19
20    return 0;
21  }
```

```
The area of the circle of radius 1 is 3.14159
The area of the circle of radius 5 is 78.5397
The area of the circle of radius 100 is 31415.9
```

There are at least two benefits for separating a class definition from implementation.

why separation?

1. It hides implementation from definition. You can feel free to change the implementation. The client program that uses the class does not need to change as long as the definition is not changed.

2. As a software vendor, you can just provide the customer with the header file and class object code without revealing the source code for implementing the class. This protects the software vendor's intellectual property.

Note

To compile a main program from the command line, you need to add all its supporting files in the command. For example, to compile TestCircleWithDefinition.cpp using a GNU C++ compiler, the command is

compile from command line

```
g++ Circle.h Circle.cpp TestCircleWithHeader.cpp -o Main
```

Note

If the main program uses other programs, all of these program source files must be present in the project pane in the IDE. Otherwise, you may get linking errors. For example, to run TestCircleWithHeader.cpp, you need to place TestCircleWithHeader.cpp, Circle.cpp, and Circle.h in the project pane in Visual C++, as shown in Figure 9.5.

compile from IDE

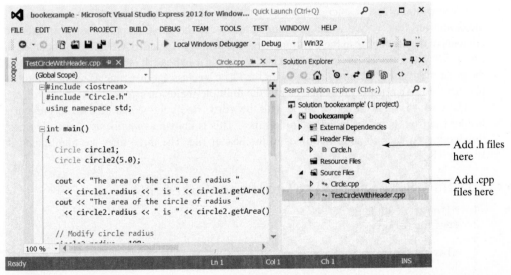

FIGURE 9.5 For the program to run, you need to place all dependent files in the project pane.

9.10 How do you separate class definition from implementation?

9.11 What is the output of the following code? (Use the `Circle` class defined in Listing 9.3, Circle.h.)

```cpp
int main()
{
  Circle c1;
  Circle c2(6);
  c1 = c2;
  cout << c1.getArea() << endl;

  return 0;
}
```

(a)

```cpp
int main()
{
  cout << Circle(8).getArea()
    << endl;

  return 0;
}
```

(b)

9.7 Preventing Multiple Inclusions

Inclusion guard prevents header files to be included multiple times.

It is a common mistake to include, inadvertently, the same header file in a program multiple times. Suppose Head.h includes `Circle.h` and TestHead.cpp includes both Head.h and `Circle.h`, as shown in Listings 9.6 and 9.7.

LISTING 9.6 Head.h

include `Circle.h`

```cpp
1  #include "Circle.h"
2  // Other code in Head.h omitted
```

LISTING 9.7 TestHead.cpp

include `Circle.h`
include Head.h

```cpp
1  #include "Circle.h"
2  #include "Head.h"
3
4  int main()
5  {
6    // Other code in TestHead.cpp omitted
7  }
```

If you compile TestHead.cpp, you will get a compile error indicating that there are multiple definitions for `Circle`. What is wrong here? Recall that the C++ preprocessor inserts the contents of the header file at the position where the header is included. `Circle.h` is included in line 1. Since the header file for `Circle` is also included in Head.h (see line 1 in Listing 9.6), the preprocessor will add the definition for the `Circle` class another time as result of including Head.h in TestHead.cpp, which causes the multiple-inclusion errors.

inclusion guard

The C++ `#ifndef` directive along with the `#define` directive can be used to prevent a header file from being included multiple times. This is known as *inclusion guard*. To make this work, you have to add three lines to the header file. The three lines are highlighted in Listing 9.8.

LISTING 9.8 CircleWithInclusionGuard.h

is symbol defined?
define symbol

```cpp
1  #ifndef CIRCLE_H
2  #define CIRCLE_H
3
4  class Circle
5  {
6  public:
```

```
7    // The radius of this circle
8    double radius;
9
10   // Construct a default circle object
11   Circle();
12
13   // Construct a circle object
14   Circle(double);
15
16   // Return the area of this circle
17   double getArea();
18 };
19
20 #endif
```
end of #ifndef

Recall that the statements preceded by the pound sign (#) are preprocessor directives. They are interpreted by the C++ preprocessor. The preprocessor directive #ifndef stands for "*if not defined*." Line 1 tests whether the symbol CIRCLE_H is already defined. If not, define the symbol in line 2 using the #define directive and the rest of the header file is included; otherwise, the rest of the header file is skipped. The #endif directive is needed to indicate the end of header file.

To avoid multiple-inclusion errors, define a class using the following template and convention for naming the symbol:

```
#ifndef ClassName_H
#define ClassName_H

A class header for the class named ClassName

#endif
```

If you replace Circle.h by CircleWithInclusionGuard.h in Listings 9.6 and 9.7, the program will not have the multiple-inclusion error.

9.12 What might cause multiple-inclusion errors? How do you prevent multiple inclusions of header files?

Check Point

9.13 What is the #define directive for?

9.8 Inline Functions in Classes

You can define short functions as inline functions to improve performance.

Key Point

Section 6.10, "Inline Functions," introduced how to improve function efficiency using inline functions. When a function is implemented inside a class definition, it automatically becomes an inline function. This is also known as *inline definition*. For example, in the following definition for class A, the constructor and function f1 are automatically inline functions, but function f2 is not.

inline definition

```
class A
{
public:
  A()
  {
    // Do something;
  }

  double f1()
  {
    // Return a number
  }
```

```
    double f2();
};
```

There is another way to define inline functions for classes. You may define inline functions in the class's implementation file. For example, to define function f2 as an inline function, precede the inline keyword in the function header as follows:

```
// Implement function as inline
inline double A::f2()
{
  // Return a number
}
```

As noted in Section 6.10, short functions are good candidates for inline functions, but long functions are not.

9.14 How do you implement all functions inline in Listing 9.4, Circle.cpp?

9.9 Data Field Encapsulation

Making data fields private protects data and makes the class easy to maintain.

The data fields radius in the Circle class in Listing 9.1 can be modified directly (e.g., circle1.radius = 5). This is not a good practice—for two reasons:

- First, data may be tampered with.

- Second, it makes the class difficult to maintain and vulnerable to bugs. Suppose you want to modify the Circle class to ensure that the radius is nonnegative after other programs have already used the class. You have to change not only the Circle class, but also the programs that use the Circle class. This is because the clients may have modified the radius directly (e.g., myCircle.radius = -5).

data field encapsulation
private

To prevent direct modifications of properties, you should declare the data field private, using the private keyword. This is known as *data field encapsulation*. Making the radius data field private in the Circle class, you can define the class as follows:

```
class Circle
{
public:
  Circle();
  Circle(double);
  double getArea();

private:
  double radius;
};
```

A private data field cannot be accessed by an object through a direct reference outside the class that defines the private field. But often a client needs to retrieve and/or modify a data field. To make a private data field accessible, provide a *get* function to return the field's value. To enable a private data field to be updated, provide a *set* function to set a new value.

Note

accessor
mutator

Colloquially, a get function is referred to as an *accessor*, and a set function is referred to as a *mutator*.

A **get** function has the following signature:

```
returnType getPropertyName()
```

If the **returnType** is **bool**, by convention the **get** function should be defined as follows: bool accessor

```
bool isPropertyName()
```

A **set** function has the following signature:

```
void setPropertyName(dataType propertyValue)
```

Let us create a new circle class with a private data field radius and its associated accessor and mutator functions. The class diagram is shown in Figure 9.6. The new circle class is defined in Listing 9.9.

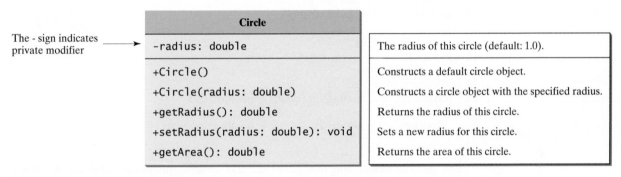

FIGURE 9.6   The `Circle` class encapsulates circle properties and provides get/set and other functions.

LISTING 9.9   CircleWithPrivateDataFields.h

```
1  #ifndef CIRCLE_H
2  #define CIRCLE_H
3
4  class Circle
5  {
6  public:                                              public
7    Circle();
8    Circle(double);
9    double getArea();
10   double getRadius();                                access function
11   void setRadius(double);                            mutator function
12
13 private:                                             private
14   double radius;
15 };
16
17 #endif
```

Listing 9.10 implements the class contract specified in the header file in Listing 9.9.

LISTING 9.10   CircleWithPrivateDataFields.cpp

```
1  #include "CircleWithPrivateDataFields.h"            include header file
2
3  // Construct a default circle object
4  Circle::Circle()                                    constructor
```

```
 5  {
 6      radius = 1;
 7  }
 8
 9  // Construct a circle object
10  Circle::Circle(double newRadius)
11  {
12      radius = newRadius;
13  }
14
15  // Return the area of this circle
16  double Circle::getArea()
17  {
18      return radius * radius * 3.14159;
19  }
20
21  // Return the radius of this circle
22  double Circle::getRadius()
23  {
24      return radius;
25  }
26
27  // Set a new radius
28  void Circle::setRadius(double newRadius)
29  {
30      radius = (newRadius >= 0) ? newRadius : 0;
31  }
```

constructor — lines 9–13
get area — lines 15–19
get radius — lines 21–25
set radius — lines 27–31

The getRadius() function (lines 22–25) returns the radius, and the setRadius (newRadius) function (line 28–31) sets a new radius into the object. If the new radius is negative, 0 is set to the radius in the object. Since these functions are the only ways to read and modify radius, you have total control over how the radius property is accessed. If you have to change the functions' implementation, you need not change the client programs. This makes the class easy to maintain.

Listing 9.11 is a client program that uses the Circle class to create a Circle object and modifies the radius using the setRadius function.

LISTING 9.11 TestCircleWithPrivateDataFields.cpp

```
 1  #include <iostream>
 2  #include "CircleWithPrivateDataFields.h"
 3  using namespace std;
 4
 5  int main()
 6  {
 7      Circle circle1;
 8      Circle circle2(5.0);
 9
10      cout << "The area of the circle of radius "
11        << circle1.getRadius() << " is " << circle1.getArea() << endl;
12      cout << "The area of the circle of radius "
13        << circle2.getRadius() << " is " << circle2.getArea() << endl;
14
15      // Modify circle radius
16      circle2.setRadius(100);
17      cout << "The area of the circle of radius "
18        << circle2.getRadius() << " is " << circle2.getArea() << endl;
19
20      return 0;
21  }
```

include header file — line 2
construct object — lines 7, 8
get radius — line 11
set radius — line 16

```
The area of the circle of radius 1 is 3.14159
The area of the circle of radius 5 is 78.5397
The area of the circle of radius 100 is 31415.9
```

The data field `radius` is declared private. Private data can be accessed only within their defining class. You cannot use `circle1.radius` in the client program. A compile error would occur if you attempted to access private data from a client.

Tip

To prevent data from being tampered with and to make the class easy to maintain, the data fields in this book will be private.

9.15 What is wrong in the following code? (Use the `Circle` class defined in Listing 9.9, CircleWithPrivateDataFields.h.)

Check
Point

```
Circle c;
cout << c.radius << endl;
```

9.16 What is an accessor function? What is a mutator function? What are the naming conventions for such functions?

9.17 What are the benefits of data field encapsulation?

9.10 The Scope of Variables

The scope of instance and static variables is the entire class, regardless of where the variables are declared.

Key
Point

Chapter 6 discussed the scope of global variables, local variables, and static local variables. Global variables are declared outside all functions and are accessible to all functions in its scope. The scope of a global variable starts from its declaration and continues to the end of the program. Local variables are defined inside functions. The scope of a local variable starts from its declaration and continues to the end of the block that contains the variable. Static local variables are permanently stored in the program so they can be used in the next call of the function.

The data fields are declared as variables and are accessible to all constructors and functions in the class. Data fields and functions can be in any order in a class. For example, all the following declarations are the same:

```
class Circle
{
public:
  Circle();
  Circle(double);
  double getArea();
  double getRadius();
  void setRadius(double);

private:
  double radius;
};
```

```
class Circle
{
public:
  Circle();
  Circle(double);

private:
  double radius;

public:
  double getArea();
  double getRadius();
  void setRadius(double);
};
```

```
class Circle
{
private:
  double radius;

public:
  double getArea();
  double getRadius();
  void setRadius(double);

public:
  Circle();
  Circle(double);
};
```

| (a) | (b) | (c) |

public first

 Tip
Though the class members can be in any order, the common style in C++ is to place public members first and then private members.

This section discusses the scope rules of all the variables in the context of a class.

You can declare a variable for data field only once, but you can declare the same variable name in a function many times in different functions.

Local variables are declared and used inside a function locally. If a local variable has the same name as a data field, the local variable takes precedence, and the data field with the same name is hidden. For example, in the program in Listing 9.12, x is defined as a data field and as a local variable in the function.

LISTING 9.12 HideDataField.cpp

```
1   #include <iostream>
2   using namespace std;
3
4   class Foo
5   {
6   public:
7     int x; // Data field
8     int y; // Data field
9
10    Foo()
11    {
12      x = 10;
13      y = 10;
14    }
15
16    void p()
17    {
18      int x = 20; // Local variable
19      cout << "x is " << x << endl;
20      cout << "y is " << y << endl;
21    }
22  };
23
24  int main()
25  {
26    Foo foo;
27    foo.p();
28
29    return 0;
30  }
```

data field x
data field y

no-arg constructor

local variable

create object
invoke function

```
x is 20
y is 10
```

Why is the printout 20 for x and 10 for y? Here is why:

- x is declared as a data field in the Foo class, but is also defined as a local variable in the function p() with an initial value of 20. The latter x is displayed to the console in line 19.

- y is declared as a data field, so it is accessible inside function p().

Tip
As demonstrated in the example, it is easy to make mistakes. To avoid confusion, do not declare the same variable name twice in a class, except for function parameters.

9.18 Can data fields and functions be placed in any order in a class?

Check Point

VideoNote
The **Loan** class

Key Point

9.11 Class Abstraction and Encapsulation

Class abstraction is the separation of class implementation from the use of a class. The details of implementation are encapsulated and hidden from the user. This is known as class encapsulation.

In Chapter 6 you learned about function abstraction and used it in stepwise program development. C++ provides many levels of abstraction. *Class abstraction* is the separation of class implementation from the use of a class. The creator of a class provides a description of the class and lets the user know how it can be used. The collection of functions and fields that are accessible from outside the class, together with the description of how these members are expected to behave, serves as the *class's contract*. As shown in Figure 9.7, the user of the class does not need to know how the class is implemented. The details of implementation are encapsulated and hidden from the user. This is known as *class encapsulation*. For example, you can create a `Circle` object and find the area of the circle without knowing how the area is computed.

class abstraction

class's contract

class encapsulation

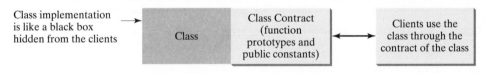

FIGURE 9.7 Class abstraction separates class implementation from the use of the class.

Class abstraction and encapsulation are two sides of the same coin. Many real-life examples illustrate the concept of class abstraction. Consider, for instance, building a computer system. Your personal computer is made up of many components, such as a CPU, CD-ROM, floppy disk, motherboard, fan, and so on. Each component can be viewed as an object that has properties and functions. To get the components to work together, all you need to know is how each component is used and how it interacts with the others. You don't need to know how it works internally. The internal implementation is encapsulated and hidden from you. You can build a computer without knowing how a component is implemented.

The computer-system analogy precisely mirrors the object-oriented approach. Each component can be viewed as an object of the class for the component. For example, you might have a class that models all kinds of fans for use in a computer, with properties like fan size and speed, functions like start, stop, and so on. A specific fan is an instance of this class with specific property values.

As another example, consider getting a loan. A specific loan can be viewed as an object of a **Loan** class. Interest rate, loan amount, and loan period are its data properties, and computing monthly payment and total payment are its functions. When you buy a car, a loan object is created by instantiating the class with your loan interest rate, loan amount, and loan period. You can then use the functions to find the monthly payment and total payment of your loan. As a user of the **Loan** class, you don't need to know how these functions are implemented.

Let us use the **Loan** class as an example to demonstrate the creation and use of classes. **Loan** has the data fields **annualInterestRate**, **numberOfYears**, and **loanAmount**, and the functions **getAnnualInterestRate**, **getNumberOfYears**, **getLoanAmount**, **setAnnualInterestRate**, **setNumberOfYears**, **setLoanAmount**, **getMonthlyPayment**, and **getTotalPayment**, as shown in Figure 9.8.

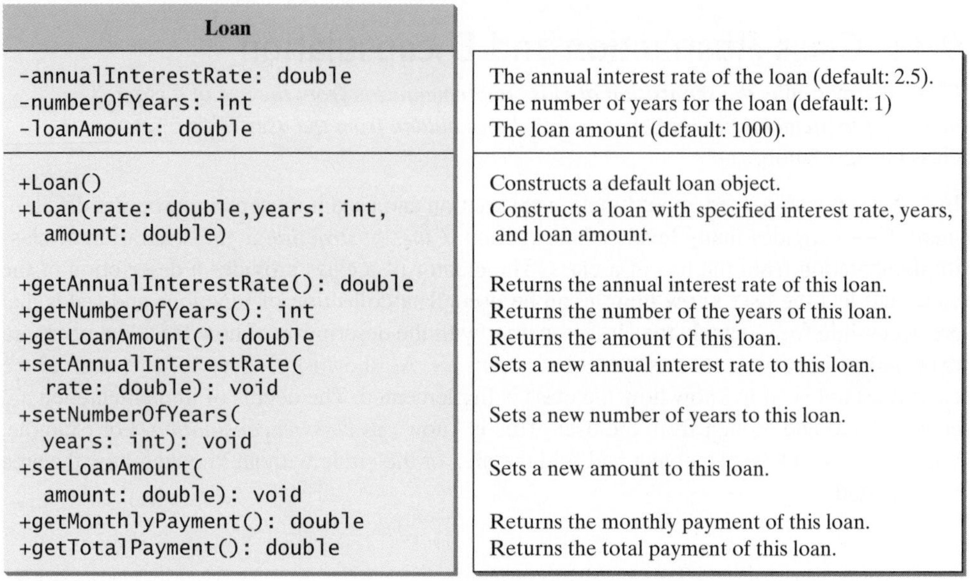

Loan	
-annualInterestRate: double -numberOfYears: int -loanAmount: double	The annual interest rate of the loan (default: 2.5). The number of years for the loan (default: 1) The loan amount (default: 1000).

+Loan()
+Loan(rate: double,years: int,
  amount: double)
 	
+getAnnualInterestRate(): double
+getNumberOfYears(): int
+getLoanAmount(): double
+setAnnualInterestRate(
  rate: double): void
+setNumberOfYears(
  years: int): void
+setLoanAmount(
  amount: double): void
+getMonthlyPayment(): double
+getTotalPayment(): double
	Constructs a default loan object.
	Constructs a loan with specified interest rate, years,
	  and loan amount.
	
	Returns the annual interest rate of this loan.
	Returns the number of the years of this loan.
	Returns the amount of this loan.
	Sets a new annual interest rate to this loan.
	
	Sets a new number of years to this loan.
	
	Sets a new amount to this loan.
	
	Returns the monthly payment of this loan.
	Returns the total payment of this loan.

FIGURE 9.8   The **Loan** class models the properties and behaviors of loans.

The UML diagram in Figure 9.8 serves as the contract for the **Loan** class. Throughout the book, you will play the role of both class user and class developer. The user can use the class without knowing how the class is implemented. Assume that the **Loan** class is available, with the header file, as shown in Listing 9.13. Let us begin by writing a test program that uses the **Loan** class, in Listing 9.14.

LISTING 9.13   Loan.h

```
1  #ifndef LOAN_H
2  #define LOAN_H
3
4  class Loan
5  {
6  public:
7    Loan();
8    Loan(double rate, int years, double amount);
9    double getAnnualInterestRate();
10   int getNumberOfYears();
11   double getLoanAmount();
12   void setAnnualInterestRate(double rate);
13   void setNumberOfYears(int years);
14   void setLoanAmount(double amount);
15   double getMonthlyPayment();
16   double getTotalPayment();
17
18 private:
19   double annualInterestRate;
```

public functions

private fields

```
20    int numberOfYears;
21    double loanAmount;
22  };
23
24  #endif
```

LISTING 9.14 TestLoanClass.cpp

```
1   #include <iostream>
2   #include <iomanip>
3   #include "Loan.h"                                                   include Loan header
4   using namespace std;
5
6   int main()
7   {
8     // Enter annual interest rate
9     cout << "Enter yearly interest rate, for example 8.25: ";
10    double annualInterestRate;
11    cin >> annualInterestRate;
12
13    // Enter number of years
14    cout << "Enter number of years as an integer, for example 5: ";
15    int numberOfYears;
16    cin >> numberOfYears;                                             input number of years
17
18    // Enter loan amount
19    cout << "Enter loan amount, for example 120000.95: ";
20    double loanAmount;
21    cin >> loanAmount;                                                input loan amount
22
23    // Create Loan object
24    Loan loan(annualInterestRate, numberOfYears, loanAmount);         create Loan object
25
26    // Display results
27    cout << fixed << setprecision(2);
28    cout << "The monthly payment is "
29       << loan.getMonthlyPayment() << endl;                           monthly payment
30    cout << "The total payment is " << loan.getTotalPayment() << endl; total payment
31
32    return 0;
33  }
34
```

The **main** function reads interest rate, payment period (in years), and loan amount (lines 8–21), creates a **Loan** object (line 24), and then obtains the monthly payment (line 29) and total payment (line 30) using the instance functions in the **Loan** class.

The **Loan** class can be implemented as in Listing 9.15.

LISTING 9.15 Loan.cpp

```
1   #include "Loan.h"
2   #include <cmath>
3   using namespace std;
4
5   Loan::Loan()                                                       no-arg constructor
6   {
7     annualInterestRate = 9.5;
8     numberOfYears = 30;
9     loanAmount = 100000;
10  }
```

	11
constructor	12 `Loan::Loan(double rate, int years, double amount)`

```
11
12  Loan::Loan(double rate, int years, double amount)
13  {
14    annualInterestRate = rate;
15    numberOfYears = years;
16    loanAmount = amount;
17  }
18
19  double Loan::getAnnualInterestRate()
20  {
21    return annualInterestRate;
22  }
23
24  int Loan::getNumberOfYears()
25  {
26    return numberOfYears;
27  }
28
29  double Loan::getLoanAmount()
30  {
31    return loanAmount;
32  }
33
34  void Loan::setAnnualInterestRate(double rate)
35  {
36    annualInterestRate = rate;
37  }
38
39  void Loan::setNumberOfYears(int years)
40  {
41    numberOfYears = years;
42  }
43
44  void Loan::setLoanAmount(double amount)
45  {
46    loanAmount = amount;
47  }
48
49  double Loan::getMonthlyPayment()
50  {
51    double monthlyInterestRate = annualInterestRate / 1200;
52    return loanAmount * monthlyInterestRate / (1 -
53      (pow(1 / (1 + monthlyInterestRate), numberOfYears * 12)));
54  }
55
56  double Loan::getTotalPayment()
57  {
58    return getMonthlyPayment() * numberOfYears * 12;
59  }
```

Margin labels (left column):
- constructor (line 12)
- accessor function (line 19)
- accessor function (line 24)
- accessor function (line 29)
- mutator function (line 34)
- mutator function (line 39)
- mutator function (line 44)
- get monthly payment (line 49)
- get total payment (line 56)

From a class developer's perspective, a class is designed for use by many different customers. In order to be useful in a wide range of applications, a class should provide a variety of ways for customization through constructors, properties, and functions.

The **Loan** class contains two constructors, three *get* functions, three *set* functions, and the functions for finding monthly payment and total payment. You can construct a **Loan** object by using the no-arg constructor or the one with three parameters: annual interest rate, number of years, and loan amount. The three *get* functions, **getAnnualInterest**, **getNumberOfYears**, and **getLoanAmount**, return annual interest rate, payment years, and loan amount, respectively.

Important Pedagogical Tip
The UML diagram for the **Loan** class is shown in Figure 9.8. Students should begin by writing a test program that uses the **Loan** class even though they don't know how the **Loan** class is implemented. This has three benefits:

■ It demonstrates that developing a class and using a class are two separate tasks.

■ It enables you to skip the complex implementation of certain classes without interrupting the sequence of the book.

■ It is easier to learn how to implement a class if you are familiar with the class through using it.

For all the examples from now on, you may first create an object from the class and try to use its functions before turning your attention to its implementation.

9.19 What is the output of the following code? (Use the **Loan** class defined in Listing 9.13, Loan.h.)

```cpp
#include <iostream>
#include "Loan.h"
using namespace std;

class A
{
public:
  Loan loan;
  int i;
};

int main()
{
  A a;
  cout << a.loan.getLoanAmount() << endl;
  cout << a.i << endl;

  return 0;
}
```

KEY TERMS

CHAPTER SUMMARY

1. A class is a blueprint for objects.

2. A class defines the data fields for storing the properties of objects and provides constructors for creating objects and functions for manipulating them.

3. Constructors must have the same name as the class itself.

4. A non-arg constructor is a constructor that does not have arguments.

5. A class is also a data type. You can use it to declare and create objects.

6. An object is an instance of a class. You use the dot (.) operator to access members of that object through its name.

7. The *state* of an object is represented by *data fields* (also known as *properties*) with their current values.

8. The *behavior* of an object is defined by a set of functions.

9. The data fields do not have initial values. They must be initialized in constructors.

10. You can separate class definition from class implementation by defining class in a header file and class implementation in a separate file.

11. The C++ `#ifndef` directive, called *inclusion guard*, can be used to prevent a header file from being included multiple times.

12. When a function is implemented inside a class definition, it automatically becomes an inline function.

13. Visibility keywords specify how the class, function, and data are accessed.

14. A `public` function or data is accessible to all clients.

15. A `private` function or data is accessible only inside the class.

16. You can provide a *get* function or a *set* function to enable clients to see or modify the data.

17. Colloquially, a *get* function is referred to as a *getter* (or *accessor*), and a *set* function is referred to as a *setter* (or *mutator*).

18. A *get* function has the signature

    `returnType getPropertyName()`

19. If the `returnType` is `bool`, the *get* function should be defined as

    bool `isPropertyName()`.

20. A *set* function has the signature

    void `setPropertyName(dataType propertyValue)`

QUIZ

Answer the quiz for this chapter online at www.cs.armstrong.edu/liang/cpp3e/quiz.html.

PROGRAMMING EXERCISES

Pedagogical Note

The exercises achieve three objectives:

three objectives

1. Design and draw UML for classes;

2. Implement classes from the UML;

3. Use classes to develop applications.

Solutions for the UML diagrams for the even-numbered exercises can be downloaded from the Companion Website and all others from the Instructor Web site.

Sections 9.2–9.11

9.1 (*The* `Rectangle` *class*) Design a class named `Rectangle` to represent a rectangle. The class contains:

- Two `double` data fields named `width` and `height` that specify the width and height of the rectangle.
- A no-arg constructor that creates a rectangle with `width 1` and `height 1`.
- A constructor that creates a default rectangle with the specified `width` and `height`.
- The accessor and mutator functions for all the data fields.
- A function named `getArea()` that returns the area of this rectangle.
- A function named `getPerimeter()` that returns the perimeter.

Draw the UML diagram for the class. Implement the class. Write a test program that creates two `Rectangle` objects. Assign width `4` and height `40` to the first object and width `3.5` and height `35.9` to the second. Display the properties of both objects and find their areas and perimeters.

9.2 (*The* `Fan` *class*) Design a class named `Fan` to represent a fan. The class contains:

- An `int` data field named `speed` that specifies the speed of the fan. A fan has three speeds indicated with a value `1`, `2`, or `3`.
- A `bool` data field named `on` that specifies whether the fan is on.
- A `double` data field named `radius` that specifies the radius of the fan.
- A no-arg constructor that creates a default fan with `speed 1`, `on false`, and `radius 5`.
- The accessor and mutator functions for all the data fields.

VideoNote
The `Fan` class

Draw the UML diagram for the class. Implement the class. Write a test program that creates two `Fan` objects. Assign speed `3`, radius `10`, and turn it on to the first object. Assign speed `2`, radius `5`, and turn it off to the second object. Invoke their accessor functions to display the fan properties.

9.3 (*The* `Account` *class*) Design a class named `Account` that contains:

- An `int` data field named `id` for the account.
- A `double` data field named `balance` for the account.
- A `double` data field named `annualInterestRate` that stores the current interest rate.

- A no-arg constructor that creates a default account with **id 0**, **balance 0**, and **annualInterestRate 0**.
- The accessor and mutator functions for **id**, **balance**, and **annualInterestRate**.
- A function named **getMonthlyInterestRate()** that returns the monthly interest rate.
- A function named **withdraw(amount)** that withdraws a specified amount from the account.
- A function named **deposit(amount)** that deposits a specified amount to the account.

Draw the UML diagram for the class. Implement the class. Write a test program that creates an **Account** object with an account ID of **1122**, a balance of **20000**, and an annual interest rate of **4.5%**. Use the **withdraw** function to withdraw $2500, use the **deposit** function to deposit $3000, and print the balance, the monthly interest.

9.4   (*The* **MyPoint** *class*) Design a class named **MyPoint** to represent a point with x- and y-coordinates. The class contains:

- Two data fields **x** and **y** that represent the coordinates.
- A no-arg constructor that creates a point (0, 0).
- A constructor that constructs a point with specified coordinates.
- Two *get* functions for data fields **x** and **y**, respectively.
- A function named **distance** that returns the distance from this point to another point of the **MyPoint** type.

Draw the UML diagram for the class. Implement the class. Write a test program that creates two points (0, 0) and (10, 30.5) and displays the distance between them.

*9.5   (*The* **Time** *class*) Design a class named **Time**. The class contains:

- Data fields **hour**, **minute**, and **second** that represent a time.
- A no-arg constructor that creates a **Time** object for the current time.
- A constructor that constructs a **Time** object with a specified elapse time since the middle of night, Jan 1, 1970, in seconds.
- A constructor that constructs a **Time** object with the specified hour, minute, and second.
- Three *get* functions for the data fields **hour**, **minute**, and **second**.
- A function named **setTime(int elapseTime)** that sets a new time for the object using the elapsed time.

Draw the UML diagram for the class. Implement the class. Write a test program that creates two **Time** objects, one using a no-arg constructor and the other using **Time(555550)**, and display their hour, minute, and second.

(*Hint*: The first two constructors will extract hour, minute, and second from the elapse time. For example, if the elapse time is **555550** seconds, the hour is **10**, the minute is **19**, and the second is **9**. For the no-arg constructor, the current time can be obtained using **time(0)**, as shown in Listing 2.9, ShowCurrentTime.cpp.)

*9.6   (*Algebra: quadratic equations*) Design a class named **QuadraticEquation** for a quadratic equation $ax^2 + bx + x = 0$. The class contains:

- Data fields **a**, **b**, and **c** that represent three coefficients.
- A constructor for the arguments for **a**, **b**, and **c**.
- Three **get** functions for **a**, **b**, and **c**.
- A function named **getDiscriminant()** that returns the discriminant, which is $b^2 - 4ac$.

- The functions named `getRoot1()` and `getRoot2()` for returning two roots of the equation:

$$r_1 = \frac{-b + \sqrt{b^2 - 4ac}}{2a} \quad \text{and} \quad r_2 = \frac{-b - \sqrt{b^2 - 4ac}}{2a}$$

These functions are useful only if the discriminant is nonnegative. Let these functions return 0 if the discriminant is negative.

Draw the UML diagram for the class. Implement the class. Write a test program that prompts the user to enter values for *a*, *b*, and *c*, and displays the result based on the discriminant. If the discriminant is positive, display the two roots. If the discriminant is 0, display the one root. Otherwise, display "The equation has no real roots".

*9.7 (*Stopwatch*) Design a class named `StopWatch`. The class contains:

- Private data fields `startTime` and `endTime` with `get` functions.
- A no-arg constructor that initializes `startTime` with the current time.
- A function named `start()` that resets the `startTime` to current time.
- A function named `stop()` that sets the `endTime` to current time.
- A function named `getElapsedTime()` that returns the elapsed time for the stop watch in milliseconds.

Draw the UML diagram for the class. Implement the class. Write a test program that measures the execution time of sorting 100000 numbers using selection sort.

*9.8 (*The* `Date` *class*) Design a class named `Date`. The class contains:

- Data fields `year`, `month`, and `day` that represent a date.
- A no-arg constructor that creates a `Date` object for the current date.
- A constructor that constructs a `Date` object with a specified elapse time since the middle of night, Jan 1, 1970, in seconds.
- A constructor that constructs a `Date` object with the specified year, month, and day.
- Three *get* functions for the data fields `year`, `month`, and `day`.
- A function named `setDate(int elapseTime)` that sets a new date for the object using the elapsed time.

Draw the UML diagram for the class. Implement the class. Write a test program that creates two `Date` objects, one using a no-arg constructor and the other using `Date(555550)`, and display their year, month, and day.

(*Hint*: The first two constructors will extract year, month, and day from the elapse time. For example, if the elapse time is 561555550 seconds, the year is 1987, the month is 10, and the day is 17. For the no-arg constructor, the current date can be obtained using `time(0)`, as shown in Listing 2.9, ShowCurrentTime.cpp.)

*9.9 (*Algebra:* 2 × 2 *linear equations*) Design a class named `LinearEquation` for a 2 × 2 system of linear equations:

$$\begin{matrix} ax + by = e \\ cx + dy = f \end{matrix} \quad x = \frac{ed - bf}{ad - bc} \quad y = \frac{af - ec}{ad - bc}$$

The class contains:

- Private data fields `a`, `b`, `c`, `d`, `e`, and `f`.
- A constructor with the arguments for `a`, `b`, `c`, `d`, `e`, and `f`.

- Six get functions for a, b, c, d, e, and f.
- A function named isSolvable() that returns true if $ad - bc$ is not 0.
- Functions getX() and getY() that return the solution for the equation.

Draw the UML diagram for the class and then implement the class. Write a test program that prompts the user to enter a, b, c, d, e, and f and displays the result. If $ad - bc$ is 0, report that "The equation has no solution." See Programming Exercise 3.3 for sample runs.

**9.10 (*Geometry: intersection*) Suppose two line segments intersect. The two endpoints for the first line segment are (x1, y1) and (x2, y2) and for the second line segment are (x3, y3) and (x4, y4). Write a program that prompts the user to enter these four endpoints and displays the intersecting point. Use the LinearEquation class in Exercise 9.9 for finding the interesting point. See Programming Exercise 3.22 for sample runs.

**9.11 (The EvenNumber class) Define the EvenNumber class for representing an even number. The class contains:

- A data field value of the int type that represents the integer value stored in the object.
- A no-arg constructor that creates an EvenNumber object for the value 0.
- A constructor that constructs an EvenNumber object with the specified value.
- A function named getValue() to return an int value for this object.
- A function named getNext() to return an EvenNumber object that represents the next even number after the current even number in this object.
- A function named getPrevious() to return an EvenNumber object that represents the previous even number before the current even number in this object.

Draw the UML diagram for the class. Implement the class. Write a test program that creates an EvenNumber object for value 16 and invokes the getNext() and getPrevious() functions to obtain and displays these numbers.

OBJECT-ORIENTED THINKING

Objectives

- To process strings using the `string` class (§10.2).

- To develop functions with object arguments (§10.3).

- To store and process objects in arrays (§10.4).

- To distinguish between instance and static variables and functions (§10.5).

- To define constant functions to prevent data fields from being modified accidentally (§10.6).

- To explore the differences between the procedural paradigm and object-oriented paradigm (§10.7).

- To design a class for body mass index (§10.7).

- To develop classes for modeling composition relationships (§10.8).

- To design a class for a stack (§10.9).

- To design classes that follow the class design guidelines (§10.10).

10.1 Introduction

Key Point

The focus of this chapter is on class design and explores the differences between procedural programming and object-oriented programming.

Chapter 9 introduced the important concept of objects and classes. You learned how to define classes, create objects, and use objects. This book's approach is to teach problem solving and fundamental programming techniques before object-oriented programming. This chapter addresses the transition from procedural to object-oriented programming. Students will see the benefits of object-oriented programming and use it effectively.

Our focus here is on class design. We will use several examples to illustrate the advantages of the object-oriented approach. The first example is the `string` class provided in the C++ library. The other examples involve designing new classes and using them in applications. We will also introduce some language features supporting these examples.

10.2 The `string` Class

VideoNote
The `string` class

Key Point

The `string` class defines the `string` type in C++. It contains many useful functions for manipulating strings.

In C++ there are two ways to process strings. One way is to treat them as arrays of characters ending with the null terminator (`'\0'`), as discussed in Section 7.11, "C-Strings." These are known as *C-strings*. The null terminator indicates the end of the string, which is important for the C-string functions to work. The other way is to process strings using the `string` class. You can use the C-string functions to manipulate and process strings, but the `string` class is easier. Processing C-strings requires the programmer to know how characters are stored in the array. The `string` class hides the low-level storage from the programmer. The programmer is freed from implementation details.

Section 4.8, "The `string` Type," briefly introduced the string type. You learned how to retrieve a string character using the `at(index)` function and the subscript operator `[]`, and use the `size()` and `length()` functions to return the number of characters in a string. This section gives a more detailed discussion on using string objects.

10.2.1 Constructing a String

You created a string using a syntax like this:

```
string s = "Welcome to C++";
```

This statement is not efficient because it takes two steps. It first creates a string object using a string literal and then copies the object to `s`.

A better way to create a string is to use the string constructor like this:

```
string s("Welcome to C++");
```

empty string

You can create an *empty string* using `string`'s no-arg constructor. For example, the following statement creates an empty string:

```
string s;
```

C-string to string

You can also create a string from a C-string using `string`'s constructor as shown in the following code:

```
char s1[] = "Good morning";
string s(s1);
```

Here `s1` is a C-string and `s` is a string object.

10.2.2 Appending to a String

You can use several overloaded functions to add new contents to a string, as shown in Figure 10.1.

string
+append(s: string): string
+append(s: string, index: int, n: int): string
+append(s: string, n: int): string
+append(n: int, ch: char): string

Appends string s into this string object.

Appends n number of characters in s starting at the position index to this string.

Appends the first n number of characters in s to this string.

Appends n copies of character ch to this string.

FIGURE 10.1 The **string** class provides the functions for appending a string.

For example:

```
string s1("Welcome");
s1.append(" to C++"); // Appends " to C++" to s1
cout << s1 << endl; // s1 now becomes Welcome to C++

string s2("Welcome");
s2.append(" to C and C++", 0, 5); // Appends " to C" to s2
cout << s2 << endl; // s2 now becomes Welcome to C

string s3("Welcome");
s3.append(" to C and C++", 5); // Appends " to C" to s3
cout << s3 << endl; // s3 now becomes Welcome to C

string s4("Welcome");
s4.append(4, 'G'); // Appends "GGGG" to s4
cout << s4 << endl; // s4 now becomes WelcomeGGGG
```

10.2.3 Assigning a String

You can use several overloaded functions to assign new contents to a string, as shown in Figure 10.2.

string
+assign(s[]: char): string
+assign(s: string): string
+assign(s: string, index: int, n: int): string
+assign(s: string, n: int): string
+assign(n: int, ch: char): string

Assigns array of characters or a string s to this string.

Assigns string s to this string.

Assigns n number of characters in s starting at the position index to this string.

Assigns the first n number of characters in s to this string.

Assigns n copies of character ch to this string.

FIGURE 10.2 The **string** class provides the functions for assigning a string.

For example:

```
string s1("Welcome");
s1.assign("Dallas"); // Assigns "Dallas" to s1
cout << s1 << endl; // s1 now becomes Dallas
```

```
string s2("Welcome");
s2.assign("Dallas, Texas", 0, 5); // Assigns "Dalla" to s2
cout << s2 << endl; // s2 now becomes Dalla

string s3("Welcome");
s3.assign("Dallas, Texas", 5); // Assigns "Dalla" to s3
cout << s3 << endl; // s3 now becomes Dalla

string s4("Welcome");
s4.assign(4, 'G'); // Assigns "GGGG" to s4
cout << s4 << endl; // s4 now becomes GGGG
```

10.2.4   Functions at, clear, erase, and empty

You can use the at(index) function to retrieve a character at a specified index, clear() to clear the string, erase(index, n) to delete part of the string, and empty() to test whether a string is empty, as shown in Figure 10.3.

string
+at(index: int): char
+clear(): void
+erase(index: int, n: int): string
+empty(): bool

Returns the character at the position index from this string.

Removes all characters in this string.

Removes n characters from this string starting at position index.

Returns true if this string is empty.

FIGURE 10.3   The string class provides the functions for retrieving a character, clearing and erasing a string, and checking whether a string is empty.

For example:

```
string s1("Welcome");
cout << s1.at(3) << endl; // s1.at(3) returns c
cout << s1.erase(2, 3) << endl; // s1 is now Weme
s1.clear(); // s1 is now empty
cout << s1.empty() << endl; // s1.empty returns 1 (means true)
```

10.2.5   Functions length, size, capacity, and c_str()

You can use the functions length(), size(), and capacity() to obtain a string's length, size, and capacity and c_str() to return a C-string, as shown in Figure 10.4. The functions length() and size() are aliases. The functions c_str() and data() are the same in the new C++11. The capacity() function returns the internal buffer size which is always greater than or equal to the actual string size.

string
+length(): int
+size(): int
+capacity(): int
+c_str(): char[]
+data(): char[]

Returns the number of characters in this string.

Same as length().

Returns the size of the storage allocated for this string.

Returns a C-string for this string.

Same as c_str().

FIGURE 10.4   The string class provides the functions for getting the length, capacity, and C-string of the string.

For example, see the following code:

```
1  string s1("Welcome");                              create string
2  cout << s1.length() << endl; // Length is 7
3  cout << s1.size() << endl; // Size is 7
4  cout << s1.capacity() << endl; // Capacity is 15
5
6  s1.erase(1, 2);                                     erase two characters
7  cout << s1.length() << endl; // Length is now 5
8  cout << s1.size() << endl; // Size is now 5
9  cout << s1.capacity() << endl; // Capacity is still 15
```

> **Note**
> The *capacity* is set to 15 when string **s1** is created in line 1. After two characters are   capacity?
> erased in line 6, the capacity is still 15, but the length and size become 5.

10.2.6 Comparing Strings

Often, in a program, you need to compare the contents of two strings. You can use the **compare** function. This function returns an **int** value greater than **0**, **0**, or less than **0** if this string is greater than, equal to, or less than the other string, as shown in Figure 10.5.

string
+compare(s: string): int
+compare(index: int, n: int, s: string): int

Returns a value greater than 0, 0, or less than 0 if this string is greater than, equal to, or less than s.
Compares this string with substring s(index, ..., index + n−1).

FIGURE 10.5   The **string** class provides the functions for comparing strings.

For example:

```
string s1("Welcome");
string s2("Welcomg");
cout << s1.compare(s2) << endl; // Returns -1
cout << s2.compare(s1) << endl; // Returns 1
cout << s1.compare("Welcome") << endl; // Returns 0
```

10.2.7 Obtaining Substrings

You can obtain a single character from a string using the **at** function. You can also obtain a substring from a string using the **substr** function, as shown in Figure 10.6.

string
+substr(index: int, n: int): string
+substr(index: int): string

Returns a substring of n characters from this string starting at position index.
Returns a substring of this string starting at position index.

FIGURE 10.6   The **string** class provides the functions for obtaining substrings.

For example:

```
string s1("Welcome");
cout << s1.substr(0, 1) << endl; // Returns W
```

```
cout << s1.substr(3) << endl; // Returns come
cout << s1.substr(3, 3) << endl; // Returns com
```

10.2.8 Searching in a String

You can use the `find` function to search for a substring or a character in a string, as shown in Figure 10.7. The function returns `string::npos` (not a position) if no match is found. `npos` is a constant defined in the `string` class.

string
+find(ch: char): unsigned
+find(ch: char, index: int): unsigned
+find(s: string): unsigned
+find(s: string, index: int): unsigned

Returns the position of the first matching character for ch.

Returns the position of the first matching character for ch at or from the position index.

Returns the position of the first matching substring s.

Returns the position of the first matching substring s starting at or from the position index.

FIGURE 10.7   The `string` class provides the functions for finding substrings.

For example:

```
string s1("Welcome to HTML");
cout << s1.find("co") << endl; // Returns 3
cout << s1.find("co", 6) << endl; // Returns string::npos
cout << s1.find('o') << endl; // Returns 4
cout << s1.find('o', 6) << endl; // Returns 9
```

10.2.9 Inserting and Replacing Strings

You can use the `insert` and `replace` functions to insert a substring and replace a substring in a string, as shown in Figure 10.8.

String
+insert(index: int, s: string): string
+insert(index: int, n: int, ch: char): string
+replace(index: int, n: int, s: string): string

Inserts the string s into this string at position index.

Inserts the character ch n times into this string at position index.

Replaces the n characters starting at position index in this string with the string s.

FIGURE 10.8   The `string` class provides the functions for inserting and replacing substrings.

Here are examples of using the `insert` and `replace` functions:

```
string s1("Welcome to HTML");
s1.insert(11, "C++ and ");
cout << s1 << endl; // s1 becomes Welcome to C++ and HTML

string s2("AA");
s2.insert(1, 4, 'B');
cout << s2 << endl; // s2 becomes to ABBBBA

string s3("Welcome to HTML");
s3.replace(11, 4, "C++");
cout << s3 << endl; // s3 becomes Welcome to C++
```

Note

A `string` object invokes the `append`, `assign`, `erase`, `replace`, and `insert` functions to change the contents of the `string` object. These functions also return the new string. For example, in the following code, `s1` invokes the `insert` function to insert "C++ and " into `s1`, and the new string is returned and assigned to `s2`.

return string

```
string s1("Welcome to HTML");
string s2 = s1.insert(11, "C++ and ");
cout << s1 << endl; // s1 becomes Welcome to C++ and HTML
cout << s2 << endl; // s2 becomes Welcome to C++ and HTML
```

Note

On most compilers, the capacity is automatically increased to accommodate more characters for the functions `append`, `assign`, `insert`, and `replace`. If the capacity is fixed and is too small, the function will copy as many characters as possible.

capacity too small?

10.2.10 String Operators

C++ supports operators to simplify string operations. Table 10.1 lists the string operators.

TABLE 10.1 String Operators

Operator	Description
[]	Accesses characters using the array subscript operator.
=	Copies the contents of one string to the other.
+	Concatenates two strings into a new string.
+=	Appends the contents of one string to the other.
<<	Inserts a string to a stream
>>	Extracts characters from a stream to a string delimited by a whitespace or the null terminator character.
==, !=, <,	Six relational operators for comparing strings.
<=, >, >=	

Here are the examples to use these operators:

```
string s1 = "ABC"; // The = operator                          =
string s2 = s1;  // The = operator
for (int i = s2.size() - 1; i >= 0; i--)
  cout << s2[i]; // The [] operator                           []

string s3 = s1 + "DEFG"; // The + operator                    +
cout << s3 << endl; // s3 becomes ABCDEFG                     <<

s1 += "ABC";                                                  +=
cout << s1 << endl; // s1 becomes ABCABC

s1 = "ABC";
s2 = "ABE";
cout << (s1 == s2) << endl; // Displays 0 (means false)       ==
cout << (s1 != s2) << endl; // Displays 1 (means true)        !=
cout << (s1 > s2) << endl; // Displays 0 (means false)        >
cout << (s1 >= s2) << endl; // Displays 0 (means false)       >=
cout << (s1 < s2) << endl; // Displays 1 (means true)         <
cout << (s1 <= s2) << endl; // Displays 1 (means true)        <=
```

10.2.11 Converting Numbers to Strings

Section 7.11.6, "Conversion between Strings and Numbers," introduced how to convert a string to an integer and a floating-point number using the functions `atoi` and `atof`. You can also use the `itoa` function to convert an integer to a string. Sometimes you need to convert a floating-point number to a string. You can write a function to perform the conversion. However, a simple approach is to use the `stringstream` class in the `<sstream>` header. `stringstream` provides an interface to manipulate strings as if they were input/output streams. One application of `stringstream` is for converting numbers to strings. Here is an example:

number to stringstream
stringstream to string

```
1  stringstream ss;
2  ss << 3.1415;
3  string s = ss.str();
```

10.2.12 Splitting Strings

Often you need to extract the words from a string. Assume that the words are separated by whitespaces. You can use the `stringstream` class discussed in the preceding section to accomplish this task. Listing 10.1 gives an example that extracts the words from a string and displays the words in separate lines.

LISTING 10.1 ExtractWords.cpp

include sstream header
include string header

create stringstream

end of stream

get data from stream

```
1  #include <iostream>
2  #include <sstream>
3  #include <string>
4  using namespace std;
5
6  int main()
7  {
8    string text("Programming is fun");
9    stringstream ss(text);
10
11   cout << "The words in the text are " << endl;
12   string word;
13   while (!ss.eof())
14   {
15     ss >> word;
16     cout << word << endl;
17   }
18
19   return 0;
20 }
```

```
The words in the text are
Programming
is
fun
```

The program creates a `stringstream` object for the text string (line 9) and this object can be used just like an input stream for reading data from the console. It sends data from the string stream to a string object `word` (line 15). The `eof()` function in the `stringstream` class returns true when all items in string stream are read (line 13).

10.2.13 Case Study: Replacing Strings

In this case study, you will write the following function that replaces the occurrence of a substring **oldSubStr** with a new substring **newSubStr** in the string **s**.

```
bool replaceString(string& s, const string& oldSubStr,
  const string& newSubStr)
```

The function returns **true** if string **s** is changed, and otherwise, it returns **false**.

Listing 10.2 gives the program.

LISTING 10.2   ReplaceString.cpp

```cpp
 1  #include <iostream>
 2  #include <string>                                      include string header
 3  using namespace std;
 4
 5  // Replace oldSubStr in s with newSubStr
 6  bool replaceString(string& s, const string& oldSubStr,  replaceString function
 7    const string& newSubStr);
 8
 9  int main()
10  {
11    // Prompt the user to enter s, oldSubStr, and newSubStr
12    cout << "Enter string s, oldSubStr, and newSubStr: ";
13    string s, oldSubStr, newSubStr;
14    cin >> s >> oldSubStr >> newSubStr;
15
16    bool isReplaced = replaceString(s, oldSubStr, newSubStr);  invoke replaceString
17
18    if (isReplaced)
19      cout << "The replaced string is " << s << endl;
20    else
21      cout << "No matches" << endl;
22
23    return 0;
24  }
25
26  bool replaceString(string& s, const string& oldSubStr,
27    const string& newSubStr)
28  {
29    bool isReplaced = false;                              isReplaced
30    int currentPosition = 0;
31    while (currentPosition < s.length())
32    {
33      int position = s.find(oldSubStr, currentPosition);  search substring
34      if (position == string::npos) // No more matches
35        return isReplaced;                                return isReplaced
36      else
37      {
38        s.replace(position, oldSubStr.length(), newSubStr);  replace substring
39        currentPosition = position + newSubStr.length();
40        isReplaced = true; // At least one match
41      }
42    }
43
44    return isReplaced;
45  }
```

```
Enter string s, oldSubStr, and newSubStr: abcdabab ab AAA
The replaced string is AAAcdAAAAAA
```

```
Enter string s, oldSubStr, and newSubStr: abcdabab gb AAA
No matches
```

The program prompts the user to enter a string, an old substring, and a new substring (line 14). The program invokes the `repalceString` function to replace all occurrences of the old substring with the new substring (line 16) and displays a message indicating whether the string has been replaced (lines 18–21).

The `replaceString` function searches for `oldSubStr` in string `s` starting from `currentPosition` starting from `0` (line 30). The `find` function in the string class is used to find a substring in a string (line 33). It returns `string::npos` if it is not found. In this case, the search ends and the function returns `isReplaced` (line 35). `isReplaced` is a `bool` variable and initially set to `false` (line 29). Whenever a match for a substring is found, it is set to `true` (line 40).

The function repeatedly finds a substring and replaces it with a new substring using the replace function (line 38) and resets the current search position (line 39) to look for a new match in the rest of the string.

✓Check Point

10.1 To create a string `"Welcome to C++"`, you may use a statement like this:

```
string s1("Welcome to C++");
```

or this:

```
string s1 = "Welcome to C++";
```

Which one is better? Why?

10.2 Suppose that `s1` and `s2` are two strings, given as follows:

```
string s1("I have a dream");
string s2("Computer Programming");
```

Assume that each expression is independent. What are the results of the following expressions?

(1) `s1.append(s2)`   (13) `s1.erase(1, 2)`
(2) `s1.append(s2, 9, 7)`   (14) `s1.compare(s3)`
(3) `s1.append("NEW", 3)`   (15) `s1.compare(0, 10, s3)`
(4) `s1.append(3, 'N')`   (16) `s1.c_str()`
(5) `s1.assign(3, 'N')`   (17) `s1.substr(4, 8)`
(6) `s1.assign(s2, 9, 7)`   (18) `s1.substr(4)`
(7) `s1.assign("NEWNEW", 3)`   (19) `s1.find('A')`
(8) `s1.assign(3, 'N')`   (20) `s1.find('a', 9)`
(9) `s1.at(0)`   (21) `s1.replace(2, 4, "NEW")`
(10) `s1.length()`   (22) `s1.insert(4, "NEW")`
(11) `s1.size()`   (23) `s1.insert(6, 8, 'N')`
(12) `s1.capacity()`   (24) `s1.empty()`

10.3 Suppose that `s1` and `s2` are given as follows:

```
string s1("I have a dream");
string s2("Computer Programming");
char s3[] = "ABCDEFGHIJKLMN";
```

Assume that each expression is independent. What are the results of **s1, s2,** and **s3** after each of the following statements?

```
(1) s1.clear()
(2) s1.copy(s3, 5, 2)
(3) s1.compare(s2)
```

10.4 Suppose that **s1** and **s2** are given as follows:

```
string s1("I have a dream");
string s2("Computer Programming");
```

Assume that each expression is independent. What are the results of the following expressions?

```
(1) s1[0]                      (6) s1 >= s2
(2) s1 = s2                    (7) s1 < s2
(3) s1 = "C++ " + s2           (8) s1 <= s2
(4) s2 += "C++ "               (9) s1 == s2
(5) s1 > s2                    (10) s1 != s2
```

10.5 Suppose you entered New York when running the following programs. What would be the printout?

```
#include <iostream>
#include <string>
using namespace std;

int main()
{
  cout << "Enter a city: ";
  string city;
  cin >> city;

  cout << city << endl;

  return 0;
}
```
(a)

```
#include <iostream>
#include <string>
using namespace std;

int main()
{
  cout << "Enter a city: ";
  string city;
  getline(cin, city);

  cout << city << endl;

  return 0;
}
```
(b)

10.6 Show the output of the following code (the **replaceString** function is defined in Listing 10.2).

```
string s("abcdabab"), oldSubStr("ab"), newSubStr("AAA");
replaceString(s, oldSubStr, newSubStr);
cout << s << endl;
```

10.7 If the **replaceString** function is returned from line 44 in Listing 10.2, is the returned value always false?

10.3 Passing Objects to Functions

Objects can be passed to a function by value or by reference, but it is more efficient to pass objects by reference.

Key Point

So far, you have learned how to pass arguments of primitive types, array types, and string types to functions. You can pass any types of objects to functions. You can pass objects by value or by reference. Listing 10.3 gives an example that passes an object by value.

LISTING 10.3 PassObjectByValue.cpp

```
1  #include <iostream>
2  // CircleWithPrivateDataFields.h is defined in Listing 9.9
3  #include "CircleWithPrivateDataFields.h"
4  using namespace std;
5
6  void printCircle(Circle c)
7  {
8    cout << "The area of the circle of "
9      << c.getRadius() << " is " << c.getArea() << endl;
10 }
11
12 int main()
13 {
14   Circle myCircle(5.0);
15   printCircle(myCircle);
16
17   return 0;
18 }
```

include header file
object parameter
access circle
create circle
pass object

The area of the circle of 5 is 78.5397

The Circle class defined CircleWithPrivateDataFields.h from Listing 9.9 is included in line 3. The parameter for the printCircle function is defined as Circle (line 6). The main function creates a Circle object myCircle (line 14) and passes it to the printCircle function by value (line 15). To pass an object argument by value is to copy the object to the function parameter. So the object c in the printCircle function is independent of the object myCircle in the main function, as shown in Figure 10.9a.

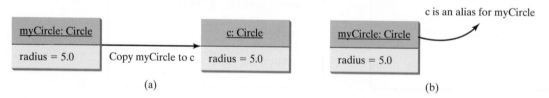

FIGURE 10.9 You can pass an object to a function (a) by value or (b) by reference.

Listing 10.4 gives an example that passes an object by reference.

LISTING 10.4 PassObjectByReference.cpp

```
1  #include <iostream>
2  #include "CircleWithPrivateDataFields.h"
3  using namespace std;
4
5  void printCircle(Circle& c)
6  {
7    cout << "The area of the circle of "
8      << c.getRadius() << " is " << c.getArea() << endl;
9  }
10
11 int main()
12 {
13   Circle myCircle(5.0);
```

include header file
reference parameter
access circle
create circle

```
14      printCircle(myCircle);
15
16      return 0;
17  }
```

pass reference

```
The area of the circle of 5 is 78.5397
```

A reference parameter of the `Circle` type is declared in the `printCircle` function (line 5). The `main` function creates a `Circle` object `myCircle` (line 13) and passes the reference of the object to the `printCircle` function (line 14). So the object `c` in the `printCircle` function is essentially an alias of the object `myCircle` in the main function, as shown in Figure 10.9b.

Though you can pass an object to a function by value or by reference, passing by reference is preferred, because it takes time and additional memory space to pass by value.

pass object by reference

10.8 Why is passing by reference preferred for passing an object to a function?

10.9 What is the printout of the following code?

✓ Check
Point

```cpp
#include <iostream>
using namespace std;

class Count
{
public:
  int count;

  Count(int c)
  {
    count = c;
  }

  Count()
  {
    count = 0;
  }
};

void increment(Count c, int times)
{
  c.count++;
  times++;
}

int main()
{
  Count myCount;
  int times = 0;

  for (int i = 0; i < 100; i++)
    increment(myCount, times);

  cout << "myCount.count is " << myCount.count;
  cout << " times is " << times;

  return 0;
}
```

10.10 If the highlighted code in Check Point 10.9 is changed to

```
void increment(Count& c, int times)
```

what will be the printout?

10.11 If the highlighted code in Check Point 10.9 is changed to

```
void increment(Count& c, int& times)
```

what will be the printout?

10.12 Can you change the highlighted code in Check Point 10.9 to the following?

```
void increment(const Count& c, int times)
```

10.4 Array of Objects

Key
Point

You can create an array of any objects just like an array of primitive values or strings.

In Chapter 7, arrays of primitive type elements and strings were created. You can create arrays of any objects. For example, the following statement declares an array of 10 `Circle` objects:

```
Circle circleArray[10]; // Declare an array of ten Circle objects
```

The name of the array is `circleArray`, and the no-arg constructor is called to initialize each element in the array. So, `circleArray[0].getRadius()` returns 1, because the no-arg constructor assigns 1 to `radius`.

You can also use the array initializer to declare and initialize an array using a constructor with arguments. For example,

```
Circle circleArray[3] = {Circle(3), Circle(4), Circle(5)};
```

Listing 10.5 gives an example that demonstrates how to use an array of objects. The program summarizes the areas of an array of circles. It creates `circleArray`, an array composed of 10 `Circle` objects; it then sets circle radii with radius 1, 2, 3, 4, . . . , and 10 and displays the total area of the circles in the array.

LISTING 10.5 TotalArea.cpp

```
 1  #include <iostream>
 2  #include <iomanip>
 3  #include "CircleWithPrivateDataFields.h"
 4  using namespace std;
 5
 6  // Add circle areas
 7  double sum(Circle circleArray[], int size)
 8  {
 9    // Initialize sum
10    double sum = 0;
11
12    // Add areas to sum
13    for (int i = 0; i < size; i++)
14      sum += circleArray[i].getArea();
15
16    return sum;
17  }
18
19  // Print an array of circles and their total area
20  void printCircleArray(Circle circleArray[], int size)
```

include header file

array of objects

get area

array of objects

```
21  {
22    cout << setw(35) << left << "Radius" << setw(8) << "Area" << endl;
23    for (int i = 0; i < size; i++)
24    {
25      cout << setw(35) << left << circleArray[i].getRadius()
26        << setw(8) << circleArray[i].getArea() << endl;
27    }
28
29    cout << "-----------------------------------------" << endl;
30
31    // Compute and display the result
32    cout << setw(35) << left << "The total area of circles is"
33      << setw(8) << sum(circleArray, size) << endl;
34  }
35
36  int main()
37  {
38    const int SIZE = 10;
39
40    // Create a Circle object with radius 1
41    Circle circleArray[SIZE];                                    create array
42
43    for (int i = 0; i < SIZE; i++)
44    {
45      circleArray[i].setRadius(i + 1);                           new radius
46    }
47
48    printCircleArray(circleArray, SIZE);                         pass array
49
50    return 0;
51  }
```

```
Radius                               Area
1                                    3.14159
2                                    12.5664
3                                    28.2743
4                                    50.2654
5                                    78.5397
6                                    113.097
7                                    153.938
8                                    201.062
9                                    254.469
10                                   314.159
-----------------------------------------
The total area of circles is         1209.51
```

The program creates an array of ten `Circle` objects (line 41). Two `Circle` classes were introduced in Chapter 9. This example uses the `Circle` class defined in Listing 9.9 (line 3).

Each object element in the array is created using the `Circle`'s no-arg constructor. A new radius for each circle is set in lines 43–46. `circleArray[i]` refers to a `Circle` object in the array. `circleArray[i].setRadius(i + 1)` sets a new radius in the `Circle` object (line 45). The array is passed to the `printCircleArray` function, which displays the radius and area of each circle and the total area of the circles (line 48).

The sum of the areas of the circle is computed using the `sum` function (line 33), which takes the array of `Circle` objects as the argument and returns a `double` value for the total area.

10.13 How do you declare an array of 10 **string** objects?

10.14 What is the output in the following code?

```
1  int main()
2  {
3    string cities[] = {"Atlanta", "Dallas", "Savannah"};
4    cout << cities[0] << endl;
5    cout << cities[1] << endl;
6
7    return 0;
8  }
```

VideoNote

static versus instance

10.5 Instance and Static Members

Key Point

A static variable is shared by all objects of the class. A static function cannot access instance members of the class.

instance data field
instance variables

The data fields used in the classes so far are known as *instance data fields,* or *instance variables.* An instance variable is tied to a specific instance of the class; it is not shared among objects of the same class. For example, suppose that you create the following objects using the **Circle** class in Listing 9.9, CircleWithPrivateDataFields.h:

```
Circle circle1;
Circle circle2(5);
```

The **radius** in **circle1** is independent of the **radius** in **circle2** and is stored in a different memory location. Changes made to **circle1**'s **radius** do not affect **circle2**'s **radius**, and vice versa.

static variable

If you want all the instances of a class to share data, use *static variables,* also known as *class variables.* Static variables store values for the variables in a common memory location. Accordingly, all objects of the same class are affected if one object changes the value of a static variable. C++ supports static functions as well as static variables. *Static functions* can be called without creating an instance of the class. Recall that *instance functions* can only be called from a specific instance.

static function
instance function

Let us modify the **Circle** class by adding a static variable **numberOfObjects** to count the number of circle objects created. When the first object of this class is created, **numberOfObjects** is 1. When the second object is created, **numberOfObjects** becomes 2. The UML of the new circle class is shown in Figure 10.10. The **Circle** class defines the instance variable **radius** and the static variable **numberOfObjects**, the instance functions **getRadius**, **setRadius**, and **getArea**, and the static function **getNumberOfObjects**. (Note that static variables and functions are underlined in the UML diagram.)

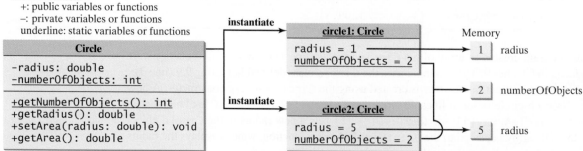

FIGURE 10.10 The instance variables, which belong to the instances, have memory storage independent of one another. The static variables are shared by all the instances of the same class.

To declare a static variable or a static function, put the modifier `static` in the variable or function declaration. So the static variable `numberOfObjects` and the static function `getNumberOfObjects()` can be declared as follows:

```
static int numberOfObjects;
static int getNumberOfObjects();
```

declare static variable
define static function

The new circle class is defined in Listing 10.6

LISTING 10.6   CircleWithStaticDataFields.h

```
1   #ifndef CIRCLE_H
2   #define CIRCLE_H
3
4   class Circle
5   {
6   public:
7     Circle();
8     Circle(double);
9     double getArea();
10    double getRadius();
11    void setRadius(double);
12    static int getNumberOfObjects();
13
14  private:
15    double radius;
16    static int numberOfObjects;
17  };
18
19  #endif
```

static function

static variable

A static function `getNumberOfObjects` is declared in line 12 and a static variable `numberOfObjects` is declared in line 16 as a private data field in the class.

Listing 10.7 gives the implementation of the `Circle` class:

LISTING 10.7   CircleWithStaticDataFields.cpp

```
1   #include "CircleWithStaticDataFields.h"
2
3   int Circle::numberOfObjects = 0;
4
5   // Construct a circle object
6   Circle::Circle()
7   {
8     radius = 1;
9     numberOfObjects++;
10  }
11
12  // Construct a circle object
13  Circle::Circle(double newRadius)
14  {
15    radius = newRadius;
16    numberOfObjects++;
17  }
18
19  // Return the area of this circle
20  double Circle::getArea()
21  {
22    return radius * radius * 3.14159;
23  }
```

include header

initialize static variable

increment
  numberOfObjects

increment
  numberOfObjects

```
24
25   // Return the radius of this circle
26   double Circle::getRadius()
27   {
28     return radius;
29   }
30
31   // Set a new radius
32   void Circle::setRadius(double newRadius)
33   {
34     radius = (newRadius >= 0) ? newRadius : 0;
35   }
36
37   // Return the number of circle objects
38   int Circle::getNumberOfObjects()
39   {
40     return numberOfObjects;
41   }
```

return numberOfObjects

The static data field **numberOfObjects** is initialized in line 3. When a **Circle** object is created, **numberOfObjects** is incremented (lines 9, 16).

Instance functions (e.g., **getArea()**) and instance data fields (e.g., **radius**) belong to instances and can be used only after the instances are created. They are accessed from a specific instance. Static functions (e.g., **getNumberOfObjects()**) and static data fields (e.g., **numberOfObjects**) can be accessed from any instance of the class, as well as from their class name.

The program in Listing 10.8 demonstrates how to use instance and static variables and functions and illustrates the effects of using them.

LISTING 10.8   TestCircleWithStaticDataFields.cpp

include header

invoke instance function

invoke static function

invoke static function

modify radius

invoke static function

```
1    #include <iostream>
2    #include "CircleWithStaticDataFields.h"
3    using namespace std;
4
5    int main()
6    {
7      cout << "Number of circle objects created: "
8        << Circle::getNumberOfObjects() << endl;
9
10     Circle circle1;
11     cout << "The area of the circle of radius "
12       << circle1.getRadius() << " is " << circle1.getArea() << endl;
13     cout << "Number of circle objects created: "
14       << Circle::getNumberOfObjects() << endl;
15
16     Circle circle2(5.0);
17     cout << "The area of the circle of radius "
18       << circle2.getRadius() << " is " << circle2.getArea() << endl;
19     cout << "Number of circle objects created: "
20        << Circle::getNumberOfObjects() << endl;
21
22     circle1.setRadius(3.3);
23     cout << "The area of the circle of radius "
24       << circle1.getRadius() << " is " << circle1.getArea() << endl;
25
26     cout << "circle1.getNumberOfObjects() returns "
27       << circle1.getNumberOfObjects() << endl;
```

```
28    cout << "circle2.getNumberOfObjects() returns "
29      << circle2.getNumberOfObjects() << endl;
30
31    return 0;
32  }
```

invoke static function

```
Number of circle objects created: 0
The area of the circle of radius 1 is 3.14159
Number of circle objects created: 1
The area of the circle of radius 5 is 78.5397
Number of circle objects created: 2
The area of the circle of radius 3.3 is 34.2119
circle1.getNumberOfObjects() returns 2
circle2.getNumberOfObjects() returns 2
```

Static variables and functions can be accessed without creating objects. Line 8 displays the number of objects, which is 0, since no objects have been created.

The `main` function creates two circles, `circle1` and `circle2` (lines 10, 16). The instance variable `radius` in `circle1` is modified to become `3.3` (line 22). This change does not affect the instance variable `radius` in `circle2`, since these two instance variables are independent. The static variable `numberOfObjects` becomes 1 after `circle1` is created (line 10), and it becomes 2 after `circle2` is created (line 16).

You can access static data fields and functions from the instances of the class—e.g., `circle1.getNumberOfObjects()` in line 27 and `circle2.getNumberOfObjects()` in line 29. But it is better to access them from the class name—e.g., `Circle::`. Note that in lines 27 and 29 `circle1.getNumberOfObjects()` and `circle2.getNumberOfObjects()` could be replaced by `Circle::getNumberOfObjects()`. This improves readability, because the reader can easily recognize the static function `getNumberOfObjects()`.

Tip
Use `ClassName::functionName(arguments)` to invoke a static function and `ClassName::staticVariable` to access static variables This improves readability, because the user can easily recognize the static function and data in the class.

use class name

Tip
How do you decide whether a variable or function should be instance or static? A variable or function that is dependent on a specific instance of the class should be an instance variable or function. A variable or function that is not dependent on a specific instance of the class should be a static variable or function. For example, every circle has its own radius. Radius is dependent on a specific circle. Therefore, `radius` is an instance variable of the `Circle` class. Since the `getArea` function is dependent on a specific circle, it is an instance function. Since `numberOfObjects` is not dependent on any specific instance, it should be declared static.

instance or static?

10.15 A data field and function can be declared as instance or static. What are the criteria for deciding?

10.16 Where do you initialize a static data field?

10.17 Suppose function `f()` is static defined in class `C` and `c` is an object of the `C` class. Can you invoke `c.f()`, `C::f()`, or `c::f()`?

Check
Point

10.6 Constant Member Functions

C++ also enables you to specify a constant member function to tell the compiler that the function should not change the value of any data fields in the object.

constant function

You used the **const** keyword to specify a constant parameter to tell the compiler that the parameter should not be changed in the function. You can also use the **const** keyword to specify a constant member function (or simply constant function) to tell the compiler that the function does not change the data fields in the object. To do so, place the **const** keyword at the end of the function header. For example, you may redefine the **Circle** class in Listing 10.6 as shown in Listing 10.9, and the header file is implemented in Listing 10.10.

LISTING 10.9 CircleWithConstantMemberFunctions.h

```
1  #ifndef CIRCLE_H
2  #define CIRCLE_H
3
4  class Circle
5  {
6  public:
7    Circle();
8    Circle(double);
9    double getArea() const;
10   double getRadius() const;
11   void setRadius(double);
12   static int getNumberOfObjects();
13
14 private:
15   double radius;
16   static int numberOfObjects;
17 };
18
19 #endif
```

const function
const function

LISTING 10.10 CircleWithConstantMemberFunctions.cpp

```
1  #include "CircleWithConstantMemberFunctions.h"
2
3  int Circle::numberOfObjects = 0;
4
5  // Construct a circle object
6  Circle::Circle()
7  {
8    radius = 1;
9    numberOfObjects++;
10 }
11
12 // Construct a circle object
13 Circle::Circle(double newRadius)
14 {
15   radius = newRadius;
16   numberOfObjects++;
17 }
18
19 // Return the area of this circle
20 double Circle::getArea() const
21 {
22   return radius * radius * 3.14159;
23 }
```

const function

```
24
25  // Return the radius of this circle
26  double Circle::getRadius() const                          const function
27  {
28    return radius;
29  }
30
31  // Set a new radius
32  void Circle::setRadius(double newRadius)
33  {
34    radius = (newRadius >= 0) ? newRadius : 0;
35  }
36
37  // Return the number of circle objects
38  int Circle::getNumberOfObjects()
39  {
40    return numberOfObjects;
41  }
```

Only instance member functions can be defined as constant functions. Like constant parameters, constant functions are for *defensive programming*. If your function mistakenly changes the value of data fields in a function, a compile error will be reported. Note that you can define only instant functions constant, not static functions. An instance get function should always be defined as a constant member function, because it does not change the contents of the object.

If a function does not change the object being passed, you should define the parameter constant using the `const` keyword like this:

defensive programming

constant parameter

```
void printCircle(const Circle& c)
{
  cout << "The area of the circle of "
    << c.getRadius() << " is " << c.getArea() << endl;
}
```

Note that this code will not compile if the `getRadius()` or `getArea()` function is not defined `const`. If you use the `Circle` class defined in Listing 9.9, the preceding function will not compile, because the `getRadius()` and `getArea()` are not defined `const`. However, if you use the `Circle` class defined in Listing 10.9, the preceding function will compile, because the `getRadius()` and `getArea()` are defined `const`.

Tip
You can use the `const` modifier to specify a constant reference parameter or a constant member function. You should use the `const` modifier *consistently* whenever appropriate.

use const consistently

10.18 True or false? Only instance member functions can be defined as constant functions.

10.19 What is wrong in the following class definition?

```
class Count
{
public:
  int count;

  Count(int c)
  {
    count = c;
  }
```

```cpp
      Count()
      {
        count = 0;
      }

      int getCount() const
      {
        return count;
      }

      void incrementCount() const
      {
        count++;
      }
};
```

10.20 What is wrong in the following code?

```cpp
#include <iostream>
using namespace std;

class A
{
public:
  A();
  double getNumber();

private:
  double number;
};

A::A()
{
  number = 1;
}

double A::getNumber()
{
  return number;
}

void printA(const A& a)
{
  cout << "The number is " << a.getNumber() << endl;
}

int main()
{
  A myObject;
  printA(myObject);

  return 0;
}
```

VideoNote

Thinking in objects

10.7 Thinking in Objects

🔑 Key
Point

The procedural paradigm focuses on designing functions. The object-oriented paradigm couples data and functions together into objects. Software design using the object-oriented paradigm focuses on objects and operations on objects.

This book has introduced fundamental programming techniques for problem solving using loops, functions, and arrays. The study of these techniques lays a solid foundation for object-oriented programming. Classes provide more flexibility and modularity for building reusable software. This section uses the object-oriented approach to improve the solution for a problem introduced in Chapter 3. Observing the improvements, you will gain insight on the differences between the procedural programming and object-oriented programming and see the benefits of developing reusable code using objects and classes.

Listing 3.2, ComputeAndInterpreteBMI.cpp, presented a program for computing body mass index. The program cannot be reused in other programs. To make the code reusable, define a function to compute body mass index as follows:

double getBMI(**double** weight, **double** height)

This function is useful for computing body mass index for a specified weight and height. However, it has limitations. Suppose you need to associate the weight and height with a person's name and birth date. You may declare separate variables to store these values. But these values are not tightly coupled. The ideal way to couple them is to create an object that contains them. Since these values are tied to individual objects, they should be stored in instance data fields. You can define a class named BMI, as shown in Figure 10.11.

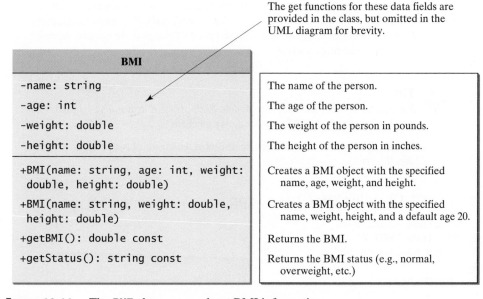

FIGURE 10.11   The BMI class encapsulates BMI information.

The BMI class can be defined as in Listing 10.11.

LISTING 10.11   BMI.h

```
1  #ifndef BMI_H
2  #define BMI_H
3
4  #include <string>
5  using namespace std;
6
7  class BMI
8  {
9  public:
```

constructors

```
10    BMI(const string& newName, int newAge,
11      double newWeight, double newHeight);
12    BMI(const string& newName, double newWeight, double newHeight);
```

functions

```
13    double getBMI() const;
14    string getStatus() const;
15    string getName() const;
16    int getAge() const;
17    double getWeight() const;
18    double getHeight() const;
19
20  private:
21    string name;
22    int age;
23    double weight;
24    double height;
25  };
26
27  #endif
```

Tip

The `string` parameter `newName` is defined as pass-by-reference using the syntax `string& newName`. This improves performance by preventing the compiler from making a copy of the object being passed into the function. Further, the reference is defined `const` to prevent `newName` from being modified accidentally. *You should always pass an object parameter by reference. If the object does not change in the function, define it as a `const` reference parameter.*

const reference parameter

Tip

If a member function does not change data fields, define it as a `const` function. All member functions in the `BMI` class are `const` functions.

const function

Assume that the `BMI` class has been implemented. Listing 10.12 is a test program that uses this class.

LISTING 10.12 UseBMIClass.cpp

```
1   #include <iostream>
2   #include "BMI.h"
3   using namespace std;
4
5   int main()
6   {
```

create object
invoke instance function

```
7     BMI bmi1("John Doe", 18, 145, 70);
8     cout << "The BMI for " << bmi1.getName() << " is "
9       << bmi1.getBMI() << " " << bmi1.getStatus() << endl;
10
```

create object
invoke instance function

```
11    BMI bmi2("Susan King", 215, 70);
12    cout << "The BMI for " << bmi2.getName() << " is "
13      << bmi2.getBMI() << " " + bmi2.getStatus() << endl;
14
15    return 0;
16  }
```

```
The BMI for John Doe is 20.8051 Normal
The BMI for Susan King is 30.849 Obese
```

Line 7 creates an object `bmi1` for John Doe and line 11 creates an object `bmi2` for Susan King. You can use the instance functions `getName()`, `getBMI()`, and `getStatus()` to return the BMI information in a `BMI` object.

The `BMI` class can be implemented as in Listing 10.13.

LISTING 10.13   BMI.cpp

```
1   #include <iostream>
2   #include "BMI.h"
3   using namespace std;
4
5   BMI::BMI(const string& newName, int newAge,              constructor
6       double newWeight, double newHeight)
7   {
8       name = newName;
9       age = newAge;
10      weight = newWeight;
11      height = newHeight;
12  }
13
14  BMI::BMI(const string& newName, double newWeight, double newHeight)   constructor
15  {
16      name = newName;
17      age = 20;
18      weight = newWeight;
19      height = newHeight;
20  }
21
22  double BMI::getBMI() const                               getBMI
23  {
24      const double KILOGRAMS_PER_POUND = 0.45359237;
25      const double METERS_PER_INCH = 0.0254;
26      double bmi = weight * KILOGRAMS_PER_POUND /
27        ((height * METERS_PER_INCH) * (height * METERS_PER_INCH));
28      return bmi;
29  }
30
31  string BMI::getStatus() const                            getStatus
32  {
33      double bmi = getBMI();
34      if (bmi < 18.5)
35        return "Underweight";
36      else if (bmi < 25)
37        return "Normal";
38      else if (bmi < 30)
39        return "Overweight";
40      else
41        return "Obese";
42  }
43
44  string BMI::getName() const
45  {
46      return name;
47  }
48
49  int BMI::getAge() const
50  {
51      return age;
52  }
```

```
53
54   double BMI::getWeight() const
55   {
56     return weight;
57   }
58
59   double BMI::getHeight() const
60   {
61     return height;
62   }
```

The mathematic formula for computing the BMI using weight and height is given in Section 3.7, "Case Study: Computing Body Mass Index." The instance function **getBMI()** returns the BMI. Since the weight and height are instance data fields in the object, the **getBMI()** function can use these properties to compute the BMI for the object.

The instance function **getStatus()** returns a string that interprets the BMI. The interpretation is also given in Section 3.7.

This example demonstrates the advantages of using the object-oriented over the procedural paradigm. The procedural paradigm focuses on designing functions. The object-oriented paradigm couples data and functions together into objects. Software design using the object-oriented paradigm focuses on objects and operations on objects. The object-oriented approach combines the power of the procedural paradigm with an added dimension that integrates data with operations into objects.

Procedural versus Object-Oriented Paradigms

In procedural programming, data and operations on the data are separate, and this methodology requires sending data to functions. Object-oriented programming places data and the operations that pertain to them within a single entity called an *object*; this approach solves many of the problems inherent in procedural programming. The object-oriented programming approach organizes programs in a way that mirrors the real world, in which all objects are associated with both attributes and activities. Using objects improves software reusability and makes programs easier to develop and easier to maintain.

Check Point

10.21 What is the output of the following code?

```cpp
#include <iostream>
#include <string>
#include "BMI.h"
using namespace std;

int main()
{
  string name("John Doe");
  BMI bmi1(name, 18, 145, 70);
  name[0] = 'P';

  cout << "name from bmil.getName() is " << bmi1.getName() <<
    endl;
  cout <<  "name is " << name << endl;

  return 0;
}
```

10.22 In the following code, what will be the output from **a.s** and **b.k** in the main function?

```cpp
#include <iostream>
#include <string>
using namespace std;
```

```
class A
{
public:
  A()
  {
    s = "John";
  }

  string s;
}

class B
{
public:
  B()
  {
    k = 4;
  };

  int k;
};

int main()
{
  A a;
  cout << a.s << endl;

  B b;
  cout << b.k << endl;

  return 0;
}
```

10.23 What is wrong in the following code?

```
#include <iostream>
#include <string>
using namespace std;

class A
{
public:
  A() { };
  string s("abc");
};

int main()
{
  A a;
  cout << a.s << endl;

  return 0;
}
```

10.24 What is wrong in the following code?

```
#include <iostream>
#include <string>
using namespace std;
class A
```

```
    {
    public:
      A() { };

    private:
      string s;
    };

    int main()
    {
      A a;
      cout << a.s << endl;

      return 0;
    }
```

10.8 Object Composition

Key Point

An object can contain another object. The relationship between the two is called composition.

In Listing 10.11, you defined the BMI class to contain a string data field. The relationship between BMI and string is composition.

aggregation

has-a relationship

Composition is actually a special case of the *aggregation* relationship. Aggregation models *has-a* relationships and represents an ownership relationship between two objects. The owner object is called an *aggregating object* and its class an *aggregating class*. The subject object is called an *aggregated object* and its class an *aggregated class*.

composition

An object may be owned by several other aggregating objects. If an object is exclusively owned by an aggregating object, the relationship between the object and its aggregating object is referred to as *composition*. For example, "a student has a name" is a composition relationship between the Student class and the Name class, whereas "a student has an address" is an aggregation relationship between the Student class and the Address class, since an address may be shared by several students. In UML, a filled diamond is attached to an aggregating class (e.g., Student) to denote the composition relationship with an aggregated class (e.g., Name), and an empty diamond is attached to an aggregating class (e.g., Student) to denote the aggregation relationship with an aggregated class (e.g., Address), as shown in Figure 10.12.

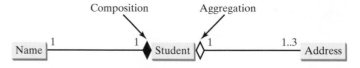

FIGURE 10.12 A student has a name and an address.

multiplicity

Each class involved in a relationship may specify a *multiplicity*. A multiplicity could be a number or an interval that specifies how many objects of the class are involved in the relationship. The character * means an unlimited number of objects, and the interval m..n means that the number of objects should be between m and n, inclusive. In Figure 10.12, each student has only one address, and each address may be shared by up to three students. Each student has one name, and a name is unique for each student.

An aggregation relationship is usually represented as a data field in the aggregating class. For example, the relationship in Figure 10.12 can be represented as follows:

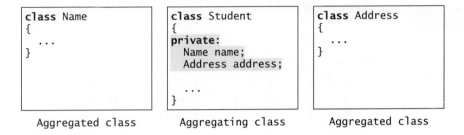

| Aggregated class | Aggregating class | Aggregated class |

Aggregation may exist between objects of the same class. For example, a person may have a supervisor. This is illustrated in Figure 10.13.

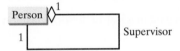

FIGURE 10.13   A person may have a supervisor.

In the relationship "a person has a supervisor," as shown in Figure 10.13, a supervisor can be represented as a data field in the **Person** class, as follows:

```
class Person
{
private:
    Person supervisor;    // The type for the data is the class itself

    ...
}
```

If a person may have several supervisors, as shown in Figure 10.14, you may use an array to store supervisors (for example, **10** supervisors).

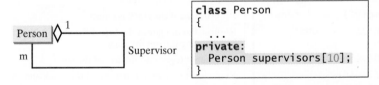

FIGURE 10.14   A person may have several supervisors.

 Note

Since aggregation and composition relationships are represented using classes in similar ways, we will not differentiate them and call both compositions.

aggregation or composition

10.25 What is object composition?

10.26 What is the difference between aggregation and composition?

10.27 What is UML notation of aggregation and composition?

10.28 Why both aggregation and composition are together referred to as composition?

10.9 Case Study: The **StackOfIntegers** Class

This section designs a class for modeling stacks.

Recall that a stack is a data structure that holds data in a last-in, first-out fashion, as shown in Figure 10.15.

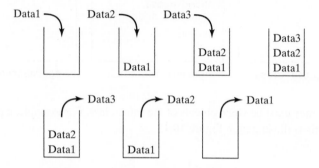

FIGURE 10.15 A stack holds data in a last-in, first-out fashion.

stack

Stacks have many applications. For example, the compiler uses a stack to process function invocations. When a function is invoked, its parameters and local variables are placed in an activation record that is pushed into a stack. When a function calls another function, the new function's parameters and local variables are placed in a new activation record that is pushed into the stack. When a function finishes its work and returns to its caller, its activation record is released from the stack.

You can define a class to model stacks. For simplicity, assume the stack holds the `int` values. So, name the stack class `StackOfIntegers`. The UML diagram for the class is shown in Figure 10.16.

StackOfIntegers	
`-elements[100]: int` `-size: int`	An array to store integers in the stack. The number of integers in the stack.

`+StackOfIntegers()`
`+isEmpty(): bool const`
`+peek(): int const`
 	
`+push(value: int): void`
`+pop(): int`
`+getSize(): int const`
	Constructs an empty stack.
	Returns true if the stack is empty
	Returns the integer at the top of the stack without
	    removing it from the stack.
	Stores an integer into the top of the stack.
	Removes the integer at the top of the stack and returns it.
	Returns the number of elements in the stack.

FIGURE 10.16 The `StackOfIntegers` class encapsulates the stack storage and provides the operations for manipulating the stack.

Suppose that the class is available, as defined in Listing 10.14. Let us write a test program in Listing 10.15 that uses the class to create a stack (line 7), stores ten integers 0, 1, 2, . . . , and 9 (lines 9–10), and displays them in reverse order (lines 12–13).

LISTING 10.14 StackOfIntegers.h

```
1  #ifndef STACK_H
2  #define STACK_H
3
```

```
 4  class StackOfIntegers
 5  {
 6  public:                                      public members
 7    StackOfIntegers();
 8    bool isEmpty() const;
 9    int peek() const;
10    void push(int value);
11    int pop();
12    int getSize() const;
13
14  private:                                     private members
15    int elements[100];                         element array
16    int size;
17  };
18
19  #endif
```

LISTING 10.15 TestStackOfIntegers.cpp

```
 1  #include <iostream>
 2  #include "StackOfIntegers.h"                  StackOfIntegers header
 3  using namespace std;
 4
 5  int main()
 6  {
 7    StackOfIntegers stack;                      create a stack
 8
 9    for (int i = 0; i < 10; i++)
10      stack.push(i);                            push to stack
11
12    while (!stack.isEmpty())                    stack empty?
13      cout << stack.pop() << " ";               pop from stack
14
15    return 0;
16  }
```

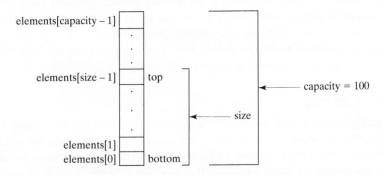

```
9 8 7 6 5 4 3 2 1 0
```

How do you implement the **StackOfIntegers** class? The elements in the stack are stored in an array named **elements**. When you create a stack, the array is also created. The no-arg constructor initializes **size** to 0. The variable **size** counts the number of elements in the stack, and **size** − 1 is the index of the element at the top of the stack, as shown in Figure 10.17. For an empty stack, **size** is 0.

elements[capacity − 1]

elements[size − 1]   top

capacity = 100

size

elements[1]

elements[0]   bottom

FIGURE 10.17   The **StackOfIntegers** class encapsulates the stack storage and provides the operations for manipulating the stack.

The `StackOfIntegers` class is implemented in Listing 10.16.

LISTING 10.16 StackOfIntegers.cpp

StackOfIntegers header

constructor

initialize size

```cpp
1  #include "StackOfIntegers.h"
2
3  StackOfIntegers::StackOfIntegers()
4  {
5      size = 0;
6  }
7
8  bool StackOfIntegers::isEmpty() const
9  {
10     return size == 0;
11 }
12
13 int StackOfIntegers::peek() const
14 {
15     return elements[size - 1];
16 }
17
18 void StackOfIntegers::push(int value)
19 {
20     elements[size++] = value;
21 }
22
23 int StackOfIntegers::pop()
24 {
25     return elements[--size];
26 }
27
28 int StackOfIntegers::getSize() const
29 {
30     return size;
31 }
```

10.29 When a stack is created, what are the initial values in the `elements` array?

10.30 When a stack is created, what is the value of variable `size`?

10.10 Class Design Guidelines

Class design guidelines are helpful for designing sound classes.

This chapter is concerned mainly with object-oriented design. While there are many object-oriented methodologies, UML has become the industry-standard notation for object-oriented modeling, and itself leads to a methodology. The process of designing classes calls for identifying the classes and discovering the relationships among them.

You have learned how to design classes from the examples from this chapter and from many other examples in the preceding chapters. Here are some guidelines.

10.10.1 Cohesion

coherent purpose

A class should describe a single entity, and all the class operations should logically fit together to support a coherent purpose. You can use a class for students, for example, but you should not combine students and staff in the same class, because students and staff are different entities.

separating responsibilities

A single entity with too many responsibilities can be broken into several classes to separate responsibilities.

10.10.2   Consistency

Follow standard programming style and naming conventions. Choose informative names for classes, data fields, and functions. A popular style in C++ is to place the data declaration after the functions, and place constructors before functions.

naming conventions

Choose names consistently. It is a good practice to choose the same names for similar operations using function overloading.

naming consistency

In general, you should consistently provide a public no-arg constructor for constructing a default instance. If a class does not support a no-arg constructor, document the reason. If no constructors are defined explicitly, a public default no-arg constructor with an empty body is assumed.

no-arg constructor

10.10.3   Encapsulation

A class should use the `private` modifier to hide its data from direct access by clients. This makes the class easy to maintain.

encapsulating data fields

Provide a `get` function only if you want the field to be readable, and provide a `set` function only if you want the field to be updateable. A class should also hide functions not intended for client use. Such functions should be defined as private.

10.10.4   Clarity

Cohesion, consistency, and encapsulation are good guidelines for achieving design clarity. Additionally, a class should have a clear contract that is easy to explain and easy to understand.

easy to explain

Users can incorporate classes in many different combinations, orders, and environments. Therefore, you should design a class that imposes no restrictions on what the user can do with it or when, design the properties in a way that lets the user set them in any order and with any combination of values, and design functions independently of their order of occurrence. For example, the `Loan` class in Listing 9.13 contains the functions `setLoanAmount`, `setNumberOfYears`, and `setAnnualInterestRate`. The values of these properties can be set in any order.

independent functions

You should not declare a data field that can be derived from other data fields. For example, the following `Person` class has two data fields: `birthDate` and `age`. Since `age` can be derived from `birthDate`, `age` should not be declared as a data field.

independent properties

```
class Person
{
public:
  ...

private:
  Date birthDate;
  int age;
}
```

10.10.5   Completeness

Classes are designed for use by many different customers. In order to be useful in a wide range of applications, a class should provide a variety of ways for customization through properties and functions. For example, the `string` class contains more than 20 functions that are useful for a variety of applications.

10.10.6   Instance vs. Static

A variable or function that is dependent on a specific instance of the class should be an instance variable or function. A variable that is shared by all the instances of a class should be declared static. For example, the variable `numberOfObjects` in `Circle` in Listing 10.9 is shared by all the objects of the `Circle` class and therefore is declared static. A function that is not dependent on a specific instance should be defined as a static function. For instance, the `getNumberOfObjects` function in `Circle` is not tied to any specific instance, and therefore is defined as a static function.

Always reference static variables and functions from a class name (rather than an object) to improve readability and avoid errors.

A constructor is always instance, because it is used to create a specific instance. A static variable or function can be invoked from an instance function, but an instance variable or function cannot be invoked from a static function.

10.31 Describe the class design guidelines.

KEY TERMS

aggregation 418	instance function 406
composition 418	instance variable 406
constant function 414	multiplicity 418
has-a relationship 418	static function 406
instance data field 406	static variable 406

CHAPTER SUMMARY

1. The C++ `string` class encapsulates an array of characters and provides many functions for processing strings such as `append`, `assign`, `at`, `clear`, `erase`, `empty`, `length`, `c_str`, `compare`, `substr`, `find`, `insert`, and `replace`.

2. C++ supports operators (`[]`, `=`, `+`, `+=`, `<<`, `>>`, `==`, `!=`, `<`, `<=`, `>`, `>=`) to simplify string operations.

3. You can use `cin` to read a string ending with a whitespace character and use `getline(cin, s, delimiterCharacter)` to read a string ending with the specified delimiter character.

4. You can pass an object to a function by value or by reference. For performance, passing by reference is preferred.

5. If the function does not change the object being passed, define the object parameter as a constant reference parameter to prevent the object's data being modified accidentally.

6. An instance variable or function belongs to an instance of a class. Its use is associated with individual instances.

7. A static variable is a variable shared by all instances of the same class.

8. A static function is a function that can be invoked without using instances.

9. Every instance of a class can access the class's static variables and functions. For clarity, however, it is better to invoke static variables and functions using `ClassName::staticVariable` and `ClassName::functionName(arguments)`.

10. If a function does not change the data fields of an object, define the function constant to prevent errors.

11. A constant function does not change the values of any data fields.

12. You can specify a member function to be constant by placing the `const` modifier at the end of the function declaration.

13. The object-oriented approach combines the power of the procedural paradigm with an added dimension that integrates data with operations into objects.

14. The procedural paradigm focuses on designing functions. The object-oriented paradigm couples data and functions together into objects.

15. Software design using the object-oriented paradigm focuses on objects and operations on objects.

16. An object can contain another object. The relationship between the two is called *composition*.

17. Some guidelines for class design are *cohesion*, *consistency*, *encapsulation*, *clarity*, and *completeness*.

QUIZ

Answer the quiz for this chapter online at www.cs.armstrong.edu/liang/cpp3e/quiz.html.

PROGRAMMING EXERCISES

Sections 10.2–10.6

*10.1 (*Anagrams*) Write a function that checks whether two words are anagrams. Two words are anagrams if they contain the same letters in any order. For example, "silent" and "listen" are anagrams. The header of the function is as follows:

bool isAnagram(**const** string& s1, **const** string& s2)

Write a test program that prompts the user to enter two strings and checks whether they are anagrams. Here are sample runs:

```
Enter a string s1: silent  ↵Enter
Enter a string s2: listen  ↵Enter
silent and listen are anagrams
```

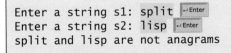

```
Enter a string s1: split  ↵Enter
Enter a string s2: lisp  ↵Enter
split and lisp are not anagrams
```

*10.2 (*Common characters*) Write a function that returns the common characters of two strings using the following header:

string commonChars(**const** string& s1, **const** string& s2)

Write a test program that prompts the user to enter two strings and display their common characters. Here are some sample runs:

```
Enter a string s1: abcd  ⏎Enter
Enter a string s2: aecaten  ⏎Enter
The common characters are ac
```

```
Enter a string s1: abcd  ⏎Enter
Enter a string s2: efg  ⏎Enter
No common characters
```

**10.3 (*Bioinformatics: find genes*) Biologists use a sequence of letters A, C, T, and G to model a *genome*. A *gene* is a substring of a genome that starts after a triplet ATG and ends before a triplet TAG, TAA, or TGA. Furthermore, the length of a gene string is a multiple of 3 and the gene does not contain any of the triplets ATG, TAG, TAA, and TGA. Write a program that prompts the user to enter a genome and displays all genes in the genome. If no gene is found in the input sequence, displays no gene. Here are the sample runs:

```
Enter a genome string: TTATGTTTTAAGGATGGGGCGTTAGTT  ⏎Enter
TTT
GGGCGT
```

```
Enter a genome string: TGTGTGTATAT  ⏎Enter
no gene is found
```

10.4 (*Sort characters in a string*) Write a function that returns a sorted string using the following header:

```
string sort(string& s)
```

Write a test program that prompts the user to enter a string and displays the new sorted string. Here is a sample run of the program:

```
Enter a string s: silent  ⏎Enter
The sorted string is eilnst
```

*10.5 (*Check palindrome*) Write the following function to check whether a string is a palindrome assuming letters are case-insensitive:

```
bool isPalindrome(const string& s)
```

Write a test program that reads a string and displays whether it is a palindrome. Here are some sample runs:

```
Enter a string s: ABa  ⏎Enter
Aba is a palindrome
```

```
Enter a string s: AcBa  ⏎Enter
Acba is not a palindrome
```

*10.6   (*Count the vowels in a string*) Write the `countVowels` function which counts the number of vowels using the string class as follows:

```
int countVowels(const string& s)
```

Write a test program that prompts the user to enter a string, invokes the `countVowels` function and displays the total number of vowels in the string.

*10.7   (*Count occurrences of each digit in an integer*) Write the `countDigits` function using the following header to count the occurrences of each digit:

```
void countDigits(const int& number, int dArray[], int size)
```

where `size` is the size of the `dArray` array. In this case, it is `10` to store the count of ten digits i.e., from `0` to `9`.

Write a test program that prompts the user to enter an integer, invokes the `countDigits` function, and displays the counts of each digit in the given integer.

*10.8   (*Financial application: monetary units*) Rewrite Listing 2.12, ComputeChange. cpp, to fix the possible loss of accuracy when converting a float value to an integer value. Enter the input as a string such as `"11.56"`. Your program should extract the dollar amount before the decimal point and the cents after the decimal amount.

**10.9   (*Guess capitals*) Write a program that repeatedly prompts the user to enter a capital for a state. Upon receiving the user input, the program reports whether the answer is correct. A sample run is shown below:

```
What is the capital of Alabama? Montgomery  ↵Enter
Your answer is correct.
What is the capital of Alaska? Anchorage  ↵Enter
The capital of Alaska is Juneau
```

Assume that fifty states and their capitals are stored in a two-dimensional array, as shown in Figure 10.18. The program prompts the user to enter ten states' capitals and displays the total correct count.

```
Alabama     Montgomery
Alaska      Juneau
Arizona     Phoenix
...         ...
```

FIGURE 10.18   A two-dimensional array stores states and their capitals.

Section 10.7

VideoNote
The `MyInteger` class

10.10   (*The `MyInteger` class*) Design a class named `MyInteger`. The class contains the following:

- An `int` data field named `value` that stores the `int` value represented by this object.
- A constructor that creates a `MyInteger` object for the specified `int` value.
- A constant get function that return the `int` value.
- Constant functions `isEven()`, `isOdd()`, `isPrime()` that return `true` if the value is even, odd, or prime, respectively.
- Static functions `isEven(int)`, `isOdd(int)`, `isPrime(int)` that return `true` if the specified value is even, odd, or prime, respectively.

- Static functions `isEven(const MyInteger&)`, `isOdd(const MyInteger&)`, `isPrime(const MyInteger&)` that return `true` if the specified value is even, odd, or prime, respectively.
- Constant functions `equals(int)` and `equals(const MyInteger&)` that return `true` if the value in the object is equal to the specified value.
- A static function `parseInt(const string&)` that converts a string to an `int` value.

Draw the UML diagram for the class. Implement the class. Write a client program that tests all functions in the class.

10.11 (*Modify the* Loan *class*) Rewrite the Loan class in Listing 9.13 to add two static functions for computing monthly payment and total payment, as follows:

```
double getMonthlyPayment(double annualInterestRate,
  int numberOfYears, double loanAmount)
```

```
double getTotalPayment(double annualInterestRate,
  int numberOfYears, double loanAmount)
```

Write a client program to test these two functions.

Sections 10.8–10.11

10.12 (*The* Stock *class*) Design a class named Stock that contains the following:

- A string data field named `symbol` for the stock's symbol.
- A string data field named `name` for the stock's name.
- A `double` data field named `previousClosingPrice` that stores the stock price for the previous day.
- A `double` data field named `currentPrice` that stores the stock price for the current time.
- A constructor that creates a stock with specified symbol and name.
- The constant accessor functions for all data fields.
- The mutator functions for `previousClosingPrice` and `currentPrice`.
- A constant function named `getChangePercent()` that returns the percentage changed from `previousClosingPrice` to `currentPrice`.

Draw the UML diagram for the class. Implement the class. Write a test program that creates a Stock object with the stock symbol MSFT, the name Microsoft Corporation, and the previous closing price of 27.5. Set a new current price to 27.6 and display the price-change percentage.

10.13 (*Geometry:* n-*sided regular polygon*) An *n*-sided regular polygon has *n* sides of the same length, and all its angles have the same degree (i.e., the polygon is both equilateral and equiangular). Design a class named RegularPolygon that contains the following:

- A private `int` data field named n that defines the number of sides in the polygon.
- A private `double` data field named side that stores the length of the side.
- A private `double` data field named x that defines the *x*-coordinate of the center of the polygon.
- A private `double` data field named y that defines the *y*-coordinate of the center of the polygon.
- A no-arg constructor that creates a regular polygon with n 3, side 1, x 0, and y 0.
- A constructor that creates a regular polygon with the specified number of sides and length of side, and centered at (0, 0).
- A constructor that creates a regular polygon with the specified number of sides, length of side, and *x*- and *y*-coordinates.

■ The constant accessor functions and mutator functions for all data fields.
■ The constant function `getPerimeter()` that returns the perimeter of the polygon.
■ The constant function `getArea()` that returns the area of the polygon. The formula for computing the area of a regular polygon is

$$Area = \frac{n \times s^2}{4 \times \tan\left(\frac{\pi}{n}\right)}.$$

Draw the UML diagram for the class. Implement the class. Write a test program that creates three `RegularPolygon` objects, using the no-arg constructor, using `RegularPolygon(6, 4)`, and using `RegularPolygon(10, 4, 5.6, 7.8)`. For each object, display its perimeter and area.

*10.14 (*Display the non-prime numbers*) Write a program that displays all the non-prime numbers less than 100 in decreasing order. Use the `StackOfIntegers` class to store the non-prime numbers (e.g., 4, 6, 8, . . .) and retrieve and display them in reverse order.

***10.15 (*Game: hangman*) Write a hangman game that randomly generates a word and prompts the user to guess one letter at a time, as shown in the sample run. Each letter in the word is displayed in an asterisk. When the user makes a correct guess, the actual letter is then displayed. When the user finishes a word, display the number of misses and ask the user whether to continue for another word. Declare an array to store words, as follows:

```
// Use any words you wish
string words[] = {"write", "that", ...};
```

```
(Guess) Enter a letter in word ******* > p ↵Enter
(Guess) Enter a letter in word p****** > r ↵Enter
(Guess) Enter a letter in word pr**r** > p ↵Enter
        p is already in the word
(Guess) Enter a letter in word pr**r** > o ↵Enter
(Guess) Enter a letter in word pro*r** > g ↵Enter
(Guess) Enter a letter in word progr** > n ↵Enter
        n is not in the word
(Guess) Enter a letter in word progr** > m ↵Enter
(Guess) Enter a letter in word progr*m > a ↵Enter
The word is program. You missed 1 time

Do you want to guess for another word? Enter y or n>
```

*10.16 (*Display the multiples*) Write a program that receives an integer and displays its first ten multiples in decreasing order. For example, if the integer is 5, he first ten multiples are displayed as 50, 45, 40, 35, 30 25, 20, 15, 10, 5. Use the `StackOfIntegers` class to store the multiples (e.g., 5, 10, . . ., 50) and retrieve and display the multiples in reverse order.

**10.17 (*The `Location` class*) Design a class named `Location` for locating a maximal value and its location in a two-dimensional array. The class contains public data fields `row`, `column`, and `maxValue` that store the maximal value and its indices in a two-dimensional array with `row` and `column` as `int` type and `maxValue` as `double` type.

Write the following function that returns the location of the largest element in a two-dimensional array. Assume that the column size is fixed.

```
const int ROW_SIZE = 3;
const int COLUMN_SIZE = 4;
Location locateLargest(const double a[][COLUMN_SIZE]);
```

The return value is an instance of **Location**. Write a test program that prompts the user to enter a two-dimensional array and displays the location of the largest element in the array. Here is a sample run:

```
Enter a 3-by-4 two-dimensional array:
23.5 35 2 10  ↵Enter
4.5 3 45 3.5  ↵Enter
35 44 5.5 9.6  ↵Enter
The location of the largest element is 45 at (1, 2)
```

POINTERS AND DYNAMIC MEMORY MANAGEMENT

Objectives

- To describe what a pointer is (§11.1).
- To learn how to declare a pointer and assign a memory address to it (§11.2).
- To access values via pointers (§11.2).
- To define synonymous types using the `typedef` keyword (§11.3).
- To declare constant pointers and constant data (§11.4).
- To explore the relationship between arrays and pointers and access array elements using pointers (§11.5).
- To pass pointer arguments to a function (§11.6).
- To learn how to return a pointer from a function (§11.7).
- To use array functions with pointers (§11.8).
- To use the `new` operator to create dynamic arrays (§11.9).
- To create objects dynamically and access objects via pointers (§11.10).
- To reference the calling object using the `this` pointer (§11.11).
- To implement the destructor for performing customized operations (§11.12).
- To design a class for students registering courses (§11.13).
- To create an object using the copy constructor that copies data from another object of the same type (§11.14).
- To customize the copy constructor for performing a deep copy (§11.15).

11.1 Introduction

Key Point

Pointer variables are also known as pointers. You can use a pointer to reference the address of an array, an object, or any variable.

why pointers?

Pointer is one of the most powerful features in C++. It is the heart and soul of the C++ programming language. Many of the C++ language features and libraries are built using pointers. To see why pointers are needed, let us consider writing a program that processes an unspecified number of integers. You would use an array to store the integers. But how do you create the array if you don't know its size? The size may change as you add or remove integers. To deal with this, your program needs the ability to allocate and release the memory for the integers on the fly at runtime. This can be accomplished using pointers.

11.2 Pointer Basics

VideoNote
Pointer basics

Key Point

*A pointer variable holds the memory address. Through the pointer, you can use the dereference operator * to access the actual value at a specific memory location.*

Pointer variables, simply called *pointers*, are declared to hold memory addresses as their values. Normally, a variable contains a data value—e.g., an integer, a floating-point value, and a character. However, a pointer contains the memory address of a variable that in turn contains a data value. As shown in Figure 11.1, pointer **pCount** contains the memory address for variable **count**.

Each byte of memory has a unique address. A variable's address is the address of the first byte allocated to that variable. Suppose three variables **count**, **status**, and **letter** are declared as follows:

```
int count = 5;
short status = 2;
char letter = 'A';
string s("ABC");
```

As shown in Figure 11.1, variable **count** is declared as an **int** type which contains four bytes, variable **status** is declared as a **short** type which contains two bytes, and variable **letter** is declared as a **char** type which contains one byte. Note that the ASCII code for **'A'** is hex 55. Variable **s** is declared as a **string** type whose memory size may change, depending on the number of the characters in the string, but the memory address for the string is fixed, once string is declared.

declare pointer

Like any other variables, pointers must be declared before they can be used. To declare a pointer, use the following syntax:

```
dataType* pVarName;
```

Each variable being declared as a pointer must be preceded by an asterisk (*). For example, the following statements declare pointers named **pCount**, **pStatus**, and **pLetter**, which can point to an **int** variable, a **short** variable, a **char** variable, and a string, respectively.

```
int* pCount;
short* pStatus;
char* pLetter;
string* pString;
```

assign address

You can now assign the address of a variable to a pointer. For example, the following code assigns the address of variable **count** to **pCount**:

```
pCount = &count;
```

address operator

The ampersand (&) symbol is called the *address operator* when placed in front of a variable. It is a unary operator that returns the variable's address. So, you may pronounce **&count** as the address of **count**.

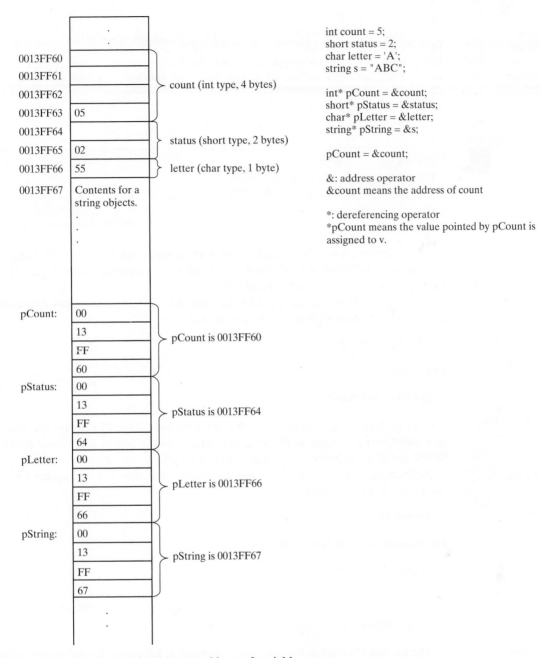

int count = 5;
short status = 2;
char letter = 'A';
string s = "ABC";

int* pCount = &count;
short* pStatus = &status;
char* pLetter = &letter;
string* pString = &s;

pCount = &count;

&: address operator
&count means the address of count

*: dereferencing operator
*pCount means the value pointed by pCount is
assigned to v.

FIGURE 11.1   **pCount** contains the memory address of variable **count**.

Listing 11.1 gives a complete example that demonstrates the use of pointers.

LISTING 11.1   TestPointer.cpp

```
1   #include <iostream>
2   using namespace std;
3
4   int main()
5   {
6     int count = 5;                    declare variable
7     int* pCount = &count;             declare pointer
```

accessing count   8
accessing &count
accessing pCount
accessing *pCount

```
8
9       cout << "The value of count is " << count << endl;
10      cout << "The address of count is " << &count << endl;
11      cout << "The address of count is " << pCount << endl;
12      cout << "The value of count is " << *pCount << endl;
13
14      return 0;
15  }
```

```
The value of count is 5
The address of count is 0013FF60
The address of count is 0013FF60
The value of count is 5
```

Line 6 declares a variable named **count** with an initial value **5**. Line 7 declares a pointer variable named **pCount** and initialized with the address of variable **count**. Figure 11.1 shows the relationship between **count** and **pCount**.

A pointer can be initialized when it is declared or by using an assignment statement. However, if you assign an address to a pointer, the syntax is

```
pCount = &count; // Correct
```

rather than

```
*pCount = &count; // Wrong
```

Line 10 displays the address of **count** using **&count**. Line 11 displays the value stored in **pCount**, which is same as **&count**. The value stored in **count** is retrieved directly from **count** in line 9 and indirectly through a pointer variable using ***pCount** in line 12.

indirect referencing

Referencing a value through a pointer is often called *indirection*. The syntax for referencing a value from a pointer is

```
*pointer
```

For example, you can increase **count** using

```
count++; // Direct reference
```

or

```
(*pCount)++; // Indirect reference
```

indirection operator
dereference operator
dereferenced

The asterisk (*) used in the preceding statement is known as the *indirection operator* or *dereference operator* (dereference means indirect reference). When a pointer is *dereferenced*, the value at the address stored in the pointer is retrieved. You may pronounce ***pCount** as the value indirectly pointed by **pCount**, or simply pointed by **pCount**.

The following points on pointers are worth noting:

* in three forms

- The asterisk (*) can be used in three different ways in C++:

  - As a multiplication operator, such as

    ```
    double area = radius * radius * 3.14159;
    ```

  - To declare a pointer variable, such as

    ```
    int* pCount = &count;
    ```

■ As the dereference operator, such as

   (*pCount)++;

Don't worry. The compiler can tell what the symbol * is used for in a program.

■ A pointer variable is declared with a type such as int or double. You have to assign   pointer type
the address of the variable of the same type. It is a syntax error if the type of the variable does not match the type of the pointer. For example, the following code is wrong:

```
int area = 1;
double* pArea = &area; // Wrong
```

You can assign a pointer to another pointer of the same type, but cannot assign a
pointer to a nonpointer variable. For example, the following code is wrong:

```
int area = 1;
int* pArea = &area;
int i = pArea; // Wrong
```

■ Pointers are variables. So, the naming conventions for variables are applied to point-   naming pointers
ers. So far, we have named pointers with prefix **p**, such as **pCount** and **pArea**. However, it is impossible to enforce this convention. Soon you will realize that an array
name is actually a pointer.

■ Like a local variable, a local pointer is assigned an arbitrary value if you don't initialize
it. A pointer may be initialized to 0, which is a special value to indicate that the pointer
points to nothing. To prevent errors, you should always initialize pointers. Dereferencing a pointer that is not initialized could cause a fatal runtime error or it could accidentally modify important data. A number of C++ libraries including <iostream> define
NULL as a constant with value 0. It is more descriptive to use NULL than 0.   NULL

Suppose **pX** and **pY** are two pointer variables for variables **x** and **y**, as shown in Figure 11.2.
To understand the relationships between the variables and their pointers, let us examine the
effect of assigning **pY** to **pX** and *pY to *pX.   effect of assignment =

The statement **pX = pY** assigns the content of **pY** to **pX**. The content of **pY** is the address
of variable **y**. So, after this assignment, **pX** and **pY** contain the same content, as pictured in
Figure 11.2a.

Now consider *pX = *pY. With the asterisk symbol in front of **pX** and **pY**, you are dealing with the variables pointed by **pX** and **pY**. *pX refers to the contents in **x** and *pY refers to
the contents in **y**. So the statement *pX = *pY assigns 6 to *pX, as pictured in Figure 11.2b.

You can declare an int pointer using the syntax

   int* p;

or

   int *p;

or

   int * p;   int* p, int *p, or int * p

All these are equivalent. Which one is better is a matter of personal preference. This book uses
the style int* p for declaring a pointer for two reasons:

1. int* p clearly separates the type int* from the identifier p. p is of the type int*, not
of the type int.

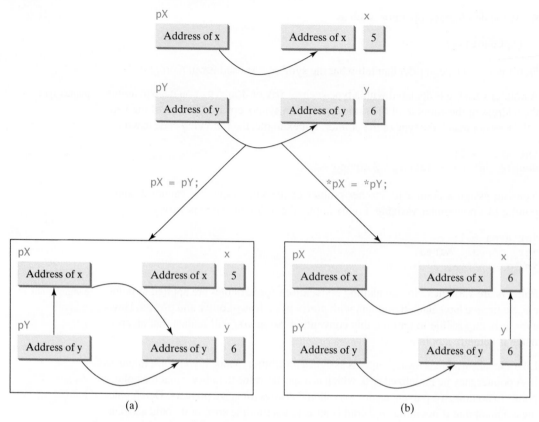

Figure 11.2 (a) **pY** is assigned to **pX**; (b) *pY is assigned to *pX.

2. Later in the book, you will see that a function may return a pointer. It is more intuitive to write the function header as

```
typeName* functionName(parameterList);
```

rather than

```
typeName *functionName(parameterList);
```

One drawback of using the `int* p` style syntax is that it may lead to a mistake like this:

```
int* p1, p2;
```

This line seems as if it declares two pointers, but it is actually same as

```
int *p1, p2;
```

We recommend that you always declare a pointer variable in a single line like this:

```
int* p1;
int* p2;
```

11.1 How do you declare a pointer variable? Does a local pointer variable have a default value?

11.2 How do you assign a variable's address to a pointer variable? What is wrong in the following code?

```
int x = 30;
int* pX = x;
cout << "x is " << x << endl;
cout << "x is " << pX << endl;
```

11.3 Show the printout of the following code:

```
int x = 30;
int* p = &x;
cout << *p << endl;

int y = 40;
p = &y;
cout << *p << endl;
```

11.4 Show the printout of the following code:

```
double x = 3.5;
double* p1 = &x;

double y = 4.5;
double* p2 = &y;

cout << *p1 + *p2 << endl;
```

11.5 Show the printout of the following code:

```
string s = "ABCD";
string* p = &s;

cout << p << endl;
cout << *p << endl;
cout << (*p)[0] << endl;
```

11.6 What is wrong in the following code?

```
double x = 3.0;
int* pX = &x;
```

11.7 Are both variables **p1** and **p2** pointers if **p1** and **p2** are defined as follows:

```
double* p1, p2;
```

11.3 Defining Synonymous Types Using the **typedef** Keyword

A synonymous type can be defined using the typedef keyword.

🔑 **Key Point**

Recall that the **unsigned** type is synonymous to **unsigned int**. C++ enables you to define custom synonymous types using the **typedef** keyword. Synonymous types can be used to simplify coding and avoid potential errors.

The syntax to define a new synonym for an existing data type is as follows:

```
typedef existingType newType;
```

For example, the following statement defines **integer** as a synonym for **int**:

```
typedef int integer;
```

So, now you can declare an `int` variable using

```
integer value = 40;
```

The `typedef` declaration does not create new data types. It merely creates a synonym for a data type. This feature is useful to define a pointer type name to make the program easy to read. For example, you can define a type named `intPointer` for `int*` as follows:

```
typedef int* intPointer;
```

An integer pointer variable can now be declared as follows:

```
intPointer p;
```

which is the same as

```
int* p;
```

One advantage of using a pointer type name is to avoid the errors involving missing asterisks. If you intend to declare two pointer variables, the following declaration is wrong:

```
int* p1, p2;
```

A good way to avoid this error is to use the synonymous type `intPointer` as follows:

```
intPointer p1, p2;
```

With this syntax, both **p1** and **p2** are declared as variables of the `intPointer` type.

11.8 How do you define a new type named `doublePointer` that is synonymous to `double*`?

11.4 Using **const** with Pointers

A constant pointer points to a constant memory location, but the actual value in the memory location can be changed.

You have learned how to declare a constant using the **const** keyword. Once it is declared, a constant cannot be changed. You can declare a constant pointer. For example:

constant pointer

```
double radius = 5;
double* const p = &radius;
```

Here **p** is a constant pointer. It must be declared and initialized in the same statement. You cannot assign a new address to **p** later. Though **p** is a constant, the data pointed to by **p** is not constant. You can change it. For example, the following statement changes radius to **10**:

```
*p = 10;
```

constant data

Can you declare that dereferenced data be constant? Yes. You can add the **const** keyword in front of the data type, as follows:

Constant data   Constant pointer

```
const double* const pValue = &radius;
```

In this case, the pointer is a constant, and the data pointed to by the pointer is also a constant.

If you declare the pointer as

```
const double* p = &radius;
```

then the pointer is not a constant, but the data pointed to by the pointer is a constant.
For example:

```
double radius = 5;
double* const p = &radius;
double length = 5;
*p = 6; // OK
p = &length; // Wrong because p is constant pointer

const double* p1 = &radius;
*p1 = 6; // Wrong because p1 points to a constant data
p1 = &length; // OK

const double* const p2 = &radius;
*p2 = 6; // Wrong because p2 points to a constant data
p2 = &length; // Wrong because p2 is a constant pointer
```

11.9 What is wrong in the following code?

Check
Point

```
int x;
int* const p = &x;
int y;
p = &y;
```

11.10 What is wrong in the following code?

```
int x;
const int* p = &x;
int y;
p = &y;
*p = 5;
```

11.5 Arrays and Pointers

A C++ array name is actually a constant pointer to the first element in the array.

Key
Point

An array without a bracket and a subscript actually represents the starting address of the array.
In this sense, an array is essentially a pointer. Suppose you declare an array of `int` values as
follows:

```
int list[6] = {11, 12, 13, 14, 15, 16};
```

The following statement displays the starting address of the array:

```
cout << "The starting address of the array is " << list << endl;
```

Figure 11.3 shows the array in the memory. C++ allows you to access the elements in the
array using the dereference operator. To access the first element, use `*list`. Other elements
can be accessed using `*(list + 1)`, `*(list + 2)`, `*(list + 3)`, `*(list + 4)`, and
`*(list + 5)`.

An integer may be added to or subtracted from a pointer. The pointer is incremented or   pointer arithmetic
decremented by that integer times the size of the element to which the pointer points.

Array `list` points to the starting address of the array. Suppose this address is `1000`. Will
`list + 1` be `1001`? No. It is `1000 + sizeof(int)`. Why? Since `list` is declared as an

list[0]	list[1]	list[2]	list[3]	list[4]	list[5]
11	12	13	14	15	16

list	list+1	list+2	list+3	list+4	list+5
↓	↓	↓	↓	↓	↓
11	12	13	14	15	16

*list   *(list+1) *(list+2)*(list+3) *(list+4) *(list+5)

FIGURE 11.3 Array `list` points to the first element in the array.

array of `int` elements, C++ automatically calculates the address for the next element by adding `sizeof(int)`. Recall that `sizeof(type)` function returns the size of a data type (see Section 2.8, "Numeric Data Types and Operations"). The size of each data type is machine dependent. On Windows, the size of the `int` type is usually 4. So, no matter how big each element of the list is, `list + 1` points to the second element of the list, and `list + 3` points to the third, and so on.

why 0-based index?

Note
Now you see why an array index starts with 0. An array is actually a pointer. `list + 0` points to the first element in the array and `list[0]` refers to the first element in the array.

Listing 11.2 gives a complete program that uses pointers to access array elements.

LISTING 11.2 ArrayPointer.cpp

declare array

incrementing address
dereference operator
array indexed variable

```
1   #include <iostream>
2   using namespace std;
3
4   int main()
5   {
6     int list[6] = {11, 12, 13, 14, 15, 16};
7
8     for (int i = 0; i < 6; i++)
9       cout << "address: " << (list + i) <<
10        " value: " << *(list + i) << " " <<
11        " value: " << list[i] << endl;
12
13    return 0;
14  }
```

```
address: 0013FF4C value: 11   value: 11
address: 0013FF50 value: 12   value: 12
address: 0013FF54 value: 13   value: 13
address: 0013FF58 value: 14   value: 14
address: 0013FF5C value: 15   value: 15
address: 0013FF60 value: 16   value: 16
```

As shown in the sample output, the address of the array `list` is 0013FF4C. So `(list + 1)` is actually 0013FF4C + 4, and `(list + 2)` is 0013FF4C + 2 * 4 (line 9). The array elements are accessed using pointer dereference `*(list + 1)` (line 10). Line 11 accesses the elements via index using `list[i]`, which is equivalent to `*(list + i)`.

operator precedence

Caution
`*(list + 1)` is different from `*list + 1`. The dereference operator (*) has precedence over +. So, `*list + 1` adds 1 with the value of the first element in the array, while `*(list + 1)` dereferences the element at address `(list + 1)` in the array.

Note

Pointers can be compared using relational operators (==, !=, <, <=, >, >=) to determine their order.

compare pointers

Arrays and pointers form a close relationship. A pointer for an array can be used just like an array. You can even use pointer with index. Listing 11.3 gives such an example.

LISTING 11.3 PointerWithIndex.cpp

```cpp
 1  #include <iostream>
 2  using namespace std;
 3
 4  int main()
 5  {
 6    int list[6] = {11, 12, 13, 14, 15, 16};
 7    int* p = list;
 8
 9    for (int i = 0; i < 6; i++)
10      cout << "address: " << (list + i) <<
11        " value: " << *(list + i) << " " <<
12        " value: " << list[i] << " " <<
13        " value: " << *(p + i) << " " <<
14        " value: " << p[i] << endl;
15
16    return 0;
17  }
```

declare array
declare pointer

incrementing address
dereference operator
array with index
dereference operator
pointer with index

```
address: 0013FF4C value: 11  value: 11  value: 11  value: 11
address: 0013FF50 value: 12  value: 12  value: 12  value: 12
address: 0013FF54 value: 13  value: 13  value: 13  value: 13
address: 0013FF58 value: 14  value: 14  value: 14  value: 14
address: 0013FF5C value: 15  value: 15  value: 15  value: 15
address: 0013FF60 value: 16  value: 16  value: 16  value: 16
```

Line 7 declares an `int` pointer `p` assigned with the address of the array.

```cpp
int* p = list;
```

Note that we do not use the address operator (&) to assign the address of the array to the pointer, because the name of the array is already the starting address of the array. This line is equivalent to

```cpp
int* p = &list[0];
```

Here, `&list[0]` represents the address of `list[0]`.

As seen in this example, for array `list`, you can access an element using array syntax `list[i]` as well as pointer syntax `*(list + i)`. When a pointer such as `p` points to an array, you can use either pointer syntax or the array syntax to access an element in the array—i.e., `*(p + i)` or `p[i]`. You can use array syntax or pointer syntax to access arrays, whichever is convenient. However, there is one difference between arrays and pointers. Once an array is declared, you cannot change its address. For example, the following statement is illegal:

```cpp
int list1[10], list2[10];
list1 = list2; // Wrong
```

An array name is actually treated as a constant pointer in C++.

constant pointer

pointer-based C-strings

C-strings are often referred to as *pointer-based strings*, because they can be conveniently accessed using pointers. For example, the following two declarations are both fine:

```
char city[7] = "Dallas"; // Option 1
char* pCity = "Dallas";   // Option 2
```

Each declaration creates a sequence that contains characters `'D'`, `'a'`, `'l'`, `'l'`, `'a'`, `'s'`, and `'\0'`.

array syntax
pointer syntax

You can access `city` or `pCity` using the array syntax or pointer syntax. For example, each of the following

```
cout << city[1] << endl;
cout << *(city + 1) << endl;
cout << pCity[1] << endl;
cout << *(pCity + 1) << endl;
```

displays character **a** (the second element in the string).

Check
Point

11.11 Assume you declared `int* p`, and p's current value is 100. What is `p + 1`?

11.12 Assume you declared `int* p`. What are the differences among `p++`, `*p++`, and `(*p)++`?

11.13 Assume you declared `int p[4] = {1, 2, 3, 4}`. What are `*p`, `*(p+1)`, `p[0]` and `p[1]`?

11.14 What is wrong in the following code?

```
char* p;
cin >> p;
```

11.15 What is the printout of the following statements?

```
char* const pCity = "Dallas";
cout << pCity << endl;
cout << *pCity << endl;
cout << *(pCity + 1) << endl;
cout << *(pCity + 2) << endl;
cout << *(pCity + 3) << endl;
```

11.16 What is the output of the following code?

```
char* city = "Dallas";
cout << city[0] << endl;

char* cities[] = {"Dallas", "Atlanta", "Houston"};
cout << cities[0] << endl;
cout << cities[0][0] << endl;
```

11.6 Passing Pointer Arguments in a Function Call

Key
Point

A C++ function may have pointer parameters.

You have learned two ways to pass arguments to a function in C++: *pass-by-value* and *pass-by-reference*. You can also pass pointer arguments in a function call. A pointer argument can be passed by value or by reference. For example, you can define a function as follows:

```
void f(int* p1, int* &p2)
```

which is equivalently to

```
typedef int* intPointer;
void f(intPointer p1, intPointer& p2)
```

Consider invoking function `f(q1, q2)` with two pointers `q1` and `q2`:

- The pointer `q1` is passed to `p1` by value. So `*p1` and `*q1` point to the same contents. If function `f` changes `*p1` (e.g., `*p1 = 20`), `*q1` is changed too. However, if function `f` changes `p1` (e.g., `p1 = somePointerVariable`), `q1` is not changed.

- The pointer `q2` is passed to `p2` by reference. So `q2` and `p2` are now aliases. They are essentially the same. If function `f` changes `*p2` (e.g., `*p2 = 20`), `*q2` is changed too. If function `f` changes `p2` (e.g., `p2 = somePointerVariable`), `q2` is changed too.

Listing 6.14, SwapByValue.cpp, demonstrated the effect of pass-by-value. Listing 6.17, SwapByReference.cpp, demonstrated the effect of pass-by-reference with reference variables. Both examples used the **swap** function to demonstrate the effect. We now give an example of passing pointers in Listing 11.4.

LISTING 11.4 TestPointerArgument.cpp

VideoNote
Pass pointer arguments

```
1   #include <iostream>
2   using namespace std;
3
4   // Swap two variables using pass-by-value
5   void swap1(int n1, int n2)                              pass-by-value
6   {
7     int temp = n1;
8     n1 = n2;
9     n2 = temp;
10  }
11
12  // Swap two variables using pass-by-reference
13  void swap2(int& n1, int& n2)                            pass-by-reference
14  {
15    int temp = n1;
16    n1 = n2;
17    n2 = temp;
18  }
19
20  // Pass two pointers by value
21  void swap3(int* p1, int* p2)                            pass a pointer by value
22  {
23    int temp = *p1;
24    *p1 = *p2;
25    *p2 = temp;
26  }
27
28  // Pass two pointers by reference
29  void swap4(int* &p1, int* &p2)                          pass a pointer by reference
30  {
31    int* temp = p1;
32    p1 = p2;
33    p2 = temp;
34  }
35
36  int main()
```

```
37  {
38    // Declare and initialize variables
39    int num1 = 1;
40    int num2 = 2;
41
42    cout << "Before invoking the swap function, num1 is "
43      << num1 << " and num2 is " << num2 << endl;
44
45    // Invoke the swap function to attempt to swap two variables
46    swap1(num1, num2);
47
48    cout << "After invoking the swap function, num1 is " << num1 <<
49      " and num2 is " << num2 << endl;
50
51    cout << "Before invoking the swap function, num1 is "
52      << num1 << " and num2 is " << num2 << endl;
53
54    // Invoke the swap function to attempt to swap two variables
55    swap2(num1, num2);
56
57    cout << "After invoking the swap function, num1 is " << num1 <<
58      " and num2 is " << num2 << endl;
59
60    cout << "Before invoking the swap function, num1 is "
61      << num1 << " and num2 is " << num2 << endl;
62
63    // Invoke the swap function to attempt to swap two variables
64    swap3(&num1, &num2);
65
66    cout << "After invoking the swap function, num1 is " << num1 <<
67      " and num2 is " << num2 << endl;
68
69    int* p1 = &num1;
70    int* p2 = &num2;
71    cout << "Before invoking the swap function, p1 is "
72      << p1 << " and p2 is " << p2 << endl;
73
74    // Invoke the swap function to attempt to swap two variables
75    swap4(p1, p2);
76
77    cout << "After invoking the swap function, p1 is " << p1 <<
78      " and p2 is " << p2 << endl;
79
80    return 0;
81  }
```

```
Before invoking the swap function, num1 is 1 and num2 is 2
After invoking the swap function, num1 is 1 and num2 is 2
Before invoking the swap function, num1 is 1 and num2 is 2
After invoking the swap function, num1 is 2 and num2 is 1
Before invoking the swap function, num1 is 2 and num2 is 1
After invoking the swap function, num1 is 1 and num2 is 2
Before invoking the swap function, p1 is 0028FB84 and p2 is 0028FB78
After invoking the swap function, p1 is 0028FB78 and p2 is 0028FB84
```

Four functions swap1, swap2, swap3, and swap4 are defined in lines 5–34. Function swap1 is invoked by passing the value of num1 to n1 and the value of num2 to n2 (line 46).

The `swap1` function swaps the values in `n1` and `n2`. `n1`, `num1`, `n2`, `num2` are independent variables. After invoking the function, the values in variables `num1` and `num2` are not changed.

The `swap2` function has two reference parameters, `int& n1` and `int& n2` (line 13). The references of `num1` and `num2` are passed to `n1` and `n2` (line 55), so `n1` and `num1` are aliases and `n2` and `num2` are aliases. `n1` and `n2` are swapped in `swap2`. After the function returns, the values in variables `num1` and `num2` are also swapped.

The `swap3` function has two pointer parameters, `p1` and `p2` (line 21). The addresses of `num1` and `num2` are passed to `p1` and `p2` (line 64), so `p1` and `&num1` refer to the same memory location and `p2` and `&num2` refer to the same memory location. `*p1` and `*p2` are swapped in `swap3`. After the function returns, the values in variables `num1` and `num2` are also swapped.

The `swap4` function has two pointer parameters, `p1` and `p2`, passed by reference (line 29). Invoking this function swaps `p1` with `p2` (line 75).

An array parameter in a function can always be replaced using a pointer parameter. For example,

array parameter or pointer parameter

`void m(int list[], int size)`	can be replaced by	`void m(int* list, int size)`
`void m(char c_string[])`	can be replaced by	`void m(char* c_string)`

Recall that a C-string is an array of characters that ends with a null terminator. The size of a C-string can be detected from the C-string itself.

If a value does not change, you should declare it `const` to prevent it from being accidentally modified. Listing 11.5 gives an example.

const parameter

LISTING 11.5 ConstParameter.cpp

```
1  #include <iostream>
2  using namespace std;
3
4  void printArray(const int*, const int);
5
6  int main()
7  {
8    int list[6] = {11, 12, 13, 14, 15, 16};
9    printArray(list, 6);
10
11   return 0;
12 }
13
14 void printArray(const int* list, const int size)
15 {
16   for (int i = 0; i < size; i++)
17     cout << list[i] << " ";
18 }
```

function prototype

declare array
invoke printArray

```
19 11 12 13 14 15 16
```

The `printArray` function declares an array parameter with constant data (line 4). This ensures that the contents of the array will not be changed. Note that the `size` parameter also is declared `const`. This usually is not necessary, since an `int` parameter is passed by value. Even though `size` is modified in the function, it does not affect the original `size` value outside this function.

11.17 What is the output of the following code?

```
#include <iostream>
using namespace std;

void f1(int x, int& y, int* z)
{
  x++;
  y++;
  (*z)++;
}

int main()
{
  int i = 1, j = 1, k = 1;
  f1(i, j, &k);

  cout << "i is " << i << endl;
  cout << "j is " << j << endl;
  cout << "k is " << k << endl;

  return 0;
}
```

11.7 Returning a Pointer from Functions

A C++ function may return a pointer.

You can use pointers as parameters in a function. Can you return a pointer from a function? Yes, you can.

Suppose you want to write a function that passes an array argument, reverses it, and returns the array. You can define a **reverse** function and implement it as shown in Listing 11.6.

LISTING 11.6 ReverseArrayUsingPointer.cpp

```
 1  #include <iostream>
 2  using namespace std;
 3
 4  int* reverse(int* list, int size)
 5  {
 6    for (int i = 0, j = size - 1; i < j; i++, j--)
 7    {
 8      // Swap list[i] with list[j]
 9      int temp = list[j];
10      list[j] = list[i];
11      list[i] = temp;
12    }
13
14    return list;
15  }
16
17  void printArray(const int* list, int size)
18  {
19    for (int i = 0; i < size; i++)
20      cout << list[i] << " ";
21  }
22
23  int main()
24  {
25    int list[] = {1, 2, 3, 4, 5, 6};
26    int* p = reverse(list, 6);
```

reverse function

swap

return list

print array

invoke reverse

```
27    printArray(p, 6);
28
29    return 0;
30  }
```
print array

```
6 5 4 3 2 1
```

The **reverse** function prototype is specified like this:

```
int* reverse(int* list, int size)
```

The return value type is an **int** pointer. It swaps the first element with the last, second element with the second last, . . . , and so on in **list**, as shown in the following diagram:

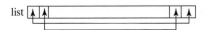

The function returns list as a pointer in line 14.

11.18 Show the output of the following code.

Check Point

```
#include <iostream>
using namespace std;

int* f(int list1[], const int list2[], int size)
{
  for (int i = 0; i <size; i++)
   list1[i]+ = list2[i];
  return list1;
}

int main()
{
  int list1[] = {1, 2, 3, 4};
  int list2[] = {1, 2, 3, 4};
  int* p = f(list1, list2, 4);
  cout << p[0] << endl;
  cout << p[1] << endl;

  return 0;
}
```

11.8 Useful Array Functions

The min_element, max_element, sort, random_shuffle, *and* find *functions can be used for arrays.*

Key Point

C++ provides several functions for manipulating arrays. You can use the **min_element** and **max_element** functions to return the pointer to the minimal and maximal element in an array, the **sort** function to sort an array, the **random_shuffle** function to randomly shuffle an array, and the **find** function to find an element in an array. All these functions use pointers in the arguments and in the return value. Listing 11.7 gives an example of using these functions.

LISTING 11.7 UsefulArrayFunctions.cpp

```
1  #include <iostream>
2  #include <algorithm>
3  using namespace std;
4
5  void printArray(const int* list, int size)
```
print array

```
 6   {
 7      for (int i = 0; i < size; i++)
 8        cout << list[i] << " ";
 9      cout << endl;
10   }
11
12   int main()
13   {
14      int list[] = {4, 2, 3, 6, 5, 1};
15      printArray(list, 6);
16
17      int* min = min_element(list, list + 6);
18      int* max = max_element(list, list + 6);
19      cout << "The min value is " << *min << " at index "
20        << (min - list) << endl;
21      cout << "The max value is " << *max << " at index "
22        << (max - list) << endl;
23
24      random_shuffle(list, list + 6);
25      printArray(list, 6);
26
27      sort(list, list + 6);
28      printArray(list, 6);
29
30      int key = 4;
31      int* p = find(list, list + 6, key);
32      if (p != list + 6)
33        cout << "The value " << *p << " is found at position "
34           << (p - list) << endl;
35      else
36        cout << "The value " << *p << " is not found" << endl;
37
38      return 0;
39   }
```

declare an array

min_element
max_element

random_shuffle

sort

find

```
4 2 3 6 5 1
The min value is 1 at index 5
The max value is 6 at index 3
5 2 6 3 4 1
1 2 3 4 5 6
The value 4 is found at position 3
```

min_element

Invoking `min_element(list, list + 6)` (line 17) returns the pointer for the smallest element in the array from `list[0]` to `list[5]`. In this case, it returns `list + 5` since value 1 is the smallest element in the array and the pointer to this element is `list + 5`. Note that the two arguments passed to the function are the pointers that specify a range and the second pointer points the end of the specified range.

random_shuffle

Invoking `random_shuffle(list, list + 6)` (line 24) randomly rearranges the elements in the array from `list[0]` to `list[5]`.

sort

Invoking `sort(list, list + 6)` (line 27) sorts the elements in the array from `list[0]` to `list[5]`.

find

Invoking `find(list, list + 6, key)` (line 31) finds the key in the array from `list[0]` to `list[5]`. The function returns the pointer that points the matching element in the array if the element is found; otherwise, it returns the pointer that points to the position after the last element in the array (i.e., `list + 6` in this case).

11.19 Show the output of the following code:

```
int list[] = {3, 4, 2, 5, 6, 1};
cout << *min_element(list, list + 2) << endl;
cout << *max_element(list, list + 2) << endl;
cout << *find(list, list + 6, 2) << endl;
cout << find(list, list + 6, 20) << endl;
sort(list, list + 6);
cout << list[5] << endl;
```

11.9 Dynamic Persistent Memory Allocation

The new operator can be used to create persistent memory at runtime for primitive type values, arrays, and objects.

Key Point

Listing 11.6 writes a function that passes an array argument, reverses it, and returns the array. Suppose you don't want to change the original array. You can rewrite the function that passes an array argument and returns a new array that is the reversal of the array argument.

new operator

An algorithm for the function can be described as follows:

1. Let the original array be `list`.

2. Declare a new array named `result` that has the same size as the original array.

3. Write a loop to copy the first element, second, . . . , and so on in the original array into the last element, second last, . . . , in the new array, as shown in the following diagram:

4. Return `result` as a pointer.

The function prototype can be specified like this:

```
int* reverse(const int* list, int size)
```

The return value type is an `int` pointer. How do you declare a new array in Step 2? You may attempt to declare it as

```
int result[size];
```

But C++ does not allow the size to be a variable. To avoid this limitation, let us assume that the array size is `6`. So, you can declare it as

```
int result[6];
```

You can now implement the code in Listing 11.8, but you will soon find out that it is not working correctly.

LISTING 11.8 WrongReverse.cpp

```
1  #include <iostream>
2  using namespace std;
3
4  int* reverse(const int* list, int size)
5  {
```

reverse function

declare result array

```
6    int result[6];
7
```

reverse to result

```
8    for (int i = 0, j = size - 1; i < size; i++, j--)
9    {
10       result[j] = list[i];
11   }
12
```

return result

```
13   return result;
14  }
15
```

print array

```
16  void printArray(const int* list, int size)
17  {
18     for (int i = 0; i < size; i++)
19        cout << list[i] << " ";
20  }
21
22  int main()
23  {
24     int list[] = {1, 2, 3, 4, 5, 6};
```

invoke reverse
print array

```
25     int* p = reverse(list, 6);
26     printArray(p, 6);
27
28     return 0;
29  }
```

```
6 4462476 4419772 1245016 4199126 4462476
```

The sample output is incorrect. Why? The reason is that the array `result` is stored in the activation record in the call stack. The memory in the call stack does not persist; when the function returns, the activation record used by the function in the call stack are thrown away from the call stack. Attempting to access the array via the pointer will result in erroneous and unpredictable values. To fix this problem, you have to allocate persistent storage for the `result` array so that it can be accessed after the function returns. We discuss the fix next.

dynamic memory allocation

C++ supports dynamic memory allocation, which enables you to allocate persistent storage dynamically. The memory is created using the `new` operator. For example,

```
int* p = new int(4);
```

Here, `new int` tells the computer to allocate memory space for an `int` variable initialized to `4` at runtime, and the address of the variable is assigned to the pointer **p**. So you can access the memory through the pointer.

You can create an array dynamically. For example,

```
cout << "Enter the size of the array: ";
int size;
cin >> size;
int* list = new int[size];
```

dynamic array

Here, `new int[size]` tells the computer to allocate memory space for an `int` array with the specified number of elements, and the address of the array is assigned to `list`. The array created using the `new` operator is also known as a *dynamic array*. Note that when you create a regular array, its size must be known at compile time. It cannot be a variable. It must be a constant. For example,

```
int numbers[40]; // 40 is a constant value
```

When you create a dynamic array, its size is determined at runtime. It can be an integer variable. For example,

```
int* list = new int[size]; // size is a variable
```

The memory allocated using the **new** operator is persistent and exists until it is explicitly deleted or the program exits. Now you can fix the problem in the preceding example by creating a new array dynamically in the **reverse** function. This array can be accessed after the function returns. Listing 11.9 gives the new program.

LISTING 11.9 CorrectReverse.cpp

```
 1  #include <iostream>
 2  using namespace std;
 3
 4  int* reverse(const int* list, int size)          reverse function
 5  {
 6    int* result = new int[size];                   create array
 7
 8    for (int i = 0, j = size - 1; i < size; i++, j--)    reverse to result
 9    {
10      result[j] = list[i];
11    }
12
13    return result;                                 return result
14  }
15
16  void printArray(const int* list, int size)       print array
17  {
18    for (int i = 0; i < size; i++)
19      cout << list[i] << " ";
20  }
21
22  int main()
23  {
24    int list[] = {1, 2, 3, 4, 5, 6};
25    int* p = reverse(list, 6);                     invoke reverse
26    printArray(p, 6);                              print array
27
28    return 0;
29  }
```

```
6 5 4 3 2 1
```

Listing 11.9 is almost identical to Listing 11.6 except that the new **result** array is created using the **new** operator dynamically. The size can be a variable when creating an array using the **new** operator.

C++ allocates local variables in the stack, but the memory allocated by the **new** operator is in an area of memory called the *freestore* or *heap*. The heap memory remains available until you explicitly free it or the program terminates. If you allocate heap memory for a variable while in a function, the memory is still available after the function returns. The **result** array is created in the function (line 6). After the function returns in line 25, the **result** array is intact. So, you can access it in line 26 to print all the elements in the **result** array.

freestore
heap

delete operator

To explicitly free the memory created by the **new** operator, use the **delete** operator for the pointer. For example,

```
delete p;
```

delete a dynamic array

The word **delete** is a keyword in C++. If the memory is allocated for an array, the [] symbol must be placed between the **delete** keyword and the pointer to the array to release the memory properly. For example,

```
delete [] list;
```

dangling pointers

After the memory pointed by a pointer is freed, the value of the pointer becomes undefined. Moreover, if some other pointer points to the same memory that was freed, this other pointer is also undefined. These undefined pointers are called *dangling pointers*. Don't apply the dereference operator * on dangling pointer. Doing so would cause serious errors.

delete dynamic memory

 Caution

Use the **delete** keyword only with the pointer that points to the memory created by the **new** operator. Otherwise, it may cause unexpected problems. For example, the following code is erroneous, because **p** does not point to a memory created using **new**.

```
int x = 10;
int* p = &x;
delete p; // This is wrong
```

You might inadvertently reassign a pointer before deleting the memory to which it points. Consider the following code:

```
1  int* p = new int;
2  *p = 45;
3  p = new int;
```

memory leak

Line 1 declares a pointer assigned with a memory address for an **int** value, as shown in Figure 11.4a. Line 2 assigns **45** to the variable pointed by **p**, as shown in Figure 11.4b. Line 3 assigns a new memory address to **p**, as shown in Figure 11.4c. The original memory space that holds value **45** is not accessible, because it is not pointed to by any pointer. This memory cannot be accessed and cannot be deleted. This is a *memory leak*.

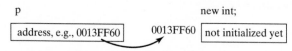

(a) **int *p = new int;** allocates memory for an int value and assigns an address to p.

(b) ***p = 45;** assigns 45 to the memory location pointed by p.

Memory at 0013FF60 is not referenced by any pointer. It is a leak.

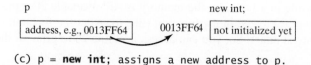

(c) p = **new int;** assigns a new address to p.

FIGURE 11.4 Unreferenced memory space causes memory leak.

Dynamic memory allocation is a powerful feature, but you must use it carefully to avoid memory leaks and other errors. As a good programming practice, every call to new should be matched by a call to `delete`.

11.20 How do you create the memory space for a `double` value? How do you access this `double` value? How do you release this memory?

11.21 Is the dynamic memory destroyed when the program exits?

11.22 Explain memory leak.

11.23 Suppose you create a dynamic array and later you need to release it. Identify two errors in the following code:

```
double x[] = new double[30];
...
delete x;
```

11.24 What is wrong in the following code:

```
double d = 5.4;
double* p1 = d;
```

11.25 What is wrong in the following code:

```
double d = 5.4;
double* p1 = &d;
delete p1;
```

11.26 What is wrong in the following code:

```
double* p1;
p1* = 5.4;
```

11.27 What is wrong in the following code:

```
double* p1 = new double;
double* p2 = p1;
*p2 = 5.4;
delete p1;
cout << *p2 << endl;
```

11.10 Creating and Accessing Dynamic Objects

To create an object dynamically, invoke the constructor for the object using the syntax `new ClassName(arguments)`.

You can also create objects dynamically on the heap using the syntax shown below.

create dynamic object

```
ClassName* pObject = new ClassName(); or
ClassName* pObject = new ClassName;
```

creates an object using the no-arg constructor and assigns the object address to the pointer.

```
ClassName* pObject = new ClassName(arguments);
```

creates an object using the constructor with arguments and assigns the object address to the pointer.

For example,

```
// Create an object using the no-arg constructor
string* p = new string(); // or string* p = new string;

// Create an object using the constructor with arguments
string* p = new string("abcdefg");
```

To access object members via a pointer, you must dereference the pointer and use the dot (.) operator to object's members. For example,

invoke substr()

invoke length()

```
string* p = new string("abcdefg");
cout << "The first three characters in the string are "
  << (*p).substr(0, 3) << endl;
cout << "The length of the string is " << (*p).length() << endl;
```

arrow operator

C++ also provides a shorthand member selection operator for accessing object members from a pointer: *arrow operator* (->), which is a dash (-) immediately followed by the greater-than (>) symbol. For example,

invoke substr()

invoke length()

```
cout << "The first three characters in the string are "
  << p->substr(0, 3) << endl;
cout << "The length of the string is " << p->length() << endl;
```

The objects are destroyed when the program is terminated. To explicitly destroy an object, invoke

delete dynamic object

```
delete p;
```

Check Point

11.28 Are the following programs correct? If not, correct them.

```
int main()
{
  string s1;
  string* p = s1;

  return 0;
}
```
(a)

```
int main()
{
  string* p = new string;
  string* p1 = new string();

  return 0;
}
```
(b)

```
int main()
{
  string* p = new string("ab");

  return 0;
}
```
(c)

11.29 How do you create an object dynamically? How do you delete an object? Why is the code in (a) wrong and in (b) correct?

```
int main()
{
  string s1;
  string* p = &s1;
  delete p;
  return 0;
}
```
(a)

```
int main()
{
  string* p = new string();
  delete p;

  return 0;
}
```
(b)

11.30 In the following code, lines 7 and 8 both create an anonymous object and print the area of the circle. Why is line 8 bad?

```
1    #include <iostream>
2    #include "Circle.h"
3    using namespace std;
4
5    int main()
6    {
7      cout << Circle(5).getArea() << endl;
8      cout << (new Circle(5))->getArea() << endl;
9
10     return 0;
11   }
```

11.11 The **this** Pointer

The **this** *pointer points to the calling object itself.*

Key Point

Sometimes you need to reference a class's hidden data field in a function. For example, a data field name is often used as the parameter name in a set function for the data field. In this case, you need to reference the hidden data field name in the function in order to set a new value to it. A hidden data field can be accessed by using the **this** keyword, which is a special built-in pointer that references the calling object. You can rewrite the `Circle` class defined in CircleWithPrivateDataFields.h in Listing 9.9 using the **this** pointer, as shown in Listing 11.10.

hidden variable

this keyword

LISTING 11.10 CircleWithThisPointer.cpp

```
1    #include "CircleWithPrivateDataFields.h"  // Defined in Listing 9.9
2
3    // Construct a default circle object
4    Circle::Circle()
5    {
6      radius = 1;
7    }
8
9    // Construct a circle object
10   Circle::Circle(double radius)
11   {
12     this->radius = radius; // or (*this).radius = radius;
13   }
14
15   // Return the area of this circle
16   double Circle::getArea()
17   {
18     return radius * radius * 3.14159;
19   }
20
21   // Return the radius of this circle
22   double Circle::getRadius()
23   {
24     return radius;
25   }
26
27   // Set a new radius
28   void Circle::setRadius(double radius)
29   {
30     this->radius = (radius >= 0) ? radius : 0;
31   }
```

include header file

this pointer

this pointer

The parameter name `radius` in the constructor (line 10) is a local variable. To reference the data field `radius` in the object, you have to use `this->radius` (line 12). The parameter name `radius` in the `setRadius` function (line 28) is a local variable. To reference the data field `radius` in the object, you have to use `this->radius` (line 30).

11.31 What is wrong in the following code? How can it be fixed?

```
// Construct a circle object
Circle::Circle(double radius)
{
  radius = radius;
}
```

VideoNote

Destructor and copy constructor

11.12 Destructors

Every class has a destructor, which is called automatically when an object is deleted.

destructor

Destructors are the opposite of constructors. A constructor is invoked when an object is created and a destructor is invoked automatically when the object is destroyed. Every class has a default destructor if the destructor is not explicitly defined. Sometimes, it is desirable to implement destructors to perform customized operations. Destructors are named the same as constructors, but you must put a tilde character (~) in front. Listing 11.11 shows a `Circle` class with a destructor defined.

LISTING 11.11 CircleWithDestructor.h

```
1  #ifndef CIRCLE_H
2  #define CIRCLE_H
3
4  class Circle
5  {
6  public:
7    Circle();
8    Circle(double);
9    ~Circle(); // Destructor
10   double getArea() const;
11   double getRadius() const;
12   void setRadius(double);
13   static int getNumberOfObjects();
14
15 private:
16   double radius;
17   static int numberOfObjects;
18 };
19
20 #endif
```

A destructor for the `Circle` class is defined in line 9. Destructors have no return type and no arguments.

Listing 11.12 gives the implementation of the `Circle` class defined in CircleWith-Destructor.h.

LISTING 11.12 CircleWithDestructor.cpp

include header

```
1  #include "CircleWithDestructor.h"
2
3  int Circle::numberOfObjects = 0;
4
5  // Construct a default circle object
```

```
 6  Circle::Circle()
 7  {
 8    radius = 1;
 9    numberOfObjects++;
10  }
11
12  // Construct a circle object
13  Circle::Circle(double radius)
14  {
15    this->radius = radius;
16    numberOfObjects++;
17  }
18
19  // Return the area of this circle
20  double Circle::getArea() const
21  {
22    return radius * radius * 3.14159;
23  }
24
25  // Return the radius of this circle
26  double Circle::getRadius() const
27  {
28    return radius;
29  }
30
31  // Set a new radius
32  void Circle::setRadius(double radius)
33  {
34    this->radius = (radius >= 0) ? radius : 0;
35  }
36
37  // Return the number of circle objects
38  int Circle::getNumberOfObjects()
39  {
40    return numberOfObjects;
41  }
42
43  // Destruct a circle object
44  Circle::~Circle()                                              implement destructor
45  {
46    numberOfObjects--;
47  }
```

The implementation is identical to CircleWithStaticDataFields.cpp in Listing 10.7, except that the destructor is implemented to decrement **numberOfObjects** in lines 44–47.

The program in Listing 11.13 demonstrates the effects of destructors.

LISTING 11.13 TestCircleWithDestructor.cpp

```
 1  #include <iostream>
 2  #include "CircleWithDestructor.h"                              include header
 3  using namespace std;
 4
 5  int main()
 6  {
 7    Circle* pCircle1 = new Circle();                             create pCircle1
 8    Circle* pCircle2 = new Circle();                             create pCircle2
 9    Circle* pCircle3 = new Circle();                             create pCircle3
10
11    cout << "Number of circle objects created: "
```

display numberOfObjects

```
12        << Circle::getNumberOfObjects() << endl;
13
14    delete pCircle1;
15
16    cout << "Number of circle objects created: "
17      << Circle::getNumberOfObjects() << endl;
18
19    return 0;
20 }
```

destroy pCircle1

display numberOfObjects

```
Number of circle objects created: 3
Number of circle objects created: 2
```

The program creates three `Circle` objects using the `new` operator in lines 7–9. Afterwards, `numberOfObjects` becomes 3. The program deletes a `Circle` object in line 14. After this, `numberOfObjects` becomes 2.

Destructors are useful for deleting memory and other resources dynamically allocated by the object, as shown in the case study in the next section.

Check Point

11.32 Does every class have a destructor? How is a destructor named? Can it be over-loaded? Can you redefine a destructor? Can you invoke a destructor explicitly?

11.33 What is the output of the following code?

```cpp
#include <iostream>
using namespace std;

class Employee
{
public:
  Employee(int id)
  {
    this->id = id;
  }

  ~Employee()
  {
    cout << "object with id " << id << " is destroyed" << endl;
  }

private:
  int id;
};

int main()
{
  Employee* e1 = new Employee(1);
  Employee* e2 = new Employee(2);
  Employee* e3 = new Employee(3);

  delete e3;
  delete e2;
  delete e1;

  return 0;
}
```

11.34 Why does the following class need a destructor? Add one.

```cpp
class Person
{
public:
  Person()
  {
    numberOfChildren = 0;
    children = new string[20];
  }

  void addAChild(string name)
  {
    children[numberOfChildren++] = name;
  }

  string* getChildren()
  {
    return children;
  }

  int getNumberOfChildren()
  {
    return numberOfChildren;
  }

private:
  string* children;
  int numberOfChildren;
};
```

11.13 Case Study: The **Course** Class

This section designs a class for modeling courses.

Key Point

Suppose you need to process course information. Each course has a name and a number of students who take the course. You should be able to add/drop a student to/from the course. You can use a class to model the courses, as shown in Figure 11.5.

Course
-courseName: string
-students: string*
-numberOfStudents: int
-capacity: int
+Course(courseName: string&, capacity: int)
+~Course()
+getCourseName(): string const
+addStudent(name: string&): void
+dropStudent(name: string&): void
+getStudents(): string* const
+getNumberOfStudents(): int const

The name of the course.

An array of students who take the course. students is a pointer for the array.

The number of students (default: 0).

The maximum number of students allowed for the course.

Creates a Course with the specified name and maximum number of students allowed.

Destructor

Returns the course name.

Adds a new student to the course.

Drops a student from the course.

Returns the array of students for the course.

Returns the number of students for the course.

FIGURE 11.5 The Course class models the courses.

A Course object can be created using the constructor Course(string courseName, int capacity) by passing a course name and the maximum number of students allowed. You can add a student to the course using the addStudent(string name) function, drop a student from the course using the dropStudent(string name) function, and return all the students for the course using the getStudents() function.

Suppose the class is defined as shown in Listing 11.14. Listing 11.15 gives a test class that creates two courses and adds students to them.

LISTING 11.14 Course.h

```
1   #ifndef COURSE_H
2   #define COURSE_H
3   #include <string>
4   using namespace std;
5
6   class Course
7   {
8   public:
9     Course(const string& courseName, int capacity);
10    ~Course();
11    string getCourseName() const;
12    void addStudent(const string& name);
13    void dropStudent(const string& name);
14    string* getStudents() const;
15    int getNumberOfStudents() const;
16
17  private:
18    string courseName;
19    string* students;
20    int numberOfStudents;
21    int capacity;
22  };
23
24  #endif
```

using string class (line 3)
Course class (line 6)
public members (line 8)
private members (line 17)

LISTING 11.15 TestCourse.cpp

```
1   #include <iostream>
2   #include "Course.h"
3   using namespace std;
4
5   int main()
6   {
7     Course course1("Data Structures", 10);
8     Course course2("Database Systems", 15);
9
10    course1.addStudent("Peter Jones");
11    course1.addStudent("Brian Smith");
12    course1.addStudent("Anne Kennedy");
13
14    course2.addStudent("Peter Jones");
15    course2.addStudent("Steve Smith");
16
17    cout << "Number of students in course1: " <<
18      course1.getNumberOfStudents() << "\n";
19    string* students = course1.getStudents();
20    for (int i = 0; i < course1.getNumberOfStudents(); i++)
21      cout << students[i] << ", ";
22
23    cout << "\nNumber of students in course2: "
```

Course header (line 2)
create course1 (line 7)
create course2 (line 8)
add a student (line 10)
number of students (line 17)
return students (line 19)
display a student (line 21)

```
24        << course2.getNumberOfStudents() << "\n";
25    students = course2.getStudents();
26    for (int i = 0; i < course2.getNumberOfStudents(); i++)
27      cout << students[i] << ", ";
28
29    return 0;
30  }
```

```
Number of students in course1: 3
Peter Jones, Brian Smith, Anne Kennedy,
Number of students in course2: 2
Peter Jones, Steve Smith,
```

The **Course** class is implemented in Listing 11.16.

LISTING 11.16   Course.cpp

```
1   #include <iostream>
2   #include "Course.h"                                       Course header
3   using namespace std;
4
5   Course::Course(const string& courseName, int capacity)
6   {
7     numberOfStudents = 0;                                   initialize data field
8     this->courseName = courseName;                          set course name
9     this->capacity = capacity;
10    students = new string[capacity];
11  }
12
13  Course::~Course()
14  {
15    delete [] students;                                     destroy dynamic array
16  }
17
18  string Course::getCourseName() const
19  {
20    return courseName;
21  }
22
23  void Course::addStudent(const string& name)               add a student
24  {
25    students[numberOfStudents] = name;
26    numberOfStudents++;                                     increase number of students
27  }
28
29  void Course::dropStudent(const string& name)
30  {
31    // Left as an exercise
32  }
33
34  string* Course::getStudents() const
35  {
36    return students;                                        return students
37  }
38
39  int Course::getNumberOfStudents() const
40  {
41    return numberOfStudents;
42  }
```

The `Course` constructor initializes `numberOfStudents` to 0 (line 7), sets a new course name (line 8), sets a capacity (line 9), and creates a dynamic array (line 10).

The `Course` class uses an array to store the students for the course. The array is created when a `Course` object is constructed. The array size is the maximum number of students allowed for the course. So, the array is created using `new string[capacity]`.

When a `Course` object is destroyed, the destructor is invoked to properly destroy the array (line 15).

throw exception

The `addStudent` function adds a student to the array (line 23). This function does not check whether the number of students in the class exceeds the maximum capacity. In Chapter 16, you will learn how to revise this function to make your program more robust by throwing an exception if the number of students in the class exceeds the maximum capacity.

The `getStudents` function (lines 34–37) returns the address of the array for storing the students.

The `dropStudent` function (lines 29–32) removes a student from the array. The implementation of this function is left as an exercise.

The user can create a `Course` and manipulate it through the public functions `addStudent`, `dropStudent`, `getNumberOfStudents`, and `getStudents`. However, the user doesn't need to know how these functions are implemented. The `Course` class encapsulates the internal implementation. This example uses an array to store students. You may use a different data structure to store students. The program that uses `Course` does not need to change as long as the contract of the public functions remains unchanged.

Note

When you create a `Course` object, an array of strings is created (line 10). Each element has a default string value created by the `string` class's no-arg constructor.

preventing memory leak

Caution

You should customize a destructor if the class contains a pointer data field that points to dynamically created memory. Otherwise, the program may have memory leak.

Check Point

11.35 When a `Course` object is created, what is the value of the `students` pointer?

11.36 Why is `delele [] students` used in the implementation of the destructor for the `students` pointer?

11.14 Copy Constructors

Key Point

Every class has a copy constructor, which is used to copy objects.

copy constructor

Each class may define several overloaded constructors and one destructor. Additionally, every class has a *copy constructor*, which can be used to create an object initialized with the data of another object of the same class.

The signature of the copy constructor is

    ClassName(const ClassName&)

For example, the copy constructor for the `Circle` class is

    Circle(const Circle&)

A default copy constructor is provided for each class implicitly, if it is not defined explicitly. The default copy constructor simply copies each data field in one object to its counterpart in the other object. Listing 11.17 demonstrates this.

LISTING 11.17 CopyConstructorDemo.cpp

```
1   #include <iostream>
2   #include "CircleWithDestructor.h" // Defined in Listing 11.11      include header
3   using namespace std;
4
5   int main()
6   {
7     Circle circle1(5);                                              create circle1
8     Circle circle2(circle1); // Use copy constructor                create circle2
9
10    cout << "After creating circle2 from circle1:" << endl;
11    cout << "\tcircle1.getRadius() returns "
12      << circle1.getRadius() << endl;                               display circle1
13    cout << "\tcircle2.getRadius() returns "
14      << circle2.getRadius() << endl;                               display circle2
15
16    circle1.setRadius(10.5);                                        modify circle1
17    circle2.setRadius(20.5);                                        modify circle2
18
19    cout << "After modifying circle1 and circle2: " << endl;
20    cout << "\tcircle1.getRadius() returns "
21      << circle1.getRadius() << endl;                               display circle1
22    cout << "\tcircle2.getRadius() returns "
23      << circle2.getRadius() << endl;                               display circle2
24
25    return 0;
26  }
```

```
After creating circle2 from circle1:
  circle1.getRadius() returns 5
  circle2.getRadius() returns 5

After modifying circle1 and circle2:
  circle1.getRadius() returns 10.5
  circle2.getRadius() returns 20.5
```

The program creates two `Circle` objects: `circle1` and `circle2` (lines 7–8). `circle2` is created using the copy constructor by copying `circle1`'s data.

The program then modifies the radius in `circle1` and `circle2` (lines 16–17) and displays their new radius in lines 20–23.

Note that the memberwise assignment operator and copy constructor are similar in the sense that both assign values from one object to the other. The difference is that a new object is created using a copy constructor. Using the assignment operator does not create new objects.

The default copy constructor or assignment operator for copying objects performs a *shallow copy*, rather than a *deep copy*, meaning that if the field is a pointer to some object, the address of the pointer is copied rather than its contents. Listing 11.18 demonstrates this.

shallow copy
deep copy

LISTING 11.18 ShallowCopyDemo.cpp

```
1   #include <iostream>
2   #include "Course.h" // Defined in Listing 11.14                   include Course header
3   using namespace std;
4
```

```
5  int main()
6  {
7    Course course1("C++", 10);
8    Course course2(course1);
9
10   course1.addStudent("Peter Pan"); // Add a student to course1
11   course2.addStudent("Lisa Ma"); // Add a student to course2
12
13   cout << "students in course1: " <<
14     course1.getStudents()[0] << endl;
15   cout << "students in course2: " <<
16     course2.getStudents()[0] << endl;
17
18   return 0;
19 }
```

create course1
create course2

add a student
add a student

get a student

get a student

```
students in course1: Lisa Ma
students in course2: Lisa Ma
```

The Course class was defined in Listing 11.14. The program creates a Course object course1 (line 7) and creates another Course object course2 using the copy constructor (line 8). course2 is a copy of course1. The Course class has four data fields: courseName, numberOfStudents, capacity, and students. The students field is a pointer type. When course1 is copied to course2 (line 8), all the data fields are copied to course2. Since students is a pointer, its value in course1 is copied to course2. Now both students in course1 and course2 point to the same array object, as shown in Figure 11.6.

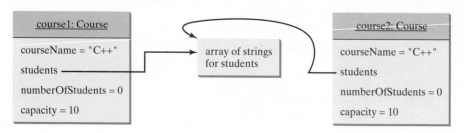

FIGURE 11.6   After course1 is copied to course2, the students data fields of course1 and course2 point to the same array.

Line 10 adds a student "Peter Pan" to course1, which is to set "Peter Pan" in the first element of the array. Line 11 adds a student "Lisa Ma" to course2 (line 11), which is to set "Lisa Ma" in the first element of the array. This in effect replaces "Peter Pan" with "Lisa Ma" in the first element of the array since both course1 and course2 use the same array to store student names. So, the student in both course1 and course2 is "Lisa Ma" (lines 13–16).

When the program terminates, course1 and course2 are destroyed. course1 and course2's destructors are invoked to delete the array from the heap (line 10 in Listing 11.16). Since both course1 and course2's students pointer point to the same array, the array will be deleted twice. This will cause a runtime error.

To avoid all these problems, you should perform a deep copy so that course1 and course2 have independent arrays to store student names.

Check Point

11.37 Does every class have a copy constructor? How is a copy constructor named? Can it be overloaded? Can you redefine a copy constructor? How do you invoke one?

11.38 What is the output of the following code?

```
#include <iostream>
#include <string>
using namespace std;

int main()
{
  string s1("ABC");
  string s2("DEFG");
  s1 = string(s2);
  cout << s1 << endl;
  cout << s2 << endl;

  return 0;
}
```

11.39 Is the highlighted code in the preceding question the same as the following?

```
s1 = s2;
```

Which is better?

11.15 Customizing Copy Constructors

You can customize the copy constructor to perform a deep copy.

Key Point

As discussed in the preceding section, the default copy constructor or assignment operator = performs a shallow copy. To perform a deep copy, you can implement the copy constructor. Listing 11.19 revises the **Course** class to define a copy constructor in line 11.

LISTING 11.19 CourseWithCustomCopyConstructor.h

```
1  #ifndef COURSE_H
2  #define COURSE_H
3  #include <string>
4  using namespace std;
5
6  class Course
7  {
8  public:
9    Course(const string& courseName, int capacity);
10   ~Course(); // Destructor
11   Course(const Course&); // Copy constructor
12   string getCourseName() const;
13   void addStudent(const string& name);
14   void dropStudent(const string& name);
15   string* getStudents() const;
16   int getNumberOfStudents() const;
17
18 private:
19   string courseName;
20   string* students;
21   int numberOfStudents;
22   int capacity;
23 };
24
25 #endif
```

copy constructor

Listing 11.20 implements the new copy constructor in lines 51–57. It copies **courseName**, **numberOfStudents**, and **capacity** from one course object to this course object (lines 53–55). A new array is created to hold student names in this object in line 56.

LISTING 11.20   CourseWithCustomCopyConstructor.cpp

include header file

```cpp
 1  #include <iostream>
 2  #include "CourseWithCustomCopyConstructor.h"
 3  using namespace std;
 4
 5  Course::Course(const string& courseName, int capacity)
 6  {
 7    numberOfStudents = 0;
 8    this->courseName = courseName;
 9    this->capacity = capacity;
10    students = new string[capacity];
11  }
12
13  Course::~Course()
14  {
15    delete [] students;
16  }
17
18  string Course::getCourseName() const
19  {
20    return courseName;
21  }
22
23  void Course::addStudent(const string& name)
24  {
25    if (numberOfStudents >= capacity)
26    {
27      cout << "The maximum size of array exceeded" << endl;
28      cout << "Program terminates now" << endl;
29      exit(0);
30    }
31
32    students[numberOfStudents] = name;
33    numberOfStudents++;
34  }
35
36  void Course::dropStudent(const string& name)
37  {
38    // Left as an exercise
39  }
40
41  string* Course::getStudents() const
42  {
43    return students;
44  }
45
46  int Course::getNumberOfStudents() const
47  {
48    return numberOfStudents;
49  }
50
```

copy constructor

```cpp
51  Course::Course(const Course& course) // Copy constructor
52  {
53    courseName = course.courseName;
```

```
54    numberOfStudents = course.numberOfStudents;
55    capacity = course.capacity;
56    students = new string[capacity];                create a new array
57  }
```

Listing 11.21 gives a program to test the custom copy constructor. The program is identical to Listing 11.18, ShallowCopyDemo.cpp, except that it uses CourseWithCustomCopyConstructor.h rather than Course.h.

LISTING 11.21 CustomCopyConstructorDemo.cpp

```
1   #include <iostream>
2   #include "CourseWithCustomCopyConstructor.h"
3   using namespace std;
4
5   int main()
6   {
7     Course course1("C++ Programming", 10);
8     Course course2(course1);                          use copy constructor
9
10    course1.addStudent("Peter Pan"); // Add a student to course1
11    course2.addStudent("Lisa Ma"); // Add a student to course2
12
13    cout << "students in course1: " <<
14      course1.getStudents()[0] << endl;
15    cout << "students in course2: " <<
16      course2.getStudents()[0] << endl;
17
18    return 0;
19  }
```

```
students in course1: Peter Pan
students in course2: Lisa Ma
```

The copy constructor constructs a new array in **course2** for storing student names that is independent of the array in **course1**. The program adds a student **"Peter Pan"** to **course1** (line 10) and a student **"Lisa Ma"** to **course2** (line 11). As you see in the output in this example, the first student in **course1** is now **"Peter Pan"** and in **course2** is **"Lisa Ma"**. Figure 11.7 shows the two **Course** objects and two arrays of strings for students.

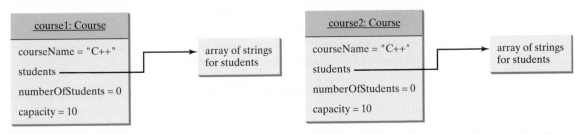

FIGURE 11.7 After **course1** is copied to **course2**, the **students** data fields of **course1** and **course2** point to two different arrays.

 Note
The custom copy constructor does not change the behavior of the memberwise copy
operator = by default. Chapter 14 will introduce how to customize the = operator.   memberwise copy

Check Point

11.40 Use the `Person` class in Check Point 11.34 to demonstrate why a deep copy is needed. Supply a customized constructor that performs a deep copy for the `children` array.

KEY TERMS

address operator (&)   432
arrow operator (->)   454
constant pointer   438
copy constructor   462
dangling pointer   452
deep copy   463
delete operator   452
dereference operator (*)   434
destructor   456

freestore   451
heap   451
indirection operator   434
memory leak   452
new operator   449
pointer   442
pointer-based string   442
shallow copy   463
`this` keyword   455

CHAPTER SUMMARY

1. Pointers are variables that store the memory address of other variables.

2. The declaration

    `int* pCount;`

    declares `pCount` to be a pointer that can point to an `int` variable.

3. The ampersand (&) symbol is called the *address operator* when placed in front of a variable. It is a unary operator that returns the address of the variable.

4. A pointer variable is declared with a type such as `int` or `double`. You have to assign it with the address of the variable of the same type.

5. Like a local variable, a local pointer is assigned an arbitrary value if you don't initialize it.

6. A pointer may be initialized to `NULL` (same as `0`), which is a special value for a pointer to indicate that the pointer points to nothing.

7. The asterisk (*) placed before a pointer is known as the indirection operator or dereference operator (dereference means indirect reference).

8. When a pointer is dereferenced, the value at the address stored in the pointer is retrieved.

9. The `const` keyword can be used to declare constant pointer and constant data.

10. An array name is actually a constant pointer that points to the starting address of the array.

11. You can access array elements using pointers or via index.

12. An integer may be added or subtracted from a pointer. The pointer is incremented or decremented by that integer times the size of the element to which the pointer points.

13. A pointer argument can be passed by value or by reference.

14. A pointer may be returned from a function. But you should not return the address of a local variable from a function, because a local variable is destroyed after the function is returned.

15. The new operator can be used to allocate persistent memory on the heap.

16. You should use the delete operator to release the memory created using the new operator, when the memory is no longer needed.

17. You can use pointers to reference an object and access object data fields and invoke functions.

18. You can create objects dynamically in a heap using the new operator.

19. The keyword this can be used as a pointer to the calling object.

20. Destructors are the opposite of constructors.

21. Constructors are invoked to create objects, and destructors are invoked automatically when objects are destroyed.

22. Every class has a default destructor, if the destructor is not explicitly defined.

23. The default destructor does not perform any operations.

24. Every class has a default copy constructor, if the copy constructor is not explicitly defined.

25. The default copy constructor simply copies each data field in one object to its counterpart in the other object.

QUIZ

Answer the quiz for this chapter online at www.cs.armstrong.edu/liang/cpp3e/quiz.html.

PROGRAMMING EXERCISES

Sections 11.2–11.11

11.1   (*Analyze input*) Write a program that first reads an integer for the array size, then reads numbers into the array, counts the even numbers and the odd numbers and displays them.

**11.2   (*Print the consonants*) Write a program that first reads an integer for the array size, then reads characters into the array, and displays the consonants (i.e., a character is displayed only if it is a consonant). (*Hint*: Read a character and store it to an array if it is not a vowel. If the character is a vowel, discard it. After the input, the array contains only the consonants.)

*11.3   (*Sort an array*) In Programming Exercise 7.14, you used bubble sort to sort an array. The bubble sort function repeatedly compares the successive neighboring pairs in the array and swaps them if they are in decreasing order. Modify the program by using the following header:

```
void bubbleSort(int* const array, int size)
```

The function returns an array that contains the sorted elements.

11.4   (*Sum of even locations*) Write two overloaded functions that return the sum of values at even locations of an array with the following headers:

```
int sumOfEven(const int* array, int size);
double sumOfEven(const double* array, int size);
```

Write a test program that reads five integers or double values, invokes this function, and displays the sum of values at even locations.

11.5   (*Find the largest element*) Use pointers to write a function that finds the largest element in an array of integers. Use {6, 7, 9, 10, 15, 3, 99, -21} to test the function.

VideoNote
Return a pointer

**11.6   (*Occurrences of each digit in a string*) Write a function that counts the occurrences of each digit in a string using the following header:

```
int* count(const string& s)
```

The function counts how many times a digit appears in the string. The return value is an array of ten elements, each of which holds the count for a digit. For example, after executing `int* counts = count("12203AB3")`, `counts[0]` is 1, `counts[1]` is 1, `counts[2]` is 2, `counts[3]` is 2.

Write a main function to display the count for "SSN is 343 32 4545 and ID is 434 34 4323".

Redesign the function to pass the `counts` array in a parameter as follows:

```
void count(const string& s, int counts[], int size)
```

where `size` is the size of the `counts` array. In this case, it is 10.

**11.7   (*Business: ATM machine*) Use the `Account` class created in Programming Exercise 9.3 to simulate an ATM machine. Create 10 accounts in an array with id 0, 1, . . . , 9, and initial balance $100. The system prompts the user to enter an id. If the id is entered incorrectly, ask the user to enter a correct one. Once an id is accepted, the main menu is displayed, as shown in the sample run. You can enter a choice 1 for viewing the current balance, 2 for withdrawing money, 3 for depositing money, and 4 for exiting the main menu. Once you exit, the system will prompt for an id again. So, once the system starts, it will not stop.

```
Enter an id: 4 ↵Enter

Main menu
1: check balance
2: withdraw
3: deposit
4: exit
Enter a choice: 1 ↵Enter
The balance is 100.0
```

```
Main menu
1: check balance
2: withdraw
3: deposit
4: exit
Enter a choice: 2 ↵Enter
Enter an amount to withdraw: 3 ↵Enter

Main menu
1: check balance
2: withdraw
3: deposit
4: exit
Enter a choice: 1 ↵Enter
The balance is 97.0

Main menu
1: check balance
2: withdraw
3: deposit
4: exit
Enter a choice: 3 ↵Enter
Enter an amount to deposit: 10 ↵Enter

Main menu
1: check balance
2: withdraw
3: deposit
4: exit
Enter a choice: 1 ↵Enter
The balance is 107.0

Main menu
1: check balance
2: withdraw
3: deposit
4: exit
Enter a choice: 4 ↵Enter
Enter an id:
```

*11.8   (*Geometry: The* Circle2D *class*) Define the Circle2D class that contains:

- Two double data fields named x and y that specify the center of the circle with constant get functions.
- A double data field radius with a constant get function.
- A no-arg constructor that creates a default circle with (0, 0) for (x, y) and 1 for radius.
- A constructor that creates a circle with the specified x, y, and radius.
- A constant function getArea() that returns the area of the circle.
- A constant function getPerimeter() that returns the perimeter of the circle.
- A constant function contains(double x, double y) that returns true if the specified point (x, y) is inside this circle. See Figure 11.8a.
- A constant function contains(const Circle2D& circle) that returns true if the specified circle is inside this circle. See Figure 11.8b.
- A constant function overlaps(const Circle2D& circle) that returns true if the specified circle overlaps with this circle. See Figure 11.8c.

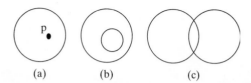

(a)   (b)   (c)

FIGURE 11.8 (a) A point is inside the circle. (b) A circle is inside another circle. (c) A circle overlaps another circle.

Draw the UML diagram for the class. Implement the class. Write a test program that creates a `Circle2D` object `c1(2, 2, 5.5)`, `c2(2, 2, 5.5)`, and `c3(4, 5, 10.5)`, displays `c1`'s area and perimeter, the result of `c1.contains(3, 3)`, `c1.contains(c2)`, and `c1.overlaps(c3)`.

*11.9 (*Geometry: The* `Rectangle2D` *class*) Define the `Rectangle2D` class that contains:

- Two `double` data fields named x and y that specify the center of the rectangle with constant `get` functions and `set` functions. (Assume that the rectangle sides are parallel to x- or y-axes.)
- The `double` data fields `width` and `height` with constant `get` functions and `set` functions.
- A no-arg constructor that creates a default rectangle with (0, 0) for (x, y) and 1 for both `width` and `height`.
- A constructor that creates a rectangle with the specified x, y, `width`, and `height`.
- A constant function `getArea()` that returns the area of the rectangle.
- A constant function `getPerimeter()` that returns the perimeter of the rectangle.
- A constant function `contains(double x, double y)` that returns `true` if the specified point (x, y) is inside this rectangle. See Figure 11.9a.
- A constant function `contains(const Rectangle2D &r)` that returns `true` if the specified rectangle is inside this rectangle. See Figure 11.9b.
- A constant function `overlaps(const Rectangle2D &r)` that returns `true` if the specified rectangle overlaps with this rectangle. See Figure 11.9c.

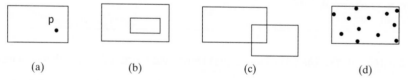

(a)   (b)   (c)   (d)

FIGURE 11.9 (a) A point is inside the rectangle. (b) A rectangle is inside another rectangle. (c) A rectangle overlaps another rectangle. (d) Points are enclosed inside a rectangle.

Draw the UML diagram for the class. Implement the class. Write a test program that creates three `Rectangle2D` objects `r1(2, 2, 5.5, 4.9)`, `r2(4, 5, 10.5, 3.2))`, and `r3(3, 5, 2.3, 5.4)`, and displays `r1`'s area and perimeter, and displays the result of `r1.contains(3, 3)`, `r1.contains(r2)`, and `r1.overlaps(r3)`.

*11.10 (*Count occurrences of each digit in an integer*) Rewrite the `countDigits` function in Programming Exercise 10.7 using the following header:

```
int* countDigits(const int& number)
```

This function returns the counts as an array of 10 elements. For example, after invoking

```
int counts[] = countDigits(11223)
```

```
counts[0] is 0, counts[1] is 2, counts[2] is 2,
counts[3] is 1, ...
```

Write a test program that prompts the user to enter an integer, invokes the count-Digits function, and displays the counts of each digit in the given integer.

*11.11 (*Geometry: find the bounding rectangle*) A bounding rectangle is the minimum rectangle that encloses a set of points in a two-dimensional plane, as shown in Figure 11.9d. Write a function that returns a bounding rectangle for a set of points in a two-dimensional plane, as follows:

```
const int SIZE = 2;
Rectangle2D getRectangle(const double points[][SIZE]);
```

The Rectangle2D class is defined in Programming Exercise 11.9. Write a test program that prompts the user to enter five points and displays the bounding rectangle's center, width, and height. Here is a sample run:

```
Enter five points: 1.0 2.5 3 4 5 6 7 8 9 10 ↵Enter
The bounding rectangle's center (5.0, 6.25), width 8.0, height 7.5
```

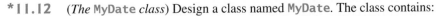

*11.12 (*The MyDate class*) Design a class named MyDate. The class contains:

- The data fields year, month, and day that represent a date. month is 0-based, i.e., 0 is for January.
- A no-arg constructor that creates a MyDate object for the current date.
- A constructor that constructs a MyDate object with a specified elapsed time since midnight, January 1, 1970, in seconds.
- A constructor that constructs a MyDate object with the specified year, month, and day.
- Three constant get functions for the data fields year, month, and day, respectively.
- Three set functions for the data fields year, month, and day, respectively.
- A function named setDate(long elapsedTime) that sets a new date for the object using the elapsed time.

Draw the UML diagram for the class and then implement the class. Write a test program that creates two MyDate objects (using MyDate() and MyDate(3435555513)) and displays their year, month, and day.

(*Hint*: The first two constructors will extract the year, month, and day from the elapsed time. For example, if the elapsed time is 561555550 seconds, the year is 1987, the month is 9, and the day is 18.)

Sections 11.12–11.15

**11.13 (*The Course class*) Revise the Course class implementation in Listing 11.16, Course.cpp, as follows:

- When adding a new student to the course, if the array capacity is exceeded, increase the array size by creating a new larger array and copying the contents of the current array to it.
- Implement the dropStudent function.
- Add a new function named clear() that removes all students from the course.
- Implement the destructor and copy constructor to perform a deep copy in the class.

Write a test program that creates a course, adds three students, removes one, and displays the students in the course.

11.14 (*Implementing the* string *class*) The string class is provided in the C++ library. Provide your own implementation for the following functions (name the new class MyString):

```
MyString();
MyString(const char* cString);
char at(int index) const;
int length() const;
void clear();
bool empty() const;
int compare(const MyString& s) const;
int compare(int index, int n, const MyString& s) const;
void copy(char s[], int index, int n);
char* data() const;
int find(char ch) const;
int find(char ch, int index) const;
int find(const MyString& s, int index) const;
```

11.15 (*Implementing the* string *class*) The string class is provided in the C++ library. Provide your own implementation for the following functions (name the new class MyString):

```
MyString(const char ch, int size);
MyString(const char chars[], int size);
MyString append(const MyString& s);
MyString append(const MyString& s, int index, int n);
MyString append(int n, char ch);
MyString assign(const char* chars);
MyString assign(const MyString& s, int index, int n);
MyString assign(const MyString& s, int n);
MyString assign(int n, char ch);
MyString substr(int index, int n) const;
MyString substr(int index) const;
MyString erase(int index, int n);
```

11.16 (*Sort characters in a string*) Rewrite the sort function in Programming Exercise 10.4 using the sort function introduced in Section 11.8. (*Hint*: Obtain a C-string from the string and apply the sort function to sort the characters in the C-string array, and obtain a string from the sorted C-string.) Write a test program that prompts the user to enter a string and displays the new sorted string. The sample run is the same as in Programming Exercise 10.4.

CHAPTER

12

TEMPLATES, VECTORS, AND STACKS

Objectives

- To know the motivation and benefits of templates (§12.2).
- To define a template function with type parameters (§12.2).
- To develop a generic sort function using templates (§12.3).
- To develop generic classes using class templates (§§12.4–12.5).
- To use the C++ `vector` class as a resizable array (§12.6).
- To replace arrays using vectors (§12.7).
- To parse and evaluate expressions using stacks (§12.8).

12.1 Introduction

You can define template functions and classes in C++ using generic types. Templates functions and classes enable programs to work on many different data types without being rewritten for each one.

what is a template?

C++ provides functions and classes for developing reusable software. Templates provide the capability to parameterize types in functions and classes. With this capability, you can define one function or one class with a generic type that the compiler can substitute for a concrete type. For example, you may define one function for finding the maximum number between two numbers of a generic type. If you invoke this function with two `int` arguments, the generic type is replaced by the `int` type. If you invoke this function with two `double` arguments, the generic type is replaced by the `double` type.

This chapter introduces the concept of templates, and you will learn how to define function templates and class templates and use them with concrete types. You will also learn a very useful generic template `vector`, which you can use to replace arrays.

12.2 Templates Basics

VideoNote
Templates basics

Templates provide the capability to parameterize types in functions and classes. You can define functions or classes with generic types that can be substituted for concrete types by the compiler.

template

Let us begin with a simple example to demonstrate the need for templates. Suppose you want to find the maximum of two integers, two doubles, two characters, and two strings. You might write four overloaded functions as follows:

int type

```
1  int maxValue(int value1, int value2)
2  {
3    if (value1 > value2)
4      return value1;
5    else
6      return value2;
7  }
8
```

double type

```
9  double maxValue(double value1, double value2)
10 {
11   if (value1 > value2)
12     return value1;
13   else
14     return value2;
15 }
16
```

char type

```
17 char maxValue(char value1, char value2)
18 {
19   if (value1 > value2)
20     return value1;
21   else
22     return value2;
23 }
24
```

string type

```
25 string maxValue(string value1, string value2)
26 {
27   if (value1 > value2)
28     return value1;
29   else
30     return value2;
31 }
```

These four functions are almost identical, except that each uses a different type. The first function uses the `int` type, the second the `double` type, the third the `char` type, and the fourth the `string` type. It would save typing, save space, and make the program easy to maintain if you could simply define one function with a generic type as follows:

```
1  GenericType maxValue(GenericType value1, GenericType value2)
2  {
3    if (value1 > value2)
4      return value1;
5    else
6      return value2;
7  }
```
generic type

This `GenericType` applies to all types such as `int`, `double`, `char`, and `string`.

C++ enables you to define a function template with generic types. Listing 12.1 defines a template function for finding a maximum value between two values of a generic type.

LISTING 12.1   GenericMaxValue.cpp

```
1  #include <iostream>
2  #include <string>
3  using namespace std;
4
5  template<typename T>
6  T maxValue(T value1, T value2)
7  {
8    if (value1 > value2)
9      return value1;
10   else
11      return value2;
12 }
13
14 int main()
15 {
16   cout << "Maximum between 1 and 3 is " << maxValue(1, 3) << endl;
17   cout << "Maximum between 1.5 and 0.3 is "
18     << maxValue(1.5, 0.3) << endl;
19   cout << "Maximum between 'A' and 'N' is "
20     << maxValue('A', 'N') << endl;
21   cout << "Maximum between \"NBC\" and \"ABC\" is "
22     << maxValue(string("NBC"), string("ABC")) << endl;
23
24   return 0;
25 }
```
template prefix
type parameter

invoke maxValue

invoke maxValue

invoke maxValue

invoke maxValue

```
Maximum between 1 and 3 is 3
Maximum between 1.5 and 0.3 is 1.5
Maximum between 'A' and 'N' is N
Maximum between "NBC" and "ABC" is NBC
```

The definition for the function template begins with the keyword `template` followed by a list of parameters. Each parameter must be preceded by the interchangeable keyword `typename` or `class` in the form `<typename typeParameter>` or `<class typeParameter>`. For example, line 5

```
template<typename T>
```

template prefix
type parameter

begins the definition of the function template for `maxValue`. This line is also known as the *template prefix*. Here T is a *type parameter*. By convention, a single capital letter such as T is used to denote a type parameter.

The `maxValue` function is defined in lines 6–12. A type parameter can be used in the function just like a regular type. You can use it to specify the return type of a function, declare function parameters, or declare variables in the function.

invoke a function

The `maxValue` function is invoked to return the maximum **int**, **double**, **char**, and **string** in lines 16–22. For the function call `maxValue(1,  3)`, the compiler recognizes that the parameter type is **int** and replaces the type parameter T with **int** to invoke the `maxValue` function with a concrete **int** type. For the function call `maxValue(string("NBC"),  string("ABC"))`, the compiler recognizes that the parameter type is **string** and replaces the type parameter T with **string** to invoke the `maxValue` function with a concrete **string** type.

C-string

What happens if you replace `maxValue(string("NBC"),  string("ABC"))` in line 22 with `maxValue("NBC",  "ABC")`? You will be surprised to see that it returns ABC. Why? "NBC" and "ABC" are C-strings. Invoking `maxValue("NBC",  "ABC")` passes the addresses of "NBC" and "ABC" to the function parameter. When comparing `value1 > value2`, the addresses of two arrays are compared, not the contents of the array!

Caution

match parameter

The generic `maxValue` function can be used to return a maximum of two values of *any type*, provided that

■ The two values have the same type;

■ The two values can be compared using the > operator.

For example, if one value is **int** and the other is **double** (e.g., `maxValue(1, 3.5)`), the compiler will report a syntax error because it cannot find a match for the call. If you invoke `maxValue(Circle(1),  Circle(2))`, the compiler will report a syntax error because the > operator is not defined in the `Circle` class.

Tip

<typename T> preferred

You can use either `<typename T>` or `<class T>` to specify a type parameter. Using `<typename T>` is better because `<typename T>` is descriptive. `<class T>` could be confused with class definition.

Note

multiple type parameters

Occasionally, a template function may have more than one parameter. In this case, place the parameters together inside the brackets, separated by commas, such as `<typename T1, typename T2, typename T3>`.

The parameters in the generic function in Listing 12.1 are defined as pass-by-value. You can modify it using pass-by-reference as shown in Listing 12.2.

LISTING 12.2   GenericMaxValuePassByReference.cpp

template prefix
type parameter

```
1   #include <iostream>
2   #include <string>
3   using namespace std;
4
5   template<typename T>
6   T maxValue(const T& value1, const T& value2)
7   {
8     if (value1 > value2)
9       return value1;
```

```
10    else
11      return value2;
12  }
13
14  int main()
15  {
16    cout << "Maximum between 1 and 3 is " << maxValue(1, 3) << endl;      invoke maxValue
17    cout << "Maximum between 1.5 and 0.3 is "
18      << maxValue(1.5, 0.3) << endl;                                       invoke maxValue
19    cout << "Maximum between 'A' and 'N' is "
20      << maxValue('A', 'N') << endl;                                       invoke maxValue
21    cout << "Maximum between \"NBC\" and \"ABC\" is "
22      << maxValue(string("NBC"), string("ABC")) << endl;                   invoke maxValue
23
24    return 0;
25  }
```

```
Maximum between 1 and 3 is 3
Maximum between 1.5 and 0.3 is 1.5
Maximum between 'A' and 'N' is N
Maximum between "NBC" and "ABC" is NBC
```

12.1 For the `maxValue` function in Listing 12.1, can you invoke it with two arguments of different types, such as `maxValue(1, 1.5)`?

12.2 For the `maxValue` function in Listing 12.1, can you invoke it with two arguments of strings, such as `maxValue("ABC", "ABD")`? Can you invoke it with two arguments of circles, such as `maxValue(Circle(2), Circle(3))`?

12.3 Can `template<typename T>` be replaced by `template<class T>`?

12.4 Can a type parameter be named using any identifier other than a keyword?

12.5 Can a type parameter be of a primitive type or an object type?

12.6 What is wrong in the following code?

```
#include <iostream>
#include <string>
using namespace std;
template<typename T>
T maxValue(T value1, T value2)
{
  int result;
  if (value1 > value2)
    result = value1;
  else
    result = value2;
  return result;
}

int main()
{
  cout << "Maximum between 1 and 3 is "
    << maxValue(1, 3) << endl;
  cout << "Maximum between 1.5 and 0.3 is "
    << maxValue(1.5, 0.3) << endl;
  cout << "Maximum between 'A' and 'N' is "
    << maxValue('A', 'N') << endl;
```

```
  cout << "Maximum between \"ABC\" and \"ABD\" is "
    << maxValue("ABC", "ABD") << endl;

  return 0;
}
```

12.7 Suppose you define the maxValue function as follows:

```
template<typename T1, typename T2>
T1 maxValue(T1 value1, T2 value2)
{
  if (value1 > value2)
    return value1;
  else
    return value2;
}
```

What would be the return value from invoking `maxValue(1, 2.5)`, `maxValue(1.4, 2.5)`, and `maxValue(1.5, 2)`?

12.3 Example: A Generic Sort

Key Point

This section defines a generic sort function.

Listing 7.11, SelectionSort.cpp, gives a function to sort an array of double values. Here is a copy of the function:

double type

double type

```
1  void selectionSort(double list[], int listSize)
2  {
3    for (int i = 0; i < listSize; i++)
4    {
5      // Find the minimum in the list[i..listSize-1]
6      double currentMin = list[i];
7      int currentMinIndex = i;
8
9      for (int j = i + 1; j < listSize; j++)
10     {
11       if (currentMin > list[j])
12       {
13         currentMin = list[j];
14         currentMinIndex = j;
15       }
16     }
17
18     // Swap list[i] with list[currentMinIndex] if necessary
19     if (currentMinIndex != i)
20     {
21       list[currentMinIndex] = list[i];
22       list[i] = currentMin;
23     }
24   }
25 }
```

It is easy to modify this function to write new overloaded functions for sorting an array of int values, char values, string values, and so on. All you need to do is to replace the word double by int, char, or string in two places (lines 1 and 6).

Instead of writing several overloaded sort functions, you can define just one template function that works for any type. Listing 12.3 defines a generic function for sorting an array of elements.

LISTING 12.3 GenericSort.cpp

```cpp
1  #include <iostream>
2  #include <string>
3  using namespace std;
4
5  template<typename T>                                       template prefix
6  void sort(T list[], int listSize)                          type parameter
7  {
8    for (int i = 0; i < listSize; i++)
9    {
10     // Find the minimum in the list[i..listSize-1]
11     T currentMin = list[i];                                type parameter
12     int currentMinIndex = i;
13
14     for (int j = i + 1; j < listSize; j++)
15     {
16       if (currentMin > list[j])
17       {
18         currentMin = list[j];
19         currentMinIndex = j;
20       }
21     }
22
23     // Swap list[i] with list[currentMinIndex] if necessary;
24     if (currentMinIndex != i)
25     {
26       list[currentMinIndex] = list[i];
27       list[i] = currentMin;
28     }
29   }
30 }
31
32 template<typename T>                                        template prefix
33 void printArray(const T list[], int listSize)              type parameter
34 {
35   for (int i = 0; i < listSize; i++)
36   {
37     cout << list[i] << " ";
38   }
39   cout << endl;
40 }
41
42 int main()
43 {
44   int list1[] = {3, 5, 1, 0, 2, 8, 7};
45   sort(list1, 7);                                          invoke sort
46   printArray(list1, 7);                                    invoke printArray
47
48   double list2[] = {3.5, 0.5, 1.4, 0.4, 2.5, 1.8, 4.7};
49   sort(list2, 7);
50   printArray(list2, 7);
51
52   string list3[] = {"Atlanta", "Denver", "Chicago", "Dallas"};
53   sort(list3, 4);
54   printArray(list3, 4);
55
56   return 0;
57 }
```

```
0 1 2 3 5 7 8
0.4 0.5 1.4 1.8 2.5 3.5 4.7
Atlanta Chicago Dallas Denver
```

Two template functions are defined in this program. The template function sort (lines 5–30) uses the type parameter T to specify the element type in an array. This function is identical to the selectionSort function except that the parameter double is replaced by a generic type T.

The template function printArray (lines 32–40) uses the type parameter T to specify the element type in an array. This function displays all the elements in the array to the console.

The main function invokes the sort function to sort an array of int, double, and string values (lines 45, 49, 53) and invokes the printArray function to display these arrays (lines 46, 50, 54).

developing generic function

 Tip
When you define a generic function, it is better to start with a nongeneric function, debug and test it, and then convert it to a generic function.

12.8 Suppose you define the swap function as follows:

```
template<typename T>
void swap(T& var1, T& var2)
{
  T temp = var1;
  var1 = var2;
  var2 = temp;
}
```

What is wrong in the following code?

```
int main()
{
  int v1 = 1;
  int v2 = 2;
  swap(v1, v2);

  double d1 = 1;
  double d2 = 2;
  swap(d1, d2);

  swap(v1, d2);
  swap(1, 2);

  return 0;
}
```

VideoNote
Templates class

template class

12.4 Class Templates

You can define generic types for a class.

In the preceding sections, you defined template functions with type parameters for the function. You also can define *template classes* with type parameters for the class. The type parameters can be used everywhere in the class where a regular type appears.

Recall that the StackOfIntegers class, defined in Section 10.9, "Case Study: The StackOfInteger Class," can be used to create a stack for int values. Here is a copy of the class with its UML class diagram, as shown in Figure 12.1a.

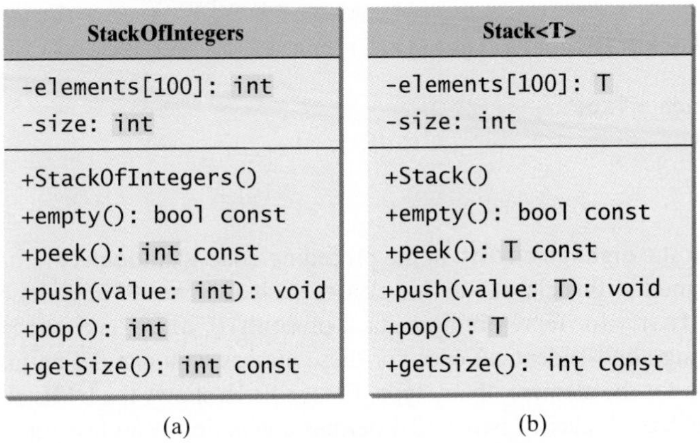

StackOfIntegers	Stack<T>
-elements[100]: int -size: int	-elements[100]: T -size: int
+StackOfIntegers() +empty(): bool const +peek(): int const +push(value: int): void +pop(): int +getSize(): int const	+Stack() +empty(): bool const +peek(): T const +push(value: T): void +pop(): T +getSize(): int const
(a)	(b)

FIGURE 12.1   Stack<T> is a generic version of the Stack class.

```
1   #ifndef STACK_H
2   #define STACK_H
3
4   class StackOfIntegers
5   {
6   public:
7     StackOfIntegers();
8     bool empty() const;
9     int peek() const;                       int type
10    void push(int value);                   int type
11    int pop();                              int type
12    int getSize() const;
13
14  private:
15    int elements[100];
16    int size;                               int type
17  };
18
19  StackOfIntegers::StackOfIntegers()
20  {
21    size = 0;
22  }
23
24  bool StackOfIntegers::empty() const
25  {
26    return size == 0;
27  }
28
29  int StackOfIntegers::peek() const
30  {
31    return elements[size - 1];
32  }
33
34  void StackOfIntegers::push(int value)
35  {
36    elements[size++] = value;
37  }
38
39  int StackOfIntegers::pop()
40  {
41    return elements[--size];
42  }
```

```
43
44   int StackOfIntegers::getSize() const
45   {
46     return size;
47   }
48
49   #endif
```

By replacing the highlighted `int` in the preceding code with `double`, `char`, or `string`, you easily can modify this class to define classes such as `StackOfDouble`, `StackOfChar`, and `StackOfString` for representing a stack of `double`, `char`, and `string` values. But, instead of writing almost identical code for these classes, you can define just one template class that works for the element of any type. Figure 12.1b shows the UML class diagram for the new generic `Stack` class. Listing 12.4 defines a generic stack class for storing elements of a generic type.

LISTING 12.4 GenericStack.h

```
 1   #ifndef STACK_H
 2   #define STACK_H
 3
 4   template<typename T>          ← template prefix
 5   class Stack
 6   {
 7   public:
 8     Stack();
 9     bool empty() const;
10     T peek() const;            ← type parameter
11     void push(T value);        ← type parameter
12     T pop();
13     int getSize() const;
14
15   private:
16     T elements[100];           ← type parameter
17     int size;
18   };
19
20   template<typename T>          ← function template
21   Stack<T>::Stack()
22   {
23     size = 0;
24   }
25
26   template<typename T>          ← function template
27   bool Stack<T>::empty() const
28   {
29     return size == 0;
30   }
31
32   template<typename T>          ← function template
33   T Stack<T>::peek() const
34   {
35     return elements[size - 1];
36   }
37
38   template<typename T>          ← function template
39   void Stack<T>::push(T value)
40   {
41     elements[size++] = value;
42   }
```

```
43
44  template<typename T>                                        function template
45  T Stack<T>::pop()
46  {
47     return elements[--size];
48  }
49
50  template<typename T>                                        function template
51  int Stack<T>::getSize() const
52  {
53     return size;
54  }
55
56  #endif
```

The syntax for class templates is basically the same as that for function templates. You place the *template prefix* before the class definition (line 4), just as you place the template prefix before the function template.

template prefix

```
template<typename T>
```

The type parameter can be used in the class just like any regular data type. Here, the type T is used to define functions peek() (line 10), push(T value) (line 11), and pop() (line 12). T also is used in line 16 to declare array elements.

The constructors and functions are defined the same way as in regular classes, except that the constructors and functions themselves are templates. So, you have to place the template prefix before the constructor and function header in the implementation. For example,

define constructors
define functions

```
template<typename T>
Stack<T>::Stack()
{
   size = 0;
}

template<typename T>
bool Stack<T>::empty()
{
   return size == 0;
}

template<typename T>
T Stack<T>::peek()
{
   return elements[size - 1];
}
```

Note also that the class name before the scope resolution operator :: is Stack<T>, not Stack.

Tip

GenericStack.h combines class definition and class implementation into one file. Normally, you put class definition and class implementation into two separate files. For class templates, however, it is safer to put them together, because some compilers cannot compile them separately.

compile issue

Listing 12.5 gives a test program that creates a stack for int values in line 9 and a stack for strings in line 18.

LISTING 12.5 TestGenericStack.cpp

```
1  #include <iostream>
2  #include <string>
```

generic Stack

```
 3  #include "GenericStack.h"
 4  using namespace std;
 5
 6  int main()
 7  {
 8    // Create a stack of int values
 9    Stack<int> intStack;
10    for (int i = 0; i < 10; i++)
11      intStack.push(i);
12
13    while (!intStack.empty())
14      cout << intStack.pop() << " ";
15    cout << endl;
16
17    // Create a stack of strings
18    Stack<string> stringStack;
19    stringStack.push("Chicago");
20    stringStack.push("Denver");
21    stringStack.push("London");
22
23    while (!stringStack.empty())
24      cout << stringStack.pop() << " ";
25    cout << endl;
26
27    return 0;
28  }
```

int stack

string stack

```
9 8 7 6 5 4 3 2 1 0
London Denver Chicago
```

declaring objects

To declare an object from a template class, you have to specify a concrete type for the type parameter T. For example,

```
Stack<int> intStack;
```

This declaration replaces the type parameter T with **int**. So, **intStack** is a stack for **int** values. The object **intStack** is just like any other object. The program invokes the **push** function on **intStack** to add ten **int** values to the stack (line 11), and displays the elements from the stack (lines 13–14).

The program declares a stack object for storing strings in line 18, adds three strings in the stack (lines 19–21), and displays the strings from the stack (line 24).

Note the code in lines 9–11:

```
while (!intStack.empty())
  cout << intStack.pop() << " ";
cout << endl;
```

and in lines 23–25:

```
while (!stringStack.empty())
  cout << stringStack.pop() << " ";
cout << endl;
```

These two fragments are almost identical. The difference is that the former operates on **intStack** and the latter on **stringStack**. You can define a function with a stack parameter to display the elements in the stack. The new program is shown in Listing 12.6.

LISTING 12.6 TestGenericStackWithTemplateFunction.cpp

```
1   #include <iostream>
2   #include <string>
3   #include "GenericStack.h"                                     GenericStack header
4   using namespace std;
5
6   template<typename T>
7   void printStack(Stack<T>& stack)                              Stack<T> parameter
8   {
9     while (!stack.empty())
10      cout << stack.pop() << " ";
11    cout << endl;
12  }
13
14  int main()
15  {
16    // Create a stack of int values
17    Stack<int> intStack;
18    for (int i = 0; i < 10; i++)
19      intStack.push(i);
20    printStack(intStack);                                       invoke printStack
21
22    // Create a stack of strings
23    Stack<string> stringStack;
24    stringStack.push("Chicago");
25    stringStack.push("Denver");
26    stringStack.push("London");
27    printStack(stringStack);                                    invoke printStack
28
29    return 0;
30  }
```

The generic class name Stack<T> is used as a parameter type in a *template function* template function
(line 7).

Note

C++ allows you to assign a *default type* for a type parameter in a class template. For   default type
example, you may assign int as a default type in the generic Stack class as follows:

```
template<typename T = int>
class Stack
{
  ...
};
```

You now can declare an object using the default type like this:

```
Stack<> stack;  // stack is a stack for int values
```

You can use default type only in class templates, not in function templates.

Note

You also can use *nontype parameters* along with type parameters in a template prefix.   nontype parameter
For example, you may declare the array capacity as a parameter for the Stack class as
follows:

```
template<typename T, int capacity>
class Stack
```

```
        {
          ...
        private:
          T elements[capacity];
          int size;
        };
```

So, when you create a stack, you can specify the capacity for the array. For example,

```
Stack<string, 500> stack;
```

declares a stack that can hold up to 500 strings.

Note
You can define static members in a template class. Each template specialization has its own copy of a static data field.

static members

12.9 Do you have to use the template prefix for each function in the class definition? Do you have to use the template prefix for each function in the class
implementation?

12.10 What is wrong in the following code?

```
template<typename T = int>
void printArray(const T list[], int arraySize)
{
  for (int i = 0; i < arraySize; i++)
  {
    cout << list[i] << " ";
  }
  cout << endl;
}
```

12.11 What is wrong in the following code?

```
template<typename T>
class Foo
{
public:
  Foo();
  T f1(T value);
  T f2();
};

Foo::Foo()
{
  ...
}

T Stack::f1(T value)
{
  ...
}

T Stack::f2()
{
  ...
};
```

12.12 Suppose the template prefix for the **Stack** class is

```
template<typename T = string>
```

Can you create a stack of strings using the following?

```
Stack stack;
```

12.5 Improving the **Stack** Class

This section implements a dynamic stack class.

Key
Point

There is a problem in the **Stack** class. The elements of the stack are stored in an array with a fixed size 100 (see line 16 in Listing 12.4). So, you cannot store more than 100 elements in a stack. You could change 100 to a larger number, but if the actual stack is small, this would waste space. One way to resolve this dilemma is to allocate more memory dynamically when needed.

The **size** property in the **Stack<T>** class represents the number of elements in the stack. Let us add a new property named **capacity** that represents the current size of the array for storing the elements. The no-arg constructor of **Stack<T>** creates an array with capacity 16. When you add a new element to the stack, you may need to increase the array size in order to store the new element if the current capacity is full.

How do you increase the array capacity? You cannot do so, once the array is declared. To circumvent this restriction, you may create a new, larger array, copy the contents of the old array to this new one, and delete the old array.

The improved **Stack<T>** class is shown in Listing 12.7.

LISTING 12.7   ImprovedStack.h

```
1   #ifndef IMPROVEDSTACK_H
2   #define IMPROVEDSTACK_H
3
4   template<typename T>
5   class Stack
6   {
7   public:
8     Stack();
9     Stack(const Stack&);
10    ~Stack();
11    bool empty() const;
12    T peek() const;
13    void push(T value);
14    T pop();
15    int getSize() const;
16
17  private:
18    T* elements;
19    int size;
20    int capacity;
21    void ensureCapacity();
22  };
23
24  template<typename T>
25  Stack<T>::Stack(): size(0), capacity(16)
26  {
27    elements = new T[capacity];
28  }
29
30  template<typename T>
31  Stack<T>::Stack(const Stack& stack)
32  {
33    elements = new T[stack.capacity];
```

define Stack class

implement Stack class
no-arg constructor

copy constructor

destructor

increase capacity if needed

create a new array

copy to the new array

destroy the old array

```
34      size = stack.size;
35      capacity = stack.capacity;
36      for (int i = 0; i < size; i++)
37      {
38        elements[i] = stack.elements[i];
39      }
40    }
41
42    template<typename T>
43    Stack<T>::~Stack()
44    {
45      delete [] elements;
46    }
47
48    template<typename T>
49    bool Stack<T>::empty() const
50    {
51      return size == 0;
52    }
53
54    template<typename T>
55    T Stack<T>::peek() const
56    {
57      return elements[size - 1];
58    }
59
60    template<typename T>
61    void Stack<T>::push(T value)
62    {
63      ensureCapacity();
64      elements[size++] = value;
65    }
66
67    template<typename T>
68    void Stack<T>::ensureCapacity()
69    {
70      if (size >= capacity)
71      {
72        T* old = elements;
73        capacity = 2 * size;
74        elements = new T[size * 2];
75
76        for (int i = 0; i < size; i++)
77          elements[i] = old[i];
78
79        delete [] old;
80      }
81    }
82
83    template<typename T>
84    T Stack<T>::pop()
85    {
86      return elements[--size];
87    }
88
89    template<typename T>
90    int Stack<T>::getSize() const
91    {
92      return size;
```

```
93   }
94
95   #endif
```

Since the internal array **elements** is dynamically created, a destructor must be provided to properly destroy the array to avoid memory leak (lines 42–46). Note that the array elements in Listing 12.4, GenericStack.h, are not allocated dynamically, so there is no need to provide a destructor in that case.

The **push(T value)** function (lines 60–65) adds a new element to the stack. This function first invokes **ensureCapacity()** (line 63), which ensures that there is a space in the array for the new element.

The **ensureCapacity()** function (lines 67–81) checks whether the array is full. If it is, create a new array that doubles the current array size, set the new array as the current array, copy the old array to the new array, and delete the old array (line 79).

Please note that the syntax to destroy a dynamically created array is

```
delete [] elements; // Line 45
delete [] old; // Line 79
```

What happens if you mistakenly write the following?

```
delete elements; // Line 45
delete old; // Line 79
```

The program will compile and run fine for a stack of primitive-type values, but it is not correct for a stack of objects. The statement **delete [] elements** first calls the destructor on each object in the **elements** array and then destroys the array, whereas the statement **delete elements** calls the destructor only on the first object in the array.

12.13 What is wrong if line 79 in Listing 12.7 ImprovedStack.h is replaced by

```
delete old;
```

Check
Point

12.6 The C++ **vector** Class

C++ contains a generic **vector** *class for storing a list of objects.*

Key
Point

You can use an array to store a collection of data such as strings and **int** values. There is a serious limitation: The array size is fixed when the array is created. C++ provides the **vector** class, which is more flexible than arrays. You can use a **vector** object just like an array, but a vector's size can grow automatically if needed.

VideoNote
The **vector** class

To create a vector, use the syntax:

```
vector<elementType> vectorName;
```

For example,

```
vector<int> intVector;
```

creates a vector to store **int** values.

```
vector<string> stringVector;
```

creates a vector to store **string** objects.

Figure 12.2 lists several frequently used functions in the vector class in a UML class diagram.

vector<elementType>	
+vector<elementType>()	Constructs an empty vector with the specified element type.
+vector<elementType>(size: int)	Constructs a vector with the initial size, filled with default values.
+vector<elementType>(size: int, defaultValue: elementType)	Constructs a vector with the initial size, filled with specified values.
+push_back(element: elementType): void	Appends the element in this vector.
+pop_back(): void	Removes the last element from this vector.
+size(): unsigned const	Returns the number of the elements in this vector.
+at(index: int): elementType const	Returns the element at the specified index in this vector.
+empty(): bool const	Returns true if this vector is empty.
+clear(): void	Removes all elements from this vector.
+swap(v2: vector): void	Swaps the contents of this vector with the specified vector.

FIGURE 12.2 The `vector` class functions as a resizable array.

You can also create a vector with the initial size, filled with default values. For example, the following code creates a vector of initial size 10 with default values 0.

```
vector<int> intVector(10);
```

A vector can be accessed using the array subscript operator [ ]. For example,

```
cout << intVector[0];
```

displays the first element in the vector.

vector index range

Caution

To use the array subscript operator [ ], the element must already exist in the vector. Like array, the index is 0-based in a vector—i.e., the index of the first element in the vector is 0 and the last one is v.size() − 1. To use an index beyond this range would cause errors.

Listing 12.8 gives an example of using vectors.

LISTING 12.8 TestVector.cpp

```cpp
1  #include <iostream>
2  #include <vector>
3  #include <string>
4  using namespace std;
5
6  int main()
7  {
8    vector<int> intVector;
9
10   // Store numbers 1, 2, 3, 4, 5, ..., 10 to the vector
11   for (int i = 0; i < 10; i++)
12     intVector.push_back(i + 1);
13
14   // Display the numbers in the vector
15   cout << "Numbers in the vector: ";
16   for (int i = 0; i < intVector.size(); i++)
17     cout << intVector[i] << " ";
```

vector header
string header

create a vector

append int value

vector size
vector subscript

```
18
19   vector<string> stringVector;                              create a vector
20
21   // Store strings into the vector
22   stringVector.push_back("Dallas");                         append string
23   stringVector.push_back("Houston");
24   stringVector.push_back("Austin");
25   stringVector.push_back("Norman");
26
27   // Display the string in the vector
28   cout << "\nStrings in the string vector: ";
29   for (int i = 0; i < stringVector.size(); i++)             vector size
30     cout << stringVector[i] << " ";                         vector subscript
31
32   stringVector.pop_back(); // Remove the last element       remove element
33
34   vector<string> v2;                                        create vector
35   v2.swap(stringVector);                                    swap vector
36   v2[0] = "Atlanta";                                        assign string
37
38   // Redisplay the string in the vector
39   cout << "\nStrings in the vector v2: ";
40   for (int i = 0; i < v2.size(); i++)                       vector size
41     cout << v2.at(i) << " ";                                 at function
42
43   return 0;
44  }
```

```
Numbers in the vector: 1 2 3 4 5 6 7 8 9 10
Strings in the string vector: Dallas Houston Austin Norman
Strings in the vector v2: Atlanta Houston Austin
```

Since the vector class is used in the program, line 2 includes its header file. Since the string class is also used, line 3 includes the string class header file.

A vector for storing int values is created in line 8. The int values are appended to the vector in line 12. There is no limit on the size of the vector. The size grows automatically as more elements are added into the vector. The program displays all the int values in the vector in lines 15–17. Note the array subscript operator [] is used to retrieve an element in line 17.

A vector for storing strings is created in line 19. Four strings are added to the vector (lines 22–25). The program displays all the strings in the vector in lines 29–30. Note the array subscript operator [] is used to retrieve an element in line 30.

Line 32 removes the last string from the vector. Line 34 creates another vector v2. Line 35 swaps v2 with stringVector. Line 36 assigns a new string to v2[0]. The program displays the strings in v2 (lines 40–41). Note that the at function is used to retrieve the elements. You can also use the subscript operator [] to retrieve the elements.

The size() function returns the size of the vector as an unsigned (i.e., unsigned integer), not int. Some compilers may warn you because an unsigned value is used with a signed int value in variable i (lines 16, 29, 40). This is just a warning and should not cause any problems, because the unsigned value is automatically promoted to a signed value in this case. To get rid of the warning, declare i to be unsigned int in line 16 as follows:

unsigned int

```
for (unsigned i = 0; i < intVector.size(); i++)
```

12.14 How do you declare a vector to store double values? How do you append a double to a vector? How do you find the size of a vector? How do you remove an element from a vector?

Check Point

12.15 Why is the code in (a) wrong, but the code in (b) correct?

```
vector<int> v;
v[0] = 4;
```
(a)

```
vector<int> v(5);
v[0] = 4;
```
(b)

12.7 Replacing Arrays Using the **vector** Class

 Key Point

A vector can be used to replace arrays. Vectors are more flexible than arrays, but arrays are more efficient than vectors.

vector

array versus vector

A **vector** object can be used like an array, but there are some differences. Table 12.1 lists their similarities and differences.

TABLE 12.1 Differences and Similarities between Arrays and vector

Operation	Array	vector
Creating an array/vector	string a[10]	vector<string> v
Accessing an element	a[index]	v[index]
Updating an element	a[index] = "London"	v[index] = "London"
Returning size		v.size()
Adding a new element		v.push_back("London")
Removing an element		v.pop_back()
Removing all elements		v.clear()

Both arrays and vectors can be used to store a list of elements. Using an array is more efficient if the size of the list is fixed. A vector is a resizable array. The **vector** class contains many member functions for accessing and manipulating a vector. Using vectors is more flexible than using arrays. In general, you can always use vectors to replace arrays. All the examples in the preceding chapters that use arrays can be modified using vectors. This section rewrites Listing 7.2, DeckOfCards.cpp, and Listing 8.1, PassTwoDimensionalArray.cpp, using vectors.

Recall that Listing 7.2 is a program that picks four cards randomly from a deck of 52 cards. We use a vector to store the 52 cards with initial values 0 to 51, as follows:

```
const int NUMBER_OF_CARDS = 52;
vector<int> deck(NUMBER_OF_CARDS);

// Initialize cards
for (int i = 0; i < NUMBER_OF_CARDS; i++)
  deck[i] = i;
```

deck[0] to deck[12] are Clubs, deck[13] to deck[25] are Diamonds, deck[26] to deck[38] are Hearts, and deck[39] to deck[51] are Spades. Listing 12.9 gives the solution to the problem.

LISTING 12.9 DeckOfCardsUsingVector.cpp

```
1  #include <iostream>
2  #include <vector>
3  #include <string>
4  #include <ctime>
```

include vector

```
 5  using namespace std;
 6
 7  const int NUMBER_OF_CARDS = 52;
 8  string suits[4] = {"Spades", "Hearts", "Diamonds", "Clubs"};        suits
 9  string ranks[13] = {"Ace", "2", "3", "4", "5", "6", "7", "8", "9",  ranks
10    "10", "Jack", "Queen", "King"};
11
12  int main()
13  {
14    vector<int> deck(NUMBER_OF_CARDS);                                 create vector deck
15
16    // Initialize cards
17    for (int i = 0; i < NUMBER_OF_CARDS; i++)                          initialize deck
18      deck[i] = i;
19
20    // Shuffle the cards
21    srand(time(0));
22    for (int i = 0; i < NUMBER_OF_CARDS; i++)
23    {
24      // Generate an index randomly                                    shuffle deck
25      int index = rand() % NUMBER_OF_CARDS;
26      int temp = deck[i];
27      deck[i] = deck[index];
28      deck[index] = temp;
29    }
30
31    // Display the first four cards
32    for (int i = 0; i < 4; i++)
33    {
34      cout << ranks[deck[i] % 13] << " of " <<                         display rank
35        suits[deck[i] / 13] << endl;                                   display suit
36    }
37
38    return 0;
39  }
```

```
4 of Clubs
Ace of Diamonds
6 of Hearts
Jack of Clubs
```

This program is identical to Listing 7.2, except that line 2 includes the vector class and line 14 uses a vector to store all cards instead of an array. Interestingly, the syntax for using arrays and vectors is very similar, because you can use indexes in the brackets to access the elements in a vector, which is the same as for accessing array elements.

You could also change the arrays suits and ranks in lines 8–10 to vectors. If so, you have to write many lines of code to insert the suits and ranks to the vector. The code is simpler and better using arrays.

Recall that Listing 8.1 creates a two-dimensional array and invokes a function to return the sum of all elements in the array. A vector of vectors can be used to represent a two-dimensional array. Here is an example to represent a two-dimensional array with four rows and three columns:

```
vector<vector<int> > matrix(4); // four rows

for (int i = 0; i < 4; i++)
```

```
matrix[i] = vector<int>(3);

matrix[0][0] = 1; matrix[0][1] = 2; matrix[0][2] = 3;
matrix[1][0] = 4; matrix[1][1] = 5; matrix[1][2] = 6;
matrix[2][0] = 7; matrix[2][1] = 8; matrix[2][2] = 9;
matrix[3][0] = 10; matrix[3][1] = 11; matrix[3][2] = 12;
```

Note

There is a space separating > and > in the line

```
vector<vector<int> > matrix(4); // Four rows
```

Without the space, some old C++ compilers may not compile.

Listing 12.10 revises Listing 8.1, PassTwoDimensionalArray.cpp, using vectors.

LISTING 12.10   TwoDArrayUsingVector.cpp

include vector

function with vector

vector for 2-D array

assign values

```
 1  #include <iostream>
 2  #include <vector>
 3  using namespace std;
 4
 5  int sum(const vector<vector<int>>& matrix)
 6  {
 7    int total = 0;
 8    for (unsigned row = 0; row < matrix.size(); row++)
 9    {
10      for (unsigned column = 0; column < matrix[row].size(); column++)
11      {
12        total += matrix[row][column];
13      }
14    }
15
16    return total;
17  }
18
19  int main()
20  {
21    vector<vector<int>> matrix(4); // Four rows
22
23    for (unsigned i = 0; i < 4; i++)
24      matrix[i] = vector<int>(3); // Each row has three columns
25
26    matrix[0][0] = 1; matrix[0][1] = 2; matrix[0][2] = 3;
27    matrix[1][0] = 4; matrix[1][1] = 5; matrix[1][2] = 6;
28    matrix[2][0] = 7; matrix[2][1] = 8; matrix[2][2] = 9;
29    matrix[3][0] = 10; matrix[3][1] = 11; matrix[3][2] = 12;
30
31    cout << "Sum of all elements is " << sum(matrix) << endl;
32
33    return 0;
34  }
```

```
Sum of all elements is 78
```

The variable `matrix` is declared as a vector. Each element of the vector `matrix[i]` is another vector. So, `matrix[i][j]` represents the *i*th row and *j*th column in a two-dimensional array.

The `sum` function returns the sum of all elements in the vector. The size of the vector can be obtained from the `size()` function in the `vector` class. So, you don't have to specify the vector's size when invoking the `sum` function. The same function for two-dimensional array requires two parameters as follows:

```
int sum(const int a[][COLUMN_SIZE], int rowSize)
```

Using vectors for representing two-dimensional arrays simplifies coding.

12.16 Write the code that represents the following array using a vector:

```
int list[4] = {1, 2, 3, 4};
```

12.17 Write the code that represents the following array using a vector:

```
int matrix[4][4] =
  {{1, 2, 3, 4},
   {5, 6, 7, 8},
   {9, 10, 11, 12},
   {13, 14, 15, 16}};
```

Check Point

12.8 Case Study: Evaluating Expressions

Stacks can be used to evaluate expressions.

Key Point

Stacks have many applications. This section gives an application of using stacks. You can enter an arithmetic expression from Google to evaluate the expression as shown in Figure 12.3.

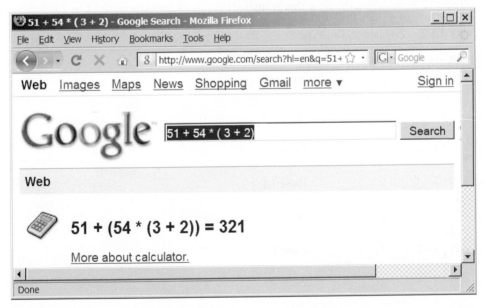

FIGURE 12.3 You can evaluate an arithmetic expression from Google.

How does Google evaluate an expression? This section presents a program that evaluates a *compound expression* with multiple operators and parentheses (e.g., `(15 + 2) * 34 - 2`). For simplicity, assume that the operands are integers and operators are of four types: +, −, *, and /.

compound expression

process an operator

The problem can be solved using two stacks, named **operandStack** and **operatorStack**, for storing operands and operators, respectively. Operands and operators are pushed into the stacks before they are processed. When an *operator is processed*, it is popped from **operatorStack** and applied on the first two operands from **operandStack** (the two operands are popped from **operandStack**). The resultant value is pushed back to **operandStack**.

The algorithm takes two phases:

Phase 1: Scanning expression

The program scans the expression from left to right to extract operands, operators, and the parentheses.

1.1 If the extracted item is an operand, push it to **operandStack**.

1.2 If the extracted item is a + or – operator, process all the operators at the top of **operatorStack** with higher or equal precedence (i.e., +, –, *, /), push the extracted operator to **operatorStack**.

1.3 If the extracted item is a * or / operator, process all the operators at the top of **operatorStack** with higher or equal precedence (i.e., *, /), push the extracted operator to **operatorStack**.

1.4 If the extracted item is a (symbol, push it to **operatorStack**.

1.5 If the extracted item is a) symbol, repeatedly process the operators from the top of **operatorStack** until seeing the (symbol on the stack.

Phase 2: Clearing stack

Repeatedly process the operators from the top of **operatorStack** until **operatorStack** is empty.

Table 12.2 shows how the algorithm is applied to evaluate the expression (1 + 2) * 4 – 3.

TABLE 12.2 Evaluate an Expression

Expression	Scan	Action	operandStack	operatorStack
(1 + 2) * 4 – 3	(	Phase 1.4		(
(1 + 2) * 4 – 3	1	Phase 1.1	1	(
(1 + 2) * 4 – 3	+	Phase 1.2	1	+ (
(1 + 2) * 4 – 3	2	Phase 1.1	2 1	+ (
(1 + 2) * 4 – 3	)	Phase 1.5	3	
(1 + 2) * 4 – 3	*	Phase 1.3	3	*
(1 + 2) * 4 – 3	4	Phase 1.1	4 3	*
(1 + 2) * 4 – 3	–	Phase 1.2	12	–
(1 + 2) * 4 – 3	3	Phase 1.1	3 12	–
(1 + 2) * 4 – 3	none	Phase 2	9	

Listing 12.11 gives the program.

LISTING 12.11 EvaluateExpression.cpp

```
1  #include <iostream>
2  #include <vector>
3  #include <string>
4  #include <cctype>
5  #include "ImprovedStack.h"
6
7  using namespace std;
8
9  // Split an expression into numbers, operators, and parentheses
10 vector<string> split(const string& expression);                          split expression
11
12 // Evaluate an expression and return the result
13 int evaluateExpression(const string& expression);                        evaluate expression
14
15 // Perform an operation
16 void processAnOperator(                                                   perform an operation
17   Stack<int>& operandStack, Stack<char>& operatorStack);
18
19 int main()
20 {
21   string expression;
22   cout << "Enter an expression: ";
23   getline(cin, expression);                                              read an expression
24
25   cout << expression << " = "
26     << evaluateExpression(expression) << endl;                          evaluate expression
27
28   return 0;
29 }
30
31 vector<string> split(const string& expression)                           split expression
32 {
33   vector<string> v; // A vector to store split items as strings
34   string numberString; // A numeric string
35
36   for (unsigned i = 0; i < expression.length(); i++)
37   {
38     if (isdigit(expression[i]))
39       numberString.append(1, expression[i]); // Append a digit            append numeral
40     else
41     {
42       if (numberString.size() > 0)
43       {
44         v.push_back(numberString); // Store the numeric string            store number
45         numberString.erase(); // Empty the numeric string
46       }
47
48       if (!isspace(expression[i]))
49       {
50         string s;
51         s.append(1, expression[i]);
52         v.push_back(s); // Store an operator and parenthesis              store operator/parenthesis
53       }
54     }
55   }
56
```

```
57       // Store the last numeric string
58       if (numberString.size() > 0)
59         v.push_back(numberString);
60
61       return v;
62     }
63
64     // Evaluate an expression
65     int evaluateExpression(const string& expression)
66     {
67       // Create operandStack to store operands
68       Stack<int> operandStack;
69
70       // Create operatorStack to store operators
71       Stack<char> operatorStack;
72
73       // Extract operands and operators
74       vector<string> tokens = split(expression);
75
76       // Phase 1: Scan tokens
77       for (unsigned i = 0; i < tokens.size(); i++)
78       {
79         if (tokens[i][0] == '+' || tokens[i][0] == '-')
80         {
81           // Process all +, -, *, / in the top of the operator stack
82           while (!operatorStack.empty() && (operatorStack.peek() == '+'
83            || operatorStack.peek() == '-' || operatorStack.peek() == '*'
84            || operatorStack.peek() == '/'))
85           {
86             processAnOperator(operandStack, operatorStack);
87           }
88
89           // Push the + or - operator into the operator stack
90           operatorStack.push(tokens[i][0]);
91         }
92         else if (tokens[i][0] == '*' || tokens[i][0] == '/')
93         {
94           // Process all *, / in the top of the operator stack
95           while (!operatorStack.empty() && (operatorStack.peek() == '*'
96            || operatorStack.peek() == '/'))
97           {
98             processAnOperator(operandStack, operatorStack);
99           }
100
101           // Push the * or / operator into the operator stack
102           operatorStack.push(tokens[i][0]);
103         }
104         else if (tokens[i][0] == '(')
105         {
106           operatorStack.push('('); // Push '(' to stack
107         }
108         else if (tokens[i][0] == ')')
109         {
110           // Process all the operators in the stack until seeing '('
111           while (operatorStack.peek() != '(')
112           {
113             processAnOperator(operandStack, operatorStack);
114           }
115
```

store last number

operandStack

operatorStack

split expression

scan each token

+ or - scanned

* or / scanned

(scanned

) scanned

```
116          operatorStack.pop(); // Pop the '(' symbol from the stack
117       }
118       else
119       { // An operand scanned. Push an operand to the stack as integer
120          operandStack.push(atoi(tokens[i].c_str()));
121       }
122    }
123
124    // Phase 2: process all the remaining operators in the stack
125    while (!operatorStack.empty())
126    {
127       processAnOperator(operandStack, operatorStack);
128    }
129
130    // Return the result
131    return operandStack.pop();
132 }
133
134 // Process one opeator: Take an operator from operatorStack and
135 // apply it on the operands in the operandStack
136 void processAnOperator(
137    Stack<int>& operandStack, Stack<char>& operatorStack)
138 {
139    char op = operatorStack.pop();
140    int op1 = operandStack.pop();
141    int op2 = operandStack.pop();
142    if (op == '+')
143       operandStack.push(op2 + op1);
144    else if (op == '-')
145       operandStack.push(op2 - op1);
146    else if (op == '*')
147       operandStack.push(op2 * op1);
148    else if (op == '/')
149       operandStack.push(op2 / op1);
150 }
```

an operand scanned (line 120)

clear operatorStack (line 127)

return result (line 131)

process + (line 143)

process - (line 145)

*process *** (line 147)

process / (line 149)

```
Enter an expression: (13 + 2) * 4 - 3 ↵Enter
(13 + 2) * 4 - 3 = 57
```

```
Enter an expression: 5 / 4 + (2 - 3) * 5 ↵Enter
5 / 4 + (2 - 3) * 5 = -4
```

The program reads an expression as a string (line 23) and invokes the `evaluateExpression` function (line 26) to evaluate the expression.

The `evaluateExpression` function creates two stacks `operandStack` and `operatorStack` (lines 68, 71) and invokes the `split` function to extract numbers, operators, and parentheses from the expression (line 74) into tokens. The tokens are stored in a vector of strings. For example, if the expression is (13 + 2) * 4 - 3, the tokens are (, 13, +, 2,), *, 4, -, and 3.

The `evaluateExpression` function scans each token in the `for` loop (lines 77–122). If a token is an operand, push it to `operandStack` (line 120). If a token is a + or – operator (line 79), process all the operators from the top of `operatorStack` if any (lines 81–87) and push the newly scanned operator to the stack (line 90). If a token is a * or / operator (line 92), process all the * and / operators from the top of `operatorStack` if any (lines 95–99) and push the newly scanned operator to the stack (line 102). If a token is a (symbol (line 104), push it to operatorStack. If a token is a) symbol (line 108), process all the operators from the top of operatorStack until seeing the) symbol (lines 111–114) and pop the) symbol from the stack (line 116).

After all tokens are considered, the program processes the remaining operators in operatorStack (lines 125–128).

The processAnOperator function (lines 136–150) processes an operator. The function pops the operator from operatorStack (line 139) and pops two operands from operandStack (lines 140–141). Depending on the operator, the function performs an operation and pushes the result of the operation back to operandStack (lines 143, 145, 147, 149).

Check Point

12.18 Trace how the expression $(3 + 4) * (1 - 3) - ((1 + 3) * 5 - 4)$ is evaluated using the program in Listing 12.11.

KEY TERMS

template 476	template prefix 478
template class 482	type parameter 478
template function 487	

CHAPTER SUMMARY

1. Templates provide the capability to parameterize types in functions and classes.

2. You can define functions or classes with generic types that can be substituted for concrete types by the compiler.

3. The definition for the function template begins with the keyword template followed by a list of parameters. Each parameter must be preceded by the interchangeable keywords class or typename in the form

   ```
   <typename typeParameter> or
   <class typeParameter>
   ```

4. When you define a generic function, it is better to start with a nongeneric function, debug and test it, and then convert it to a generic function.

5. The syntax for class templates is basically the same as that for function templates. You place the template prefix before the class definition, just as you place the template prefix before the function template.

6. If the elements need to be processed in a last-in first-out fashion, use a stack to store the elements.

7. The array size is fixed after it is created. C++ provides the vector class, which is more flexible than arrays.

8. The vector class is a generic class. You can use it to create objects for concrete types.

9. You can use a vector object just like an array, but a vector's size can grow automatically if needed.

Quiz

Answer the quiz for this chapter online at www.cs.armstrong.edu/liang/cpp3e/quiz.html.

Programming Exercises

Sections 12.2–12.3

12.1 (*Minimum in array*) Design a generic function that returns a minimum element from an array. The function should have two parameters. One is the array of a generic type, and the other is the size of the array. Test the function with an array of `int`, `double`, and `string` values.

12.2 (*Selection Sort*) Rewrite the selection sort function in Listing 7.11, `SelectionSort.cpp`, to use a generic type for array elements. Test the function with an array of `int`, `double`, and `string` values.

12.3 (*Bubble Sort*) Rewrite the bubble sort function in Programming Exercise 7.14, to use a generic type for array elements. Test the function with an array of `int`, `double`, and `string` values.

12.4 (*Are strictly identical?*) Write the following function to check if the two arrays are strictly identical

```
template<typename T>
bool areStrictlyIdentical(const T list1[], const T list2[], int size)
```

Test the function with an array of `int`, `double`, and `string` values.

12.5 (*Largest values*) Write a generic function that finds the largest among the three values. Your function should have three parameters of the same type. Test the function with `int`, `double`, and `string` values.

Sections 12.4–12.5

*12.6 (*Function* `printStack`) Add the `printStack` function into the `Stack` class as an instance function to display all the elements in the stack. The `Stack` class was introduced in Listing 12.4, GenericStack.h.

*12.7 (*Function* `position`) Add the `position(T element)` function into the `Stack` class as an instance function to find the position of the element in the stack. The `Stack` class was introduced in Listing 12.4, `GenericStack.h`.

Sections 12.6–12.7

**12.8 (*Implement* `vector` *class*) The `vector` class is provided in the standard C++ library. Implement the `vector` class as an exercise. The standard vector class has many functions. For this exercise, implement only the functions defined in the UML class diagram, as shown in Figure 12.2.

12.9 (*Implement a stack class using a vector*) In Listing 12.4, `GenericStack` is implemented using arrays. Implement it using a vector.

12.10 (*The* `Course` *class*) Rewrite the `Course` class in Listing 11.19, CourseWithCustomCopyConstructor.h. Use a `vector` to replace an array to store students.

VideoNote
Use vector to replace arrays

**12.11 (*Simulation: coupon collector's problem*) Rewrite Programming Exercise 7.21 using vectors to represent arrays.

**12.12 (*Geometry: same line?*) Rewrite Programming Exercise 8.16 using vectors to represent arrays.

Section 12.8

**12.13 (*Evaluate expression*) Modify Listing 12.11 EvaluateExpression.cpp to add operators ∧ for exponent and % for modulus. For example, 3 ∧ 2 is 9 and 3 % 2 is 1. The ∧ operator has the highest precedence and the & operator has the same precedence as the * and / operators. Here is a sample run of the program:

```
Enter an expression: (5 * 2 ∧ 3 + 2 * 3 % 2) * 4  ↵Enter
(5 * 2 ∧ 3 + 2 * 3 % 2) * 4 = 160
```

*12.14 (*Closest pair*) Listing 8.3 finds a closest pair of two points. The program prompts the user to enter 8 points. The number 8 is fixed. Rewrite the program. First, prompt the user to enter the number of points, and then prompt the user to enter all the points.

**12.15 (*Match grouping symbols*) A C++ program contains various pairs of grouping symbols, such as the following:

Parentheses: (and).

Braces: { and }.

Brackets: [and].

Note that the grouping symbols cannot overlap. For example, (a{b)} is illegal. Write a program that checks whether a C++ source-code file has correct pairs of grouping symbols. The file is read by the program using input redirection using the following command:

Exercise12_15 < file.cpp

**12.16 (*Postfix notation*) Postfix notation is a way of writing expressions without using parentheses. For example, the expression (1 + 2) * 3 would be written as 1 2 + 3 *. A postfix expression is evaluated using a stack. Scan a postfix expression from left to right. A variable or constant is pushed to the stack. When an operator is encountered, apply the operator with the top two operands in the stack and replace the two operands with the result. The following diagram shows how to evaluate 1 2 + 3 *.

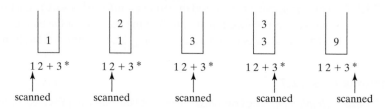

Write a program that prompts the user to enter a postfix expression and evaluates it.

***12.17 (*Test 24*) Write a program that prompts the user to enter four numbers between 1 and 13 and tests whether these four numbers can form an expression that yields 24. The expression can use the operators (addition, subtraction, multiplication, and division) and parentheses in any combination. Each number must be used once and only once. Here is a sample run of the program:

```
Enter four numbers (between 1 and 13): 5 4 12 13  ↵Enter
The solution is 4+12+13-5
```

```
Enter four numbers (between 1 and 13): 5 6 5 12 ↵Enter
There is no solution
```

**12.18 (*Convert infix to postfix*) Write a function that converts an infix expression into a postfix expression using the following header.

```
string infixToPostfix(const string& expression)
```

For example, the function should convert the infix expression (1 + 2) * 3 to 1 2 + 3 * and 2 * (1 + 3) to 2 1 3 + *.

***12.19 (*Game: the 24-point card game*) The 24-point card game is to pick any four cards from 52 cards (note two Jokers are excluded). Each card represents a number. An Ace, King, Queen, and Jack represent 1, 13, 12, and 11, respectively. Write a program that randomly picks four cards and prompts the user to enter expression that uses the four numbers from the selected cards. Each number must be used once and only once. You can use the operators (addition, subtraction, multiplication, and division) and parentheses in any combination in the expression. The expression must evaluate to 24. If such an expression does not exist, enter 0. Here is a sample run of the program:

```
4 of Clubs
Ace (1) of Diamonds
6 of Hearts
Jack (11) of Clubs
Enter an expression: (11 + 1 - 6) * 4 ↵Enter
Congratulations! You got it!
```

```
Ace (1) of Diamonds
5 of Diamonds
9 of Spades
Queen (12) of Hearts
Enter an expression: (13 - 9) * (1 + 5) ↵Enter
Congratulations! You got it!
```

```
6 of Clubs
5 of Clubs
Jack (11) of Clubs
5 of Spades
Enter an expression: 0 ↵Enter
Sorry, one correct expression would be (5 * 6) - (11 - 5)
```

```
6 of Clubs
5 of Clubs
Queen (12) of Clubs
5 of Spades
Enter an expression: 0 ↵Enter
Yes. No 24 points
```

**12.20 (*Add vector*) Write a function that adds the contents of two vectors using the following header:

```
template<typename T>
void addvector(vector<T> &v1, vector<T> &v2)
```

Write a test program that reads in **6 int** values in two vector, adds both and displays the result.

**12.21 (*Game: no solution ratio for 24-point game*) For the 24-point game, introduced in Programming Exercise 12.19, write a program to find out the no solution ratio for the 24-point game, i.e., number of no solutions / number of solutions, among all possible four card combinations.

*12.22 (*Are strictly identical?: two vectors*) Write the following function to check if the two vectors are strictly identical

```
template<typename T>
bool areStrictlyIdentical(vector<T> &v1, vector<T> &v2)
```

Write a program that reads the elements of two vectors, invokes the are **StrictlyIdentical** function and displays whether both are strictly identical.

12.23 (*Pattern recognition: consecutive four equal numbers*) Rewrite the **isConsecutiveFour function in Programming Exercise 8.21 using a vector as follows:

```
bool isConsecutiveFour(const vector<vector<int>>& values)
```

Write a test program like the one in Programming Exercise 8.21.

*12.24 (*Algebra: solve* 3×3 *linear equations*) You can use the following computations to solve a 3×3 system of linear equation:

$$a_{11}x + a_{12}y + a_{13}z = b_1$$
$$a_{21}x + a_{22}y + a_{23}z = b_2$$
$$a_{31}x + a_{32}y + a_{33}z = b_3$$

$$x = \frac{(a_{22}a_{33}-a_{23}a_{32})b_1 + (a_{13}a_{32}-a_{12}a_{33})b_2 + (a_{12}a_{23}-a_{13}a_{22})b_3}{|A|}$$

$$y = \frac{(a_{23}a_{31}-a_{21}a_{33})b_1 + (a_{11}a_{33}-a_{13}a_{31})b_2 + (a_{13}a_{21}-a_{11}a_{23})b_3}{|A|}$$

$$z = \frac{(a_{21}a_{32}-a_{22}a_{31})b_1 + (a_{12}a_{31}-a_{11}a_{32})b_2 + (a_{11}a_{22}-a_{12}a_{21})b_3}{|A|}$$

$$|A| = \begin{vmatrix} a_{11} & a_{12} & a_{13} \\ a_{21} & a_{22} & a_{23} \\ a_{31} & a_{32} & a_{33} \end{vmatrix} = a_{11}a_{22}a_{33} + a_{31}a_{12}a_{23} + a_{13}a_{21}a_{32}$$

$$- a_{13}a_{22}a_{31} - a_{11}a_{23}a_{32} - a_{33}a_{21}a_{12}.$$

Write a program that prompts the user to enter $a_{11}, a_{12}, a_{13}, a_{21}, a_{22}, a_{23}, a_{31}, a_{32}, a_{33}, b_1, b_2$, and b_3, and displays the result. If $|A|$ is **0**, report that "The equation has no solution."

```
Enter a11, a12, a13, a21, a22, a23, a31, a32, a33:
  1 2 1 2 3 1 4 5 3  ↵Enter
Enter b1, b2, b3: 2 5 3  ↵Enter
The solution is 0 3 -4
```

```
Enter a11, a12, a13, a21, a22, a23, a31, a32, a33:
  1 2 1 0.5 1 0.5 1 4 5  ↵Enter
Enter b1, b2, b3: 2 5 3  ↵Enter
No solution
```

**12.25 (*New* `Account` *class*) An `Account` class was specified in Programming Exercise 9.3. Modify the `Account` class as follows:

- Assume that the interest rate is same for all accounts. So, the `annualInterestRate` property should be static.
- Add a new data field `name` of the `string` type to store the name of the customer.
- Add a new constructor that constructs an account with the specified name, id, and balance.
- Add a new data field named `transactions` whose type is `vector<Transaction>` that stores the transaction for the accounts. Each transaction is an instance of the `Transaction` class. The `Transaction` class is defined as shown in Figure 12.4.
- Modify the `withdraw` and `deposit` functions to add a transaction to the `transactions` vector.
- All other properties and functions are same as in Programming Exercise 9.3.

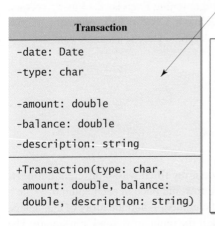

The get and set functions for these data fields are provided in the class, but omitted in the UML diagram for brevity.

Transaction	
-date: Date	The date of this transaction. Date is defined in Exercise 9.8.
-type: char	The type of the transaction, such as 'W' for withdrawal, 'D' for deposit, etc.
-amount: double	The amount of the transaction.
-balance: double	The new balance after this transaction.
-description: string	The description of this transaction.
+Transaction(type: char, amount: double, balance: double, description: string)	Construct a Transaction with the specified date, type, balance, and description.

FIGURE 12.4   The `Transaction` class describes a transaction for a bank account.

Write a test program that creates an `Account` with annual interest rate `1.5%`, balance `1000`, id `1122`, and name `George`. Deposit $30, $40, $50 to the account and withdraw $5, $4, $2 from the account. Print account summary that shows account holder name, interest rate, balance, and all transactions.

*12.26 (*New* `Location` *class*) Revise Programming Exercise 10.17 to define the `locateLargest` function as

```
Location locateLargest(const vector<vector<double>> v);
```

Where `v` is vector representing a two-dimensional array. Write a test program that prompts the user to enter the number of rows and columns of a two-dimensional array and displays the location of the largest element in the array. A sample run is the same as in Programming Exercise 10.17.

**12.27 (*Largest block*) Given a square matrix with elements 0 or 1, write a program to find a maximum square submatrix whose elements are all 1s. Your program should prompt the user to enter the number of rows in the matrix and then the matrix and displays the location of the first element in the maximum square submatrix and the number of the rows in the submatrix. Assume the maximum number of rows is 100. Here is a sample run:

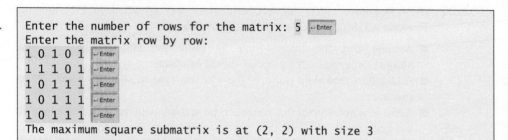

```
Enter the number of rows for the matrix: 5 ↵Enter
Enter the matrix row by row:
1 0 1 0 1 ↵Enter
1 1 1 0 1 ↵Enter
1 0 1 1 1 ↵Enter
1 0 1 1 1 ↵Enter
1 0 1 1 1 ↵Enter
The maximum square submatrix is at (2, 2) with size 3
```

Your program should implement and use the following function to find the maximum square submatrix:

vector<**int**> findLargestBlock(**const** vector<vector<**int**>>& m)

The return value is a vector that consists of three values. The first two values are the row and column indices for the first element in the submatrix and the third value is the number of the rows in the submatrix.

*12.28 (*Smallest rows and columns*) Rewrite Programming Exercise 8.14 using vectors. The program randomly fills in 0s and 1s into a 5 × 5 matrix, prints the matrix, and finds the rows and columns with the least 1s. Here is a sample run:

```
00110
00101
11100
11101
01001
The smallest row's index: 0, 1, 4
The smallest column's index: 3
```

**12.29 (*Latin square*) A Latin square is an n by n array filled with n different Latin letters, each occurring exactly once in each row and once in each column. Write a program that prompts the user to enter the number n and the array of characters, as shown in the sample output and check if the input array is a Latin square. The characters are the first n characters starting from A.

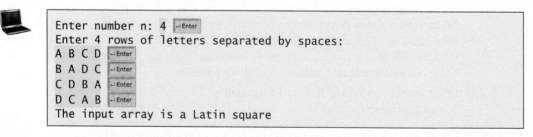

```
Enter number n: 4 ↵Enter
Enter 4 rows of letters separated by spaces:
A B C D ↵Enter
B A D C ↵Enter
C D B A ↵Enter
D C A B ↵Enter
The input array is a Latin square
```

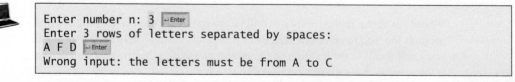

```
Enter number n: 3 ↵Enter
Enter 3 rows of letters separated by spaces:
A F D ↵Enter
Wrong input: the letters must be from A to C
```

**12.30 (*Explore matrix*) Rewrite Programming Exercise 8.7 using vectors. The program prompts the user to enter the length of a square matrix, randomly fills in 0s and 1s into the matrix, prints the matrix, and finds the rows, columns, and diagonals with all 0s or 1s. Here is a sample run:

```
Enter the size for the matrix: 4  ↵Enter
1111
0000
0100
1111
All 0s on row 1
All 1s on row 1, 3
No same numbers on a column
No same numbers on the major diagonal
No same numbers on the subdiagonal
```

**12.31 (*Intersection*) Write a function that returns the intersection of two vectors using the following header:

```
template<typename T>
vector<T> intersect(const vector<T>& v1, const vector<T>& v2)
```

The intersection of two vectors contains the common elements that appear in both vectors. For example, the intersection of two vectors {2, 3, 1, 5} and {3, 4, 5} is {3, 5}. Write a test program that prompts the user to enter two vectors, each with five strings, and displays their intersection. Here is a sample run:

```
Enter five strings for vector1:
  Atlanta Dallas Chicago Boston Denver  ↵Enter
Enter five strings for vector2:
  Dallas Tampa Miami Boston Richmond  ↵Enter
The common strings are Dallas Boston
```

**12.32 (*Remove duplicates*) Write a function that removes the duplicate elements from a vector using the following header:

```
template<typename T>
void removeDuplicate(vector<T>& v)
```

Write a test program that prompts the user to enter 10 integers to a vector and displays the distinct integers. Here is a sample run:

```
Enter ten integers: 34 5 3 5 6 4 33 2 2 4  ↵Enter
The distinct integers are 34 5 3 6 4 33 2
```

*12.33 (*Area of a polygon*) Revise Programming Exercise 7.29 to prompt the user to enter the number of points in a convex polygon, then enter the points clockwise, and display the area of the polygon. Here is a sample run of the program:

```
Enter the number of the points: 7  ↵Enter
Enter the coordinates of the points:
  -12 0 -8.5 10 0 11.4 5.5 7.8 6 -5.5 0 -7 -3.5 -3.5  ↵Enter
The total area is 250.075
```

12.34   (*Subtraction quiz*) Rewrite Listing 5.1 RepeatSubtractionQuiz.cpp to alert the user if a same answer is entered again. *Hint: use a vector to store answers.* Here is a sample run:

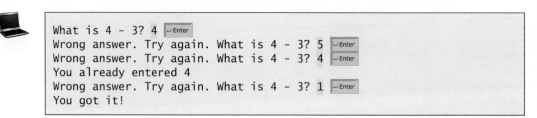

```
What is 4 - 3? 4  ↵Enter
Wrong answer. Try again. What is 4 - 3? 5  ↵Enter
Wrong answer. Try again. What is 4 - 3? 4  ↵Enter
You already entered 4
Wrong answer. Try again. What is 4 - 3? 1  ↵Enter
You got it!
```

**12.35   (*Algebra: perfect square*) Write a program that prompts the user to enter an integer m and find the smallest integer n such that m * n is a perfect square. (*Hint:* Store all smallest factors of m into a vector. n is the product of the factors that appear an odd number of times in the vector. For example, consider m = 90, store the factors 2, 3, 3, 5 in a vector. 2 and 5 appear an odd number of times in the vector. So, n is 10.) Here are sample runs:

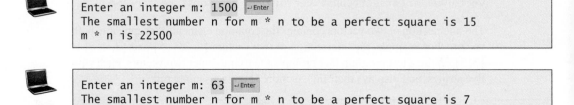

```
Enter an integer m: 1500  ↵Enter
The smallest number n for m * n to be a perfect square is 15
m * n is 22500
```

```
Enter an integer m: 63  ↵Enter
The smallest number n for m * n to be a perfect square is 7
m * n is 441
```

***12.36   (*Game: connect four*) Rewrite the Connect Four game in Programming Exercise 8.22 using vectors.

FILE INPUT AND OUTPUT

Objectives

- To use `ofstream` for output (§13.2.1) and `ifstream` for input (§13.2.2).

- To test whether a file exists (§13.2.3).

- To test the end of a file (§13.2.4).

- To let the user enter a file name (§13.2.5).

- To write data in a desired format (§13.3).

- To read and write data using the `getline`, `get`, and `put` functions (§13.4).

- To use an `fstream` object to read and write data (§13.5).

- To open a file with specified modes (§13.5).

- To use the `eof()`, `fail()`, `bad()`, and `good()` functions to test stream states (§13.6).

- To understand the difference between text I/O and binary I/O (§13.7).

- To write binary data using the `write` function (§13.7.1).

- To read binary data using the `read` function (§13.7.2).

- To cast primitive type values and objects to byte arrays using the `reinterpret_cast` operator (§13.7).

- To read/write arrays and objects (§§13.7.3–13.7.4).

- To use the `seekp` and `seekg` functions to move the file pointers for random file access (§13.8).

- To open a file for both input and output to update files (§13.9).

13.1 Introduction

You can read/write data from/to a file using the functions in the `ifstream`, `ofstream`, *and* `fstream` *classes.*

Data stored in variables, arrays, and objects are temporary; they are lost when the program terminates. To store the data created in a program permanently, you must save them in a file on a permanent storage medium, such as a disk. The file can be transported and can be read later by other programs. Section 4.11, "Simple File Input and Output," introduced simple text I/O involving numeric values. This chapter introduces I/O in detail.

C++ provides the `ifstream`, `ofstream`, and `fstream` classes for processing and manipulating files. These classes are defined in the `<fstream>` header file. The `ifstream` class is for reading data from a file, the `ofstream` class is for writing data to a file, and the `fstream` class can be used for reading and writing data in a file.

C++ uses the term *stream* to describe a flow of data. If it flows to your program, the stream is called an *input stream*. If it flows out from your program, it is called an *output stream*. C++ uses objects to read/write a stream of data. For convenience, an input object is called an *input stream* and an output object is called an *output stream*.

input stream
output stream

cin stream
cout stream

You have already used the input stream and output stream in your programs. `cin` (console input) is a predefined object for reading input from the keyboard, and `cout` (console output) is a predefined object for outputting characters to the console. These two objects are defined in the `<iostream>` header file. In this chapter, you will learn how to read/write data from/to files.

13.2 Text I/O

Data in a text file can be read by a text editor.

This section demonstrates how to perform simple text input and output.

absolute file name

Every file is placed in a directory in the file system. An *absolute file name* contains a file name with its complete path and drive letter. For example, **c:\example\scores.txt** is the absolute file name for the file **scores.txt** on the Windows operating system. Here **c:\example** is referred to as the *directory path* for the file. Absolute file names are machine dependent. On UNIX, the absolute file name may be **/home/liang/example/scores.txt**, where **/home/liang/example** is the directory path for the file **scores.txt**.

directory path

relative file name

A *relative file name* is relative to its current working directory. The complete directory path for a relative file name is omitted. For example, **scores.txt** is a relative file name. If its current working directory is **c:\example**, the absolute file name would be **c:\example\scores.txt**.

13.2.1 Writing Data to a File

The `ofstream` class can be used to write primitive data-type values, arrays, strings, and objects to a text file. Listing 13.1 demonstrates how to write data. The program creates an instance of `ofstream` and writes two lines to the file **scores.txt**. Each line consists of first name (a string), middle name initial (a character), last name (a string), and score (an integer).

LISTING 13.1 TextFileOutput.cpp

include `fstream` header

```
1  #include <iostream>
2  #include <fstream>
3  using namespace std;
4
5  int main()
6  {
```

```
7    ofstream output;                                              declare object
8
9    // Create a file
10   output.open("scores.txt");                                    open file
11
12   // Write two lines
13   output << "John" << " " << "T" << " " << "Smith"              output to file
14     << " " << 90 << endl;
15   output << "Eric" << " " << "K" << " " << "Jones"
16     << " " << 85 << endl;
17
18   output.close();                                               close file
19
20   cout << "Done" << endl;
21
22   return 0;
23 }
```

scores.txt

| John T Smith 90 |
| Eric K Jones 85 |

Since the **ofstream** class is defined in the **fstream** header file, line 2 includes this header file.
(include <fstream> header)

Line 7 creates an object, **output**, from the **ofstream** class using its no-arg constructor.
(create object)

Line 10 opens a file named scores.txt for the **output** object. If the file does not exist, a new file is created. If the file already exists, its contents are destroyed without warning.
(open file)

You can write data to the **output** object using the stream insertion operator (<<) in the same way that you send data to the **cout** object. Lines 13–16 write strings and numeric values to **output**, as shown in Figure 13.1.
(cout)

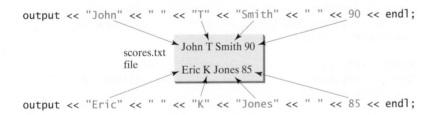

FIGURE 13.1 The output stream sends data to the file.

The **close()** function (line 18) must be used to close the stream for the object. If this function is not invoked, the data may not be saved properly in the file.
(close file)

You may open an output stream using the following constructor:
(alternative syntax)

```
ofstream output("scores.txt");
```

This statement is equivalent to

```
ofstream output;
output.open("scores.txt");
```

Caution

If a file already exists, its contents will be destroyed without warning.
(file exists?)

Caution

The directory separator for Windows is a backslash (\). The backslash is a special escape character and should be written as \\ in a string literal (see Table 4.5). For example,
(\ in file names)

```
output.open("c:\\example\\scores.txt");
```

relative file name

Note

An absolute file name is platform dependent. It is better to use a *relative file name* without drive letters. If you use an IDE to run C++, the directory of the relative file name can be specified in the IDE. For example, the default directory for data files is the same directory with the source code in Visual C++.

VideoNote

Text I/O

13.2.2 Reading Data from a File

The `ifstream` class can be used to read data from a text file. Listing 13.2 demonstrates how to read data. The program creates an instance of `ifstream` and reads data from the file scores.txt, which was created in the preceding example.

LISTING 13.2 `TextFileInput.cpp`

include `fstream` header

input object

input from file

input from file

close file

```cpp
 1  #include <iostream>
 2  #include <fstream>
 3  #include <string>
 4  using namespace std;
 5
 6  int main()
 7  {
 8    ifstream input("scores.txt");
 9
10    // Read data
11    string firstName;
12    char mi;
13    string lastName;
14    int score;
15    input >> firstName >> mi >> lastName >> score;
16    cout << firstName << " " << mi << " " << lastName << " "
17      << score << endl;
18
19    input >> firstName >> mi >> lastName >> score;
20    cout << firstName << " " << mi << " " << lastName << " "
21      << score << endl;
22
23    input.close();
24
25    cout << "Done" << endl;
26
27    return 0;
28  }
```

```
John T Smith 90
Eric K Jones 85
Done
```

include <fstream> header

Since the `ifstream` class is defined in the `fstream` header file, line 2 includes this header file.

Line 8 creates an object, **input**, from the `ifstream` class for file **scores.txt**.

cin

You can read data from the **input** object using the stream extraction operator (`>>`) in the same way that you read data from the `cin` object. Lines 15 and 19 read strings and numeric values from the input file, as shown in Figure 13.2.

close file

The `close()` function (line 23) is used to close the stream for the object. It is not necessary to close the input file, but doing so is a good practice in order to release the resources occupied by the file.

alternative syntax

You may open an input stream using the following constructor:

```cpp
ifstream input("scores.txt");
```

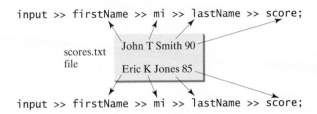

FIGURE 13.2 The input stream reads data from the file.

This statement is equivalent to

```
ifstream input;
input.open("scores.txt");
```

 Caution
To read data correctly, you need to know exactly how data are stored. For example, the   know data format
program in Listing 13.2 would not work if the file contained score as a **double** value
with a decimal point.

13.2.3 Testing File Existence

If the file does not exist when reading a file, your program will run and produce incorrect
results. Can your program check whether a file exists? Yes. You can invoke the **fail()** func-   file not exist?
tion immediately after invoking the **open** function. If **fail()** returns **true**, it indicates that
the file does not exist.

```
1  // Open a file
2  input.open("scores.txt");
3
4  if (input.fail())
5  {
6    cout << "File does not exist" << endl;
7    cout << "Exit program" << endl;
8
9    return 0;
10 }
```
check file operation

13.2.4 Testing End of File

Listing 13.2 reads two lines from the data file. If you don't know how many lines are in the
file and want to read them all, how do you recognize the end of file? You can invoke the
eof() function on the input object to detect it, as discussed in Listing 5.6, ReadAllData.cpp.   eof function
However, this program will not work if there are extra blank characters after the last number.
To understand this, let us look at the file that contains the numbers shown in Figure 13.3. Note
there is an extra blank character after the last number.

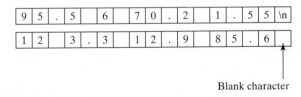

Blank character

FIGURE 13.3 The file contains numbers separated by spaces.

If you use the following code to read all data and add the total, the last number will be
added twice.

```
ifstream input("score.txt");

double sum = 0;
double number;
while (!input.eof()) // Continue if not end of file
{
  input >> number;   // Read data
  cout << number << " ";   // Display data
  sum += number;
}
```

The reason for this is that when the last number 85.6 is read, the file system does not know it is the last number because there are blank characters after the last number. So, the eof() function returns false. When the program reads the number again, the eof() function returns true, but the variable number is not changed, because nothing is read from the file. The variable number still contains the value 85.6, which is added again to sum.

There are two ways to fix this problem. One is to check the eof() function right after reading a number. If the eof() function returns true, exit the loop, as shown in the following code:

```
ifstream input("score.txt");

double sum = 0;
double number;
while (!input.eof()) // Continue if not end of file
{
  input >> number;   // Read data
  if (input.eof()) break;
  cout << number << " ";   // Display data
  sum += number;
}
```

The other way to fix this problem is to write the code like this:

```
while (input >> number) // Continue to read data until it fails
{
  cout << number << " ";   // Display data
  sum += number;
}
```

The statement input >> number is actually to invoke an operator function. Operator functions will be introduced in Chapter 14. This function returns an object if a number is read; otherwise it returns NULL. NULL is a constant value 0. C++ automatically casts it to a bool value false when it is used as a condition in a loop statement or a selection statement. If no number is read from the input stream, input >> number returns NULL and the loop terminates.

Listing 13.3 gives a complete program that reads numbers from the file and displays their sum.

LISTING 13.3 TestEndOfFile.cpp

```
1  #include <iostream>
2  #include <fstream>
3  using namespace std;
4
5  int main()
6  {
7    // Open a file
8    ifstream input("score.txt");
9
```

include fstream header

create input object

```
10    if (input.fail())                                                file exists?
11    {
12      cout << "File does not exist" << endl;
13      cout << "Exit program" << endl;
14      return 0;
15    }
16
17    double sum = 0;
18    double number;
19    while (input >> number) // Continue if not end of file           end of file?
20    {
21      cout << number << " ";   // Display data
22      sum += number;
23    }
24
25    input.close();                                                   close file
26
27    cout << "\nSum is " << sum << endl;                              display data
28
29    return 0;
30  }
```

```
95.5 6 70.2 1.55 12 3.3 12.9 85.6
Total is 287.05
```

The program reads data in a loop (lines 19–23). Each iteration of the loop reads one number and adds it to sum. The loop terminates when the input reaches the end of file.

13.2.5 Letting the User Enter a File name

In the preceding examples, the file names are string literals hard-coded in the program. In many cases, it is desirable to let the user enter the name of a file at runtime. Listing 13.4 gives an example that prompts the user to enter a file name and checks whether the file exists.

LISTING 13.4 CheckFile.cpp

```
1  #include <iostream>
2  #include <fstream>                                                 include fstream header
3  #include <string>                                                  include string header
4  using namespace std;
5
6  int main()
7  {
8    string filename;                                                 create input object
9    cout << "Enter a file name: ";
10   cin >> filename;                                                 enter file
11
12   ifstream input(filename.c_str());
13
14   if (input.fail())                                                file exists?
15     cout << filename << " does not exist" << endl;
16   else
17     cout << filename << " exists" << endl;
18
19   return 0;
20 }
```

```
Enter a file name: c:\example\Welcome.cpp  ⏎ Enter
c:\example\Welcome.cpp exists
```

```
Enter a file name: c:\example\TTTT.cpp  ⏎ Enter
c:\example\TTTT.cpp does not exist
```

The program prompts the user to enter a file name as a string (line 10). However, the file name passed to the input and output stream constructor or to the **open** function must be a C-string in the standard C++. So, the **c_str()** function in the **string** class is invoked to return a C-string from a **string** object (line 12).

> **Note**
>
> Some compilers such as Visual C++ allow you to pass a filename as a **string** to the input and output stream constructor or to the **open** function. To enable your program to work on all C++ compilers, pass a filename as a C-string.

13.1 How do you declare and open a file for output? How do you declare and open a file for input?

13.2 Why should you always close a file after it is processed?

13.3 How do you detect whether a file exists?

13.4 How do you detect whether the end of file is reached?

13.5 Should you pass a filename as a string or a C-string to create an input and output stream object or to the **open** function?

13.3 Formatting Output

The stream manipulators can be used to format console output as well as file output.

You have used the stream manipulators to format output to the console in Section 4.10, "Formatting Console Output." You can use the same stream manipulator to format output to a file. Listing 13.5 gives an example that formats the student records to the file named **formattedscores.txt**.

LISTING 13.5 WriteFormattedData.cpp

include **iomanip** header
include **fstream** header

declare object

output with format

output with format

```
1  #include <iostream>
2  #include <iomanip>
3  #include <fstream>
4  using namespace std;
5
6  int main()
7  {
8    ofstream output;
9
10   // Create a file
11   output.open("formattedscores.txt");
12
13   // Write two lines
14   output << setw(6) << "John" << setw(2) << "T" << setw(6) << "Smith"
15     << " " << setw(4) << 90 << endl;
16   output << setw(6) << "Eric" << setw(2) << "K" << setw(6) << "Jones"
```

```
17        << " " << setw(4) << 85;
18
19     output.close();
20
21     cout << "Done" << endl;
22
23     return 0;
24 }
```

close file

The contents of the file are shown below:

| | | J | o | h | n | | T | | S | m | i | t | h | | | 9 | 0 | \n |
| | | E | r | i | c | | K | | J | o | n | e | s | | | 8 | 5 | |

13.6   Can you use the stream manipulators to format text output?

Check Point

13.4 Functions: **getline**, **get**, and **put**

The getline function can be used to read a string that includes whitespace characters and the get/put function can be used to read and write a single character.

Key Point

There is a problem in reading data using the stream extraction operator (>>). Data are delimited by whitespace. What happens if the whitespace characters are part of a string? In Section 4.8.4, "Reading Strings," you learned how to use the getline function to read a string with whitespace. You can use the same function to read strings from a file. Recall that the syntax for the getline function is

```
getline(ifstream& input, int string s, char delimitChar)
```

The function stops reading characters when the delimiter character or end-of-file mark is encountered. If the delimiter is encountered, it is read but not stored in the array. The third argument delimitChar has a default value ('\n'). The getline function is defined in the iostream header file.

getline

Suppose a file named **state.txt** is created that contains the state names delimited by the pound (#) symbol. The following diagram shows the contents in the file:

| N | e | w | | Y | o | r | k | # | N | e | w | | M | e | x | i | c | o |
| # | T | e | x | a | s | # | I | n | d | i | a | n | a | | | | | |

Listing 13.6 gives a program that reads the states from the file.

LISTING 13.6   ReadCity.cpp

```
1  #include <iostream>
2  #include <fstream>
3  #include <string>
4  using namespace std;
5
6  int main()
7  {
8     // Open a file
9     ifstream input("state.txt");
10
11    if (input.fail())
```

include **fstream** header

input object

input file exist?

```
12    {
13      cout << "File does not exist" << endl;
14      cout << "Exit program" << endl;
15      return 0;
16    }
17
18    // Read data
19    string city;
20
21    while (!input.eof()) // Continue if not end of file
22    {
23      getline(input, city, '#');
24      cout << city << endl;
25    }
26
27    input.close();
28
29    cout << "Done" << endl;
30
31    return 0;
32  }
```

string city → line 19
end of file? → line 21
input from file → line 23
display data → line 24
close file → line 27

```
New York
New Mexico
Texas
Indiana
Done
```

Invoking `getline(input, state, '#')` (line 23) reads characters to the array `state` until it encounters the # character or the end-of-file.

Two other useful functions are `get` and `put`. You can invoke the `get` function on an input object to read a character and invoke the `put` function on an output object to write a character.

get function

The `get` function has two versions:

```
char get() // Return a char
ifstream* get(char& ch) // Read a character to ch
```

The first version returns a character from the input. The second version passes a character reference argument, reads a character from the input, and stores it in `ch`. This function also returns the reference to the input object being used.

put function

The header for the `put` function is

```
void put(char ch)
```

It writes the specified character to the output object.

Listing 13.7 gives an example of using these two functions. The program prompts the user to enter a file and copies it to a new file.

LISTING 13.7 CopyFile.cpp

```
1  #include <iostream>
2  #include <fstream>
3  #include <string>
4  using namespace std;
5
6  int main()
7  {
```

include `fstream` header → line 2

```
 8    // Enter a source file
 9    cout << "Enter a source file name: ";
10    string inputFilename;
11    cin >> inputFilename;                              enter input file name
12
13    // Enter a target file
14    cout << "Enter a target file name: ";
15    string outputFilename;
16    cin >> outputFilename;                             enter output file name
17
18    // Create input and output streams
19    ifstream input(inputFilename.c_str());             input object
20    ofstream output(outputFilename.c_str());           output object
21
22    if (input.fail())                                  file exist?
23    {
24      cout << inputFilename << " does not exist" << endl;
25      cout << "Exit program" << endl;
26      return 0;
27    }
28
29    char ch = input.get();
30    while (!input.eof()) // Continue if not end of file    end of file?
31    {
32      output.put(ch);                                  put function
33      ch = input.get(); // Read next character         get function
34    }
35
36    input.close();                                     close file
37    output.close();                                    close file
38
39    cout << "\nCopy Done" << endl;
40
41    return 0;
42  }
```

```
Enter a source file name: c:\example\CopyFile.cpp ↵Enter
Enter a target file name: c:\example\temp.txt ↵Enter
Copy Done
```

The program prompts the user to enter a source file name in line 11 and a target file name in line 16. An input object for **inputFilename** is created in line 19 and an output object for **outputFilename** in line 20. File names must be C-strings. **inputFilename.c_str()** returns a C-string from string **inputFilename**.

Lines 22–27 check whether the input file exists. Lines 30–34 read characters repeatedly one at a time using the **get** function and write the character to the output file using the **put** function.

Suppose lines 29–34 are replaced by the following code:

```
while (!input.eof()) // Continue if not end of file
{
  output.put(input.get());
}
```

What will happen? If you run the program with this new code, you will see that the new file is one byte larger than the original one. The new file contains an extra garbage character at the end. This is because when the last character is read from the input file using **input.get()**, `input.eof()` is still `false`. Afterward, the program attempts to read another character; `input.eof()` now becomes `true`. However, the extraneous garbage character has already been sent to the output file.

The correct code in Listing 13.7 reads a character (line 29) and checks `eof()` (line 30). If `eof()` is `true`, the character is not put to `output`; otherwise, it is copied (line 32). This process continues until `eof()` returns `true`.

13.7 What are the differences between `getline` and `get` functions?

13.8 What function do you use to write a character?

13.5 `fstream` and File Open Modes

You can use `fstream` to create a file object for both input and output.

In the preceding sections, you used the `ofstream` to write data and the `ifstream` to read data. Alternatively, you can use the `fstream` class to create an input or output stream. It is convenient to use `fstream` if your program needs to use the same stream object for both input and output. To open an `fstream` file, you have to specify a *file open mode* to tell C++ how the file will be used. The file modes are listed in Table 13.1.

file open mode

TABLE 13.1 File Modes

Mode	Description
`ios::in`	Opens a file for input.
`ios::out`	Opens a file for output.
`ios::app`	Appends all output to the end of the file.
`ios::ate`	Opens a file for output. If the file already exists, move to the end of the file. Data can be written anywhere in the file.
`ios::truct`	Discards the file's contents if the file already exists. (This is the default action for `ios:out`.)
`ios::binary`	Opens a file for binary input and output.

Note

Some of the file modes also can be used with `ifstream` and `ofstream` objects to open a file. For example, you may use the `ios:app` mode to open a file with an `ofstream` object so that you can append data to the file. However, for consistency and simplicity, it is better to use the file modes with the `fstream` objects.

Note

combine modes

Several modes can be combined using the | operator. This is a bitwise inclusive-OR operator. See Appendix E for more details. For example, to open an output file named city.txt for appending data, you can use the following statement:

```
stream.open("city.txt", ios::out | ios::app);
```

Listing 13.8 gives a program that creates a new file named **city.txt** (line 11) and writes data to the file. The program then closes the file and reopens it to append new data (line 19), rather than overriding it. Finally, the program reads all data from the file.

LISTING 13.8 AppendFile.cpp

```
1  #include <iostream>
2  #include <fstream>                                          include fstream header
3  #include <string>
4  using namespace std;
5
6  int main()
7  {
8    fstream inout;                                            fstream object
9
10   // Create a file
11   inout.open("city.txt", ios::out);                         open output file
12
13   // Write cities
14   inout << "Dallas" << " " << "Houston" << " " << "Atlanta" << " ";   write data
15
16   inout.close();                                            close stream
17
18   // Append to the file
19   inout.open("city.txt", ios::out | ios::app);              open output for append
20
21   // Write cities
22   inout << "Savannah" << " " << "Austin" << " " << "Chicago";   write data
23
24   inout.close();                                            close stream
25
26   string city;
27
28   // Open the file
29   inout.open("city.txt", ios::in);                          open for input
30   while (!inout.eof()) // Continue if not end of file       end of file?
31   {
32     inout >> city;                                          read data
33     cout << city << " ";
34   }
35
36   inout.close();                                            close stream
37
38   return 0;
39 }
```

```
Dallas Houston Atlanta Savannah Austin Chicago
```

The program creates an **fstream** object in line 8 and opens the file **city.txt** for output using the file mode **ios::out** in line 11. After writing data in line 14, the program closes the stream in line 16.

The program uses the same stream object to reopen the text file with the combined modes **ios::out | ios::app** in line 19. The program then appends new data to the end of the file in line 22 and closes the stream in line 24.

Finally, the program uses the same stream object to reopen the text file with the input mode **ios::in** in line 29. The program then reads all data from the file (lines 30–34).

13.9 How do you open a file so that you can append data into the file?

13.10 What is the file open mode **ios::truct**?

Check Point

VideoNote

Test stream states

Key Point

13.6 Testing Stream States

The functions eof(), fail(), good(), *and* bad() *can be used to test the states of stream operations.*

stream state

You have used the eof() function and fail() function to test the states of a stream. C++ provides several more functions in a stream for testing *stream states*. Each stream object contains a set of bits that act as flags. These bit values (0 or 1) indicate the state of a stream. Table 13.2 lists these bits.

TABLE 13.2 Stream State Bit Values

Bit	Description
ios::eofbit	Set when the end of an input stream is reached.
ios::failbit	Set when an operation has failed.
ios::hardfail	Set when an unrecoverable error has occurred.
ios::badbit	Set when an invalid operation has been attempted.
ios::goodbit	Set if none of the preceding bits is set.

The states of the I/O operations are represented in these bits. It is not convenient to directly access these bits. C++ provides member functions in the I/O stream object to test them. These functions are listed in Table 13.3.

TABLE 13.3 Stream State Functions

Function	Description
eof()	Returns true if the eofbit flag is set.
fail()	Returns true if the failbit or hardfail flag is set.
bad()	Returns true if the badbit is set.
good()	Returns true if the goodbit is set.
clear()	Clears all flags.

Listing 13.9 gives an example to detect the stream states.

LISTING 13.9 ShowStreamState.cpp

include fstream header

function prototype

input object

open input file

show state
close file

```
 1  #include <iostream>
 2  #include <fstream>
 3  #include <string>
 4  using namespace std;
 5
 6  void showState(const fstream&);
 7
 8  int main()
 9  {
10    fstream inout;
11
12    // Create an output file
13    inout.open("temp.txt", ios::out);
14    inout << "Dallas";
15    cout << "Normal operation (no errors)" << endl;
16    showState(inout);
17    inout.close();
18
```

```
19    // Create an input file
20    inout.open("temp.txt", ios::in);                              open output file
21
22    // Read a string
23    string city;
24    inout >> city;                                                read city
25    cout << "End of file (no errors)" << endl;
26    showState(inout);                                             show state
27
28    inout.close();                                                close file
29
30    // Attempt to read after file closed
31    inout >> city;
32    cout << "Bad operation (errors)" << endl;
33    showState(inout);                                             show state
34
35    return 0;
36  }
37
38  void showState(const fstream& stream)                          show state
39  {
40    cout << "Stream status: " << endl;
41    cout << "  eof(): " << stream.eof() << endl;
42    cout << "  fail(): " << stream.fail() << endl;
43    cout << "  bad(): " << stream.bad() << endl;
44    cout << "  good(): " << stream.good() << endl;
45  }
```

```
Normal operation (no errors)
Stream status:
  eof(): 0
  fail(): 0
  bad(): 0
  good(): 1
End of file (no errors)

Stream status:
  eof(): 1
  fail(): 0
  bad(): 0
  good(): 0

Bad operation (errors)
Stream status:
  eof(): 1
  fail(): 1
  bad(): 0
  good(): 0
```

The program creates a `fstream` object using its no-arg constructor in line 10, opens **temp.txt** for output in line 13, and writes a string Dallas in line 14. The state of the stream is displayed in line 15. There are no errors so far.

The program then closes the stream in line 17, reopens **temp.txt** for input in line 20, and reads a string Dallas in line 24. The state of the stream is displayed in line 26. There are no errors so far, but the end of file is reached.

Finally, the program closes the stream in line 28 and attempts to read data after the file is closed in line 31, which causes an error. The state of the stream is displayed in line 33.

When invoking the `showState` function in lines 16, 26, and 33, the stream object is passed to the function by reference.

Check Point

13.11 How do you determine the state of I/O operations?

VideoNote

Binary I/O

Key Point

13.7 Binary I/O

The `ios::binary` *mode can be used to open a file for binary input and output.*

So far, you have used text files. Files can be classified into text and binary. A file that can be processed (read, created, or modified) using a text editor such as Notepad on Windows or vi on UNIX is called a *text file*. All the other files are called *binary files*. You cannot read binary files using a text editor. They are designed to be read by programs. For example, the C++ source programs are stored in text files and can be read by a text editor, but the C++ executable files are stored in binary files and are read by the operating system.

text file
binary file
why binary file?

Although it is not technically precise and correct, you can envision a text file as consisting of a sequence of characters and a binary file as consisting of a sequence of bits. For example, the decimal integer **199** is stored as the sequence of the three characters, `'1'`, `'9'`, `'9'`, in a text file, and the same integer is stored as an integer **C7** in a binary file, because decimal **199** equals hex **C7** ($199 = 12 \times 16^1 + 7$). The advantage of binary files is that they are more efficient to process than text files.

> **Note**
>
> Computers do not differentiate binary files and text files. All files are stored in binary format, and thus all files are essentially binary files. Text I/O is built upon binary I/O to provide a level of abstraction for character encoding and decoding.

text versus binary I/O

Binary I/O does not require conversions. If you write a numeric value to a file using binary I/O, the exact value in the memory is copied into the file. To perform binary I/O in C++, you have to open a file using the binary mode `ios::binary`. By default, a file is opened in text mode.

ios::binary

You used the `<<` operator and **put** function to write data to a text file and the `>>` operator, **get**, and **getline** functions to read data from a text file. To read/write data from/to a binary file, you have to use the **read** and **write** functions on a stream.

13.7.1 The **write** Function

The syntax for the **write** function is

write function

```
streamObject.write(const char* s, int size)
```

which writes an array of bytes in the type `char*`. Each character is a byte.

Listing 13.10 shows an example of using the **write** function.

LISTING 13.10 BinaryCharOutput.cpp

```cpp
 1  #include <iostream>
 2  #include <fstream>
 3  #include <string>
 4  using namespace std;
 5
 6  int main()
 7  {
 8      fstream binaryio("city.dat", ios::out | ios::binary);
 9      string s = "Atlanta";
10      binaryio.write(s.c_str(), s.size()); // Write s to file
11      binaryio.close();
12
```

fstream object
string
write data
close file

```
13    cout << "Done" << endl;
14
15    return 0;
16  }
```

Line 8 opens the binary file **city.dat** for output. Invoking `binaryio.write(s.c_str(),` `s.size())` (line 10) writes string `s` to the file.

Often you need to write data other than characters. How can you accomplish this? You can use the `reinterpret_cast` operator. The `reinterpret_cast` operator can cast any pointer type to another pointer type of unrelated classes. It simply performs a binary copy of the value from one type to the other without altering the data. The syntax of using the `reinterpret_cast` operator is as follows:

```
reinterpret_cast<dataType*>(address)
```

reinterpret_cast

Here, `address` is the starting address of the data (primitive, array, or object) and `dataType` is the data type you are casting to. In this case for binary I/O, it is `char*`.

For example, see the code in Listing 13.11.

LISTING 13.11   BinaryIntOutput.cpp

```
1   #include <iostream>
2   #include <fstream>
3   using namespace std;
4
5   int main()
6   {
7     fstream binaryio("temp.dat", ios::out | ios::binary);     fstream object
8     int value = 199;                                          int value
9     binaryio.write(reinterpret_cast<char*>(&value), sizeof(value));  binary output
10    binaryio.close();                                         close file
11
12    cout << "Done" << endl;
13
14    return 0;
15  }
```

Line 9 writes the content in variable `value` to the file. `reinterpret_cast<char*>` `(&value)` cast the address of the `int` value to the type `char*`. `sizeof(value)` returns the storage size for the value variable, which is `4`, since it is an `int` type variable.

Note

For consistency, this book uses the extension `.txt` to name text files and `.dat` to name binary files.

.txt and .dat

13.7.2   The **read** Function

The syntax for the `read` function is

```
streamObject.read(char* address, int size)
```

read function

The `size` parameter indicates the maximum number of bytes read. The actual number of bytes read can be obtained from a member function `gcount`.

Assume the file **city.dat** was created in Listing 13.10. Listing 13.12 reads the bytes using the `read` function.

LISTING 13.12 BinaryCharInput.cpp

fstream object
byte array
read data
gcount()

close file

```
1   #include <iostream>
2   #include <fstream>
3   using namespace std;
4
5   int main()
6   {
7     fstream binaryio("city.dat", ios::in | ios::binary);
8     char s[10]; // Array of 10 bytes. Each character is a byte.
9     binaryio.read(s, 10);
10    cout << "Number of chars read: " << binaryio.gcount() << endl;
11    s[binaryio.gcount()] = '\0'; // Append a C-string terminator
12    cout << s << endl;
13    binaryio.close();
14
15    return 0;
16  }
```

```
number of chaps read: 7
Atlanta
```

Line 7 opens the binary file **city.dat** for input. Invoking `binaryio.read(s, 10)` (line 9) reads up to **10** bytes from the file to the array. The actual number of bytes read can be determined by invoking `binaryio.gcount()` (line 11).

Assume that the file **temp.dat** was created in Listing 13.11. Listing 13.13 reads the integer using the **read** function.

LISTING 13.13 BinaryIntInput.cpp

open binary file

binary output

close file

```
1   #include <iostream>
2   #include <fstream>
3   using namespace std;
4
5   int main()
6   {
7     fstream binaryio("temp.dat", ios::in | ios::binary);
8     int value;
9     binaryio.read(reinterpret_cast<char*>(&value), sizeof(value));
10    cout << value << endl;
11    binaryio.close();
12
13    return 0;
14  }
```

```
199
```

The data in the file **temp.dat** were created in Listing 13.11. The data consisted of an integer and were cast to bytes before stored. This program first read the data as bytes and then used the `reinterpret_cast` operator to cast bytes into an **int** value (line 9).

13.7.3 Example: Binary Array I/O

You can use the `reinterpret_cast` operator to cast data of any type to bytes and vice versa. This section gives an example in Listing 13.14 to write an array of `double` values to a binary file and read it back from the file.

LISTING 13.14 BinaryArrayIO.cpp

```cpp
1  #include <iostream>
2  #include <fstream>
3  using namespace std;
4
5  int main()
6  {
7    const int SIZE = 5; // Array size
8
9    fstream binaryio; // Create stream object
10
11   // Write array to the file
12   binaryio.open("array.dat", ios::out | ios::binary);
13   double array[SIZE] = {3.4, 1.3, 2.5, 5.66, 6.9};
14   binaryio.write(reinterpret_cast<char*>(&array), sizeof(array));
15   binaryio.close();
16
17   // Read array from the file
18   binaryio.open("array.dat", ios::in | ios::binary);
19   double result[SIZE];
20   binaryio.read(reinterpret_cast<char*>(&result), sizeof(result));
21   binaryio.close();
22
23   // Display array
24   for (int i = 0; i < SIZE; i++)
25     cout << result[i] << " ";
26
27   return 0;
28 }
```

(margin notes:) constant array size · fstream object · open binary file · create array · write to file · close file · open input file · create array · read from file · close file

```
3.4 1.3 2.5 5.66 6.9
```

The program creates a stream object in line 9, opens the file **array.dat** for binary output in line 12, writes an array of `double` values to the file in line 14, and closes the file in line 15.

The program then opens the file **array.dat** for binary input in line 18, reads an array of `double` values from the file in line 20, and closes the file in line 21.

Finally, the program displays the contents in the array `result` (lines 24–25).

13.7.4 Example: Binary Object I/O

This section gives an example of writing objects to a binary file and reading the objects back from the file.

Listing 13.1 writes student records into a text file. A student record consists of first name, middle initial, last name, and score. These fields are written to the file separately. A better way of processing is to define a class to model records. Each record is an object of the `Student` class.

Let the class be named `Student` with the data fields `firstName`, `mi`, `lastName`, and `score`, their supporting accessors and mutators, and two constructors. The class UML diagram is shown in Figure 13.4.

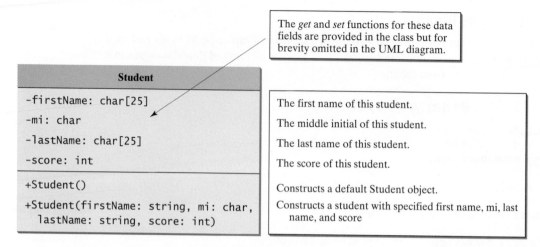

FIGURE 13.4   The Student class describes student information.

Listing 13.15 defines the Student class in the header file, and Listing 13.16 implements the class. Note that the first name and last name are stored in two arrays of characters with a fixed-length 25 internally (lines 22, 24), so that every student record will have the same size. This is necessary to ensure that students can be read from the file correctly. Since it is easier to use the string type than C-string, the string type is used in the get and set functions for firstName and lastName (lines 12, 14, 16, 18).

LISTING 13.15   Student.h

```
1   #ifndef STUDENT_H
2   #define STUDENT_H
3   #include <string>
4   using namespace std;
5
6   class Student
7   {
8   public:
9     Student();
10    Student(const string& firstName, char mi,
11      const string& lastName, int score);
12    void setFirstName(const string& s);
13    void setMi(char mi);
14    void setLastName(const string& s);
15    void setScore(int score);
16    string getFirstName() const;
17    char getMi() const;
18    string getLastName() const;
19    int getScore() const;
20
21  private:
22    char firstName[25];
23    char mi;
24    char lastName[25];
25    int score;
26  };
27
28  #endif
```

public members — line 8
no-arg constructor — line 9
constructor — lines 10–11
mutator function — line 12
accessor function — line 16
private data fields — line 21

LISTING 13.16   Student.cpp

```cpp
1  #include "Student.h"
2  #include <cstring>
3
4  // Construct a default student
5  Student::Student()
6  {
7  }
8
9  // Construct a Student object with specified data
10  Student::Student(const string& firstName, char mi,
11     const string& lastName, int score)
12  {
13    setFirstName(firstName);
14    setMi(mi);
15    setLastName(lastName);
16    setScore(score);
17  }
18
19  void Student::setFirstName(const string& s)
20  {
21    strcpy(firstName, s.c_str());
22  }
23
24  void Student::setMi(char mi)
25  {
26    this->mi = mi;
27  }
28
29  void Student::setLastName(const string& s)
30  {
31      strcpy(lastName, s.c_str());
32  }
33
34  void Student::setScore(int score)
35  {
36    this->score = score;
37  }
38
39  string Student::getFirstName() const
40  {
41    return string(firstName);
42  }
43
44  char Student::getMi() const
45  {
46    return mi;
47  }
48
49  string Student::getLastName() const
50  {
51    return string(lastName);
52  }
53
54  int Student::getScore() const
55  {
56    return score;
57  }
```

include header file

no-arg constructor

constructor

setFirstName

getMi()

Listing 13.17 gives a program that creates four Student objects, writes them to a file named **student.dat**, and reads them back from the file.

Listing 13.17 BinaryObjectIO.cpp

```
 1  #include <iostream>
 2  #include <fstream>
 3  #include "Student.h"
 4  using namespace std;
 5
 6  void displayStudent(const Student& student)
 7  {
 8    cout << student.getFirstName() << " ";
 9    cout << student.getMi() << " ";
10    cout << student.getLastName() << " ";
11    cout << student.getScore() << endl;
12  }
13
14  int main()
15  {
16    fstream binaryio; // Create stream object
17    binaryio.open("student.dat", ios::out | ios::binary);
18
19    Student student1("John", 'T', "Smith", 90);
20    Student student2("Eric", 'K', "Jones", 85);
21    Student student3("Susan", 'T', "King", 67);
22    Student student4("Kim", 'K', "Peterson", 95);
23
24    binaryio.write(reinterpret_cast<char*>
25      (&student1), sizeof(Student));
26    binaryio.write(reinterpret_cast<char*>
27      (&student2), sizeof(Student));
28    binaryio.write(reinterpret_cast<char*>
29      (&student3), sizeof(Student));
30    binaryio.write(reinterpret_cast<char*>
31      (&student4), sizeof(Student));
32
33    binaryio.close();
34
35    // Read student back from the file
36    binaryio.open("student.dat", ios::in | ios::binary);
37
38    Student studentNew;
39
40    binaryio.read(reinterpret_cast<char*>
41      (&studentNew), sizeof(Student));
42
43    displayStudent(studentNew);
44
45    binaryio.read(reinterpret_cast<char*>
46      (&studentNew), sizeof(Student));
47
48    displayStudent(studentNew);
49
50    binaryio.close();
51
52    return 0;
53  }
```

Margin notes (left column):

include Student header

display Student data

fstream object
open output file

create student1
create student2
create student3
create student4

write student1

write student2

write student3

write student4

close file

open input file

create student

read from file

display student

```
John T Smith 90
Eric K Jones 85
```

The program creates a stream object in line 16, opens the file **student.dat** for binary output in line 17, creates four `Student` objects in lines 19–22, writes them to the file in lines 24–31, and closes the file in line 33.

The statement to write an object to the file is

```
binaryio.write(reinterpret_cast<char*>
  (&student1), sizeof(Student));
```

The address of object `student1` is cast into the type `char*`. The size of an object is determined by the data fields in the object. Every student has the same size, which is `sizeof(Student)`.

The program opens the file **student.dat** for binary input in line 36, creates a `Student` object using its no-arg constructor in line 38, reads a `Student` object from the file in lines 40–41, and displays the object's data in line 43. The program continues to read another object (lines 45–46) and displays its data in line 48.

Finally, the program closes the file in line 50.

13.12 What is a text file, and what is a binary file? Can you view a text file or a binary file using a text editor?

Check Point

13.13 How do you open a file for binary I/O?

13.14 The `write` function can write only an array of bytes. How do you write a primitive-type value or an object into a binary file?

13.15 If you write string `"ABC"` to an ASCII text file, what values are stored in a file?

13.16 If you write string `"100"` to an ASCII text file, what values are stored in a file? If you write a numeric byte-type value `100` using binary I/O, what values are stored in a file?

13.8 Random Access File

The functions `seekg()` *and* `seekp()` *can be used to move file pointer to any position in a random-access file for input and output.*

Key Point

A file consists of a sequence of bytes. A special marker called *file pointer* is positioned at one of these bytes. A read or write operation takes place at the location of the file pointer. When a file is opened, the file pointer is set at the beginning of the file. When you read or write data to the file, the file pointer moves forward to the next data item. For example, if you read a byte using the `get()` function, C++ reads one byte from the file pointer, and now the file pointer is 1 byte ahead of the previous location, as shown in Figure 13.5.

file pointer

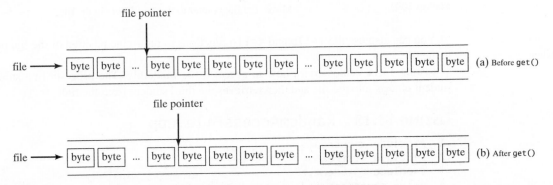

FIGURE 13.5   After a byte is read, the file pointer is moved one byte ahead.

sequential access file

All the programs you have developed so far read/write data sequentially. This is called *sequential access file*. That is, the file pointer always moves forward. If a file is open for input, it starts to read data from the beginning to the end. If a file is open for output, it writes data one item after the other from the beginning or from the end (with the append mode `ios::app`).

random access file
seekp function
seekg function

The problem with sequential access is that in order to read a byte in a specific location, all the bytes that precede it must be read. This is not efficient. C++ enables the file pointer to jump backward or forward freely using the **seekp** and **seekg** member functions on a stream object. This capability is known as *random access file*.

The **seekp** ("seek put") function is for the output stream, and the **seekg** ("seek get") function is for the input stream. Each function has two versions with one argument or two arguments. With one argument, the argument is the absolute location. For example,

```
input.seekg(0);
output.seekp(0);
```

moves the file pointer to the beginning of the file.

With two arguments, the first argument is a long integer that indicates an offset, and the second argument, known as the *seek base*, specifies where to calculate the offset from. Table 13.4 lists the three possible seek base arguments.

TABLE 13.4 Seek Base

Seek Base	Description
ios::beg	Calculates the offset from the beginning of the file.
ios::end	Calculates the offset from the end of the file.
ios::cur	Calculates the offset from the current file pointer.

Table 13.5 gives some examples of using the **seekp** and **seekg** functions.

TABLE 13.5 seekp and seekg Examples

Statement	Description
seekg(100, ios::beg);	Moves the file pointer to the 100th byte from the beginning of the file.
seekg(-100, ios::end);	Moves the file pointer to the 100th byte backward from the end of the file.
seekp(42, ios::cur);	Moves the file pointer to the 42nd byte forward from the current file pointer.
seekp(-42, ios::cur);	Moves the file pointer to the 42nd byte backward from the current file pointer.
seekp(100);	Moves the file pointer to the 100th byte in the file.

tellp function
tellg function

You can also use the **tellp** and **tellg** functions to return the position of the file pointer in the file.

Listing 13.18 demonstrates how to access a file randomly. The program first stores 10 student objects into the file and then retrieves the third student from the file.

LISTING 13.18 RandomAccessFile.cpp

```
1  #include <iostream>
2  #include <fstream>
3  #include "Student.h"
4  using namespace std;
5
```

```
 6  void displayStudent(const Student& student)
 7  {
 8    cout << student.getFirstName() << " ";
 9    cout << student.getMi() << " ";
10    cout << student.getLastName() << " ";
11    cout << student.getScore() << endl;
12  }
13
14  int main()
15  {
16    fstream binaryio; // Create stream object
17    binaryio.open("student.dat", ios::out | ios::binary);        open output file
18
19    Student student1("FirstName1", 'A', "LastName1", 10);        create students
20    Student student2("FirstName2", 'B', "LastName2", 20);
21    Student student3("FirstName3", 'C', "LastName3", 30);
22    Student student4("FirstName4", 'D', "LastName4", 40);
23    Student student5("FirstName5", 'E', "LastName5", 50);
24    Student student6("FirstName6", 'F', "LastName6", 60);
25    Student student7("FirstName7", 'G', "LastName7", 70);
26    Student student8("FirstName8", 'H', "LastName8", 80);
27    Student student9("FirstName9", 'I', "LastName9", 90);
28    Student student10("FirstName10", 'J', "LastName10", 100);
29
30    binaryio.write(reinterpret_cast<char*>                       write students
31      (&student1), sizeof(Student));
32    binaryio.write(reinterpret_cast<char*>
33      (&student2), sizeof(Student));
34    binaryio.write(reinterpret_cast<char*>
35      (&student3), sizeof(Student));
36    binaryio.write(reinterpret_cast<char*>
37      (&student4), sizeof(Student));
38    binaryio.write(reinterpret_cast<char*>
39      (&student5), sizeof(Student));
40    binaryio.write(reinterpret_cast<char*>
41      (&student6), sizeof(Student));
42    binaryio.write(reinterpret_cast<char*>
43      (&student7), sizeof(Student));
44    binaryio.write(reinterpret_cast<char*>
45      (&student8), sizeof(Student));
46    binaryio.write(reinterpret_cast<char*>
47      (&student9), sizeof(Student));
48    binaryio.write(reinterpret_cast<char*>
49      (&student10), sizeof(Student));
50
51    binaryio.close();                                            close file
52
53    // Read student back from the file
54    binaryio.open("student.dat", ios::in | ios::binary);         open input file
55
56    Student studentNew;                                          create student
57
58    binaryio.seekg(2 * sizeof(Student));                         move to third student
59
60    cout << "Current position is " << binaryio.tellg() << endl;
61
62    binaryio.read(reinterpret_cast<char*>                        read student
63      (&studentNew), sizeof(Student));
64
65    displayStudent(studentNew);                                  display student
66
```

```
67        cout << "Current position is " << binaryio.tellg() << endl;
68
69        binaryio.close();
70
71        return 0;
72   }
```

```
Current position is 112
FirstName3 C LastName3 30
Current position is 168
```

The program creates a stream object in line 16, opens the file **student.dat** for binary output in line 17, creates ten `Student` objects in lines 19–28, writes them to the file in lines 30–49, and closes the file in line 51.

The program opens the file **student.dat** for binary input in line 54, creates a `Student` object using its no-arg construction in line 56, and moves the file pointer to the address of the third student in the file in line 58. The current position is now at 112. (Note that `sizeof(Student)` is 56.) After the third object is read, the file pointer is moved to the fourth object. So, the current position becomes 168.

13.17 What is the file pointer?

13.18 What are the differences between `seekp` and `seekg`?

13.9 Updating Files

You can update a binary file by opening a file using the mode `ios::in | ios:out | ios::binary`.

Often you need to update the contents of the file. You can open a file for both input and output. For example,

```
binaryio.open("student.dat", ios::in | ios::out | ios::binary);
```

This statement opens the binary file **student.dat** for both input and output.

Listing 13.19 demonstrates how to update a file. Suppose file **student.dat** already has been created with ten `Student` objects from Listing 13.18. The program first reads the second student from the file, changes the last name, writes the revised object back to the file, and reads the new object back from the file.

LISTING 13.19 UpdateFile.cpp

include header file

```
1   #include <iostream>
2   #include <fstream>
3   #include "Student.h"
4   using namespace std;
5
6   void displayStudent(const Student& student)
7   {
8     cout << student.getFirstName() << " ";
9     cout << student.getMi() << " ";
10    cout << student.getLastName() << " ";
11    cout << student.getScore() << endl;
12  }
13
14  int main()
```

```
15  {
16      fstream binaryio; // Create stream object                                    open input/output
17
18      // Open file for input and output
19      binaryio.open("student.dat", ios::in | ios::out | ios::binary);
20
21      Student student1;                                                            student1
22      binaryio.seekg(sizeof(Student));                                             move to second student
23      binaryio.read(reinterpret_cast<char*>                                        read student1
24          (&student1), sizeof(Student));
25      displayStudent(student1);                                                    display student1
26
27      student1.setLastName("Yao");
28      binaryio.seekp(sizeof(Student));
29      binaryio.write(reinterpret_cast<char*>                                       update student1
30          (&student1), sizeof(Student));
31
32      Student student2;                                                            student2
33      binaryio.seekg(sizeof(Student));                                             move to second student
34      binaryio.read(reinterpret_cast<char*>                                        read student2
35          (&student2), sizeof(Student));
36      displayStudent(student2);                                                    display student2
37
38      binaryio.close();
39
40      return 0;
41  }
```

```
FirstName2 B LastName2 20
FirstName2 B Yao 20
```

The program creates a stream object in line 16 and opens the file **student.dat** for binary input and output in line 19.

The program moves to the second student in the file (line 22) and reads the student (lines 23–24), displays it (line 25), changes its last name (line 27), and writes the revised object back to the file (lines 29–30).

The program then moves to the second student in the file again (line 33) and reads the student (lines 34–35) and displays it (line 36). You will see that the last name of this object has been changed in the sample output.

KEY TERMS

absolute file name   512
binary file   526
file open mode   522
file pointer   533
input stream   512
output stream   512

random access file   534
relative file name   512
sequential access file   534
stream state   524
text file   526

CHAPTER SUMMARY

1. C++ provides the classes `ofstream`, `ifstream`, and `fstream` for facilitating file input and output.

2. You can use the `ofstream` class to write data to a file, use `ifstream` to read data from a file, and use the `fstream` class to read and write data.

3. You can use the **open** function to open a file, the **close** function to close a file, the **fail** function to test whether a file exists, the **eof** function to test whether the end of the file is reached.

4. The stream manipulators (e.g., **setw**, **setprecision**, **fixed**, **showpoint**, **left**, and **right**) can be used to format output.

5. You can use the **getline** function to read a line from a file, the **get** function to read a character from a file, and the **put** function to write a character to a file.

6. The file open modes (**iso::in**, **iso::out**, **iso::app**, **iso::truct**, and **iso::binary**) can be used to specify how a file is opened.

7. File I/O can be classified into text I/O and binary I/O.

8. Text I/O interprets data in sequences of characters. How text is stored in a file is dependent on the encoding scheme for the file. C++ automatically performs encoding and decoding for text I/O.

9. Binary I/O interprets data as raw binary values. To perform binary I/O, open the file using the **iso::binary** mode.

10. For binary output, use the **write** function. For binary input, use the **read** function.

11. You can use the **reinterpret_cast** operator to cast any type of data into an array of bytes for binary input and output.

12. You can process a file sequentially or in a random manner.

13. The **seekp** and **seekg** functions can be used to move the file-access pointer anywhere in the file before invoking the **put**/**write** and **get**/**read** functions.

QUIZ

Answer the quiz for this chapter online at www.cs.armstrong.edu/liang/cpp3e/quiz.html.

PROGRAMMING EXERCISES

Sections 13.2–13.6

*13.1 (*Print in a file*) Write a program that reads characters from a file named **Exercise13_1.txt** if it exists. If it does exist, the program counts the total numbers of characters in the file and prints the count by appending it to the same file.

*13.2 (*Count vowels*) Write a program that prompts the user to enter a file name and displays the number of vowels in the file.

*13.3 (*Sum, average and product of numbers in a file*) Suppose that a text file **Exercise13_3.txt** contains six integers. Write a program that reads integers from the file and displays their sum, average and product. Integers are separated by blanks.

*13.4 (*Sort in reverse order/Replace*) Suppose that a text file **Exercise13_4.txt** contains 20 integers. Write a program that reads the integers from the file, sort the integers in reverse order, and replaces the unsorted numbers by sorted numbers in the file.

*13.5 (*Baby name popularity ranking*) The popularity ranking of baby names from years 2001 to 2010 are downloaded from www.ssa.gov/oact/Babynames and stored in files named **Babynameranking2001.txt**, **Babynameranking2002.txt**, . . . , and **Babynameranking2010.txt**. Each file contains one thousand lines. Each line contains a ranking, a boy's name, number for the boy's name, a girl's name, and the number for the girl's name. For example, the first two lines in the file **Babynameranking2010.txt** are as follows:

```
1  Jacob   21,875      Isabella  22,731
2  Ethan   17,866      Sophia    20,477
```

So, the boy's name Jacob and girl's name Isabella are ranked #1 and the boy's name Ethan and girl's name Sophia are ranked #2. 21,875 boys are named Jacob and 22,731 girls are named Isabella. Write a program that prompts the user to enter the year, gender, followed by a name, and displays the ranking of the name for the year. Here is a sample run:

```
Enter the year: 2010 ↵Enter
Enter the gender: M ↵Enter
Enter the name: Javier ↵Enter
Javier is ranked #190 in year 2010
```

```
Enter the year: 2010 ↵Enter
Enter the gender: F ↵Enter
Enter the name: ABC ↵Enter
The name ABC is not ranked in year 2010
```

*13.6 (*Name for both genders*) Write a program that prompts the user to enter one of the file names described in Programming Exercise 13.5 and displays the names that are used for both genders in the file. Here is a sample run:

```
Enter a file name for baby name ranking: Babynameranking2001.txt ↵Enter
69 names used for both genders
They are Tyler Ryan Christian ...
```

*13.7 (*Sort names without duplicates*) Write a program that reads the names from the 10 files described in Programming Exercise 13.5, sorts all names (boy and girl names together, duplicates removed), and stores the sorted names in one file, 10 per line.

*13.8 (*Sort names with duplicates*) Write a program that reads the names from the 10 files described in Programming Exercise 13.5, sorts all names (boy and girl names together, duplicates allowed), and stores the sorted names in one file, 10 per line.

*13.9 (*Cumulative ranking*) Write a program that obtains the cumulative ranking for the names in the 10 years using the data from the 10 files described in Programming Exercise 13.5. Your program should display the cumulative ranking for boy's names and girl's names separately. For each name, display its ranking, name, and its cumulative count.

*13.10 (*Remove ranking*) Write a program that prompts the user to enter one of the file names described in Programming Exercise 13.5, reads the data from the file, and stores the data in a new file without the rankings. The new file is the same as the original file except that it does not have the ranking for each row. The new file is named as the input file with the extension **.new**.

*13.11 (*Data sorted?*) Write a program that reads the strings from file **SortedStrings.txt** and report whether the strings in the files are stored in ascending order. If the strings are not sorted in the file, display the first two strings that are out of order.

*13.12 (*Ranking summary*) Write a program that uses the files described in Programming Exercise 13.5 and displays a ranking summary table for the first five girl's and boy's names as follows:

Year	Rank 1	Rank 2	Rank 3	Rank 4	Rank 5	Rank 1	Rank 2	Rank 3	Rank 4	Rank 5
2010	Isabella	Sophia	Emma	Olivia	Ava	Jacob	Ethan	Michael	Jayden	William
2009	Isabella	Emma	Olivia	Sophia	Ava	Jacob	Ethan	Michael	Alexander	William
...										
2001	Emily	Madison	Hannah	Ashley	Alexis	Jacob	Michael	Matthew	Joshua	Christopher

Section 13.7

*13.13 (*Write/Read: binary data file*) Write a program that creates a binary file **Exercise13_13.dat** and prompts the user to write data to it. The program then reads the written data from the file and displays it back.

*13.14 (*Store **Loan** objects*) Write a program that creates five **Loan** objects and stores them in a file named **Exercise13_14.dat**. The **Loan** class was introduced in Listing 9.13.

*13.15 (*Restore objects from a file*) Suppose a file named **Exercise13_15.dat** has been created from the preceding exercise. Write a program that reads the **Loan** objects from the file and computes the total of the loan amount. Suppose you don't know how many **Loan** objects are in the file. Use the **eof()** to detect the end of the file.

*13.16 (*Copy files*) Listing 13.7, CopyFile.cpp, copies files using text I/O. Revise the program that copies files using binary I/O. Here is a sample run of the program:

```
Enter a source file name: c:\exercise.zip  ↵Enter
Enter a target file name: c:\exercise.bak  ↵Enter
Copy Done
```

VideoNote

Split a large file

*13.17 (*Split files*) Suppose you wish to back up a huge file (e.g., a 10-GB AVI file) to a CD-R. You can do this by splitting the file into smaller pieces and backing up these pieces separately. Write a utility program that splits a large file into smaller ones. Your program should prompt the user to enter a source file and the number of bytes in each smaller file. Here is a sample run of the program:

```
Enter a source file name: c:\exercise.zip  ↵Enter
Enter the number of bytes in each smaller file: 9343400  ↵Enter
File c:\exercise.zip.0 produced
File c:\exercise.zip.1 produced
File c:\exercise.zip.2 produced
File c:\exercise.zip.3 produced
Split Done
```

*13.18 (*Combine files*) Write a utility program that combines the files into a new file. Your program should prompt the user to enter the number of source files, each source-file name, and the target file name. Here is a sample run of the program:

```
Enter the number of source files: 4 ↵Enter
Enter a source file: c:\exercise.zip.0 ↵Enter
Enter a source file: c:\exercise.zip.1 ↵Enter
Enter a source file: c:\exercise.zip.2 ↵Enter
Enter a source file: c:\exercise.zip.3 ↵Enter
Enter a target file: c:\temp.zip ↵Enter
Combine Done
```

13.19 (*Encrypt files*) Encode the file by adding the index of each byte to that byte, for every byte. Write a program that prompts the user to enter an input file name, an output file name, and saves the encrypted version in the output file.

13.20 (*Decrypt files*) Suppose a file is encrypted using the scheme in Programming Exercise 13.19. Decode the file by subtracting the index of each byte from that byte, for every byte. Write a program that reads the name of an encrypted file and the name of an output file, and saves the decrypted version in the output file.

*****13.21** (*Game: hangman*) Rewrite Programming Exercise 10.15. The program reads the words stored in a text file, named **Exercise13_21.txt**. Words are delimited by spaces. *Hint*: Read the words from the file and store them in a vector.

Section 13.8

***13.22** (*Update count*) Suppose you want to track how many times a program has been executed. You may store an `int` to count the file. Increase the count by 1 each time this program is executed. Let the program be **Exercise13_22** and store the count in **Exercise13_22.dat**.

OPERATOR OVERLOADING

Objectives

- To understand operator overloading and its benefits (§14.1).
- To define the `Rational` class for creating rational numbers (§14.2).
- To discover how an operator can be overloaded in C++ using a function (§14.3).
- To overload the relational operators (<, <=, ==, !=, >=, >) and arithmetic operators (+, -, *, /) (§14.3).
- To overload the subscript operator [] (§14.4).
- To overload the augmented assignment operators +=, -=, *=, and /= (§14.5).
- To overload the unary operators + and - (§14.6).
- To overload the prefix and postfix ++ and -- operators (§14.7).
- To enable `friend` functions and `friend` classes to access a class's private members (§14.8).
- To overload the stream insertion and extraction operators << and >> as `friend` nonmember functions (§14.9).
- To define operator functions to perform object conversions to a primitive type (§14.10.1).
- To define appropriate constructors to perform conversions from a numeric value to an object type (§14.10.2).
- To define nonmember functions to enable implicit type conversions (§14.11).
- To define a new `Rational` class with overloaded operators (§14.12).
- To overload the = operator to perform a deep copy (§14.13).

14.1 Introduction

C++ allows you to define functions for operators. This is called operator overloading.

In Section 10.2.10, "String Operators," you learned how to use operators to simplify string operations. You can use the + operator to concatenate two strings, the relational operators (==, !=, <, <=, >, >=) to compare two strings, and the subscript operator [] to access a character. In Section 12.6, "The C++ `vector` Class," you learned how to use the [] operator to access an element in a vector. For example, the following code uses the [] operator to return a character from a string (line 3), the + operator to combine two strings (line 4), the < operator to compare two strings (line 5), the [] operator to return an element from a vector (line 10).

[] operator
+ operator
< operator

[] operator

```
1   string s1("Washington");
2   string s2("California");
3   cout << "The first character in s1 is " << s1[0] << endl;
4   cout << "s1 + s2 is " << (s1 + s2) << endl;
5   cout << "s1 < s2? " << (s1 < s2) << endl;
6
7   vector<int> v;
8   v.push_back(3);
9   v.push_back(5);
10  cout << "The first element in v is " << v[0] << endl;
```

The operators are actually functions defined in a class. These functions are named with keyword `operator` followed by the actual operator. For example, you can rewrite the preceding code using the function syntax as follows:

[] operator function

+ operator function
< operator function

[] operator function

```
1   string s1("Washington");
2   string s2("California");
3   cout << "The first character in s1 is " << s1.operator[](0)
        << endl;
4   cout << "s1 + s2 is " << operator+(s1, s2) << endl;
5   cout << "s1 < s2? " << operator<(s1, s2) << endl;
6
7   vector<int> v;
8   v.push_back(3);
9   v.push_back(5);
10  cout << "The first element in v is " << v.operator[](0) << endl;
```

The `operator[]` function is a member function in the `string` class, and the `vector` class and `operator+` and `operator<` are nonmember functions in the `string` class. Note that a member function must be invoked by an object using the syntax `objectName.functionName(...)`, such as `s1.operator[](0)`. Obviously, it is more intuitive and convenient to use the operator syntax `s1[0]` than the function syntax `s1.operator[](0)`.

operator overloading

Defining functions for operators is called *operator overloading*. Operators such as +, ==, !=, <, <=, >, >=, and [] are overloaded in the `string` class. How do you overload operators in your custom classes? This chapter uses the `Rational` class as an example to demonstrate how to overload a variety of operators. First, you will learn how to design a `Rational` class for supporting rational-number operations and then overload the operators to simplify these operations.

14.2 The **Rational** Class

This section defines the Rational class for modeling rational numbers.

A rational number has a numerator and a denominator in the form a/b, where a is the numerator and b is the denominator. For example, 1/3, 3/4, and 10/4 are rational numbers.

A rational number cannot have a denominator of 0, but a numerator of 0 is fine. Every integer i is equivalent to a rational number i/1. Rational numbers are used in exact computations involving fractions—for example, 1/3 = 0.33333.... This number cannot be precisely represented in floating-point format using data type `double` or `float`. To obtain the exact result, we must use rational numbers.

C++ provides data types for integers and floating-point numbers but not for rational numbers. This section shows how to design a class to represent rational numbers.

A `Rational` number can be represented using two data fields: `numerator` and `denominator`. You can create a `Rational` number with specified numerator and denominator or create a default `Rational` number with numerator 0 and denominator 1. You can add, subtract, multiply, divide, and compare rational numbers. You can also convert a rational number into an integer, floating-point value, or string. The UML class diagram for the `Rational` class is given in Figure 14.1.

Rational	
-numerator: int	The numerator of this rational number.
-denominator: int	The denominator of this rational number.
+Rational()	Creates a rational number with numerator 0 and denominator 1.
+Rational(numerator: int, denominator: int)	Creates a rational number with specified numerator and denominator.
+getNumerator(): int const	Returns the numerator of this rational number.
+getDenominator(): int const	Returns the denominator of this rational number.
+add(secondRational: Rational): Rational const	Returns the addition of this rational with another.
+subtract(secondRational: Rational): Rational const	Returns the subtraction of this rational with another.
+multiply(secondRational: Rational): Rational const	Returns the multiplication of this rational with another.
+divide(secondRational: Rational): Rational const	Returns the division of this rational with another.
+compareTo(secondRational: Rational): int const	Returns an int value −1, 0, or 1 to indicate whether this rational number is less than, equal to, or greater than the specified number.
+equals(secondRational: Rational): bool const	Returns true if this rational number is equal to the specified number.
+intValue(): int const	Returns the numerator / denominator.
+doubleValue(): double const	Returns the 1.0 * numerator / denominator.
+toString(): string const	Returns a string in the form "numerator / denominator." Returns numerator if denominator is 1.
-gcd(n: int, d: int): int	Returns the greatest common divisor between n and d.

FIGURE 14.1   The properties, constructors, and functions of the `Rational` class are illustrated in UML.

A rational number consists of a numerator and a denominator. There are many equivalent rational numbers; for example, 1/3 = 2/6 = 3/9 = 4/12. For convenience, we use 1/3 to represent all rational numbers that are equivalent to 1/3. The numerator and the denominator of 1/3 have no common divisor except 1, so 1/3 is said to be in *lowest terms*.

lowest term

To reduce a rational number to its lowest terms, you need to find the greatest common divisor (GCD) of the absolute values of its numerator and denominator and then divide both numerator and denominator by this value. You can use the function for computing the GCD of two integers **n** and **d**, as suggested in Listing 6.4, GreatestCommonDivisor.cpp. The numerator and denominator in a **Rational** object are reduced to their lowest terms.

As usual, we first write a test program to create **Rational** objects and test the functions in the **Rational** class. Listing 14.1 shows the header file for the **Rational** class, and Listing 14.2 is a test program.

LISTING 14.1   Rational.h

```
1   #ifndef RATIONAL_H
2   #define RATIONAL_H
3   #include <string>
4   using namespace std;
5
6   class Rational
7   {
8   public:
9     Rational();
10    Rational(int numerator, int denominator);
11    int getNumerator() const;
12    int getDenominator() const;
13    Rational add(const Rational& secondRational) const;
14    Rational subtract(const Rational& secondRational) const;
15    Rational multiply(const Rational& secondRational) const;
16    Rational divide(const Rational& secondRational) const;
17    int compareTo(const Rational& secondRational) const;
18    bool equals(const Rational& secondRational) const;
19    int intValue() const;
20    double doubleValue() const;
21    string toString() const;
22
23  private:
24    int numerator;
25    int denominator;
26    static int gcd(int n, int d);
27  };
28
29  #endif
```

include guard
define constant

public members

private members

static function

LISTING 14.2   TestRationalClass.cpp

```
1   #include <iostream>
2   #include "Rational.h"
3   using namespace std;
4
5   int main()
6   {
7     // Create and initialize two rational numbers r1 and r2
8     Rational r1(4, 2);
9     Rational r2(2, 3);
10
11    // Test toString, add, subtract, multiply, and divide
12    cout << r1.toString() << " + " << r2.toString() << " = "
13      << r1.add(r2).toString() << endl;
14    cout << r1.toString() << " - " << r2.toString() << " = "
15      << r1.subtract(r2).toString() << endl;
16    cout << r1.toString() << " * " << r2.toString() << " = "
```

include Rational

create Rational

invoke toString
invoke add

invoke subtract

```
17            << r1.multiply(r2).toString() << endl;
18       cout << r1.toString() << " / " << r2.toString() << " = "
19            << r1.divide(r2).toString() << endl;
20
21       // Test intValue and double
22       cout << "r2.intValue()" << " is " << r2.intValue() << endl;
23       cout << "r2.doubleValue()" << " is " << r2.doubleValue() << endl;
24
25       // Test compareTo and equal
26       cout << "r1.compareTo(r2) is " << r1.compareTo(r2) << endl;
27       cout << "r2.compareTo(r1) is " << r2.compareTo(r1) << endl;
28       cout << "r1.compareTo(r1) is " << r1.compareTo(r1) << endl;
29       cout << "r1.equals(r1) is "
30            << (r1.equals(r1) ? "true" : "false") << endl;
31       cout << "r1.equals(r2) is "
32            << (r1.equals(r2) ? "true" : "false") << endl;
33
34       return 0;
35    }
```

invoke multiply

invoke divide

invoke intValue
invoke doubleValue

invoke compareTo

invoke equal

```
2 + 2/3 = 8/3
2 - 2/3 = 4/3
2 * 2/3 = 4/3
2 / 2/3 = 3
r2.intValue() is 0
r2.doubleValue() is 0.666667
r1.compareTo(r2) is 1
r2.compareTo(r1) is -1
r1.compareTo(r1) is 0
r1.equals(r1) is true
r1.equals(r2) is false
```

The `main` function creates two rational numbers, `r1` and `r2` (lines 8–9), and displays the results of `r1 + r2`, `r1 - r2`, `r1 x r2`, and `r1 / r2` (lines 12–19). To perform `r1 + r2`, invoke `r1.add(r2)` to return a new `Rational` object. Similarly, `r1.subtract(r2)` returns a new `Rational` object for `r1 - r2`, `r1.multiply(r2)` for `r1 x r2`, and `r1.divide(r2)` for `r1 / r2`.

The `intValue()` function displays the `int` value of `r2` (line 22). The `doubleValue()` function displays the `double` value of `r2` (line 23).

Invoking `r1.compareTo(r2)` (line 26) returns 1, since `r1` is greater than `r2`. Invoking `r2.compareTo(r1)` (line 27) returns -1, since `r2` is less than `r1`. Invoking `r1.compareTo(r1)` (line 28) returns 0, since `r1` is equal to `r1`. Invoking `r1.equals(r1)` (line 29) returns `true`, since `r1` is equal to `r1`. Invoking `r1.equals(r2)` (line 30) returns `false`, since `r1` are `r2` are not equal.

The `Rational` class is implemented in Listing 14.3.

LISTING 14.3 Rational.cpp

```
1    #include "Rational.h"
2    #include <sstream> // Used in toString to convert numbers to strings
3    #include <cstdlib> // For the abs function
4    Rational::Rational()
5    {
6       numerator = 0;
7       denominator = 1;
```

Rational header

no-arg constructor

initialize data fields

```
  8  }
  9
 10  Rational::Rational(int numerator, int denominator)
 11  {
 12    int factor = gcd(numerator, denominator);
 13    this->numerator = ((denominator > 0) ? 1 : -1) * numerator / factor;
 14    this->denominator = abs(denominator) / factor;
 15  }
 16
 17  int Rational::getNumerator() const
 18  {
 19    return numerator;
 20  }
 21
 22  int Rational::getDenominator() const
 23  {
 24    return denominator;
 25  }
 26
 27  // Find GCD of two numbers
 28  int Rational::gcd(int n, int d)
 29  {
 30    int n1 = abs(n);
 31    int n2 = abs(d);
 32    int gcd = 1;
 33
 34    for (int k = 1; k <= n1 && k <= n2; k++)
 35    {
 36      if (n1 % k == 0 && n2 % k == 0)
 37        gcd = k;
 38    }
 39
 40    return gcd;
 41  }
 42
 43  Rational Rational::add(const Rational& secondRational) const
 44  {
 45    int n = numerator * secondRational.getDenominator() +
 46      denominator * secondRational.getNumerator();
 47    int d = denominator * secondRational.getDenominator();
 48    return Rational(n, d);
 49  }
 50
 51  Rational Rational::subtract(const Rational& secondRational) const
 52  {
 53    int n = numerator * secondRational.getDenominator()
 54      - denominator * secondRational.getNumerator();
 55    int d = denominator * secondRational.getDenominator();
 56    return Rational(n, d);
 57  }
 58
 59  Rational Rational::multiply(const Rational& secondRational) const
 60  {
 61    int n = numerator * secondRational.getNumerator();
 62    int d = denominator * secondRational.getDenominator();
 63    return Rational(n, d);
 64  }
 65
 66  Rational Rational::divide(const Rational& secondRational) const
```

constructor

initialize data fields

gcd

add

$\frac{a}{b} + \frac{c}{d} = \frac{ad + bc}{bd}$

subtract

$\frac{a}{b} - \frac{c}{d} = \frac{ad - bc}{bd}$

multiply

$\frac{a}{b} \times \frac{c}{d} = \frac{ac}{bd}$

divide

```
67  {
68      int n = numerator * secondRational.getDenominator();
69      int d = denominator * secondRational.numerator;
70      return Rational(n, d);
71  }
72
73  int Rational::compareTo(const Rational& secondRational) const         compareTo
74  {
75      Rational temp = subtract(secondRational);
76      if (temp.getNumerator() < 0)
77        return -1;
78      else if (temp.getNumerator() == 0)
79        return 0;
80      else
81        return 1;
82  }
83
84  bool Rational::equals(const Rational& secondRational) const            equals
85  {
86      if (compareTo(secondRational) == 0)
87        return true;
88      else
89        return false;
90  }
91
92  int Rational::intValue() const                                         intValue
93  {
94      return getNumerator() / getDenominator();
95  }
96
97  double Rational::doubleValue() const                                   doubleValue
98  {
99      return 1.0 * getNumerator() / getDenominator();
100 }
101
102 string Rational::toString() const                                      toString
103 {
104     stringstream ss;
105     ss << numerator;
106
107     if (denominator > 1)
108       ss << "/" << denominator;
109
110     return ss.str();
111 }
```

$$\frac{a}{b} \div \frac{c}{d} = \frac{ad}{bc}$$

The rational number is encapsulated in a `Rational` object. Internally, a rational number is represented in its lowest terms (lines 13–14), and the numerator determines its sign (line 13). The denominator is always positive (line 14).

The `gcd()` function (lines 28–41) is private; it is not intended for use by clients. The `gcd()` function is only for internal use by the `Rational` class. The `gcd()` function is also static, since it is not dependent on any particular `Rational` object.

The `abs(x)` function (lines 30–31) is defined in the standard C++ library that returns the absolute value of `x`.

Two `Rational` objects can perform add, subtract, multiply, and divide operations. These functions return a new `Rational` object (lines 43–71).

The `compareTo(&secondRational)` function (lines 73–82) compares this rational number to the other rational number. It first subtracts the second rational from this rational and saves the result in `temp` (line 75). Return -1, 0, or 1, if `temp`'s numerator is less than, equal to, or greater than 0.

The `equals(&secondRational)` function (lines 84–90) utilizes the `compareTo` function to compare this rational number to the other one. If this function returns 0, the `equals` function returns `true`; otherwise, it returns `false`.

The functions `intValue` and `doubleValue` return an `int` and a `double` value, respectively, for this rational number (lines 92–100).

The `toString()` function (lines 102–111) returns a string representation of a `Rational` object in the form `numerator/denominator` or simply `numerator` if `denominator` is 1. The string stream is used here to convert a number into a string, which was introduced in Section 10.2.11, "Converting Numbers to Strings."

Tip

encapsulation

The numerator and denominator are represented using two variables. We can represent them also using an array of two integers. See Programming Exercise 14.2. The signatures of the public functions in the **Rational** class are not changed, although the internal representation of a rational number is changed. This is a good illustration of the idea that the data fields of a class should be kept private so as to *encapsulate* the implementation of the class from the use of the class.

14.3 Operator Functions

VideoNote

Overload the < operator

🔑 **Key Point**

Most of the operators in C++ can be defined as functions to perform desirable operations.

It is convenient to compare two string objects using an intuitive syntax like

```
string1 < string2
```

Can you compare two `Rational` objects using a similar syntax like the following?

```
r1 < r2
```

how to overload operators?

Yes. You can define a special function called the *operator function* in the class. The operator function is just like a regular function except that it must be named with keyword `operator` followed by the actual operator. For example, the following function header

```
bool operator<(const Rational& secondRational) const
```

defines the < operator function that returns `true` if this `Rational` object is less than `secondRational`. You can invoke the function using

```
r1.operator<(r2)
```

or simply

```
r1 < r2
```

overload operator<

To use this operator, you have to add the function header for `operator<` in the public section in Listing 14.1 Rational.h and implement the function in the Rational.cpp in Listing 14.3 as follows:

function operator

invoke compareTo

```
1  bool Rational::operator<(const Rational& secondRational) const
2  {
3      // compareTo is already defined Rational.h
4      if (compareTo(secondRational) < 0)
5          return true;
6      else
7          return false;
8  }
```

The following code

```
Rational r1(4, 2);
Rational r2(2, 3);
cout << "r1 < r2 is " << (r1.operator<(r2) ? "true" : "false");
cout << "\nr1 < r2 is " << ((r1 < r2) ? "true" : "false");
cout << "\nr2 < r1 is " << (r2.operator<(r1) ? "true" : "false");
```

displays

```
r1 < r2 is false
r1 < r2 is false
r2 < r1 is true
```

Note that `r1.operator<(r2)` is same as `r1 < r2`. The latter is simpler and therefore preferred.

C++ allows you to overload the operators listed in Table 14.1. Table 14.2 shows the four operators that cannot be overloaded. C++ does not allow you to create new operators.

overloadable operators

TABLE 14.1   Operators That Can Be Overloaded

+	−	*	/	%	∧	&	|	~	!	=
<	>	+=	−=	*=	/=	%=	∧=	&=	|=	<<
>>	>>=	<<=	==	!=	<=	>=	&&	||	++	--
->*	,	->	[]	()	new	delete				

TABLE 14.2   Operators That Cannot Be Overloaded

?:	.	.*	::

Note

C++ defines the operator precedence and associativity (see Section 3.15, "Operator Precedence and Associativity"). You cannot change the operator precedence and associativity by overloading.

precedence and associativity

Note

Most operators are binary operators. Some are unary. You cannot change the number of operands by overloading. For example, the `/` divide operator is binary and `++` is unary.

number of operands

Here is another example that overloads the binary + operator in the `Rational` class. Add the following function header in Rational.h in Listing 14.1.

overload binary +

```
Rational operator+(const Rational& secondRational) const
```

Implement the function in Rational.cpp in Listing 14.3 as follows:

```
1  Rational Rational::operator+(const Rational& secondRational) const
2  {
3    // add is already defined Rational.h
4    return add(secondRational);
5  }
```

+ function operator

invoke

The following code

```
Rational r1(4, 2);
Rational r2(2, 3);
cout << "r1 + r2 is " << (r1 + r2).toString() << endl;
```

displays

```
r1 + r2 is 8/3
```

Check
Point

14.1   How do you define an operator function for overloading an operator?

14.2   List the operators that cannot be overloaded.

14.3   Can you change the operator precedence or associativity by overloading?

14.4 Overloading the Subscript Operator []

The subscript operator [] is commonly defined to access and modify a data field or an element in an object.

subscript operator

In C++, the pair of square brackets [] is called the *subscript operator*. You have used this operator to access array elements and the elements in a **string** object and a **vector** object. You can overload this operator to access the contents of the object if desirable. For example, you may wish to access the numerator and denominator of a **Rational** object r using r[0] and r[1].

We first give an incorrect solution to overload the [] operator. We will then identify the problem and give a correct solution. To enable a **Rational** object to access its numerator and denominator using the [] operator, define the following function header in the Rational.h header file:

```
int operator[](int index);
```

Implement the function in Rational.cpp as follows:

[] function operator

access numerator

access denominator

```
1    int Rational::operator[](int index)   ◄──────── Partially correct
2    {
3      if (index == 0)
4        return numerator;
5      else
6        return denominator;
7    }
```

The following code

```
Rational r(2, 3);
cout << "r[0] is " << r[0] << endl;
cout << "r[1] is " << r[1] << endl;
```

displays

```
r[0] is 2
r[1] is 3
```

Can you set a new numerator or denominator like an array assignment such as the following?

```
r[0] = 5;
r[1] = 6;
```

If you compile it, you will get the following error:

```
Lvalue required in function main()
```

In C++, *Lvalue* (short for left value) refers to anything that can appear on the left side of the   Lvalue
assignment operator (=) and *Rvalue* (short for right value) refers to anything that can appear   Rvalue
on the right side of the assignment operator (=). How can you make `r[0]` and `r[1]` an Lvalue
so that you can assign a value to `r[0]` and `r[1]`? The answer is that you can define the `[]`
operator to return a reference of the variable.

Add the following correct function header in Rational.h:

```cpp
int& operator[](int index);
```

Implement the function in Rational.cpp:

```cpp
int& Rational::operator[](int index)  ◄──────  Correct
{
  if (index == 0)
    return numerator;
  else
    return denominator;
}
```
correct function header

You are familiar with pass-by-reference. *Return-by-reference* and pass-by-reference are   return-by-reference
the same concept. In pass-by-reference, the formal parameter and the actual parameter are
aliases. In return-by-reference, the function returns an alias to a variable.

In this function, if `index` is `0`, the function returns an alias of variable `numerator`. If
index is `1`, the function returns an alias of variable `denominator`.

Note that this function does not check the bounds of the index. In Chapter 16, you will
learn how to revise this function to make your program more robust by throwing an exception
if the index is not `0` or `1`.

The following code

```cpp
1  Rational r(2, 3);
2  r[0] = 5; // Set numerator to 5
3  r[1] = 6; // Set denominator to 6
4  cout << "r[0] is " << r[0] << endl;
5  cout << "r[1] is " << r[1] << endl;
6  cout << "r.doubleValue() is " << r.doubleValue() << endl;
```
assign to r[0]
assign to r[1]

displays

```
r[0] is 5
r[1] is 6
r.doubleValue() is 0.833333
```

In `r[0]`, r is an object and `0` is the argument to the member function `[]`. When `r[0]` is used
as an expression, it returns a value for the numerator. When `r[0]` is used on the left side of
the assignment operator, it is an alias for variable `numerator`. So, `r[0] = 5` assigns `5` to
`numerator`.

The `[]` operator functions as both accessor and mutator. For example, you use `r[0]` as an   [] accessor and mutator
accessor to retrieve the numerator in an expression, and you use `r[0] = value` as a mutator.

For convenience, we call a function operator that returns a reference an *Lvalue operator*.   Lvalue operator
Several other operators such as +=, -=, *=, /=, and %= are also Lvalue operators.

Check Point

14.4 What is an Lvalue? What is an Rvalue?

14.5 Explain pass-by-reference and return-by-reference.

14.6 What should be the function signature for the [] operator?

14.5 Overloading Augmented Assignment Operators

Key Point

You can define the augmented assignment operators as functions to return a value by reference.

C++ has augmented assignment operators +=, -=, *=, /=, and %= for adding, subtracting, multiplying, dividing, and modulus a value in a variable. You can overload these operators in the `Rational` class.

Note that the augmented operators can be used as Lvalues. For example, the code

```
int x = 0;
(x += 2) += 3;
```

is legal. So augmented assignment operators are Lvalue operators and you should overload them to return by reference.

Here is an example that overloads the addition assignment operator +=. Add the function header in Listing 14.1, Rational.h.

```
Rational& operator+=(const Rational& secondRational)
```

Implement the function in Listing 14.3, Rational.cpp.

+= function operator

add to calling object
return calling object

```
1  Rational& Rational::operator+=(const Rational& secondRational)
2  {
3    *this = add(secondRational);
4    return *this;
5  }
```

Line 3 invokes the **add** function to add the calling `Rational` object with the second `Rational` object. The result is copied to the calling object `*this` in line 3. The calling object is returned in line 4.

For example, the following code

+= function operator

```
1  Rational r1(2, 4);
2  Rational r2 = r1 += Rational(2, 3);
3  cout << "r1 is " << r1.toString() << endl;
4  cout << "r2 is " << r2.toString() << endl;
```

displays

```
r1 is 7/6
r2 is 7/6
```

Check Point

14.7 When you overload an augmented operator such as +=, should the function be void or nonvoid?

14.8 Why should the functions for augmented assignment operators return a reference?

14.6 Overloading the Unary Operators

The unary + and − operators can be overloaded.

The + and − are unary operators. They can be overloaded, too. Since the unary operator operates on one operand that is the calling object itself, the unary function operator has no parameters.

Here is an example that overloads the − operator. Add the function header in Listing 14.1, Rational.h.

```
Rational operator-()
```

Implement the function in Listing 14.3, Rational.cpp.

```
1  Rational Rational::operator-()
2  {
3      return Rational(-numerator, denominator);
4  }
```

negate numerator
return calling object

Negating a **Rational** object is the same as negating its numerator (line 3). Line 4 returns the calling object. Note that the negating operator returns a new **Rational**. The calling object itself is not changed.

The following code

```
1  Rational r2(2, 3);
2  Rational r3 = -r2;   // Negate r2
3  cout << "r2 is " << r2.toString() << endl;
4  cout << "r3 is " << r3.toString() << endl;
```

unary - operator

displays

```
r2 is 2/3
r3 is -2/3
```

14.9 What should be the function signature for the unary + operator?

14.10 Why is the following implementation for the unary − operator wrong?

```
Rational Rational::operator-()
{
    numerator *= -1;
    return *this;
}
```

14.7 Overloading the ++ and −− Operators

The preincrement, predecrement, postincrement, and postdecrement operators can be overloaded.

The ++ and −− operators may be prefix or postfix. The prefix **++var** or **--var** first adds or subtracts 1 from the variable and then evaluates to the new value in the **var**. The postfix **var++** or **var--** adds or subtracts 1 from the variable, but evaluates to the old value in the **var**.

If the ++ and −− are implemented correctly, the following code

```
1  Rational r2(2, 3);
2  Rational r3 = ++r2; // Prefix increment
3  cout << "r3 is " << r3.toString() << endl;
4  cout << "r2 is " << r2.toString() << endl;
```

assign to r2[0]
assign to r2[1]

```
5
6   Rational r1(2, 3);
7   Rational r4 = r1++; // Postfix increment
8   cout << "r1 is " << r1.toString() << endl;
9   cout << "r4 is " << r4.toString() << endl;
```

should display

```
r3 is 5/3
r2 is 5/3
r1 is 5/3
r4 is 2/3  ◄──────── r4 stores the original value of r1
```

How does C++ distinguish the prefix ++ or -- function operators from the postfix ++ or -- function operators? C++ defines postfix ++/-- function operators with a special dummy parameter of the `int` type and defines the prefix ++ function operator with no parameters as follows:

prefix ++ operator

```
Rational& operator++();
```

postfix ++ operator

```
Rational operator++(int dummy)
```

Note that the prefix ++ and -- operators are Lvalue operators, but the postfix ++ and -- operators are not. These prefix and postfix ++ operator functions can be implemented as follows:

$\frac{a}{b} + 1 = \frac{a + b}{b}$
return calling object

```
1   // Prefix increment
2   Rational& Rational::operator++()
3   {
4       numerator += denominator;
5       return *this;
6   }
7
8   // Postfix increment
9   Rational Rational::operator++(int dummy)
10  {
11      Rational temp(numerator, denominator);
12      numerator += denominator;
13      return temp;
14  }
```

create temp
$\frac{a}{b} + 1 = \frac{a + b}{b}$
return temp object

In the prefix ++ function, line 4 adds the denominator to the numerator. This is the new numerator for the calling object after adding 1 to the `Rational` object. Line 5 returns the calling object.

In the postfix ++ function, line 11 creates a temporary `Rational` object to store the original calling object. Line 12 increments the calling object. Line 13 returns the original calling object.

14.11 What should be the function signature for the prefix ++ operator? for the postfix ++ operator?

14.12 Suppose you implement the postfix ++ as follows

```
Rational Rational::operator++(int dummy)
{
    Rational temp(*this);
    add(Rational(1, 0));
    return temp;
}
```

Is this implementation correct? If so, compare it with the implementation in the text; which one is better?

14.8 **friend** Functions and **friend** Classes

You can define a **friend** *function or a* **friend** *class to enable it to access private members in another class.*

Key Point

C++ allows you to overload the stream insertion operator (<<) and the stream extraction operator (>>). These operators must be implemented as **friend** nonmember functions. This section introduces **friend** functions and **friend** classes to prepare you to overload these operators.

Private members of a class cannot be accessed from outside the class. Occasionally, it is convenient to allow some trusted functions and classes to access a class's private members. C++ enables you to use the **friend** keyword to define **friend** functions and **friend** classes so that these trusted functions and classes can access another class's private members.

Listing 14.4 gives an example that defines a **friend** class.

friend class

LISTING 14.4 Date.h

```
1  #ifndef DATE_H
2  #define DATE_H
3  class Date
4  {
5  public:
6    Date(int year, int month, int day)
7    {
8      this->year = year;
9      this->month = month;
10     this->day = day;
11   }
12
13   friend class AccessDate;
14
15  private:
16    int year;
17    int month;
18    int day;
19  };
20
21  #endif
```

a friend class

The AccessDate class (line 4) is defined as a **friend** class. So, you can directly access private data fields year, month, and day from the AccessDate class in Listing 14.5.

LISTING 14.5 TestFriendClass.cpp

```
1  #include <iostream>
2  #include "Date.h"
3  using namespace std;
4
5  class AccessDate
6  {
7  public:
8    static void p()
9    {
10     Date birthDate(2010, 3, 4);
11     birthDate.year = 2000;
```

header Date1.h

static function

create a Date
modify private data

access private data

```
12        cout << birthDate.year << endl;
13      }
14  };
15
16  int main()
17  {
```

invoke static function

```
18      AccessDate::p();
19
20      return 0;
21  }
```

The AccessDate class is defined in lines 5–14. A Date object is created in the class. Since AccessDate is a friend class of the Date class, the private data in a Date object can be accessed in the AccessDate class (lines 11–12). The main function invokes the static function AccessDate::p() in line 18.

friend function

Listing 14.6 gives an example of how to use a friend function. The program defines the Date class with a friend function p (line 13). Function p is not a member of the Date class but can access the private data in Date. In function p, a Date object is created in line 23, and the private field data year is modified in line 24 and retrieved in line 25.

LISTING 14.6 TestFriendFunction.cpp

```
1  #include <iostream>
2  using namespace std;
3
4  class Date
5  {
6  public:
7    Date(int year, int month, int day)
8    {
9      this->year = year;
10     this->month = month;
11     this->day = day;
12    }
```

define friend function

```
13    friend void p();
14
15  private:
16    int year;
17    int month;
18    int day;
19  };
20
21  void p()
22  {
23    Date date(2010, 5, 9);
```

modify private data
access private data

```
24    date.year = 2000;
25    cout << date.year << endl;
26  }
27
28  int main()
29  {
```

invoke friend function

```
30    p();
31
32    return 0;
33  }
```

14.13 How do you define a friend function to access a class's private members?

14.14 How do you define a friend class to access a class's private members?

14.9 Overloading the << and >> Operators

The stream extraction (>>) and insertion (<<) operators can be overloaded for performing input and output operations.

So far, in order to display a `Rational` object, you invoke the `toString()` function to return a string representation for the `Rational` object and then display the string. For example, to display a `Rational` object `r`, you write

```
cout << r.toString();
```

Wouldn't it be nice to be able to display a `Rational` object directly using a syntax like the following?

```
cout << r;
```

The stream insertion operator (<<) and the stream extraction operator (>>) are just like other binary operators in C++. `cout << r` is actually the same as `<<(cout, r)` or `operator<<(cout, r)`.

Consider the following statement:

```
r1 + r2;
```

The operator is + with two operands `r1` and `r2`. Both are instances of the `Rational` class. So, you can overload the + operator as a member function with `r2` as the argument. However, for the statement

```
cout << r;
```

the operator is << with two operands `cout` and `r`. The first operand is an instance of the `ostream` class, not the `Rational` class. So, you cannot overload the << operator as a member function in the `Rational` class. However, you can define the function as a `friend` function of the `Rational` class in the Rational.h header file:

why nonmember function for <<?

```
friend ostream& operator<<(ostream& out, const Rational& rational);
```

Note that this function returns a reference of `ostream`, because you may use the << operator in a chain of expressions. Consider the following statement:

chains of <<

```
cout << r1 << " followed by " << r2;
```

This is equivalent to

```
((cout << r1) << " followed by ") << r2;
```

For this to work, `cout << r1` must return a reference of `ostream`. So, the function << can be implemented as follows:

```
ostream& operator<<(ostream& out, const Rational& rational)
{
  out << rational.numerator << "/" << rational.denominator;
  return out;
}
```

Similarly, to overload the >> operator, define the following function header in the Rational.h header file:

```
friend istream& operator>>(istream& in, Rational& rational);
```

Implement this function in Rational.cpp as follows:

```
istream& operator>>(istream& in, Rational& rational)
{
  cout << "Enter numerator: ";
  in >> rational.numerator;

  cout << "Enter denominator: ";
  in >> rational.denominator;
  return in;
}
```

The following code gives a test program that uses the overloaded << and >> functions operators.

```
1  Rational r1, r2;
2  cout << "Enter first rational number" << endl;
3  cin >> r1;
4
5  cout << "Enter second rational number" << endl;
6  cin >> r2;
7
8  cout << r1 << " + " << r2 << " = " << r1 + r2 << endl;
```

>> operator (line 3)

>> operator (line 6)

<< operator (line 8)

```
Enter first rational number
Enter numerator: 1 ⏎Enter
Enter denominator: 2 ⏎Enter
Enter second rational number
Enter numerator: 3 ⏎Enter
Enter denominator: 4 ⏎Enter
1/2 + 3/4 is 5/4
```

Line 3 reads values to a rational object from **cin**. In line 8, **r1 + r2** is evaluated to a new rational number, which is then sent to **cout**.

Check Point

14.15 What should be the function signature for the << operator? for the >> operator?

14.16 Why should the << and >> operators be defined as nonmember functions?

14.17 Suppose you overload the << operator as follows:

```
ostream& operator<<(ostream& stream, const Rational& rational)
{
  stream << rational.getNumerator() << " / "
    << rational.getDenominator();
  return stream;
}
```

Do you still need to define

```
friend ostream& operator<<(ostream& stream, Rational& rational)
```

in the **Rational** class?

14.10 Automatic Type Conversions

You can define functions to perform automatic conversion from an object to a primitive type value and vice versa.

Key Point

C++ can perform certain type conversions automatically. You can define functions to enable conversions from a `Rational` object to a primitive type value or vice versa.

14.10.1 Converting to a Primitive Data Type

You can add an `int` value with a `double` value such as

```
4 + 5.5
```

In this case, C++ performs automatic type conversion to convert an `int` value `4` to a double value `4.0`.

Can you add a rational number with an `int` or a `double` value? Yes. You have to define a function operator to convert an object into `int` or `double`. Here is the implementation of the function to convert a `Rational` object to a `double` value.

```
Rational::operator double()
{
  return doubleValue(); // doubleValue() already in Rational.h
}
```

Don't forget that you have to add the member function header in the Rational.h header file.

```
operator double();
```

This is a special syntax for defining conversion functions to a primitive type in C++. There is no return type like a constructor. The function name is the type that you want the object to be converted to.

So, the following code

```
1  Rational r1(1, 4);
2  double d = r1 + 5.1;
3  cout << "r1 + 5.1 is " << d << endl;
```

conversion function syntax

add rational with double

displays

```
r1 + 5.1 is 5.35
```

The statement in line 2 adds a rational number `r1` with a `double` value `5.1`. Since the conversion function is defined to convert a rational number to a `double`, `r1` is converted to a `double` value `0.25`, which is then added with `5.1`.

14.10.2 Converting to an Object Type

A `Rational` object can be automatically converted to a numeric value. Can a numeric value be automatically converted to a `Rational` object? Yes, it can.

To achieve this, define the following constructor in the header file:

```
Rational(int numerator);
```

and implement it in the implementation file as follows:

```
Rational::Rational(int numerator)
{
  this->numerator = numerator;
  this->denominator = 1;
}
```

Provided that the + operator is also overloaded (see Section 14.3), the following code

```
Rational r1(2, 3);
Rational r = r1 + 4; // Automatically converting 4 to Rational
cout << r << endl;
```

displays

```
14 / 3
```

When C++ sees r1 + 4, it first checks to see if the + operator has been overloaded to add a **Rational** with an integer. Since no such function is defined, the system next searches for the + operator to add a **Rational** with another **Rational**. Since **4** is an integer, C++ uses the constructor that constructs a **Rational** object from an integer argument. In other words, C++ performs an automatic conversion to convert an integer to a **Rational** object. This automatic conversion is possible because the suitable constructor is available. Now two **Rational** objects are added using the overloaded + operator to return a new **Rational** object (**14 / 3**).

A class can define the conversion function to convert an object to a primitive type value or define a conversion constructor to convert a primitive type value to an object, but not both simultaneously in the class. If both are defined, the compiler will report an ambiguity error.

14.18 What should be the function signature for converting an object to the **int** type?

14.19 How do you convert a primitive type value to an object?

14.20 Can a class define the conversion function to convert an object to a primitive type value and define a conversion constructor to convert a primitive type value to an object simultaneously in the class?

14.11 Defining Nonmember Functions for Overloading Operators

If an operator can be overloaded as a nonmember function, define it as a nonmember function to enable implicit type conversions.

C++ can perform certain type conversions automatically. You can define functions to enable conversions.

You can add a **Rational** object **r1** with an integer like this:

```
r1 + 4
```

Can you add an integer with a **Rational** object **r1** like this?

```
4 + r1
```

Naturally you would think the + operator is symmetric. However, it does not work, because the left operand is the calling object for the + operator and the left operand must be a **Rational** object. Here, 4 is an integer, not a `Rational` object. C++ does not perform automatic conversion in this case. To circumvent this problem, take the following two steps:

1. Define and implement the following constructor, as discussed in the preceding section.

```
Rational(int numerator);
```

This constructor enables the integer to be converted to a `Rational` object.

2. Define the + operator as a nonmember function in the Rational.h header file as follows:

```
Rational operator+(const Rational& r1, const Rational& r2)
```

Implement the function in Rational.cpp as follows:

```
1  Rational operator+(const Rational& r1, const Rational& r2)
2  {
3    return r1.add(r2);
4  }
```

+function operator

invoke add

Automatic type conversion to the user-defined object also works for comparison operators (<, <=, ==, !=, >, >=).

Note that the examples for the `operator<` and `operator+` are defined as member functions in Section 14.3. From now on, we will define them as nonmember functions.

14.21 Why defining a nonmember function for an operator is preferred?

Check
Point

14.12 The **Rational** Class with Overloaded Function Operators

This section revises the `Rational` *class with overloaded function operators.*

Key
Point

The preceding sections introduced how to overload function operators. The following points are worth noting:

- Conversion functions from a class type to a primitive type or from a primitive type to a class type cannot both be defined in the same class. Doing so would cause ambiguity errors, because the compiler cannot decide which conversion to perform. Often converting from a primitive type to a class type is more useful. So, we will define our `Rational` class to support automatic conversion from a primitive type to the `Rational` type.

automatic type conversion

- Most operators can be overloaded either as member or nonmember functions. However, the =, [], ->, and () operators must be overloaded as member functions and << and >> operators must be overloaded as nonmember functions.

member versus nonmember

- If an operator (i.e., +, -, *, /, %, <, <=, ==, !=, >, and >=) can be implemented either as a member or nonmember function, it is better to overload it as a nonmember function to enable automatic type conversion with symmetric operands.

nonmember preferred

- If you want the returned object to be used as an Lvalue (i.e., used on the left-hand side of the assignment statement), you need to define the function to return a reference. The augmented assignment operators +=, -=, *=, /=, and %=, the prefix ++ and -- operators, the subscript operator [], and the assignment operators = are Lvalue operators.

Lvalue

Listing 14.7 gives a new header file named RationalWithOperators.h for the `Rational` class with function operators. Lines 10–22 in the new file are the same as in Listing 14.1 Rational.h. The functions for augmented assignment operators (+=, -=, *=, /=), subscript operator [], prefix ++, and prefix -- are defined to return a reference (lines 27–37). The stream extraction << and stream insertion >> operators are defined in lines 48–49. The nonmember functions for comparison operators (<, <=, >, >=, ==, !=) and arithmetic operators (+, -, *, /) are defined in lines 57–69.

LISTING 14.7 `RationalWithOperators.h`

```
1   #ifndef RATIONALWITHOPERATORS_H
2   #define RATIONALWITHOPERATORS_H
3   #include <string>
4   #include <iostream>
5   using namespace std;
6
7   class Rational
8   {
9   public:
10    Rational();
11    Rational(int numerator, int denominator);
12    int getNumerator() const;
13    int getDenominator() const;
14    Rational add(const Rational& secondRational) const;
15    Rational subtract(const Rational& secondRational) const;
16    Rational multiply(const Rational& secondRational) const;
17    Rational divide(const Rational& secondRational) const;
18    int compareTo(const Rational& secondRational) const;
19    bool equals(const Rational& secondRational) const;
20    int intValue() const;
21    double doubleValue() const;
22    string toString() const;
23
24    Rational(int numerator); // Suitable for type conversion
25
26    // Define function operators for augmented operators
27    Rational& operator+=(const Rational& secondRational);
28    Rational& operator-=(const Rational& secondRational);
29    Rational& operator*=(const Rational& secondRational);
30    Rational& operator/=(const Rational& secondRational);
31
32    // Define function operator []
33    int& operator[](int index);
34
35    // Define function operators for prefix ++ and --
36    Rational& operator++();
37    Rational& operator--();
38
39    // Define function operators for postfix ++ and --
40    Rational operator++(int dummy);
41    Rational operator--(int dummy);
42
43    // Define function operators for unary + and -
44    Rational operator+();
45    Rational operator-();
46
47    // Define the << and >> operators
48    friend ostream& operator<<(ostream& , const Rational&);
49    friend istream& operator>>(istream& , Rational&);
50
51  private:
52    int numerator;
```

constructor for type conversion (line 24)

augmented operators (line 27)

subscript operator (line 33)

prefix ++ operator (line 36)
prefix -- operator (line 37)

postfix ++ operator (line 40)
postfix -- operator (line 41)

unary + operator (line 44)

<< operator (line 48)
>> operator (line 49)

```
53     int denominator;
54     static int gcd(int n, int d);
55   };
56
57   // Define nonmember function operators for relational operators
58   bool operator<(const Rational& r1, const Rational& r2);
59   bool operator<=(const Rational& r1, const Rational& r2);
60   bool operator>(const Rational& r1, const Rational& r2);
61   bool operator>=(const Rational& r1, const Rational& r2);
62   bool operator==(const Rational& r1, const Rational& r2);
63   bool operator!=(const Rational& r1, const Rational& r2);
64
65   // Define nonmember function operators for arithmetic operators
66   Rational operator+(const Rational& r1, const Rational& r2);
67   Rational operator-(const Rational& r1, const Rational& r2);
68   Rational operator*(const Rational& r1, const Rational& r2);
69   Rational operator/(const Rational& r1, const Rational& r2);
70
71   #endif
```

nonmember functions

nonmember functions

Listing 14.8 implements the header file. The member functions for augmented assignment operators +=, -=, *=, and /= change the contents of the calling object (lines 120–142). You have to assign the result of the operation to `this`. The comparison operators are implemented by invoking `r1.compareTo(r2)` (lines 213–241). The arithmetic operators +, -, *, and / are implemented by invoking the functions `add`, `subtract`, `multiply`, and `divide` (lines 244–262).

LISTING 14.8 RationalWithOperators.cpp

```
1    #include "RationalWithOperators.h"
2    #include <sstream>
3    #include <cstdlib> // For the abs function
4    Rational::Rational()
5    {
6      numerator = 0;
7      denominator = 1;
8    }
9
10   Rational::Rational(int numerator, int denominator)
11   {
12     int factor = gcd(numerator, denominator);
13     this->numerator = (denominator > 0 ? 1 : -1) * numerator / factor;
14     this->denominator = abs(denominator) / factor;
15   }
16
17   int Rational::getNumerator() const
18   {
19     return numerator;
20   }
21
22   int Rational::getDenominator() const
23   {
24     return denominator;
25   }
26
27   // Find GCD of two numbers
28   int Rational::gcd(int n, int d)
29   {
30     int n1 = abs(n);
31     int n2 = abs(d);
```

include header

```
32    int gcd = 1;
33
34    for (int k = 1; k <= n1 && k <= n2; k++)
35    {
36      if (n1 % k == 0 && n2 % k == 0)
37        gcd = k;
38    }
39
40    return gcd;
41  }
42
43  Rational Rational::add(const Rational& secondRational) const
44  {
45    int n = numerator * secondRational.getDenominator() +
46      denominator * secondRational.getNumerator();
47    int d = denominator * secondRational.getDenominator();
48    return Rational(n, d);
49  }
50
51  Rational Rational::subtract(const Rational& secondRational) const
52  {
53    int n = numerator * secondRational.getDenominator()
54      - denominator * secondRational.getNumerator();
55    int d = denominator * secondRational.getDenominator();
56    return Rational(n, d);
57  }
58
59  Rational Rational::multiply(const Rational& secondRational) const
60  {
61    int n = numerator * secondRational.getNumerator();
62    int d = denominator * secondRational.getDenominator();
63    return Rational(n, d);
64  }
65
66  Rational Rational::divide(const Rational& secondRational) const
67  {
68    int n = numerator * secondRational.getDenominator();
69    int d = denominator * secondRational.numerator;
70    return Rational(n, d);
71  }
72
73  int Rational::compareTo(const Rational& secondRational) const
74  {
75    Rational temp = subtract(secondRational);
76    if (temp.getNumerator() < 0)
77      return -1;
78    else if (temp.getNumerator() == 0)
79      return 0;
80    else
81      return 1;
82  }
83
84  bool Rational::equals(const Rational& secondRational) const
85  {
86    if (compareTo(secondRational) == 0)
87      return true;
88    else
89      return false;
90  }
91
```

```
92   int Rational::intValue() const
93   {
94     return getNumerator() / getDenominator();
95   }
96
97   double Rational::doubleValue() const
98   {
99     return 1.0 * getNumerator() / getDenominator();
100  }
101
102  string Rational::toString() const
103  {
104    stringstream ss;
105    ss << numerator;
106
107    if (denominator > 1)
108      ss << "/" << denominator;
109
110    return ss.str();
111  }
112
113  Rational::Rational(int numerator) // Suitable for type conversion       constructor
114  {
115    this->numerator = numerator;
116    this->denominator = 1;
117  }
118
119  // Define function operators for augmented operators
120  Rational& Rational::operator+=(const Rational& secondRational)          augmented assignment
121  {                                                                            operators
122    *this = add(secondRational);
123    return *this;
124  }
125
126  Rational& Rational::operator-=(const Rational& secondRational)
127  {
128    *this = subtract(secondRational);
129    return *this;
130  }
131
132  Rational& Rational::operator*=(const Rational& secondRational)
133  {
134    *this = multiply(secondRational);
135    return *this;
136  }
137
138  Rational& Rational::operator/=(const Rational& secondRational)
139  {
140    *this = divide(secondRational);
141    return *this;
142  }
143
144  // Define function operator []
145  int& Rational::operator[](int index)                                   [] operator
146  {
147    if (index == 0)
148      return numerator;
149    else
150      return denominator;
151  }
```

prefix ++

postfix ++

unary + operator

<< operator

```
152
153    // Define function operators for prefix ++ and --
154    Rational& Rational::operator++()
155    {
156      numerator += denominator;
157      return *this;
158    }
159
160    Rational& Rational::operator--()
161    {
162      numerator -= denominator;
163      return *this;
164    }
165
166    // Define function operators for postfix ++ and --
167    Rational Rational::operator++(int dummy)
168    {
169      Rational temp(numerator, denominator);
170      numerator += denominator;
171      return temp;
172    }
173
174    Rational Rational::operator--(int dummy)
175    {
176      Rational temp(numerator, denominator);
177      numerator -= denominator;
178      return temp;
179    }
180
181    // Define function operators for unary + and -
182    Rational Rational::operator+()
183    {
184      return *this;
185    }
186
187    Rational Rational::operator-()
188    {
189      return Rational(-numerator, denominator);
190    }
191
192    // Define the output and input operator
193    ostream& operator<<(ostream& out, const Rational& rational)
194    {
195      if (rational.denominator == 1)
196        out << rational.numerator;
197      else
198        out << rational.numerator << "/" << rational.denominator;
199      return out;
200    }
201
202    istream& operator>>(istream& in, Rational& rational)
203    {
204      cout << "Enter numerator: ";
205      in >> rational.numerator;
206
207      cout << "Enter denominator: ";
208      in >> rational.denominator;
209      return in;
210    }
211
```

```
212   // Define function operators for relational operators
213   bool operator<(const Rational& r1, const Rational& r2)
214   {
215      return r1.compareTo(r2) < 0;
216   }
217
218   bool operator<=(const Rational& r1, const Rational& r2)
219   {
220      return r1.compareTo(r2) <= 0;
221   }
222
223   bool operator>(const Rational& r1, const Rational& r2)
224   {
225      return r1.compareTo(r2) > 0;
226   }
227
228   bool operator>=(const Rational& r1, const Rational& r2)
229   {
230      return r1.compareTo(r2) >= 0;
231   }
232
233   bool operator==(const Rational& r1, const Rational& r2)
234   {
235      return r1.compareTo(r2) == 0;
236   }
237
238   bool operator!=(const Rational& r1, const Rational& r2)
239   {
240      return r1.compareTo(r2) != 0;
241   }
242
243   // Define nonmember function operators for arithmetic operators
244   Rational operator+(const Rational& r1, const Rational& r2)
245   {
246      return r1.add(r2);
247   }
248
249   Rational operator-(const Rational& r1, const Rational& r2)
250   {
251      return r1.subtract(r2);
252   }
253
254   Rational operator*(const Rational& r1, const Rational& r2)
255   {
256      return r1.multiply(r2);
257   }
258
259   Rational operator/(const Rational& r1, const Rational& r2)
260   {
261      return r1.divide(r2);
262   }
```

relational operators

arithmetic operators

Listing 14.9 gives a program for testing the new **Rational** class.

LISTING 14.9 TestRationalWithOperators.cpp

```
1   #include <iostream>
2   #include <string>
3   #include "RationalWithOperators.h"
4   using namespace std;
```

include new Rational

```
 5
 6   int main()
 7   {
 8       // Create and initialize two rational numbers r1 and r2.
 9       Rational r1(4, 2);
10       Rational r2(2, 3);
11
12       // Test relational operators
13       cout << r1 << " > " << r2 << " is " <<
14         ((r1 > r2) ? "true" : "false") << endl;
15       cout << r1 << " < " << r2 << " is " <<
16         ((r1 < r2) ? "true" : "false") << endl;
17       cout << r1 << " == " << r2 << " is " <<
18         ((r1 == r2) ? "true" : "false") << endl;
19       cout << r1 << " != " << r2 << " is " <<
20         ((r1 != r2) ? "true" : "false") << endl;
21
22       // Test toString, add, subtract, multiply, and divide operators
23       cout << r1 << " + " << r2 << " = " << r1 + r2 << endl;
24       cout << r1 << " - " << r2 << " = " << r1 - r2 << endl;
25       cout << r1 << " * " << r2 << " = " << r1 * r2 << endl;
26       cout << r1 << " / " << r2 << " = " << r1 / r2 << endl;
27
28       // Test augmented operators
29       Rational r3(1, 2);
30       r3 += r1;
31       cout << "r3 is " << r3 << endl;
32
33       // Test function operator []
34       Rational r4(1, 2);
35       r4[0] = 3; r4[1] = 4;
36       cout << "r4 is " << r4 << endl;
37
38       // Test function operators for prefix ++ and --
39       r3 = r4++;
40       cout << "r3 is " << r3 << endl;
41       cout << "r4 is " << r4 << endl;
42
43       // Test function operator for conversion
44       cout << "1 + " << r4 << " is " << (1 + r4) << endl;
45
46       return 0;
47   }
```

Margin annotations:
- relational operator
- arithmetic operator
- subscript operator []
- postfix ++
- type conversion

```
2 > 2/3 is true
2 < 2/3 is false
2 == 2/3 is false
2 != 2/3 is true
2 + 2/3 = 8/3
2 - 2/3 = 4/3
2 * 2/3 = 4/3
2 / 2/3 = 3
r3 is 5/2
r4 is 3/4
r3 is 3/4
r4 is 7/4
1 + 7/4 is 11/4
```

14.22 Can the [] operator be defined as a nonmember function?

14.23 What is wrong if the function + is defined as follows:

```
Rational operator+(const Rational& r1, const Rational& r2) const
```

14.24 If you remove the constructor `Rational(int numerator)` from both RationalWithOperators.h and RationalWithOperators.cpp, will there be a compile error in line 44 in TestRationalWithOperators.cpp? What will be the error?

14.25 Can the `gcd` function in the `Rational` class be defined as a constant function?

14.13 Overloading the = Operators

You need to overload the = operator to perform a customized copy operation for an object.

By default, the = operator performs a memberwise copy from one object to the other. For example, the following code copies `r2` to `r1`.

```
1  Rational r1(1, 2);
2  Rational r2(4, 5);
3  r1 = r2;
4  cout << "r1 is " << r1 << endl;
5  cout << "r2 is " << r2 << endl;
```

copy r2 to r1

So, the output is

```
r1 is 4/5
r2 is 4/5
```

The behavior of the = operator is the same as that of the default copy constructor. It performs a *shallow copy*, meaning that if the data field is a pointer to some object, the address of the pointer is copied rather than its contents. In Section 11.15, "Customizing Copy Constructors," you learned how to customize the copy constructor to perform a deep copy. However, customizing the copy constructor does not change the default behavior of the assignment copy operator =. For example, the **Course** class defined in Listing 11.19, CourseWithCustomCopyConstructor.h, has a pointer data field named **students** which points to an array of **string** objects. If you run the following code using the assignment operator to assign **course1** to **course2**, as shown in line 9 in Listing 14.10, you will see that both **course1** and **course2** have the same **students** array.

shallow copy

LISTING 14.10 DefaultAssignmentDemo.cpp

```
1  #include <iostream>
2  #include "CourseWithCustomCopyConstructor.h" // See Listing 11.19
3  using namespace std;
4
5  int main()
6  {
7    Course course1("Java Programming", 10);
8    Course course2("C++ Programming", 14);
9    course2 = course1;
10
11   course1.addStudent("Peter Pan"); // Add a student to course1
12   course2.addStudent("Lisa Ma"); // Add a student to course2
```

include Course header

create course1
create course2
assign to course2

add a student
add a student

get a student

get a student

```
13
14    cout << "students in course1: " <<
15      course1.getStudents()[0] << endl;
16    cout << "students in course2: " <<
17      course2.getStudents()[0] << endl;
18
19    return 0;
20  }
```

```
students in course1: Lisa Ma
students in course2: Lisa Ma
```

To change the way the default assignment operator = works, you need to overload the = operator, as shown in line 17 in Listing 14.11.

LISTING 14.11 CourseWithEqualsOperatorOverloaded.h

```
1   #ifndef COURSE_H
2   #define COURSE_H
3   #include <string>
4   using namespace std;
5
6   class Course
7   {
8   public:
9     Course(const string& courseName, int capacity);
10    ~Course(); // Destructor
11    Course(const Course&); // Copy constructor
12    string getCourseName() const;
13    void addStudent(const string& name);
14    void dropStudent(const string& name);
15    string* getStudents() const;
16    int getNumberOfStudents() const;
17    const Course& operator=(const Course& course);
18
19  private:
20    string courseName;
21    string* students;
22    int numberOfStudents;
23    int capacity;
24  };
25
26  #endif
```

overload = operator

In Listing 14.11, we define

```
const Course& operator=(const Course& course);
```

Why is the return type Course not void? C++ allows expressions with multiple assignments, such as:

```
course1 = course2 = course3;
```

In this statement, course3 is copied to course2, and then returns course2, and then course2 is copied to course1. So the = operator must have a valid return value type.

The implementation of the header file is given in Listing 14.12.

LISTING 14.12 CourseWithEqualsOperatorOverloaded.cpp

```cpp
1  #include <iostream>
2  #include "CourseWithEqualsOperatorOverloaded.h"
3  using namespace std;
4
5  Course::Course(const string& courseName, int capacity)
6  {
7    numberOfStudents = 0;
8    this->courseName = courseName;
9    this->capacity = capacity;
10   students = new string[capacity];
11 }
12
13 Course::~Course()
14 {
15   delete [] students;
16 }
17
18 string Course::getCourseName() const
19 {
20   return courseName;
21 }
22
23 void Course::addStudent(const string& name)
24 {
25   if (numberOfStudents >= capacity)
26   {
27     cout << "The maximum size of array exceeded" << endl;
28     cout << "Program terminates now" << endl;
29     exit(0);
30   }
31
32   students[numberOfStudents] = name;
33   numberOfStudents++;
34 }
35
36 void Course::dropStudent(const string& name)
37 {
38   // Left as an exercise
39 }
40
41 string* Course::getStudents() const
42 {
43   return students;
44 }
45
46 int Course::getNumberOfStudents() const
47 {
48   return numberOfStudents;
49 }
50
51 Course::Course(const Course& course) // Copy constructor
52 {
53   courseName = course.courseName;
54   numberOfStudents = course.numberOfStudents;
55   capacity = course.capacity;
56   students = new string[capacity];
57 }
58
```

overload = operator

copy courseName
copy numberofStudents
copy capacity
create array

return calling object

```
59  const Course& Course::operator=(const Course& course)
60  {
61      courseName = course.courseName;
62      numberOfStudents = course.numberOfStudents;
63      capacity = course.capacity;
64      students = new string[capacity];
65
66      return *this;
67  }
```

Line 66 returns the calling object using `*this`. Note that `this` is the pointer to the calling object, so `*this` refers to the calling object.

Listing 14.13 gives you a new test program that uses the overloaded = operator to copy a **Course** object. As shown in the sample output, the two courses have different **students** array.

LISTING 14.13   CustomAssignmentDemo.cpp

include Course header

```
1   #include <iostream>
2   #include "CourseWithEqualsOperatorOverloaded.h"
3   using namespace std;
4
5   int main()
6   {
```

create course1
create course2
assign to course2

```
7       Course course1("Java Programming", 10);
8       Course course2("C++ Programming", 14);
9       course2 = course1;
10
```

add a student
add a student

```
11      course1.addStudent("Peter Pan"); // Add a student to course1
12      course2.addStudent("Lisa Ma"); // Add a student to course2
13
14      cout << "students in course1: " <<
```

get a student

```
15        course1.getStudents()[0] << endl;
16      cout << "students in course2: " <<
```

get a student

```
17        course2.getStudents()[0] << endl;
18
19      return 0;
20  }
```

```
students in course1: Peter Pan
students in course2: Lisa Ma
```

Note

rule of three

The copy constructor, the = assignment operator, and the destructor are called the *rule of three*, or *the Big Three*. If they are not defined explicitly, all three are created by the compiler automatically. You should customize them if a data field in the class is a pointer that points to a dynamic generated array or object. If you have to customize one of the three, you should customize the other two as well.

14.26 In what situation should you overload the = operator?

KEY TERMS

CHAPTER SUMMARY

1. C++ allows you to overload operators to simplify operations for objects.

2. You can overload nearly all operators except ?:, ., .*, and ::.

3. You cannot change the operator precedence and associativity by overloading.

4. You can overload the subscript operator [] to access the contents of the object if desirable.

5. A C++ function may return a reference, which is an alias for the returned variable.

6. The augmented assignment operators (+=, -=, *=, /=), subscript operator [], prefix ++, and prefix -- operators are Lvalue operators. The functions for overloading these operators should return a reference.

7. The **friend** keyword can be used to give the trusted functions and classes access to a class's private members.

8. The operators [], ++, --, and () should be overloaded as member functions.

9. The << and >> operators should be overloaded as nonmember **friend** functions.

10. The arithmetic operators (+, -, *, /) and comparison operators (>, >=, ==, !=, <, <=) should be implemented as nonmember functions.

11. C++ can perform certain type conversions automatically if appropriate functions and constructors are defined.

12. By default, the memberwise shallow copy is used for the = operator. To perform a deep copy for the = operator, you need to overload the = operator.

QUIZ

Answer the quiz for this chapter online at www.cs.armstrong.edu/liang/cpp3e/quiz.html.

PROGRAMMING EXERCISES

Section 14.2

14.1 (*Use the* **Rational** *class*) Write a program that computes the following summation series using the **Rational** class:

$$\frac{1}{2} + \frac{2}{3} + \frac{3}{4} + \ \dots \ + \frac{98}{99} + \frac{99}{100}$$

*14.2 (*Demonstrate the benefits of encapsulation*) Rewrite the **Rational** class in Section 14.2 using a new internal representation for the numerator and denominator. Declare an array of two integers as follows:

```
int r[2];
```

Use **r[0]** to represent the numerator and **r[1]** to represent the denominator. The signatures of the functions in the **Rational** class are not changed, so a client application that uses the previous `Rational` class can continue to use this new `Rational` class without any modification.

Sections 14.3–14.13

*14.3 (*The* `Circle` *class*) Implement the relational operators (`<, <=, ==, !=, >, >=`) in the `Circle` class in Listing 10.9, CircleWithConstantMemberFunctions.h, to order the `Circle` objects according to their radii.

*14.4 (*The* `StackOfIntegers` *class*) Section 10.9, "Case Study: The `StackOfIntegers` Class," defined the `StackOfIntegers` class. Implement the subscript operator `[]` in this class to access the elements via the `[]` operator.

**14.5 (*Implement* `string` *operators*) The `string` class in the C++ standard library supports the overloaded operators, as shown in Table 10.1. Implement the following operators: `>>, ==, !=, >, >=` in the `MyString` class in Programming Exercise 11.15.

**14.6 (*Implement* `string` *operators*) The `string` class in the C++ standard library supports the overloaded operators, as shown in Table 10.1. Implement the following operators: `[]`, `+`, and `+=` in the `MyString` class in Programming Exercise 11.14.

VideoNote

The `Complex` class

*14.7 (*Math: The* `Complex` *class*) A complex number has the form $a + bi$, where a and b are real numbers and i is $\sqrt{-1}$. The numbers a and b are known as the real part and imaginary part of the complex number, respectively. You can perform addition, subtraction, multiplication, and division for complex numbers using the following formulas:

$$a + bi + c + di = (a + c) + (b + d)i$$
$$a + bi - (c + di) = (a - c) + (b - d)i$$
$$(a + bi) * (c + di) = (ac - bd) + (bc + ad)i$$
$$(a + bi) / (c + di) = (ac + bd) / (c^2 + d^2) + (bc - ad)i / (c^2 + d^2)$$

You can also obtain the absolute value for a complex number using the following formula:

$$|a + bi| = \sqrt{a^2 + b^2}$$

(A complex number can be interpreted as a point on a plane by identifying the (a, b) values as the coordinates of the point. The absolute value of the complex number corresponds to the distance of the point to the origin, as shown in Figure 14.2.)

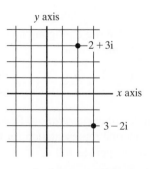

Figure 14.2 A complex number can be interpreted as a point in a plane.

Design a class named **Complex** for representing complex numbers and the functions **add**, **subtract**, **multiply**, **divide**, **abs** for performing complex-number operations, and the **toString** function for returning a string representation for a complex number. The **toString** function returns **a + bi** as a string. If b is **0**, it simply returns **a**.

Provide three constructors **Complex(a, b)**, **Complex(a)**, and **Complex()**. **Complex()** creates a **Complex** object for number **0** and **Complex(a)** creates a **Complex** object with **0** for **b**. Also provide the **getRealPart()** and **getImaginaryPart()** functions for returning the real and imaginary part of the complex number, respectively.

Overload the operators +, -, *, /, +=, -=, *=, /=, [], unary + and -, prefix ++ and --, postfix ++ and --, <<, >>.

Overload the operators +, -, *, / as nonmember functions. Overload [] so that **[0]** returns **a** and **[1]** returns **b**.

Write a test program that prompts the user to enter two complex numbers and display the result of their addition, subtraction, multiplication, and division. Here is a sample run:

```
Enter the first complex number: 3.5 5.5  ↵Enter
Enter the second complex number: -3.5 1  ↵Enter
(3.5 + 5.5i) + (-3.5 + 1.0i) = 0.0 + 6.5i
(3.5 + 5.5i) - (-3.5 + 1.0i) = 7.0 + 4.5i
(3.5 + 5.5i) * (-3.5 + 1.0i) = -17.75 + -15.75i
(3.5 + 5.5i) / (-3.5 + 1.0i) = -0.5094 + -1.7i
|3.5 + 5.5i| = 6.519202405202649
```

*14.8 (*Mandelbrot set*) A Mandelbrot set, named after Benoît Mandelbrot, is a set of points in the complex plane, defined using the following iteration:

$$z_{n+1} = z_n^2 + c$$

c is a complex number and the starting point of iteration is $z_0 = 0$. For a given c, the iteration will produce a sequence of complex numbers: $\{z_0, z_1, \ldots, z_n, \ldots\}$. It can be shown that the sequence either tends to infinity or stays bounded, depending on the value of c. For example, if c is 0, the sequence is $\{0, 0, \ldots\}$, which is bounded. If c is i, the sequence is $\{0, i, -1 + i, -i, -1 + i, \ldots\}$, which is bounded. If c is $1 + i$, the sequence is $\{0, 1 + i, 1 + 3i, \ldots\}$, which is unbounded. It is known that if the absolute value of a complex value z_i in the sequence is greater than 2, then the sequence is unbounded. The Mandelbrot set consists of the c value such that the sequence is bounded. For example, 0 and i are in the Mandelbrot set.

Write a program that prompts the user to enter a complex number c and determines if it is in the Mandelbrot set. Your program should compute $z1, z2, \ldots$, $z60$. If none of their absolute value exceeds **2**, we assume c is in the Mandelbrot set. Of course, there is always an error, but **60** iterations usually are enough. You can use the **Complex** class defined in Programming Exercise 14.7 or use the C++ **complex** class. The C++ **complex** class is a template class defined in the header file **<complex>**. You should use **complex<double>** to create a complex number in this program.

**14.9 (*The* EvenNumber *class*) Revise the EvenNumber class in Programming Exercise 9.11 to implement the preincrement, predecrement, postincrement, and postdecrement operators for getNext() and getPrevious() functions. Write a test program that creates an EvenNumber object for value 16 and invokes the ++ and -- operators to obtain next and previous even numbers.

**14.10 (*Convert decimals to fractions*) Write a program that prompts the user to enter a decimal number and display the number in a fraction. (*Hint*: read the decimal number as a string, extract the integer part and fractional part from the string, and use the Rational class to obtain a rational number for the decimal number.) Here are some sample runs:

```
Enter a decimal number: 3.25 ↵Enter
The fraction number is 13/4
```

```
Enter a decimal number: 0.45452 ↵Enter
The fraction number is 11363/25000
```

CHAPTER

15

INHERITANCE AND POLYMORPHISM

Objectives

- To define a derived class from a base class through inheritance (§15.2).

- To enable generic programming by passing objects of a derived type to a parameter of a base class type (§15.3).

- To know how to invoke the base class's constructors with arguments (§15.4.1).

- To understand constructor and destructor chaining (§15.4.2).

- To redefine functions in the derived class (§15.5).

- To distinguish between redefining and overloading functions (§15.5).

- To define generic functions using polymorphism (§15.6).

- To enable dynamic binding using virtual functions (§15.7).

- To distinguish between redefining and overriding functions (§15.7).

- To distinguish between static matching and dynamic binding (§15.7).

- To access protected members of a base class from derived classes (§15.8).

- To define abstract classes with pure virtual functions (§15.9).

- To cast an object of a base class type to a derived class type using the `static_cast` and `dynamic_cast` operators and know the differences between the two operators (§15.10).

15.1 Introduction

inheritance

Object-oriented programming allows you to define new classes from existing classes. This is called inheritance.

why inheritance?

Inheritance is an important and powerful feature in C++ for reusing software. Suppose you are to define classes to model circles, rectangles, and triangles. These classes have many common features. What is the best way to design them to avoid redundancy? The answer is to use inheritance—the subject of this chapter.

15.2 Base Classes and Derived Classes

VideoNote

Define derived classes

Inheritance enables you to define a general class (i.e., a base class) and later extend it to more specialized classes (i.e., derived classes).

You use a class to model objects of the same type. Different classes may have some common properties and behaviors, which can be generalized in a class that can be shared by other classes. Inheritance enables you to define a general class and later extend it to more specialized ones. The specialized classes inherit properties and functions from the general class.

Consider geometric objects. Suppose you want to design the classes to model geometric objects like circles and rectangles. Geometric objects have many common properties and behaviors. They can be drawn in a certain color, filled or unfilled. Thus, a general class `GeometricObject` can be used to model all geometric objects. This class contains the properties `color` and `filled` and their appropriate `get` and `set` functions. Assume that this class also contains the `toString()` function, which returns a string representation for the object. Since a circle is a special type of geometric object, it shares common properties and functions with other geometric objects. Thus, it makes sense to define the `Circle` class that extends the `GeometricObject` class. Likewise, `Rectangle` can also be defined as a derived class of `GeometricObject`. Figure 15.1 shows the relationships among these classes. A triangle pointing to the base class is used to denote the inheritance relationship between the two classes involved.

derived class
base class
parent class
superclass
child class
subclass

In C++ terminology, a class `C1` extended from another class `C2` is called a *derived class*, and `C2` is called a *base class*. We also refer to a base class as a *parent class* or a *superclass* and to a derived class as a *child class* or a *subclass*. A derived class inherits accessible data fields and functions from its base class and may also add new data fields and functions.

The `Circle` class inherits all accessible data fields and functions from the `GeometricObject` class. In addition, it has a new data field, `radius`, and its associated `get` and `set` functions. It also contains the `getArea()`, `getPerimeter()`, and `getDiameter()` functions for returning the area, perimeter, and diameter of the circle.

The `Rectangle` class inherits all accessible data fields and functions from the `GeometricObject` class. In addition, it has data fields `width` and `height` and its associated `get` and `set` functions. It also contains the `getArea()` and `getPerimeter()` functions for returning the area and perimeter of the rectangle.

The class definition for `GeometricObject` is shown in Listing 15.1. The preprocessor directives in lines 1 and 2 guard against multiple inclusions. The C++ `string` class header is included in line 3 to support the use of the `string` class in `GeometricObject`. The `isFilled()` function is the accessor for the `filled` data field. Since this data field is the `bool` type, the accessor function is named `isFilled()` by convention.

LISTING 15.1   GeometricObject.h

inclusion guard

```
1  #ifndef GEOMETRICOBJECT_H
2  #define GEOMETRICOBJECT_H
3  #include <string>
4  using namespace std;
```

```
5
6   class GeometricObject
7   {
8   public:                                                public members
9     GeometricObject();
10    GeometricObject(const string& color, bool filled);
11    string getColor() const;
12    void setColor(const string& color);
13    bool isFilled() const;
14    void setFilled(bool filled);
15    string toString() const;
16
17  private:                                               private members
18    string color;
19    bool filled;
20  }; // Must place semicolon here
21
22  #endif
```

GeometricObject	
-color: string -filled: bool	The color of the object (default: white). Indicates whether the object is filled with a color (default: false).
+GeometricObject() +GeometricObject(color: string, filled: bool) +getColor(): string const +setColor(color: string): void +isFilled(): bool const +setFilled(filled: bool): void +toString(): string const	Creates a GeometricObject. Creates a GeometricObject with the specified color and filled values. Returns the color. Sets a new color. Returns the filled property. Sets a new filled property. Returns a string representation of this object.

Circle	Rectangle
-radius: double	-width: double -height: double
+Circle() +Circle(radius: double) +Circle(radius: double, color: string, filled: bool) +getRadius(): double const +setRadius(radius: double): void +getArea(): double const +getPerimeter(): double const +getDiameter(): double const +toString(): string const	+Rectangle() +Rectangle(width: double, height: double) +Rectangle(width: double, height: double, color: string, filled: bool) +getWidth(): double const +setWidth(width: double): void +getHeight(): double const +setHeight(height: double): void +getArea(): double const +getPerimeter(): double const +toString(): string const

FIGURE 15.1 The GeometricObject class is the base class for Circle and Rectangle.

The GeometricObject class is implemented in Listing 15.2. The toString function (lines 35–38) returns a string that describes the object. The string operator + is used to concatenate two strings and returns a new string object.

LISTING 15.2 GeometricObject.cpp

header file

```
 1  #include "GeometricObject.h"
 2
```

no-arg constructor

```
 3  GeometricObject::GeometricObject()
 4  {
 5    color = "white";
 6    filled = false;
 7  }
 8
```

constructor

```
 9  GeometricObject::GeometricObject(const string& color, bool filled)
10  {
11    this->color = color;
12    this->filled = filled;
13  }
14
```

getColor

```
15  string GeometricObject::getColor() const
16  {
17    return color;
18  }
19
```

setColor

```
20  void GeometricObject::setColor(const string& color)
21  {
22    this->color = color;
23  }
24
```

isFilled

```
25  bool GeometricObject::isFilled() const
26  {
27    return filled;
28  }
29
```

setFilled

```
30  void GeometricObject::setFilled(bool filled)
31  {
32    this->filled = filled;
33  }
34
```

toString

```
35  string GeometricObject::toString() const
36  {
37    return "Geometric Object";
38  }
```

The class definition for `Circle` is shown in Listing 15.3. Line 5 defines that the `Circle` class is derived from the base class `GeometricObject`. The syntax

tells the compiler that the class is derived from the base class. So, all public members in `GeometricObject` are inherited in `Circle`.

LISTING 15.3 DerivedCircle.h

inclusion guard

```
 1  #ifndef CIRCLE_H
 2  #define CIRCLE_H
 3  #include "GeometricObject.h"
 4
```

extends GeometricObject

```
 5  class Circle: public GeometricObject
```

```
6   {
7   public:                                                              public members
8     Circle();
9     Circle(double);
10    Circle(double radius, const string& color, bool filled);
11    double getRadius() const;
12    void setRadius(double);
13    double getArea() const;
14    double getPerimeter() const;
15    double getDiameter() const;
16    string toString() const;
17
18  private:                                                             private members
19    double radius;
20  }; // Must place semicolon here
21
22  #endif
```

The `Circle` class is implemented in Listing 15.4.

LISTING 15.4 DerivedCircle.cpp

```
1   #include "DerivedCircle.h"                                           Circle header
2
3   // Construct a default circle object
4   Circle::Circle()                                                     no-arg constructor
5   {
6     radius = 1;
7   }
8
9   // Construct a circle object with specified radius
10  Circle::Circle(double radius)                                        constructor
11  {
12    setRadius(radius);
13  }
14
15  // Construct a circle object with specified radius,
16  //   color and filled values
17  Circle::Circle(double radius, const string& color, bool filled)      constructor
18  {
19    setRadius(radius);
20    setColor(color);
21    setFilled(filled);
22  }
23
24  // Return the radius of this circle
25  double Circle::getRadius() const                                     getRadius
26  {
27    return radius;
28  }
29
30  // Set a new radius
31  void Circle::setRadius(double radius)                                setRadius
32  {
33    this->radius = (radius >= 0) ? radius : 0;
34  }
35
36  // Return the area of this circle
37  double Circle::getArea() const                                       getArea
```

```
38   {
39       return radius * radius * 3.14159;
40   }
41
42   // Return the perimeter of this circle
43   double Circle::getPerimeter() const
44   {
45       return 2 * radius * 3.14159;
46   }
47
48   // Return the diameter of this circle
49   double Circle::getDiameter() const
50   {
51       return 2 * radius;
52   }
53
54   // Redefine the toString function
55   string Circle::toString() const
56   {
57       return "Circle object";
58   }
```

getPerimeter

getDiameter

The constructor `Circle(double radius, const string& color, bool filled)` is implemented by invoking the `setColor` and `setFilled` functions to set the `color` and `filled` properties (lines 17–22). These two public functions are defined the base class `GeometricObject` and are inherited in `Circle`. So, they can be used in the derived class.

You might attempt to use the data fields `color` and `filled` directly in the constructor as follows:

private member in base class

```
Circle::Circle(double radius, const string& c, bool f)
{
    this->radius = radius; // This is fine
    color = c; // Illegal since color is private in the base class
    filled = f; // Illegal since filled is private in the base class
}
```

This is wrong, because the private data fields `color` and `filled` in the `GeometricObject` class cannot be accessed in any class other than in the `GeometricObject` class itself. The only way to read and modify `color` and `filled` is through their `get` and `set` functions.

The class `Rectangle` is defined in Listing 15.5. Line 5 defines that the `Rectangle` class is derived from the base class `GeometricObject`. The syntax

Derived class   Base class

class Rectangle: **public** GeometricObject

tells the compiler that the class is derived from the base class. So, all public members in `GeometricObject` are inherited in `Rectangle`.

LISTING 15.5 DerivedRectangle.h

inclusion guard

```
1   #ifndef RECTANGLE_H
2   #define RECTANGLE_H
3   #include "GeometricObject.h"
4
```

```
5   class Rectangle: public GeometricObject          extends GeometricObject
6   {
7   public:                                          public members
8     Rectangle();
9     Rectangle(double width, double height);
10    Rectangle(double width, double height,
11      const string& color, bool filled);
12    double getWidth() const;
13    void setWidth(double);
14    double getHeight() const;
15    void setHeight(double);
16    double getArea() const;
17    double getPerimeter() const;
18    string toString() const;
19
20  private:                                          private members
21    double width;
22    double height;
23  };  // Must place semicolon here
24
25  #endif
```

The **Rectangle** class is implemented in Listing 15.6.

LISTING 15.6   DerivedRectangle.cpp

```
1   #include "DerivedRectangle.h"                     Rectangle header
2
3   // Construct a default rectangle object
4   Rectangle::Rectangle()                            no-arg constructor
5   {
6     width = 1;
7     height = 1;
8   }
9
10  // Construct a rectangle object with specified width and height
11  Rectangle::Rectangle(double width, double height)   constructor
12  {
13    setWidth(width);
14    setHeight(height);
15  }
16
17  Rectangle::Rectangle(                              constructor
18    double width, double height, const string& color, bool filled)
19  {
20    setWidth(width);
21    setHeight(height);
22    setColor(color);
23    setFilled(filled);
24  }
25
26  // Return the width of this rectangle
27  double Rectangle::getWidth() const                 getWidth
28  {
29    return width;
30  }
31
32  // Set a new radius
```

setWidth

```
33  void Rectangle::setWidth(double width)
34  {
35    this->width = (width >= 0) ? width : 0;
36  }
37
```

getHeight

```
38  // Return the height of this rectangle
39  double Rectangle::getHeight() const
40  {
41    return height;
42  }
43
```

setHeight

```
44  // Set a new height
45  void Rectangle::setHeight(double height)
46  {
47    this->height = (height >= 0) ? height : 0;
48  }
49
```

getArea

```
50  // Return the area of this rectangle
51  double Rectangle::getArea() const
52  {
53    return width * height;
54  }
55
```

getPerimeter

```
56  // Return the perimeter of this rectangle
57  double Rectangle::getPerimeter() const
58  {
59    return 2 * (width + height);
60  }
61
62  // Redefine the toString function, to be covered in Section 15.5
63  string Rectangle::toString() const
64  {
65    return "Rectangle object";
66  }
```

Listing 15.7 gives a test program that uses these three classes—GeometricObject, Circle, and Rectangles.

LISTING 15.7   TestGeometricObject.cpp

GeometricObject header
Circle header
Rectangle header

create a GeometricObject

create a Circle

```
1   #include "GeometricObject.h"
2   #include "DerivedCircle.h"
3   #include "DerivedRectangle.h"
4   #include <iostream>
5   using namespace std;
6
7   int main()
8   {
9     GeometricObject shape;
10    shape.setColor("red");
11    shape.setFilled(true);
12    cout << shape.toString() << endl
13      << " color: " << shape.getColor()
14      << " filled: " << (shape.isFilled() ? "true" : "false") << endl;
15
16    Circle circle(5);
17    circle.setColor("black");
18    circle.setFilled(false);
19    cout << circle.toString()<< endl
20      << " color: " << circle.getColor()
```

```
21          << " filled: " << (circle.isFilled() ? "true" : "false")
22          << " radius: " << circle.getRadius()
23          << " area: " << circle.getArea()
24          << " perimeter: " << circle.getPerimeter() << endl;
25
26      Rectangle rectangle(2, 3);
27      rectangle.setColor("orange");
28      rectangle.setFilled(true);
29      cout << rectangle.toString()<< endl
30          << " color: " << circle.getColor()
31          << " filled: " << (circle.isFilled() ? "true" : "false")
32          << " width: " << rectangle.getWidth()
33          << " height: " << rectangle.getHeight()
34          << " area: " << rectangle.getArea()
35          << " perimeter: " << rectangle.getPerimeter() << endl;
36
37      return 0;
38  }
```

create a Rectangle

```
Geometric Object
  color: red filled: true
Circle object
  color: black filled: false radius: 5 area: 78.5397 perimeter: 31.4159
Rectangle object
  color: black filled: false width: 2 height: 3 area: 6 perimeter: 10
```

The program creates a `GeometricObject` and invokes its functions `setColor`, `setFilled`, `toString`, `getColor`, and `isFilled` in lines 9–14.

The program creates a `Circle` object and invokes its functions `setColor`, `setFilled`, `toString`, `getColor`, `isFilled`, `getRadius`, `getArea`, and `getPerimeter` in lines 16–24. Note that the `setColor` and `setFilled` functions are defined in the `GeometricObject` class and inherited in the `Circle` class.

The program creates a `Rectangle` object and invokes its functions `setColor`, `setFilled`, `toString`, `getColor`, `isFilled`, `getWidth`, `getHeight`, `getArea`, and `getPerimeter` in lines 26–35. Note that the `setColor` and `setFilled` functions are defined in the `GeometricObject` class and inherited in the `Rectangle` class.

Note the following points about inheritance:

- Private data fields in a base class are not accessible outside the class. Therefore, they cannot be used directly in a derived class. They can, however, be accessed/mutated through public accessor/mutator if defined in the base class. *private data fields*

- Not all *is-a* relationships should be modeled using inheritance. For example, a square is a rectangle, but you should not define a `Square` class to extend a `Rectangle` class, because there is nothing to extend (or supplement) from a rectangle to a square. Rather you should define a `Square` class to extend the `GeometricObject` class. For class A to extend class B, A should contain more detailed information than B. *nonextensible is-a*

- Inheritance is used to model the *is-a* relationship. Do not blindly extend a class just for the sake of reusing functions. For example, it makes no sense for a `Tree` class to extend a `Person` class, even though they share common properties such as height and weight. A derived class and its base class must have the *is-a* relationship. *no blind extension*

- C++ allows you to derive a derived class from several classes. This capability is known as *multiple inheritance*, which is discussed in Supplement IV.A. *multiple inheritance*

Check Point

15.1 True or false? A derived class is a subset of a base class.

15.2 Can a class be derived from multiple base classes in C++?

15.3 Identify the problems in the following classes.

```cpp
class Circle
{
public:
  Circle(double radius)
  {
    radius = radius;
  }

  double getRadius()
  {
    return radius;
  }

  double getArea()
  {
    return radius * radius * 3.14159;
  }

private:
  double radius;
};

class B: Circle
{
public:
  B(double radius, double length)
  {
    radius = radius;
    length = length;
  }

  // Returns Circle's getArea() * length
  double getArea()
  {
    return getArea() * length;
  }

private:
  double length;
};
```

15.3 Generic Programming

Key Point

An object of a derived class can be passed wherever an object of a base type parameter is required. Thus a function can be used generically for a wide range of object arguments. This is known as generic programming.

generic programming

If a function's parameter type is a base class (e.g., `GeometricObject`), you may pass an object to this function of any of the parameter's derived classes (e.g., `Circle` or `Rectangle`).

For example, suppose you define a function as follows:

```cpp
void displayGeometricObject(const GeometricObject& shape)
{
  cout << shape.getColor() << endl;
}
```

The parameter type is `GeometricObject`. You can invoke this function in the following code:

```
displayGeometricObject(GeometricObject("black", true));
displayGeometricObject(Circle(5));
displayGeometricObject(Rectangle(2, 3));
```

Each statement creates an anonymous object and passes it to invoke `displayGeometricObject`. Since `Circle` and `Rectangle` are derived from `GeometricObject`, you can pass a `Circle` object or a `Rectangle` object to the `GeometricObject` parameter type in the `displayGeometricObject` function.

15.4 Constructors and Destructors

The constructor of a derived class first calls its base class's constructor before it executes its own code. The destructor of a derived class executes its own code then automatically calls its base class's destructor.

Key Point

A derived class inherits accessible data fields and functions from its base class. Does it inherit constructors or destructors? Can base class constructors and destructors be invoked from derived classes? We now consider these questions and their ramifications.

15.4.1 Calling Base Class Constructors

A constructor is used to construct an instance of a class. Unlike data fields and functions, the constructors of a base class are not inherited in the derived class. They can only be invoked from the constructors of the derived classes to initialize the data fields in the base class. You can invoke the base class's constructor from the constructor initializer list of the derived class. The syntax is as follows:

```
DerivedClass(parameterList): BaseClass()
{
  // Perform initialization
}
```

or

```
DerivedClass(parameterList): BaseClass(argumentList)
{
  // Perform initialization
}
```

The former invokes the no-arg constructor of its base class, and the latter invokes the base class constructor with the specified arguments.

A constructor in a derived class always invokes a constructor in its base class explicitly or implicitly. If a base constructor is not invoked explicitly, the base class's no-arg constructor is invoked by default. For example,

```
public Circle()
{
  radius = 1;
}
```

is equivalent to

```
public Circle(): GeometricObject()
{
  radius = 1;
}
```

```
public Circle(double radius)
{
  this->radius = radius;
}
```

is equivalent to

```
public Circle(double radius)
  : GeometricObject()
{
  this->radius = radius;
}
```

The `Circle(double radius, const string& color, bool filled)` constructor (lines 17–22) in Listing 15.4, DerivedCircle.cpp, can also be implemented by invoking the base class's constructor `GeometricObject(const string& color, bool filled)` as follows:

<table>
<tr><td style="text-align:right">invoke base constructor</td><td>

```
1  // Construct a circle object with specified radius, color and filled
2  Circle::Circle(double radius, const string& color, bool filled)
3    : GeometricObject(color, filled)
4  {
5    setRadius(radius);
6  }
```

</td></tr>
</table>

or

<table>
<tr><td style="text-align:right">initialize data field</td><td>

```
1  // Construct a circle object with specified radius, color and filled
2  Circle::Circle(double radius, const string& color, bool filled)
3    : GeometricObject(color, filled), radius(radius)
4  {
5  }
```

</td></tr>
</table>

The latter also initializes the data field `radius` in the constructor initializer. `radius` is a data field defined in the `Circle` class.

15.4.2 Constructor and Destructor Chaining

Constructing an instance of a class invokes the constructors of all the base classes along the inheritance chain. When constructing an object of a derived class, the derived class constructor first invokes its base class constructor before performing its own tasks. If a base class is derived from another class, the base class constructor invokes its parent class constructor before performing its own tasks. This process continues until the last constructor along the inheritance hierarchy is called. This is called *constructor chaining*. Conversely, the destructors are automatically invoked in reverse order. When an object of a derived class is destroyed, the derived class destructor is called. After it finishes its tasks, it invokes its base class destructor. This process continues until the last destructor along the inheritance hierarchy is called. This is called *destructor chaining*.

constructor chaining

destructor chaining

Consider the following code in Listing 15.8:

LISTING 15.8 ConstructorDestructorCallDemo.cpp

Person class

Employee class

```
1  #include <iostream>
2  using namespace std;
3
4  class Person
5  {
6  public:
7    Person()
8    {
9      cout << "Performs tasks for Person's constructor" << endl;
10   }
11
12   ~Person()
13   {
14     cout << "Performs tasks for Person's destructor" << endl;
15   }
16 };
17
18 class Employee: public Person
```

```
19  {
20  public:
21    Employee()
22    {
23      cout << "Performs tasks for Employee's constructor" << endl;
24    }
25
26    ~Employee()
27    {
28      cout << "Performs tasks for Employee's destructor" << endl;
29    }
30  };
31
32  class Faculty: public Employee                                    Faculty class
33  {
34  public:
35    Faculty()
36    {
37      cout << "Performs tasks for Faculty's constructor" << endl;
38    }
39
40    ~Faculty()
41    {
42      cout << "Performs tasks for Faculty's destructor" << endl;
43    }
44  };
45
46  int main()
47  {
48    Faculty faculty;                                               create a Faculty
49
50    return 0;
51  }
```

```
Performs tasks for Person's constructor
Performs tasks for Employee's constructor
Performs tasks for Faculty's constructor
Performs tasks for Faculty's destructor
Performs tasks for Employee's destructor
Performs tasks for Person's destructor
```

The program creates an instance of Faculty in line 48. Since Faculty is derived from Employee and Employee is derived from Person, Faculty's constructor invokes Employee's constructor before it performs its own task. Employee's constructor invokes Person's constructor before it performs its own task, as shown in the following figure:

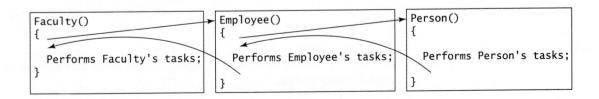

```
Faculty()                    Employee()                   Person()
{                            {                            {
    Performs Faculty's tasks;    Performs Employee's tasks;   Performs Person's tasks;
}                            }                            }
```

When the program exits, the **Faculty** object is destroyed. So the **Faculty**'s destructor is called, then **Employee**'s, and finally **Person**'s, as shown in the following figure:

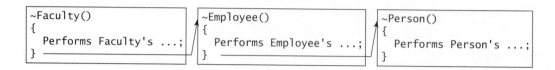

no-arg constructor

 Caution

If a class is designed to be extended, it is better to provide a *no-arg constructor* to avoid programming errors. Consider the following code:

```cpp
class Fruit
{
public:
  Fruit(int id)
  {
  }
};
```

```cpp
class Apple: public Fruit
{
public:
  Apple()
  {
  }
};
```

Since no constructor is explicitly defined in **Apple**, **Apple**'s default no-arg constructor is defined implicitly. Since **Apple** is a derived class of **Fruit**, **Apple**'s default constructor automatically invokes **Fruit**'s no-arg constructor. However, **Fruit** does not have a no-arg constructor, because **Fruit** has an explicit constructor defined. Therefore, the program cannot be compiled.

copy constructor
assignment operator

Note

If the base class has a customized copy constructor and assignment operator, you should customize these in the derived classes to ensure that the data fields in the base class are properly copied. Suppose class **Child** is derived from **Parent**. The code for the copy constructor in **Child** would typically look like this:

```cpp
Child::Child(const Child& object): Parent(object)
{
  // Write the code for copying data fields in Child
}
```

The code for the assignment operator in **Child** would typically look like this:

```cpp
Child& Child::operator=(const Child& object)
{
  Parent::operator(object);
  // Write the code for copying data fields in Child
}
```

destructor

When a destructor for a derived class is invoked, it automatically invokes the destructor in the base class. The destructor in the derived class only needs to destroy the dynamically created memory in the derived class.

15.4 True or false? When invoking a constructor from a derived class, its base class's no-arg constructor is always invoked.

✓ Check Point

15.5 What is the printout of running the program in (a)? What problem arises in compiling the program in (b)?

```cpp
#include <iostream>
using namespace std;

class Parent
{
public:
  Parent()
  {
    cout <<
      "Parent's no-arg constructor is invoked";
  }
};

class Child: public Parent
{
};

int main()
{
  Child c;

  return 0;
}
```
(a)

```cpp
#include <iostream>
using namespace std;

class Parent
{
public:
  Parent(int x)
  {
  }
};

class Child: public Parent
{
};

int main()
{
  Child c;

  return 0;
}
```
(b)

15.6 Show the output of the following code:

```cpp
#include <iostream>
using namespace std;

class Parent
{
public:
  Parent()
  {
    cout << "Parent's no-arg constructor is invoked" << endl;
  }

  ~Parent()
  {
    cout << "Parent's destructor is invoked" << endl;
  }
};

class Child: public Parent
{
public:
  Child()
```

```
                             {
                               cout << "Child's no-arg constructor is invoked" << endl;
                             }

                             ~Child()
                             {
                               cout << "Child's destructor is invoked" << endl;
                             }
                           };

                           int main()
                           {
                             Child c1;
                             Child c2;

                             return 0;
                           }
```

15.7   If a base class has a customized copy constructor and assignment operator, how should you define the copy constructor and the assignment operator in the derived class?

15.8   If a base class has a customized destructor, are you required to implement the destructor in the derived class?

15.5 Redefining Functions

Key Point

A function defined in the base class can be redefined in the derived classes.

The `toString()` function is defined in the `GeometricObject` class to return a string `"Geometric object"` (lines 35–38 in Listing 15.2) as follows:

```
string GeometricObject::toString() const
{
  return "Geometric object";
}
```

To redefine a base class's function in the derived class, you need to add the function's prototype in the derived class's header file, and provide a new implementation for the function in the derived class's implementation file.

The `toString()` function is redefined in the `Circle` class (lines 55–58 in Listing 15.4) as follows:

```
string Circle::toString() const
{
  return "Circle object";
}
```

The `toString()` function is redefined in the `Rectangle` class (lines 63–66 in Listing 15.6) as follows:

```
string Rectangle::toString() const
{
  return "Rectangle object";
}
```

So, the following code

create GeometricObject
invoke toString

```
1  GeometricObject shape;
2  cout << "shape.toString() returns " << shape.toString() << endl;
3
```

```
4  Circle circle(5);
5  cout << "circle.toString() returns " << circle.toString() << endl;
6
7  Rectangle rectangle(4, 6);
8  cout << "rectangle.toString() returns "
9    << rectangle.toString() << endl;
```

create Circle

invoke toString

create Rectangle

invoke toString

displays:

```
shape.toString() returns Geometric object
circle.toString() returns Circle object
rectangle.toString() returns Rectangle object
```

The code creates a `GeometricObject` in line 1. The `toString` function defined in `GeometricObject` is invoked in line 2, since `shape`'s type is `GeometricObject`.

The code creates a `Circle` object in line 4. The `toString` function defined in `Circle` is invoked in line 5, since `circle`'s type is `Circle`.

The code creates a `Rectangle` object in line 7. The `toString` function defined in `Rectangle` is invoked in line 9, since `rectangle`'s type is `Rectangle`.

If you wish to invoke the `toString` function defined in the `GeometricObject` class on the calling object `circle`, use the scope resolution operator (`::`) with the base class name. For example, the following code

invoke function in the base

```
Circle circle(5);
cout << "circle.toString() returns " << circle.toString() << endl;
cout << "invoke the base class's toString() to return "
  << circle.GeometricObject::toString();
```

displays

```
circle.toString() returns Circle object
invoke the base class's toString() to return Geometric object
```

 Note

In Section 6.7, "Overloading Functions," you learned about overloading functions. Overloading a function is a way to provide more than one function with the same name but with different signatures to distinguish them. To redefine a function, the function must be defined in the derived class using the same signature and same return type as in its base class.

redefining versus overloading

15.9 What is the difference between overloading a function and redefining a function?

 Check Point

15.10 True or false? (1) You can redefine a private function defined in a base class. (2) You can redefine a static function defined in a base class. (3) You can redefine a constructor.

15.6 Polymorphism

Polymorphism means that a variable of a supertype can refer to a subtype object.

The three pillars of object-oriented programming are encapsulation, inheritance, and polymorphism. You have already learned the first two. This section introduces polymorphism.

First, let us define two useful terms: subtype and supertype. A class defines a type. A type defined by a derived class is called a *subtype*, and a type defined by its base class is called a *supertype*. Therefore, you can say that `Circle` is a subtype of `GeometricObject` and `GeometricObject` is a supertype for `Circle`.

 Key Point

 VideoNote

Polymorphism and virtual functions

subtype
supertype

The inheritance relationship enables a derived class to inherit features from its base class with additional new features. A derived class is a specialization of its base class; every instance of a derived class is also an instance of its base class, but not vice versa. For example, every circle is a geometric object, but not every geometric object is a circle. Therefore, you can always pass an instance of a derived class to a parameter of its base class type. Consider the code in Listing 15.9.

LISTING 15.9 PolymorphismDemo.cpp

```cpp
1   #include <iostream>
2   #include "GeometricObject.h"
3   #include "DerivedCircle.h"
4   #include "DerivedRectangle.h"
5
6   using namespace std;
7
8   void displayGeometricObject(const GeometricObject& g)
9   {
10      cout << g.toString() << endl;
11  }
12
13  int main()
14  {
15      GeometricObject geometricObject;
16      displayGeometricObject(geometricObject);
17
18      Circle circle(5);
19      displayGeometricObject(circle);
20
21      Rectangle rectangle(4, 6);
22      displayGeometricObject(rectangle);
23
24      return 0;
25  }
```

displayGeometricObject

invoke toString

pass a GeometricObject

pass a Circle

pass a Rectangle

```
Geometric object
Geometric object
Geometric object
```

The function **displayGeometricObject** (line 8) takes a parameter of the **Geometric-Object** type. You can invoke **displayGeometricObject** by passing any instance of **GeometricObject**, **Circle**, and **Rectangle** (lines 16, 19, 22). An object of a derived class can be used wherever its base class object is used. This is commonly known as *polymorphism* (from a Greek word meaning "many forms"). In simple terms, polymorphism means that a variable of a supertype can refer to a subtype object.

polymorphism

15.11 What is a subtype and a supertype? What is polymorphism?

15.7 Virtual Functions and Dynamic Binding

A function can be implemented in several classes along the inheritance chain. Virtual functions *enable the system to decide which function is invoked at runtime based on the actual type of the object.*

The program in Listing 15.9 defines the **displayGeometricObject** function that invokes the **toString** function on a **GeometricObject** (line 10).

The `displayGeometricObject` function is invoked in lines 16, 19, 22 by passing an object of `GeometricObject`, `Circle`, and `Rectangle`, respectively. As shown in the output, the `toString()` function defined in class `GeometricObject` is invoked. Can you invoke the `toString()` function defined in `Circle` when executing `display-GeometricObject(circle)`, the `toString()` function defined in `Rectangle` when executing `displayGeometicObject(rectangle)`, and the `toString()` function defined in `GeometricObject` when executing `displayGeometricObject(geometricObject)`? You can do so simply by declaring `toString` as a virtual function in the base class `GeometricObject`.

virtual function

Suppose you replace line 15 in Listing 15.1 with the following function declaration:

```
virtual string toString() const;
```

define virtual function

Now if you rerun Listing 15.9, you will see the following output:

```
Geometric object
Circle object
Rectangle object
```

With the `toString()` function defined as `virtual` in the base class, C++ dynamically determines which `toString()` function to invoke at runtime. When invoking `displayGeometricObject(circle)`, a `Circle` object is passed to g by reference. Since g refers to an object of the `Circle` type, the `toString` function defined in class `Circle` is invoked. The capability of determining which function to invoke at runtime is known as *dynamic binding*.

virtual

dynamic binding

> **Note**
> In C++, *redefining* a virtual function in a derived class is called *overriding a function*.

overriding a function

To enable dynamic binding for a function, you need to do two things:

- The function must be defined `virtual` in the base class.

- The variable that references the object must be passed by reference or passed as a pointer in the virtual function.

Listing 15.9 passes the object to a parameter by reference (line 8); alternatively, you can rewrite lines 8–11 by passing a pointer, as in Listing 15.10:

LISTING 15.10 VirtualFunctionDemoUsingPointer.cpp

```
1  #include <iostream>
2  #include "GeometricObject.h" // toString() is defined virtual now
3  #include "DerivedCircle.h"
4  #include "DerivedRectangle.h"
5
6  using namespace std;
7
8  void displayGeometricObject(const GeometricObject* g)
9  {
10    cout << (*g).toString() << endl;
11  }
12
13  int main()
```

pass a pointer

invoke `toString`

```
14  {
15    displayGeometricObject(&GeometricObject());
16    displayGeometricObject(&Circle(5));
17    displayGeometricObject(&Rectangle(4, 6));
18
19    return 0;
20  }
```

pass a GeometricObject
pass a Circle
pass a Rectangle

```
Geometric object
Circle object
Rectangle object
```

However, if the object argument is passed by value, the virtual functions are not bound dynamically. As shown in Listing 15.11, even though the function is defined to be virtual, the output is the same as it would be without using the virtual function.

LISTING 15.11 VirtualFunctionDemoPassByValue.cpp

```
1  #include <iostream>
2  #include "GeometricObject.h"
3  #include "DerivedCircle.h"
4  #include "DerivedRectangle.h"
5
6  using namespace std;
7
8  void displayGeometricObject(GeometricObject g)
9  {
10   cout << g.toString() << endl;
11  }
12
13  int main()
14  {
15    displayGeometricObject(GeometricObject());
16    displayGeometricObject(Circle(5));
17    displayGeometricObject(Rectangle(4, 6));
18
19    return 0;
20  }
```

pass object by value

invoke toString

pass a GeometricObject
pass a Circle
pass a Rectangle

```
Geometric object
Geometric object
Geometric object
```

Note the following points regarding virtual functions:

virtual

- If a function is defined **virtual** in a base class, it is automatically **virtual** in all its derived classes. The keyword **virtual** need not be added in the function declaration in the derived class.

- Matching a function signature and binding a function implementation are two separate issues. The *declared type* of the variable decides which function to match at compile time. This is *static binding*. The compiler finds a matching function according to parameter type, number of parameters, and order of the parameters at compile time. A virtual function may be implemented in several derived classes. C++ dynamically binds the implementation of the function at runtime, decided by the *actual class* of the object referenced by the variable. This is *dynamic binding*.

static binding versus dynamic binding

- If a function defined in a base class needs to be redefined in its derived classes, you should define it virtual to avoid confusions and mistakes. On the other hand, if a function will not be redefined, it is more efficient not to declare it virtual, because more time and system resource are required to bind virtual functions dynamically at runtime. We call a class with a virtual function a *polymorphic type*.

polymorphic type

15.12 Answer the following questions for the program below:

```
1   #include <iostream>
2   using namespace std;
3
4   class Parent
5   {
6   public:
7     void f()
8     {
9       cout << "invoke f from Parent" << endl;
10    }
11  };
12
13  class Child: public Parent
14  {
15  public:
16    void f()
17    {
18      cout << "invoke f from Child" << endl;
19    }
20  };
21
22  void p(Parent a)
23  {
24    a.f();
25  }
26
27  int main()
28  {
29    Parent a;
30    a.f();
31    p(a);
32
33    Child b;
34    b.f();
35    p(b);
36
37    return 0;
38  }
```

a. What is the output of this program?

b. What will be the output if line 7 is replaced by `virtual void f()`?

c. What will be the output if line 7 is replaced by `virtual void f()` and line 22 is replaced by `void p(Parent& a)`?

15.13 What is static binding and what is dynamic binding?

15.14 Is declaring virtual functions enough to enable dynamic binding?

15.15 Show the output of the following code:

```
#include <iostream>
#include <string>
using namespace std;

class Person
{
public:
  void printInfo()
  {
    cout << getInfo() << endl;
  }

  virtual string getInfo()
  {
    return "Person";
  }
};

class Student: public Person
{
public:
  virtual string getInfo()
  {
    return "Student";
  }
};

int main()
{
  Person().printInfo();
  Student().printInfo();
}
```

(a)

```
#include <iostream>
#include <string>
using namespace std;

class Person
{
public:
  void printInfo()
  {
    cout << getInfo() << endl;
  }

  string getInfo()
  {
    return "Person";
  }
};

class Student: public Person
{
public:
  string getInfo()
  {
    return "Student";
  }
};

int main()
{
  Person().printInfo();
  Student().printInfo();
}
```

(b)

15.16 Is it a good practice to define all functions virtual?

15.8 The **protected** Keyword

Key Point

A protected member of a class can be accessed from a derived class.

So far, you have used the **private** and **public** keywords to specify whether data fields and functions can be accessed from outside the class. Private members can be accessed only from inside the class or from **friend** functions and **friend** classes, and public members can be accessed from any other classes.

Often it is desirable to allow derived classes to access data fields or functions defined in the base class but not allow nonderived classes to do so. For this purpose, you can use the **protected** keyword. A protected data field or a protected function in a base class can be accessed in its derived classes.

protected

visibility keyword

The keywords **private**, **protected**, and **public** are known as *visibility* or *accessibility keywords* because they specify how class and class members are accessed. Their visibility increases in this order:

Visibility increases
→
private, protected, public

Listing 15.12 demonstrates the use of **protected** keywords.

LISTING 15.12 VisibilityDemo.cpp

```cpp
1  #include <iostream>
2  using namespace std;
3
4  class B
5  {
6  public:
7    int i;
8
9  protected:
10   int j;
11
12 private:
13   int k;
14 };
15
16 class A: public B
17 {
18 public:
19   void display() const
20   {
21     cout << i << endl; // Fine, can access it
22     cout << j << endl; // Fine, can access it
23     cout << k << endl; // Wrong, cannot access it
24   }
25 };
26
27 int main()
28 {
29   A a;
30   cout << a.i << endl; // Fine, can access it
31   cout << a.j << endl; // Wrong, cannot access it
32   cout << a.k << endl; // Wrong, cannot access it
33
34   return 0;
35 }
```

public

protected

private

Since A is derived from B and j is protected, j can be accessed from class A in line 22. Since k is private, k cannot be accessed from class A.

Since i is public, i can be accessed from a.i in line 30. Since j and k are not public, they cannot be accessed from the object a in lines 31–32.

15.17 If a member is declared private in a class, can it be accessed from other classes? If a member is declared protected in a class, can it be accessed from other classes? If a member is declared public in a class, can it be accessed from other classes?

Check Point

15.9 Abstract Classes and Pure Virtual Functions

An abstract class cannot be used to create objects. An abstract class can contain abstract functions, which are implemented in concrete derived classes.

VideoNote
Abstract classes

Key Point

In the inheritance hierarchy, classes become more specific and concrete *with each new derived class*. If you move from a derived class back up to its parent and ancestor classes, the classes become more general and less specific. Class design should ensure that a base class contains

abstract class

common features of its derived classes. Sometimes a base class is so abstract that it cannot have any specific instances. Such a class is referred to as an *abstract class*.

In Section 15.2, `GeometricObject` was defined as the base class for `Circle` and `Rectangle`. `GeometricObject` models common features of geometric objects. Both `Circle` and `Rectangle` contain the `getArea()` and `getPerimeter()` functions for computing the area and perimeter of a circle and a rectangle. Since you can compute areas and perimeters for all geometric objects, it is better to define the `getArea()` and `getPerimeter()` functions in the `GeometricObject` class. However, these functions cannot be implemented in the `GeometricObject` class, because their implementation is dependent on the specific type of geometric object. Such functions are referred to as *abstract functions*. After you define the abstract functions in `GeometricObject`, `GeometricObject` becomes an abstract class. The new `GeometricObject` class is shown in Figure 15.2. In UML graphic notation, the names of abstract classes and their abstract functions are italicized, as shown in Figure 15.2.

abstract function

pure virtual function

In C++, abstract functions are called *pure virtual functions*. A class that contains pure virtual functions becomes an abstract class. A pure virtual function is defined this way:

Place optional **const** for ———————————┐   ┌——— Indicates pure virtual function
constant function here.   │   │

```
virtual double getArea() = 0;
```

The `= 0` notation indicates that `getArea` is a pure virtual function. A pure virtual function does not have a body or implementation in the base class.

Listing 15.13 defines the new abstract `GeometricObject` class with two pure virtual functions in lines 18–19.

LISTING 15.13 AbstractGeometricObject.h

```
1   #ifndef GEOMETRICOBJECT_H
2   #define GEOMETRICOBJECT_H
3   #include <string>
4   using namespace std;
5
6   class GeometricObject
7   {
8   protected:
9     GeometricObject();
10    GeometricObject(const string& color, bool filled);
11
12  public:
13    string getColor() const;
14    void setColor(const string& color);
15    bool isFilled() const;
16    void setFilled(bool filled);
17    string toString() const;
18    virtual double getArea() const = 0;
19    virtual double getPerimeter() const = 0;
20
21  private:
22    string color;
23    bool filled;
24  }; // Must place semicolon here
25
26  #endif
```

pure virtual function
pure virtual function

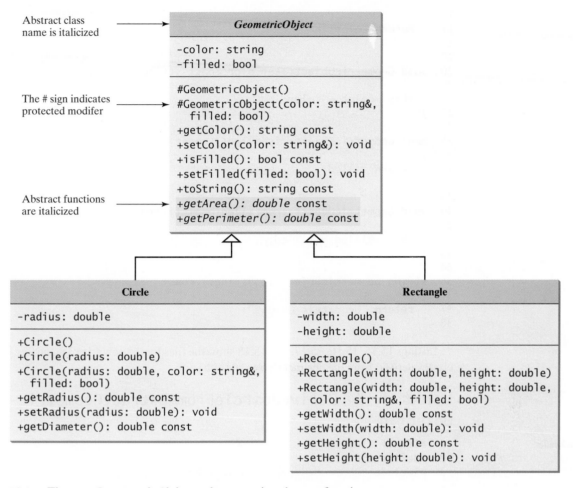

FIGURE 15.2   The new `GeometricObject` class contains abstract functions.

`GeometricObject` is just like a regular class, except that you cannot create objects from it because it is an abstract class. If you attempt to create an object from `GeometricObject`, the compiler will report an error.

Listing 15.14 gives an implementation of the `GeometricObject` class.

LISTING 15.14   AbstractGeometricObject.cpp

```
1  #include "AbstractGeometricObject.h"                              include header
2
3  GeometricObject::GeometricObject()
4  {
5    color = "white";
6    filled = false;
7  }
8
9  GeometricObject::GeometricObject(const string& color, bool filled)
10  {
11    setColor(color);
12    setFilled(filled);
13  }
14
15  string GeometricObject::getColor() const
```

```
16  {
17    return color;
18  }
19
20  void GeometricObject::setColor(const string& color)
21  {
22    this->color = color;
23  }
24
25  bool GeometricObject::isFilled() const
26  {
27    return filled;
28  }
29
30  void GeometricObject::setFilled(bool filled)
31  {
32    this->filled = filled;
33  }
34
35  string GeometricObject::toString() const
36  {
37    return "Geometric Object";
38  }
```

Listings 15.15, 15.16, 15.17, and 15.18 show the files for the new `Circle` and `Rectangle` classes derived from the abstract `GeometricObject`.

LISTING 15.15   DerivedCircleFromAbstractGeometric-Object.h

include header

```
1   #ifndef CIRCLE_H
2   #define CIRCLE_H
3   #include "AbstractGeometricObject.h"
4
5   class Circle: public GeometricObject
6   {
7   public:
8     Circle();
9     Circle(double);
10    Circle(double radius, const string& color, bool filled);
11    double getRadius() const;
12    void setRadius(double);
13    double getArea() const;
14    double getPerimeter() const;
15    double getDiameter() const;
16
17  private:
18    double radius;
19  };  // Must place semicolon here
20
21  #endif
```

LISTING 15.16   DerivedCircleFromAbstractGeometric-Object.cpp

inclusion guard

AbstractGeometric-
Object header

```
1   #include "DerivedCircleFromAbstractGeometricObject.h"
2
3   // Construct a default circle object
4   Circle::Circle()
```

```
 5  {
 6     radius = 1;
 7  }
 8
 9  // Construct a circle object with specified radius
10  Circle::Circle(double radius)
11  {
12     setRadius(radius);
13  }
14
15  // Construct a circle object with specified radius, color, filled
16  Circle::Circle(double radius, const string& color, bool filled)
17  {
18     setRadius(radius);
19     setColor(color);
20     setFilled(filled);
21  }
22
23  // Return the radius of this circle
24  double Circle::getRadius() const
25  {
26     return radius;
27  }
28
29  // Set a new radius
30  void Circle::setRadius(double radius)
31  {
32     this->radius = (radius >= 0) ? radius : 0;
33  }
34
35  // Return the area of this circle
36  double Circle::getArea() const
37  {
38     return radius * radius * 3.14159;
39  }
40
41  // Return the perimeter of this circle
42  double Circle::getPerimeter() const
43  {
44     return 2 * radius * 3.14159;
45  }
46
47  // Return the diameter of this circle
48  double Circle::getDiameter() const
49  {
50     return 2 * radius;
51  }
```

LISTING 15.17 DerivedRectangleFromAbstractGeometric-Object.h

```
1  #ifndef RECTANGLE_H
2  #define RECTANGLE_H
3  #include "AbstractGeometricObject.h"
4
5  class Rectangle: public GeometricObject
6  {
7  public:
8     Rectangle();
```

inclusion guard

AbstractGeometric-Object header

```
 9      Rectangle(double width, double height);
10      Rectangle(double width, double height,
11          const string& color, bool filled);
12      double getWidth() const;
13      void setWidth(double);
14      double getHeight() const;
15      void setHeight(double);
16      double getArea() const;
17      double getPerimeter() const;
18
19   private:
20      double width;
21      double height;
22   };   // Must place semicolon here
23
24   #endif
```

LISTING 15.18 DerivedRectangleFromAbstractGeometric-Object.cpp

inclusion guard

AbstractGeometric-
Object header

```
 1   #include "DerivedRectangleFromAbstractGeometricObject.h"
 2
 3   // Construct a default retangle object
 4   Rectangle::Rectangle()
 5   {
 6     width = 1;
 7     height = 1;
 8   }
 9
10   // Construct a rectangle object with specified width and height
11   Rectangle::Rectangle(double width, double height)
12   {
13     setWidth(width);
14     setHeight(height);
15   }
16
17   // Construct a rectangle object with width, height, color, filled
18   Rectangle::Rectangle(double width, double height,
19       const string& color, bool filled)
20   {
21     setWidth(width);
22     setHeight(height);
23     setColor(color);
24     setFilled(filled);
25   }
26
27   // Return the width of this rectangle
28   double Rectangle::getWidth() const
29   {
30     return width;
31   }
32
33   // Set a new radius
34   void Rectangle::setWidth(double width)
35   {
36     this->width = (width >= 0) ? width : 0;
37   }
38
39   // Return the height of this rectangle
```

```
40  double Rectangle::getHeight() const
41  {
42    return height;
43  }
44
45  // Set a new height
46  void Rectangle::setHeight(double height)
47  {
48    this->height = (height >= 0) ? height : 0;
49  }
50
51  // Return the area of this rectangle
52  double Rectangle::getArea() const
53  {
54    return width * height;
55  }
56
57  // Return the perimeter of this rectangle
58  double Rectangle::getPerimeter() const
59  {
60    return 2 * (width + height);
61  }
```

You may be wondering whether the abstract functions `getArea` and `getPerimeter` should be removed from the `GeometricObject` class. The following example in Listing 15.19 shows the benefits of defining them in the `GeometricObject` class.

This example presents a program that creates two geometric objects (a circle and a rectangle), invokes the `equalArea` function to check whether the two objects have equal areas, and invokes the `displayGeometricObject` function to display the objects.

LISTING 15.19 TestAbstractGeometricObject.cpp

```
1  #include "AbstractGeometricObject.h"                            include header file
2  #include "DerivedCircleFromAbstractGeometricObject.h"
3  #include "DerivedRectangleFromAbstractGeometricObject.h"
4  #include <iostream>
5  using namespace std;
6
7  // A function for comparing the areas of two geometric objects
8  bool equalArea(const GeometricObject& g1,
9    const GeometricObject& g2)
10 {
11   return g1.getArea() == g2.getArea();                          dynamic binding
12 }
13
14 // A function for displaying a geometric object
15 void displayGeometricObject(const GeometricObject& g)
16 {
17   cout << "The area is " << g.getArea() << endl;                dynamic binding
18   cout << "The perimeter is " << g.getPerimeter() << endl;      dynamic binding
19 }
20
21 int main()
22 {
23   Circle circle(5);
24   Rectangle rectangle(5, 3);
25
26   cout << "Circle info: " << endl;
27   displayGeometricObject(circle);
```

```
28
29    cout << "\nRectangle info: " << endl;
30    displayGeometricObject(rectangle);
31
32    cout << "\nThe two objects have the same area? " <<
33      (equalArea(circle, rectangle) ? "Yes" : "No") << endl;
34
35    return 0;
36  }
```

```
Circle info:
The area is 78.5397
The perimeter is 31.4159

Rectangle info:
The area is 15
The perimeter is 16

The two objects have the same area? No
```

The program creates a `Circle` object and a `Rectangle` object in lines 23–24.

The pure virtual functions `getArea()` and `getPerimeter()` defined in the `GeometricObject` class are overridden in the `Circle` class and the `Rectangle` class.

When invoking `displayGeometricObject(circle1)` (line 27), the functions `getArea` and `getPerimeter` defined in the `Circle` class are used, and when invoking `displayGeometricObject(rectangle)` (line 30), the functions `getArea` and `getPerimeter` defined in the `Rectangle` class are used. C++ dynamically determines which of these functions to invoke at runtime, depending on the type of object.

Similarly, when invoking `equalArea(circle, rectangle)` (line 33), the `getArea` function defined in the `Circle` class is used for `g1.getArea()`, since `g1` is a circle. Also, the `getArea` function defined in the `Rectangle` class is used for `g2.getArea()`, since `g2` is a rectangle.

why abstract functions?

Note that if the `getArea` and `getPerimeter` functions were not defined in `GeometricObject`, you cannot define the `equalArea` and `displayObject` functions in this program. So, you now see the benefits of defining the abstract functions in `GeometricObject`.

15.18 How do you define a pure virtual function?

15.19 What is wrong in the following code?

```
class A
{
public:
  virtual void f() = 0;
};

int main()
{
  A a;

  return 0;
}
```

15.20 Can you compile and run the following code? What will be the output?

```cpp
#include <iostream>
using namespace std;

class A
{
public:
  virtual void f() = 0;
};

class B: public A
{
public:
  void f()
  {
    cout << "invoke f from B" << endl;
  }
};

class C: public B
{
public:
  virtual void m() = 0;
};

class D: public C
{
public:
  virtual void m()
  {
    cout << "invoke m from D" << endl;
  }
};

void p(A& a)
{
  a.f();
}

int main()
{
  D d;
  p(d);
  d.m();

  return 0;
}
```

15.21 The **getArea** and **getPerimeter** functions may be removed from the **GeometricObject** class. What are the benefits of defining **getArea** and **getPerimeter** as abstract functions in the **GeometricObject** class?

15.10 Casting: **static_cast** versus **dynamic_cast**

*The **dynamic_cast** operator can be used to cast an object to its actual type at runtime.*

Key
Point

Suppose you wish to rewrite the **displayGeometricObject** function in Listing 15.19, TestAbstractGeometricObject.cpp, to display the radius and diameter for a circle object and the width and height for a rectangle object. You may attempt to implement the function as follows:

```cpp
void displayGeometricObject(GeometricObject& g)
{
  cout << "The raidus is " << g.getRadius() << endl;
  cout << "The diameter is " << g.getDiameter() << endl;

  cout << "The width is " << g.getWidth() << endl;
  cout << "The height is " << g.getHeight() << endl;

  cout << "The area is " << g.getArea() << endl;
  cout << "The perimeter is " << g.getPerimeter() << endl;
}
```

There are two problems with this code. First, the code cannot be compiled because **g**'s type is **GeometricObject**, but the **GeometricObject** class does not contain the **getRadius()**, **getDiameter()**, **getWidth()**, and **getHeight()** functions. Second, your code should detect whether the geometric object is a circle or a rectangle and then display radius and diameter for a circle and width and height for a rectangle.

static_cast operator

The problems may be fixed by casting **g** into **Circle** or **Rectangle**, as shown in the following code:

```cpp
void displayGeometricObject(GeometricObject& g)
{
  GeometricObject* p = &g;
  cout << "The raidus is " <<
    static_cast<Circle*>(p)->getRadius() << endl;
  cout << "The diameter is " <<
    static_cast<Circle*>(p)->getDiameter() << endl;

  cout << "The width is " <<
    static_cast<Rectangle*>(p)->getWidth() << endl;
  cout << "The height is " <<
    static_cast<Rectangle*>(p)->getHeight() << endl;

  cout << "The area is " << g.getArea() << endl;
  cout << "The perimeter is " << g.getPerimeter() << endl;
}
```

casting to Circle*

Static casting is performed on **p** that points to a **GeometricObject g** (line 3). This new function can compile but is still incorrect. A **Circle** object may be cast to **Rectangle** to invoke **getWidth()** in line 10. Likewise, a **Rectangle** object may be cast to **Circle** to invoke **getRadius()** in line 5. We need to ensure that the object is indeed a **Circle** object before invoking **getRadius()**. This can be done using **dynamic_cast**.

why dynamic casting?
dynamic_cast operator

The **dynamic_cast** works like the **static_cast**. Additionally, it performs runtime checking to ensure that casting is successful. If casting fails, it returns **NULL**. So, if you run the following code,

```cpp
1  Rectangle rectangle(5, 3);
2  GeometricObject* p = &rectangle;
3  Circle* p1 = dynamic_cast<Circle*>(p);
4  cout << (*p1).getRadius() << endl;
```

NULL

p1 will be **NULL**. A runtime error will occur when running the code in line 4. Recall that **NULL** is defined as **0**, which indicates that a pointer does not point to any object. The definition of **NULL** is in a number of standard libraries including **<iostream>** and **<cstddef>**.

Note

Assigning a pointer of a derived class type to a pointer of its base class type is called *upcasting*, and assigning a pointer of a base class type to a pointer of its derived class type is called *downcasting*. Upcasting can be performed implicitly without using the static_cast or dynamic_cast operator. For example, the following code is correct:

upcasting and downcasting

```
GeometricObject* p = new Circle(1);
Circle* p1 = new Circle(2);
p = p1;
```

However, downcasting must be performed explicitly. For example, to assign **p** to **p1**, you have to use

```
p1 = static_cast<Circle*>(p);
```

or

```
p1 = dynamic_cast<Circle*>(p);
```

Note

dynamic_cast can be performed only on the pointer or the reference of a polymorphic type; i.e., the type contains a virtual function. dynamic_cast can be used to check whether casting is performed successfully at runtime. static_cast is performed at compile time.

dynamic_cast for virtual function

Now you can rewrite the displayGeometricObject function using dynamic casting, as in Listing 15.20, to check whether casting is successful at runtime.

LISTING 15.20 DynamicCastingDemo.cpp

```
 1  #include "AbstractGeometricObject.h"
 2  #include "DerivedCircleFromAbstractGeometricObject.h"
 3  #include "DerivedRectangleFromAbstractGeometricObject.h"
 4  #include <iostream>
 5  using namespace std;
 6
 7  // A function for displaying a geometric object
 8  void displayGeometricObject(GeometricObject& g)
 9  {
10    cout << "The area is " << g.getArea() << endl;
11    cout << "The perimeter is " << g.getPerimeter() << endl;
12
13    GeometricObject* p = &g;
14    Circle* p1 = dynamic_cast<Circle*>(p);
15    Rectangle* p2 = dynamic_cast<Rectangle*>(p);
16
17    if (p1 != NULL)
18    {
19      cout << "The radius is " << p1->getRadius() << endl;
20      cout << "The diameter is " << p1->getDiameter() << endl;
21    }
22
23    if (p2 != NULL)
24    {
25      cout << "The width is " << p2->getWidth() << endl;
26      cout << "The height is " << p2->getHeight() << endl;
27    }
28  }
29
30  int main()
31  {
32    Circle circle(5);
```

include header file

casting to Circle
casting to Rectangle

```
33      Rectangle rectangle(5, 3);
34
35      cout << "Circle info: " << endl;
36      displayGeometricObject(circle);
37
38      cout << "\nRectangle info: " << endl;
39      displayGeometricObject(rectangle);
40
41      return 0;
42    }
```

```
Circle info:
The area is 78.5397
The perimeter is 31.4159
The radius is 5
The diameter is 10

Rectangle info:
The area is 15
The perimeter is 16
The width is 5
The height is 3
```

Line 13 creates a pointer for a `GeometricObject` g. The `dynamic_cast` operator (line 14) checks whether pointer p points to a `Circle` object. If so, the object's address is assigned to p1; otherwise p1 is NULL. If p1 is not NULL, the `getRadius()` and `getDiameter()` functions of the `Circle` object (pointed by p1) are invoked in lines 19–20. Similarly, if the object is a rectangle, its width and height are displayed in lines 25–26.

The program invokes the `displayGeometricObject` function to display a `Circle` object in line 36 and a `Rectangle` object in line 39. The function casts the parameter g into a `Circle` pointer p1 in line 14 and a `Rectangle` pointer p2 in line 15. If it is a `Circle` object, the object's `getRadius()` and `getDiameter()` functions are invoked in lines 19–20. If it is a `Rectangle` object, the object's `getWidth()` and `getHeight()` functions are invoked in lines 25–26.

The function also invokes `GeometricObject`'s `getArea()` and `getPerimeter()` functions in lines 10–11. Since these two functions are defined in the `GeometricObject` class, there is no need to downcast the object parameter to `Circle` or `Rectangle` in order to invoke them.

Tip

typeid operator

Occasionally, it is useful to obtain information about the class of the object. You can use the `typeid` operator to return a reference to an object of class `type_info`. For example, you can use the following statement to display the class name for object x:

```
string x;
cout << typeid(x).name() << endl;
```

It displays string, because x is an object of the **string** class. To use the **typeid** operator, the program must include the **<typeinfo>** header file.

Tip

It is good practice to always define destructors virtual. Suppose class **Child** is derived
from class **Parent** and destructors are not virtual. Consider the following code:

define destructor virtual

```
Parent* p = new Child;
...
delete p;
```

When **delete** is invoked with **p**, **Parent**'s destructor is called, since **p** is declared a
pointer for **Parent**. **p** actually points to an object of **Child**, but **Child**'s destructor
is never called. To fix the problem, define the destructor virtual in class **Parent**. Now,
when **delete** is invoked with **p**, **Child**'s destructor is called and then **Parent**'s
destructor is called, since constructors are virtual.

15.22 What is upcasting? What is downcasting?

**Check
Point**

15.23 When do you need to downcast an object from a base class type to a derived
class type?

15.24 What will be the value in **p1** after the following statements?

```
GeometricObject* p = new Rectangle(2, 3);
Circle* p1 = new Circle(2);
p1 = dynamic_cast<Circle*>(p);
```

15.25 Analyze the following code:

```
#include <iostream>
using namespace std;

class Parent
{
};

class Child: public Parent
{
public:
  void m()
  {
    cout << "invoke m" << endl;
  }
};

int main()
{
  Parent* p = new Child();

  // To be replaced in the questions below

  return 0;
}
```

a. What compile errors will you get if the highlighted line is replaced by the following
code?

```
(*p).m();
```

b. What compile errors will you get if the highlighted line is replaced by the following code?

```
Child* p1 = dynamic_cast<Child*>(p);
(*p1).m();
```

c. Will the program compile and run if the highlighted line is replaced by the following code?

```
Child* p1 = static_cast<Child*>(p);
(*p1).m();
```

d. Will the program compile and run if `virtual void m() { }` is added in the `Parent` class and the highlighted line is replaced `dynamic_cast<Child*>(p)->m();`?

15.26 Why should you define a destructor virtual?

KEY TERMS

abstract class 602
abstract function 602
base class 580
child class 580
constructor chaining 590
derived class 580
destructor chaining 590
downcasting 611
dynamic binding 597
generic programming 588
inheritance 580
override function 597

parent class 580
polymorphic type 599
polymorphism 595
protected 600
pure virtual function 602
subclass 580
subtype 595
superclass 580
supertype 595
upcasting 611
virtual function 597

CHAPTER SUMMARY

1. You can derive a new class from an existing class. This is known as *class inheritance*. The new class is called a *derived class*, *child class*, or *subclass*. The existing class is called a *base class*, *parent class*, or *superclass*.

2. An object of a derived class can be passed wherever an object of a base type parameter is required. Then a function can be used generically for a wide range of object arguments. This is known as *generic programming*.

3. A constructor is used to construct an instance of a class. Unlike data fields and functions, the constructors of a base class are not inherited in the derived class. They can only be invoked from the constructors of the derived classes to initialize the data fields in the base class.

4. A derived class constructor always invokes its base class constructor. If a base constructor is not invoked explicitly, the base class no-arg constructor is invoked by default.

5. Constructing an instance of a class invokes the constructors of all the base classes along the inheritance chain.

6. A base class constructor is called from a derived class constructor. Conversely, the destructors are automatically invoked in reverse order, with the derived class's destructor invoked first. This is called *constructor and destructor chaining*.

7. A function defined in the base class may be redefined in the derived class. A redefined function must match the signature and return type of the function in the base class.

8. A virtual function enables dynamic binding. A virtual function is often redefined in the derived classes. The compiler decides which function implementation to use dynamically at runtime.

9. If a function defined in a base class needs to be redefined in its derived classes, you should define it virtual to avoid confusions and mistakes. On the other hand, if a function will not be redefined, it is more efficient not to declare it virtual, because more time and system resource are required to bind virtual functions dynamically at runtime.

10. A protected data field or a protected function in a base class can be accessed in its derived classes.

11. A pure virtual function is also called an abstract function.

12. If a class contains a pure virtual function, the class is called an abstract class.

13. You cannot create instances from an abstract class, but abstract classes can be used as data types for parameters in a function to enable generic programming.

14. You can use the `static_cast` and `dynamic_cast` operators to cast an object of a base class type to a derived class type. `static_cast` is performed at compile time and `dynamic_cast` is performed at runtime for runtime type checking. The `dynamic_cast` operator can only be performed on a polymorphic type (i.e., the type with virtual functions).

QUIZ

Answer the quiz for this chapter online at www.cs.armstrong.edu/liang/cpp3e/quiz.html.

PROGRAMMING EXERCISES

Sections 15.2–15.4

15.1 (*The* `Triangle` *class*) Design a class named `Triangle` that extends `GeometricObject`. The class contains the following:

- Three `double` data fields named `side1`, `side2`, and `side3` to denote three sides of the triangle.
- A no-arg constructor that creates a default triangle with each side `1.0`.
- A constructor that creates a rectangle with the specified `side1`, `side2`, and `side3`.
- The constant accessor functions for all three data fields.
- A constant function named `getArea()` that returns the area of this triangle.
- A constant function named `getPerimeter()` that returns the perimeter of this triangle.

Draw the UML diagram that involves the classes `Triangle` and `Geometric-Object`. Implement the class. Write a test program that prompts the user to enter three sides of the triangle, enter a color, and enter `1` or `0` to indicate whether the triangle is filled. The program should create a `Triangle` object with these sides and set the color and filled properties using the input. The program should display the area, perimeter, color, and true or false to indicate whether filled or not.

Sections 15.5–15.10

15.2 (*The* `Person`, `Student`, `Employee`, `Faculty`, *and* `Staff` *classes*) Design a class named `Person` and its two derived classes named `Student` and `Employee`. Make `Faculty` and `Staff` derived classes of `Employee`. A person has a name, address, phone number, and e-mail address. A student has a class status (freshman, sophomore, junior, or senior). An employee has an office, salary, and date-hired. Define a class named `MyDate` that contains the fields `year`, `month`, and `day`. A faculty member has office hours and a rank. A staff member has a title. Define a constant virtual `toString` function in the `Person` class and override it in each class to display the class name and the person's name.

Draw the UML diagram for the classes. Implement the classes. Write a test program that creates a `Person`, `Student`, `Employee`, `Faculty`, and `Staff`, and invokes their `toString()` functions.

VideoNote
The `MyPoint` class

15.3 (*Extend* `MyPoint`) In Programming Exercise 9.4, the `MyPoint` class was created to model a point in a two-dimensional space. The `MyPoint` class has the properties `x` and `y` that represent `x`- and `y`-coordinates, two `get` functions for `x` and `y`, and the function for returning the distance between two points. Create a class named `ThreeDPoint` to model a point in a three-dimensional space. Let `ThreeDPoint` be derived from `MyPoint` with the following additional features:

- A data field named `z` that represents the `z`-coordinate.
- A no-arg constructor that constructs a point with coordinates (0, 0, 0).
- A constructor that constructs a point with three specified coordinates.
- A constant `get` function that returns the `z` value.
- A constant `distance(const MyPoint&)` function to return the distance between this point and the other point in the three-dimensional space.

Draw the UML diagram for the classes involved. Implement the classes. Write a test program that creates two points (0, 0, 0) and (10, 30, 25.5) and displays the distance between them.

15.4 (*Derived classes of* `Account`) In Programming Exercise 9.3, the `Account` class was created to model a bank account. An account has the properties account number, balance, and annual interest rate, date created, and functions to deposit and withdraw. Create two derived classes for checking and saving accounts. A checking account has an overdraft limit, but a savings account cannot be over-drawn. Define a constant virtual `toString()` function in the `Account` class and override it in the derived classes to return the account number and balance as a string.

Draw the UML diagram for the classes. Implement the classes. Write a test program that creates objects of `Account`, `SavingsAccount`, and `CheckingAccount` and invokes their `toString()` functions.

15.5 (*Implement a stack class using inheritance*) In Listing 12.4, `GenericStack` is implemented using arrays. Create a new stack class that extends `vector`. Draw the UML diagram for the classes. Implement it.

EXCEPTION HANDLING

Objectives

- To get an overview of exceptions and exception handling (§16.2).
- To know how to throw an exception and how to catch it (§16.2).
- To explore the advantages of using exception handling (§16.3).
- To create exceptions using C++ standard exception classes (§16.4).
- To define custom exception classes (§16.5).
- To catch multiple exceptions (§16.6).
- To explain how an exception is propagated (§16.7).
- To rethrow exceptions in a `catch` block (§16.8).
- To declare functions with an exception specification (§16.9).
- To use exception handling appropriately (§16.10).

16.1 Introduction

Exception handling enables a program to deal with exceptional situations and continue its normal execution.

An exception indicates an unusual situation that occurs during a program's execution. For example, suppose your program uses a vector **v** to store elements. The program accesses an element in the vector using **v[i]**, assuming that the element at the index **i** exists. The exceptional situation occurs when the element at the index **i** does not exist. You should write the code in the program to deal with exceptions. This chapter introduces the concept of exception handling in C++. You will learn how to throw, catch, and process an exception.

16.2 Exception-Handling Overview

An exception is thrown using a **throw** *statement and caught in a* **try-catch** *block.*

To demonstrate exception handling including how an exception is created and thrown, let us begin with an example that reads in two integers and displays their quotient, as shown in Listing 16.1.

LISTING 16.1   Quotient.cpp

```
1  #include <iostream>
2  using namespace std;
3
4  int main()
5  {
6    // Read two integers
7    cout << "Enter two integers: ";
8    int number1, number2;
9    cin >> number1 >> number2;
10
11    cout << number1 << " / " << number2 << " is "
12      << (number1 / number2) << endl;
13
14    return 0;
15  }
```

reads two integers

integer division

```
Enter two integers: 5 2 ↵Enter
5 / 2 is 2
```

If you enter **0** for the second number, a runtime error occurs, because you cannot divide an integer by **0**. (*Recall that a floating-point number divided by 0 does not raise an exception.*) A simple way to fix the error is to add an **if** statement to test the second number, as shown in Listing 16.2.

LISTING 16.2   QuotientWithIf.cpp

```
1  #include <iostream>
2  using namespace std;
3
4  int main()
5  {
6    // Read two integers
7    cout << "Enter two integers: ";
8    int number1, number2;
```

```
9     cin >> number1 >> number2;                              reads two integers
10
11    if (number2 != 0)                                       test number2
12    {
13      cout << number1 << " / " << number2 << " is "
14        << (number1 / number2) << endl;
15    }
16    else
17    {
18      cout << "Divisor cannot be zero" << endl;
19    }
20
21    return 0;
22  }
```

```
Enter two integers: 5 0  ↵Enter
Divisor cannot be zero
```

To demonstrate the concept of exception handling including how to create, throw, catch, and handle an exception, we rewrite Listing 16.2 as shown in Listing 16.3.

LISTING 16.3 QuotientWithException.cpp

```
1   #include <iostream>
2   using namespace std;
3
4   int main()
5   {
6     // Read two integers
7     cout << "Enter two integers: ";
8     int number1, number2;
9     cin >> number1 >> number2;                              reads two integers
10
11    try                                                     try block
12    {
13      if (number2 == 0)
14        throw number1;
15
16      cout << number1 << " / " << number2 << " is "
17        << (number1 / number2) << endl;
18    }
19    catch (int ex)                                          catch block
20    {
21      cout << "Exception: an integer " << ex <<
22        " cannot be divided by zero" << endl;
23    }
24
25    cout << "Execution continues ..." << endl;
26
27    return 0;
28  }
```

```
Enter two integers: 5 3  ↵Enter
5 / 3 is 1
Execution continues ...
```

```
Enter two integers: 5 0 ↵Enter
Exception: an integer 5 cannot be divided by zero
Execution continues . . .
```

The program contains a `try` block and a `catch` block. The `try` block (lines 11–18) contains the code that is executed in normal circumstances. The `catch` block contains the code that is executed when `number2` is zero. When `number2` is zero, the program throws an exception by executing

throw statement

```
throw number1;
```

exception
throwing exception

The value thrown, in this case `number1`, is called an *exception*. The execution of a throw statement is called *throwing an exception*. You can throw a value of any type. In this case, the value is of the `int` type.

When an exception is thrown, the normal execution flow is interrupted. As the name suggests, to "throw an exception" is to pass the exception from one place to another. The excep-

handle exception

tion is caught by the `catch` block. The code in the `catch` block is executed to *handle the exception*. Afterward, the statement (line 25) after the `catch` block is executed.

The `throw` statement is analogous to a function call, but instead of calling a function, it calls a `catch` block. In this sense, a `catch` block is like a function definition with a parameter that matches the type of the value being thrown. However, after the `catch` block has been executed, the program control does not return to the `throw` statement; instead, it executes the next statement after the `catch` block.

The identifier `ex` in the `catch` block header

```
catch (int ex)
```

catch block parameter

acts very much like a parameter in a function. So, it is referred to as a `catch` block parameter. The type (e.g., `int`) preceding `ex` specifies the kind of exception the `catch` block can catch. Once the exception is caught, you can access the thrown value from this parameter in the body of a catch block.

In summary, a template for a `try-throw-catch` block may look like this:

```
try
{
  Code to try;
  Throw an exception with a throw statement or
    from function if necessary;
  More code to try;
}
catch (type ex)
{
  Code to process the exception;
}
```

An exception may be thrown directly using a `throw` statement in a `try` block, or a function may be invoked that throws an exception.

omit catch block parameter

Note

If you are not interested in the contents of an exception object, the `catch` block parameter may be omitted. For example, the following `catch` block is legal.

```
try
{
  // ...
}
```

```
catch (int)
{
  cout << "Error occurred " << endl;
}
```

16.1 Show the output of the following code with input 120.

Check
Point

```
#include <iostream>
using namespace std;

int main()
{
  cout << "Enter a temperature: ";
  double temperature;
  cin >> temperature;

  try
  {
    cout << "Start of try block ..." << endl;

    if (temperature > 95)
      throw temperature;

    cout << "End of try block ..." << endl;
  }
  catch (double temperature)
  {
    cout << "The temperature is " << temperature << endl;
    cout << "It is too hot" << endl;
  }

  cout << "Continue ..." << endl;

  return 0;
}
```

16.2 What would be the output for the preceding code if the input were 80?

16.3 Would it be an error if you changed

```
catch (double temperature)
{
  cout << "The temperature is " << temperature << endl;
  cout << "It is too hot" << endl;
}
```

in the preceding code to the following?

```
catch (double)
{
  cout << "It is too hot" << endl;
}
```

16.3 Exception-Handling Advantages

*Exception handling enables the caller of the function to process the exception thrown
from a function.*

Key
Point

Listing 16.3 demonstrates how an exception is created, thrown, caught, and handled. You may
wonder about the benefits. To see them, we rewrite Listing 16.3 to compute a quotient using
a function as shown in Listing 16.4.

VideoNote

Exception-handling advantages

LISTING 16.4 QuotientWithFunction.cpp

```cpp
1  #include <iostream>
2  using namespace std;
3
4  int quotient(int number1, int number2)
5  {
6    if (number2 == 0)
7      throw number1;
8
9    return number1 / number2;
10 }
11
12 int main()
13 {
14   // Read two integers
15   cout << "Enter two integers: ";
16   int number1, number2;
17   cin >> number1 >> number2;
18
19   try
20   {
21     int result = quotient(number1, number2);
22     cout << number1 << " / " << number2 << " is "
23       << result << endl;
24   }
25   catch (int ex)
26   {
27     cout << "Exception from function: an integer " << ex <<
28       " cannot be divided by zero" << endl;
29   }
30
31   cout << "Execution continues ..." << endl;
32
33   return 0;
34 }
```

quotient function

throw exception

reads two integers

try block

invoke function

catch block

```
Enter two integers: 5 3 ↵Enter
5 / 3 is 1
Execution continues ...
```

```
Enter two integers: 5 0 ↵Enter
Exception from function: an integer 5 cannot be divided by zero
Execution continues ...
```

Function quotient (lines 4–10) returns the quotient of two integers. If number2 is 0, it cannot return a value. So, an exception is thrown in line 7.

The main function invokes the quotient function (line 21). If the quotient function executes normally, it returns a value to the caller. If the quotient function encounters an exception, it throws the exception back to its caller. The caller's catch block handles the exception.

advantage

Now you see the *advantages* of using exception handling. It enables a function to throw an exception to its caller. Without this capability, a function must handle the exception or terminate the program. Often, the called function does not know what to do in case of error. This is typically the case for the library function. The library function can detect the error, but only the caller knows what needs to be done when an error occurs. The fundamental idea of exception handling is to separate error detection (done in a called function) from error handling (done in the calling function).

16.4   What is advantage of using exception handling?

Check
Point

16.4 Exception Classes

You can use C++ standard exception classes to create exception objects and throw exceptions.

Key
Point

The `catch` block parameter in the preceding examples is the `int` type. A class type is often more useful, because an object can contain more information that you want to throw to a `catch` block. C++ provides a number of standard classes that can be used for creating exception objects. These classes are shown in Figure 16.1.

VideoNote
C++ exception classes

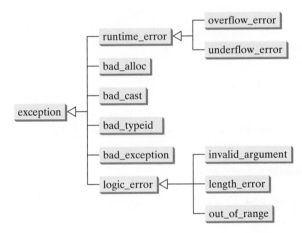

FIGURE 16.1   You can use standard library classes to create exception objects.

The root class in this hierarchy is `exception` (defined in header `<exception>`). It contains the virtual function `what()` that returns an exception object's error message.

The `runtime_error` class (defined in header `<stdexcept>`) is a base class for several *standard exception* classes that describes runtime errors. Class `overflow_error` describes an arithmetic overflow—i.e., a value is too large to be stored. Class `underflow_error` describes an arithmetic underflow—i.e., a value is too small to be stored.

The `logic_error` class (defined in header `<stdexcept>`) is a base class for several standard exception classes that describes logic errors. Class `invalid_argument` indicates that an invalid argument has been passed to a function. Class `length_error` indicates that an object's length has exceeded the maximum allowed length. Class `out_of_range` indicates that a value has exceeded its allowed range.

Classes `bad_alloc`, `bad_cast`, `bad_typeid`, and `bad_exception` describe the exceptions thrown by C++ operators. For example, a `bad_alloc` exception is thrown by the `new` operator if the memory cannot be allocated. A `bad_cast` exception is thrown by the `dynamic_cast` operator as the result of a failed cast to a reference type. A `bad_typeid` exception is thrown by the `typeid` operator when the operand for `typeid` is a `NULL` pointer. The `bad_exception` class is used in the exception-specification of a function, which will be discussed in Section 16.9.

exception
what()
runtime_error
standard exception

logic_error

bad_alloc
bad_cast
bad_typeid
bad_exception

These classes are used by some functions in the C++ standard library to throw exceptions. You also can use these classes to throw exceptions in your programs. Listing 16.5 rewrites Listing 16.4, QuotientWithFunction.cpp, by throwing a **runtime_error**.

LISTING 16.5 QuotientThrowRuntimeError.cpp

```cpp
1   #include <iostream>
2   #include <stdexcept>
3   using namespace std;
4
5   int quotient(int number1, int number2)
6   {
7     if (number2 == 0)
8       throw runtime_error("Divisor cannot be zero");
9
10    return number1 / number2;
11  }
12
13  int main()
14  {
15    // Read two integers
16    cout << "Enter two integers: ";
17    int number1, number2;
18    cin >> number1 >> number2;
19
20    try
21    {
22      int result = quotient(number1, number2);
23      cout << number1 << " / " << number2 << " is "
24        << result << endl;
25    }
26    catch (runtime_error& ex)
27    {
28      cout << ex.what() << endl;
29    }
30
31    cout << "Execution continues ..." << endl;
32
33    return 0;
34  }
```

quotient function

throw exception

reads two integers

try block

invoke function

catch block

```
Enter two integers: 5 3  ↵Enter
5 / 3 is 1
Execution continues ...
```

```
Enter two integers: 5 0  ↵Enter
Divisor cannot be zero
Execution continues ...
```

The **quotient** function in Listing 16.4 throws an **int** value, but the function in this program throws a **runtime_error** object (line 8). You can create a **runtime_error** object by passing a string that describes the exception.

The catch block catches a **runtime_error** exception and invokes the **what** function to return a string description of the exception (line 28).

Listing 16.6 shows an example of handling the **bad_alloc** exception.

LISTING 16.6 BadAllocExceptionDemo.cpp

```
1  #include <iostream>
2  using namespace std;
3
4  int main()
5  {
6    try                                                          try block
7    {
8      for (int i = 1; i <= 100; i++)
9      {
10       new int[70000000];                                      create a large array
11       cout << i << " arrays have been created" << endl;
12     }
13   }
14   catch (bad_alloc& ex)                                        catch block
15   {
16     cout << "Exception: " << ex.what() << endl;                invoke ex.what()
17   }
18
19   return 0;
20 }
```

```
1 arrays have been created
2 arrays have been created
3 arrays have been created
4 arrays have been created
5 arrays have been created
6 arrays have been created
Exception: bad alloc exception thrown
```

The output shows that the program creates six arrays before it fails on the seventh **new** operator. When it fails, a **bad_alloc** exception is thrown and caught in the **catch** block, which displays the message returned from **ex.what()**.

Listing 16.7 shows an example of handling the **bad_cast** exception.

LISTING 16.7 BadCastExceptionDemo.cpp

```
1  #include <typeinfo>                                            include typeinfo
2  #include "DerivedCircleFromAbstractGeometricObject.h"          see Listing 15.15
3  #include "DerivedRectangleFromAbstractGeometricObject.h"       see Listing 15.17
4  #include <iostream>
5  using namespace std;
6
7  int main()
8  {
9    try                                                          try block
10   {
11     Rectangle r(3, 4);
12     Circle&  c = dynamic_cast<Circle&>(r);                     cast
13   }
14   catch (bad_cast& ex)                                         catch block
```

invoke ex.what()

```
15    {
16      cout << "Exception: " << ex.what() << endl;
17    }
18
19    return 0;
20  }
```

Output from VC++

```
Exception: Bad Dynamic_cast!
```

Dynamic casting was introduced in Section 15.10, "Casting: static_cast versus dynamic_cast." In line 12, a reference of a Rectangle object is cast to a Circle reference type, which is illegal, and a bad_cast exception is thrown. The exception is caught in the catch block in line 14.

Listing 16.8 shows an example of throwing and handling an invalid_argument exception.

LISTING 16.8   InvalidArgumentExceptionDemo.cpp

```
1  #include <iostream>
2  #include <stdexcept>
3  using namespace std;
4
5  double getArea(double radius)
6  {
7    if (radius < 0)
8      throw invalid_argument("Radius cannot be negative");
9
10    return radius * radius * 3.14159;
11  }
12
13  int main()
14  {
15    // Prompt the user to enter radius
16    cout << "Enter radius: ";
17    double radius;
18    cin >> radius;
19
20    try
21    {
22      double result = getArea(radius);
23      cout << "The area is " << result << endl;
24    }
25    catch (exception& ex)
26    {
27      cout << ex.what() << endl;
28    }
29
30    cout << "Execution continues ..." << endl;
31
32    return 0;
33  }
```

getArea function

throw exception

reads radius

try block

invoke function

catch block

```
Enter radius: 5 ⏎Enter
The area is 78.5397
Execution continues ...
```

```
Enter radius: -5  ↵Enter
Radius cannot be negative
Execution continues ...
```

In the sample output, the program prompts the user to enter radius, 5 and −5. Invoking `getArea(-5)` (line 22) causes an `invalid_argument` exception to be thrown (line 8). This exception is caught in the `catch` block in line 25. Note that the catch-block parameter type `exception` is a base class for `invalid_argument`. So, it can catch an `invalid_argument`.

16.5 Describe the C++ `exception` class and its derived classes. Give examples of using `bad_alloc` and `bad_cast`.

16.6 Show the output of the following code with input 10, 60, and 120, respectively.

```cpp
#include <iostream>
using namespace std;

int main()
{
  cout << "Enter a temperature: ";
  double temperature;
  cin >> temperature;

  try
  {
    cout << "Start of try block ..." << endl;

    if (temperature > 95)
      throw runtime_error("Exceptional temperature");

    cout << "End of try block ..." << endl;
  }
  catch (runtime_error& ex)
  {
    cout << ex.what() << endl;
    cout << "It is too hot" << endl;
  }

  cout << "Continue ..." << endl;

  return 0;
}
```

16.5 Custom Exception Classes

You can define custom exception classes to model exceptions that cannot be adequately represented using C++ standard exception classes.

C++ provides the exception classes listed in Figure 16.1. Use them whenever possible instead of creating your own exception classes. However, if you run into a problem that cannot be adequately described by the standard exception classes, you can create your own exception class. This class is just like any C++ class, but often it is desirable to derive it from `exception` or a derived class of `exception` so you can utilize the common features (e.g., the `what()` function) in the `exception` class.

VideoNote
Create custom exception classes

Let us consider the `Triangle` class for modeling triangles. The class UML diagram is shown in Figure 16.2. The class is derived from the `GeometricObject` class, which is an abstract class introduced in Section 15.9, "Abstract Classes and Pure Virtual Functions."

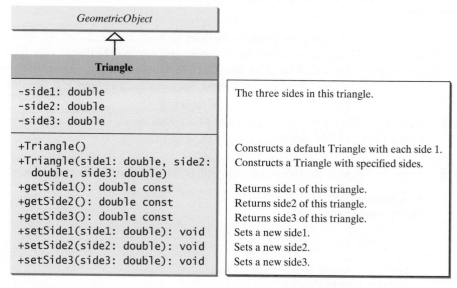

FIGURE 16.2 The `Triangle` class models triangles.

A triangle is valid if the sum of any two sides is greater than the third side. When you attempt to create a triangle, or change a side of a triangle, you need to ensure that this property is not violated. Otherwise, an exception should be thrown. You can define the `TriangleException` class as in Listing 16.9 to model this exception.

LISTING 16.9 TriangleException.h

```
1  #ifndef TRIANGLEEXCEPTION_H
2  #define TRIANGLEEXCEPTION_H
3  #include <stdexcept>
4  using namespace std;
5
6  class TriangleException: public logic_error
7  {
8  public:
9    TriangleException(double side1, double side2, double side3)
10     : logic_error("Invalid triangle")
11   {
12     this->side1 = side1;
13     this->side2 = side2;
14     this->side3 = side3;
15   }
16
17   double getSide1() const
18   {
19     return side1;
20   }
21
22   double getSide2() const
23   {
24     return side2;
25   }
```

include `stdexcept`

extend `logic_error`

invoke base constructor

```
26
27    double getSide3() const
28    {
29      return side3;
30    }
31
32  private:
33    double side1, side2, side3;
34  }; // Semicolon required
35
36  #endif
```

The `TriangleException` class describes a logic error, so it is appropriate to define this class to extend the standard `logic_error` class in line 6. Since `logic_error` is in the `<stdexcept>` header file, this header is included in line 3.

Recall that if a base constructor is not invoked explicitly, the base class's no-arg constructor is invoked by default. However, since the base class `logic_error` does not have a no-arg constructor, you must invoke a base class's constructor to avoid compile errors in line 10. Invoking `logic_error("Invalid triangle")` sets an error message, which can be returned from invoking `what()` on an `exception` object.

Note
A custom exception class is just like a regular class. Extending from a base class is not necessary, but it is a good practice to extend from the standard **exception** or a derived class of **exception** so your custom exception class can use the functions from the standard classes.

Note
The header file TriangleException.h contains the implementation for the class. Recall that this is the inline implementation. For short functions, using inline implementation is efficient.

The `Triangle` class can be implemented as follows in Listing 16.10.

LISTING 16.10 Triangle.h

```
1   #ifndef TRIANGLE_H                                              header for
2   #define TRIANGLE_H                                                GeometricObject
3   #include "AbstractGeometricObject.h" // Defined in Listing 15.13  header for
4   #include "TriangleException.h"                                    TriangleException
5   #include <cmath>                                               header for cmath
6
7   class Triangle: public GeometricObject                         extend GeometricObject
8   {
9   public:
10    Triangle()                                                   no-arg constructor
11    {
12      side1 = side2 = side3 = 1;
13    }
14
15    Triangle(double side1, double side2, double side3)           constructor
16    {
17      if (!isValid(side1, side2, side3))
18        throw TriangleException(side1, side2, side3);            throw TriangleException
19
20      this->side1 = side1;
21      this->side2 = side2;
```

```
22          this->side3 = side3;
23        }
24
25        double getSide1() const
26        {
27          return side1;
28        }
29
30        double getSide2() const
31        {
32          return side2;
33        }
34
35        double getSide3() const
36        {
37          return side3;
38        }
39
40        void setSide1(double side1)
41        {
42          if (!isValid(side1, side2, side3))
```
throw TriangleException
```
43            throw TriangleException(side1, side2, side3);
44
45          this->side1 = side1;
46        }
47
48        void setSide2(double side2)
49        {
50          if (!isValid(side1, side2, side3))
```
throw TriangleException
```
51            throw TriangleException(side1, side2, side3);
52
53          this->side2 = side2;
54        }
55
56        void setSide3(double side3)
57        {
58          if (!isValid(side1, side2, side3))
```
throw TriangleException
```
59            throw TriangleException(side1, side2, side3);
60
61          this->side3 = side3;
62        }
63
```
override getPerimeter()
```
64        double getPerimeter() const
65        {
66          return side1 + side2 + side3;
67        }
68
```
override getArea()
```
69        double getArea() const
70        {
71          double s = getPerimeter() / 2;
72          return sqrt(s * (s - side1) * (s - side2) * (s - side3));
73        }
74
75      private:
76        double side1, side2, side3;
77
```
check sides
```
78        bool isValid(double side1, double side2, double side3) const
```

```
79   {
80     return (side1 < side2 + side3) && (side2 < side1 + side3) &&
81        (side3 < side1 + side2);
82   }
83 };
84
85 #endif
```

The `Triangle` class extends `GeometricObject` (line 7) and overrides the pure virtual functions `getPerimeter` and `getArea` defined in the `GeometricObject` class (lines 64–73).

The `isValid` function (lines 78–83) checks whether a triangle is valid. This function is defined private for use inside the `Triangle` class.

When constructing a `Triangle` object with three specified sides, the constructor invokes the `isValid` function (line 17) to check validity. If not valid, a `TriangleException` object is created and thrown in line 18. Validity also is checked when the functions `setSide1`, `setSide2`, and `setSide3` are invoked. When invoking `setSide1(side1)`, `isValid(side1, side2, side3)` is invoked. Here `side1` is the new `side1` to be set, not the current `side1` in the object.

Listing 16.11 gives a test program that creates a `Triangle` object using its no-arg constructor (line 9), displays its perimeter and area (lines 10–11), and changes its `side3` to 4 (line 13), which causes a `TriangleException` to be thrown. The exception is caught in the `catch` block (lines 17–22).

LISTING 16.11   TestTriangle.cpp

```
1  #include <iostream>
2  #include "Triangle.h"                                          Triangle header
3  using namespace std;
4
5  int main()
6  {
7    try
8    {
9      Triangle triangle;                                         create object
10     cout << "Perimeter is " << triangle.getPerimeter() << endl;
11     cout << "Area is " << triangle.getArea() << endl;
12
13     triangle.setSide3(4);                                      set new side
14     cout << "Perimeter is " << triangle.getPerimeter() << endl;
15     cout << "Area is " << triangle.getArea() << endl;
16   }
17   catch (TriangleException& ex)                                catch block
18   {
19     cout << ex.what();                                         invoke ex.what()
20     cout << " three sides are " << ex.getSide1() << " "        invoke ex.getSide1()
21        << ex.getSide2() << " " << ex.getSide3() << endl;
22   }
23
24   return 0;
25 }
```

```
Perimeter is 3
Area is 0.433013
Invalid triangle three sides are 1 1 4
```

The `what()` function is defined in the `exception` class. Since `TriangleException` is derived from `logic_error`, which is derived from `exception`, you can invoke `what()` (line 19) to display an error message on a `TriangleException` object. The `TriangleException` object contains the information pertinent to a triangle. This information is useful for handling the exception.

16.7 What is the benefit of defining a custom exception class to be derived from the `exception` class?

16.6 Multiple Catches

A `try-catch` block may contain multiple catch clauses to deal with different exceptions thrown in the `try` clause.

Usually a `try` block should run without exceptions. Occasionally, though, it may throw an exception of one type or another. For example, a nonpositive value for a side in a triangle in Listing 16.11 may be considered a type of exception different from a `TriangleException`. So, the `try` block may throw a nonpositive-side exception or a `TriangleException`, depending on the occasion. One `catch` block can catch only one type of exception. C++ allows you to add multiple `catch` blocks after a `try` block in order to catch multiple types of exceptions.

Let us revise the example in the preceding section by creating a new exception class named `NonPositiveSideException` and incorporating it in the `Triangle` class. The `NonPositiveSideException` class is shown in Listing 16.12 and the new `Triangle` class in Listing 16.13.

LISTING 16.12 NonPositiveSideException.h

```
1   #ifndef NonPositiveSideException_H
2   #define NonPositiveSideException_H
3   #include <stdexcept>
4   using namespace std;
5
6   class NonPositiveSideException: public logic_error
7   {
8   public:
9     NonPositiveSideException(double side)
10      : logic_error("Non-positive side")
11    {
12      this->side = side;
13    }
14
15    double getSide()
16    {
17      return side;
18    }
19
20  private:
21    double side;
22  };
23
24  #endif
```

include `stdexcept`

extend `logic_error`

invoke base constructor

The `NonPositiveSideException` class describes a logic error, so it is appropriate to define this class to extend the standard `logic_error` class in line 6.

LISTING 16.13 NewTriangle.h

```
1  #ifndef TRIANGLE_H
2  #define TRIANGLE_H
3  #include "AbstractGeometricObject.h"
4  #include "TriangleException.h"
5  #include "NonPositiveSideException.h"
6  #include <cmath>
7
8  class Triangle: public GeometricObject
9  {
10 public:
11   Triangle()
12   {
13     side1 = side2 = side3 = 1;
14   }
15
16   Triangle(double side1, double side2, double side3)
17   {
18     check(side1);
19     check(side2);
20     check(side3);
21
22     if (!isValid(side1, side2, side3))
23       throw TriangleException(side1, side2, side3);
24
25     this->side1 = side1;
26     this->side2 = side2;
27     this->side3 = side3;
28   }
29
30   double getSide1() const
31   {
32     return side1;
33   }
34
35   double getSide2() const
36   {
37     return side2;
38   }
39
40   double getSide3() const
41   {
42     return side3;
43   }
44
45   void setSide1(double side1)
46   {
47     check(side1);
48     if (!isValid(side1, side2, side3))
49       throw TriangleException(side1, side2, side3);
50
51     this->side1 = side1;
52   }
53
54   void setSide2(double side2)
55   {
56     check(side2);
57     if (!isValid(side1, side2, side3))
```

header for GeometricObject

header for
  TriangleException

NonPositiveSide-
  Exception

header for cmath

extend GeometricObject

no-arg constructor

constructor

check side1

throw TriangleException

check side1

```
58              throw TriangleException(side1, side2, side3);
59
60          this->side2 = side2;
61      }
62
63      void setSide3(double side3)
64      {
65          check(side3);
66          if (!isValid(side1, side2, side3))
67              throw TriangleException(side1, side2, side3);
68
69          this->side3 = side3;
70      }
71
72      double getPerimeter() const
73      {
74          return side1 + side2 + side3;
75      }
76
77      double getArea() const
78      {
79          double s = getPerimeter() / 2;
80          return sqrt(s * (s - side1) * (s - side2) * (s - side3));
81      }
82
83  private:
84      double side1, side2, side3;
85
86      bool isValid(double side1, double side2, double side3) const
87      {
88          return (side1 < side2 + side3) && (side2 < side1 + side3) &&
89              (side3 < side1 + side2);
90      }
91
92      void check(double side) const
93      {
94          if (side <= 0)
95              throw NonPositiveSideException(side);
96      }
97  };
98
99  #endif
```

throw NonPositiveSide-Exception *(margin note aligned to lines 94–95)*

The new `Triangle` class is identical to the one in Listing 16.10, except that it also checks nonpositive sides. When a `Triangle` object is created, all of its sides are checked by invoking the `check` function (lines 18–20). The `check` function checks whether a side is nonpositive (line 94); it throws a `NonPositiveSideException` (line 95).

Listing 16.14 gives a test program that prompts the user to enter three sides (lines 9–11) and creates a `Triangle` object (line 12).

LISTING 16.14 MultipleCatchDemo.cpp

new `Triangle` class *(margin note)*

```
1  #include <iostream>
2  #include "NewTriangle.h"
3  using namespace std;
4
5  int main()
6  {
7      try
```

```
8   {
9       cout << "Enter three sides: ";
10      double side1, side2, side3;
11      cin >> side1 >> side2 >> side3;
12      Triangle triangle(side1, side2, side3);                     create object
13      cout << "Perimeter is " << triangle.getPerimeter() << endl;
14      cout << "Area is " << triangle.getArea() << endl;
15  }
16  catch (NonPositiveSideException& ex)                            catch block
17  {
18      cout << ex.what();
19      cout << " the side is " << ex.getSide() << endl;
20  }
21  catch (TriangleException& ex)                                   catch block
22  {
23      cout << ex.what();
24      cout << " three sides are " << ex.getSide1() << " "
25          << ex.getSide2() << " " << ex.getSide3() << endl;
26  }
27
28      return 0;
29  }
```

```
Enter three sides: 2 2.5 2.5  ↵Enter   ◄─────────  Normal execution
Perimeter is 7
Area is 2.29129

Enter three sides: -1 1 1  ↵Enter   ◄─────────  Nonpositive side –1
Nonpositive side the side is -1

Enter three sides: 1 2 1  ↵Enter   ◄─────────  Invalid triangle
Invalid triangle three sides are 1 2 1
```

As shown in the sample output, if you enter three sides 2, 2.5, and 2.5, it is a legal triangle. The program displays the perimeter and area of the triangle (lines 13–14). If you enter -1, 1, and 1, the constructor (line 12) throws a NonPositiveSideException. This exception is caught by the catch block in line 16 and processed in lines 18–19. If you enter 1, 2, and 1, the constructor (line 12) throws a TriangleException. This exception is caught by the catch block in line 21 and processed in lines 23–25.

Note

Various exception classes can be derived from a common base class. If a catch block   catch block
catches exception objects of a base class, it can catch all the exception objects of the
derived classes of that base class.

Note

The order in which exceptions are specified in catch blocks is important. A catch   order of exception handlers
block for a base class type should appear after a catch block for a derived class
type. Otherwise, the exception of a derived class is always caught by the catch block
for the base class. For example, the ordering in (a) below is erroneous, because
TriangleException is a derived class of logic_error. The correct ordering
should be as shown in (b). In (a), a TriangleException occurred in the try block
is caught by the catch block for logic_error.

```
try                              try
{                                {
   ...                              ...
}                                }
catch (logic_error& ex)          catch (logic_error& ex)
{                                {
   ...                              ...
}                                }
catch (TriangleException& ex)    catch (logic_error& ex)
{                                {
   ...                              ...
}                                }
```

(a) Wrong order   (b) Correct order

catch all exceptions

You may use an ellipsis (...) as the parameter of catch, which will catch any exception no matter what the type of the exception that was thrown. This can be used as a default handler that catches all exceptions not caught by other handlers if it is specified last, as shown in the following example:

```
try
{
   Execute some code here
}
catch (Exception1& ex1)
{
   cout << "Handle Exception1" << endl;
}
catch (Exception2& ex2)
{
   cout << "Handle Exception2" << endl;
}
catch (...)
{
   cout << "Handle all other exceptions" << endl;
}
```

Check Point

16.8 Can you throw multiple exceptions in one throw statement? Can you have multiple catch blocks in a try-catch block?

16.9 Suppose that statement2 causes an exception in the following try-catch block:

```
try
{
   statement1;
   statement2;
   statement3;
}
catch (Exception1& ex1)
{
}
catch (Exception2& ex2)
{
}

statement4;
```

Answer the following questions:

- Will `statement3` be executed?
- If the exception is not caught, will `statement4` be executed?
- If the exception is caught in the `catch` block, will `statement4` be executed?

16.7 Exception Propagation

An exception is thrown through a chain of calling functions until it is caught or it reaches to the main function.

 Key Point

You now know how to declare an exception and how to throw an exception. When an exception is thrown, it can be caught and handled in a `try-catch` block, as follows:

```
try
{
  statements;  // Statements that may throw exceptions
}
catch (Exception1& ex1)
{
  handler for exception1;
}
catch (Exception2& ex2)
{
  handler for exception2;
}
...
catch (ExceptionN& exN)
{
  handler for exceptionN;
}
```

If no exceptions arise during the execution of the `try` block, the `catch` blocks are skipped.

If one of the statements inside the `try` block throws an exception, C++ skips the remaining statements in the `try` block and starts the process of finding the code to handle the exception. This code, called the *exception handler,* is found by propagating the exception backward through a chain of function calls, starting from the current function. Each `catch` block is examined in turn, from first to last, to see whether the type of the exception object is an instance of the exception class in the `catch` block. If so, the exception object is assigned to the variable declared, and the code in the `catch` block is executed. If no handler is found, C++ exits this function, passes the exception to the function that invoked the function, and continues the same process to find a handler. If no handler is found in the chain of functions being invoked, the program prints an error message on the console and terminates. The process of finding a handler is called *catching an exception.*

exception handler

catching exception

Suppose the `main` function invokes `function1`, `function1` invokes `function2`, `function2` invokes `function3`, and `function3` throws an exception, as shown in Figure 16.3. Consider the following scenario:

- If the exception type is `Exception3`, it is caught by the `catch` block for handling exception `ex3` in `function2`. `statement5` is skipped, and `statement6` is executed.
- If the exception type is `Exception2`, `function2` is aborted, the control is returned to `function1`, and the exception is caught by the `catch` block for handling exception `ex2` in `function1`. `statement3` is skipped, and `statement4` is executed.

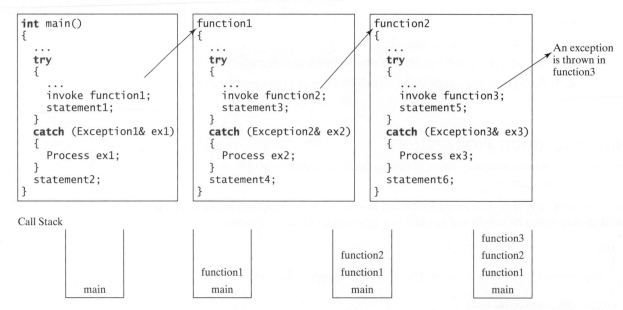

Call Stack

FIGURE 16.3 If an exception is not caught in the current function, it is passed to its caller. The process is repeated until the exception is caught or passed to the `main` function.

- If the exception type is `Exception1`, `function1` is aborted, the control is returned to the `main` function, and the exception is caught by the `catch` block for handling exception `ex1` in the `main` function. `statement1` is skipped, and `statement2` is executed.

- If the exception is not caught in `function2`, `function1`, and `main`, the program terminates. `statement1` and `statement2` are not executed.

16.8 Rethrowing Exceptions

Key Point

After an exception is caught, it can be rethrown to the caller of the function.

C++ allows an exception handler to rethrow the exception if it cannot process it or simply wants to let its caller be notified. The syntax may look like this:

```
try
{
  statements;
}
catch (TheException& ex)
{
  perform operations before exits;
  throw;
}
```

rethrow exception

The statement `throw` rethrows the exception so that other handlers get a chance to process it. Listing 16.15 gives an example that demonstrates how to *rethrow exceptions*.

LISTING 16.15 RethrowExceptionDemo.cpp

```
1  #include <iostream>
2  #include <stdexcept>
3  using namespace std;
4
```

```
5   int f1()
6   {
7     try
8     {
9       throw runtime_error("Exception in f1");          throw an exception
10    }
11    catch (exception& ex)                              catch block
12    {
13      cout << "Exception caught in function f1" << endl;
14      cout << ex.what() << endl;
15      throw; // Rethrow the exception                  rethrow exception
16    }
17  }
18
19  int main()
20  {
21    try
22    {
23      f1();                                            invoke f1
24    }
25    catch (exception& ex)                              catch block
26    {
27      cout << "Exception caught in function main" << endl;
28      cout << ex.what() << endl;
29    }
30
31    return 0;
32  }
```

```
Exception caught in function f1       ◀──────  Handler in function f1
Exception in f1

Exception caught in function main     ◀──────  Handler in function main
Exception in f1
```

The program invokes function **f1** in line 23, which throws an exception in line 9. This exception is caught in the **catch** block in line 11, and it is rethrown to the main function in line 15. The **catch** block in the main function catches the rethrown exception and processes it in lines 27–28.

16.10 Suppose that **statement2** causes an exception in the following statement:

Check
Point

```
try
{
  statement1;
  statement2;
  statement3;
}
catch (Exception1& ex1)
{
}
catch (Exception2& ex2)
{
}
catch (Exception3& ex3)
{
  statement4;
```

```
        throw;
    }
    statement5;
```

Answer the following questions:

■ Will `statement5` be executed if the exception is not caught?

■ If the exception is of type `Exception3`, will `statement4` be executed, and will `statement5` be executed?

16.9 Exception Specification

Key Point

You can declare potential exceptions a function may throw in the function header.

exception specification
throw list

An *exception specification,* also known as *throw list,* lists exceptions that a function can throw. So far, you have seen the function defined without a throw list. In this case, the function can throw any exception. So, it is tempting to omit exception specification. However, this is not a good practice. A function should give warning of any exceptions it might throw, so that programmers can write a robust program to deal with these potential exceptions in a `try-catch` block.

The syntax for exception specification is as follows:

```
returnType functionName(parameterList) throw (exceptionList)
```

The exceptions are declared in the function header. For example, you should revise the `check` function and the `Triangle` constructor in Listing 16.13 to specify appropriate exceptions as follows:

throw list

throw NonPositiveSide-
Exception

throw list

throw TriangleException

```
1  void check(double side) throw (NonPositiveSideException)
2  {
3    if (side <= 0)
4      throw NonPositiveSideException(side);
5  }
6
7  Triangle(double side1, double side2, double side3)
8    throw (NonPositiveSideException, TriangleException)
9  {
10   check(side1);
11   check(side2);
12   check(side3);
13
14   if (!isValid(side1, side2, side3))
15     throw TriangleException(side1, side2, side3);
16
17   this->side1 = side1;
18   this->side2 = side2;
19   this->side3 = side3;
20 }
```

Function `check` declares that it throws `NonPositiveSideException` and constructor `Triangle` declares that it throws `NonPositiveSideException` and `TriangleException`.

empty exception specification

Note

Placing `throw()` after a function header, known as an *empty exception specification,* declares that the function does not throw any exceptions. If a function attempts to throw an exception, a standard C++ function **unexpected** is invoked, which normally terminates the program. In Visual C++, however, the empty exception specification is treated as if no exception list is present.

Note

Throwing an exception that is not declared in the throw list will cause the function **unexpected** to be invoked. However, a function without exception specification can throw any exception and will not cause **unexpected** to be invoked.

undeclared exception

Note

If a function specifies **bad_exception** in its throw list, the function will throw a **bad_exception** if an unspecified exception is thrown from the function.

bad_exception

16.11 What is the purpose of exception specifications? How do you declare a throw list? Can you declare multiple exceptions in a function declaration?

Check Point

16.10 When to Use Exceptions

Use exceptions for exceptional circumstances, not for simple logic errors that can be caught easily using an **if** *statement.*

Key Point

The **try** block contains the code that is executed in normal circumstances. The **catch** block contains the code that is executed in exceptional circumstances. Exception handling separates error-handling code from normal programming tasks, thus making programs easier to read and to modify. Be aware, however, that exception handling usually requires more time and resources, because it requires instantiating a new exception object, rolling back the call stack, and propagating the exception through the chain of functions invoked to search for the handler.

An exception occurs in a function. If you want the exception to be processed by its caller, you should throw it. If you can handle the exception in the function where it occurs, there is no need to throw or use exceptions.

In general, common exceptions that may occur in multiple classes in a project are candidates for exception classes. Simple errors that may occur in individual functions are best handled locally without throwing exceptions.

Exception handling is for dealing with unexpected error conditions. Do not use a **try-catch** block to deal with simple, expected situations. Which situations are exceptional and which are expected is sometimes difficult to decide. The point is not to abuse exception handling as a way to deal with a simple logic test.

A general paradigm for exception handling is that you declare to throw an exception in a function as shown in (a) below, and use the function in a **try-catch** block as shown in (b).

```
returnType function1(parameterList)
  throw (exceptionList)
{
  ...
  if (an exception condition)
    throw AnException(arguments);
  ...
}
```

(a)

```
returnType function2(parameterList)
{
  try
  {
    ...
    function1 (arguments);
    ...
  }
  catch (AnException& ex)
  {
    Handler;
  }
  ...
}
```

(b)

16.12 What exceptions should be used in a program?

Check Point

KEY TERMS

exception 620	standard exception 623
exception specification 640	throw exception 623
rethrow exception 638	throw list 640

CHAPTER SUMMARY

1. Exception handling makes programs robust. Exception handling separates error-handling code from normal programming tasks, thus making programs easier to read and modify. Another important advantage of exception handling is that it enables a function to throw an exception to its caller.

2. C++ allows you to use the `throw` statement to throw a value of any type (primitive or class type) when an exception occurs. This value is passed to a `catch` block as an argument so that the `catch` block can utilize this value to process the exception.

3. When an exception is thrown, the normal execution flow is interrupted. If the exception value matches a `catch` block parameter type, the control is transferred to a `catch` block. Otherwise, the function is exited and the exception is thrown to the function's caller. If the exception is not handled in the `main` function, the program is aborted.

4. C++ provides a number of standard exception classes that can be used for creating exception objects. You can use the `exception` class or its derived classes `runtime_error` and `logic_error` to create exception objects.

5. You also can create a custom exception class if the standard exception classes cannot adequately describe exceptions. This class is just like any C++ class, but often it is desirable to derive it from `exception` or a derived class of `exception` so you can utilize the common features (e.g., the `what()` function) in the `exception` class.

6. A `try` block may be followed by multiple `catch` blocks. The order in which exceptions are specified in `catch` blocks is important. A `catch` block for a base class type should appear after a `catch` block for a derived class type.

7. If a function throws an exception, you should declare the exception's type in the function header to warn programmers to deal with potential exceptions.

8. Exception handling should not be used to replace simple tests. You should test simple exceptions whenever possible and reserve exception handling for dealing with situations that cannot be handled with `if` statements.

QUIZ

Answer the quiz for this chapter online at www.cs.armstrong.edu/liang/cpp3e/quiz.html.

PROGRAMMING EXERCISES

Sections 16.2–16.4

*16.1 (invalid_argument) Listing 6.18 gives the hex2Dec(const string& hexString) function that returns a decimal number from a hex string. Implement the hex2Dec function to throw a invalid_argument exception if the string is not a hex string. Write a test program that prompts the user to enter a hex number as a string and display the number in decimal.

*16.2 (*invalid_argument*) Programming Exercise 6.40 specifies the bin2Octal(const string& binaryString) function that returns an octal number from a binary string. Implement the bin2Octal function to throw an invalid_argument exception if the string is not a binary string. Write a test program that prompts the user to enter a binary number as a string and displays the octal number.

*16.3 (*Modify the* Course *class*) Rewrite the addStudent function in the Course class in Listing 11.16, Course.cpp to throw a runtime_error if the number of students exceeds the capacity.

*16.4 (*Modify the* Rational *class*) Rewrite the subscript operator function in the Rational class in Listing 14.8, RationalWithOperators.cpp to throw a runtime_error if the index is not 0 or 1.

Sections 16.5–16.10

*16.5 (HexFormatException) Implement the hex2Dec function in Programming Exercise 16.1 to throw a HexFormatException if the string is not a hex string. Define a custom exception class named HexFormatException. Write a test program that prompts the user to enter a hex number as a string and displays the number in decimal.

VideoNote
The HexFormatException class

*16.6 (*BinaryFormatException*) Implement the bin2Octal function in Programming Exercise 16.2 to throw a BinaryFormatException if the string is not a binary string. Define a custom exception class named BinaryFormatException. Write a test program that reads a binary number as a string, invokes the bin2Octal function, and displays the octal number.

*16.7 (*Modify* Rational *class*) Section 14.4, "Overloading the Subscript Operator []," introduced how to overload the subscript operator [] in the Rational class. If the subscript is neither 0 nor 1, the function throws a runtime_error exception. Define a custom exception called IllegalSubscriptException and let the function operator throw an IllegalSubscriptException if the subscript is neither 0 nor 1. Write a test program with a try-catch block to handle this type of exception.

*16.8 (*Modify* StackOfIntegers *class*) In Section 10.9, "Case Study: The StackOfIntegers Class," you defined a stack class for integers. Define a custom exception class named EmptyStackException and let the pop and peek functions throw an EmptyStackException if the stack is empty. Write a test program with a try-catch block to handle this type of exception.

*16.9 (*Algebra: solve* 3 × 3 *linear equations*) Programming Exercise 12.24 solves a 3 × 3 system of linear equation. Write the following function to solve the equation.

```
vector<double> solveLinearEquation(
    vector<vector<double>> a, vector<double> b)
```

The parameter **a** stores $\{\{a_{11}, a_{12}, a_{13}\}, \{a_{21}, a_{22}, a_{23}\}, \{a_{31}, a_{32}, a_{33}\}\}$ and **b** stores $\{b_1, b_2, b_3\}$. The solution for $\{x, y, z\}$ is returned in a vector of three elements. The function throws a **runtime_error** if $|A|$ is **0** and an **invalid_argument** if the size of **a**, **a[0]**, **a[1]**, **a[2]**, and **b** is not **3**.

Write a program that prompts the user to enter $a_{11}, a_{12}, a_{13}, a_{21}, a_{22}, a_{23}, a_{31}, a_{32}, a_{33}, b_1, b_2,$ and b_3, and displays the result. If $|A|$ is **0**, report that "The equation has no solution". The sample runs are the same as in Programming Exercise 12.24.

RECURSION

Objectives

- To describe what a recursive function is and the benefits of using recursion (§17.1).

- To develop recursive programs for recursive mathematical functions (§§17.2–17.3).

- To explain how recursive function calls are handled in a call stack (§§17.2–17.3).

- To think recursively (§17.4).

- To use an overloaded helper function to derive a recursive function (§17.5).

- To solve selection sort using recursion (§17.5.1).

- To solve binary search using recursion (§17.5.2).

- To solve the Towers of Hanoi problem using recursion (§17.6).

- To solve the Eight Queens problem using recursion (§17.7).

- To understand the relationship and difference between recursion and iteration (§17.8).

- To know tail-recursive functions and why they are desirable (§17.9).

17.1 Introduction

Key Point

Recursion is a technique that leads to elegant solutions to problems that are difficult to program using simple loops.

string permutations

Suppose you wish to print all permutations of a string. For example, for a string **abc**, its permutations are **abc**, **acb**, **bac**, **bca**, **cab**, and **cba**. How do you solve this problem? There are several ways to do so. An intuitive and effective solution is to use recursion.

Eight Queens problem

The classic Eight Queens puzzle is to place eight queens on a chessboard such that no two can attack each other (i.e., no two queens are on the same row, same column, or same diagonal), as shown in Figure 17.1. How do you write a program to solve this problem? There are several ways to solve this problem. An intuitive and effective solution is to use recursion.

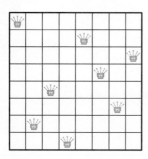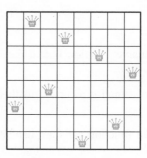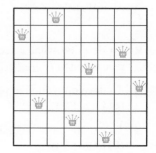

FIGURE 17.1 The Eight Queens problem can be solved using recursion.

recursive function

To use recursion is to program using *recursive functions*—functions that invoke themselves. Recursion is a useful programming technique. In some cases, it enables you to develop a natural, straightforward, simple solution to an otherwise difficult problem. This chapter introduces the concepts and techniques of recursive programming and illustrates by examples how to "think recursively."

17.2 Example: Factorials

Key Point

A recursive function is one that invokes itself.

Many mathematical functions are defined using recursion. We begin with a simple example that illustrates recursion.

The factorial of a number **n** can be recursively defined as follows:

```
0! = 1;
n! = n × (n - 1)!; n > 0
```

How do you find **n!** for a given **n**? It is easy to find **1!** because you know that **0!** is **1** and **1!** is **1 × 0!**. Assuming you know that **(n - 1)!**, **n!** can be obtained immediately using **n × (n - 1)!**. Thus, the problem of computing **n!** is reduced to computing **(n - 1)!**. When computing **(n - 1)!**, you can apply the same idea recursively until **n** is reduced to **0**.

Let **factorial(n)** be the function for computing **n!**. If you call the function with **n = 0**, it immediately returns the result. The function knows how to solve the simplest case, which is referred to as the *base case* or the *stopping condition*. If you call the function with **n > 0**, it reduces the problem into a subproblem for computing the factorial of **n - 1**. The subproblem is essentially the same as the original problem but is simpler or smaller than the original. Because the subproblem has the same property as the original, you can call the function with a different argument, which is referred to as a *recursive call*.

base case or stopping condition

recursive call

The recursive algorithm for computing `factorial(n)` can be simply described as follows:

```
if (n == 0)
  return 1;
else
  return n * factorial(n - 1);
```

A recursive call can result in many more recursive calls, because the function is dividing a subproblem into new subproblems. For a recursive function to terminate, the problem must eventually be reduced to a stopping case. At this point the function returns a result to its caller. The caller then performs a computation and returns the result to its own caller. This process continues until the result is passed back to the original caller. The original problem can now be solved by multiplying n by the result of `factorial(n - 1)`.

Listing 17.1 is a complete program that prompts the user to enter a nonnegative integer and displays the factorial for the number.

LISTING 17.1 ComputeFactorial.cpp

```cpp
1   #include <iostream>
2   using namespace std;
3
4   // Return the factorial for a specified index
5   int factorial(int);
6
7   int main()
8   {
9     // Prompt the user to enter an integer
10    cout << "Please enter a non-negative integer: ";
11    int n;
12    cin >> n;
13
14    // Display factorial
15    cout << "Factorial of " << n << " is " << factorial(n);
16
17    return 0;
18  }
19
20  // Return the factorial for a specified index
21  int factorial(int n)
22  {
23    if (n == 0) // Base case                                      base case
24      return 1;
25    else
26      return n * factorial(n - 1); // Recursive call              recursion
27  }
```

```
Please enter a nonnegative integer: 5 [↵Enter]
Factorial of 5 is 120
```

The `factorial` function (lines 21–27) is essentially a direct translation of the recursive mathematical definition for the factorial into C++ code. The call to `factorial` is recursive because it calls itself. The parameter passed to `factorial` is decremented until it reaches the base case of `0`.

You see how to write a recursive function. How does recursion work? Figure 17.2 illus-   how does it work?
trates the execution of the recursive calls, starting with n = 4. The use of stack space for recursive calls is shown in Figure 17.3.

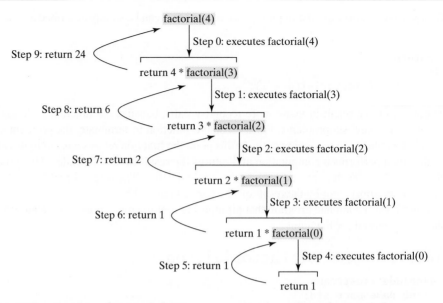

Figure 17.2 Invoking `factorial(4)` spawns recursive calls to `factorial`.

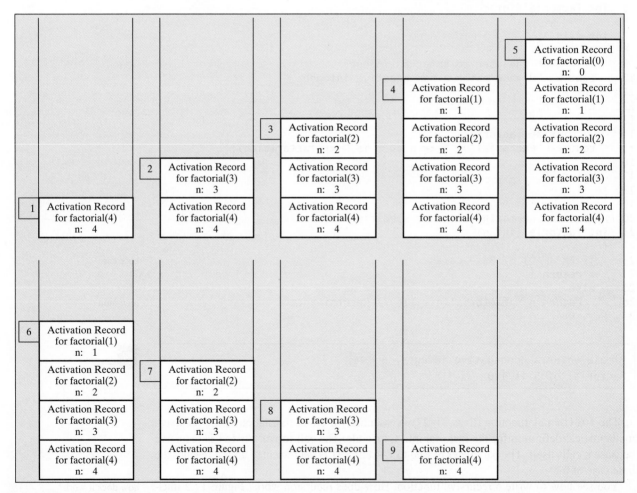

Figure 17.3 When `factorial(4)` is being executed, the `factorial` function is called recursively, causing memory space to dynamically change.

Caution

infinite recursion

Infinite recursion can occur if recursion does not reduce the problem in a manner that allows it to eventually converge into the base case or a base case is not specified. For example, suppose you mistakenly write the `factorial` function as follows:

```cpp
int factorial(int n)
{
  return n * factorial(n - 1);
}
```

The function runs infinitely and causes the stack overflow.

Pedagogical Note

It is simpler and more efficient to implement the `factorial` function using a loop. However, the recursive `factorial` function is a good example to demonstrate the concept of recursion.

Note

The example discussed so far shows a recursive function that invokes itself. This is known as *direct recursion*. It is also possible to create *indirect recursion*. This occurs when function **A** invokes function **B**, which in turn invokes function **A**. There can even be several more functions involved in the recursion. For example, function **A** invokes function **B**, which invokes function **C**, which invokes function **A**.

direct recursion
indirect recursion

17.1 What is a recursive function? Describe the characteristics of recursive functions. What is an infinite recursion?

17.2 Show the output of the following programs and identify base cases and recursive calls.

```cpp
#include <iostream>
using namespace std;

int f(int n)
{
  if (n == 1)
    return 1;
  else
    return n + f(n - 1);
}

int main()
{
  cout << "Sum is " << f(5) << endl;

  return 0;
}
```

```cpp
#include <iostream>
using namespace std;

void f(int n)
{
  if (n > 0)
  {
    cout << n % 10;
    f(n / 10);
  }
}

int main()
{
  f(1234567);

  return 0;
}
```

17.3 Write a recursive mathematical definition for computing 2^n for a positive integer n.

17.4 Write a recursive mathematical definition for computing x^n for a positive integer n and a real number x.

17.5 Write a recursive mathematical definition for computing $1 + 2 + 3 + \ldots + n$ for a positive integer.

17.6 How many times is the `factorial` function in Listing 17.1 invoked for `factorial(6)`?

17.3 Case Study: Fibonacci Numbers

Key Point

In some cases, recursion enables you to create an intuitive, straightforward, simple solution to a problem.

The `factorial` function in the preceding section easily could be rewritten without using recursion. In some cases, however, using recursion enables you to give a natural, straightforward, simple solution to a program that would otherwise be difficult to solve. Consider the well-known Fibonacci series problem, as follows:

```
The series: 0  1  1  2  3  5  8  13  21  34  55  89 . . .
   Indices: 0  1  2  3  4  5  6  7   8   9  10  11
```

The Fibonacci series begins with 0 and 1, and each subsequent number is the sum of the preceding two numbers in the series. The series can be defined recursively as follows:

```
fib(0) = 0;
fib(1) = 1;
fib(index) = fib(index - 2) + fib(index - 1); index >= 2
```

The Fibonacci series was named for Leonardo Fibonacci, a medieval mathematician, who originated it to model the growth of the rabbit population. It can be applied in numeric optimization and in various other areas.

How do you find `fib(index)` for a given `index`? It is easy to find `fib(2)` because you know `fib(0)` and `fib(1)`. Assuming that you know `fib(index - 2)` and `fib(index - 1)`, `fib(index)` can be obtained immediately. Thus, the problem of computing `fib(index)` is reduced to computing `fib(index - 2)` and `fib(index - 1)`. When computing `fib(index - 2)` and `fib(index - 1)`, you apply the idea recursively until `index` is reduced to 0 or 1.

The base case is `index = 0` or `index = 1`. If you call the function with `index = 0` or `index = 1`, it immediately returns the result. If you call the function with `index >= 2`, it divides the problem into two subproblems for computing `fib(index - 1)` and `fib(index - 2)` using recursive calls. The recursive algorithm for computing `fib(index)` can be simply described as follows:

```
if (index == 0)
  return 0;
else if (index == 1)
  return 1;
else
  return fib(index - 1) + fib(index - 2);
```

Listing 17.2 is a complete program that prompts the user to enter an index and computes the Fibonacci number for the index.

LISTING 17.2 ComputeFibonacci.cpp

```cpp
1   #include <iostream>
2   using namespace std;
3
4   // The function for finding the Fibonacci number
5   int fib(int);
6
7   int main()
8   {
9     // Prompt the user to enter an integer
10    cout << "Enter an index for the Fibonacci number: ";
11    int index;
```

```
12     cin >> index;
13
14     // Display factorial
15     cout << "Fibonacci number at index " << index << " is "
16       << fib(index) << endl;
17
18     return 0;
19   }
20
21   // The function for finding the Fibonacci number
22   int fib(int index)
23   {
24     if (index == 0) // Base case                                   base case
25       return 0;
26     else if (index == 1) // Base case                              base case
27       return 1;
28     else // Reduction and recursive calls
29       return fib(index - 1) + fib(index - 2);                      recursion
30   }
```

```
Enter an index for the Fibonacci number: 7 ↵Enter
Fibonacci number at index 7 is 13
```

The program does not show the considerable amount of work done behind the scenes by the computer. Figure 17.4, however, shows successive recursive calls for evaluating `fib(4)`. The original function, `fib(4)`, makes two recursive calls, `fib(3)` and `fib(2)`, and then returns `fib(3)` + `fib(2)`. But in what order are these functions called? In C++, operands for the binary + operator may be evaluated in any order. Assume it is evaluated from the left to right. The labels in Figure 17.4 show the order in which functions are called.

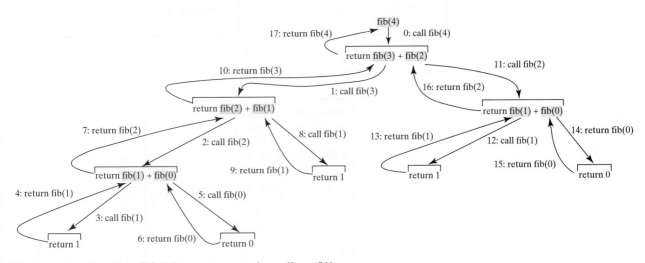

FIGURE 17.4 Invoking `fib(4)` spawns recursive calls to `fib`.

As shown in Figure 17.4, there are many duplicated recursive calls. For instance, `fib(2)` is called twice, `fib(1)` three times, and `fib(0)` twice. In general, computing `fib(index)` requires twice as many recursive calls as are needed for computing `fib(index - 1)`. As you try larger index values, the number of calls substantially increases, as shown in Table 17.1.

TABLE 17.1 Number of Recursive Calls in `fib (index)`

index	2	3	4	10	20	30	40	50
# of calls	3	5	9	177	21891	2,692,537	331,160,281	2,075,316,483

Pedagogical Note

The recursive implementation of the `fib` function is very simple and straightforward, but not efficient. See Programming Exercise 17.2 for an efficient solution using loops. The recursive `fib` function is a good example to demonstrate how to write recursive functions, though it is not practical.

17.7 How many times is the `fib` function in Listing 17.2 invoked for `fib(6)`?

17.8 Show the output of the following two programs:

```cpp
#include <iostream>
using namespace std;

void f(int n)
{
  if (n > 0)
  {
    cout << n << " ";
    f(n - 1);
  }
}

int main()
{
  f(5);

  return 0;
}
```

```cpp
#include <iostream>
using namespace std;

void f(int n)
{
  if (n > 0)
  {
    f(n - 1);
    cout << n << " ";
  }
}

int main()
{
  f(5);

  return 0;
}
```

17.9 What is wrong in the following function?

```cpp
#include <iostream>
using namespace std;

void f(double n)
{
  if (n != 0)
  {
    cout << n;
    f(n / 10);
  }
}

int main()
{
  f(1234567);

  return 0;
}
```

17.4 Problem Solving Using Recursion

If you think recursively, you can solve many problems using recursion.

Key Point

The preceding sections presented two classic recursion examples. All recursive functions have the following characteristics:

recursion characteristics

- The function is implemented using an `if-else` or a `switch` statement that leads to different cases.

if-else

- One or more *base cases* (the simplest case) are used to stop recursion.

base cases

- Every recursive call reduces the original problem, bringing it increasingly closer to a base case until it becomes that case.

reduction

In general, to solve a problem using recursion, you break it into subproblems. If a subproblem resembles the original problem, you can apply the same approach to solve the subproblem recursively. This subproblem is almost the same as the original problem in nature with a smaller size.

Recursion is everywhere. It is fun to *think recursively*. Consider drinking coffee. You may describe the procedure recursively as follows:

think recursively

```
void drinkCoffee(Cup& cup)
{
  if (!cup.isEmpty())
  {
    cup.takeOneSip(); // Take one sip
    drinkCoffee(cup);
  }
}
```

Assume **cup** is an object for a cup of coffee with the instance functions `isEmpty()` and `takeOneSip()`. You can break the problem into two subproblems: one is to drink one sip of coffee and the other is to drink the rest of the coffee in the cup. The second problem is the same as the original problem but smaller in size. The base case for the problem is when **cup** is empty.

Let us consider a simple problem of printing a message for **n** times. You can break the problem into two subproblems: one is to print the message one time and the other is to print the message **n - 1** times. The second problem is the same as the original problem with a smaller size. The base case for the problem is **n == 0**. You can solve this problem using recursion as follows:

```
void nPrintln(const string& message, int times)
{
  if (times >= 1)
  {
    cout << message << endl;
    nPrintln(message, times - 1);
  } // The base case is times == 0
}
```

recursive call

Note that the `fib` function in Listing 17.2 returns a value to its caller, but the `nPrintln` function is `void` and does not return a value to its caller.

think recursively

Many of the problems presented in the early chapters can be solved using recursion if you *think recursively*. Consider the palindrome problem in Listing 5.16, TestPalindrome.cpp. Recall that a string is a palindrome if it reads the same from the left and from the right. For example, mom and dad are palindromes, but uncle and aunt are not. The problem to check whether a string is a palindrome can be divided into two subproblems:

■ Check whether the first character and the last character of the string are equal.

■ Ignore these two end characters and check whether the rest of the substring is a palindrome.

The second subproblem is the same as the original problem with a smaller size. There are two base cases: (1) the two end characters are not the same; (2) the string size is 0 or 1. In case 1, the string is not a palindrome; and in case 2, the string is a palindrome. The recursive function for this problem can be implemented in Listing 17.3.

LISTING 17.3 RecursivePalindrome.cpp

include header file

function header

string length

recursive call

input string

```cpp
 1  #include <iostream>
 2  #include <string>
 3  using namespace std;
 4
 5  bool isPalindrome(const string& s)
 6  {
 7    if (s.size() <= 1) // Base case
 8      return true;
 9    else if (s[0] != s[s.size() - 1]) // Base case
10      return false;
11    else
12      return isPalindrome(s.substr(1, s.size() - 2));
13  }
14
15  int main()
16  {
17    cout << "Enter a string: ";
18    string s;
19    getline(cin, s);
20
21    if (isPalindrome(s))
22      cout << s << " is a palindrome" << endl;
23    else
24      cout << s << " is not a palindrome" << endl;
25
26    return 0;
27  }
```

```
Enter a string: aba  ↵Enter
aba is a palindrome
```

```
Enter a string: abab  ↵Enter
abab is not a palindrome
```

The `isPalindrome` function checks whether the size of the string is less than or equal to 1 (line 7). If so, the string is a palindrome. The function checks whether the first and the last elements of the string are the same (line 9). If not, the string is not a palindrome. Otherwise, obtain a substring of `s` using `s.substr(1, s.size() - 2)` and recursively invoke `isPalindrome` with the new string (line 12).

17.5 Recursive Helper Functions

Sometimes you can find a solution to the original problem by defining a recursive function to a problem similar to the original problem. This new function is called a recursive helper function. The original problem can be solved by invoking the recursive helper function.

The preceding recursive `isPalindrome` function is not efficient, because it creates a new string for every recursive call. To avoid creating new strings, you can use the `low` and `high` indices to indicate the range of the substring. These two indices must be passed to the recursive function. Since the original function is `isPalindrome(const string& s)`, you have to create a new function `isPalindrome(const string& s, int low, int high)` to accept additional information on the string, as shown in Listing 17.4.

LISTING 17.4 RecursivePalindromeUsingHelperFunction.cpp

```
1  #include <iostream>
2  #include <string>
3  using namespace std;
4
5  bool isPalindrome(const string& s, int low, int high)          helper function
6  {
7    if (high <= low) // Base case
8      return true;
9    else if (s[low] != s[high]) // Base case
10     return false;
11   else
12     return isPalindrome(s, low + 1, high - 1);               recursive call
13 }
14
15 bool isPalindrome(const string& s)                             function header
16 {
17   return isPalindrome(s, 0, s.size() - 1);                    invoke helper function
18 }
19
20 int main()
21 {
22   cout << "Enter a string: ";
23   string s;
24   getline(cin, s);                                            input string
25
26   if (isPalindrome(s))
27     cout << s << " is a palindrome" << endl;
28   else
29     cout << s << " is not a palindrome" << endl;
30
31   return 0;
32 }
```

```
Enter a string: aba  ⏎Enter
aba is a palindrome

Enter a string: abab  ⏎Enter
abab is not a palindrome
```

Two overloaded `isPalindrome` functions are defined. The function `isPalin drome(const string& s)` (line 15) checks whether a string is a palindrome, and the second function `isPalindrome(const string& s, int low, int high)` (line 5) checks whether a substring `s(low..high)` is a palindrome. The first function passes the string `s` with `low = 0` and `high = s.size() - 1` to the second function. The second function can be invoked recursively to check a palindrome in an ever-shrinking substring. It is a common design technique in recursive programming to define a second function that receives additional parameters. Such a function is known as a *recursive helper function*.

recursive helper function

Helper functions are very useful to design recursive solutions for problems involving strings and arrays. The sections that follow present two more examples.

17.5.1 Selection Sort

Selection sort was introduced in Section 7.10, "Sorting Arrays." Now we introduce a recursive selection sort for characters in a string. A variation of selection sort works as follows. It finds the largest element in the list and places it last. It then finds the largest element remaining and places it next to last, and so on until the list contains only a single element. The problem can be divided into two subproblems:

■ Find the largest element in the list and swap it with the last element.

■ Ignore the last element and sort the remaining smaller list recursively.

The base case is that the list contains only one element.

Listing 17.5 gives the recursive sort function.

LISTING 17.5 RecursiveSelectionSort.cpp

helper sort function

recursive call

sort function

```cpp
 1   #include <iostream>
 2   #include <string>
 3   using namespace std;
 4
 5   void sort(string& s, int high)
 6   {
 7     if (high > 0)
 8     {
 9       // Find the largest element and its index
10       int indexOfMax = 0;
11       char max = s[0];
12       for (int i = 1; i <= high; i++)
13       {
14         if (s[i] > max)
15         {
16           max = s[i];
17           indexOfMax = i;
18         }
19       }
20
21       // Swap the largest with the last element in the list
22       s[indexOfMax] = s[high];
23       s[high] = max;
24
25       // Sort the remaining list
26       sort(s, high - 1);
27     }
28   }
29
30   void sort(string& s)
```

```
31   {
32      sort(s, s.size() - 1);                                    invoke helper function
33   }
34
35   int main()
36   {
37      cout << "Enter a string: ";
38      string s;
39      getline(cin, s);                                          input string
40
41      sort(s);
42
43      cout << "The sorted string is " << s << endl;
44
45      return 0;
46   }
```

```
Enter a string: ghfdacb ⏎Enter
The sorted string is abcdfgh
```

Two overloaded **sort** functions are defined. The function **sort(string& s)** sorts characters in **s[0..s.size() - 1]** and the second function **sort(string& s, int high)** sorts characters in **s[0..high]**. The helper function can be invoked recursively to sort an ever-shrinking substring.

17.5.2 Binary Search

VideoNote
Binary search

Binary search was introduced in Section 7.9.2, "The Binary Search Approach." For binary search to work, the elements in the array must already be ordered. The binary search first compares the key with the element in the middle of the array. Consider the following cases:

- Case 1: If the key is less than the middle element, recursively search the key in the first half of the array.

- Case 2: If the key is equal to the middle element, the search ends with a match.

- Case 3: If the key is greater than the middle element, recursively search the key in the second half of the array.

Case 1 and Case 3 reduce the search to a smaller list. Case 2 is a base case when there is a match. Another base case is that the search is exhausted without a match. Listing 17.6 gives a clear, simple solution for the binary search problem using recursion.

LISTING 17.6 RecursiveBinarySearch.cpp

```
1    #include <iostream>
2    using namespace std;
3
4    int binarySearch(const int list[], int key, int low, int high)     helper function
5    {
6       if (low > high)  // The list has been exhausted without a match
7          return -low - 1; // key not found, return the insertion point   base case
8
9       int mid = (low + high) / 2;
10      if (key < list[mid])
11         return binarySearch(list, key, low, mid - 1);               recursive call
12      else if (key == list[mid])
```

base case

recursive call

binarySearch function

call helper function

```
13        return mid;
14     else
15        return binarySearch(list, key, mid + 1, high);
16  }
17
18  int binarySearch(const int list[], int key, int size)
19  {
20    int low = 0;
21    int high = size - 1;
22    return binarySearch(list, key, low, high);
23  }
24
25  int main()
26  {
27    int list[] = { 2, 4, 7, 10, 11, 45, 50, 59, 60, 66, 69, 70, 79};
28    int i = binarySearch(list, 2, 13); // Returns 0
29    int j = binarySearch(list, 11, 13); // Returns 4
30    int k = binarySearch(list, 12, 13); // Returns -6
31
32    cout << "binarySearch(list, 2, 13) returns " << i << endl;
33    cout << "binarySearch(list, 11, 13) returns " << j << endl;
34    cout << "binarySearch(list, 12, 13) returns " << k << endl;
35
36    return 0;
37  }
```

```
binarySearch(list, 2, 13) returns 0
binarySearch(list, 11, 13) returns 4
binarySearch(list, 12, 13) returns -6
```

The binarySearch function in line 18 finds a key in the whole list. The helper binarySearch function in line 4 finds a key in the list with index from low to high.

The binarySearch function in line 18 passes the initial array with low = 0 and high = size - 1 to the helper binarySearch function. The helper function is invoked recursively to find the key in an ever-shrinking subarray.

Check Point

17.10 Show the call stack for isPalindrome("abcba") using the functions defined in Listings 17.3 and 17.4, respectively.

17.11 Show the call stack for selectionSort("abcba") using the function defined in Listing 17.5.

17.12 What is a recursive helper function?

VideoNote
Towers of Hanoi

17.6 Towers of Hanoi

Key Point

The classic Towers of Hanoi problem can be solved easily using recursion, but it is difficult to solve otherwise.

The Towers of Hanoi problem is a classic recursion example. It can be solved easily using recursion but is difficult to solve otherwise.

The problem involves moving a specified number of disks of distinct sizes from one tower to another while observing the following rules:

■ There are *n* disks labeled 1, 2, 3, . . . , *n,* and three towers labeled A, B, and C.

■ No disk can be on top of a smaller disk at any time.

- All the disks are initially placed on tower A.

- Only one disk can be moved at a time, and it must be the top disk on the tower.

The objective is to move all the disks from A to B with the assistance of C. For example, if you have three disks, the steps to move all of the disks from A to B are shown in Figure 17.5.

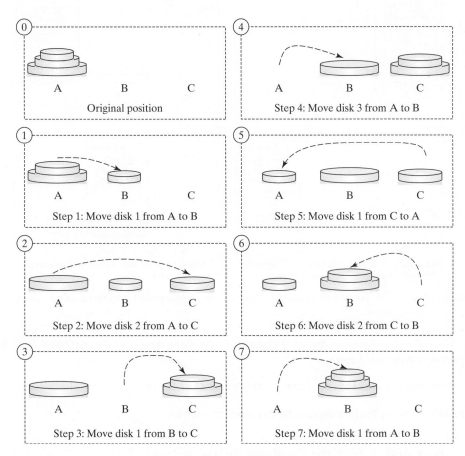

Figure 17.5   The goal of the Towers of Hanoi problem is to move disks from tower A to tower B without breaking the rules.

Note
The Towers of Hanoi is a classic computer science problem. Many websites are devoted to this problem. The website www.cut-the-knot.com/recurrence/hanoi.shtml is worth a look.

In the case of three disks, you can find the solution manually. For a larger number of disks, however—even for four—the problem is quite complex. Fortunately, the problem has an inherently recursive nature, which leads to a straightforward recursive solution.

The base case for the problem is n = 1. If n == 1, you could simply move the disk from A to B. When n > 1, you could split the original problem into three subproblems and solve them sequentially.

1. Move the first n - 1 disks from A to C recursively with the assistance of tower B, as shown in Step 1 in Figure 17.6.

2. Move disk n from A to B, as shown in Step 2 in Figure 17.6.

3. Move **n** - **1** disks from C to B recursively with the assistance of tower A, as shown in Step 3 in Figure 17.6.

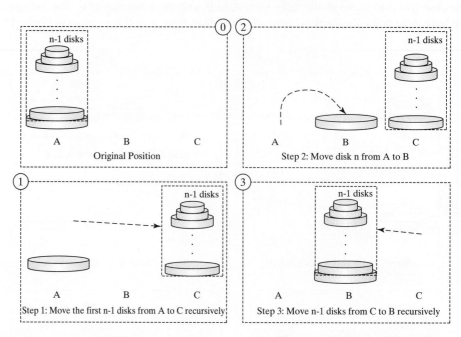

FIGURE 17.6   The Towers of Hanoi problem can be decomposed into three subproblems.

The following function moves *n* disks from the `fromTower` to the `toTower` with the assistance of the `auxTower`:

```
void moveDisks(int n, char fromTower, char toTower, char auxTower)
```

The algorithm for the function can be described as follows:

```
if (n == 1) // Stopping condition
  Move disk 1 from the fromTower to the toTower;
else
{
  moveDisks(n - 1, fromTower, auxTower, toTower);
  Move disk n from the fromTower to the toTower;
  moveDisks(n - 1, auxTower, toTower, fromTower);
}
```

Listing 17.7 prompts the user to enter the number of disks and invokes the recursive function `moveDisks` to display the solution for moving the disks.

LISTING 17.7   TowersOfHanoi.cpp

```
1  #include <iostream>
2  using namespace std;
3
4  // The function for finding the solution to move n disks
5  // from fromTower to toTower with auxTower
```

```
6  void moveDisks(int n, char fromTower,                    recursive function
7      char toTower, char auxTower)
8  {
9    if (n == 1) // Stopping condition
10       cout << "Move disk " << n << " from " <<
11         fromTower << " to " << toTower << endl;
12   else
13   {
14     moveDisks(n - 1, fromTower, auxTower, toTower);       recursion
15     cout << "Move disk " << n << " from " <<
16       fromTower << " to " << toTower << endl;
17     moveDisks(n - 1, auxTower, toTower, fromTower);       recursion
18   }
19 }
20
21 int main()
22 {
23   // Read number of disks, n
24   cout << "Enter number of disks: ";
25   int n;
26   cin >> n;
27
28   // Find the solution recursively
29   cout << "The moves are: " << endl;
30   moveDisks(n, 'A', 'B', 'C');
31
32   return 0;
33 }
```

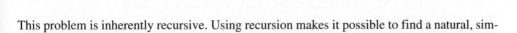

```
Enter number of disks: 4  ↵Enter
The moves are:
Move disk 1 from A to C
Move disk 2 from A to B
Move disk 1 from C to B
Move disk 3 from A to C
Move disk 1 from B to A
Move disk 2 from B to C
Move disk 1 from A to C
Move disk 4 from A to B
Move disk 1 from C to B
Move disk 2 from C to A
Move disk 1 from B to A
Move disk 3 from C to B
Move disk 1 from A to C
Move disk 2 from A to B
Move disk 1 from C to B
```

This problem is inherently recursive. Using recursion makes it possible to find a natural, simple solution. It would be difficult to solve the problem without using recursion.

Consider tracing the program for $n = 3$. The successive recursive calls are shown in Figure 17.7. As you can see, writing the program is easier than tracing the recursive calls. The system uses stacks to trace the calls behind the scenes. To some extent, recursion provides a level of abstraction that hides iterations and other details from the user.

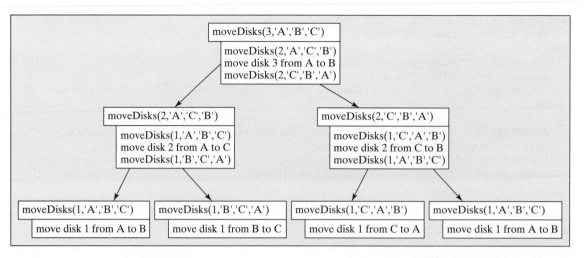

FIGURE 17.7 Invoking `moveDisks(3, 'A', 'B', 'C')` spawns calls to `moveDisks` recursively.

17.13 How many times is the `moveDisks` function in Listing 17.7 invoked for `moveDisks(5, 'A', 'B', 'C')`?

17.7 Eight Queens

The Eight Queens problem can be solved using recursion.

This section gives a recursive solution to the Eight Queens problem presented earlier. The task is to place a queen in each row on a chessboard in such a way that no two queens can attack each other. You may use a two-dimensional array to represent a chessboard. However, since each row can have only one queen, it is sufficient to use a one-dimensional array to denote the position of the queen in the row. So, let us declare array **queens** as follows:

```
int queens[8];
```

Assign `j` to `queens[i]` to denote that a queen is placed in row `i` and column `j`. Figure 17.8a shows the contents of array **queens** for the chessboard in Figure 17.8b.

queens[0]	0
queens[1]	6
queens[2]	4
queens[3]	7
queens[4]	1
queens[5]	3
queens[6]	5
queens[7]	2

(a)   (b)

FIGURE 17.8 `queens[i]` denotes the position of the queen in row i.

Listing 17.8 is a program that finds a solution for the Eight Queens problem.

LISTING 17.8 EightQueen.cpp

```cpp
1  #include <iostream>
2  using namespace std;
```

```
3
4    const int NUMBER_OF_QUEENS = 8; // Constant: eight queens
5    int queens[NUMBER_OF_QUEENS];
6
7    // Check whether a queen can be placed at row i and column j
8    bool isValid(int row, int column)                                    check if valid
9    {
10     for (int i = 1; i <= row; i++)
11       if (queens[row - i] == column       // Check column
12          || queens[row - i] == column - i  // Check upper left diagonal
13          || queens[row - i] == column + i) // Check upper right diagonal
14         return false; // There is a conflict
15     return true;  // No conflict
16   }
17
18   // Display the chessboard with eight queens
19   void printResult()
20   {
21     cout << "\n--------------------------------\n";
22     for (int row = 0; row < NUMBER_OF_QUEENS; row++)
23     {
24       for (int column = 0; column < NUMBER_OF_QUEENS; column++)
25         printf(column == queens[row] ? "| Q " : "|   ");
26       cout << "|\n--------------------------------\n";
27     }
28   }
29
30   // Search to place a queen at the specified row
31   bool search(int row)                                                  search this row
32   {
33     if (row == NUMBER_OF_QUEENS) // Stopping condition
34       return true; // A solution found to place 8 queens in 8 rows
35
36     for (int column = 0; column < NUMBER_OF_QUEENS; column++)          search columns
37     {
38       queens[row] = column; // Place a queen at (row, column)
39       if (isValid(row, column) && search(row + 1))                     search next row
40         return true; // Found, thus return true to exit for loop        found
41     }
42
43     // No solution for a queen placed at any column of this row
44     return false;                                                      not found
45   }
46
47   int main()
48   {
49     search(0); // Start search from row 0. Note row indices are 0 to 7
50     printResult(); // Display result
51
52     return 0;
53   }
```

```
--------------------------------
| Q |   |   |   |   |   |   |   |
--------------------------------
|   |   |   |   | Q |   |   |   |
--------------------------------
|   |   |   |   |   |   |   | Q |
--------------------------------
```

(continued)

```
|   |   |   |   |   | Q |   |   |
---------------------------------
|   |   | Q |   |   |   |   |   |
---------------------------------
|   |   |   |   |   |   | Q |   |
---------------------------------
|   | Q |   |   |   |   |   |   |
---------------------------------
|   |   |   | Q |   |   |   |   |
---------------------------------
```

The program invokes `search(0)` (line 49) to start a search for a solution at row 0, which recursively invokes `search(1)`, `search(2)`, ..., and `search(7)` (line 39).

The recursive `search(row)` function returns `true` if all rows are filled (lines 39–40). The function checks whether a queen can be placed in column 0, 1, 2, ..., and 7 in a `for` loop (line 36). Place a queen in the column (line 38). If the placement is valid, recursively search for the next row by invoking `search(row + 1)` (line 39). If search is successful, return `true` (line 40) to exit the `for` loop. In this case, there is no need to look for the next column in the row. If there is no solution for a queen to be placed on any column of this row, the function returns `false` (line 44).

Suppose you invoke `search(row)` for `row` is 3, as shown in Figure 17.9a. The function tries to fill in a queen in column 0, 1, 2, and so on in this order. For each trial, the `isValid(row, column)` function (line 39) is called to check whether placing a queen at the specified position causes a conflict with the queens placed before this row. It ensures that no queen is placed in the same column (line 11), no queen is placed in the upper left diagonal (line 12), and no queen is placed in the upper right diagonal (line 13), as shown in Figure 17.9a. If `isValid(row, column)` returns `false`, check the next column, as shown Figure 17.9b. If `isValid(row, column)` returns `true`, recursively invoke `search(row + 1)`, as shown in Figure 17.9d. If `search(row + 1)` returns `false`, check the next column on the preceding row, as shown Figure 17.9c.

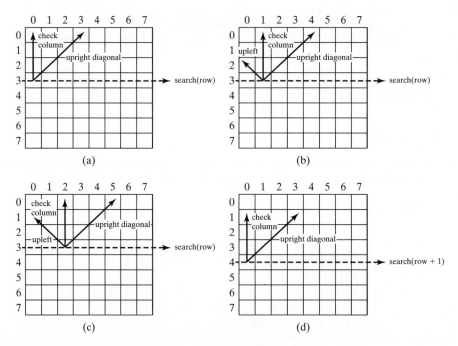

FIGURE 17.9 Invoking `search(row)` fills in a queen in a column on the row.

17.8 Recursion versus Iteration

Recursion is an alternative form of program control. It is essentially repetition without a loop.

Key Point

Recursion is an alternative form of program control. It is essentially repetition without a loop control. When you use loops, you specify a loop body. The repetition of the loop body is controlled by the loop-control structure. In recursion, the function itself is called repeatedly. A selection statement must be used to control whether to call the function recursively or not.

Recursion bears substantial overhead. Each time the program calls a function, the system must assign space for all of the function's local variables and parameters. This can consume considerable memory and requires extra time to manage the additional space.

recursion overhead

Any problem that can be solved recursively can be solved nonrecursively with iterations. Recursion has some negative aspects: It uses too much time and too much memory. Why, then, should you use it? In some cases, using recursion enables you to specify a clear, simple solution for an inherent recursive problem that would otherwise be difficult to obtain. The Towers of Hanoi problem is such an example, which is rather difficult to solve without using recursion.

recursion advantages

The decision whether to use recursion or iteration should be based on the nature of the problem you are trying to solve and your understanding of it. The rule of thumb is to use whichever of the two approaches can best develop an intuitive solution that naturally mirrors the problem. If an iterative solution is obvious, use it. It generally will be more efficient than the recursive option.

recursion or iteration?

Note
Your recursive program could run out of memory, causing a *stack overflow* runtime error.

stack overflow

Tip
If you are concerned about your program's performance, avoid using recursion, because it takes more time and consumes more memory than iteration.

performance concern

17.9 Tail Recursion

A tail recursive function is efficient for reducing stack space.

Key Point

A recursive function is said to be *tail recursive* if there are no pending operations to be performed on return from a recursive call, as illustrated in Figure 17.10a. However, function **B** in Figure 17.10b is not tail recursive because there are pending operations after a function call is returned.

tail recursion

```
Recursive function A
    ...
    ...
    ...
    Invoke function A recursively
```

```
Recursive function B
    ...
    ...
    Invoke function B recursively
    ...
    ...
```

(a) Tail Recursion   (b) Nontail Recursion

FIGURE 17.10 A tail-recursive function has no pending operations after a recursive call.

For example, the recursive `isPalindrome` function (lines 5–13) in Listing 17.4 is tail recursive because there are no pending operations after recursively invoking `isPalindrome` in line 12. However, the recursive `factorial` function (lines 21–27) in Listing 17.1 is not tail recursive, because there is a pending operation, namely multiplication, to be performed on return from each recursive call.

Tail recursion is desirable, because the function ends when the last recursive call ends. So there is no need to store the intermediate calls in the stack. Some compilers can optimize tail recursion to reduce stack space.

A nontail-recursive function can often be converted to a tail-recursive function by using auxiliary parameters. These parameters are used to contain the result. The idea is to incorporate the pending operations into the auxiliary parameters in such a way that the recursive call no longer has a pending operation. You may define a new auxiliary recursive function with the auxiliary parameters. This function may overload the original function with the same name but a different signature. For example, the `factorial` function in Listing 17.1 can be written in a tail-recursive way as follows:

original function

invoke auxiliary function

auxiliary function

recursive call

```
1   // Return the factorial for a specified number
2   int factorial(int n)
3   {
4     return factorial(n, 1); // Call auxiliary function
5   }
6
7   // Auxiliary tail-recursive function for factorial
8   int factorial(int n, int result)
9   {
10    if (n == 1)
11      return result;
12    else
13      return factorial(n - 1, n * result); // Recursive call
14  }
```

The first `factorial` function simply invokes the second auxiliary function (line 4). The second function contains an auxiliary parameter `result` that stores the result for factorial of `n`. This function is invoked recursively in line 13. There is no pending operation after a call is returned. The final result is returned in line 11, which is also the return value from invoking `factorial(n, 1)` in line 4.

17.14 Which of the following statements are true?

- Any recursive function can be converted into a nonrecursive function.
- A recursive function takes more time and memory to execute than a nonrecursive function.
- Recursive functions are *always* simpler than nonrecursive functions.
- There is always a selection statement in a recursive function to check whether a base case is reached.

17.15 What is the cause for the stack overflow exception?

17.16 Identify tail-recursive functions in this chapter.

17.17 Rewrite the `fib` function in Listing 17.2 using tail recursion.

KEY TERMS

CHAPTER SUMMARY

1. A recursive function is one that invokes itself directly or indirectly. For a recursive function to terminate, there must be one or more base cases.

2. Recursion is an alternative form of program control. It is essentially repetition without a loop control. It can be used to write simple, clear solutions for inherently recursive problems that would otherwise be difficult to solve.

3. Sometimes the original function needs to be modified to receive additional parameters in order to be invoked recursively. A recursive helper function can be defined for this purpose.

4. Recursion bears substantial overhead. Each time the program calls a function, the system must assign space for all of the function's local variables and parameters. This can consume considerable memory and requires extra time to manage the additional space.

5. A recursive function is said to be *tail recursive* if there are no pending operations to be performed on return from a recursive call. Some compilers can optimize tail recursion to reduce stack space.

QUIZ

Answer the quiz for this chapter online at www.cs.armstrong.edu/liang/cpp3e/quiz.html.

PROGRAMMING EXERCISES

Sections 17.2–17.3

17.1 (*Linear search*) Rewrite the linear search function in Listing 7.9 using recursion.

*17.2 (*Fibonacci numbers*) Rewrite the `fib` function in Listing 17.2 using iterations.

Hint: To compute `fib(n)` without recursion, you need to obtain `fib(n - 2)` and `fib(n - 1)` first. Let `f0` and `f1` denote the two previous Fibonacci numbers. The current Fibonacci number would then be `f0 + f1`. The algorithm can be described as follows:

```
f0 = 0; // For fib(0)
f1 = 1; // For fib(1)

for (int i = 2; i <= n; i++)
{
  currentFib = f0 + f1;
  f0 = f1;
  f1 = currentFib;
}

// After the loop, currentFib is fib(n)
```

Write a test program that prompts the user to enter an index and displays its Fibonacci number.

*17.3 (*Compute greatest common divisor using recursion*) The `gcd(m, n)` can also be defined recursively as follows:

- If `m % n` is `0`, `gcd (m, n)` is `n`.
- Otherwise, `gcd(m, n)` is `gcd(n, m % n)`.

VideoNote
The GCD problem

Write a recursive function to find the GCD. Write a test program that prompts the user to enter two integers and displays their GCD.

17.4 (*Sum series*) Write a recursive function to compute the following series:

$$f(n) = 1 + \frac{1}{4} + \frac{1}{9} + \ldots + \frac{1}{n^2}$$

Write a test program that displays f(n) for n = 1, 2, ..., 15.

17.5 (*Sum series*) Write a recursive function to compute the following series:

$$f(n) = \frac{1}{3} + \frac{1}{8} + \frac{1}{15} + \ldots + \frac{1}{n(n + 2)}$$

Write a test program that displays f(n) for n = 1, 2, ..., 15.

**17.6 (*Sum series*) Write a recursive function to compute the following series:

$$f(n) = 1 + \frac{3}{4} + \frac{3}{5} + \frac{1}{2} + \ldots + \frac{3}{n + 2}$$

Write a test program that displays f(n) for n = 1, 2, ..., 15.

*17.7 (*Palindrome string*) Modify Listing 17.3, `RecursivePalindrome.cpp`, so that the program finds the number of times the `isPalindrome` function is called. (*Hint:* Use a global variable and increment it every time the function is called.)

Section 17.4

**17.8 (*Count even and odd digits*) Write a recursive function that displays the number of even and odd digits in an integer using the following header:

`void evenAndOddCount(int value)`

Write a test program that prompts the user to enter an integer and displays the number of even and odd digits in it.

**17.9 (*Print the characters in a string reversely*) Write a recursive function that displays a string reversely on the console using the following header:

`void reverseDisplay(const string& s)`

For example, `reverseDisplay("abcd")` displays `dcba`. Write a test program that prompts the user to enter a string and displays its reversal.

*17.10 (*Occurrences of a specified character in a string*) Write a recursive function that finds the number of occurrences of a specified letter in a string using the following function header.

`int count(const string& s, char a)`

For example, `count("Welcome", 'e')` returns 2. Write a test program that prompts the user to enter a string and a character, and displays the number of occurrences for the character in the string.

**17.11 (*Product of digits in an integer using recursion*) Write a recursive function that computes the product of the digits in an integer. Use the following function header:

`int productDigits(int n)`

For example, `productDigits(912)` returns 9 * 1 * 2 = 18. Write a test program that prompts the user to enter an integer and displays the product of digits.

VideoNote

Count occurrence

Section 17.5

**17.12 (*Print the characters in a string reversely*) Rewrite Programming Exercise 17.9 using a helper function to pass the substring high index to the function. The helper function header is as follows:

```
void reverseDisplay(const string& s, int high)
```

**17.13 (*Find the smallest number in an array*) Write a recursive function that returns the smallest integer in an array. Write a test program that prompts the user to enter a list of five integers and displays the smallest integer.

*17.14 (*Find the number of lowercase letters in a string*) Write a recursive function to return the number of lowercase letters in a string. You need to define the following two functions. The second one is a recursive helper function.

```
int getNumberOfLowercaseLetters(const string& s)
int getNumberOfLowercaseLetters(const string& s, int low)
```

Write a test program that prompts the user to enter a string and displays the number of lowercase letters in the string.

*17.15 (*Occurrences of the space character in a string*) Write a recursive function to return the total number of space characters in a string. You need to define the following two functions. The second one is a recursive helper function.

```
int numberOfSpaces(const string& s)
int numberOfSpaces(const string& s, int i)
```

Write a test program that prompts the user to enter a string, invokes the function, and displays the number of spaces in the string.

Section 17.6

*17.16 (*Towers of Hanoi*) Modify Listing 17.7, TowersOfHanoi.cpp, so that the program finds the number of moves needed to move *n* disks from tower A to tower B. (*Hint:* Use a global variable and increment it every time the function is called.)

Comprehensive

***17.17 (*String permutations*) Write a recursive function to print all permutations of a string. For example, for a string abc, the permutation is

```
abc
acb
bac
bca
cab
cba
```

(*Hint:* Define the following two functions. The second is a helper function.)

```
void displayPermuation(const string& s)
void displayPermuation(const string& s1, const string& s2)
```

The first function simply invokes displayPermuation("", s). The second function uses a loop to move a character from s2 to s1 and recursively invoke it with a new s1 and s2. The base case is that s2 is empty and prints s1 to the console.

Write a test program that prompts the user to enter a string and displays all its permutations.

***17.18 (*Game: Sudoku*) Supplement VI.A gives a program to find a solution for a Sudoku problem. Rewrite it using recursion.

***17.19 (*Game: multiple Eight Queens solutions*) Rewrite Listing 17.8 using recursion.

***17.20 (*Game: multiple Sudoku solutions*) Modify Programming Exercise 17.18 to display all possible solutions for a Sudoku puzzle.

*17.21 (*Decimal to binary*) Write a recursive function that converts a decimal number into a binary number as a string. The function header is:

```
string decimalToBinary(int value)
```

Write a test program that prompts the user to enter a decimal number and displays its binary equivalent.

*17.22 (*Decimal to hex*) Write a recursive function that converts a decimal number into a hex number as a string. The function header is:

```
string decimalToHex(int value)
```

Write a test program that prompts the user to enter a decimal number and displays its hex equivalent.

*17.23 (*Binary to decimal*) Write a recursive function that parses a binary number as a string into a decimal integer. The function header is:

```
int binaryToDecimal(const string& binaryString)
```

Write a test program that prompts the user to enter a binary string and displays its decimal equivalent.

*17.24 (*Hex to decimal*) Write a recursive function that parses a hex number as a string into a decimal integer. The function header is:

```
int hexToDecimal(const string& hexString)
```

Write a test program that prompts the user to enter a hex string and displays its decimal equivalent.

APPENDIXES

C++ Keywords

The following keywords are reserved for use by the C++ language. They should not be used for anything other than their predefined purposes in C++.

asm	do	inline	short	typeid
auto	double	int	signed	typename
bool	dynamic_cast	long	sizeof	union
break	else	mutable	static	unsigned
case	enum	namespace	static_cast	using
catch	explicit	new	struct	virtual
char	extern	operator	switch	void
class	false	private	template	volatile
const	float	protected	this	wchar_t
const_cast	for	public	throw	while
continue	friend	register	true	
default	goto	reinterpret_cast	try	
delete	if	return	typedef	

Note that the following eleven C++ keywords are not essential. Not all C++ compilers support them. However, they provide more readable alternatives to some C++ operators.

Keyword	Equivalent Operator
and	&&
and_eq	&=
bitand	&
bitor	|
compl	~
not	!
not_eq	!=
or	||
or_eq	|=
xor	^
xor_eq	^=

The ASCII Character Set

Tables B.1 and B.2 show ASCII characters and their respective decimal and hexadecimal codes. The decimal or hexadecimal code of a character is a combination of its row index and column index. For example, in Table B.1, the letter A is at row 6 and column 5, so its decimal equivalent is 65; in Table B.2, letter A is at row 4 and column 1, so its hexadecimal equivalent is 41.

TABLE B.1 ASCII Character Set in the Decimal Index

	0	1	2	3	4	5	6	7	8	9
0	nul	soh	stx	etx	eot	enq	ack	bel	bs	ht
1	nl	vt	ff	cr	so	si	dle	dc1	dc2	dc3
2	dc4	nak	syn	etb	can	em	sub	esc	fs	gs
3	rs	us	sp	!	"	#	$	%	&	'
4	(	)	*	+	,	-	.	/	0	1
5	2	3	4	5	6	7	8	9	:	;
6	<	=	>	?	@	A	B	C	D	E
7	F	G	H	I	J	K	L	M	N	O
8	P	Q	R	S	T	U	V	W	X	Y
9	Z	[	\	]	^	_	`	a	b	c
10	d	e	f	g	h	i	j	k	l	m
11	n	o	p	q	r	s	t	u	v	w
12	x	y	z	{	|	}	~	del		

TABLE B.2 ASCII Character Set in the Hexadecimal Index

	0	1	2	3	4	5	6	7	8	9	A	B	C	D	E	F
0	nul	soh	stx	etx	eot	enq	ack	bel	bs	ht	nl	vt	ff	cr	so	si
1	dle	dc1	dc2	dc3	dc4	nak	syn	etb	can	em	sub	esc	fs	gs	rs	us
2	sp	!	"	#	$	%	&	'	(	)	*	+	,	-	.	/
3	0	1	2	3	4	5	6	7	8	9	:	;	<	=	>	?
4	@	A	B	C	D	E	F	G	H	I	J	K	L	M	N	O
5	P	Q	R	S	T	U	V	W	X	Y	Z	[	\	]	^	_
6	`	a	b	c	d	e	f	g	h	i	j	k	l	m	n	o
7	p	q	r	s	t	u	v	w	x	y	z	{	|	}	~	del

Operator Precedence Chart

The operators are shown in decreasing order of precedence from top to bottom. Operators in the same group have the same precedence, and their associativity is shown in the table.

Operator	Type	Associativity
::	binary scope resolution	left to right
::	unary scope resolution	
.	object member access via object	left to right
->	object member access via pointer	
()	function call	
[]	array subscript	
++	postfix increment	
--	postfix decrement	
typeid	runtime type information	
dynamic_cast	dynamic cast (runtime)	
static_cast	static cast (compile time)	
reinterpret_cast	cast for nonstandard conversion	
++	prefix increment	right to left
--	prefix decrement	
+	unary plus	
-	unary minus	
!	unary logical negation	
~	bitwise negation	
sizeof	size of a type	
&	address of a variable	
*	pointer of a variable	
new	dynamic memory allocation	
new[]	dynamic array allocation	
delete	dynamic memory deallocation	
delete[]	dynamic array deallocation	
(type)	C-Style cast	right to left
*	multiplication	left to right
/	division	
%	modulus	

Operator	Type	Associativity
+	addition	left to right
-	subtraction	
<<	output or bitwise left shift	left to right
>>	input or bitwise right shift	
<	less than	left to right
<=	less than or equal to	
>	greater than	
>=	greater than or equal to	
==	equal	left to right
!=	not equal	
&	bitwise AND	left to right
^	bitwise exclusive OR	left to right
|	bitwise inclusive OR	left to right
&&	Boolean AND	left to right
||	Boolean OR	left to right
?:	ternary operator	right to left
=	assignment	right to left
+=	addition assignment	
-=	subtraction assignment	
*=	multiplication assignment	
/=	division assignment	
%=	modulus assignment	
&=	bitwise AND assignment	
^=	bitwise exclusive OR assignment	
|=	bitwise inclusive OR assignment	
<<=	bitwise left-shift assignment	
>>=	bitwise right-shift assignment	

APPENDIX D

Number Systems

D.1 Introduction

Computers use binary numbers internally, because computers are made naturally to store and process 0s and 1s. The binary number system has two digits, 0 and 1. A number or character is stored as a sequence of 0s and 1s. Each 0 or 1 is called a *bit* (binary digit).

binary numbers

In our daily life we use decimal numbers. When we write a number such as 20 in a program, it is assumed to be a decimal number. Internally, computer software is used to convert decimal numbers into binary numbers, and vice versa.

decimal numbers

We write computer programs using decimal numbers. However, to deal with an operating system, we need to reach down to the "machine level" by using binary numbers. Binary numbers tend to be very long and cumbersome. Often hexadecimal numbers are used to abbreviate them, with each hexadecimal digit representing four binary digits. The hexadecimal number system has 16 digits: 0–9 and A–F. The letters A, B, C, D, E, and F correspond to the decimal numbers 10, 11, 12, 13, 14, and 15.

hexadecimal number

The digits in the decimal number system are 0, 1, 2, 3, 4, 5, 6, 7, 8, and 9. A decimal number is represented by a sequence of one or more of these digits. The value that each digit represents depends on its position, which denotes an integral power of 10. For example, the digits 7, 4, 2, and 3 in decimal number 7423 represent 7000, 400, 20, and 3, respectively, as shown below:

$$\boxed{7\ |\ 4\ |\ 2\ |\ 3} = 7 \times 10^3 + 4 \times 10^2 + 2 \times 10^1 + 3 \times 10^0$$

$$10^3\ 10^2\ 10^1\ 10^0 = 7000 + 400 + 20 + 3 = 7423$$

The decimal number system has ten digits, and the position values are integral powers of 10. We say that 10 is the *base* or *radix* of the decimal number system. Similarly, since the binary number system has two digits, its base is 2, and since the hex number system has 16 digits, its base is 16.

base
radix

If 1101 is a binary number, the digits 1, 1, 0, and 1 represent $1 \times 2^3, 1 \times 2^2, 0 \times 2^1$, and 1×2^0, respectively:

$$\boxed{1\ |\ 1\ |\ 0\ |\ 1} = 1 \times 2^3 + 1 \times 2^2 + 0 \times 2^1 + 1 \times 2^0$$

$$2^3\ 2^2\ 2^1\ 2^0 = 8 + 4 + 0 + 1 = 13$$

If 7423 is a hex number, the digits 7, 4, 2, and 3 represent $7 \times 16^3, 4 \times 16^2, 2 \times 16^1$, and 3×16^0, respectively:

$$\boxed{7\ |\ 4\ |\ 2\ |\ 3} = 7 \times 16^3 + 4 \times 16^2 + 2 \times 16^1 + 3 \times 16^0$$

$$16^3\ 16^2\ 16^1\ 16^0 = 28672 + 1024 + 32 + 3 = 29731$$

D.2 Conversions Between Binary and Decimal Numbers

binary to decimal

Given a binary number $b_n b_{n-1} b_{n-2} \ldots b_2 b_1 b_0$, the equivalent decimal value is

$$b_n \times 2^n + b_{n-1} \times 2^{n-1} + b_{n-2} \times 2^{n-2} + \ldots + b_2 \times 2^2 + b_1 \times 2^1 + b_0 \times 2^0$$

Here are some examples of converting binary numbers to decimals:

Binary	Conversion Formula	Decimal
10	$1 \times 2^1 + 0 \times 2^0$	2
1000	$1 \times 2^3 + 0 \times 2^2 + 0 \times 2^1 + 0 \times 2^0$	8
10101011	$1 \times 2^7 + 0 \times 2^6 + 1 \times 2^5 + 0 \times 2^4 + 1 \times 2^3 + 0 \times 2^2 +$ $1 \times 2^1 + 1 \times 2^0$	171

decimal to binary

To convert a decimal number d to a binary number is to find the bits b_n, b_{n-1}, $b_{n-2}, \ldots, b_2, b_1,$ and b_0 such that

$$d = b_n \times 2^n + b_{n-1} \times 2^{n-1} + b_{n-2} \times 2^{n-2} + \ldots + b_2 \times 2^2 + b_1 \times 2^1 + b_0 \times 2^0$$

These bits can be found by successively dividing d by 2 until the quotient is 0. The remainders are $b_0, b_1, b_2, \ldots, b_{n-2}, b_{n-1},$ and b_n.

For example, the decimal number 123 is 1111011 in binary. The conversion is done as follows:

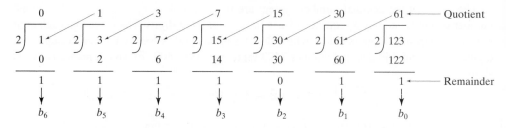

 Tip
The Windows Calculator, as shown in Figure D.1, is a useful tool for performing number conversions. To run it, search for *Calculator* from the *Start* button and launch Calculator, then under *View* select *Scientific*.

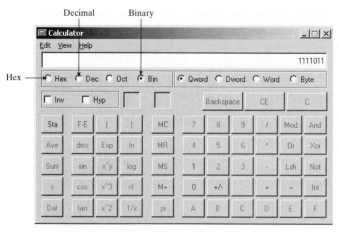

FIGURE D.1   You can perform number conversions using the Windows Calculator.

D.3 Conversions Between Hexadecimal and Decimal Numbers

Given a hexadecimal number $h_n h_{n-1} h_{n-2} \ldots h_2 h_1 h_0$, the equivalent decimal value is

hex to decimal

$$h_n \times 16^n + h_{n-1} \times 16^{n-1} + h_{n-2} \times 16^{n-2} + \ldots + h_2 \times 16^2 + h_1 \times 16^1 + h_0 \times 16^0$$

Here are some examples of converting hexadecimal numbers to decimals:

Hexadecimal	Conversion Formula	Decimal
7F	$7 \times 16^1 + 15 \times 16^0$	127
FFFF	$15 \times 16^3 + 15 \times 16^2 + 15 \times 16^1 + 15 \times 16^0$	65535
431	$4 \times 16^2 + 3 \times 16^1 + 1 \times 16^0$	1073

To convert a decimal number d to a hexadecimal number is to find the hexadecimal digits $h_n, h_{n-1}, h_{n-2}, \ldots, h_2, h_1$, and h_0 such that

decimal to hex

$$d = h_n \times 16^n + h_{n-1} \times 16^{n-1} + h_{n-2} \times 16^{n-2} + \ldots + h_2 \times 16^2$$
$$+ h_1 \times 16^1 + h_0 \times 16^0$$

These numbers can be found by successively dividing d by 16 until the quotient is 0. The remainders are $h_0, h_1, h_2, \ldots, h_{n-2}, h_{n-1}$, and h_n.

For example, the decimal number 123 is 7B in hexadecimal. The conversion is done as follows:

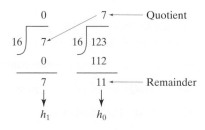

D.4 Conversions Between Binary and Hexadecimal Numbers

To convert a hexadecimal to a binary number, simply convert each digit in the hexadecimal number into a four-digit binary number, using Table D.1.

hex to binary

For example, the hexadecimal number 7B is 1111011, where 7 is 111 in binary, and B is 1011 in binary.

To convert a binary number to a hexadecimal, convert every four binary digits from right to left in the binary number into a hexadecimal number.

binary to hex

For example, the binary number 1110001101 is 38D, since 1101 is D, 1000 is 8, and 11 is 3, as shown below.

TABLE D.1 Converting Hexadecimal to Binary

Hexadecimal	Binary	Decimal
0	0000	0
1	0001	1
2	0010	2
3	0011	3
4	0100	4
5	0101	5
6	0110	6
7	0111	7
8	1000	8
9	1001	9
A	1010	10
B	1011	11
C	1100	12
D	1101	13
E	1110	14
F	1111	15

Note

Octal numbers are also useful. The octal number system has eight digits, 0 to 7. A decimal number 8 is represented in the octal system as 10.

Here are some good online resources for practicing number conversions:

- http://forums.cisco.com/CertCom/game/binary_game_page.htm

- http://people.sinclair.edu/nickreeder/Flash/binDec.htm

- http://people.sinclair.edu/nickreeder/Flash/binHex.htm

MyProgrammingLab™

D.1 Convert the following decimal numbers into hexadecimal and binary numbers:

100; 4340; 2000

D.2 Convert the following binary numbers into hexadecimal and decimal numbers:

1000011001; 100000000; 100111

D.3 Convert the following hexadecimal numbers into binary and decimal numbers:

FEFA9; 93; 2000

APPENDIX E

Bitwise Operations

To write programs at the machine-level, often you need to deal with binary numbers directly and perform operations at the bit-level. C++ provides the bitwise operators and shift operators defined in the following table.

Operator	Name	Example	Description
&	bitwise AND	10101110 & 10010010 yields 10000010	The AND of two corresponding bits yields a 1 if both bits are 1.
|	Bitwise inclusive OR	10101110 | 10010010 yields 10111110	The OR of two corresponding bits yields a 1 if either bit is 1.
^	Bitwise exclusive OR	10101110 ^ 10010010 yields 00111100	The XOR of two corresponding bits yields a 1 only if two bits are different.
~	One's complement	~10101110 yields 01010001	The operator toggles each bit from 0 to 1 and from 1 to 0.
<<	Left shift	10101110 << 2 yields 10111000	Shift bits in the first operand left by the number of the bits specified in the second operand, filling with 0s on the right.
>>	Right shift for unsigned integer	1010111010101110 >> 4 yields 0000101011101010	Shift bit in the first operand right by the number of the bits specified in the second operand, filling with zeros on the left.
>>	Right shift for signed integer		The behavior depends on the platform. Therefore, you should avoid right shift signed integers.

All the bitwise operators can form bitwise assignment operators such as ^=, |= <<=, and >>=.

INDEX

Symbols

`--` (decrement operator). *see* Decrement operator (`--`)

`""` (quotation marks)
  missing quotation marks causing error, 43
  use of special characters in C++, 36

`-` (subtraction) operator, 63, 555

`/` (division) operator, 63

`//` (double slashes), use of special characters in C++, 36

`/=` (division assignment operator), 69, 553

`::` (binary scope resolution operator), 372

`;` (semicolon)
  common errors in selection statements, 100
  missing semicolon causing error, 43
  use of special characters in C++, 36

(escape character), 143

`||` (or) operator, 111, 113, 131

`+` (addition) operator. *see* Addition operator (`+`)

`+` (concatenation operator), 156, 397

`++` (increment operator). *see* Increment operator (`++`)

`+=` (addition assignment operator). *see* Addition
  assignment
  operator (`+=`)

`=` (assignment operator). *see* Assignment operator (`=`)

`-=` (subtraction assignment operator), 69, 553

`==` (equality operator), 100, 397

`->` (arrow operator), accessing object members from
  pointers, 454

`!` (not) operator, 111

`!=` (not equal to) operator, 397

`#` (pound sign), use of special characters in C++, 36

`%` (modulus) operator, 63

`%=` (modulus assignment operator), 69, 553

`&` (address operator), variable addresses, 432

`&&` (and) operator. *see* And (`&&`) operator

`()` (parentheses), use of special characters in C++, 36

`*` (dereference operator)
  operator precedence and, 440
  referencing values with pointers, 434

`*` (multiplication) operator, 37, 63, 434

`*=` (multiplication assignment operator)
  augmented assignment operators, 69
  overloading, 553

`[]` (subscript operator). *see* Subscript operator (`[]`)

`{}` (braces)
  common errors in selection statements, 99–100

missing braces causing error, 43
  use of special characters in C++, 36

`~` (tilde), use with destructors, 456

`<` (less than operator), 397, 544

`<<` (stream insertion operator). *see* Stream insertion
  operator (`<<`)

`<=` (less than or equal to) operator, 397

`<>` (angle brackets), use of special characters in C++, 36

`>` (greater than) operator, 397

`>=` (greater than or equal to) operator, 397

`>>` (stream extraction operator). *see* Stream extraction
  operator (`>>`)

Numbers

8-bit encoding, ASCII, 142

24-point card game, 505–506

1000BaseT NIC, 28

A

`abs()` function, 140, 549

Absolute file names, 512

Abstract classes
  `AbstractGeometricObject.cpp`, 603–604
  `DerivedCircleFromAbstractGeometricObject`
    `.cpp`, 604–605
  `DerivedRectangleFromAbstractGeometric`
    `Object.cpp`, 606–607
  overview of, 601–602
  `TestGeometricObject.cpp`, 607–609

Abstract functions
  benefits of, 608
  implementing in concrete derived classes, 601–602

Acceleration
  computing runway length for airfield, 87
  relationship to velocity, 86

Accessibility keywords, 600

Accessors
  `get` function, 376–378
  making private data fields accessible outside class, 587
  subscript operator as, 553

`action-after-each-iteration`, in `for` loops,
  192–193

Actions (behavior), object, 362

Activation record (or frame), invoking functions and,
  231–232

CREDITS